D1242679

The Field of Yiddish

LINGUISTIC CIRCLE OF NEW YORK

PUBLICATIONS

---

1. Uriel Weinreich: *Languages in Contact; Findings and Problems* (1953)
2. *Linguistics Today*, edited by the editors of *Word* (1954)
3. *The Field of Yiddish* (1954)

Publications of the Linguistic Circle of New York——Number 3

The Field of Yiddish

Studies in Yiddish Language, Folklore, and Literature

Published on the Occasion of the Bicentennial of Columbia University

Edited by

URIEL WEINREICH
Assistant Professor of Yiddish Language, Literature and Culture on the Atran Chair, Columbia University

NEW YORK
1954

Published by the
Linguistic Circle of New York
Columbia University
New York 27, New York
With the Aid of Grants From
Columbia University and The Atran Foundation, Inc.
and Gifts From
Harry A. Abramson and L. M. Stein

Library of Congress Catalogue Card
Number 54-12380

All communications to the Editor or, through him, to the individual contributors should be addressed to: Uriel Weinreich, Department of General and Comparative Linguistics, Columbia University, New York 27, New York.

PREFACE

The Field of Yiddish marks the first attempt to present to the scholarly world, in a medium other than Yiddish, a sampling of Yiddish linguistic, folkloristic, and literary research combined in a single volume. At the same time, it is the first collection representing the three disciplines to appear in any language, including Yiddish, since World War II. The German massacre of the larger part of Yiddish-speaking Jewry also destroyed the bulk of its scholarly personnel and the network of its institutions, drastically reducing the possibilities of specialized publication in the field. In the Soviet Union, too, Yiddish studies have lain fallow since the War, with the outlook even more somber after the 1949 ban on Yiddish publishing in that country. Consequently, the present book constitutes a much needed fresh start. It is intended as the first in a series of volumes of increasing size and broadening scope.

The field of Yiddish contains a wealth of material on many fundamental processes of culture and language formation and functioning. It is of substantial significance not only to the study of Jewish civilization, but also to the humanities and general social science. The broad implications of Yiddish research have served as the premise of such previous works as the English-language publications of the Yiddish Scientific Institute—Yivo. To the neighboring disciplines of Germanic, Romance, Slavic, and Hebrew scholarship, the pertinence of Yiddish materials should be particularly evident. Yet the importance of Yiddish research has not been equally appreciated with respect to all subfields involved. The relevance of Yiddish linguistics for the general science of language has been explicitly formulated before; the understanding of the evidence offered by Jewish folklore to folklore theory has been growing; in the present volume, Mr. Hrushovski makes a pioneering contribution by outlining the position of Yiddish letters from a comparative-literature point of view.

The finished collection does not in all details conform to the Editor's original plans. In particular, literary research is not represented by as many studies as had been anticipated because several scholars could not, unfortunately, accept the deadline for papers. Regarding the unequal length of the articles, it should be stated that because of the limitations imposed by the budget, the expense of printing papers which exceeded the standard space assigned had to be covered by the authors themselves or by special gifts from sources other than the institutions which granted the original funds for the book.

With the workers in the field of Yiddish widely scattered and differently trained, a certain diversity of methodology and scholarly style was taken for granted. Indeed, the volume in part reflects approaches and schools of thought not often represented in the publications of the Linguistic Circle of New York.

When, in 1952, the late Frank Z. Atran made it possible to establish the Atran Chair in Yiddish Language, Literature, and Culture at Columbia University, it was the hope of all concerned that Columbia would become a focus of research, as well as a center of training, in Yiddish studies. The acceptance by so many scholars of the invitation to dedicate papers to the University's Bicentennial in 1954 is a welcome indication that the hope is materializing.

NOTE ON TRANSCRIPTION, TRANSLITERATION, AND CITATION OF TITLES

No uniform system of transcription of Yiddish and Hebrew could be used in this volume, since the requirements vary too substantially from one instance to another. The following desiderata frequently conflict: (1) readability of transcribed forms without ambiguity as to the sound value of the Latin letters; (2) definite correspondence of the transcribed form with the Jewish graphic form where the latter is significant for etymological or other purposes; (3) accommodation of existing habits, good or bad, of librarians and bibliographers. Finally, there are occasions on which written forms have to be cited whose pronunciation is unknown or uncertain; there the editor passes on the burden of decoding to the reader.

The following paragraphs serve to explain and justify the use of the several systems in this book. Discussion of the problem by interested scholars will be welcome.[1]

1. Yiddish

a. Modern Standard Yiddish is rendered in the so-called Yivo system. This is essentially a phonemic transcription of Standard Yiddish, worked out by the Yiddish Scientific Institute in New York. It bases itself on the conventions of standard Yiddish orthography in matters of spacing, hyphenation, and the like. Forms appear in italics. The digraph *sh* stands for I.P.A. /ʃ/ , *zh* for I.P.A. /ʒ/, *kh* for the spirant /x/; *y* stands for the semivowel /j/, and hence *ay* is /aj/ and *ey* is /ej/. Palatalization may be indicated by an accent mark, thus: *n′*, *l′*. Stress is indicated in polysyllabic words by an accent when it falls on a syllable other than the penult (syllables without vowels are included in the count): *ózere* 'lake', *geyég* 'hunting', *lóshekl* 'filly', *óvntn* 'evenings'. In the article on stress problems (pp. 1ff.), the more detailed treatment of the stress is explained separately. Superior hyphens are used to break up digraphs if necessary: *k˗h* = /kh/ but *kh* = /x/.

The Yivo system is applied to citations from the whole period of modern Standard Yiddish, i.e. beginning with the 19th century, since most writing of this period is directly legible and recognizable as one's own to the modern Yiddish reader. Gross dialectal deviants, on the phonemic level, are also rendered in

[1] Previous transcriptions of Yiddish, mostly non-scholarly, were analyzed by Solomon A. Birnbaum: [Transcriptions of Yiddish], *Filologishe shriftn* [*fun Yivo*] 2 (1929) 485–496. Birnbaum's own proposed transcription, discussed in his article, "Die Umschrift des Jiddischen," *Teuthonista* 9 (1933) 90–105, is not adequate for the differentiated needs of a volume like the present one.

this transcription whenever possible; more subtle subphonemic variations, on the other hand, are noted in the phonetic transcription (1b). When references are made to orthography as such, the transliteration (1c) is used.

Bibliographical references to Yiddish works also make use of the Yivo system. Titles of articles, when followed by a reference to the journal or collection, are given in English translation in square brackets.

Hebrew titles of traditional Yiddish books are cited in their standard Yiddish pronunciation, the first citation being followed, for purposes of bibliographical identification, by the Hebrew transcription (see 2a), e.g. *Simkhas hanefesh* (*Šimḥat hanefeš*).

b. PHONETIC AND PHONEMIC FORMS, whenever necessary, are cited in [brackets] or /slashes/, respectively, in a transcription which follows the I.P.A. system or is, in deviant cases, identified ad-hoc. In the article on Swiss Yiddish (pp. 48ff.), long sequences in phonetic transcription are rendered in italics without slashes or brackets.

c. PRE-19TH-CENTURY YIDDISH FORMS are rendered in an exact transliteration, each such citation being preceded by the symbol ♮. The reason for using this system is that the pronunciation of older Yiddish in its various stages has not been reconstructed to the satisfaction of all, and the problem of further decoding (especially insofar as the value of the vowels is concerned) must be reserved for future study. References to modern orthography as such may also make use of this transliteration. The main features of the system are the following: (1) one-to-one correspondence between Jewish letters and transliteration symbols; (2) use of consonant letters for the Jewish letters, but vowel letters for the Jewish vowel points; (3) use of diacritics in the transliteration to correspond exactly to their use in the Jewish script, except that ′ is used as a designation of the final variant of the letters kaf, mem, nun, peh, and ṣadi.

The correspondences in the transliteration are as follows:[2]

א	*ʔ*	ז	*z*	מ	*m*	ק	*q*
ב	*b*	ח	*x*	נ	*n*	ר	*r*
ג	*g*	ט	*t*	ס	*σ*	ש	*s*
ד	*d*	י	*y*	ע	*ʕ*	ת	*θ*
ה	*h*	כ	*k*	פ	*p*		
ו	*v*	ל	*l*	צ	*c*		

The final letters are: ך *ḱ*, ם *ḿ*, ן *ń*, ף *ṕ*, ץ *ć*.

The letters שׁ and שׂ, in the rare cases when they are so marked in the Jewish text, are designated by *s˙* and *˙s*, respectively.

Dageš, šureḳ, and mappiḳ are represented by a dot over the transliteration symbol: בּ *ḃ*, הּ *ḣ*, וּ *v̇*, כּ *k̇*, מּ *ṁ*, פּ *ṗ*, תּ *θ̇*, etc. A distinction between dagesh forte and dagesh lene of course has no place in a transliteration.

[2] Several of the principles of the present transliteration are derived from that used by Solomon A. Birnbaum in his paper, "Umschrift des ältesten datierten jiddischen Schriftstücks," *Teuthonista* 8 (1931/32) 197–207. The editor has also profited greatly from discussions with two contributors, Professors Judah A. Joffe and Herbert H. Paper.

Rafeh (bar) is represented by a bar over the corresponding symbol in the transliteration, as in the Jewish alphabet: בֿ b̄, כֿ k̄, פֿ p̄, תֿ θ̄.

The vowel point occurring under or over a Jewish letter is represented by the following superior signs after the corresponding letter in the transliteration: pataḥ ᵃ, ḥaṭef pataḥ ă, ḳameṣ ᵒ, ḥaṭef ḳameṣ ŏ, segol ᵉ, ḥaṭef segol ĕ, ṣereh ê, ḥolem ô, ḥiriḳ ⁱ, ḳibbuṣ ᵘ, sheva' ᵊ.

2. Hebrew

The citation of Hebrew forms in scholarly Yiddish studies using the Latin alphabet presents difficult problems, too. The following solution has been adopted by the editor:

a. Hebrew forms as a rule are cited in the CUSTOMARY SYSTEM, a mixture of transcription and transliteration used by American Judaistic publications. It is used for isolated words, connected discourse, and bibliographical references where (1) a Sefardic pronunciation is the basis or (2) nothing in particular is implied about pronunciation. ' stands for 'alef, ' for 'ayin, *ḥ* for ḥet, *ṭ* for ṭet, *ṣ* for ṣadi, *ḳ* for ḳuf, *š* for šin, *s* for samek, *ś* for śin; *u* stands for ḳibbuṣ and šureḳ. In the following pairs of vowels, the latter may, if necessary, be distinguished by a circumflex accent: *a* for pataḥ and long ḳameṣ, *o* for short ḳameṣ and ḥolem, *e* for segol and ṣereh. Double letters are used for dagesh forte; *kh* = kaf lene.

b. Hebrew forms in their Eastern European Ashkenazic pronunciation are transcribed in the same (Yivo) system as that used for modern Standard Yiddish (1a). If it is not clear from the context that this transcription is being used, the symbol AH is placed before the cited form. Thus *raṣon* 'will' = AH *rotsoyn* = ♮*racôn̂*.

c. If necessary, transliterations of Hebrew are given according to the Yiddish system (1c), and are preceded by ♮.

In bibliographic references, titles of Hebrew articles are cited in English translation in square brackets.

3. Anglicized Forms

Yiddish and Hebrew words which have entered the English language and are listed by large English dictionaries are cited in their accepted forms, e.g. Torah, seder, vav, Mishnah, Nissan, Sefardic. Words stemming specifically from the Yiddish-language sphere are cited in their Yiddish forms, e.g. yeshive, kheyder. First names of Yiddish-speaking persons are also generally cited in their Yiddish forms, e.g. Avrohom, Yitskhok.

4. Russian and Ukrainian

References to forms or book titles in languages using the Cyrillic alphabet follow the transcription system of *The American Slavic and East European Review*, in which *y* stands for Russian ы, Ukrainian и; *j* stands for consonantal *i*; *kh* stands for /x/; ′ denotes the palatalization of a pre-consonantal or final consonant.

THE EDITOR

CONTENTS

*Translated from the manuscript

STRESS AND WORD STRUCTURE IN YIDDISH

URIEL WEINREICH (New York)

0. The present paper examines the functioning of stress in spoken Yiddish. It also explores the possibility of utilizing stress as the basis of a definition of the word in its phonic aspect and of correlating the phonic and grammatical aspects of the word.[1]

1. The connection between stress and words has been asserted by many writers. To quote only two: Bloomfield states that "in English and many other languages, each word is marked by containing one and only one high stress,"[2] while Trubetzkoy in discussing the "culminative" function of stress declares that "it is phonemically essential to languages with free stress [of which Yiddish is one] that . . . such an emphasis [by stress] takes place only once in each word, and in a way such that the prosodeme . . . in question [i.e. the significant stress] predominates over all other prosodemes of the same word and is not predominated over by any other prosodemes of the same word."[3] It is our task to determine what kind of "words" can be arrived at by reference to stress, and how "words" defined in this way correspond to "words" defined by other criteria.

STRESS AND THE PHONIC WORD

2. The description of stress is complicated because the same phonetic signal, namely relative loudness,[4] serves a number of different functions. De Groot classifies them into non-conventional (expressive and esthetic) and conventional (semantic or sign-distinguishing, syntactic, and "énonciatifs");[5] Trager speaks of "prosodemes . . . affecting the syllable and the word" and of "prosodemes . . . affecting groups of words."[6] This writer feels that the several functions of stress should be studied separately, and noted separately in an analytic transcription, not on the same level as is sometimes done in more recent work on American English (cf. §4.2, end).

[1] In a somewhat different version, this paper was presented to the Linguistic Circle of the Yiddish Scientific Institute—Yivo in New York on January 10, 1954, under the title "Words, Quasi-Words, and Non-Words." If the revised conclusions offered here, especially in criticism of Zaretski, are more satisfactory than those contained in the original paper, credit is due to the members of the Circle, and particularly to Yudel Mark, for their enlightening suggestions.

[2] Leonard Bloomfield: *Language*, New York, 1933, p. 182.

[3] N. S. Trubetzkoy: *Grundzüge der Phonologie*, Prague, 1939, p. 186; French ed., Paris, 1949, p. 221.

[4] We take it for granted that stress involves not only loudness but also intensity, pitch, and other phonetic characteristics. This caution applies to all further references to loudness.

[5] A. W. de Groot: "L'accent en allemand et en néerlandais," *Travaux du Cercle linguistique de Prague* 7 (1939) 149–172.

[6] George L. Trager: "The Theory of Accentual Systems," *Language, Culture and Personality; Essays in Memory of Edward Sapir*, Menasha, Wis., 1941, pp. 131–145; idem and Henry Lee Smith, Jr.: *An Outline of English Structure* (=Studies in Linguistics, Occasional Papers 3), Norman, Okla., 1951, p. 57: "word superfixes" vs. "phrase superfixes."

Phonemic Stress

3. Every Yiddish morpheme which consists of more than one syllable may receive a stress on one of the syllables, but not on others. Thus, in *mame* 'mother', stress if realized must fall on the first syllable; in *aher* 'hither', it must fall on the second. In the present paper, we designate this fact by writing *máme, ahér*.

The distinguishing value of stress within the morpheme is almost nil; differently stated, there are practically no pairs of morphemes which are distinguished by nothing except the place of stress. One minimal pair is formed by the nouns *kúpe* 'heap'—*kupé* 'railroad compartment'; a few near-minimal pairs are *múze* 'muse'—*muzéy* 'museum', *díre* 'apartment'—*tiré* 'dash', *káve* 'coffee'—*kafé* 'café', *znákher* 'quack'—*nakhér* '(substandard) later', and a somewhat marginal minimal pair is *róman* (man's name)—*román* 'novel'. Yet the place of the stress is very firmly fixed: **mamé*, **áher* are completely impossible.[7] This remains a fact despite the existence of a few lexical variants in the standard language, due either to dialect differences (e.g. NE Yiddish *kapóte*, Central Yid. *kápote* 'capote') or to the intersecting routes of borrowing (e.g. *kárete* or *karéte* 'chariot', *revólver* or *revolvér* 'revolver', *mágistrat* or *magistrát* 'city hall (in Europe)'). The fact is not invalidated, either, by the existence of morpheme alternants which differ as to place of stress, e.g. in the singular and plural pairs *pólyak—polyák-n* 'Pole(s)', *profésor—profesór-n* 'professor(s)', *gádlen—gadlón-im* 'boaster(s), conceited person(s)'. These variants are of the same type as others in which segmental phonemes are involved, e.g. *tlúmik* or *klúmik* 'bag'; *shtarb—shtorb* (in *geshtorbn*) 'die(d)'.

3.1. It should be pointed out that the stress so marked is not an obligatory loudness at all, but rather a place where relative loudness occurs if the morpheme is to be emphasized in the text. We could pronounce *vu árbet di máme* 'where does mother work' with or without emphasis on any one of the elements (see below, §5.2); but if the element *árbet* is to be emphasized, it will be the greater relative loudness of the syllable *ár* that will signify this emphasis; if *máme* is to be emphasized, it will be the loudness of *má* that will do it. We can therefore consider phonemic stress within the morpheme as the place at which relative loudness occurs if the morpheme is emphasized.[8] But if no emphasis falls on these morphemes, then *ár* will not be any louder than *bet* nor *má* than *me*.

[7] It was André Martinet who vividly pointed out this discrepancy between rigid rendering and extremely low functional yield of stress in many languages ("Accents et tons," *Miscellanea phonetica*, 1954). On German and Dutch specifically, see de Groot (p. 157): "The stress of the radical as such has no semantic function." R. Jakobson ("Über die Beschaffenheit der prosodischen Gegensätze," *Mélanges . . . van Ginneken*, Paris, 1937, 25–33) speaks of the semantic function of the accent within the word as marginal, but far more widespread in some languages than in others.

[8] Roman Jakobson: "Die Betonung und ihre Rolle in der Wort- und Syntagmaphonologie," *Travaux du Cercle linguistique de Prague* 4 (1931) 164–182, pp. 164f. The same principle was also considered by Rulon S. Wells ("Immediate Constituents," *Language* 23 [1947] 81–117, p. 109) when he postulated, for English, an emphatic morpheme consisting of primary stress /ʹ/; if he felt that the marking of the place of potential stress "has no phonemic value whatever" (*ibid.*, footnote 47), it is probably because he thought that in an actual

3.2. Syllables which have no vowels are automatically unstressable and the indication of stress place on the other syllable can be dispensed with. We therefore write *ovnt* for [ˈovn̥t] 'evening', not *óvnt,* in a disyllabic word.

3.3. Do additional ("secondary") stresses occur in the morpheme? Perhaps they do, but if so they are automatically governed by the sonority of the vowels and have no distinctive status. It is possible, for instance, that in *karosérye* '(automobile) body' there is a somewhat greater loudness on *ka-* than on *-ro-*, but if this is so, it is due only to the greater sonority of *a* and has no distinctive value. As a check on this assertion, we could test morphemes like *katastrófe,* which should have equally slight loudness on *ka-* and *-ta-*.[9] The phonemic irrelevance of minor loudness differences among unstressed syllables of a morpheme is illustrated by the fact that in Yiddish metric verse, *katastrófe* could equally well fill two iambic measures (⏑́ ⏑ | ⏑́ ⏑) or the end of one dactyl and the beginning of another (.. ⏑ ⏑ | ⏑́ ⏑ ..).

Constructive Stress

4. We come now to another function of stress. We may call a STRESS CONSTRUCTION a sequence of morphemes which stand in a fixed stress relationship to each other. In the sequence *tog-shul* '(all-)day school', the first morpheme must receive greater stress than the second. We may call this stress CONSTRUCTIVE and designate it by ˈ before the morpheme on which it falls: *ˈtog-shul.* The fixed stress relationship will be understood to pertain to all morphemes connected by hyphens. Apparently this function of stress should also be interpreted as a facultative relative loudness, actualized only if the construction as a whole is emphasized in the sentence. To this writer's ear, the sequence *DI ˈtog-shul BOYT men itst* 'this day school is now being built' could be pronounced with great relative loudness on *di* and *boyt.* In these circumstances, with *ˈtog-shul* receiving no sentence stress, the syllable *tog* is no louder (to this writer's ear) than *shul;* but instrumental and statistical tests must be instituted to check this point.

For the sake of an orderly argument, this section on constructive stress deals with examples taken out of the context of sentences with their interfering factors of sentence stress (see §5). Furthermore, the examples of this section

---

rendition of the text, stress may or may not be there. This writer feels that facultative properties of morphemes or other units of a language can and should be noted in a lexical listing.

[9] Caution should be exercised against transferring the concept of so-called "tertiary stress" from English to Yiddish. The English tertiary stress, designated by a grave accent, as in *lògarìthmic,* seems to be due sometimes to rhythmic reasons and sometimes to the sonority of the vowels, but since it is determined automatically, from a phonemic point of view there is no stress there. In addition to this theoretical consideration, there is the fact that probably the first syllable of a Yiddish word like *logarítmish* is not any louder, in phonetic fact, than the second—unless English influence is strong. This point has also been well stated about German, in contrast to English, by Hugo Mueller: "Stress Phonemes in German," *Studies in Linguistics* 8 (1950) 82–87, p. 83, example *Sĕntĭmĕntălĭtắt;* yet George O. Curme (*A Grammar of the German Language*, New York, $_2$1952, §§45, 3; 48, 2) does find "important" rhythmical secondary accents in "foreign" words like *Àktivitắt.*

consist of constructions which are composed of bases and affixes, to the exclusion of clitics (see §13).

4.1. Certain constructions include morphemes which have no vowels; those cannot be stressed, and the other morpheme, which does have a vowel, automatically has greater loudness, just as in the case of certain phonemic stresses (cf. §3.2). The indication of morphological stress in such constructions may be dispensed with: in this paper we write *tish-l* 'little table' (not *ˈtish-l*), *shrayb-st* '(you) write' (not *ˈshrayb-st*), *shnur-s* 'daughter-in-law's' (not *ˈshnur-s*).

4.2. If the constructive stress falls on a morpheme which itself consists of more than one syllable, it is rendered on the syllable which has phonemic stress: in *ˈkhúpe-kleyd* 'wedding dress' (literally 'wedding-canopy dress'), the syllable of greater relative loudness is *khu-*. No significant stress difference between *-pe-* and *-kleyd* exists; any non-significant differences would have to be instrumentally and statistically determined.[10] This does not mean, of course, that the stress on *khu-* is necessarily greater than on *tog-* in the example of §4 because of the existence of two stresses. We are dealing rather with two functions of the same phonetic loudness. The symbol ˈ means that the loudness affects the morpheme *khúpe* rather than *kleyd*, while the symbol ´ means that within *khúpe*, the constructive stress, if any, falls on the syllable *khu-*. Thus stress is analyzed according to its functions, not simply according to its substantial manifestation.

4.21. The statement about the lack of a loudness difference between *-pe-* and *-kleyd* would have to be qualified in the case of constructions of two morphemes in which the first, stressed morpheme is so long that two or more unstressed syllables intervene between the stressed syllable and the morpheme boundary: e.g. *khásene-kleyd* 'wedding dress', *késhene-gelt* 'spending (literally 'pocket') money'. In these cases, a secondary stress, consisting of loudness of the second morpheme intermediate between that of the unstressed and stressed syllables of the first morpheme, seems to be manifested: [ˈxaseneˌklejd], [ˈkešeneˌgelt]. In metric verse, these forms could only be used in triple meters, e.g. filling a dactylic measure and the beginning of another (⏊ ⏑ ⏑ | ⏊ .. ..). Since this secondary stress can be predicted automatically according to a rhythmic principle, it need not be marked in an analytic transcription.

[10] In English the second element of the equivalent construction would characteristically be marked by a secondary stress: *wédding drêss* (see Trager and Smith, *op. cit.;* Wells, *op. cit.*, p. 109). Stanley S. Newman ("On the Stress System of English," *Word* 2 [1946] 171–187, p. 180) calls it "middle stress." Curme (*op. cit.*) also postulates a secondary stress in equivalent cases in German: *Ấbgrùnd* (§45), *lébhàft* (§48, 1 B *b*) as against *Bắcker*. William G. Moulton ("Juncture in Standard German," *Language* 23 [1947] 212–226, p. 215) does likewise: e.g. /ˈʔainˌflus/ *Einfluss* 'influence'. Mueller (*op. cit.*, p. 82) proceeds in the same way: he contrasts the unstressed second syllable of *Schúlĕ* with a secondarily-stressed second element in *Schúl-gèld*. In Dutch, according to de Groot (*op. cit.*, p. 157), it is possible to distinguish between *dráagbaar* 'bearable' and *dráagbáar* (*dráagbàar?*) 'stretcher'. Even if these analyses are phonemically correct (which is doubtful at least for English and German, since the sonority of the unstressed syllables seems to be the automatically determining factor), they do not seem applicable to Yiddish. If Yid. *ˈtsol-n-dik* 'paying' is distinguished from *ˈtsol-n-ˈdik* 'inches thick', it is because the second element in the latter form has a full stress equal to that of the first; cf. §4.73.

4.3. If a polysyllabic morpheme enters into a stress construction in the unstressed position, the needs of constructive stress (i.e. lack of stress) and of phonemic stress seem to be adjusted as follows:

1. If the unstressed polysyllabic morpheme precedes the stressed morpheme, it seems to be completely devoid of any relative loudness: *táte-ˈmáme* 'parents' (literally 'father-mother') = [tateˈmame], with the syllables *ta-*, *-te-*, and *-me* equally unstressed; *órem-ˈman* 'poor man' = [oreˈman], with *o* and *rem* equally unstressed.

2. If the unstressed polysyllabic morpheme follows the stressed morpheme and:
   a. if it has initial phonemic stress, it is completely devoid of relative loudness provided the constructive stress occurs in the syllable immediately before the morpheme boundary: *ˈpost-márke* 'postage stamp' = [ˈpostmarke], *ˈshul-yóntev* 'school holiday' = [ˈšuljontev], *ˈbyuró-árbet* 'office work' = [bjuˈroarbet];
   b. if the place of phonemic stress in the unstressed morpheme is two or more syllables away from the syllable bearing the constructive stress of the construction, whether the intervening unstressed syllables belong to the stressed or the unstressed morpheme, a loudness intermediate between that of the stressed syllable in the stressed morpheme and the unstressed syllables appears to be realized in the place of phonemic stress of the unstressed morpheme. Thus, *ˈpost-byuró* 'post office' = [ˈpostbjuˌro], *ˈshul-statút* 'school bylaws' = [ˈšulstaˌtut], *ˈtsayt-sufíks* 'tense suffix' = [ˈtsajtsuˌfiks]; *yeshíve-bókher* 'yeshive student' = [jeˈšiveˌboxer], *ˈmelúkhe-aparát* 'state machinery' = [meˈluxeapaˌrat], *ˈdróshe-geshánk* 'wedding present' = [ˈdrošegeˌšank].[11]

Since the intermediate degree of loudness due to the rhythmic reasons described above is automatically predictable from the existence of a construction (symbolized by hyphens) and the distance between the two places of phonemic stress, it has no functional status and need not be noted in a transcription.[12]

4.4. We may define a stress construction OF THE FIRST DEGREE as consisting of one and only one stressed morpheme and one or more unstressed morphemes. So far we have considered only constructions having one unstressed morpheme. Such sequences as *far-ˈzunk-en* 'sunk', *af-dos-ˈnay* 'anew', *ˈnay-ink-er* 'new (masc. sg. nom. endearing)', *ˈkrenk-lekh-er-e* 'sicklier (pl.)', exemplify first-degree constructions containing each one stressed morpheme and several unstressed ones.[13]

4.5. In constructions involving more than two morphemes, we find that morphemes containing no vowels at all may be simply disregarded in the stress analysis: *ˈárbet-s-man* is equivalent in this analysis to *ˈárbet-man* (both forms of

[11] In German, Curme finds (*op. cit.*, §48, 2*a*) that "the intensity of all secondary accents increases with their distance from the principal accent."

[12] We may say formulaically that in a construction ˈ– - - –́(– – . . .), we find –́ = [ˌ].

[13] No analysis of the polymorphemic constructions into immediate constituents is necessary for this purpose. In other words, *ˈkrenk-lekh-er-e* may be considered a "flat" string of morphemes rather than a nucleus, *krenk-*, with a "periphery," *-lekh*, the two being together the nucleus for the further "periphery," *-er*, etc.

'working man' occur); ˈ*gas-n-lomp* 'street lamp' functions exactly like ˈ*gaz-lomp* 'gas lamp'. The constructions are describable in terms of morphemes containing vowels alone, with the vowelless ones being "skipped." Cf. §§3.2 and 4.1 above.

4.6. A stress construction, which by definition contains a stressed morpheme, may become part of a larger construction (OF THE SECOND DEGREE) in which another morpheme requires the principal constructive stress.

4.61. Let us consider the case of *folk-shprakh-khush.*[14] Here an analysis into immediate constituents (ICs) is necessary; let us designate the more immediate cut by ═. We may analyze the construction as ˈ*folk-shprakh═khush*, i.e. ˈ*folk-shprakh* 'popular language' combined with *khush* 'sense', yielding 'sense for the popular language'. Or else we may analyze it as *folk* combined with ˈ*shprakh-khush*, meaning 'popular sense of the language'. The first element of these second-degree constructions, whatever it be, must be stressed. In ˈ*folk-sphrakh═khush* the constructive stress of the whole construction coincides with that of the first IC; in ˈ*folk═ˌshprakh-khush*, the two do not coincide, and we designate the stress of the second IC, which is "demoted" by that of the entire construction, by ˌ. This seems to be realized as intermediate loudness: ˈ*folk═ˌshprakh-khush* = [ˈfolkˌšpraxxuš], while in the type ˈ*folk-shprakh═khush* no intermediate loudness occurs. The rule might be formulated as follows: if a construction enters into a larger construction in which it functions as the unstressed element, its own constructive stress is manifested as a secondary stress. Note the distinctive value of the secondary stress: [ˈonˌtsukern̥] = ˈ*on═ˌtsúker-n* 'to cover with sugar', but [ˈontsuˌkern̥] = ˈ*on═tsu-ˌker-n* 'to sweep into a pile'.

4.62. This would be true, mutatis mutandis, where an unstressed polysyllabic IC contains predictable intermediate loudness due to phonemic stress (of the type ˈ*post-byuró* [ˈpostbjuˌro], ˈ*dróshe-geshánk* [ˈdrošegeˌšank]; see §4.3, 2b). If such a construction entered a larger construction as the unstressed element (e.g. ˈ*hoypt═ˌpost-byuró* 'main post office'), the originally secondary stress would be "demoted" to a tertiary loudness, to be designated by ː, e.g. [ˈhojptˌpostbju-ːro].[15] But this tertiary loudness is also predictable and need not be transcribed.

4.63. There are stress constructions in which one of the elements itself consists of coordinated subelements: e.g. *zumer- un vinter-mantl* 'summer and winter coat'. We may transcribe it as ˈ*(zúmer-un-vínter)═mantl* or simply as ˈ*zúmer-un-*ˈ*vínter═mantl*; likewise for ˈ*zúmer═oybs-un-yágde-s* 'summer fruit and berries', where the unstressed element is the composite one.

4.64. The above remarks apply to the vast majority of second-degree stress constructions in which the unstressed construction of the first degree follows the

[14] The example, but not the analysis, is due to A. Zaretski: *Yidishe gramatik*, Vilna, 1929, p. 287. (A first edition of the book, *Praktishe gramatik*, appeared in Moscow in 1927; all citations in this paper are from the second and revised edition.)

[15] For the equivalent case in German, Mueller suggests (*op. cit.*, p. 83) an analysis whereby equal subordinate (in this case, "tertiary") stresses would be placed on all but the first element: *Kammerunteroffizier* = *Kámmer*+*ùnter*+*offizìer*. I would analyze the Yiddish equivalent as follows: ˈ*kámer* ═ ˌ*únter-ofitsír* = [ˈkamerˌunterofiːtsir], where ː stands for a tertiary degree of loudness, weaker than secondary and stronger than "lack of stress," and has no distinctive value.

stressed element. However, there are also cases in which it precedes the stressed element. Consider *shnayderay* 'tailoring', which may be analyzed as *ˌshnayd-er=ˈay*. In such cases no intermediate loudness on ˌ seems to be realized; in other words, *ˌshnayd-er=ˈay* [šnajdeˈraj] has the same phonetic loudness pattern as the constructions of the first degree *stólyer-ˈay* [stoʎeˈraj] 'carpentry' (cf. *órem-ˈman* in §4.3, 1) or *af-dos-ˈnay* [afdosˈnaj], which does not consist of stress constructions of a lower level, but is a "flat" string of three morphemes.

Among the stressed morphemes which occur last in second-degree constructions are *-al* or *-el* (*form-ˈal* 'formal', *funktsyon-ˈel* 'functional'), *-ant* (*kurs-ˈant* 'student at courses'), *-ent* (*absolv-ˈent* 'alumnus'), *-ir* (*kontról-ˈir-n* 'to check'), *-ist* (*telefón-ˈist* 'telephone operator'), *-izm* (*bund-ˈizm* 'ideology of the Jewish Socialist Labor Bund'), *-ur* (*aparát-ˈur* 'apparatus'), and the contemptuous suffixes *-ets* (*bókher-ˈets*), *-nyak* (*treyf-ˈnyak* 'eater of forbidden foods'), *-uk* (*shúster-ˈuk* 'contemptible cobbler').[16] Final stressed elements consisting of several morphemes seem to be rare, but cf. *ˌkhsid-ey=beys-ˈHílel* 'followers of the House of Hillel'.

4.65. There is a possibility, largely in theory, of making up constructions of the third or even higher degrees, in which a significant tertiary stress would be manifested. Thus, if we were to make up a compound ˈ(ˈ*melúkhe=ˌshul-yóntev*)-(ˈ*gas-n-parád*) 'state school holiday street parade', the syllable *ga* would have to receive a stress which would be tangibly weaker than the secondary stress of *shul*, yet stronger than the unstressed *me*, *khe*, and *tev;* and *rad* would, on the principle set forth in §4.3, 2 above, have a theoretical (non-significant) quaternary loudness. But in practice such subtleties of loudness appear not to be distinguished, and it is partly for this reason that excessively long compounds are avoided in Yiddish.[17]

4.7. Fixed stress relationships in morphological constructions seem to belong to three types. The examples which follow are intended to be illustrative, not exhaustive.

4.71. One element of the construction EXCEEDS the other in loudness. We may analyze this type as consisting of a stressed and an unstressed element. We find this relation in inflected forms (ˈ*gut-e* 'good (*pl.*)', ˈ*kind-er* 'children'), in derivations (ˈ*árbet-er* 'worker', ˈ*knekht-shaft* 'slavery', *ge-ˈfor-n* 'traveled', ˈ*kónter-revolútsye* 'counter-revolution', ˈ*shtif-máme* 'stepmother', ˈ*vítse-prezidént* 'vice president', ˈ*kind-vayz* 'while a child', ˈ*levóne-dik* 'moonlit'), derivations from constructions (*af-dos-ˈnay* 'anew', *fun-der-ˈvayt-ns* 'from afar', ˈ*nit-yid* 'non-Jew', ˈ*far-zikh-dik* 'separate', ˈ*shtik-n-zikh* 'to choke (*intrans.*)', *grob-er-ˈyung* 'boor', *gut-er-ˈbrúder* 'chum', *yung-er-ˈman* 'young man', *fri-ˈmorgn* 'morning', *órem-*

[16] Zaretski, *op. cit.*, p. 287.

[17] This is in contrast to English, where compounds do NOT have a similar hierarchy of stresses, and where *Port of New York Authority Ticket Book Sales Office* is not unfeasible. Of course, under the influence of English in America, one hears such un-Yiddish constructions as ˈ*kultúr* ˈ*rádyo* ˈ*prográm* 'cultural radio program', which should be ˈ*kultúr* = ˌ*rádyo-prográm*. Under Russian influence, Yiddish speakers have been led to mishandle fixed stress relations in compounds corresponding to Russian phrases, e.g. ˈ*klas-n-*ˈ*kamf* 'class struggle' for ˈ*klas-n-kamf* (Russian *klassovaja bor'ba*); see Zaretski, *op. cit.*, p. 56.

ˈmentsh '(dial.) poor woman', *ˈyen-e-velt* 'the other world'), and many compounds, both coordinative (*táte-ˈmáme* 'parents', *khosn-ˈkále* 'bride and groom', *shver-un-ˈshvíger* 'parents-in-law', *punkt-ˈkome* 'semicolon', *tint-un-ˈféder* 'pen and ink', *Kháne-ˈLéye* woman's name, *Árye-ˈLeyb* man's name) and subordinative (*ˈzup-lefl* 'soup spoon', *ˈkunst-histórish* 'of art history', *kleyn-ˈbírger-lekh* 'petty bourgeois', *éster-ˈtónes* 'fast of Esther', *bal-ˈakhsánye* 'innkeeper', *bney-ˈyisróel* 'sons of Israel, Jews', *ˈshábes-shir* 'Sabbath song', *shábes-ˈshíre* 'the Sabbath on which Moses' Song (Deut. 32:1–43) is recited', *bes-ˈmédresh* 'house of study', *rosh-ˈkhóydesh* 'beginning of the (Jew.) month'; *ben-ˈméylekh* or *ˈben-méylekh* 'prince', *bukh-ˈhalt-er* or *ˈbukh-halt-er* 'bookkeeper', *mas-ˈshtab* or *ˈmos-shtab* 'scale').[18]

4.72. Both elements of the construction are of equal[19] loudness, i.e. they are both stressed. The presence of an unstressed connective element need not disturb this relation. We find this type in certain cases of prefixation (*ˈum-ˈmíglekh* 'impossible', *ˈum=ge-ˈvash-n* '(with hands) unwashed', *ˈánti=komun-ˈist* 'anti-Communist', *ˈpro=ˈaráb-ish* 'pro-Arab', *ˈnéo=ˈkhsid-es* 'neo-hassidism', *ˈóyser=ge-ˈveyn-lekh* 'extraordinary', *ˈon-ˈrakhmónes-dik* 'pitiless'), a few kinds of suffixation (*ˈkrank-ˈerhéyt* 'while sick', *ˈfártik-ˈerhéyt* 'in a ready state'), and certain compounds (*ˈtunkl-ˈbloy* 'dark blue',[20] *ˈfitsh-ˈnas* 'wringing wet', *ˈhalb-ˈzeks* 'half past five', *ˈdray-un-ˈtsvantsik* 'twenty-three', *ˈénglish-ˈdaytsh* 'Anglo-German', *ˈshlílas-ha-ˈgóles* 'negation of the Diaspora', *ˈshíve-ˈmedúre-ˈgehénem* 'seven divisions of hell', *ˈkélev-she-be-ˈklov-im* 'dog of dogs, contemptible cur', *ˈgóles-ˈdátshe* 'sufferings of (summer) country life', *be-ˈsod=ˈsoyd-es* 'in utmost secrecy', *ˈyid-n=ˈsokhr-im* 'Jews (who are) merchants', *ˈvayt-ˈvayt* 'very far'.[21]

4.73. Of the two elements in the construction, one has a stress which is lesser than, or equal to, the stress of the other element, but not greater than that of the other. We may designate the element whose stress varies from lesser to equal by a preceding ˥. Thus *˥óyneg-ˈshábes* 'enjoyment of the Sabbath' means that [ojnegˈšabes] and [ˌojnegˈšabes] and [ˈojnegˈšabes] all occur, but not [ˈojnegšabes] etc. Some other examples of this stress relation are common compounds of Hebrew-Aramaic origin: *˥Móyshe-ˈrabéynu* 'Moses our teacher', *˥Dóvid-ha-*

[18] The existence of doublets does not, of course, invalidate the fact of a fixed stress relation. Concerning stress doublets in German (e.g. *Infinitív-Ínfinitiv, nótwendig-notwéndig*) see Curme, *op. cit.*, §§47, 2 A *c*; 47, 3 A *a*, etc. Words formed as abbreviations, if considered as constructions, also have a fixed stress relation; cf. *ˈra-sh-e* 'RaShI' (Rabbi Shlomo Iṣḥaḳi), *ta-sh-ˈya-d* 'the year (5)714'; also new abbreviations like *y-i-v-ˈo* (*yidisher visnshaftlekher institut* 'Yiddish Scientific Institute'), varying with *ˈy-i-v-o*.

[19] The range of loudness which would be perceived as equal stress needs instrumental investigation.

[20] Zaretski (*op. cit.*, p. 109) analyzes this as *ˈtunkl-bloy*. Mueller (*op. cit.*, p. 86) interprets the equivalent German cases as *tîef+schwárz, hâlb+gár*, with weaker stress on the first element; Curme finds the German compounds to have equal stresses: *blútrót, féderléicht, héllgélb* (*op. cit.*, §47, 3 A *b*).

[21] On even stress in German, see Curme, *loc. cit.* (footnote 20); English "even accent" (*whíte hót, úp-stáirs, ápple píe*) is discussed by John Samuel Kenyon: *American Pronunciation*, Ann Arbor, Mich., ₉1943, pp. 77f.

ˈméylekh 'King David',[22] *⌝góles-ˈbovl* 'the Babylonian exile', *⌝óylom-ho-ˈémes* 'the True World (hereafter)', *me-⌝mále=ˈmókem* 'substitute', *⌝nis-im=ve-ˈniflóes* 'miracles and wonders', *ˈkoydem-⌝kol* 'first of all', *be-⌝oys-es=u-ˈmofs-im* 'by signs and miracles', *⌝kúdshe-brikh-ˈhu* 'the Holy One, blessed be He', *be-ˈze=ha-⌝loshn* 'in these words', *⌝aséres=ha-ˈdíbres* 'the ten commandments'; also sequences like *⌝hob-un-ˈgut-s* 'property', *⌝toyb-ˈshtum* 'deaf and dumb', *⌝mer-ˈvéynik-er* 'more or less', *ˈal-⌝erléy* 'of all kinds', *ˈkol-⌝erléy* 'id.', *ˈdray-⌝erléy* 'of three kinds', etc.[23]

It might be suggested that these sequences with variable stress be considered sometimes as stress constructions (when the stresses are unequal) and sometimes as free syntactic sequences (when the stresses are equal). Yet the variability of stress from less to equal in one of the elements is so characteristic of a large group of Yiddish morpheme sequences that it seems advisable to classify them as a special kind of stress construction. The partly variable stress pattern cannot be equated with a free stress relationship because the element marked ⌝ never has stronger stress than that marked ˈ.

4.8. The contrast between stress constructions and sequences in which the stress relation is free is brought out by such pairs (impossible in the languages from which the Yiddish morphemes are derived) as *ˈshmek-tábek* (construction) 'snuff' vs. (*a*) *shmek tábek* (free) 'a pinch of snuff'; *ˈmas-n-arést-n* (construction) 'mass arrests' vs. *mas-n arést-n* (free) 'masses (i.e. large numbers) of arrests'; *ˈsof-zats* (construction) 'final sentence' vs. *sof zats* (free) 'end of sentence'.

4.9. Is it possible to subsume the phonemic and constructive stresses under a single function?[24] The answer to this question depends entirely on the status which one wishes to give the category of construction in one's descriptive system.[25] If both the construction and the sequential order are considered as given entities, the "constructive" stress plays the same function within the construction as the phonemic stress within the morpheme. For example, given the morphemes *sof* and *zats* placed in a construction in that order, the only possible stress scheme is *ˈsof-zats;* given the same two morphemes in a construction in the reverse order, the only possible stress scheme is *ˈzats-sof* 'sentence end'. In the same way, given the syllables *be* and *re* in a single morpheme in that order, the only possible stress is *Bére* (man's name); in the reverse order, only *rébe* 'master, teacher' is possible. Hence, if construction and order are given, neither phonemic nor constructive stress conveys meaning and both can be grouped together. When that is done, a great many minimal pairs of words can be developed which are distinguished only by the place of this generalized single stress, e.g. *génetst* 'yawns'—*genétst* 'wetted' (*ˈgénets-t—ge-ˈnets-t*), *yeníke* 'livelihood'—(*di*) *yénike*

[22] Zaretski analyzes this and similar items as belonging to the preceding type: *ˈdóvid-ha-ˈméylekh* (*op. cit.*, pp. 79f.)

[23] For German parallels (*úngezógen* or *úngezogen*), see Curme, *op. cit.*, §45, 2; for English parallels (*clóse-físted* or *clóse-fisted*, where there seems to be a functional difference connected with the stress variation), see Kenyon, *op. cit.*, p. 88.

[24] As does de Groot, *op. cit.*, p. 156, for German and Dutch.

[25] On the necessity of treating constructions as an irreducible descriptive category, see Charles F. Hockett: "Two Models of Grammatical Description," *Word* 10 (1954), pp. 221f.

'those' (*yeníke—ˈyen-ik-e*), *úmetik* 'sad'—*úmétik* 'unethicalness' (*ˈúmet-ik—um-ˈét-ik*), etc. On the other hand, it is theoretically possible to consider two other factors, e.g. order and stress, as prior to construction. Then, given the order *sof, zats*, it is the stress which determines whether we have *ˈsof-zats* 'final sentence' or *ˈsof ˈzats* 'end of sentence'. The constructive stress then is significant in distinguishing free sequences from compounds and is, unlike the phonemic stress, the bearer of a meaning, i.e. it functions not like a phoneme, but like a morpheme.

The Phonic Word in Its Syntactic Environment

5. As we pass from the handpicked examples of the preceding section to an examination of larger segments of speech, we get an opportunity to test the possibilities and limitations of a definition of the phonic word based on fixed stress relations.

5.1. Before the phonic word can be defined, we must consider the problem of phonic boundaries between adjoining stress constructions. Given the sentence [ˈkind er ˈken en far ˈštej n meˈšol im] 'children can understand parables', in which morpheme boundaries are marked by spaces, there is no question that in a "normal" rendering, the morphemes *kind*, *ken*, *shtey*, and *meshól* would be stressed, while *er*, *en*, *far*, *n*, and *im* would be fixed in a relationship of lesser stress to the rest. But we face at least the theoretical question whether *er*, for example, is to be grouped with the preceding *kind* or the following *ken*, or whether *far* belongs in a stress construction with preceding *en* or the following *shtey*.

Stress criteria alone do not suffice for the establishment of these boundaries, and we need to explore the possibility that stress constructions in Yiddish are bounded by phonetically observable signals ("junctures") of the type which, according to some scholars, exist in English.[26] It turns out that the phonetic characteristics of phonemes near possible boundaries between stress constructions are in Yiddish exceedingly ill defined. Aspiration of stops, for example, is rare even sentence-initially; glottal stops before initial vowels are entirely sporadic, so that the saying *a nemer iz nit keyn geber* 'a taker is not a giver' is sometimes parodied as *an emer iz nit keyn tseber* 'a pail is not a tub'; unvoicing of "word"-final consonants does not take place in the standard language.[27] Nothing like English "plus-juncture" could be discovered on phonetic grounds.

5.11. We might do better by looking for a construction boundary at a place where facultative pauses occur in a text, or where they *may* occur (as shown by alternate renditions of the same text) without changing the meaning.[28] Even

[26] Trager and Smith, *op. cit.* (see footnote 6), p. 50.

[27] Skepticism about phonetic boundary signals, with regard to Yiddish as well as other languages, is voiced by N. Guralnik: [The Concept of the Individual Word in the Light of [Marr's] New Doctrine of Language], *Fragn fun yidisher shprakh*, ed. M. Viner and A. Zaretski (= Moscow State Pedagogical Institute, Katedre far yidisher shprakh un literatur, *Visnshaftlekhe zamlbikher I*), Moscow, 1938, 143–155, p. 148. Zaretski (*op. cit.*, p. 284) speaks of the "frequent" mistakes of school children who write *a nayzn* for *an ayzn* 'an iron', *a narbet* for *an arbet* 'a piece of work'.

[28] Cf. A. M. Peškovskij: "Slovo otdel'noje" [Word, Separate], in *Literaturnaja entsiklopedija; slovar' literaturnykh terminov*, Moscow–Leningrad, 1925, p. 824: "Portions of a

assuming, however, that "changing the meaning" could be so defined as to exclude indications of hesitation (these could be put aside as "symptomatic" rather than "symbolic"), it still would be possible to place pauses at many different points between stressed morphemes: in *er* | *ˈvoyn-t* | *bay* | *zayn* | *ˈbrúder* 'he lives with his brother', we could visualize pauses at any of the bars.

Occasionally we *can* distinguish between more and less likely places of pause. In the example of §5.1, a pause is far more likely after than before *en;* the *k* of *kind, ken* might conceivably be aspirated, but a glottal stop would hardly precede *en*. While the precise nature of these highly ephemeral juncture phenomena remains to be investigated, it is likely that more of a break will be discovered between *en* and what follows than what precedes, and so forth for the rest of the sentence; hence, given two peaks of stress, we would be justified in placing the boundary of the constructions between *en* and *far*, and so on. Using a space to mark a construction boundary and hyphens to mark its absence, we have: *ˈkind-er ˈken-en far-ˈshtey-n ˈmeshól-im*. But we reiterate: the boundries are extremely vague.

5.12. A stress construction between such boundaries may be defined as a PHONIC WORD in Yiddish.[29] The syllable in which the constructive stress is manifested may be called the PEAK of the phonic word. A morpheme which is not part of a stress construction is a SIMPLE phonic word. The relation of the word defined phonically to other types of word-like units has to be investigated separately (see §§7.2, 13); but before we discuss that problem, a few additional properties of stress must be considered.

5.121. Incidentally, in accordance with the facts presented in §§4.72f., some phonic words have or may have two peaks (*ˈkrank-ˈerhḗyt*, *⌝toyb-ˈshtum*). Sometimes unstressed morphemes are found intercalated between the two peaks of a word; we then have what has been called a "Distanzkompositum,"[30] or—in our terminology—an extended two-peaked construction. The most frequent cases in Yiddish are finite verbs with their complements (*ˈtu-ˈoys: ⌝tu-zikh-shoyn-ˈoys* 'get undressed, now'). How these are to be analyzed when fully stressed words are intercalated (e.g. *⌝tu-zikh tḗykef ˈoys*) is a question whose solution depends on a fuller description of the grammar (see §13); it is possible that the definition of constructions as *sequences* (cf. §4) may have to be modified.

5.2. In the terms of our definitions, what is linguistically significant about stress is the relations within the stress construction. Comparing the loudness of the peaks of stress constructions in a sentence or longer utterance is one aspect of stress with which we are not concerned. Their loudness appears to vary in pro-

sentence which have their own stress . . . and permit a stoppage of speech before and after them . . ." are words. The possibility of pause also seems to underlie Bloomfield's conception of the "free" form (*op. cit.*, pp. 159f.). Note also the use of "facultative pause" and of minimal pause-groups as an approach to the word in Japanese by Bernard Bloch: "Studies in Colloquial Japanese II," *Language* 22 (1946) 200–245, p. 201.

[29] Zaretski (*op. cit.*, p. 283) calls a segment of speech "grouped about one stress" a measure (*takt*), but he does not discuss the problem of its delimitation.

[30] Walter Henzen: *Deutsche Wortbildung*, Halle/S., 1947, pp. 10, 45, after Brugmann; also called "tmesis."

portion to the emphasis desired on the particular phonic word, and it is impossible to prove that there are discrete levels of loudness (i.e. there is no 'first', 'second', 'third' level of loudness); the relation between emphasis and loudness, from this point of view, is beyond the realm of grammar.[31] Accordingly, every form not connected by hyphens to its context is a fullfledged word and is to be read with the proper stress; all stress marks refer only to relations within the word (ˈ, ˌ, ˥) or the morpheme (′).

One phenomenon which deserves further study is the reduction in loudness of phonic peaks for the purposes of de-emphasis. A fresh utterance might be stressed [ˈdovid ˈšrajb t a ˈbriv] 'David is writing a letter', but in answer to the question, "What is David doing?" the text would most likely be rendered without stress on *Dovid*. The lack of stress in an anaphoric element (i.e. one which is repeated from the preceding context) is apparently due not to its relation to its immediate neighbors, but to something in a much larger environment.

5.3. Of greater pertinence to our problem is the contrastive function of stress.[32] When the loudness of a peak is increased beyond a certain point (to be instrumentally investigated), an effect of contrast with some other word, either previously uttered or understood, is achieved. We may postulate a morpheme of contrast[33] and designated it *!;* its phonetic value (when combined with a phonic word) is a marked prominence of stress in the peak. In the example of §5.1, *!kind-er* = [ˈˈkinder] implies 'children (not adults)'; *!ken-en* = [ˈˈkenen] implies 'can (not do)'; and so forth.

Of course, since it is only relative loudness that matters, the contrastive morpheme can also be rendered by reducing the stress of all other peaks; if *!kind-er* were pronounced [ˌkinder] in an environment of nearly inaudible [. . . kenenfarštejn. . .], the effect of contrast would be achieved perfectly.

[31] Some analyses of American English have postulated a fixed stress relationship in noun phrases and others; cf. Bernard Bloch and George L. Trager: *Outline of Linguistic Analysis*, Baltimore, 1942, p. 48: *vôcal ârbitrary sýmbols* (more fully developed in Trager and Smith, *op. cit.*, pp. 70ff.). For German, too, Curme finds (*op. cit.*, §50 A 6 *b*) that "an adjective usually receives less stress than the noun which it limits." Mueller makes the surprising finding (*op. cit.*, p. 84) that in German a stress ratio holds which is the reverse of English; he contrasts English *The Nèw Wórld is for me a nêw Wòrld* with German *Die Nêue Wélt ist für mich eine nèue Wélt*. This writer feels that these analyses are on the wrong track, and finds the description given by Newman (see footnote 10) to be truer to the facts. Newman distinguishes between two varieties of primary "heavy" stresses, nuclear and subordinate. In a phrase like *ánnual méeting*, both stresses are "heavy"; if the second is, in phonetic fact, somewhat louder, this is due to its coincidence with the intonation peak, and it is not distinctive in any way. The distinctions between "heavy" and non-"heavy" stresses, on one hand, and between nuclear vs. subordinate "heavy" stresses, on the other, are on a different plane and should not be confused. In the Yiddish analysis, presented here, an effort was made to avoid such a confusion.

[32] Cf. Jakobson, "Die Betonung . . .," p. 165; Curme (*op. cit.*, §50 A 6) speaks of "distinguishing stress," de Groot (*op. cit.*, p. 165) of "accent d'opposition." Best discussion for English is apparently by Wells, *op. cit.*, p. 110; see also Newman, *op. cit.*, p. 172.

[33] Some linguists would have misgivings about a morpheme consisting of no segmental phonemes, but in one way or another, the facts presented here must be fitted into a description.

There appears to be no possibility in Yiddish of differentiating between the placement of *!* on a phonic word as a whole and its placement on the stressed morpheme of a polymorphemic word. For example, in *ˈkoyf-mir !ˈmel-tsúker* 'buy me granulated sugar', it is impossible to tell whether the burden of the contrast is 'granulated (not diced, powdered . . .) sugar' or 'granulated sugar (not molasses, honey . . .)'.

5.4. The effects of applying stress to unstressed morphemes of a construction (alternately phrased: of making parts of phonic words into words) are peculiar and far from uniform.

5.41. With one group of unstressed parts of constructions, the effect of stress would be contrast. Compare *er-iz-ˈalt ˈakht-tsik yor* 'he is eighty years old' with *ot gey-t léye mit dóvid-n; !er-iz-ˈalt ˈakht-tsik yor* (alternately transcribed: . . . *er iz-ˈalt ˈakht-tsik yor*) 'there go Leah and David; *he* is eighty years old'. Here the stress on *er* serves to contrast it with an understood *zi* 'she'. (Of course, since the usual form of *er* is unstressed, only a "normal," and not necessarily an excessive loudness constitutes the contrastive morpheme.) In *yítskhok iz-ge-ˈvor-n a-ˈler-er-!kandidát* 'Isaac became a teacher candidate', there is an implied contrast with *ˈler-er=ge-ˌhilf* 'teaching assistant' and the like, or simply with *ˈler-er* 'teacher'. Since the constructive stress relation is upset by the application of the contrastive morpheme to an unstressed element of a word, this phenomenon seems to occur only in contexts where the reference of the contrast is sufficiently apparent.[34]

An interesting problem is raised by the contrastive stressing of auxiliary verbs. It appears that in idiomatic Yiddish, the contrast of *er-!vet-ˈgey-n* 'he *will* go', for example, is with the same principal verb in another tense (e.g. after a question such as "Did he go?"). The contrastive morpheme is *not* applied to the auxiliary verb to stress the affirmativeness of the statement in response to an expected negative one (as in English: "Won't he go?" "He *will* go"). Affirmativeness in Yiddish is produced by a special word, *yo* (*er-vet-ˈyo geyn*).[35]

5.42. A second group of unstressed morphemes, if subjected to stress, produces a hypostatic effect. Hypostasis is the reference to a linguistic sign rather than the use of that sign for its extra-linguistic reference. For example, in the expression *I don't like all those buts*, *but* is used hypostatically.[36] This stress takes the place, as it were, of vocal quotation marks. In *kh-hob-im-ge-ˈze-n* 'I saw him', for instance, the stressing of *ge* would only take place if one were correcting a child or a student of the language who had in some way mispronounced or omitted that morpheme, or if one were trying to assert that one had not just mispronounced it oneself. The significant point here is that no contrast with anything

[34] In the case of some unstressed morphemes, contrastive stressing is usually or invariably accompanied by other phenomena, such as order transposition; cf. *ˈdank-mir-nit* 'don't thank me' with *ˈdank-nit-!mir* 'don't thank *me!*'. **ˈDank-!mir-nit* is impossible except with a hypostatic effect (see §5.42).

[35] The contrastive stressing of the auxiliary verb as a sign of positive affirmation in American Yiddish appears to be the result of the interference of the English system.

[36] See Bloomfield, *op. cit.*, p. 148; Wells, *op. cit.*, p. 110.

else can be effected by stressing such a morpheme, and only an echo of a previous version of the same text results. Thus, to stress *zikh* in *er-'frey-t-zikh* 'he is glad' does not produce contrast with anything, only a possible echo.[37]

In a transcription which reflects an accurate analysis of stress functions, it is desirable to distinguish unstressed morphemes which are subject to contrastive stress from those which are not. In the remaining remarks of this chapter and the sample text, italics will be used for stressed morphemes and unstressed ones capable of carrying contrastive stress, while roman script will be used for unstressed morphemes which are not stressable for contrast, only for hypostasis.[38]

5.43. There exist in Yiddish pairs of otherwise homophonous morphemes of which the stressed member (a phonic word) has a meaning different from that of the unstressed member (not a phonic word). Thus, *far mir* = ['far 'mir] means 'before me (with respect to time)', while *far-'mir* = [far 'mir] means 'for me'; similarly, *íber der-'tsol* 'above of the number', but *íber-der-'tsol* 'because of the number'; *er-'vil alts léyen*-en 'he wants to read everything', but *er-'vil-alts léyen*-en 'he constantly wants to read'; *nor er 'ken-nit* 'only he can't', but *nor-er-'ken-nit* 'but he can't; *nokh*-n *nómen* 'after the name', but *nokh*-n-*'nómen* 'according to the name'; *der rov* 'this rabbi', but *der-'rov* 'the rabbi';[39] *ven ikh-'kum 'veyn*-t-*zi* 'whenever I come she cries', but *ven-ikh-'kum 'veyn*-t-*zi* 'when I come, she cries'.[40]

The application of contrastive stress to the unstressed member of any of these pairs is a highly delicate matter and can only take place in a context in which it is clear that it is not the regular meaning of the stressed member of the pair that is intended. A distinction corresponding to that between English "*the* expert" and "this expert," for example, is difficult to make in Yiddish, since 'the expert' is *der-'múmkhe*, 'this expert' is *der múmkhe*, while '*the* expert' would be *!der-'múmkhe* = *der múmkhe*. The context must identify the intended meaning; for example, in ['der 'mumxe, 'nit 'jener 'mumxe] 'this expert, not that expert' we have the demonstrative; in ['der 'mumxe, 'nit 'a 'mumxe] '*the* expert, not *an* expert' we have the definite article with contrastive stress.

To identify unstressed morphemes which have stressed homophones with different meanings, and which can therefore receive contrastive stress only in highly specialized contexts, we will transcribe them with a preceding °, thus: *°far-'mir* 'for me'; *fargés °on-'mir* 'forget me' (because *fargés on mir* would mean 'forget without me').

[37] For this reason, *freyen-zikh* might be classified as a "medial" verb in Yiddish, distinct from true reflexives like *vashn-zikh*, where *zikh* can be stressed for contrast: *er-'vash-t-!zikh* 'he washes himself (not the baby . . .)'.

[38] Contrast can occasionally be applied even to less than a morpheme: *!pa-ríz* 'Paris (not Poris. . .)'.

[39] In his analysis of German, Moulton (*op. cit.*, p. 215) makes a similar finding; but the details differ. Moulton contrasts /ʔain'flus/ *ein Fluss* 'a river', bearing no (or "weak") stress on *ein*, with /ˌʔain'flus/ 'one river', bearing secondary stress on *ein*. In my opinion, in the second example *ein* should be marked with the same stress as *Fluss*. Any difference in loudness—even in German, and certainly in the comparable cases in Yiddish—is, I believe, a concomitant of the intonational curve and has no functional value; cf. footnote 31.

[40] A Yiddish-influenced speaker of English has been heard to say: *Whén you cóme, she mákes it*, meaning 'whenever you come . . .'.

5.5. Purely "expressive" stress seems to be a separate function which together with stretching, special pitch contours, and other voice modifications can be classed as voice gestures. For example, [erhotimderˈlangt ˈˈa: ˈˈz:ets] 'he hit him' (more literally 'he let him have a blow') is an utterance in which the stress and lengthening hint at the strength of the blow in an extra-linguistic way.

5.6. Certain texts whose structure is equivocal if the stress is not indicated become unambiguous as soon as the stress is made explicit. Thus, in *af*-n-*ˈfront* *⌝vaks*-n-*ˈtsu °di-ˈshtivl tsu-°di-ˈfis* means 'at the front, one's boots grow (*⌝vaks*-n-*ˈtsu*) to one's feet', while the same sequence of morphemes stressed as follows: *af*-n-*ˈfront ⌝vaks*-n *tsu-°di-ˈshtivl ˈtsu °di-ˈfis* means 'at the front one's feet grow (*⌝vaks*-n . . . *ˈtsu*) to one's boots' (with a so-called extended two-peak word; see §5.121).[41]

5.61. While the subtleties of stress make possible a great many variations in the meaning of a text, some writers have tended to exaggerate its distinctive value for certain constructions which, as a matter of fact, remain ambiguous even when the stress is considered. Zaretski (*op. cit.*, p. 286) cites the newspaper headline *tsu fil erd vert opgenumen* 'excessive (amounts of) land are seized'. This could imply that (1) 'less land should be seized' or, as intended, that (2) 'surplus of land is seized from those who have too much'. Zaretski is wrong in thinking that the two meanings are distinguished by the place of the "logical stress" on *erd* in (1) and on *opgenumen* in (2). Without the context no manipulation of stress could produce the distinction.

An interesting case is the quadruply ambiguous text *zi shikt im nokh kozakn.*[42] Only one half of the ambiguity is resolved by the alternative stressing, for *zi-ˈshik*-t-*im nokh kozák*-n still means either 'she sends him more cossacks' or 'she sends cossacks after him', while *zi-ˈshik*-t-*im °nokh-ˈkozák*-n still means either 'she sends him after cossacks' or 'to top it off (*nokh*), she sends him cossacks.'[43]

Text

6. By way of summary of the principles discussed, we present a text with "normal" stressing. The bracketed lines show a phonemic transcription with loudness indicated in three degrees, unanalyzed as to their function: [ˈ, ˌ], and no mark; spaces stand for morpheme boundaries. The other lines represent the text analyzed in terms of phonic words and the functions of stress.

[ˈxotš ˈsender iz kejn ˈgrojs er ˈtsadik nit ge ˈven hot er fun ˈdest vegn ˈmojre ge
khotsh sénder iz-keyn-ˈgroys-er *tsádik nit*-ge-*ˈven hot-er*-fun-*ˈdest*-vegn *ˈmóyre*=ge-

[ˌhat far ˈgot, ge ˈtsiter t far ˈdem vos ˈzits t ˌergets in di far ˈrejx er t e ˈhiml]
ˌhat °far-ˈgot, ge-*ˈtsíter*-t *°far-ˈdem °vos-ˈzits*-t *érgets in-°di*-far-*ˈreykh*-er-t-e *ˈhiml*-

[41] E. Falkovitsh: *Yidish; fonetik, grafik, leksik, gramatik*, Moscow, 1940, 384 pp., pp. 293f.

[42] After Y. L. Peretz: "An opkumenish" (see e.g. *Ale verk*, New York, 1947, vol. 5, p. 99), where the sentence is *zi shikt im nokh di kozaklekh*, and the second of the possible meanings is intended. Incidentally, in German only the second meaning is possible.

[43] Concerning the problem of ambiguous constructions, see Hockett, *op. cit.*, p. 219.

[en ˌvelx e ˈšprejt n zix ˌiber der ˈjid iš er ˈgegnt in ˈvarše].
en °*velkh*-e-ˈ*shpreyt*-n-*zikh íber* °*der*-ˈ*yid*-ish-er *gegnt in*-ˈ*várshe.*[44]

Research Problems

7.1. We have shown the possibility (§5.12) of defining phonic words as sequences of morphemes in fixed stress relations to each other (with the proviso of §5.121 concerning "sequences") and have shown how the vagueness of phonetic junctures and positions of facultative pause acts as a limitation on this definition (§§5.1 and 5.11). Among the research tasks which emerge from the preceding discussion are the following:

1. Further testing of the manifestations of stress to confirm the functions elicited and to examine in detail the adjustments in the conflicts of functions.
2. Comparison of phonic words as defined in §5.12 with orthographic conventions of hyphenation and separation.
3. Investigation of the origins of the Yiddish stress patterns and of the integration of elements of heterogeneous origin in a unified stress system.
4. Study of dialect differences in the functions of stress as such and in the utilization of this or that function for specific grammatical purposes.[45]
5. Detailed analysis of the recent interference of English, Spanish, spoken Hebrew, and other foreign stress patterns with Yiddish and vice versa.[46]
6. Study of prose rhythm, which is meaningless without a full analysis of the functions and manifestations of stress.
7. In the analysis of metric verse, a correlation between the phonic word and the colon, and a detailed examination of the conflicts between metric and linguistic (functional) stress, especially of "secondary" stresses, and the resolution of these conflicts in the poetics of Yiddish literature of various periods.

7.2. One major research problem concerns the correspondence between phonic words, defined in terms of stress and possibly juncture (see §5.1), and words defined grammatically, semantically, or otherwise. It has been asserted repeatedly, on a general basis as well as with reference to specific languages, that the word as a phonic category and as a grammatical category (not to speak of semantic criteria) do not always coincide.[47] The same has been stated about Yiddish.[48] But the detailed analysis of the congruence and non-congruence of

[44] "Although Sender was no great saint, he nevertheless feared God; he trembled before Him who sits somewhere in the smoky skies which spread over the Jewish quarter of Warsaw." From Y. Y. Zinger: "Sender Prager," in his *Dertseylungen*, New York, 1949, p. 119.

[45] For example, in Central Yiddish prepositions combined with personal pronouns into phonic words bear the stress on the preposition (ˈ*mit-n* 'with him'), while in the other dialects it is the pronoun which bears the stress (*mit*-ˈ*em, mit*-ˈ*im*).

[46] Cf. Uriel Weinreich: *Languages in Contact*, New York, 1953, pp. 38f.

[47] For a general linguistic discussion, see A. W. de Groot: "Wort und Wortstruktur," *Neophilologus* 24 (1938–39) 221–233; for English, see Smith and Trager (*op. cit.*, p. 59), where *taker* is given as an example of a phonemic word which is also a morphemic word, while *take 'er* (*take her*) is cited as a phonemic word which is a morphemic phrase; and so forth.

[48] Zaretski, *op. cit.*, 283: "The grammatical division of speech [operates with] phrase, *baheft* ['joining', after Russian *slovosočetanije*], word, morpheme; phonetically speech is

phonic and grammatical words in Yiddish has not yet been made, and we are not prepared to make it here because a satisfactory definition of a grammatical word in Yiddish is not yet available.

The Search for Grammatical Words

8. The majority of works on Yiddish grammar have taken the grammatical word for granted and have passed over the problem of its definition in silence. A number of writers did acknowledge the existence of the problem but felt nevertheless that orthographic rules for hyphenation and separation, with which they were concerned, could be better formulated on a basis other than strictly grammatical analysis.[49] Some scholars have wondered whether the word ought not for purposes of scientific description be abandoned altogether. Several grammarians, however, did make attempts at exhaustive definitions; unfortunately, they did not, in this writer's opinion, succeed.

As far as this author knows, every published attempt, both prior and subsequent to the period of research covered here, of a rigorous universal definition of the grammatical word, to hold good for all languages, has been shown to be untenable.[50] Since there is no general prescription which can be applied, ready-made, to the special case of Yiddish, the work has to continue to revolve about the Yiddish material proper.

The existing analyses of a related and grammatically similar language, Standard German, are not of an impressive completeness or validity, and do not seem to merit adoption (see §12), even though the German and Yiddish patterns show

---

divided differently: phrases . . ., *shtiker* ['pieces'] . . ., measures . . ., syllables . . ., sounds." " 'Measure' and 'word' do not coincide" (p. 287).

[49] It has been stated, for example, that "a classification [of the various types of compounds] had better not be transferred from grammar into orthography" (Max Weinreich, [Proposal for a Unified Yiddish Spelling], *Der eynheytlekher yidisher oysleyg; materyaln tsu der ortografisher konferents fun Yivo*, Vilna, 1930, 22–65, §214). Even two scholars who did attempt definitions of the word—A. Zaretski (*op. cit.*, p. 14) and N. Guralnik (*op. cit.* [footnote 27], p. 159)—admitted that the orthography cannot be based on a rigorous grammatical definition. The now standard ("Yivo") spelling rules handle the problem of compounding in a way which is admittedly independent of a grammatical definition of the word; cf. Max Weinreich, [What Is the Matter with Yiddish Spelling?], *Yidishe shprakh* 9 (1949) 1–21, p. 17. On the other hand, some critics of the standard orthography have urged that the spelling be changed to reflect the grammatical definition of compounds (see Yudel Mark, [Notes on the Spelling Rules], *Yidishe shprakh* 7 [1947] 1–29, p. 18 and passim). Zaretski, in his later works, also argued that "syntax should serve . . . the orthography (e.g. in regard to word boundaries)" ([On the Syntax of Soviet Yiddish], *Afn shprakhfront, zamlung* no. 3–4, Kiev, 1935, 170–191, p. 187).

[50] For example, in the recent effort by Knud Togeby: "Qu'est-ce qu'un mot?" (*Travaux du Cercle linguistique de Copenhague* 5 [1949], 97–111) a number of loopholes were discovered by A. Nehring, *Word* 9 (1952), 164. Another reviewer of the same study (Rulon Wells in *Language* 27 [1951], 569) voiced his skepticism as to the possibility of a universal definition. Recent research by Joseph H. Greenberg ("The Word as a Linguistic Unit," in *Psycholinguistics: a Survey of Theory and Research Problems*, Indiana University Publications in Anthropology and Linguistics, Memoir number 10, 1954, pp. 66–71) deals with this problem in the affirmative; while I have profited greatly from discussions with Greenberg, I cannot judge the universal validity of his results. The literature until 1947 is reviewed in A. Rosetti: *Le mot; esquisse d'une théorie générale*, Copenhagen–Bucharest, 1947.

sufficient prima facie resemblance to justify the consideration of transferring the analysis from the one language to the other.

In delimiting the word grammatically, there are easy and difficult cases. It is generally agreed that in the "easy" instances, at least, a rigorous scientific definition of the word should yield items which are words in the layman's intuitive or conventional conception, too. The problem amounts to determining the criteria by which words are defined in the unequivocal cases and applying those criteria systematically and consistently to the difficult cases. If linguistic analysis should be unable to improve upon the layman's conception, i.e. if the difficult cases should have to be analyzed in an arbitrary way, then the grammatical word in Yiddish would be without scientific status and would remain a concept of folk linguistics.

Zaretski's Word as a Mobile Unit

9. A bold attempt to define the grammatical word by criteria of mobility was offered by the outstanding linguist A. Zaretski.[51] His definition runs as follows: "A word is a part of speech which can be separated [*opraysn*] from the surrounding parts and cannot itself be divided [*tseraysn*]. If it can be divided, it is more than a word; if it cannot be separated, it is less than a word. 'Dividing' means transposing the parts or interposing other words[52] between them."

It should be noted that at the point where this definition is introduced in the grammar, Zaretski has not yet defined the morpheme. He proceeds from larger units ("phrase") to smaller ones, and the word is the result of his breaking up the "phrase." Therefore, in the illustration of his definition, Zaretski shows the non-divisibility both of *fun* (a single morpheme) and of *brisk-er* ('of Brest-Litovsk'; two morphemes but one word). Separability in the sequence *funbriskerov . . . hotiravadegehert*[53] ('you have certainly heard of the rabbi of Brest-

[51] *Op. cit.*, p. 13. Zaretski claims to have adopted his definition essentially from A. M Peškovskij, referring to his article [The Concept of the Separateness of the Word] in *Sbornik statjej* (Leningrad, 1925, pp. 130ff.) and to his pertinent articles, [Word] and [Word, Separate], in the two-volume *Literaturnaja entsiklopedija* of 1925 (see footnote 28). In the 1930's, under the pressure of Marrist "anti-formalist" linguistic dogma in the Soviet Union, Zaretski repented for "operating . . . with the concept 'word,' which has not been thoroughly examined critically (and which in the last analysis is based on orthography)"—see his own article, [Against Formal Grammar], *Ratn-bildung* 1931, no. 7–8, p. 54. Later he proclaimed that the word was "not a central concept of syntax" ([On the Syntax of Soviet Yiddish], cited in footnote 49, p. 188) and that to consider "the word—a formal category" as a central concept of syntax "was absurd" ([Grammatical Classes], *Fragn fun yidisher shprakh* (see footnote 27), 156–187, p. 187). Although he did retain the view that the word is an essential unit in the analysis of order ([On the Syntax . . .], p. 190) he never returned to the problems of its identification. Today the tables have again been turned; according to Smirnitskij, writing in 1952 (see footnote 57), the word is again "the central, crucial unit of language in general" (p. 183). Alas, there is no more Soviet Yiddish linguistics to profit from the new course; since 1949 all scholarly publication in or about Yiddish has been suppressed in the Soviet Union.

[52] "Segments of speech," or any simple expression other than "words," would have avoided an unnecessary and merely superficial circularity in the definition.

[53] The beginning sentence of "Tsvishn tsvey berg" ('Between Two Mountains'), a famous story by Y. L. Peretz (see e.g. his *Ale verk*, New York, 1947, vol. 4, pp. 103–117).

Litovsk') is shown by interpositions, for example: *fun|dem|briskerov, funbrisker|groysn|rov*, etc. A difficulty arises with the sequence . . . *hotir* . . ., for in Yiddish a pronoun subject, if it follows the finite verb, must come immediately after it. Here separability is proved by transposition: *ir hot* is also possible—hence *hot|ir* is two words.

9.1. Upon close examination, Zaretski's definition turns out to be practically unworkable as well as theoretically unsuited to the structure of Yiddish. Let us show first that it does not work in practice and then (§9.2) discuss its theoretical unsuitedness to the language.

We may be permitted to simplify the problem by assuming that the morpheme is defined *before* the word;[54] thus the question of a word boundary at the bar in *fu|nbriskerov* would not arise, because no morpheme boundary exists there. The question should be put thus: which morpheme boundaries are also word boundaries?

If the sign of a word boundary is to be the possibility of interposing additional material, then one type of interposition would have be to ruled out from the start. Consider this example: At the vertical bar in *ikh hob ge|zen* 'I saw', one might interpose the sequence . . . *hert ober nit ge* . . . to yield *ikh hob ge|hert ober nit ge|zen* 'I heard but did not see'. What is characteristic of this interposed stretch is that it ends in the same morpheme as that which preceded the vertical bar (*ge*) and begins with a morpheme of the same class as the morpheme which followed the bar (*her, ze:* verb stems). This type of interposition is possible at every morpheme boundary (except near so-called "unique constituents," such as *bilkh* in *bilkh-er* 'preferable', or *mage-* in *mage-ˈmase* 'business, intercourse', which do not occur alone or in any other combination) and would obliterate the difference between word and morpheme. A definition based on separability must therefore be qualified as follows: ". . . except that a boundary between morphemes *p* and *q* is not a word boundary if the only texts which can be interposed are those which begin with a morpheme of the same class as *q* and end with a morpheme of the same class as *p*."[55]

We must also decide that we are looking for boundaries in a specific text,[56] not for a finding of whether *X* is a word in the language generally.[57] Otherwise

[54] Nothing in Zaretski's definition of a morpheme (*Gramatik*, p. 15) requires that the word be previously completely defined. We are speaking, of course, of the morpheme as a syntagmatic unit, for which the term "morph" is often used (cf. Charles F. Hockett: "Problems of Morphemic Analysis," *Language* 23 [1947] 321–343, p. 322).

[55] I am indebted for this formulation to Joseph H. Greenberg (see footnote 50), who uses a somewhat different terminology in the framework of his general theory of the word.

[56] "Text" in this paper refers primarily to spoken texts. We expect, of course, that the boundaries will be found not merely in a single utterance of the text, but every time the text is pronounced.

[57] The definition of the word has a syntagmatic and a paradigmatic aspect. The syntagmatic problem concerns the delimitation of words as "concrete entities" in the spoken chain, and it is with this that we are concerned here; the paradigmatic problem deals with the grouping of the delimited concrete entities into classes, e.g. the assignment of all occurrences of *drive* and all those of *drives, drove, driven, driving* into a single class (word as an "abstract entity"). Concerning this theoretical distinction, see Ferdinand de Saussure: *Cours de linguistique générale*, Paris, $_4$1949, pp. 146–149, 189–192; A. M. Peškovskij: "Slovo"

contradictions will result. For example, in analyzing *er|shpil-t|fidl* 'he plays the violin', we want to have a boundary before *|shpil*, but in *er|ho-t|ge-shpil-t|fidl* 'he played the violin', we do not want a word boundary to precede *shpil*. Now, "is" *shpil* a separate word in Yiddish? Clearly, the problem must be stated syntagmatically and the answer can be valid only for a given text, although we might find units which are always separate words in all texts (e.g. *oder* 'or'), some which are words only in some texts (e.g. *shpil*, *fidl*), and some which are never words (e.g. *-t*).[58]

Even thus amended, however, Zaretski's definition still breaks down in practice. Consider four cases.

1. At the bar in *ikh es di royt|e karshn* 'I am eating the red cherries', one of the following morphemes may be interposed: *-er-* (comparative), *-st-* (superlative), *-lekh-* ("attenuative": 'reddish'), *-ink-* or *-itshk-* (endearing). Similarly, at the bar in *dos kind vil shlof|n* 'the child wants to sleep', a morpheme signifying endearment, *-ele-* or *-inke-*, may be introduced (*shlof-inke-n*, *shlof-ele-n*). At the bar in *ikh heyb on op|etem-en* 'I am beginning to catch my breath', the morpheme *tsu* may be inserted as a matter of free or dialectal variation.[59] The possibility of these interpositions must be excluded lest the same suffix appear as a separate word with some adjectives or infinitives and not as a word with others (where these interpositions happen to be impossible).

The qualification needed to rule out these cases could be either specific or general in form. Specifically, it might run thus: "... except that the morpheme boundary between an adjective stem and the inflectional suffix or between a verb stem and the infinitive suffix is not a word boundary." This specific form, though it has the defect of implying a previous grammatical classification of morphemes, does sum up the data satisfactorily, but gives the appearance of an extravagantly arbitrary statement. A more general form would be: "... except

---

('Word') in *Literaturnaja entsiklopedija* (see footnote 28), p. 823; V. V. Vinogradov: [On the Forms of the Word], *Izvestija Akademii Nauk S. S. S. R., Otdelenije literatury i jazyka* 3 (1944) 31–44; and the most extensive recent discussion by A. I. Smirnitskij: [On the Question of the Word; the Problem of the "Separateness of the Word"], in *Voprosy teorii i istorii jazyka v svete trudov I. V. Stalina po jazykozaniju*, Moscow, 1952, pp. 182–203.

[58] In his later works, Zaretski himself became aware of the necessity of distinguishing the syntagmatic from the paradigmatic problem; in his paper on grammatical classes (see footnote 51) he introduces the term "vocable" (*vokabl*) for a paradigmatic family of word occurrences (p. 160). Guralnik (*op. cit.*, p. 154) also distinguishes a "word as a type" from "a word as a segment of an utterance." However, since Zaretski never returned to the problem of the word, he did not elaborate on the consequences of this limitation.

[59] Two more marginal cases might be listed in this category. (1) In complemented "strong" verbs whose past-participle stem happens to be identical with the infinitive stem (e.g. *shlof-*, *grob-* 'to dig'), the possibility of using either the past participle or the infinitive in conditional clauses allows an "optional" interposition of the morpheme *ge*: *ikh volt oys(ge)grobn* 'I would dig up'. (2) In the possessive form of singular nouns, there is room for the interposition of a plural suffix: *kind(er)s* 'child(ren)'s', *froy(en)s* 'woman's—women's'; yet it is difficult to think of a concrete context where both the singular and the plural possessive can occur. In *tish-lekh* 'tables (diminutive)', as contrasted with *tish-ele-kh* 'id. (endearing)', we have a different arrangement of morphemes rather than the interposition of an *-e-*.

that the possibility of interposing one specific morpheme (e.g. *-ele-*) or a morpheme of one specific small class (e.g. the class composed of *-er-*, *-st-*, *-lekh-*, *-ink-/-itshk-*) does not constitute a word boundary." The latter, general form of the qualification sounds better theoretically,[60] provided it is not too roundabout a statement of a rather simple point. But although there are several practical ways of qualifying Zaretski's definition to exclude these interpositions, the theoretical objections to the definition (§9.2) would still remain.

2. At the bar in *do farkoyft men zumer|mantlen* 'summer coats are sold here', which should not in Yiddish be a word boundary, sequences like the following may be inserted: *oder vinter* 'or winter', *un vinter* 'and winter', *ober nit vinter* 'but not winter', *vinter un friling* 'winter and spring', *hit un* 'hats and', *hit nit* 'hats, not'. In terms of traditional grammar, we are dealing here with compounds in which one of the elements is itself a coordinated series of nouns (see §4.63). This type of interposition should be disqualified as a word boundary signal, else no noun compounds could be single words. Again, the qualification might take a specific or a general form, each involving the methodological advantages and disadvantages discussed under (1) above. The specific form would be: "... except that the possibility of interposing one or more nouns in a coordinate construction with a noun at the morpheme boundary (i.e. governed by the conjunctions *un*, *oder*, *ober*, and/or *nit*) does not constitute a word boundary." The general form would replace "nouns" by "... base morphemes (with their suffixes) parallel in construction to one of the base morphemes (with its suffixes) at the boundary." Again neither makeshift solution would invalidate the theoretical objections of §9.2.

3. We revert now to the curious case of *hotir*. Let us take the example *itst voyn|ikh do* 'now I live here', where nothing can be interposed at the bar. And yet Yiddish orthography as well as some hard-to-define *Sprachgefühl* militates for a word boundary at this point. Zaretski himself got around the difficulty by saying that the verb and pronoun can be transposed to *ir hot*. But, in fact, in any concrete text in which *hot ir* or *voyn ikh* occurs, the transposed forms, *ir hot* and *ikh voyn*, CANNOT appear.[61] Therefore the test of transposability is ruled out by the qualification already introduced into the definition on pp. 19–20 above, that only one concrete text be considered at a time. This leads to a dilemma for which I could find no practical solution; but as is shown in §9.2, the entire question should be reformulated.

4. We face a rather similar paradox in the next case, *af|ot-o|dem bild* 'on this picture'. At the first bar, nothing can be interposed.[62] This would indicate that *af* is part of the same word as that which follows. But in slightly different con-

[60] It is along these lines that André Martinet proposes to rule out the separability of French *dorm-ons* by *-i-* (Sixth International Congress of Linguists, 1948, *Proceedings*, Paris, 1949, p. 293).

[61] This is due to the fact that only one "unit" can precede the finite verb in a Yiddish sentence. If the first sentence position were occupied by some other element, the subject pronoun could not precede the verb. For a brief exposition in English of Yiddish word order, see Uriel Weinreich: *College Yiddish*, New York, $_2$1953, p. 330.

[62] Elements like *nor* 'only', according to my feeling, should precede *af*.

texts, e.g. *af|dem bild*, there are possibilities of interposition (*af ot dem bild, af grod dem bild* 'on precisely this picture', etc.), and *af* there—though apparently in an identical syntactic function—would be a separate word. Again a practical solution does not seem feasible, but the problem itself is improperly put (see §9.2).

9.2. There are weighty theoretical objections to Zaretski's definition which result from the facts of Yiddish structure as even Zaretski himself described them, and which invalidate not only his definition but also the qualifications suggested in §9.1 to plug the loopholes.

Yiddish "word" order is admittedly not free. It is rather strictly organized in terms of "positions" and the units which may fill the several positions. The following facts are pertinent:[63]

1. Order is not organized on a single, "flat" level, in such a way that the order of the ultimate constituents—the morphemes—is determined in the framework of the highest structure—the sentence. Rather, there is a hierarchy of levels *sui generis*. The clause contains a number of positions which may be filled by certain units.[64] These units may themselves be of a certain complexity and may contain subunits (again in a prescribed order), but for describing the clause, the internal makeup of its constituent units of order is irrelevant. For example, one position in the clause is reserved for the unit "finite verb." Within this unit, morphemes must appear in the order: (prefix) + stem + (personal suffix), but on the clause level this internal order is irrelevant because the "finite verb" can be moved to other positions only as a whole, never piecemeal. Other "units" capable of occupying "positions" in the clause are "noun constructions," "personal pronouns," the negative element *nit*, and so forth. While "noun constructions" allow for numerous subunits (also in a determined order), "personal pronouns" do not. On the clause level, this difference is immaterial because a "noun construction" and a "personal pronoun" can each occupy approximately the same position. Yet for the problem of interposing new material, this difference becomes essential.

2. In certain parts of the clause, the number of positions is restricted, while in others the number and order of units is grammatically free. The end of the restricted series of positions is, in many clauses, marked by the last pronoun which has a direct relation to the verb (i.e. which is not governed by a preposition). Thus, in *nekhtn | hot | er | mikh | in klas | umgerikht | farvorfn | mit shayles* 'yesterday he unexpectedly pelted me with questions in class', the units after

[63] For a fuller account than that in *College Yiddish* (see footnote 61), see Zaretski, *Gramatik*, 230–245; Yudel Mark: [The Place of the Inflected Verb in the Sentence], *Yidishe shprakh* 6 (1946) 1–15; *idem*, [Word Order in a Simple Sentence], *ibid.*, 6 (1946) 84–105. A number of complicated problems of Yiddish order have not yet been descriptively solved.

[64] It would be interesting to explore the difference between the units of order and the "immediate constituents" (ICs) postulated by general grammar; cf. Rulon S. Wells' paper cited in footnote 8. They are certainly not identical. The immediate constituents of a Yiddish clause are often the subject group and the predicate group, while its chief order units are rather the finite verb as against everything else. But this problem is beyond the scope of the present paper.

mikh are more or less freely transposable (only a shift of emphasis would result); also, more units could be added there. Up to *mikh*, only certain transpositions are possible (*er hot mikh nekhtn . . .*, *mikh hot er nekhtn . . .*), while *nekhtn hot* cannot, in the sample text, be transposed or separated by additional clause-level units.

3. Finally, if we undertook a "reduction" of Yiddish order from the sentence through units and subunits of an ever lower level until we reached the morpheme, no level would reveal any kind of break which would require us to postulate "words." For example, in analyzing the clause-level unit "finite verb" into its subunits of order (see above), we are already on the morpheme (sub-word) level; but in analyzing a prepositional phrase like that in example 4 of §9.1, we deal with "words" like *af*, *ot-o*, *dem*, and *bild* as the immediate subunits of order in the clause.[65]

The facts of Yiddish structure being what they are, a text can be viewed as a series of units-of-order filling a restricted number of positions. Hence the possibility of interposing additional stretches of text must be viewed in the light of the question: What position are they to fill? And because of the fact that not all positions and not all units are alike in flexibility and complexity, the possibilities of interposing material will differ according to the circumstances. We must ask every time into what position and at what level of order the material is to be introduced.

In the sentence *der* ¦ *lerer* $|_1$ *shraybt* $|_2$ *afn* ¦ *tovl* 'the teacher writes on the blackboard', we can interpose additional material at several places, but note the different conditions. At unit boundary $|_2$, some material that could be inserted would constitute a new unit, or several units, on the highest level—that of the clause itself: *der lerer* $|_1$ *shraybt* $|_2$ *keseyder* | *mit krayd* | *far di kinder* $|_2$ *afn tovl* '. . . continuously in chalk for the children'. Other kinds of interpositions would make new subunits within the last existing unit: . . .$|_2$ *nor* ¦ *afn* ¦ *tovl* 'only on the blackboard', . . .$|_2$ *davke* ¦ *afn* ¦ *groysn* ¦ *tovl* 'on the large blackboard and none other', etc.; similarly within the first clause-level unit: *der* ¦ *khóshever* ¦ *lerer* $|_1$ 'the respected teacher', and the like. The dotted bar ¦, it is evident, is not the boundary of a unit on the clause level, but of a subunit within the clause-level unit. At clause-position boundary $|_1$ no new units can enter at the clause level in the way that they were interposed at $|_2$; this means that only such material can be interposed there as can be made a part of the existing clause-level units. The only thing by which the second unit could be expanded would be a prefix, e.g. $|_1$ *far-shraybt* $|_2$. All other material which is interposed there must become part of the preceding clause-level unit; the possibilities include an appositional noun

[65] Some scholars feel that the constructions of morphemes into words, in some languages at least, are recognizably "different in kind" from the constructions of words into larger units; thus, for Japanese, Bernard Bloch, *op. cit.* (see footnote 28), p. 208: states "We regard the analysis of the sentence . . . as complete when further analysis would reveal only constructions different in kind from all constructions established up to that point. An element that emerges from the analysis as an ultimate constituent is typically a word." In the case of Yiddish, I could find no such recognizable difference that could be stated in a general way, i.e. a way other than a listing of all the infra-word and supra-word constructions which occur.

(*der lerer Kaplan*), a prepositional construction (*der lerer fun der shul*), a possessive (*der lerer dayner*), a relative clause (*der lerer vos voynt bay undz*), etc. But all of these stand in a determined syntactic relation and in a fixed order position as subunits within the first clause-level unit.

It should be clear by now that we cannot test separability at certain morpheme boundaries by working with unanalyzed "raw" sentences taken as strings of morphemes. The hierarchy of order units has to be considered. And since the units of the clause and their subunits in turn show dissimilar internal organization, it is impossible to devise a definition of grammatical words or a test of separability that would in essence be anything but an additive summary of the types of units and subunits which occur. A "word" so defined would be aposterioric; it could not be derived from syntagmatic analysis. Zaretski's attempt did not just break down at the case of *hotir*, which is a limiting instance of the restrictions of word order, but was doomed from the beginning. A unit "word" definable in terms of mobility alone does not exist in Yiddish.

Falkovitsh's Word as a Grammatical-Semantic Unit

10.1. One other writer to deal with the problem has been E. Falkovitsh. In his earlier works[66] he was concerned with practical pedagogical problems, yet he worked with at least an implicit definition of the word when he tried to give a grammatical justification for the rules of hyphenating and separating. Falkovitsh's criteria are mixed. On a semantic basis he first distinguishes between affixes (which have "formal meaning") and roots (which have "material meaning"). Implied is the view (pp. 20f.) that a word is a root with its pertinent affixes (if any). But he also introduces the formal tests of separability and transposability which he may have adopted from Zaretski. "That which can be separated or transposed in the phrase is not a prefix or a suffix [but a separate word] and is [therefore] to be written separately" (p. 27). When he comes to the problem of the subject pronoun which is inseparable from the preceding verb (faced by Zaretski in the case of *hot ir*), he determines the existence of a word boundary in two ways: (a) by the possibility of transposition, suggested by Zaretski; (b) by the possibility of commutation: *bet er* 'so he asks' (like *hot ir*) contains a word boundary because you can have *bet zi* 'so she asks' (p. 28). That the transposability test is invalid has been shown on p. 21; the proposal of commutation is no improvement, since commutation can affect affixes, too (cf. *di shen*-er-*e meydlekh* 'the prettier girls'—*di shen*-st-*e meydlekh* 'the prettiest girls'). The possibilities of interposition are explored by Falkovitsh more fully than by his predecessor. For example, at the boundary in *ikh vel far | makhn di tir zikh nemen ersht morgn* 'I will set out to make the door only tomorrow', he admits that it is possible but "slightly unnatural" to interpose additional elements (e.g. *gut* 'well'; p. 29). And so, in order to define a word boundary at the bar (in contrast to the place of the bar in *ikh vel far|makhn di tir* 'I will close the door'), Falkovitsh urges that the meaning of *far* be considered, although he does not indicate in what way.

[66] See his *Gramatik far dervaksene*, vol. 1, Moscow, $_2$1930, 208 pp., esp. pp. 16–57.

10.2. In a later and more theoretically inclined work[67] Falkovitsh undertakes a slightly more refined treatment of the problem. He first separates, on a semantic basis, roots on one hand and affixes as well as "auxiliary words" on the other. Affixes and auxiliary words furnish "supplementary meanings" to those carried by the roots. But what distinguishes an auxiliary word from an affix is a formal characteristic: the former is a "movable part of speech; it can usually be separated and additional words can be inserted between it and the following words. But an affix cannot be separated; it is 'glued on' " (p. 63).

There are elements, according to Falkovitsh, which sometimes appear as auxiliary words, but which in other contexts lose the possibility of being separated from what follows, and are prefixed. There are prefixed prepositions: *far*, *in*, *bay* in *far-tog* 'at daybreak', *in-gantsn* 'entirely', *bay-nakht* 'at night'; prefixed articles: *a-ponim* 'apparently', *der-iker* 'principally'; both articles and prepositions: *iber-a-yor* 'next year', *fun-dos-nay* 'anew'; particles: (*arayn-*)*tsu-geyn* 'to enter'; *nit-guter* 'demon' (pp. 76f., 98; some auxiliary words which are not prefixes seem to be conjunctions and interjections). If it is occasionally difficult in practice to say whether an element is a separate (auxiliary) word or a prefix, it is because the transition to the prefixed state is a slow one and may still be in the process.

Falkovitsh's analysis contains several valuable contributions. He shows the dependence of the grammatical word on a prior definition of roots and affixes and cites a number of interesting instances of "ultimate inseparability" of morphemes. He is not to blame for the incompleteness of his work because in his system the syntagmatic problem of the separate word was not important (cf. Zaretski's more or less contemporary disclaimers of primary interest in the word cited in footnote 51). But there are many unsolved odds and ends. Roots and affixes are distinguished on rather shaky semantic grounds. The thorny question of *hot ir* is not considered. A word consisting of more than one root is called a compound (p. 66), but how it is distinguished from a sequence of two words is not made clear. Extensive tests of separability are not carried out, and the theoretical objections to a crude application of this test, as set forth in §9.2, remain unanswered.

Guralnik's "Marrist" Approach

11. Of the several definitions of the word in Yiddish which have been offered, the one which is least workable is by N. Guralnik. According to him, "a word is an operational unit of speech and hence the bearer of a syntactically limited real meaning or of a syntactically limited structural meaning, expressed by a sound or sequence of sounds which can be moved [*iz baveglekh*] without changing [its] meaning."[68] But Guralnik is not seriously concerned with the division of texts into words; on the contrary, he says that "one can analyze a text into words [in contrast to morphemes] without any special theoretical preparation" (p. 151) and allows for doubtful cases without limit (p. 153). He does not see the problem

[67] E. Falkovitsh: *Yidish* . . . (see footnote 41).

[68] N. Guralnik, *op. cit.* (see footnote 27), p. 153.

of the discrepancy between the layman's and the analyst's conception of the word (cf. editor Zaretski's note, p. 155); rather, he is interested in placing the word as a "well-known" concept into the framework of the Marrist doctrine (now defunct, but at that time obligatory in the Soviet Union) of the "stadial" development of languages. Hence, he does not test his definition on any concrete material, since all difficult cases are to him simply transitional (e.g. *in droysn* 'out of doors': one word or two?). Without knowing precisely what he means by "syntactically limited" or "operational unit," and especially without a clarification of what "can be moved," we are hardly enlightened by Guralnik's definition.

Lack of German Parallels

12. Traditional German grammars take the word for granted, except as an orthographic problem; this is true even of Curme's brilliant work. The Duden definition of a word as "a syllable or a sequence of syllables which arouses a certain image"[69] is obviously not what we are after. A modern, scientifically critical description like Hans Glinz's[70] is not helpful in defining a word as "the smallest unit of content or of meaning." The problem of German word definition has been considered by Walter Henzen (*op. cit.*, pp. 7–12). Henzen is well aware of the inadequacy of the usual definitions and adapts (pp. 10f.) a suggestion by A. Noreen that a word is an independent linguistic form which is considered in our linguistic feeling as a unit in respect to its sound and meaning, because one does not *wish* to decompose it into smaller forms.[71] Independence is specified as the ability to be inflected or to convey meaning even when detached (in contrast to affixes), and to be so movable as to be able to change positions in the sentence according to syntactic needs. Neither criterion seems any more adequate for rigorous analysis of Yiddish than of German itself. A prefix like *trans-*, a suffix like *-ele* seem to convey their meanings perfectly well even "unattached," while the difficulties of "movability" in a language of fixed order are insurmountable, as shown in §9.2.

A study by A. W. de Groot,[72] working largely with German illustrative material, distinguishes phonetic, phonological, semantic, syntactic, identificatory, and interpretational words, and convincingly shows their non-congruence, but since it is concerned mainly with the theoretical principles, it only scratches the descriptive surface of German.

The Outlook

13. At the present state of research, the work on a grammatical definition of the word should begin by concentrating on distinguishing between bases, affixes, and possibly additional large distributional classes of morphemes. It may be

[69] *Der grosse Duden; Grammatik der deutschen Sprache*, ed. Otto Basler, Swiss ed., Zurich, *s. a.*, p. 20.

[70] *Die innere Form des Deutschen; eine neue deutsche Grammatik*, Berne, 1952, p. 79.

[71] A. Noreen: *Einführung in die wissenschaftliche Betrachtung der Sprache*, transl. H. W. Pollak, Halle/S., 1923, p. 446.

[72] "Wort und Wortstruktur" (see footnote 47).

fruitful, for instance, to work with "clitics";[73] in a sequence like *di-ˈkhéyder-ying-l-ekh* 'the kheyder [traditional school] boys', *khéyder* and *ying* would be bases, *l* and *ekh* affixes (suffixes), and *di* a clitic (proclitic). The grammatical functioning of nearly homophonous pairs of morphemes whose meaning differs according to the stress (§5.43) might well be formulated in terms of clitics, affixes, and bases. The combinatorial possibilities (with reference to affixes and clitics) of noun bases, verb bases, adjective and other bases might be compared and stated in the most general terms possible as properties of the grammatical word.

When the broad grammatical classification of morphemes will have been carried out and the canonical types of morpheme sequences established, it will be a promising further task to describe them in terms of their stress and possible junctural properties. The role of stress in derivation and composition should be delineated and the substantial part played by stress (in conjunction with pitch) in Yiddish syntax should be detailed. The layman's intuitive conception of word peaks and boundaries might then be analyzed to see if it does not emerge most clearly where phonic, grammatical, and semantic word peaks and boundaries coincide.

[73] The term is due to Eugene Nida: *Morphology; the Descriptive Analysis of Words*, Ann Arbor, Mich., 1949, pp. 97, 106, 261.

A STUDY OF THE FREQUENCY OF HEBRAISMS IN YIDDISH: PRELIMINARY REPORT

YUDEL MARK (New York)

INTRODUCTION

By Hebraisms we mean all the Yiddish words and expressions that are derived from Hebrew or Aramaic. These two languages were not always and not definitely separated in the linguistic conception of the Jewish people: a more or less strongly Aramaicized Hebrew was treated as *loshn-koydesh* ('the holy language', although the original meaning is 'the language of holiness', 'the language of the Torah'). Hebraisms are the most conspicuous part of the *loshn-koydesh* element in Yiddish; the influence of *loshn-koydesh* on morphology and syntax is partially hidden, so that the superficial observer sometimes acquires the impression that the impact of *loshn-koydesh* on Yiddish is lexical only.

For the student of Yiddish, Hebraisms are a heavy burden. He has to learn separately how to read and write them, because they are spelled in their traditional way: almost without vowels, with letters not used in other Yiddish words (♮*b̄*, *x*, ˙*s*, *θ̇*, *θ*) and with specific applications of some letters (♮*ʔ*, *h*, *v*, *j*, *℘*).[1]

Since 1910, the teachers of Yiddish schools have struggled with the problem of how to teach the reading and writing of Hebraisms and—what is more important—which Hebraisms to teach. The existing graded lists of Hebraisms were compiled on a subjective basis, from the point of view of the simplicity of the spelling. In 1933, I. Steinbaum published[2] a list of Hebraisms based upon a frequency count; but this study included only 460,000 running words from a very limited sampling. Consequently, this list could not impress the teachers as a reliable source, and had no practical value. In 1938 I began a more ambitious project. After studying the frequency counts for English, German, French and Spanish and their critical evaluation, I drafted my plan for a quantitative study of Hebraisms of a wider scope (three million running words) and based on more diverse sources. Unfortunately I was able to complete this work only fifteen years after the plan was made. There were no special funds allotted for the project. During the first years I was assisted by a group of students from the Workmen's Circle Teachers' Courses and the Jewish Teachers' Seminary, and since 1948 my assistant, J. Noskowitz, has been working with me.[3] The long hiatus caused some defects in the study; for example, it reflects the language of the Yiddish press at the end of the thirties and beginning of the forties, but not the current language. On the other hand, this long period has given me a chance to work out the details with greater care.

[1] According to the transliteration system explained on p. vii.

[2] I. Shteynboym: [The Hebrew Element in Yiddish: Attempt at a Word Scale], *Yivo-bleter* 5 (1933) 304–320.

[3] Public acknowledgment is due the Jewish Education Committee of New York for encouraging the completion of this study by permitting me and my assistant to devote some of our working hours to it.

The results of the research cover various fields. The count was primarily undertaken in order to compile a reliable frequency list of Hebraisms for the teacher of Yiddish. The study, however, not only yielded important primary results, but also developed secondary findings which afford a detailed insight into the *loshn-koydesh* component of Yiddish. In order to avoid returning to the practical school aspect of the results of my study later on, I deem it necessary to emphasize here that the high frequency of the word is only *one* of the aspects to be taken into consideration in compiling word lists for the teachers. We must also be concerned with the function of the word in sentence construction, its range of meaning, and above all, the concept it expresses. Names of Jewish holidays, names of heroes of Jewish history, the most important biblical names as well as the names of very important objects connected with ceremonies, customs, and rituals have to be included in the teaching material, regardless of their frequency in this study. Still a frequency list is of great importance because it indicates the frequency of the Hebraisms which are devoid of emotional and historical function, such as *ponim* 'face', *afile* 'even', *efsher* 'perhaps', *yam* 'sea', and many others which should be taught only because of their high frequency.

Students of the theory of word frequency have observed that if the actual frequency of words is plotted against their frequency-rank (e.g., for a given text, most frequent—3500 times, 2nd most frequent—3450 times, 3rd most frequent—3280 times, etc.), a certain type of normal curve is obtained, but of all languages tested, Yiddish alone turned out to be an exception.[4] This finding has to be investigated further, and if it is verified, the explanation by Zipf that the alleged abnormality of Yiddish is due to the fusion character of the language should be checked. The word-frequency problems of Yiddish have a great interest for general lexicological theory, but the study of this aspect of Yiddish vocabulary requires specialized counts and we cannot go into it here.

The Sixty Groups

The three million running words[5] of Yiddish text were divided into sixty special groups. Each group consisted of fifty thousand words. The detailed description of each group would take up more space than was allotted to this report; the description is therefore given in a condensed form without regard to details. The sixty groups are:

1. Mendele Moykher-Sforim (every 12th page of his prose);
2. Y. L. Peretz (two different counts, as explained later);
3. Sholom Aleichem (every 24th page of his short stories and novels);
4. Sholem Asch (every 20th page of 10 volumes of the 1921 edition, plus the books *Varshe* and *Der thilim-yid*);

[4] George K. Zipf: *Human Behavior and the Principle of Least Effort*, Cambridge, Mass., 1949, pp. 120, 125f.; Benoit Mandelbrot: "Structure formelle des textes et communication," *Word* 10 (1954) 1–27, p. 25.

[5] According to the original plan of the study, the number of running words included should have been exactly three million. In practice, however, this was impossible to carry out. In many instances it was necessary to include additional words in order to complete the reading of a page, a column, or even a sentence. Group 17 has less than 50,000 words because *Khumesh far kinder* is only 47,158 words long.

5. A. Reyzin; Z. Libin; and L. Kobrin (every 22nd page of their short stories);
6. Yoysef Opatoshu (every 16th page of 16 volumes of the Kletskin edition);
7. Dovid Bergelson (every 10th page of the Kletskin edition);
8. Y. Y. Zinger (every 12th page of *Di brider Ashkenazi, Yoshe Kalb, Perl, Shtol un ayzn, Khaver Nakhmen*);
9. Nomberg; Vaysnberg; Horontshik; Perle; Kassel (a group of writers from Poland);
10. Z. Shneyer (every 10th page from the Warsaw Jubilee edition);
11. B. Glazman, A. Raboy, D. Ignatov; Sh. Miller; M. Nadir and others (a group of ten writers in America);
12. A group of 15 writers in the Soviet Union;
13. Twelve translations of novels published in Europe and America;
14. The most recent poetry (27 poets);
15. Yiddish poetry—to approximately 1914 (from Basin's anthology, *Finf hundert yor yidishe poezye*);
16. Modern poetry—approximately from 1914 to 1939;
17. *Khumesh far kinder*—in its entirety ('Pentateuch for Children,' compiled by S. Simon, edited by Yudel Mark);
18. The Bible in Yehoash's translation (from 23 different sections);
19. Twenty-seven different sources of drama;
20. Dovid Pinski's dramatic works;
21. H. Leyvik's dramatic works;
22. The dramatic works of F. Bimko and twelve others;
23. The dramatic works of Yankev Gordin, L. Kobrin and Z. Libin;
24. The dramatic works of Perets Hirshbeyn, H. Sekler and Sholem Asch;
25. The first 19 chapters of Sholem Aleichem's *Motl Peysi dem khazns;*
26. Y. Dinezon's *Yosele* and eight other books for children, published in Europe;
27. Leon Elbe's *Yingele Ringele* and four other books for children, published in the United States;
28. The magazine *Kinder-zhurnal;*
29. The magazine *Kinder-tsaytung;*
30. Thirteen books for children, published in the United States;
31. Three children's books by S. Simon, Litman, Y. Metsker;
32. Folk songs;
33. Folk tales;
34. Folk tales and folk-like tales about hassidic rabbis and pious men, primarily those published in the second half of the 19th century;
35. Six primers;
36. Ten textbooks for grades 2–5;
37. Twelve history textbooks originally written in Yiddish, and four translations;
38. Literary criticism (seven sources);
39. *Forverts*, New York daily, from issues in March 1939 and June 1943;
40. *Der tog*, New York daily, approximately the same dates;
41. *Der morgn-zhurnal*, New York daily, approximately the same dates;
42. *Di morgn-frayhayt*, New York daily, approximately the same dates;
43. Two dailies of Buenos Aires: *Yidishe tsaytung* and *Yidishe prese*, March, 1944;
44. The Yiddish press of Kaunas, Lithuania, and Vilna, Poland, March, 1939;
45. The Yiddish press of the Soviet Union: *Der emes, Oktyabr, Shtern*, 1937–1939;
46. The Warsaw press, March, 1939;
47. Weeklies and monthlies of Europe (18 sources);
48. Weeklies and monthlies of the U. S. (nine sources);
49. Books on social problems (14 sources);
50. Books on history and economics (9 sources);
51. Works on popular science (11 sources);

52. *Yivo-bleter*, a scholarly journal (1931–1935–1937–1939–1941);
53. Khayim Zhitlovski (every 23rd page of his works);
54. Trade journals;
55. "Grandmother's bookshelf": *Tsene-rene* (*Ṣe'ena-ure'ena*) and *muser* (edifying) books;
56. S. Petrushka's translation of the Mishnah;
57. Compositions by pupils of sixteen elementary schools, not corrected by the teachers;
58. Compositions by pupils from twenty published elementary-school journals;
59. Compositions by high school students, not corrected by teachers;
60. Compositions by high school students, published in ten school journals.

The first twelve groups consist of representative samples of Yiddish belles-lettres; the thirteenth group consists of translations. Together they total 650,000 running words of creative prose. There are three groups from the works of Yiddish poets and one group from folk-songs; together, a total of 200,000 words of poetry.

Drama is represented by six groups. Though this is proportionately a greater representation than a reader would normally encounter, drama was emphasized in an effort to get a better picture of the spoken language. Unfortunately, the study shows that there is very little difference between drama and novel in the range and frequency of Hebraisms. This leads to the conclusion that this indirect effort to study Hebraisms in the spoken language did not succeed.

In addition to the group of folk songs, folklore is represented by one group of folktales and one group of folk-like tales which are linguistically similar to folktales.

The Yiddish press plays a prominent role in this study, ten groups being devoted to it. Of these, eight groups consist of samplings from the daily press and two from other periodicals. In this way the importance of the press in actual reading is stressed.

There are six groups of scientific prose, popular science, trade publications, and social studies. A whole group is devoted to the works of Dr. Zhitlovski, who had a considerable influence on the language of the popular social-studies literature. Another group consists of *Yivo-bleter*, the periodical publication of the Yiddish Scientific Institute—Yivo.

Since the primary purpose of this study was to compile a frequency list for use in the Yiddish schools, a considerable amount of the source material had to be taken from the reading matter specially designed for children and usually read by the pupils. For this reason, seven groups are devoted to juvenile literature, three groups to text-books and one group to *Khumesh far kinder* (Children's Bible). There are also four groups of school children's compositions for a total of 750,000 words from sources connected with the reading materials for the pupils of Yiddish schools.

In order to balance the study, which would have been uneven as a result of the inclusion of so much material for children, two groups which were a priori known to contain a superabundance of Hebraisms were included. These are no. 55, listed as "Grandmothers bookshelf," and no. 56, the translation of the Mishnah.

The organization of the study in this specific manner is based on the opinion of the researcher who conducted it, that in commencing a research study all the previous facts and information known to the researcher should be put to use. For this reason a well grounded knowledge of the various literary forms and their respective weight in the whole area of reading matter was taken into consideration. Also considered before the commencement of the study was all the information previously compiled in the area of Hebraisms.

Delimitation of the Word

Back in 1935, George K. Zipf[6] differentiated between words and lexical units (*give, gives, given*). In this study, when we refer to words, we actually mean lexical units. The singular, plural and diminutive of a noun are for our purposes taken to be one word. The same applies to the conjugation of verbs and the agreement of adjectives, as well as their comparative and superlative forms. Thus, *simkhe* 'joy', *símkhele* (diminutive), *símkhelekh* (dim. pl.) are counted as one word; but *símkhedik* 'joyous' together with its comparative and superlative forms is another word. Similarly all forms of *mesameyakh zayn* 'to rejoice' are also counted as one separate word. All compound words and expressions which were taken from Hebrew in an unmodified form are considered to be one word, even where the components of the expressions can be found separately in Yiddish. For example, Yiddish has the word *keyver* 'grave' and the word *oves* 'ancestors', but *keyver-oves* is counted as a word apart from *keyver* and *oves*. Compound expressions are always considered to be separate words, i.e. *toyre-shebal-pé* 'unwritten Torah', *toyre-shebiksáv* 'written Torah', *toyre-shebelév* 'law of the heart', *toyre-veavoyde* 'study and religious service', etc. Each of these combinations represents a different item.

However, in addition to all these separate words, the list prepared for the teacher will contain what we call SYNTHETIC WORDS; that is, a compilation of all the cases in which the primary word occurs. Here are two examples: (1) *simkhe* occurred 471 times in 57 groups; its Frequency Range Indicator[7] (FRI) is 5.40, but in its synthesized form, with *símkhedik* added, and with the compound expressions of which *simkhe* or *simkhes* are parts, it occurred 518 times in 58 groups and its FRI is 5.47; (2) *emes* 'truth' occurred 1,207 times in 59 groups with an FRI of 6.17, but synthesized with the adjectives *émeser* 'true' and *émesdik* 'truthful', and with other expressions compounded with *emes*, it occurred 1,815 times in 59 groups with an FRI of 6.50.

Compound expressions which are not present in Hebrew or were not developed in the manner of Hebrew, but along Germanic lines, are not counted as one word, but as two separate words. For example: *khósn-bokher* 'young man of marriageable age' is not one unit but *khosn* is added to the total incidence of *khosn* 'bridegroom', and *bokher* 'young man' is added to the total of the word *bokher*. Similarly *dróshe-geshank* 'wedding present' is not considered as a separate word, but the Hebraic component is added to the total of the word *droshe* 'speech'. Complete phrases and quotations are considered separate units.

[6] George K. Zipf: *Psycho-Biology of Language*, Boston, 1935, pp. 39f.

[7] See p. 33f.

The words *keyser* 'emperor' and *kundes* 'prankster' are not included as Hebraisms, regardless of their traditional Hebraicized spelling. *Tomer* 'in case' was also excluded, but *balebós* 'proprietor, boss' was included. The totals for words like *klezmer* 'musician', *min* 'kind, type', *shum* 'whatsoever', *din* 'religious law', *mum* 'deformity' are not reliable because they are not distinguished orthographically from non-Hebraisms in Yiddish.

Proper names were not included in the original plan for the study. They were added later when it was realized that they represent the same difficulties in teaching as the other Hebraisms, and that many of them are actually meaningful words. For example, *Meylekh* means 'king' and *Malke* means 'queen', but both are also names; as a result it was impossible to be sure that the proper names were not included in the count of the words for 'king' and 'queen'. The same is true for the male names *Sholem* 'peace', *Simkhe* 'joy', *Borukh* 'blessed', *Peysakh* 'Passover', etc., and the female names: *Brokhe* 'blessing', *Khaye* 'animal', *Nekhome* 'consolation', etc. When all this was taken into consideration it was decided to include the proper names. This required that several groups be counted again, in order to add the proper names. Except for groups 17 and 18 which contain texts from the Bible, no appreciable change resulted. The accidental high frequency of certain names in a given text which depended on the author's choice of names was counteracted by the great variety of sources. As a by-product of the study we were able to compile a list of the most frequent names. Their order of frequency is as follows: Moyshe, Yisroel, Avrohom, Khaye, Sore, Dovid, Shloyme, Sholem, Simkhe, Rokhl, Khayim, Eliyohu, Yitskhok, Yankev, Peysakh, Yoysef, Brokhe, Khane, Mitsrayim, Yerusholayim.

The proper names Sholem, Simkhe, Peysakh and others which are also meaningful words appear with a higher frequency because of the aforementioned reason.

THE FREQUENCY RANGE INDICATOR (FRI)

In tabulating the results of this study we must constantly deal with two figures: one indicates frequency (F), that is, the number of times that a word was encountered in the three million running words, and the other indicates range (R), that is, the number of groups in which the word occurred. In order to arrive at one index combining both figures, it was necessary to devise a system combining both range and frequency in one number, so as to be able to compare the words for both factors in the final listing. In compiling the Spanish frequency list[8] the following method was used: the number of groups in which the word appeared was added to one-tenth of the total number of times it occurred. Thus, too much emphasis was placed on certain extremes. For example: if a word occurs five times in five groups, its index number is 5.5, and if a word occurs four times in four groups its index number is 4.4, while a word which occurs twenty times in two groups has an index number of 4.0. Here the variation in range is not great enough to obscure the much greater variation in frequency. Incidentally, this method was much criticized. Other methods investigated also proved faulty.

[8] M. A. Buchanan: *A Graded Spanish Word Book*, Toronto, 1927, p. 10.

It therefore became necessary to devise another system of indicating frequency and range. Statisticians offered various systems. The system finally adopted was suggested by Mendel Mark and is as follows: establish the first figure as the numerical expression of one leg of a right triangle, and the second as the other leg, and the numerical value of the hypotenuse as the frequency range indicator. This system met with the approval of the mathematician, Professor L. Berz. Through the application of the Pythagorean theorem we arrived at the formula $a = \sqrt{b^2 + c^2}$. However, the range must be given more weight than the frequency. How much more, must be based on a subjective evaluation. On these grounds it was decided to multiply the numbers of groups by three. The formula finally used thus became $a = \sqrt{9b^2 + c^2}$. In order to avoid the use of large and unwieldly numbers, logarithms were utilized, making the formula $\log a = \frac{1}{2} \log (9b^2 + c^2)$. The order, of course, remains the same if all figures are multiplied by two, and so $FRI = \log (9R^2 + F^2)$. Therefore, if a word occurs once in one group the frequency range indicator is 1. For the sequence of indicators it is sufficient to take only the characteristic of the logarithm and the first two digits of the mantissa. A word which occurs twice in one group has as its indicator the logarithm of 13, or 1.11; a word which occurs

Table 1. FREQUENCY OF HEBRAISMS BY GROUPS

Group	*Running Words*	*All Hebraisms*	*Number of Different Hebraisms*	*% of Hebraisms*	*Group*	*Running Words*	*All Hebraisms*	*Number of Different Hebraisms*	*% of Hebraisms*
1	50,000	4,526	1,268	9.05	32	50,022	2,622	535	5.24
2	50,858	4,584	1,251	9.01	33	50,093	3,167	794	6.32
3	50,000	3,859	949	7.73	34	50,014	5,030	1,210	10.06
4	50,040	2,634	693	5.26	35	50,038	760	218	1.52
5	50,031	2,218	636	4.43	36	52,709	2,319	553	4.39
6	50,000	2,700	796	5.40	37	50,020	4,325	728	8.65
7	50,000	2,551	526	5.12	38	50,149	3,572	975	7.12
8	50,210	2,330	585	4.64	39	50,002	1,540	413	3.08
9	50,007	2,699	772	5.40	40	50,023	1,824	540	3.64
10	50,000	2,596	763	5.19	41	50,075	2,185	623	4.36
11	50,048	2,135	632	4.27	42	50,147	1,516	354	3.02
12	50,088	2,086	511	4.14	43	50,005	1,851	555	3.70
13	50,130	1,650	527	3.29	44	50,180	2,288	622	4.56
14	50,157	3,902	1,211	7.58	45	50,034	1,481	193	2.96
15	50,146	2,368	637	4.72	46	50,015	2,641	717	5.28
16	50,098	1,565	498	3.12	47	50,000	2,827	753	5.65
17	47,058	3,953	376	8.41	48	50,020	2,987	951	5.97
18	51,400	3,780	591	7.36	49	50,026	2,924	780	5.84
19	50,008	3,582	814	7.16	50	50,000	2,072	530	4.14
20	51,287	2,832	593	5.52	51	50,162	1,556	445	3.11
21	50,354	3,675	624	7.29	52	50,000	2,706	695	5.41
22	50,300	3,151	744	6.26	53	50,000	2,614	730	5.23
23	50,042	2,750	698	5.50	54	51,576	1,974	368	3.83
24	50,047	2,947	604	5.89	55	50,161	6,397	1,295	12.75
25	51,719	3,465	610	6.71	56	50,027	8,038	1,182	16.07
26	50,004	2,808	549	5.62	57	50,141	1,227	230	2.44
27	50,000	2,188	308	4.38	58	50,034	1,469	279	2.93
28	50,000	1,910	301	3.82	59	49,968	1,480	315	2.96
29	50,000	1,064	204	2.13	60	49,992	1,659	374	3.31
30	50,851	1,645	385	3.24					
31	50,000	924	179	1.85	All groups	3,010,511	162,128	603[9]	5.38

[9] The average has no special meaning and is of no importance.

twice in two groups has as its indicator the logarithm of 40, or 1.60, etc. The word *afile* 'even' has the frequency range indicator 6.73 and is first on the frequency list; and the common word *soyne* 'enemy' has the frequency range indicator 5.68. The 34 words with the highest FRI have the highest frequency index as well. For the first 100 words the difference between the FRI and frequency index is very slight, but the further down on the list the word, the greater the discrepancy between these two figures. For the third and fourth hundred words the discrepancy is considerable. The FRI is quite convenient, but this does not imply that we must adhere to it, since not only is the FRI listed for every word, but the frequency and range are given as well, and the critic of the FRI can disregard it entirely if he so desires. For our purposes, however, it proved very useful. In the instances where two or even more words have the same FRI the difference in frequency is overcome by the difference in range.

When the words are listed in alphabetical order, the FRI affords us an easy means of quickly ascertaining the importance of the word on the frequency list. In this the characteristic of the logarithm is most important. Only 16 words have an FRI of 6 or higher, 96 words range from 5.99 to 5, and 354 words range from 4.99 to 4. These 466 words constitute almost all the Hebraisms necessary for the Yiddish school. They occurred 118,050 times, which is 72.81 per cent of the total incidence of Hebraisms. If high school graduates would really have a thorough knowledge of these 466 words, they would have no practical difficulty reading and understanding the Hebrew element of the Yiddish vocabulary.

Percentage of Hebraisms

The overall percentage of Hebraisms is 5.38%. This figure is the result of dividing the total incidence of Hebraisms by the total number of Yiddish words counted. This would indicate that the average percentage of Hebraisms in all kinds and types of texts would probably be very close to this figure.

The range of percentages according to groups is as follows:

Table 2. PERCENTAGE OF HEBRAISMS BY TYPES OF TEXT

Group	*Percentage*	*Group*	*Percentage*	*Group*	*Percentage*	*Group*	*Percentage*
35	1.52	43	3.70	53	*5.23*	33	6.32
31	1.85	28	3.82	32	*5.24*	25	6.71
29	2.13	54	3.83	4	*5.26*	38	7.12
57	2.44	50	4.14	46	*5.28*	19	7.16
58	2.93	12	4.14	9	*5.40*	21	7.29
59	2.96	11	4.27	6	*5.40*	18	7.36
45	2.96	41	4.36	52	5.41	14	7.58
42	3.02	27	4.38	23	5.50	3	7.73
39	3.08	36	4.39	20	5.52	17	8.41
51	3.11	5	4.43	26	5.62	37	8.65
16	3.12	44	*4.56*	47	5.65	2	9.01
30	3.24	8	*4.64*	49	5.84	1	9.05
13	3.29	15	*4.72*	24	5.89	34	10.06
60	3.31	7	*5.12*	48	5.97	55	12.75
40	3.64	10	*5.19*	22	6.26	56	16.07

The median is 5.21% and the most characteristic percentages are the ten between 4.56% and 5.40%.

The mean average of the percentages in the 60 groups is 5.39%, i.e. .01% higher than the overall percentage, 5.38. This only concerns us as a check on the accuracy of the overall average, and is only incidental to the primary concern: the figure 5.38%, which gives a theoretical average of the proportion of Hebraisms in all Yiddish texts, and the figure 5.21%, the median, which is important and indicative for practical purposes.

The Surprising Result

That there were only approximately 160,000 Hebraisms among three million running words and that they amounted to only 5.38% was at first sight surprising. All the previous studies in this area[10] which were based on general impressions variously estimated that Hebraisms constituted ten to twenty per cent of Yiddish. Before arriving at the results this researcher anticipated approximately ten per cent, certainly no less than eight per cent. Why is the result so different from the general impression one derives from reading various kinds of Yiddish texts?

The answer is not difficult to find. When we read we pay very little attention to the connective words which constitute a large part of all language. When we take into account such groups of words as the definite and indefinite article, auxiliary verbs, the most frequent prepositions and conjunctions, etc., we find that they make up no less than a third, and possibly even forty per cent, of all running words in a given text. In reading they are scarcely noticeable, and the previous estimates of the percentage and role of Hebraisms were probably based on words that convey lexical meanings.

This is the reason that the estimates mentioned above were so high. The study, however, clarified this situation. This is also the reason why a very slightly higher percentage of Hebraisms in the language of a writer may indicate a richer vocabulary of Hebraisms. The difference between four and five per cent is, therefore, very great, and reflects the vocabulary, style and cultural level of a book or an author. This necessitated the Richness Quotient (*RQ*) which gives a much better indication of these differences.[11]

On the other hand, we must keep in mind that in a complete dictionary of the Yiddish language, the percentage of Hebraisms would be much higher than their frequency among running words. If we were able to discover 6,307 different Hebraisms in three million running words, then we must assume that

[10] The literature on the subject of Hebraisms in Yiddish is far too large to be cited here, but the only actual count except Steinbaum's (see footnote 3) seems to have been E. Spivak's based on two issues of a Soviet Yiddish newspaper ten years apart; see his [About Dehebraization and About the Hebrew "Element" in Yiddish], *Afn shprakhfront*, *zamlung* 2 (1934), Kiev, 1935, 3–22, esp. pp. 4f. A study by Leibush Lehrer in 1927 was based on a very small sample.

[11] See p. 40.

the total number of Hebraisms in Yiddish must be at least ten thousand and perhaps even twelve thousand.

Factors Determining the Frequency of Hebraisms

Only a relatively small number of Hebraisms, which are not directly related to the traditional way of life, have no synonyms and cannot be avoided in expressing the concepts which they convey. Such words are, for example, *afile* 'even', *yam* 'sea', *sho* 'hour', *ganev* 'thief', *levone* 'moon', etc. The large remainder can be divided into:

(a) Words necessary as names of things and concepts that are closely connected with religious studies or worship, or directly or indirectly with ritual, customs, folkways and forms of inner Jewish life;

(b) Words for which synonyms can be found in other elements of Yiddish, i.e. the Germanic or Slavic.

It is therefore understandable why certain postulates dealing with factors determining the percentage of Hebraisms which could have been arrived at a priori are confirmed by the results of the study. There can be no doubt that the primary factors determining the frequency of Hebraisms are these:

1. The THEME or the SUBJECT MATTER with which the author deals. If he is dealing with internal Jewish materials, way of life, religious studies, religious concepts and problems, configurations from the traditionally established Jewish world—he naturally uses more Hebraisms. The originally planned selection of groups which was made, confirmed this assumption. Those groups which were at the outset thought to be heavily laden with Hebraisms were actually so laden and the results are not at all surprising. Of particular interest is the case of Y. L. Peretz. Everyone who has ever read his works knows how full of Hebraisms they are. Peretz's language was subjected to a dual count:

(a) Samples from all his works, such as were taken from other writers, and which included those dealing with hassidic and religious life as well as those which were in no way related to it. This aspect of the study showed that the percentage of Hebraisms was 9.01 and the overall incidence was 4,584 (these figures are included in the results of the study in the overall table and in all other totals);

(b) Only from the hassidic and folk-like tales, which showed a percentage of 9.76 and the total incidence of 4,879; the difference between the general and the special language of Peretz is therefore .75%. This difference is, of course, the result of the difference in the subject matter dealt with. But this figure does not indicate the whole story. Actually a third study of Peretz's works ought to be made which would only include those works which do not contain a specific Jewish element (they are very difficult to find) and the results of such a third study should be compared with the other two figures. Only then would we be able to discover the great difference in the Hebraisms which is dependent on subject matter.

There are also two separate counts for Khayim Zhitlovski:

(a) All his works, giving 5.23% and a total incidence of 2,614;

(b) All his works except those volumes where Hebraisms appear rarely (for example, the volume on Einstein's theory). Here the percentage rose to 6.5, and the number of Hebraisms to 3,228. This resulted in a greater variation than in the case of Peretz, but the procedure is more open to question.

2. The WRITER'S EDUCATION and how deeply rooted he is in Jewish life. The more Jewish education the writer has had, the more his language is related to the speech of the talmudic scholar, the more Hebrew and religious literature he has absorbed, the greater the percentage of Hebraisms in his language. It isn't always convenient to give examples, but the attentive reader can reach his own conclusions about given writers on the basis of the tables.

3. The readers to whom the writer directed his work, the ADDRESSEE of the writer. If the writer clearly knew (or was under the impression) that the reader whom he was trying to reach would have difficulty with Hebraisms and he wanted to avoid them, he attempted or made an effort to replace Hebraisms with other words. This pertains not only to the language of beginners (group 35) or to materials that were written for children (group 31), but even to the daily press in America. This explains the noticeable difference between the number of Hebraisms in the daily press in America and the number of Hebraisms in the other periodicals (compare, for example, groups 39 and 48). Also, the fact that the most modern poetry contains more Hebraisms then the poetry written between 1910 and 1939 and the poetry written before World War I (7.58% compared with 3.12% and 4.72%), can in a large measure be explained by the fact that most modern poets no longer worry about the readers' ability to understand.

Some Results Derived From an Analysis of the Sixty Groups[12]

Just as there are two figures for each word, there are two figures for each group: the total incidence of Hebraisms in the group and the number of separate words. Both figures could be combined in the same manner as was used for the words, but then the differences would not be sufficiently clear to indicate the richness of Hebraisms for each separate group. For this reason another system was utilized. Group 35, which has the lowest percentage of Hebraisms, was considered the basic unit. This means that 1 equals the total incidence of Hebraisms multiplied by the number of separate Hebraisms. All the products

[12] The study includes calculations on the different literary types, i.e. for all belles-lettres, poetry, drama, press, and reading material for children. This kind of grouping together has not proven too useful (with the exception of the grouping "material for children"), because in every compilation of this kind there are diverse groups with high and low RQs. In the inclusive and extensive count of Puerto-Rican Spanish, headed by Ismail Rodriguez Bou (*Recuento de Vocabulario Español*, San Juan, P. R., 1952), the results are given according to groupings; four groups deal with oral language, four with printed material and radio, two groupings with supplementary reading material; alongside are given the summaries for these three types and finally the grand total for every word. The present writer, however, had in mind the tabulation of the results of the frequency count of Hebraisms in a manner enabling him to characterize each of the sixty groups separately.

Table 3. THE 100 MOST FREQUENT HEBRAISMS

Word	*Meaning*	*Frequency*	*Range*	*FRI*
afile	even	2,307	59	6.73
(*a*) *sakh*	much, many	1,967	60	6.59
ponim	face	1,704	60	6.47
r'	abbreviation of *reb*	1,546	40	6.38
rebe	teacher, rabbi	1,509	54	6.36
kedéy	in order to	1,448	57	6.33
milkhome	war	1,427	58	6.31
efsher	perhaps	1,402	59	6.29
mayse	story	1,380	57	6.29
Moyshe	Moses	1,366	40	6.27
khaver	friend	1,340	60	6.26
emes	truth	1,207	59	6.17
moyre	fear	1,173	59	6.15
meylekh	king	1,085	45	6.08
shabes	Sabbath	1,065	59	6.08
Yisroel	Israel	1,023	38	6.03
khásene	wedding	977	55	5.99
yam	sea	927	60	5.95
kol	voice	914	54	5.93
sof	end	889	60	5.92
koyakh	strength	815	60	5.84
neshome	soul	807	57	5.83
sho	hour	764	57	5.79
toyre	Torah	754	56	5.78
kimát	almost	727	57	5.74
yontev	holiday	688	59	5.70
soyne	enemy	666	58	5.68
oylom	public, crowd	657	57	5.66
rov	rabbi	641	49	5.63
bokher	young man	612	56	5.60
Avrohom	Abraham	607	35	5.58
Erets-Yisroel	land of Israel	592	46	5.57
kholem	dream	582	55	5.57
khoydesh	month	575	58	5.56
khaye	animal	570	56	5.55
Sore	Sarah	590	32	5.55
melukhe	state, land	570	48	5.54
Dovid	David	577	33	5.53
avade	sure, certainly	565	53	5.52
tsore	trouble, misfortune	540	59	5.51
balebós	owner, boss	529	51	5.48
Shloyme	Solomon	521	31	5.45
hárgenen	to kill	500	55	5.44
(*keyn*) *shum*	whatsoever	495	48	5.42
sholem	peace	484	57	5.42
rakhmones	pity, mercy	481	52	5.41
simkhe	joy, celebration, party	471	57	5.40
kheyder	classroom, room	471	50	5.39
poshet	simple	461	54	5.38
seyfer	book	459	52	5.37
Rokhl	Rachel	468	31	5.36
Khayim	Haim	464	30	5.35
dor	generation	449	51	5.35
kale	bride, fiancée	450	49	5.35
reb	(title)	459	29	5.34
tomid	always	437	55	5.34
khosn	bridegroom, fiancé	443	43	5.33
Eliyohu	Elijah	451	18	5.31
Yitskhok	Isaac	444	29	5.31
Yankev	Jacob	435	32	5.30
keyver	grave	421	51	5.30
beheyme	head of cattle	420	51	5.30
oyfn	manner	421	46	5.29
korbn	sacrifice	416	51	5.29
shokhn	neighbor	412	55	5.29
emes (adj.)	true	411	49	5.28
mishpokhe	family	398	59	5.28
min	kind	410	46	5.27
kaas	anger	404	51	5.27
peysakh	Passover	403	49	5.27
levone	moon	391	51	5.25
soykher	merchant	383	53	5.24
inyen	matter	382	47	5.22
gánvenen	to steal	376	53	5.22
skhoyre	merchandise	373	54	5.22
davke	necessarily	381	47	5.22
khuts	except	368	51	5.20
Yoysef	Joseph	387	32	5.20
koved	respect, honor	357	54	5.19
brokhe	blessing	361	51	5.18
mistome	perhaps	352	51	5.17
sod	secret	339	57	5.16
bik(*h*)*lál*	in general	355	41	5.15
talmid	pupil	351	46	5.15
mizrakh	east	338	53	5.14
porets	lord, squire	342	47	5.14
besmedresh	house of study (prayer)	343	43	5.13
eytse	advice	318	58	5.12
malakh	angel	342	41	5.12
Khane	Hannah	350	26	5.11
beshás	while	330	48	5.11
ganev	thief	335	43	5.11
Mitsrayim	Egypt	346	26	5.10
keseyder	constantly	315	50	5.09
mitsve	good deed, commandment	325	42	5.08
kholile	God forbid	316	44	5.07
simen	sign	304	54	5.07
khevre	group, society, gang	325	44	5.05
matone	gift	291	55	5.05
goy	gentile	315	37	5.05

The one hundred most frequent words occur 63,434 times in the whole count; that is, they constitute 39.74% of the 162,128 Hebraisms encountered.

Table 4. RICHNESS QUOTIENTS OF GROUPS

Group 1—34.64	Group 16— 4.6	Group 31— 1.0	Group 46—11.4
Group 2—34.61	Group 17— 9.0	Group 32— 8.5	Group 47—12.8
Group 3—22.1	Group 18—13.5	Group 33—15.7	Group 48—17.1
Group 4—11.0	Group 19—17.6	Group 34—36.7	Group 49—13.8
Group 5— 8.5	Group 20—11.2	Group 35— 1.0	Group 50— 6.6
Group 6—13.0	Group 21—13.8	Group 36— 7.7	Group 51— 4.2
Group 7— 8.1	Group 22—14.1	Group 37—19.0	Group 52—11.4
Group 8— 8.2	Group 23—12.2	Group 38—21.2	Group 53—11.5
Group 9—12.6	Group 24—10.7	Group 39— 5.0	Group 54— 4.4
Group 10—12.0	Group 25—12.8	Group 40— 5.9	Group 55—50.0
Group 11— 8.1	Group 26— 9.3	Group 41— 8.2	Group 56—57.3
Group 12— 6.4	Group 27— 4.1	Group 42— 3.2	Group 57— 1.7
Group 13— 5.3	Group 28— 3.5	Group 43— 6.3	Group 58— 2.5
Group 14—22.5	Group 29— 1.3	Group 44— 8.6	Group 59— 2.8
Group 15— 9.1	Group 30— 3.8	Group 45— 1.7	Group 60— 3.7

of such a multiplication are divided by the products of the multiplication in group 35. This gives us the following equation: let a and b be the figures for group 35 and let x and y be the figures for any other given group; then $RQ = xy/ab$. RQ stands for richness quotient. We arrive at the results shown in table 4.

There is a specific difference between the sequence according to the percentage of Hebraisms and the sequence according to the richness quotient. The first five and the last four on the two lists coincide, but all the cases in between diverge. For example, Group 6 is seventh according to its richness quotient and 25th according to percentage; group 17 is 31st according to RQ and 7th according to percentage. The difference is due to the fact that the richness quotient also includes the number of different Hebraisms that occur in the group. Therefore according to the richness quotient, the sequence of groups is as follows: 56, 55, 34, 1, 2, 14, 3, 38, 37, 19, 48, 33, 22, 21, 49, 18, 6, 47, 25, 9, 23, 10, 53, 52, 46, 20, 4, 24, 26, 15, 17, 44, 5, 32, 8, 41, 11, 7, 36, 50, 12, 43, 40, 13, 39, 16, 54, 51, 27, 30, 60, 28, 42, 59, 58, 45, 57, 29, 31, 35. Table 4 lists the groups according to percentage.

This analysis offers materials for interesting comparisons between one writer and another, but is still in the realm of quantitative research. We have, however, sufficient material for a qualitative comparison of the language of the writers and the groups as well, because there is a summary for every single group which contains all the Hebraisms that occurred in the group five times and more. (If one wants to ascertain further details and is interested in the words that occur in a group less than five times, one must go through the original work sheets for each separate word.)

There can be no doubt that the words most characteristic for a writer are the keys to many piquant and hidden attributes of the writer's style and even his whole personality. We have, therefore, an opportunity to discover qualitative characteristics. We shall refer to only a few instances:

Mendele Moykher-Sforim, who is known as the grandfather of modern Yiddish literature, describes the Jewish way of life realistically. The most frequent words that he uses are those that are generally more frequently used. For example: *afile*, *r'*, *ponim*, *oylom*, *reb*, *mayse*, *nishkoshe*, *neshome*, *kol*, *beheyme*, *beshás*, *tomid*, *bokher*, *koved*, *Moyshe*, *tsore* (the first word in this series occurs sixty times and the others progressively less, with the last four words occurring only 30 times). It is worthwhile to point out that the word *nishkoshe*, which occurs 41 times and is especially characteristic of Mendele, is up in the three hundreds on the main list. It is also noteworthy that *beheyme* occurs 31 times in Mendele's writings, because here it frequently has the meaning 'fool' and is not infrequently a form of address between man and wife. Now let us turn to Y. L. Peretz. The group containing his writings has an RQ which is almost the same as Mendele's (it was necessary to extend this figure to two decimal places in order to show a difference), but the most frequent words are quite different: *rebe, neshome, kol, porets, malakh* (as many as 54 times, whereas the word is 89th on the general frequency list), *reb, zikhroyne livrokhe* 'of blessed memory', *toyre, balshém* 'Baal Shem', *ponim, nign* 'melody', *reboyne-shel-oylom* 'Lord of the world', *ishe* 'female', *simkhe, avade, mitsve, tsadik* 'saint', *Shloyme, besmedresh, rosh-yeshive* 'head of a yeshive'. These words lead us into an entirely different world when compared with the most frequent words used by Mendele.

The comparison of the RQ's of the three groups of poetry is very instructive. The older poets (group 15), approximately to 1914, have an RQ of 9.1—an average similar to prose; the most frequent words here were: *yam, keyver, kholem* 'dream', *neshome, malakh, ponim, kale, levone, sod, tsore*. Group 16, modern poetry, approximately 1915 to 1939, has the much lower RQ of 4.6 (this is explained by the different backgrounds of the poets, a greater richness of subject matter, and the lessening emphasis on materials that deal only with the narrow field of internal Jewish life). The most frequent words here are somewhat different: *yam, levone, sho, efsher, kol, dor, khaver, kholem, soyne, tsaar* 'grief'. The third group, poetry written between 1940–1950, the years of the destruction of European Jewry and the moods which followed the catastrophe in which six million Jews perished, has a very high RQ, 22.5 (sixth on the RQ list), because there is a tendency to embrace the forms and words of the old way of life and to emphasize Jewish values and penitential moods. In addition the factor of intelligibility, which we have already mentioned (p. 38), also plays a part in this high RQ. Here the most frequent words are: *kholem, yam, ponim, keyver, guf* 'body', *sho, dor, nign, kol, Yankev*. When we compare all three of these groups of individually created poetry with group 32 (folksongs) we find an RQ which is 8.5, closest to the older poets who to a certain extent maintained the forms and the content of the folksong. The folksong group has these most frequent Hebraisms: *rebe, shabes, kale, khosn, toyre, khosid* 'hassid', *Avrohom, khásene, melamed* 'teacher', *khupe* 'wedding canopy'—words from the pious way of life.

When we compare the eight groups that deal with the daily press, the results (see table 5) can teach us certain things. Most apparent is the poverty of Hebraisms in the Soviet press. In Russia the orthography of the Hebraisms was "naturalized" (they were written like other Yiddish words), in order to make it easier for the less educated to read Yiddish. But it turned out that this did not prevent the impoverishment of the language, because it seems that the reform was influenced not by the above-mentioned practical motive, but

Table 5. HEBRAISMS IN YIDDISH NEWSPAPERS

	RQ	*Percentage*
Yiddish press in Poland (first half of 1939)	11.4	5.28
Yiddish press in Vilna and Kaunas (same period)	8.6	4.56
New York *Morgn-zhurnal* (primarily 1943)	8.2	4.36
Yiddish press in Argentina (from 1944)	6.3	3.70
New York *Tog* (primarily from 1943)	5.9	3.64
New York *Forverts* (same period)	5.0	3.08
New York *Morgn-frayhayt* (same period)	3.2	3.02
Soviet press (years 1937–1939)	1.7	2.96

by the direct antagonism to everything that was connected with the Jewish way of life. The Communist New York *Morgn-frayhayt* stands close to the Soviet press. It is even more interesting that the Orthodox New York *Morgn-zhurnal* contains fewer Hebraisms than the various newspapers in Lithuania and Poland, where the language of the press was much richer.

The analysis of the ten most frequent words in these eight groups leads to the discovery of the most characteristic Hebraisms in the press (such words as *milkhome*, *sholem* 'peace', *kedéy*, (*a*) *sakh*, *soyne*, *Erets-Yisroel*, etc.). It is interesting to note that of the ten most frequent Hebraisms in the *Morgn-frayhayt* and in the Soviet press, six are the same: *afile*, *melukhe*, *soyne*, *milkhome*, *kedéy*, *khoydesh*. The word *kosher* is only found among the ten most frequent words in the *Morgn-zhurnal*. When we compare the Hebraisms in weeklies and magazines (groups 47 and 48) that were published in Europe and America, we find an opposite tendency: in America the RQ is 17.1 and in Europe 12.8. This can be explained, on the one hand, by the difference in the years when the respective counts were made and the differences in subject matter, and on the other hand by the fact that in America magazine writers are more careful of their language, perhaps because they have fewer pretentions of reaching the mass of the people.

There have been certain complaints that the publications of the Yiddish Scientific Institute—Yivo, especially the journal *Yivo-bleter*, are written in very difficult language. But this cannot apply to Hebraisms because the RQ of group 52 is 11.4 and almost coincides with the RQ 11.5 of Dr. Khayim Zhitlovski's works, which are held to be models of the language of journalism and popular science.

We could cite many such instances comparing groups and combinations of groups. We must, however, be satisfied with only a few examples which serve to illustrate the great number of possible conclusions which can be derived from the material collected for this study. We should like to make one more point. Certain words sometimes characterize a whole group: *kholem*, *yam*, *levone* are typical of poetry: *milkhome*, *sholem*, *melukhe*—of the daily press; *emes*, *kedéy*, *efsher*, *oyfn*, *shaykhes* 'connection', *lemoshl* 'for example'—of journalism and scientific prose; (*a*) *sakh*, *mayse*, *khaver*, *yontev*—of the language of children, etc. We can also characterize a group by the most frequent ten or even five words. The fact that the first six words of group 55 (Grandmother's bookshelf) are *Yisroel*, *toyre*, *mitsve*, *aveyre* 'sin', *rebe*, *posek* '(biblical) verse', and that the first six words in groups 11 and 12 (modern narrative) are *afile*, *ponim*, *efsher*, (*a*) *sakh*, *kedéy*, *khaver*, speaks volumes of Jewish cultural history.

תורה (תורות, תורהלע) — 754 צאָל מאָל — 56 צאָל גרופּעס — 578 ווערט

Count	Group	Count	Group	Count	Group
14	1	9	19	2	39
39	2	24	20	—	40
3	3	4	21	19	41
13	4	7	22	—	42
2	5	5	23	6	43
6	6	6	24	2	44
—	7			—	45
21	8	1	25	2	46
1	9	26	26	4	47
4	10	2	27	12	48
1	11	25	28		
1	12	5	29	7	49
6	13	1	30	4	50
8	14	2	31	16	51
		53	32	6	52
14	15	10	33	2	53
7	16	32	34	2	54
				134	55
11	17	8	35	49	56
12	18	11	36		
		22	37	14	57
		34	38	6	58
				8	59
				9	60

באַמערקונגען: סינטאַקס: 580-56-791 (תורה שבכתב, תורה שבעל־פה, תורת חיים, תורה אור, תורה זו לנו, תורה ודעת, תורה הקדושה, תורה ומצוות, תורה שבלב, תורה ועבודה, תורת משה, תורת ה׳ תמימה, תורה נמשלה לאש, תורה נמשלה למים)

בדעה (האָבן) — 54 צאָל מאָל — 25 צאָל גרופּעס — 393 ווערט

Count	Group	Count	Group	Count	Group
	1	1	19	3	39
1	2		20	2	40
1	3		21		41
1	4	1	22	1	42
2	5		23	3	43
1	6		24	2	44
	7				45
	8		25	7	46
4	9		26	2	47
	10		27		48
	11		28		
	12		29	2	49
2	13		30	4	50
	14		31	2	51
			32	3	52
	15		33		53
	16	1	34	2	54
				4	55
	17		35		56
	18		36		
		1	37		57
			38		58
					59
				1	60

באַמערקונגען: פֿאַרבינדן מיט דעה

Original work sheets for the words *toyre* 'Torah, learning' and *bedeye* 'in mind'. To the left of each group number appears the number of times the particular Hebraism was encountered in that group. Similar sheets were compiled for each of the 3,577 Hebraisms that turned up in more than one group or more than twice in one group.

Analysis of Individual Words

More than a frequency list of Hebraisms resulted from this study. The elicited information yielded a complete picture of each word and of the role it plays in the language generally, in every literary form, in every kind of literature, partially even in given periods of time (at least the last 100 years). The function of each word is clearly indicated.

Altogether 6,307 separate words were encountered; of these 2,368 occurred only once. They were recorded on cards with indications of the group in which they appeared. 362 words occurred twice in one group. All the remaining 3,577 words were recorded each on a separate sheet indicating the numbers of the groups in which they were encountered. Thus, if a student has one of these sheets before him, he can clearly and positively identify the function of the word in the language: where, i.e. in what kind of literature, the word occurred, where one can be expected to find it, etc.

Attention is called to the sheet for the word *toyre*. It occurs most frequently in pious literature: 134 times in fifty thousand words. Then come folk-songs, Mishnah translation, literary criticism (because here the word was used primarily to mean 'philosophy, system, world outlook'), folk-like stories. Among the writers the most conspicuous is Y. L. Peretz (group 2)—39 times, and then in decreasing order the authors who described contemporary life, in whose writings the word occurs only once in fifty thousand. In the daily press the word *toyre* appears rarely, except in the Orthodox *Morgn-zhurnal*. It occurs more frequently in the pupils' compositions than in the press, because it is connected with their life as far as it is related to the Jewish school, and the fact that it does not occur even once in the Soviet and in the American Communist press is not accidental.

It would be possible to include illustrations of a great many words that are interesting and afford an insight not only into linguistic, but also into social and psychological aspects of Jewish life. That one of the most frequent words, *efsher* 'perhaps', the eighth most frequent word, occurs many times in all groups but not once in group 55 (pious literature) is highly significant. Of the 3,577 words for which separate sheets were prepared, much can be said about at least a thousand. These are materials for the psychologist, not only for the linguist.

The more detailed a study becomes, the more conclusions can be reached from the materials to be found in it. Primarily our work can be useful for the historian of culture, since Yiddish went through complicated developmental stages in the last 100 years, stages which lasted much longer in other languages. All these transitions from the traditional way of life to the libertarian, and the internal innovations in groupings and established concepts, can be illustrated by the accessible, almost symbolic pictures that we receive from the individual word sheets. This study permits us to analyze the introduction, use and obsolescence of fashionable words and expressions. Certain words are especially favored by the writers of a given period. Afterwards they are relegated to a rare and half-forgotten place in the language. If the full results of this research were to be published, it would be necessary to include the individual sheets not only for two words, as is being done here, but for a thousand, in order that others besides this researcher be able to develop their own interpretations and not be dependent only on one researcher's ability to understand and comment on the sheets for each word. The other 2,577 sheets must also be preserved for those who will at one time or another be interested in the smaller details.

The record for each individual word is the lasting and variegated contribution of this study. This leads us far afield, away from quantitative research, and places us in a domain where the quantitative acts only as a foundation or a basis for qualitative study in many areas.

One who is conscious of his attitude toward his own language, and is aware of a number of Hebraisms which he uses quite frequently, has before him in the result of this study a way of knowing whom he emulates or fails to emulate in a particular instance. Thus, an opportunity is afforded for checking up on oneself. I, for example, was surprised to discover that *hekhrakh* 'compulsion', a word which I use not infrequently, occurred only twice in one group. The same pertains to certain groups of words. It can be clearly seen that certain Hebraisms are encountered frequently in the works of writers from one dialect area and rarely or never in the works of writers from another area. The difference between *mistame* 'probably' of Lithuanian writers and *minastám* (also 'probably') of Polish writers is extremely clear. The word *rak* 'only, constantly', which occurs quite frequently in the Lithuanian dialect, is almost never found in the other dialects of Eastern Europe. These individual and dialectal characteristics are clearly indicated and can be ascertained without difficulty and with sufficient assurance. The history of the language is also reflected here, at least the history of the last three generations. In this connection the prepositions and conjunctions are of special interest. Such "little" words as *alpi* 'according to, as', *heyóys* 'whereas', *leshém* 'for the sake of', *mitsád* 'on the part of', *mikoyakh* 'concerning', etc. have had a rather unhappy fate in the last twenty or thirty years, while the words *be-éys* 'while, during', *beshás* 'id.', *kedéy* 'in order to', *khuts* 'except', have had sufficient strength to survive in the struggle for popularity and use. All these connective words are particularly interesting to the grammarian, because they are, in the final analysis, grammatical forms.

The great role of the compound verbs in Yiddish, such as *maskim zayn* 'to agree', *goyver zayn* 'to overcome', *mekuyem vern* 'to materialize', *bedeye hobn* 'to intend' and hundreds of others, play a great role which the study conspicuously points up. These verbs constitute a great segment of the Hebraisms and add a special coloring to the Yiddish verb.

The student of the semantic aspects of Yiddish has a tremendous amount of material for a profound study of groups of synonyms. If we compare the individual sheets for the synonyms of 'joy, pleasure': *simkhe*, *tayneg*, *oyneg*, *nakhes*, *nekhome*, *gdule*, *hanoe*, etc., or synonyms for 'shame': *kharpe*, *bushe*, *bizoyen*, *bize-bizoyen*, *úmkoved*, etc., or the synonyms for 'sorrow': *tsaar*, *shivre-lév*, *yesurim*, *inuyim*, etc., we get information not only about the words which occurred more frequently, but also about the tendencies of writers and types of literature, partly also about the generation of the writers, in selecting one or another synonym from a group.

The sheets for each word also give us a conception of the importance of the Hebraisms in the sphere of emotional life and abstract thinking. These words, together with all the words that are directly related to the Jewish way of life and to Jewishness generally, constitute the major component of all the Hebraisms. Here too the quantitative naturally leads to the qualitative and in certain cases even to the intuitive evaluation of the functions and the role of special groups of words, and of single words which were laden with meaning for generations of Yiddish-speaking people.

The Grammatical Analysis

Of the 6,307 separate Hebraisms that were encountered in this study, 2,368 occurred once, and 362 occured twice in one group. The total amount of other occurrences was 3,577. If we exclude the words that occurred only once, there were 3,939 words. These approximately four thousand words were classified grammatically according to the system of word classes which I have developed.[13]

Table 6. HEBRAISMS BY GRAMMATICAL CLASSES

Nouns	2,790	Prepositions	27
Adjectives	257	Conjunctions	29
Participles	13	Word Elements	18
Pronouns	11	Sententives[14]	83
Simple Verbs	89	Phrases	194
Compound Verbs	339	Quotations	29
Adverbs	161	Abbreviations	48
Adverbial Phrases	77		
		Total	4,165

This total exceeds by 226 the total number of Hebraisms analyzed because there are naturally some words that have more than one classification.

In order to clarify the principles of this analysis, let us point out that those compound words which are developed according to the Hebrew grammatical pattern of *semikut* must be classified in Yiddish as nouns, e.g. *kabolas-ponim* 'welcome, reception'; *simkhas-toyre* '(literally: joy in the Torah) the name of a holiday'. Moreover, a great many other combinations of words which consist of nouns and adjectives according to Hebrew grammar, are nouns in Yiddish, e.g. *tales-kotn* 'ritual male undergarment'; *dover-akher* '(literally: another thing) swine'; similarly for combinations variously classified in Hebrew grammar, e.g. *al-khēt* 'penance', *kezayis* 'a small piece', *loy-yutslakh* 'ne'er-do-well'. Among adjectives there are both those with suffixes, e.g. *am-harátsish* 'ignorant', *le-*

[13] [Word Classes in the Grammar of Yiddish], *Yidishe shprakh* 8 (1948), 1–11.

[14] This term was especially coined from *sentent-* + *-ive,* as in *adjective* and *substantive.* Perhaps, "sentential" would be more apt. At any rate this group of words cannot be included with the adverbs, simply because they are not adverbs, but are words which are sentences per se. In English the following words are examples of sententives: *yes, no, maybe, perhaps, certainly, of course,* etc.

vónedik 'moonlike, moonlit', and those without suffixes, e.g. *boylet* 'clear', *khoshev* 'respected', *shofl* 'lowly'.

Only participles whose roots are never used as verbs are included in the class of participles, e.g. *faryosemt* 'orphaned', *fardalest* 'impoverished'. Simple verbs include forms like *pátern* 'to waste', *eytsen* 'to advise', *míshpetn* 'to judge'; compound verbs are those that consist of a Hebrew component and an auxiliary verb, e.g. *maskim zayn* 'to agree', *poter vern* 'to get rid of', *oyker-min-hashoyresh zayn* 'to root out'. Sententives are those words that are sentences in themselves, e.g. *loy* 'no', *kholile* 'God forbid', *avade* 'certainly', *efsher* 'perhaps', *mírtseshem* 'God willing', etc. The following are examples of word elements: *shebe: yid shebe-yidn* 'a real Jew', *ha* (the definite article in Hebrew): *meylekh hageto* 'king of the ghetto'.

Abbreviations had to be classified separately because they are unique, e.g. *R-Kh-Sh*, pronounced *rakhásh*, the abbreviation which stands for 'rabbi, cantor, sexton', and means the gratuity given at a party, primarily a wedding, to the three functionaries of a Jewish community. Such names as *Rambam* or *Rashi* were not considered abbreviations.

When all the words were classified, the phrases, quotations, and abbreviations remained apart; they are listed separately in the grammatical classification list, although they are not parts of speech.

From the viewpoint of Yiddish grammar, the prepositions, conjunctions and word elements are especially interesting. The great role of compound verbs also becomes very apparent. If this analysis included the words that only occurred once, the number of compound verbs would be very great, but this reflects a language condition which was characteristic of the Jewish talmudic scholar a generation or two ago, and would not be in accord with the present status of literary Yiddish.

Of course, the grammatical analysis is not related to primary aims of the study. It is, however, important for the grammarian and to a limited extent for the historian of the Yiddish language. The figures presented here also illustrate the process of impoverishment of the language in the last generation, which ceased to use a considerable number of prepositions, conjunctions, and compound verbs. These have now become rarer than they were in the Yiddish of the nineteenth century.

A complete report of the study will include a list of the conjunctions, prepositions, word elements and sententives encountered, and a detailed analysis of the compound verbs.

THE HORSE DEALERS' LANGUAGE OF THE SWISS JEWS IN ENDINGEN AND LENGNAU

FLORENCE GUGGENHEIM-GRÜNBERG (Zurich)[1]

The oldest communities of modern Swiss Jewry were those of the two villages, Lengnau and Endingen, in the valley of the river Surb (Surbtal), near Baden in the Canton of Aargau. Their origin dates back to the beginning of the 17th century. For more than 200 years these were the only places in Switzerland where Jewish families were allowed to settle, and even this permission had to be renewed every 16 years by the Swiss Landvogt who ruled over the county of Baden in the 17th and 18th centuries.

These Swiss Jews had close family and trade relations with the Jews living in the southwest of Germany and in Alsace. They all spoke nearly the same Yiddish dialect, similar to the so-called "western Yiddish" described by Matthias Mieses[2] and Salomo Birnbaum.[3] Recently Max Weinreich included Surbtal Yiddish among the Western Yiddish dialects.[4]

Living in a kind of rural ghetto, the Surbtal Jews preserved this language nearly unchanged down to the 20th century.[5] But in the course of the emancipation of Swiss Jewry they gradually adopted the Swiss dialect spoken by their environment, and when most of them left their native villages for bigger cities like Baden and Zurich, they forgot—or tried to forget—their old idiom. Today one has great difficulty in finding older members of Jewish Surbtal families—their most frequent names are Bollag, Braunschweig, Dreifuss, Guggenheim, Moos, Wyler—who speak *jiddiʃdaitʃ* (as they call it themselves) when they are together, reminiscing about old times.

Specialists in Swiss dialectology, especially Professor R. Hotzenköcherle of Zurich University, director of the *Sprachatlas der deutschen Schweiz*, are interested in the old idiom of the Surbtal Jews as one of the various dialects spoken in Switzerland. On the present author's initiative, the Phonogramm-Archiv of Zurich University, under the direction of Professor E. Dieth and Dr. R. Brunner, made a record[6] spoken by several characteristic Jewish Surbtal speakers, to complete its series of spoken Swiss dialects. One side of the record contains the story

[1] I would like to express my gratitude to Dr. Uriel Weinreich for his kind help in translating the article into English, and to Dr. Rudolf Brunner, Zurich, for his valuable aid in phonologizing.

[2] *Die jiddische Sprache*, Berlin, 1924.

[3] *Jüdisches Lexikon*, vol. 3, 1929, s.v. Jiddische Sprache; *Encyclopaedia Judaica*, ed. Jakob Klatzkin, vol. 9, 1932, s.v. Jiddisch.

[4] "Roshe-prokim vegn mayrevdikn yidish" [Outlines of Western Yiddish], *Yidishe shprakh* 13 (1953), 35–69.

[5] See Fl. Guggenheim-Grünberg: *Die Sprache der Schweizer Juden von Endingen und Lengnau*, 1950, and *Aus einem alten Endinger Gemeindebuch*, 1952 (both published by Jüdische Buch-Gemeinde, Zurich).

[6] Number ZA 150/151.

"Simches Thore im alten Endinge"; on the other side we have a dialogue between two Jewish horse dealers.

Horse trade as well as cattle trade was one of the most important business specialties of German and Swiss Jews in the 17th and 18th centuries. In that period of unceasing wars and conflicts, the countrywide and even international connections of the Jews equipped them well for horse trading, just as for banking and jewel trade. Since horses were then the chief means of transportation, the German dukes used the Jews as suppliers of riding and carriage horses. The regents of Zurich, too—although they refused to let the Jews come within the walls of the city—permitted Jewish horse dealers from Surbtal to come to a place near the city and offer their horses for sale there.

Among themselves, the Jewish horse dealers used their Yiddish dialect, augmented by many special expressions of their profession. Those technical terms were adapted mostly from Hebrew. Thus they created a kind of professional or special language[7] for their own purposes, and this became a kind of secret language of the trade. It was secret not only from the point of view of non-Jews who understood no Yiddish, but also from the point of view of Jews who were not horse dealers. It was comparable to hunters' slang or to any other special language.

Naturally non-Jewish horse dealers tried to understand and to learn the horse dealers' Yiddish. In a rare book of 1764, entitled *Der vollkommene Pferde-Kenner*, by Wolf E. von Reizenstein, printed in Uffenheim, Germany, we find a large chapter: "Anhang, woraus diejenigen Redens-Arten können erlernet werden, deren sich die Juden in ihrem Umgang gegen einander und sonderlich auf Ross-Märkten bedienen."[8] It offers the reader a large vocabulary and several dialogues on matters of horse trade, accompanied by German translations. The pronunciation of Yiddish in this book is that of the Jews of central Germany—a western Yiddish dialect, too, but different from Swiss Yiddish.

Living in the family of an Endingen horse dealer whose father and ancestors were horse dealers in the same village for more than 200 years, I have had the opportunity to hear this language spoken by H. G. He is truly the last of the Mohicans, for he is the only person today who knows this professional language by continuous transmission from father to son.

There is another group of Jewish horse dealers in Switzerland, a group descended from immigrants from Alsace. I have discovered by interviewing them that they know many of the same professional terms, but render them in the Alsatian pronunciation of Yiddish, which has remarkably changed in the last 150 years, probably under the influence of French. Some of the non-Jewish horse dealers in Switzerland also make occasional use of Yiddish expressions

[7] One is reminded of popular neologisms in present-day Hebrew. Thus, in Israel I heard the expression *ˈʃlaif supaˈpim*, derived from German *schleifen* and French *souspape*, for 'grinding valves', in place of the expression *lṭš šstmym*, created by the official language makers.

[8] "Appendix, from which those expressions may be learned which the Jews make use of in their dealings with each other and especially at horse markets."

which they—or their fathers—learned from the Jews. Such words may eventually be incorporated into the Swiss dialects, just as the Yiddish *malauchen* became a technical term of veterinary medicine (see the vocabulary under *məlɔ:xə*), while Yiddish *mies* 'ugly', *pleite* 'bankrupt', and others have penetrated into German.

The specific horse dealers' language differs from ordinary Swiss Yiddish not only in the specialized expressions, but also in a general excess of words derived from Hebrew roots[9] and used in place of the usual Yiddish words of Germanic derivation.[10] To be sure, the ordinary vernacular of the Surbtal Jews also contained numerous words of Hebrew derivation,[11] but not quite so many as the horse dealers' language; and even these have tended to be progressively replaced by the corresponding German words. The process of de-Hebraization is handsomely illustrated by the so-called *Pinkas Guggenheim of Lengnau.*[12] This is an account book of a family fund, the entries of which, made by eight different writers, extend over a period of as many as 84 years (1750–1834).[13] The inventories of property taken after the death of various Lengnau citizens, extant from

[9] Nouns have not only been adopted as such, but have also served as bases for the derivation of verbs (*xelkənə* 'to divide', *xeʃbənə* 'to reckon', *xiləfə* 'to exchange', *ge:ʃəmə* 'to rain', *gɔrlə* 'to draw lots', *injənə* 'to deal', *məlɔ:xənə* 'to work', *mi:sənə* 'to die', *miʃpətə* 'to be at law'). The formation of periphrastic verbs composed of the Hebrew participle and the auxiliary *saĭ* 'to be' (*makir saĭ* 'to know', *ma:mən saĭ* 'to trust', *mərammə saĭ* 'to cheat'), possibly also in reflexive form (*siç məhanə saĭ* 'to enjoy', *siç məragəs saĭ* 'to be angry'), has receded in comparison with the more productive derivations directly from the Hebrew participle (*hɔuləxə* 'to go', *nɔussənə* 'to give', *ɔumərə* 'to count', *rɔjnə* 'to see', *məˈʃulləmə* 'to pay', *məʃilˈlɛ:xə* 'to dispatch', *mɛjməsə* 'to kill'). The derivatives are often extended by prefixes of Germanic derivation, especially *fər-* (*fərxiləfə*, cf. *ver+tauschen* 'to exchange'; *fərɔumədə*, cf. *ver+stehen* 'to understand'; *fərrɛbəsə*, cf. *ver+zinsen* 'to pay interest for'; *ˈabməgainə*, cf. *ab+schlagen* 'to become cheaper'; *ˈaĭməgainə*, cf. *ein+schlagen* 'to conclude a sale by shaking hands'). Derivations from what are finite verb forms in Hebrew are rather rare; they seem to go back to particularly familiar passages in the Bible or the prayers; cf. *diplə* 'to fall' (*tpl*, Exodus 15:16), *fi:əfrəxə* 'to flee' (*wybrḥ*, Genesis 31:21), *tsifənə* 'to bid' (*w-ṣwnw* 'and has bidden', in many benedictions; interpreted as *geboten*, past participle of both *bieten* and *gebieten*), and so forth.

[10] It is interesting to examine the new formations which arise as a result of expansions and shifts of meaning, i.e. as calques of German or preexisting Yiddish words; cf. *ˈabʃef* 'spavin', formed from G. *ab-* and H. *šb* 'sit' on the model of German *Absatz*; *ˈibərbɔu* 'to receive', formed from G. *ibər-* and H. *b'* 'come', on the model of Sw. *übercho* 'to receive'.

[11] Whether the names of Hebrew letters were formerly used as numerals in ordinary speech, in the way the horse dealers use them to this day, seems uncertain. They are so used in the early written documents (cf. footnotes 12 and 14) almost throughout, and frequently they are even spelled out in full, e.g. *ywm gyml* 'Tuesday', *ṭyt zhb' wyw pṣ wḥṣy* 'nine gulden and 6½ Batzen', *lmd dnryn* 'thirty dinars', *dlt l'pl'r* 'four spoons'. In the Zurich synagogue it was customary until about twenty years ago to announce pledges in this fashion, e.g. *kafhɛj frã: ləaˈnijm* 'twenty-five francs for the poor'.

[12] See my paper, "Der Pinkas Guggenheim von Lengnau," *Schweizerisches Archiv für Volkskunde* 49 (1953) 201–206.

[13] In 1752, 'bought' is still frequently rendered as *ḳwnh gww'zn* as well as by *ḳwypṭ* (using the Hebrew transliteration). Later on, only the latter form is attested. In the earlier years one constantly reads *'ḥy* 'my brother' and *gysy* 'my brother-in-law'; later on only the equivalents of Germanic origin appear.

the years 1788–1835, also illustrate the decreasing use of words of Hebrew origin.[14] In contrast to this process, the horse dealers to this day prefer expressions of Hebrew origin which are unintelligible to the uninitiated. Other Surbtal Jews, who are not horse dealers, occasionally may make use of such expressions, too, for confidential remarks in the presence of non-Jews.[15] This secret language is still called *loʃən əkoudəʃ*, in opposition to *ˈjiddiʃdaitʃ*, the ordinary vernacular.

Following is a conversation of two horse dealers which I have recorded and transcribed, accompanied by an English translation.

Note on Transcription and Pronunciation

Vowels.

a is a central vowel; only in the sequence *ai* is it slightly fronted.

The pronunciation of the remaining vowels differs, sometimes quite markedly, from one informant to the other, even in the same word or in similar positions in another word.[16] The following variations may be noted:

(1) Between close *e* and open *ɪ*, e.g. *hen* or *hɪn* 'have (pl.)', *men* or *mɪn* 'must (pl.)'.

(2) Between close *i* or open *ɪ* up to open *ɛ*, e.g. *ˈjidɪʃ* or *ˈjɪdɪʃ* or *ˈjɛdɪʃ* 'Yiddish, Jewish', *missə* or *mɪssə* or *mɛssə* 'must (infin.)', but especially before *r*, e.g. *virt* or *vɪrt* or *vɛrt* 'host'.[17]

(3) Between close *o* and open *ʊ*, e.g. *xo:xəm* or *xʊ:xəm* 'wise man', *jontəf* or *jʊntəf* 'holiday'. In the glossary we transcribe regularly *o*.

(4) Between *ɔu* and *ɒu*, e.g. *kɔunə* or *kɒunə* 'buyer'.

The masculine plural suffix of Hebrew origin, *-ɪm*, is unstressed and has a tendency to be weakened to *-əm*.

Nasalization of vowels where a following *n* has been dropped is indicated, e.g.

[14] The early (1788) inventories, for example, have *bdyl, nḥšt, mṭlṭlyn* 'tin, copper, chattel', whereas the later ones (1813) write *ṣyn, ḳwbp'r, p'rwns* (Sw. *Fahrnis*).

[15] Thus boys would warn each other when a guard was about to surprise them in a forbidden spot: *həuləx fi·əfrəx dər ʃoumər is bəka:n!* 'beat it, the policeman is here!'.

[16] Reizenstein made similar observations in 1764. He writes: "NB. Bey dem Aufsuchen der Wörter kan man sich nicht allemal nach dem Aussprechen der Juden richten, indem solches unter ihnen selbst sehr verschieden ist, sie sprechen öfters das *a* wie *o*, und das *e* wie *i* aus, das *au* wie *ou*, oder wie *o*, das *v* manchmal wie *f* manchmal wie ein *w*, das *ch* manchmal wie ein *k* u.s.w. öfters lassen sie ganze Silben gar weg, daher ist es gut, dass man sich gleich Anfangs so wohl aus diesem Wörter-Buch, als auch aus denen nachfolgenden Gesprächen ihre Haupt-Wörter bekannt mache, und hernach bey Gelegenheit nur Acht gebe, wie solche von denen Juden ausgesprochen werden." ("In looking up the words one cannot always rely on the pronunciation of the Jews, for it differs even among them; they frequently pronounce *a* as *o*, and *e* as *i*, *au* as *ou* or as *o*, *v* sometimes like *f* and sometimes like *w*, *ch* sometimes like *k*, etc. Frequently they omit entire syllables altogether; hence it is well to familiarize oneself from the very beginning with their principal words, from this dictionary as well as from the following conversational texts, and hereafter merely to note on occasion, how they are pronounced by the Jews.")

[17] The *ɛ*-pronunciation is old. In a lease for the Jewish cemetery given to the Surbtal Jews by the town of Waldshut in 1747, the representative Pickart of Endingen, who is mentioned in the German text as *Beckharth*, signed his name in Hebrew letters as *pyḳrt*.

ˈbã:ho·f 'railroad station', *ˈaĩda:nə* 'argue'; but before preserved *n*, where it is automatic, it is not indicated, e.g. *ˈabməgaint* = [ˈabmegaĩnt] 'fallen in price'.[18]

Consonants.

The lenis sounds *b*, *d*, *g*, *z*, *ʒ* are always voiceless, as is common in Swiss, South German, and Central German dialects; they are transcribed here without the diacritic [̥]. The characteristic semi-fortes are designated by a bar under the consonant (*d̠*, *t̠*, *b̠*, *p̠*, *f̠*, *g̠*, *k̠*).

In root-initial position before vowels, *k* is an aspirated velar stop; intervocalically it is unaspirated. Thus *kʰatsəf* 'butcher', *kʰats* 'cat', *fərkʰanjənə* 'to sell', but *sik̠k̠ə* 'Tabernacle', *ʃuk* 'market'. Quite frequently unaspirated *k* is lenicized to the semi-fortis *k̠*, e.g. *jɔuk̠ər*; initially before consonants also to the even weaker semi-fortis *g̠*, e.g. *g̠lɔufɪm*, plural of *kʰɛiləf* 'dog'.

x designates generally the strong velar fricative; before *a* and *ɔ* it stands for a uvular fricative.

g indicates the lenis equivalent of *x*, e.g. *lɛ:gəm* 'bread'.

The pronunciation of the stops *b—p*, *d—t*, vacillates on the part of the individual informants from voiceless lenis *b*, *d* through the semi-fortis stages *b̠*, *d̠* and *p̠*, *t̠*, to the voiceless fortes *p*, *t*. All speakers display variants in word-initial position which are more fortis than those in intervocalic position: e.g. *b̠ɛjgərə* > *gəbɛjgərt* 'to die' or *p̠ɛjgərə* > *gəb̠ɛjgərt*; *ta:m* 'taste' > *ˈu:t̠a:m* 'clumsy person' or *t̠a:m* > *ˈu:d̠a:m*. In the phonetic transcription of the conversation we note the degrees of tenseness *b̠*, *d̠*, and *g̠*, while in the glossary we let a more generalized *b*, *d*, and *g* stand for the voiceless lenis as well as for the slightly more fortis *b̠*, *d̠*, and *g̠*; the even more fortis *p̠*, *t̠*, *k̠* are noted in this way both in the text and in the glossary.[19]

The symbol *v* indicates the voiced labiodental lenis. The equivalent voiceless sound is represented by the symbol for the semi-fortis *f̠*, to which it is practically not opposed.

The fricatives *ʃ* and *ç* are audibly distinguished only in intensity; *ʃ* sounds fuller and more intense as a result of a slight protrusion of the lips during its articulation. The palatogram shows that the point of articulation of *ç* lies slightly further back than that of *ʃ*.[20] *ç* appears in words in which it corresponds etymo-

[18] Short, normally unstressed words like *dra* (G. *dran*) or the possessives *mai, dai, sai,* have nasalized vowels only when they receive sentence emphasis, e.g. *ˈmaĩ hɔuz* 'my house (not another's)'. Some informants also nasalize the diphthongs in *gɛjʃ* 'go (2. sg.)', *fərʃtejʃ* 'understand (2. sg.)'.

[19] The distribution of lenis and fortis consonants in words of Germanic derivation corresponds, according to my observations, to their status in the dialects of northwestern Switzerland (cf. E. Dieth: *Vademekum der Phonetik*, Berne, 1950, p. 360). Whether an original initial fortis in a word of Hebrew derivation is lenicized more or less (e.g. *p̠ɛjsəx* or *b̠ɛjsəx* 'Passover') seems to depend on the speaker's knowledge of Hebrew or his familiarity with the liturgy. In contrast to Surbtal Yiddish, the language of the Alsatian Jews, especially that of Lower Alsace, is marked by a far more extensive lenicization of original fortes.

[20] The palatogramm for *ç* shows the front of the tongue to be in a position similar to that of *ʃ*, while the dorsum is raised as much as for the Standard German *ich*-sound, but shows an additional rise at the forward boundary of the soft palate.

logically to the standard German *ich*-sound. (In Alsatian Yiddish, *ʃ* and *ç* have merged into a single phoneme, *ʃ*.)

The vibrant, represented by *r*, is always uvular.

The values of other symbols are those of the I.P.A.

Stress.

The reduced vowel *ə* is never stressed. In the glossary we indicate the stress only in words containing more than one syllable with vowels other than *ə*. In the transcribed conversational text we have placed the stress symbol near the center of each stress group.

Transliteration of Hebrew Roots.

The Hebrew roots are cited according to the system explained on p. viii (§ 2a).

Abbreviations.

dim. = diminutive; fem. = feminine; Fr. = French; G. = German(ic); H. = Hebrew; pl. = plural; sg. = singular; st. Y. = standard (East European) Yiddish; Sw. = Swiss German.

TEXT	TRANSLATION
ˈʃmu:lə und ˈaɪzɪg trefəd siç ˈtsba:də am ˈbã:ho·f	Shmule and Ayzig Meet at the Railroad Station in Baden
ʃ. ʃumˈlɛ:gəm ˈaɪzɪg | ˈa:x ʃɔũ uf? gɛjʃ ˈa:x ʊf ˈsolədɔrn?	S.: Hello, Ayzig! Already up, too? Are you also going to Solothurn?
a. hoʃ gəˈrɔutə ‖ də ˈfebrʊar ʃuk̲ ɪʒ ˈaləvail də ˈbeʃt ʃuk̲ ˈtsolədɔrn.	A.: You've guessed it. The February fair is always the best fair in Solothurn.
ʃ. bəˈhɛjməz hod̲s ˈmɛj vi ˈsus·ɪm | abər ɪç vɔr ˈdɔx ə pa:r ˈgatiŋi ˈmɛrəs nɪd ˈtsjɔuk̲ər bəkumə.	S.: There will be more cattle than horses, but anyhow I'll get some usable mares [that will be] not too expensive.
a. di ˈsus·ɪm hen ˈo:sər nɪd ˈabməgaint ‖ di ˈtofi ʃuk̲əd ˈharbə | un di ˈg̲lɔufɪm sɪn ˈo:sər tsfərˈkinjənə.	A.: The horses have certainly not become cheaper; the good ones cost a lot and the bad ones can't be sold.
ʃ. di ˈjanigɪ ˈsus·ɪm ʊs ˈtsarfəs sin ˈtsjɔuk̲ər ‖ di ˈvatlendər und ˈbɛrnər ˈinjəniʃɪm hen ˈa:x tsɔ:rəs ə tof sus ˈaĩtsxiləfə un kenəd ˈka:ni məˈtsi:əs fərkanjənə.	S.: The young horses from France are too expensive. Dealers in [the cantons of] Vaud and Berne also have difficulties in exchanging a good horse [for a foal] and cannot sell any bargains.
a. hoʃ daini tsvai ˈaĩgəxiləfdɪ ˈnabəlsus·ɪm əm ˈkatsəf tsbruk̲ fərˈka:ft?	A.: Have you sold the two exchanged neckers to the [horse] butcher at Brugg?
ʃ. ɪç hab əm si ʊm bɛjs ˈmɛjəs gəˈnɔusənt ‖ zi zɪn mənəˈʃʊmə zol | abər iç va:s ˈʊ:sər kan andərə ˈkɔunə ‖ ˈnabəlsus·ɪm sin kan mazəˈmatən fɔr miç.	S.: I gave them to him for two hundred [francs]. They are cheap, by God, but I don't know of any other buyer. Neckers are no business for me.

a. un di ˈʃo:xər ˈmɛrə fʊn arˈbɛrg | hoʃ di fərˈkinjənt?

A.: And the black mare of Aarberg, have you sold her?

ʃ. ˈʊ:sər ‖ mai ˈkɔunə hod si də ˈrɔufə ˈrɔijnə losə ‖ dem hen di ˈne:ləmər un di rəgˈlaijm lɔu gəd̲ipəlt ‖ də ˈʃo:l fom ˈfro:mələ iʃ ˈtsro:sən gəve: un ˈtsṯɔufəl | und di ˈtse:fə d̲ipəlt əm ˈa:x lɔu ‖ di ˈaltɪ hen ˈjʊ:ʃər ghet | ven dər mazəˈmatən ˈhɔuləxt | iʃ ə ˈfigslən ə ˈfug̲s | un ven ˈnig̲s gɛjt | iʃ ə ˈfug̲s ə ˈfig̲slə.

S.: Oh, no. My customer showed her to the veterinarian. He disliked the hoofs and legs. The chestnut from Fromele was too poor and too old, and he didn't like the color, either. The old ones [i.e. our fathers] were right: when business is good, a small chestnut is a big one; when there is no trade, a big one is a small one.

a. vil də ˈfu:rmə ˈzimxə sai məˈkeds ˈmɛ·rlə nid fərˈxiləfə? ɪç hed̲ mənəˈ-ʒʊmə ə ˈvolfəl ˈsislə fɔr sai agəl ‖ ə ˈtɔufəl ˈkɛjləflə | das tof ˈhɔuləxt un ˈlɔu harbə ˈmispə axəlt | und ˈaləvail ˈjɔufə blaibt.

A.: Doesn't drayman Simkhe like to trade in his broken-winded little mare? By God, I have a cheap cob for his carriage. An old animal that trots well, and does not eat much hay and always remains good-looking.

ʃ. ɪç ˈgla:b | fɔr ˈdem sai mazəˈmatən | das bislə ˈdsxɔ:rə fʊm ˈsik̲kəta·l uf ˈendiŋə dsfi·ərə | gɛjt sai ˈk̲laftələ nɔx gut gəˈnug ‖ ˈd̲e·r hot ˈa:x ə mazəˈmatən tsʊm məˈxulə gɛj ‖ ˈʊ:sər məˈfi·əxt ər ˈzaxlə dəmit.

S.: I think for his job—bringing the few goods from Siggental to Endingen—his old beast will be good enough. He, too, has a business [good] for going broke; he hardly earns [enough for] his food from it.

a. mit di ˈsus·ɪm iz ˈa:x nɔx ˈka:nər ə ˈko:tsən vɔrə ‖ mə hɔd tsfi:l jəˈtsʊ:əz ʊnd tsfi:l ˈhɛzɪg.

A.: Horses also have yet to make anyone rich. One has too many expenses and too much risk.

ʃ. hɔʃ ˈjʊ:ʃər ‖ də bəˈhɛjməz handəl iz ˈt̲eʃər.

S.: You are right, cattle trade is better.

a. ˈjɒʊ | a·bər mit di ˈsus·ɪm iz əz bəˈko:ʃətigər.

A.: Yes, but the business of horses is more respectable.

ʃ. fiˈlaiçt | ˈsrɔuxənt ve:nigər.

S.: Perhaps. It stinks less.

a. ˈro:jn əmvʊl də ˈgo·j bəˈka:n | biʃ dər ɛ:rəl ˈmak̲ə?

A.: Look at the [gentile] chap there, do you know him?

ʃ. ˈde·r iʃ mər nɔx ə ˈsus xajəf | abər də ˈxɔf iʃ ˈtof | ər məˈʃʊləmt ɪmə ˈʃo:nə | mit ˈhɛiləmɛjə[21] ˈrɛbəz | iç habs gut kesˈfaint.

S.: He still owes me a horse, but the debt is good. He will pay within a year, with five percent interest. I put it in writing properly.

a. ər iz ˈbai mər gəˈve: vegə dər ˈʃo:xər ˈmɛrə fɔm ˈʃa·jə ˈtsbɔrdləf.

A.: He has been at my place about the black mare from Shaye in Burgdorf.

ʃ. vɔz hɔd ər gəˈdsifənt?

S.: What did he bid?

a. ˈfo:f ˈmɛjəs ka·fˈhɛj ‖ iç hab ən

A.: Six hundred twenty-five. I wanted

[21] On the record: *hɛiləmɛjəs* (a slip of the tongue).

fɔr ˈzo·jn mɛjəs ˈnʊʊs·ənə velə ‖ abər də ˈgo·j vo ˈmit əm gəˈve:[22] *iz | hot ˈkaljəs gəmaxt | sus sai*[23] *ə ˈtaljən | ə ˈkɛjləf ‖ iç bɪn ˈɛ:rəf | der bəkunt sasˈro:əs fʊm ˈrossfro:mələ.*

to give her to him for seven hundred. But the [gentile] man who was with him spoiled it. Said the horse was a sorry jade, a necker. I guarantee he is getting commission from Horse-Fromele [a dealer].

ʃ. ˈjɔu | der hot̲ uf ˈali andərɪ kinəˈzinə ‖ hoʃ ka·n ˈãməgain fɔr ə ˈtɔufəl ˈgatiŋ ˈminiʃlə | ˈtof in dər məˈlɔ:xə | ˈvolfəl | iç ˈnɔusəns fɔr ˈkaf gəˈd̲i:xəliç | abər ˈo:ni ɛˈrufəs | fərˈʃtɛjʃ?

S.: Yes, that chap is envious of everybody. You have no customer for a nice old little gelding, good at work, cheap? I'll let him go for twenty guineas, but without guarantee, you understand.

a. iç vil dra ˈdengə ‖ ˈjɒjɒu | mər hot̲ sai ˈgsɛ:rəs mit di ɛˈrufəs..

A.: I'll think about it. Yes, yes, one has one's troubles with guarantees.

ʃ. ˈjets mus iç dər nɔx ə ˈtof ˈmɔuʃələ fərˈtsɛjlə ‖ də letʃt ˈsʊnt̲ɪg hot̲ də ˈnuməfa:l əmə ˈkɔunə ə ˈb̲ɔ:rə ˈrɔijnə lɔsə ‖ sai ˈɛifədlə | das ˈʃɔutələ fʊ ˈti:ŋə | hod̲ si ɔuzəm ˈxɛidər ˈɔussə ləˈkɛ:xt ‖ di ˈb̲ɔrə hod̲ ə ˈjɔufə ˈb̲ɪ:nəmlə | abər ən ˈmi:sə ˈtʊ:xəs ghet ‖ das ˈɛif̲ədlə ʃtelt di ˈb̲ɔrə ˈjuʃt mit əm ˈtʊ:xəs gegə də ˈkɔunən anə ‖ dɔ ˈʃrait də ˈnuməfa:l ‖ du ˈʃɔutə | los də ˈrɔʃ roijnə ‖ vas ˈtu·t də ˈxamər fɔmən ˈɛif̲əd? ər tsi:t ˈsai kap fʊn ˈsaim rɔʃ.

S.: Now I still have to tell you a funny story. Last Sunday Numefahl was showing a cow to a customer. His farmhand, that little fool from Tiengen, took her out of the stable. The cow had a nice head but a bad rear. The boy placed the cow precisely with her rear to the customer. Numefahl yelled: "You fool, let [him] see the head!" What does the ass of a cowhand do? He takes his cap off his [own] head!

a. ˈhaha | ˈɛigəl blaibt ˈɛigəl ‖ abər ˈjets ˈd̲axləs | hoʃ ep̲əs ˈtsaxlə bai dər? iç ˈkent̲ mənəˈʒʊmə ep̲əs ˈesə | iç hab ˈro:f.

A.: Haha, a calf [i.e. a fool] remains a calf! But now, let's be serious. Have you anything to eat with you? I could eat something, by God. I am hungry.

ʃ. ˈeməs | iç hab ə bəˈko:fət̲ig ʃtik ˈsupəfla:ʃ bai mər | und ə ˈknobliʒ-vɔrʃt fʊm ˈʃma:jə ‖ kanʃ ˈa:x dərfo hɔũ ‖ ˈlɛ:gəm hab iç ˈa:x.

S.: Sure. I have a nice piece of boiled beef and a garlic sausage from Shmaye. You might have some of it, too. I also have bread.

a. un ˈiç hab ə fleʃ ˈjaijn bai mər ‖ ləˈxaijm ˈʒmu:lə.

A.: And I have a bottle of wine with me. Cheers, Shmule!

Glossary

The following glossary lists difficult words occurring in the conversation, words which would not be intelligible to readers with a knowledge of standard

[22] On the record: *gəve:zə* (influenced by standard German).
[23] On the record: *sɛig* (influenced by Swiss German).

Yiddish or German. Certain additional items of this horse dealers' language are also included. As a rule, only those meanings are cited which are relevant to horse trade. German translations have been included for the benefit of Swiss readers as well as indications of the models in the case of calques, as in the first word. Because of the not entirely stable distinctions between fortes and lenes (see p. 52 above), words beginning in p̲ have been put immediately after those in b; similarly for t̲ after d. The letter x comes in the alphabetical place of *ch*.

ˈabʃef (G. *ab-*, H. *šb* 'sit') 'spavin; Absatz, Spat beim Pferd'

axlə (H. *'kl*) 'to eat, to feed; essen, fressen' (st. Y. *akhlen* '(slang) to eat') *aˈxi:lə* 'eating; Essen'

agəl (H. *'gl*) 'carriage; Wagen' (st. Y. *agole* 'hearse') *ˈagəl-sus* 'carriage horse; Wagenpferd' *aglə* 'to go (by vehicle); fahren' *aglər* 'drayman, driver; Fuhrmann, Fahrer'

ˈaĩda:nə (G. *ein-*, H. *ṭ'n*) 'to discuss; unterhandeln, diskutieren' (st. Y. *ayntaynen*)

ˈã:məgain (G. *an-*, H. see *məgainə*) 'offer, buyer; Anschlag, Käufer'

assgənə (H. *'sḳ*) 'to trade, to deal; handeln'

badsəf (H. *prṣwp*) 'face; Gesicht' (st. Y. *partsef*)

baifə, ba:fə (Fr. *boire* ?) 'to drink (of men or cattle); trinken (Mensch oder Tier)' *ˈbafme·s*, *ˈba:fmo:mən* 'tip; Trinkgeld'

baiʃən (H. *byšn*) 'bashful; schüchtern' (st. Y. *bayshn* 'bashful person') *siç baiʃənə* 'to be bashful; sich genieren'

balˈbos (H. *b'l byt*) '(house) owner, boss; Hausherr, Chef' (st. Y. *balebós*)

battərə (H. *pṭr*) 'to get rid of, to sell out; loswerden, ausverkaufen' (st. Y. *patern*)

ˈbatiʃ, battərʃ (H. *pṭr*, G. *-isch*) 'pregnant; trächtig' *ˈbatiʃə, battərʃə* 'to give birth to (of cattle); werfen, gebären (vom Vieh)'

bəxinəm (H. *b-ḥnm*) 'free of charge; umsonst, unentgeltlich' (st. Y. *bekhinem*)

bət̲e·ikə (H. *b-dywḳ*) 'completed; in order; abgeschlossen, in Ordnung'

bəhɛimə, pl. *bəhɛiməs* (H. *bhmh*) 'animal, cattle; Tier, Rindvieh' (st. Y. *beheyme*)

bɛjgərə (H. *pgr*) 'to die; verenden' *makəs un ˈbɛjgəri fiʃ* 'blows and rotten fish (rubbing it in); Prügel und faule Fische (wenn man zum Schaden noch den Spott hat)' (st. Y. *peygern*)

bɛj (H. *ph*) '(animal) mouth; Maul' *er hod ka simən im bɛj* '(the horse) has no marks in its mouth (to indicate age); (das Pferd) hat keine Kennzeichen im Maul (zur Bestimmung des Alters)'

bɛjs (H. *byt*) 'two; zwei' *bɛjsˈmɛjəs* 'two hundred; zweihundert'

bəka:n (H. *b+k'n*) 'here; hier'

bəˈkʊ:fət̲ig (H. *b+kbwd*, G. *-ig*) 'respectable, presentable; vornehm, ansehnlich' (st. Y. *bekóvedik*)

bətu:əx (H. *bṭwḥ*) 'well-to-do, deserving credit; wohlhabend, kreditfähig' (st. Y. *botuakh* 'convinced')

bilbəl (H. *blbwl*) 'pretext, complaint; Vorwand, Reklamation' (st. Y. *bilbl* 'false accusation')

bɔrə (H. *prh*) 'cow; Kuh' *bɔrəsər* 'cattle dealer, "Cowman" (sobriquet given to Surbtal Jews by the Jews of the province of Baden); Viehhändler, "Küher" (Uebername für die Surbtaler Juden im Munde der badischen Juden)'

bɔu (H. *ph* and *bw'*) 'here, arrived; da, gekommen' *ˈibərbɔu saĩ* 'to receive; bekommen' (analogically with Sw. *übercho*)

brɛ:rə (H. *brrh*) 'choice, alternative; Wahl, Auswahl' (st. Y. *breyre*)

bri·jəs (H. *bry'wt*) 'guarantee, security (in cattle trade); Garantie, Währschaft im Viehhandel'

plɛitə (H. *plṭh*) 'flight; bankruptcy; Flucht, Bankrott' *plɛitə hɔuləxə* 'take flight; die Flucht ergreifen' (st. Y. *pleyte* 'flight')

po:nəm, pl. *pɪ:nəmər*, dim. *pɪ:nəmlə*, pl. *ˈpɪ:nəmliç* (H. *pnym*) 'face; Gesicht' (st. Y. *ponim*) *ləˈhaxləs-po:nəm* 'spiteful person; einer, der andere ärgern will'

pəuʃət, pl. *pʃitəm* (H. *pšwṭ*) 'cent; 'Rappe (coin)' *er is kan pəuʃət ʃoufə* 'he isn't worth a damn; er ist keinen Pfifferling wert'

pʃɔ:rə (H. *pšrh*) 'settlement, compromise; Vergleich, Kompromiss' (st. Y. *pshore*)

ˈxadiʃ (H. *ḥdš*) 'new; neu' *balˈxidiʃ* 'curious; neugierig' *siç fərˈxiddiʃə* 'to be surprised; sich verwundern' (st. Y. *zikh farkhídeshn*)

xafər (H. *ḥbr*) '1. friend; Genosse, Freund; 2. match horse; Passpferd' (st. Y. *khaver* 'friend') *ˈkipə-xafər* 'business partner; Geschäftsteilhaber'

xaj (H. *ḥy*) 'eighteen; achtzehn' (st. Y. *khay*) *xaj tsal* '18 Kreuzer = 65 Rappen'

xajəf (H. *ḥyb*) 'owing; schuldig' (st. Y. *khayev* 'guilty')

xajəˈrəuʃə (H. *ḥyy r'šy*) 'upon my head! (oath); 'bei meinem Kopf! (Bekräftigung)' pl. *xajˈrəuʃəs*, dim. *xajˈrəuʃələ* 'sobriquet for inhabitants of Endingen and Lengnau; Uebername für Endinger und Lengnauer'

xajəs (H. *ḥywt*) 'life, temperament; Leben, Temperament' (st. Y. *khayes, khiyes*) *fərˈxajəsd* 'in love; verliebt'

xaˈla:s (H. *ḥl'wt*) 'dirty thing, bad luck; schmutzige Sache, Pech, Missgeschick' (st. Y. *khalaas* 'disease')

xaləf (H. *ḥlp*) '(slaughtering) knife; Messer, Schächtmesser' (st. Y. *khalef*)

xaˈlɔuʃəs (H. *ḥlšwt*) 'faint, nauseous; ohnmächtig, übel' (st. Y. *khaloshes* 'faint')

xamər (H. *ḥmwr*) 'donkey; Esel' (st. Y. *khamer* '(slang) ass')

xazən (H. *ḥzn*) 'cantor; Vorsinger' (st. Y. *khazn*) *sus is ə xazən* 'the horse is a whistler; das Pferd ist Rohrer'

xaˈzɔ:rən (H. *ḥsrwn*) '(human or animal) defect; Fehler, Makel (an Tier und Menschen)' (st. Y. *khisorn*)

xɛidər (H. *ḥdr*) 'stable; Stall' (st. Y. *kheyder* 'room; school')

xɛiləf (H. *ḥlb*) 'fat; Fett' (st. Y. *kheylev* 'tallow')

xɛilək (H. *ḥlk*) 'part, share; Teil, Anteil' (st. Y. *kheylek*) *xelkənə* 'to divide; teilen'

ˈxɛiʃig (H. *ḥšk*) 'eager to buy; kauflustig' (st. Y. *kheyshek* 'desire')

xərɔutə ta:nə (H. *ḥrṭh, ṭ'n*) 'to regret, to change one's mind; Reue haben, sich anders besinnen' (st. Y. *kharote* 'remorse')

xəʃad (H. *ḥšd*) 'assumption, doubt; Vermutung, Zweifel' (st. Y. *khshad* 'suspicion')

xeʃbən, pl. *xeʃˈbɔunɪm* (H. *ḥšbwn*) 'account; Rechnung' (st. Y. *kheshbn*, pl. *kheshboynes*) *xeʃbənə* 'to calculate; rechnen' (st. Y. *khéshbenen*) *xigər* (H. *ḥgr*) 'lame, limping; lahm, hinkend' *ˈtsɛiləm-xigər* 'lame in the hip; kreuzlahm'

xiləf (H. *ḥlwp*) 'barter, exchange; Tausch, Wechsel' (st. Y. *khilef* '(money) exchange') *ˈxiləf-sus* 'exchange (i.e. traded) horse; Tauschpferd' *xiləfə* 'to exchange; tauschen' *ˈaĩxiləfə* 'to exchange (*perfective*); eintauschen' *fərˈxiləfə* 'to switch; vertauschen'

ˈxilɪk̲ (H. *ḥlwk̲*) 'division, difference; Teilung, Differenz, Unterschied' (st. Y. *khilek*) *ə ˈxilɪk̲ for ən ˈunterʃi:d* 'it's no difference; es ist kein Unterschied' *xelk̲ənəd də ˈxilɪk̲* 'cut the difference; teilt die Differenz'

xo:xəm (H. *ḥkm*) 'wise, clever; gescheit, klug' (st. Y. *khokhem* 'wise man') *ˈfaixo:xəm* (H. *w-ḥkm*) 'overly clever, crafty; überklug, spitzfindig' *xɔxmə*, pl. *-s* 'wisdom; cleverness' (st. Y. *khokhme*) *xo:xəmə*, *ˈɔusxo:-xəmə* 'to puzzle out; austüfteln' (st. Y. *khokhmen zikh* 'to joke')

xɔf, pl. *xɔuf̲əs* (H. *ḥwb*) 'debt; Schuld' (st. Y. *khoyv*)

xɔljəs (H. *ḥlywt*) 'disease; Krankheit' *er hot ə xɔljəs po:nəm* 'he looks ill; er sieht schlecht aus'

xo:ʃəf (H. *ḥšwb*) 'well liked, suitable, proper; beliebt, passend, anständig' (st. Y. *khoshev* 'respected')

xɔulə (H. *ḥwlh*) 'sick; krank' (st. Y. *khoyle* 'sick person')

xʊtsə (H. *ḥṣy*) 'half; halb' (st. Y. *khotsi*—in special expressions) *xʊtsə-ˈmɛjə* 'fifty; fünfzig'

daj (H. *dy*) 'enough; genug'—used in the following expressions: *los es daj saĩ* 'let that be enough; lass es genug sein' *daˈjɛinə* 'enough; genug' *ẓman daˈjɛinə* 'plenty of time; Zeit genug'

daĩŋə (H. *d'gh*) 'worry; Sorge' (st. Y. *dayge*) *daĩŋəs fɔr ˈungəle:gtɪ ajər* 'worries about unlaid eggs, idle worries; unnütze Sorgen'

dalə (H. *dlg*) 'to jump, to run (horse); springen, laufen (vom Pferd)'

daləs (H. *dlwt*) 'poverty; Armut' (st. Y. *dales*) *er hot də daləs* 'he is penniless; er ist ohne Geld'

dam (H. *dm*) 'blood, temper; Blut, Temperament'

diplə (H. *tpl*, see footnote 9) 'to fall, to please; fallen, gefallen' *di ɛrəxər sin gədipəlt* 'the prices have fallen; die Preise sind gefallen' *es dipəlt mər lɔu* 'I don't like it; es gefällt mir nicht' *dippəl* 'fall; Fall' *di bəhɛiməs hen dər dippəl* 'cattle prices are falling; die Viehpreise fallen'

dsxɔ:rə (H. *sḥwrh*) 'goods; Ware' (st. Y. *skhoyre*) *ˈdsxɔ:rə-hendlər* 'yard-goods merchant; Tuchhändler'

t̲axləs (H. *tklyt*) 'to the point; sachlich, zur Sache' (st. Y. *takhles* 'serious business')

taljən (H. *tlyn*) 'sorry jade; Schindmähre' (st. Y. 'hangman')

tof (H. *ṭwb*), comparative: *tefər* 'good; gut'

to:mə (H. *ṭm'*) 'glanders; Rotzkrankheit (beim Pferd)' (st. Y. 'ritually unclean')

tɔufəl (H. *ṭpl*?) 'old; alt'

tsafər (H. *ṣw'r*) 'neck, throat; Hals'

tsarfəs (H. *ṣrpt*) 'France; Frankreich' (st. Y.—only in a Jewish historical sense)

tse:fə (H. *ṣb'*) 'color; Farbe'

tsɛjləmər, *ˈtsɛjləmdigər* (H. *ṣlm*) 'Kreuzer (coin)' (st. Y. *tseylem* 'cross')

tse:k̲ənə (H. *ṣ'k̲*) 'yell, complain; schreien, reklamieren' *er tse:k̲ənt um lɔu* 'he is complaining about nothing; er reklamiert grundlos' *gətse:k̲*, pl. *gətse:k̲əs* 'complaint; Reklamation'

tsifənə (H. *ṣwh*, see footnote 9) 'to bid; bieten (im Handel)'

tsifəs'jad (H. *ktybt yd*), pl. *tsifəs'jɔudəs* 'promissory note; Schuldverschreibung'

tsɔrə (H. *ṣrh*) 'worry; Sorge' (st. Y. *tsore* 'trouble')

tʃu:fə (H. *tšwbh*) 'answer; Antwort' (st. Y. *tshuve*)

tʊ:xəs (H. *tḥt*) 'hindquarters; Hinterteil' (st. Y. *tokhes*) *vo tʊ:xəs is, is brɔ:xə* 'where there is [big] hindquarters, there is blessing, i.e. wide hindquarters are appreciated; ein breites Hinterteil (am Pferd) gefällt'

tu:ə, siç tu:ə saĩ (H. *ṭ'h*) 'to be mistaken; sich irren' (st. Y. *toe zayn zikh*) *tu:əs maxə* 'to cheat; Betrügereien machen'

ɛifəd, pl. *a'fɔudɪm*, dim. *ɛifədlə* (H. *'bd*) 'farmhand, cowhand; Knecht'

ɛigəl (H. *'gl*) 'calf; Kalb'

ɛ:rəf, pl. *ɛ'ru:fɪm* (H. *'rb*) 'pledge; Bürge' (st. Y. *orev zayn* 'to pledge') *ɛ'rufəs* 'pledge, guarantee; Bürgschaft, Garantie' (st. Y. *orves*)

ɛ:rəl, pl. *ɛ'ri·lɪm* (H. *'rl*) 'non-Jew; Nichtjude' (st. Y. *orl*)

fərmassərə (H. *msr*) 'to betray; verraten' (st. Y. [*far*]*masern* 'to denounce')

fərmaslə (H. *mzl*) 'to frustrate, to abolish; vereiteln, zunichtemachen'

fərɔumədə (H. *'md*) 'to understand; verstehen'

fi·əfrəx hɔuləxə (H. *w-ybrḥ*; see footnote 9) 'to flee, to get away; flüchten, sich davon machen' (st. Y. *makhn vayivrakh*)

'gatiŋ (G.) 'presentable, good-looking; ansehnlich, hübsch'

gədi:xələ, pl. *gə'di:xəliç* (H. *ḥtykh*) '20-franc gold piece; Goldstück zu 20 Fr.'

go·j, pl. *gʊ:jəm* (H. *gwy*) 'non-Jew; Nichtjude' (st. Y. *goy*)

gsɛ:rə, pl. *-s* (H. *gzrh*) 'disagreement, dispute; Widerwärtigkeit, Disput' (st. Y. *gzeyre* 'evil decree')

gsɔ:rlə, pl. *gsɔ:rəm* (H. *ktrym*) 'crown, franc (coin); Krone, Franken' (st. Y. *ksorim* 'ornamental crowns on Torah scrolls')

hamtənə (H. *hmtn*) 'to wait; warten' *uf hamti:nə* 'on credit; auf Borg'

harbə (H. *hrbh*) 'many, much; viel'

hɛjər (H. *h'*) '5-franc piece; Fünffrankenstück' *hɛjlə'mɛjə* 'five percent; fünf Prozent'

'hɛzik̲ (H. *hzḳ*) 'loss, risk; Schaden, Risiko' (st. Y. 'loss')

hiləx (H. *hlwk*) 'pace; Gang' *hɔuləxə* 'to go; gehen' (st. Y. *hilekh* 'get-up, appearance'; *hoylekhn* '(humorous) to walk')

'injən-iʃ, pl. *'injən-iʃəm* (H. *'nyn, 'yš*) 'dealer; Händler' *'sussəm-injən-iš* 'horse dealer; Pferdehändler'

ivər (H. *'wr*) 'blind'

'jaijn (H. *yyn*) 'wine; Wein'

'jakrɪs (H. *yḳrwt*) 'expensive; teuer' (st. Y. 'dearth') *'jakrɪs da'jɛinə* 'expensive enough; teuer genug'

'janig, dim. pl. *'janigliç* (H. *ynyḳ*) 'young, young one; jung, Junges'

jətsʊ·əs, ətsʊ·əs (H. *hwṣ'wt*) 'expenses; (Geld-)Auslagen' (st. Y. *hoytsoes*)

jidʃə (G. *jüdisch, -en*) 'to circumcise; beschneiden' (st. Y. *yidishn*) *di bɔrə is gəjidʃd* 'the cow's horns have been trimmed; der Kuh sind die Hörner gestutzt worden'

jiʃ'kɔ:x (H. *yyšr kḥk*) 'thanks; danke' (st. Y. *yisher-koyakh*)

jɔufə (H. *yph*) 'beautiful; schön' *'jɔufənɪ dsxɔ:rə* 'handsome goods; schöne Ware' *jɔuḵər* (H. *yḳr*) 'expensive; teuer' *iç ka:fs jɔuḵər* 'I won't bet on it, I don't believe it; ich gebe nichts darauf, ich glaube es nicht'

jo:ʃər (H. *yšr*) 'right; recht' (st. Y. *yoysher* 'justice')

ju:zərlə (H. *ywd*? *'śr* ?) '10-franc piece; Zehnfrankenstück'

kaljəs maxə (H. *klywt*?) 'to dissuade, to frustrate; abraten, vereiteln' (st. Y. *kalye makhn* 'to spoil')

kanjənə, kinjənə (H. *ḳnyn*) 'to buy; kaufen' *fərkanjənə* 'to sell; verkaufen'

katsəf (H. *ḳṣb*) 'butcher; Metzger' (st. Y. *katsev*) *kaˈdsɔufəs* 'butchery; Metzgerei'

kɛiləf, pl. *ˈglɔufɪm*, fem. *ḵlaftə* (H. *klb*) 'dog, poor goods; Hund, Hundware'

kɛ:rən (H. *ḳrn*) 'purchase price; Ankaufspreis' (st. Y. 'capital investment')

kəsfainə (Aramaic *ktb'* ?) 'to write, to agree in writing; schreiben, schriftlich abmachen'

kinəˈsinə (H. *ḳn'h, śn'h*) 'envy, grudge; Neid, Missgunst' (st. Y. *kine-sine* 'envy and hatred')

kipə maxə (H. *ḳph*) 'to do business jointly; gemeinsam Geschäfte machen' *ˈkipə-xafər* 'partner; Teilhaber' *ˈʃtʊ:fəs-kipə* 'common treasury; gemeinsame Kasse'

ko:tsən (H. *ḳṣyn*) 'rich man; reicher Mann' *kəˈtsi:nəmliç* 'like rich people; wie reiche Leute'

kɔunə (H. *ḳwnh*) 'buyer; Käufer' (st. Y. *koyne*)

ksa:f (H. *ktb*) 'contract; Vertrag' (st. Y. *ksav* 'written document')

laxrən (H. *l-'ḥrwn*) 'behind; hinten'

ləxa·jm (H. *l-ḥyym*) 'cheers!; zum Wohl!' (st. Y. *lekhayim*)

lə:gəm (H. *lḥm*) 'bread; Brot'

ləfat (H. *lbd*) 'alone (e.g. in harness); allein, einspännig'

ləkɛ:xə (H. *lḳḥ*) 'to take, to snatch; to take bribes; nehmen, erwischen, sich bestechen lassen' (st. Y. *lakkhenen* 'to snatch')

lodlə (G.) 'to sway, to shake; wackeln, schwabbeln' *ˈlodlig* 'fat; fett' *lodlər* 'horse lame in the hip; kreuzlahmes Pferd'

lo:fən (H. *lbn*) 'white horse; Schimmel'

lo:ʃən (H. *lšwn*) '1. tongue, language; Zunge, Sprache; 2. hoof and mouth disease; Maul- und Klauenseuche' (st. Y. *loshn* 'language') *lo:ʃənə-ˈkɔudəʃ* '1. Hebrew; Hebräisch; 2. horse dealers' language; Pferdehändlersprache' (st. Y. *loshn-koydesh* 'the sacred language (Hebrew)')

lɔu (H. *l'*) 'not, no; nicht, nein' *lɔu-ˈlo:nu* 'out of the question; kommt nicht in Frage' *ˈlɔuʃɔufə* 'good-for-nothing; Nichtsnutz' *ˈlɔumɛjzər*, *ˈhodlɔu* 'destitute person; Habenichts'

maḵə (H. *mkh*; *mg'* ?[24]) sg. 'defect; Makel, Fehler' pl. *maḵəs* 'blows; Schläge' (st. Y. *make* 'boil; trouble') *maḵəs nɔussənə, maḵəsə, fərmaḵəsə* 'to beat; schlagen, verprügeln'

makə saĩ (H. *mkyr*) 'to know; kennen'

ˈmasɪḵ, fem. *maˈsi:ḵə* (H. *mzyḳ*) '1. malevolent; bösartig; 2. (of a horse) one which bites and kicks; (beim Pferd) Schläger und Beisser' (st. Y. *mazik* 'skillful fellow')

mat (H. *m't*) 'little; wenig' *ə matlə* 'a little; ein wenig' *tsmat* 'too little; zu wenig'

mazəˈmatən (H. *mś' w-mtn*) 'deal, trade; Geschäft, Handel' (st. Y.

[24] *mg'* 'touch' may have merged with *mkh* 'blow'; this might explain the semantic difference between singular and plural.

masematn) *mi:sɪ mazə'matən* > *mi:sɪ'matən*

məbɛjə (H. *mṭb'*) 'small coin; kleine Münze' (st. Y. *matbeye* 'coin') *xutsə-mə'bɛjə* 'less than nothing; weniger als nichts'

məxullə (H. *mkwlh*) 'bankrupt; bankrott' (st. Y. *mekhule* 'spoiled')

mədibbərə (H. *mdbr*) 'to speak, to say; reden, sagen' (st. Y. *dabern* 'to babble')

məfi·jəxə (H. *mrwyḥ*) 'to earn; verdienen' (st. Y. *marviakh zayn* 'to profit')

məgainə (H. *mnkh*?[25]) 'to beat, to shoe (a horse); schlagen, beschlagen (Hufe)'; *'abməgainə* 'to become cheaper; billiger werden, abschlagen' *'aĩməgainə* 'to conclude a deal; einschlagen' *'ã:məgain* 'offer, buyer; Anschlag, Käufer'

mɛjə (H. *m'h*) 'one hundred; hundert' *bɛjs'mɛjəs* '200' *mitə mɛjəs kunt dər gɛjəs* 'money brings conceit; mit dem Gelde kommt der Hochmut' (st. Y. *meye* 'hundred (of money)')

me:kəx (H. *mkḥ*) 'purchase price; Kaufpreis' (st. Y. *mekakh* 'price')

me:kər (H. *mkr*) 'tip; Trinkgeld'

məkeds, *məkʊtsər-ruəx* (H. *mkṣr rwḥ*) 'broken winded; dämpfig'

məlɔ:xə (H. *ml'kh*) 'work; Arbeit' (st. Y. *melokhe* 'craft') *məlɔ:xənə* '1. to do physical work; körperlich arbeiten; 2. to treat a horse's teeth in a way that would disguise its true age; künstlich die Zähne des Pferdes verändern, um sein Alter zu verschleiern' *malauchen*—a term of veterinary medicine in Switzerland

[25] Perhaps the development was as follows: H. *mənakɛh* 'reduce prices' > *abme akajenet* '*abgeschlagen* [fallen in price]' (cited by Reizenstein) > *abməgaint*.

mənəʃʊmə, *məʃʊmə* (G. *meine*, H. *nšmh*) 'upon my soul!; meiner Seel!'

mərammə saĩ (H. *mrmh*) 'to cheat, to be cheated; betrügen, betrogen werden' (st. Y. *merame zayn* '(learned) to cheat')

mɛrə (G.), pl. *-s*, dim. *mɛrlə* 'mare; Mähre, Stute'

me:s (H. *m'wt*) 'money; Geld' (st. Y. *moes* '(slang) money')

məʃil'lɛ:xə (H. *mšlḥ*) 'to send; schicken' (st. Y. *meshaleyakh zayn* '(humorous) to dispatch')

məʃɔ:rəs (H. *mšrt*) 'personal servant, farmhand, cowhand; persönlicher Diener, Knecht' (st. Y. *meshores* 'servant')

məʃʊlləmə (H. *mšlm*) 'to pay; bezahlen' (st. Y. *meshalem zayn* 'to remunerate')

mətsi:jə (H. *mṣy'h*) 'bargain; billiger Kauf' (st. Y. *metsie*)

məzumən (H. *mzwmn*) 'in cash; bar' (st. Y. *mezumen*) *mə'zumən me:s* 'cash; Bargeld'

mi:əs (H. *m'ws*) 'repulsive, ugly; widerlich, hässlich' (st. Y. *mies*) *'mi:smaxər* 'pessimist, wet blanket; Pessimist, Spielverderber'

'miniç (G. *Mönch*) '1. gelding; Wallach; 2. ritually neither meat nor milk; rituell nicht Milchding und nicht Fleischding'

mispə (H. *mspw'*) 'hay, straw; Heu, Stroh' *mispənə* 'to feed animals; Tiere füttern'

məuʃələ, pl. *'məuʃəliç* (H. *mšl*) '(funny) story; Geschichtchen' (st. Y. *moshl* 'parable')

nablə (H. *nbl*) 'to slaughter in a nonritual way; nicht rituell schlachten' *'nabəl-sus* 'necker; Schlachtpferd' *'nabəl-bəhɛjməs* 'slaughtering cattle; Schlachtvieh' *ne:ləmər* (H. *n'lym*) 'shoes, hoofs; Schuhe, Hufe'

ˈnɛ:rigə (H. *nhrg*) 'to flay to death; zutode schinden' (st. Y. *hárgenen* 'to kill, (dial.) to beat'; dial. *nerikn* 'to injure')

nɔussənə (H. *ntn*) 'to give; geben' (st. Y. (slang) *nasenen* 'to give')

ɔxəlˈets (H. *'wkl 'ṣ*) 'crib biter (horse); Krippenbeisser'

o:sər (H. *'swr*) '1. forbidden; verboten; 2. truly not; wahrhaftig nicht' *iç dir o:sər* 'I forbid it to you!; ich verbiete es dir' (st. Y. *oser*)

rafgənə (H. *rkb*) 'to ride; reiten' *ˈrafgən-sus* 'riding horse; Reitpferd' *rafgənər* 'rider; Reiter'

rat (abbreviation composed of initials *r, t*) 'Reichstaler (coin)' *ˈxadiʃ-rat* 'Neutaler (coin)'

rɛbəs, pl. *rəˈbʊ:sɪm* (H. *rbyt*) (analogically to H. *rwḥym*?) 'interest; Zins' *fərˈrɛbəsə* 'to pay interest; verzinsen'

rəgˈlajɪm (H. *rglym*) 'feet, legs; Füsse, Beine' (st. Y. (slang) *raglayim*)

rɛifəx (H. *rwḥ*) 'profit, use; Gewinn, Nutzen' (st. Y. *revakh*)

ro:f (H. *r'b*) 'hunger; Hunger'

rɔjnə (H. *r'h*) 'to see; sehen'

rɔʃ (H. *r'š*) 'head; Kopf'

rɔufə (H. *rwp'*) 'doctor, veterinary; Arzt, Tierarzt' (st. Y. *royfe* '(traditionally trained) doctor')

ro:sən (H. *rzwn*) 'slim; mager'

sarfə (H. *śrp*) 'to burn; brennen' (st. Y. (slang) *sarfen*) *ə sarf, ə brand* 'too expensive a buy; ein zu teurer Kauf' *ˈbrandjɔuk̲ər* 'very expensive; sehr teuer'

sassər, balˈsassər (H. *srswr*) 'agent, broker; Vermittler, Makler' (st. Y. *sarser*) *sasˈro:əs* 'brokerage, commission; Vermittlung, -sgebühr' *sassərə* 'to mediate, to act as an agent; vermitteln'

sgo:nə (H. *sknh*) 'risk, danger; Risiko, Gefahr' (st. Y. *sakone*)

sol, bəsol (H. *zwl*) 'cheap; billig, wohlfeil' (st. Y. *zol* 'time of low prices', *bezól* 'cheaply')

srɔ:xə (H. *srḥ*) 'stench; Gestank' (st. Y. *(ge)srokhe*) *srɔ:xənə* 'to stink; stinken'

sus, dim. *sislə*, pl. *ˈsisliç* (H. *sws*) 'horse; Pferd' (st. Y. (slang) *sus*)

ʃaləf (H. *ṣlp*?) '1. whip; Peitsche; 2. gentile boy; nicht jüdischer Jüngling'

ʃefə (H. *šb*) 'to lie (down); liegen, sich niederlegen'

ʃmadə (H. *šmd*) 'to baptize, to bribe; taufen, bestechen' (st. Y. *shmadn* 'to baptize')

ʃo:xər (H. *šḥwr*) '1. black; schwarz; 2. 'black horse; Rappe'

ʃo:l (H. *šw'l*) 'chestnut(-colored); Fuchs, fuchsfarben'

ʃo:nə (H. *šnh*) 'year; Jahr'

ʃɔufə (H. *šwh*) 'worth, deserving of credit; wert, kreditfähig'

ʃɔufəl (H. *špl*) 'poor, slight; schlecht, gering' (st. Y. *shofl* 'inferior')

ʃɔutə (H. *šwṭh*) 'simpleton; allzu Gutmütiger' (st. Y. *shoyte*) *ʃɔutəl* 'feeble-minded person; Schwachsinniger'

ʃti:k̲ə (H. *štykh*): *in dər ʃt.* 'in secret; im Geheimen' (st. Y. *beshtike*) *ʃti:k̲ənə* 'to be silent; schweigen'

ʃuk̲ (H. *šwk*) '1. market; Markt; 2. Mark (coin)' *ʃuk̲ə* 'to cost; kosten'

ʃumˈlɛ:xəm (H. *šlwm 'lykm*) 'hello; Grüss Gott' (st. Y. *sholem-aleykhem*)

ʊ:dsəl (H. *'ṣl*) 'lazy; faul'

u:dsə (H.?) 'to cheat; foppen, betrügen'

TWO PROBLEMS OF YIDDISH LINGUISTICS[1]

SOLOMON A. BIRNBAUM (London)

I. THE ORIGINS OF THE GERMAN ELEMENTS IN YIDDISH

Did Yiddish spring from Standard German or from the dialects? And if from the dialects—then which of them?

Middle High German

If by Standard German we mean New High German, then it is easy to see that Yiddish cannot be derived from this. For this Standard N.H.G. is much younger than Yiddish. A large number of Jews had left Germany many centuries before New High German, that creation of German Protestantism, had become the medium of conversation. Phonological tests, too, confirm the fact that their tongue cannot have its source in "Luther's German."

Standard German is characterized by the unification of different Middle High German vowels and diphthongs. For instance, New High German *Taube* corresponds to two M.H.G. equivalents, one *toube*, an inflected form of *toup* 'deaf', the other *tûbe* 'dove'. In (East) Yiddish there is no unification, the old distinction being maintained (with new sounds): *toib** 'deaf' –*toub* 'dove'. Or again: Standard German has the form *weiss*, where Yiddish has two forms, *vaas* 'white' and *vais* 'know', because in M.H.G. there were two different words: *wîz* and *weiz*.

Let us go farther back to Middle High German. At that time there is a sort of standard language, but only in literature. And Yiddish as a spoken language is not, of course, derived from a written language.

Hence, there is no doubt that we must look for its source amongst the German dialects. In doing this we shall come upon the reason why certain elements are identical in Yiddish and in Standard German. The explanation is that these two have a common factor. In other words, the common element in both languages goes back to the same dialectal German sources.

Which are they?

Central and Upper German

Phonological tests indicate that Yiddish—we are referring here to East Yiddish only—is strongly connected with the Thuringian-Upper Saxonian dialect, and that, in addition, a number of characteristic features point also to the Bavarian-Austrian dialect. The Thuringian-Upper Saxonian dialect belongs

[1] The following pages contain two chapters from my book, *The Yiddish Language*, which had already been set up in type, early in the recent War, when it was destroyed by German bombs.

* [At the author's wish, Yiddish forms cited in this article appear in his own transcription, which is not the same as in the rest of the present volume. *é* stands for open [ɛ], *i* = *ı* stands for open [ɪ], *ii* = *ıı* for long, closed [i], *y* for unstressed open [ɪ]; doubling of vowels indicates length.—ED.]

to the Central German group, the Bavarian-Austrian dialect to the Upper German group.

Central German

Certain Upper German diphthongs are represented by monophthongs in Central German. E.g., the equivalents of the vowels in the English words *foot, green, knee,* are diphthongs in Upper German, to-day as in the past: M.H.G. *vuoz, grüene, knie,* whilst Central German had and has monophthongs: [fu·s], [grü·n], [kni·]—and the same is the case in Yiddish: *fíís, griin, knii.*

The Yiddish equivalents of Germanic *p* likewise point to Central German. At the beginning of the stem it is *f*, in Yiddish as in East Central German, e.g., *fínt* 'pound' from O.H.G. and M.H.G. *pfunt* (cp. Gothic and Old English *pund*), *féfer* 'peper' from O.H.G. *pfëffar,* M.H.G. *pfëffer* (cp. Latin *piper,* Old Engl. *pipor*). Germanic *pp* has not been shifted in Yiddish and in Central German, in contrast with Upper German, e.g. *épl* 'apple', *štípn* 'to push', as against M.H.G. *apfel* (Old Engl. *æppel*), *stupfen.*

The characteristic referred to in the first example is to be met with in Standard German, too: *Fuss, schiessen, grüssen* = [fūs, šīsən, grūsən]. We have, however, some Old Central German features which are characteristic of Yiddish but not of Standard German, as, e.g., the unification of certain vowels and diphthongs. In German *Unter einem Baume in Rom stehen sie auf einem Steine,* the vowels of 'Baum, Rom, stehen, Stein' conform to M.H.G. conditions: *Under einem boume in Rôme stên si ûf einem steine.* In place of the four different sets (*ou/au, ô/o, ê/e, ei/ei*), there are only two (*oi, ai*) in Yiddish: *ínter a boim in roim štaiyn zai of a štain.* That can only be explained by the existence of a former stage, where the M.H.G. *ou* and *ei* had been monophthongized: *bôm, štên.* This, in fact, took place in Central German as early as in the M.H.G. period, from the 13th century onward.

In addition, the following features point to Central German:

¶ mutated forms like *laikynyn* 'to deny', *glaibn* 'to believe' (M.H.G. *löugen* and *leuken, gelöuben*);

¶ the preservation of a vowel in the prefixes *be* and *ge*, e.g., *bavíst* 'well known', *gytsoign* 'drawn';

¶ the splitting up of words having initial *b* into two groups, with *b* and *p*, e.g., *bouyn* 'to build' (M.H.G. *bûwen*), *blít* 'blood' (M.H.G. *bluot*), as against *pouer* 'peasant' (M.H.G. *gebûre*), *píter* 'butter' (M.H.G. *buter*);

¶ the forms *gyhat* (M.H.G. *gehât, gehat*); *fréign* 'to ask' (M.H.G. *vrëgen*); *tsí* 'to' (M.H.G. *ze*); *kaign* or *kéign* 'against' (M.H.G. *gegen*); *bréngyn* 'to bring' (M.H.G. *brėngen*);

¶ perhaps mention may be made in this connection that the lengthening of the old short vowels is older in Central than in Upper German: *fuuern* < [*fārən*] < M.H.G. *varn* 'to ride'; *féider* < [fêdər] < M.H.G. *vëder* 'feather'; *hoif* < [hōf] < M.H.G. *hof* 'court'; *miil* < M.H.G. *mül* 'mill';

¶ the same would apply to the shortening of vowels: *lozn* < M.H.G. *lâzen* 'to let'; *gybraxt* < M.H.G. *brâht* 'brought'; and to

¶ the assimilation *mb* (*mp*) > *mm*, e.g., *krím* 'crooked' < M.H.G. *krump*;

¶ the neuter adjective has no endings when it is used attributively in front of its noun: *a klain haazl* 'a little house', *mit a ziis luušn* 'with sweet language';

¶ the vocabulary contains words pointing to Central German, e.g., *fiiln* 'to feel', *héiern* 'to hear', *koul* 'ball', *zaiger* 'clock, watch', *horxn* 'to hearken', *plímp* 'a pump', *alts* 'always', *hofn* 'to hope'.

Upper German

Turning to the Upper German group we find that the Alemannic and Swabian dialects are not represented in East Yiddish.[2] The Bavarian-Austrian group seems to be the source of the following features:

¶ Continuation of an earlier *u* in certain combinations: *zín* < M.H.G. *sunne* 'sun', *zíín* < M.H.G. *sun* 'son', *tríkn* < M.H.G. *trucken* 'dry', in contrast with Central German *o*, which became also the pronunciation of Standard German: *Sonne, Sohn, trocken*;

¶ the loss of the ending *e* in nouns, e.g., *kép* < M.H.G. *köpfe* 'heads', *haix* < M.H.G. *hoehe* 'height';

¶ the *l*-diminutive: *baiml* 'a little tree';

¶ the loss of mutation in the present of the verb, e.g., *dí trugst* 'thou carriest', *er trugt* 'he carries';

¶ the fact that (*a*) diphthongization of the old long vowels and (*b*) the unrounding appear very early in Bavarian, and might therefore have come into Yiddish from here; (*a*) M.H.G. *mûs* > [mous] > Y. *mouz* 'mouse'; (*b*) M.H.G. *möuse* > [maise] > Y. *maiz* > *maaz* 'mice';

¶ vowel-lengthening through the influence of *r:* M.H.G. *arm* > [ārm] > Y. *uurym*;

¶ absence of mutation, e.g., *zoumyn zex* (M.H.G. *sûmen*) 'to tarry', *arím* (M.H.G. *umbe*), *koifn* (M.H.G. *koufen*) 'to buy';

¶ avoidance of the hiatus: *an of* [anof] 'a fowl', in contrast with *a lomp* 'a lamp';

¶ the development of *d* between *n* and *l*: *xazndl* 'a little cantor' < **xaznl*;

¶ the *t* in words like *tínkl* < M.H.G. *tunkel* 'dark', *taatš* 'meaning' < M.H.G. *tiutsch* 'German', *títs* < M.H.G. *totzên* 'dozen', *taatn* < M.H.G. *diuten* 'to point';

¶ the fact that *b* and *g* are always—also intervocalically—pronounced as stops: *huber* 'oats', *štaiger* 'manner';

¶ the preservation of final *m*, e.g. *bíízym* 'bosom', *boidym* 'attic' (cp. Engl. *bottom*), *béizym* 'broom' (cp. Engl. *besom*), *fuudym* 'thread' (cp. Engl. *fathom*);

¶ the absence of *t*-epithesis: *oips* 'fruits';

¶ the forms of the personal pronouns, 2nd pers. pl., in an extensive part of the Yiddish speech territory: *éts* 'you' (nominative), *énk* 'you' (dative/accusative), *énker* 'your';

¶ the use of the auxiliary 'to be' for the perfect of verbs of movement, e.g.

[2] The second diminutive, ending in a vowel, is to be attributed to the East Franconian source which has (today) *la* or *le*.

zai zényn gyzésn, gyléign, gyšvímyn, gyštanyn, gyšlufn 'they sat/have sat, lain, swum, stood, slept';

¶ the somewhat more frequent use of the article: *der taty ot mir ys dertsailt* 'Father told me it';

¶ the gender, e.g., *der zok* 'the sock', *der haišerik* 'the grasshopper';

¶ vocabulary, e.g. *farzííexn* 'to taste food', *préiglyn* 'to fry'.

Synthesis of German Elements

All this implies a twofold source for the German element in Yiddish. The explanation evidently is that there were two main groups amongst the Jews who emigrated to Poland, the one coming from central and the other from southern Germany, and that in their new country a welding together of their dialects took place.

In German, the Silesian dialect offers an interesting parallel. It came into being in the second half of the thirteenth century by the synthesis of dialects belonging to the same main groups as those from which the Yiddish synthesis originated, viz., the Central and the Upper German dialects. The resulting languages are, however, totally different in their phonology.

But even amongst the Jews who did not emigrate to the east of Europe, a similar development can be traced.

The economic life which the Jews were compelled to lead was very different from that of their surroundings. Circumstances forced them to engage in occupations far removed from the soil, and hence they constituted, of necessity, a much more fluctuating element than the non-Jews. A normal feature in Jewish life was therefore frequency of migration, which, in addition to economic causes, was not too rarely due to expulsion. As a result, individuals and even communities speaking a different dialect were brought into close contact with each other. In this way a synthesis of elements originating from various German dialects took place. Thus the German element in Yiddish within Germany became a synthesis distinctly different from any German dialect. This does not mean that the Jewish speech of a given region was absolutely divorced from its Christian surroundings. But it formed a distinct unity with the Jewish speech of other regions in Germany—it was a Jewish synthesis, a Jewish *koiné*.

This is a reconstruction, of course. But that it is correct seems very probable, since the main historical facts are more or less known to us. We have even an outside testimony to the existence of this Jewish *koiné*, although from a late period. It is a remark by an Alsatian scholar of the sixteenth century: 'You must know that nearly all of them pronounce the vowels in the Nuremberg or Franconian way, especially the *a* which is almost like an *o*.'[3]

If such a development was strong enough to shape a Jewish tongue in the midst of the linguistic territory of German, it is self-evident that it must have been still more powerful in eastern Europe, where there was little or no influence

[3] Elias Schade: *Mysterium etc. . . . Bericht von der Juden Teutsch-Hebreischer Schrifft* (1592).

at all from German-speaking communities. And it was in proportion to its growth that the momentum of independent development increased.

New High German: Beginnings

English, Lithuanian, Lettish, Rumanian, Slovak, and Hungarian cannot be said to have affected literary Yiddish. But this was done, and very considerably so, by a language whose territory is geographically separated from that of (East) Yiddish. I am speaking of New High German. The pioneers of the Jewish Enlightenment in the East of Europe looked upon the German Jewish Enlightenment as their spiritual home. They adopted also its attitude towards Yiddish, and to them it seemed quite natural to replace 'Jargon' by German. The protagonists of the new movement generally used Hebrew for literary purposes. The masses of the people did not, however, know it well enough for that. Hence, in propagating their ideas in the fight against the old ways of life, they were compelled to use the despised 'gibberish' itself. Already in the first stages of their work of 'educating' the people—of 'civilizing' them, as they called it—they turned their attention to the language. As they could not abolish it to order, they tried at least to Germanize it as much as possible. They did this to the vocabulary, phraseology, grammar, style, and even to the spelling. I say 'even' because this is particularly striking, since the alphabets of German and Yiddish differ. As an example I shall mention only the introduction of ayin, in imitation of the German *e*, in unstressed syllables, e.g., *gezugt*, instead of the traditional 'i': *gizugt*.

The process of Germanization went furthest in the north among the writers of Vilna. In the south, the instinct for good language was stronger, and representatives of the Enlightenment themselves wrote in pure and popular Yiddish. Only a small circle in Eastern Europe was reached by modern ideas and writings and the written and spoken language of the vast majority remained unaffected. But that circle was gradually extended. Their language was of the Germanized type.

New High German: The Present Time

The next stage was not, however, the adoption of German, but a conscious revolt against the whole trend, due to the nationalism, which, coming in the train of Europeanization, was actually basing itself upon Yiddish. Being essentially secular, it did not aim at all at returning to the old Yiddish, nor at continuing in its footsteps on new lines. This linguistic revolt, which began late in the 19th century and gained great momentum in the 20th, effected the removal of Germanisms mainly from accidence. In all other linguistic spheres (except phonetics, which had not been affected) it resulted rather in the exchange of new Germanisms for old, than in their elimination.

A few examples will suffice:—

There was not, of course, formerly a word in Yiddish for the modern idea of 'development'. No attempt was made to create such a word, not even in the shape of a translation from another language. A word was simply adopted. There is nothing unusual in this for a philologist, of course. The source from which it was taken was German and thus modern Yiddish had the word *entvikling*. The parts of this word have their Yiddish equivalents: *ant, viklyn* and *ing*, but there was no verb *antviklyn*, either in an abstract or in a concrete sense, from which to construct a noun by use of the ending *ing*. Recently, the German form of the prefix has been abandoned in favor of the Yiddish one, *antvikling*; but, up to this day, no attempt has been made to Yiddicize the word completely, in which case it would have been *antvikyling*. In this particular example a new idea was the reason for borrowing.

In other instances a new shade of thought was responsible for the adoption of such words. But very often no such explanation seems appropriate. The Yiddish word for 'danger' is *sakuuny*. In Modern Yiddish there is also *gefar*. There are a very great number of words of both categories. In some cases a rather funny reason seems to be at the root of such borrowings: poets and rimesters made use of German to increase their supply of rimes. As there are, for instance, very few rimes with the word for 'light' in the northern dialect (*lixt*), they simply appropriated the German word *Gesicht*—pronouncing it *gyzixt*—when they needed it for a rime.

No less than vocabulary, phraseology is affected. German idioms are translated literally, and part of the new idiom is often a New High German word, e.g. *diinyn als bavaaz* from German *als Beweis dienen*. Finally an example from syntax: *A fín rísiś ibergyzétsty bamérkíng*. Such a construction is impossible in real Yiddish, just as it is in English: we cannot say 'a from Russian translated note'. In Yiddish the article cannot be severed from its noun except by attributive adjectives. The correct position would be: *a bamérkíng ibergyzétst fín rísiś*, exactly as in English: 'a note translated from Russian'. The modern literary Yiddish construction just referred to is, of course, borrowed from German: *eine aus dem Russischen übersetzte Bemerkung*.

These examples from different spheres of the language will perhaps suffice to show the influence of New High German, which cannot be said to have been checked by nationalism, for where this restricted and regulated, on the one side, its influence was opposite in effect, on the other.

There is one domain only where this type of language has not gained ascendancy, that is the traditional religious literature: biblical and other translations, edifying and Khassidic writings, etc. Here the old type of Yiddish from before the advent of the Enlightenment is maintained, although the spelling is much influenced by the secularized type. The press of the religious section of East European Jewry and the rest of their literary production has, however, entirely succumbed to the secularized language. It is only amongst the adherents of a traditionalist linguistic movement[4] that the incongruity between

[4] It is based on the realization that Yiddish, like all the other Jewish languages, owes its existence to Judaism, i.e., the Jewish religion. Religion is everywhere group-forming and thus language-shaping. Cf. M. Mieses, *Die Entstehungsursache der jüdischen Dialekte*, Vienna, 1915; N. Birnbaum, *Gottes Volk*, p. 46, 1918; my Die jiddische Sprache (*Germ.-Rom.*

religious traditionalism on the one hand and secularized language on the other, is recognized. They aim at shaping a language built upon the foundation of traditional Yiddish and adapted to present needs, without however identifying those needs with the ideas of the secularized world. The result, as far as the New High German element is concerned, amounts to its complete rejection, although success in the practical execution of this aim varies of course in individual writers.

II. Standard Language

When we say or hear the word dialect, most of us think of something rather unimportant, and many people still, consciously or unconsciously, regard it as a corrupted form of the language proper. They do not realize that the speech of the overwhelming majority of human beings is dialectal and that this is largely the case also in English, French, and especially German, even though the speakers have at their disposal a standard language with a standard pronunciation. For a layman, such an interdialectal form of a language is *the* language, the 'real' language. Now, how about a standard form of Yiddish?

As to the earlier period, although the field is unexplored, this much is clear: there was a more or less common form of a literary language. In more recent times—in the sixteenth or seventeenth centuries, for instance—it must already have differed considerably from the spoken language, i.e., from the dialects. Nevertheless, books printed in western and eastern Europe are in the same type of language. This is not surprising, since the written word is always far more conservative than the spoken one.

How is present-day literary Yiddish connected with this old type? Is it a continuation of it or is it of independent growth? At present all we can say is that there is a connection between the older and the modern period, the exact nature of which has, however, yet to be worked out. On the whole, modern literary Yiddish has its main source in the modern spoken language. It has the same accidence and syntax, vocabulary, style and phonetics.

Monatsschrift, 11:151), 1923; Iîdiś ín Iîdiśkait (*Iubiléium-bíix . . . N. Biirnboim*, 147–157), 1925; Jiddische Sprache (*Religion in Geschichte und Gegenwart*, 3:175), 1929; Jiddische Sprache (*Jüdisches Lexikon*, 3:270), 1929; Iîdiś (*Bais Iaankyv Jurnal*, No. 48:4), 1929; Mytodik ín asimilatsiy (*Dus Iîdiśy Vort*, 2:6:3), 1929; Helf dym haant ín dym morgn! (*Bais Iaankyv Jurnal*, No. 55:1), 1930; *Iîdiśkait ín luuśn*, 1930; Assimilation (*Der Aufstieg*, 1:81), 1930; Jiddische Rechtschreibung und Judentum (*Der Aufstieg*, 1:114), 1930; Der ortodoksiśer ous-laig (*Oilim-Bléter*, 1:1:4), 1930; Traditsiy kaign traditsiy (*Dus Iîdiśy Tug-Blat*, 3:No. 27), 1930; Far vuus a naaer ous-laig? (*Bais Iaankyv*, No. 59:1), 1930; Jiddisch (*Der Grosse Brockhaus* 9:420), 1931; Pliśtim uléixu, iîdiśizm! (*Voxnśrift*, 27.3.), 1931; Krii ín ksiv fín iîdiś (*Dus Vort*, No. 344), 1931; *Gíly fín luuśn*, 1931; Dus iîdiśy luuśn—a hilf farn iîdiśkait (*Kinder-Guurtn*, No. 34), 1931; Toixn ín lyvíś (*Bais Iaankyv*, No. 71:1), 1931; Der nitsuxn fín índzer ous-laig (*ibid.*, p. 40); Di iííd nébex (*Dus Vort*, No. 348), 1931; Iîdiśistiś oder iîdiś? (*Ortodoksiśy Iugnt-Bléter*, No. 22), 1931; Jiddisch (*Encyclopaedia Judaica*, 9:116), 1932; Ain korbn éily luuśn tsuury (*Bais Iaankyv*, No. 101:49), 1933; Luuśn koidyś ín ivrit (*Bais Iaankyv*, No. 133:3), 1936; Jewish Languages (*Essays Presented to J. H. Hertz*, 51–67), 1944.

The Dialectal Basis of Literary Yiddish

The standard form of a language is either based on a certain dialect or on a mixture of dialects. What is the relationship between present day literary Yiddish and the dialects? Is it based on one of them or is it a mixture?

There has been a popular attempt to solve this question by reference to the spelling. The argument runs thus: 'The Hebrew letter *vav* means [u]. Literary spelling has *vav* in all words where the "Lithuanian" dialect pronounces [u]. This proves that the literary language is identical with this dialect. The "Polish" dialect is ruled out, as its pronunciation [i] contradicts the spelling.'

It is evident that such an argument is fallacious. *Vav* is not [u]. It is not [u] as, e.g., in the northern [fus] 'foot'; it is not [i·] as in the southern [fi·s]; it is not [ü·] as in Central Yiddish or Alsatian [fü·s]. It is all of them. The belief that alphabetic signs denote something absolute is untenable. The idea that the letter *u*, for instance, is only a relative symbol presents no difficulty to an Englishman who uses the same letter *u* with such different meanings as in *fun*, *full*, *blue*, *burn*, etc., but it is not so obvious to people whose language happens to be Yiddish, German, Polish, Russian, etc., where the spelling is more 'phonetic'. In short, there is no clue as to how the symbol in question should be pronounced and as to the relation between literary Yiddish and the dialects. The same applies to nearly all letters denoting vowels and diphthongs, which are the most obvious characteristics marking the dialectal differences of Yiddish.

Hence, we should not get any nearer answering our question as to whether the literary language of Yiddish is based on one of the dialects, if we made a phonological examination of the written form of Yiddish words. The reason is clear: the spelling of Yiddish is historical—it is as old as the language itself, because at the time of its birth the Jews were not an illiterate people but an old and civilized community, where practically everybody could read and write. Changes in the language naturally caused changes in the spelling too. But as the dialectal developments spring from a common source, the new sounds always appear in parallel series. Instead, for instance, of the old words with *oi*, we now have two series: one with [oi], and one with [ẹi], e.g., [azoi]/[azẹi]. The speakers of the northern dialect had no reason to change their spelling. People did not, of course, realize that phonetic development was constantly taking place, so they continued to use a certain symbol for a certain sound, even though the same symbol had signified a different sound a hundred years previously. The new sounds they produced were naturally connected with the spelling acquired at school. For them the symbol in question *was* [ẹi], not [oi], as for the southerners, or for their own ancestors. Thus, up to this day, the same Yiddish text is read differently by speakers of different dialects. Hence we could not, by the application of this method of investigation, determine the dialectal basis of literary Yiddish. We must, therefore, turn to the vocabulary and grammar. As to the former, there are as yet no dialect dictionaries, and if there were, it is doubtful whether counting up lists of words would be of great help in this connection. Grammar, on the other hand, provides us with two important clues.

Literary Yiddish has three genders: *der tuul* 'the valley' is masculine; *di muus* 'the measure' is feminine; *dus xaider* 'the room' is neuter. The same is the case in the southern dialect, but the northern has only two genders, there is no neuter: e.g., *iingl* 'boy' and *réitynis̀* 'riddle' are masculine and feminine respectively, instead of neuter, as in the south. Hence it becomes clear that the literary language had its origin in the southern dialect. The fact that the old literary language had likewise three genders may also have played a role. But there can hardly be any doubt that the neuter would have disappeared from the literary language, had the latter sprung from the northern dialect.

The following is another proof. Literary Yiddish has the construction: *er zéit zi* 'he sees her' and *er zugt ir* 'he tells her'. *Zi* is accusative, *ir* is dative. There are not many such forms in Yiddish but they include some of the most common words in the language. Consequently, the syntactical categories of the two cases remain perfectly clear in the consciousness of the speakers, even in words where there is no differentiation in the forms of the accusative and dative. People who are used to the difference in two sentences like *er dertsailt der iîdyny* 'he tells the woman' but *er fréigt di iîdyny* 'he asks the woman,' will be conscious that in sentences like *er git dym xaver* 'he gives to his friend,' and *er fréigt dym xaver* 'he asks his friend,' the identity of *dym*, none the less, covers a difference in syntax.

If we compare this with the state of affairs prevalent in the dialects, we notice the following: the northern dialect knows of no difference between accusative and dative, either in form or in syntax. Here there are only two cases, the nominative and the objective; *er zéit ir* is constructed exactly like *er zugt ir*. This shows that in the consciousness of the speaker there cannot be any difference between accusative and dative.

In the southern dialect, however, we meet with precisely the same facts as in the literary language. The two are therefore intimately connected. What we have already said before about the possible influence of the old literary language applies here, too: it might have played a rôle but would have disappeared if modern literary Yiddish had been a development from the northern dialect.

On the strength of these two important grammatical characteristics, it is possible to say that modern literary Yiddish corresponds to the southern dialect. It is not difficult to understand why, seeing that nearly all the early makers of modern Yiddish literature as well as the triad of modern classical writers and most of the great living authors belong to the south.

Standard Pronunciation

English, French and German have developed, in addition to the standard written language, a standard pronunciation, which—it is perhaps not generally realized—remains, in practice, strongly under the influence of the speakers' native dialects. Often—and this is particularly the case in South German regions —the standard pronunciation, and even the standard language itself, are wholly abandoned in conversation. There is nothing unusual in the spectacle of a German Swiss professor stepping down from his college platform to talk pure dialect to his students.

A Yiddish professor has no choice. He has no standard pronunciation at his disposal. Undesirable as this state of affairs would appear to be to a proper highbrow, or egghead, in actual practice it offers few difficulties.

Prospects and Facts

The problems connected with the creation of a standard language are being much discussed by Yiddish philologists of the present. As to a standard pronunciation, neither the complete adoption of any one dialect nor an artificial mixture of the main ones would appear to offer good prospects of finding acceptance, since very few people would consent to relearn the pronunciation of their mother tongue. In the literary language, however, such adoption has long been an accomplished fact. In writing, no 'Lithuanian' would think of refusing to use the accusative and the neuter, hard as it might seem to him to deprive even a woman of her natural gender when, contrary to his own dialect, he has to write *dus maidl* 'it/the girl'.

PREHISTORY AND EARLY HISTORY OF YIDDISH: FACTS AND CONCEPTUAL FRAMEWORK

MAX WEINREICH (New York)

1. It was a turning point in Yiddish studies when the Landau school[1] back in the eighties arrived at the conclusion that Yiddish stemmed from Middle High German (1100–1500). Until then it had been felt that Yiddish stemmed from German, i.e. from modern German, and whatever deviation Yiddish showed was due to "corruption." Linguistic evidence plainly militated against such naïve reasoning, and MHG seemed to offer the solution.

For instance, there is a correspondence in Yiddish to the German contrast *a* : *ā*; Y. *bakn* 'to bake'. *faln* 'to fall' are *backen*, *fallen* in German, while G. *Vater*, *Hahn* appear in Yiddish as *foter* 'father', *hon* 'rooster'.[2] But this general vowel correspondence is upset in cases like G. *Jammer* ~ Y. *yomer* 'lamentation'. MHG actually had *jâmer*, with a long *a*; thus Yiddish follows the rule, and corruption, if that's what we choose to call it, must be laid at the doorsteps of modern German. The Yiddish two-pronged development, as in *mayn* 'my' and (*ikh*) *meyn* '(I) think' and in *hoyt*/*hout* 'skin' vs. *leyfn*/*loyfn* 'to run', where standard German has only one diphthong in each pair, *ei* and *au*, is easily explained as soon as we move back to MHG: there we trace the Yiddish oppositions in the shape of *î* ~ *ei* and *û* ~ *ou*, respectively. On that basis, a German speaker might be tempted to construe the equivalent of G. *Gaumen* with either *oy*/*ou* or *ey*/*oy*, but the actual Yiddish word for 'palate' is *gumen*, and it matches MHG *guome*; in other words, the Yiddish form is just as "lawful" as G. *Gaumen* which corresponds to a parallel MHG *gûme*.

Simple as this discovery seems to us now, it opened up not only a new vein of phonological equations but, even more important, new perspectives. It was the first step in establishing for Yiddish a historical context in place of a hunt for haphazard resemblances and it has proven to be a lasting achievement in defining the linguistic position of Yiddish.

2. Landau himself, however, with his great skill and admirable power of discrimination, was quick to discover that the newly found approach to Yiddish through Middle High German was not an absolute blessing. As early as 1892 he wrote Sainéan:

"The comparison with the MHG sound system, customary in the presenta-

[1] Alfred Landau (1850–1935), a recluse far removed from any teaching activities, certainly never thought of himself as a leader of any kind. Moreover, L. Sainéan = Şaineanu, in his Rumanian study on Yiddish, had come out with similar ideas, at least in print, a few years earlier. [See pp.ff. 147 of the present volume.—*Editor*] Still, there can be no doubt that Landau by his persistent devotion to the field must be considered the head of the school which brought Yiddish studies into the orbit of Germanics.—On the schools in Yiddish studies, cf. the present writer's [Yiddish Philology] in *Algemeyne yidishe entsiklopedye*, supplementary volume, *Yidn B* (Paris, 1940), pp. 101–108.

[2] For simplicity's sake, no cognizance is taken here of the vocalic alternations between the different Yiddish regional groups. Except when conditions within Yiddish are discussed, transcriptions like *foter*/*futer*, *meyn*/*mayn*, *mayn*/*maan* etc. are avoided.

tion of the German dialects, with regard to Yiddish is, to be sure, valuable in some cases, but in other cases it is useless and not justified historically either, because the language of the Jews drew [its material] from old German dialects, of which just MHG as a language of literature certainly was the most foreign to them."[3]

Thus, in actual performance Landau and his disciples did not limit themselves to Middle High German comparative material. They also dug deeply into the Early New High German writings of the sixteenth and seventeenth centuries and into the German dialects of the nineteenth and the twentieth. But the theoretical difficulties of the situation had thereby become even harder to surmount.

3. Today, with our knowledge of both earlier Yiddish and earlier German so much enlarged and linguistic tools—among which concepts rank high—so much refined, the statement that Yiddish "stems" from MHG is even less satisfactory than it seemed to Landau sixty years ago. It is by now generally recognized that MHG, as we know it from the critical editions of the texts, mostly poetic, that have come down to us, is a linguistic entity thrice removed from the actual German language of the Middle Ages.

The first coat of paint, thickly as it has been laid on by the editors of the Benecke-Lachmann school in their quest for consistency, can be scraped off rather easily if recourse is had to the original manuscripts. Then we are confronted with a highly stylized language which, like any literary medium, only imperfectly reflects the actual speech of its own creators and inspirers. This second paint coat is much more difficult to remove because there are no records of actual speech from that period which the linguist could utilize for comparative purposes. In using his devices he will be able to lay his fingers on more regional peculiarities than the Middle High German authors had cared to betray, though not nearly as often as he might need to arrive at exact conclusions. But besides, the ground underneath, to sustain the metaphor, is known to have been the possession of only a small segment of the population, that of the higher strata in which the small-court environment was prominent. As O. Mausser puts it:

"The cleric, the knight and the young lady of noble rank, since the late thirteenth century the townsman of more refined culture, perhaps even with a broad mental outlook—all of them WITHIN their stratum probably spoke the dialect of their locality, district or province in a form that was weeded in a gardenerlike manner as it were: up to a certain degree phonically and inflectionally, mainly however lexically differentiated from the dialect of the populace. . . ."[4]

Bringing in the language of official records, chronicles, etc., does help somewhat, but not much, because in that material other denaturants were operative.

3.1. Now, within the universe of German studies there is no basis for deprecat-

[3] Ch. Gininger: [The Correspondence A. Landau—L. Şaineanu], *Yivo-bleter* 13 (1938) 275–300.

[4] *Mittelhochdeutsche Grammatik*, 1374 pp. (Munich, 1933), p. 150.

ing that "artificial creation" called Middle High German because, the reluctance of many contemporary linguists notwithstanding, a literary language, for more reasons than one, is a legitimate concern of the linguistic historian. But it so happens that the linguistic "raw material" which the Jews acquired upon coming into German language territory in the centuries around the year 1000 was taken neither from the written "Standessprache" nor even from the speech of those high-placed social groups whose purposes the German written language served. Historical evidence confirms what might have been presumed, namely, that the dealings of the Jews were with non-sophisticated small townspeople, with petty officials, with domestic servants and nurses. Those people had no literary spokesmen and it is a safe guess that, as a rule, they knew about Middle High German literature as little as their Jewish neighbors and were affected by it only a tiny bit more.[5]

By way of analogy, one may think of the English that the Yiddish speakers were exposed to on the New York East side during the great immigration. But there is one outstanding difference: in the Rhineland of the Middle Ages there was no policy on the part of the dominant group to teach the new arrivals correct German nor was there any of the instrumentalities, such as a compulsory school system, to feed correct German to them. There was no concept of German linguistic correctness in the first place, and if there had been, the new settlers had other things to worry about.

Thus, if we are to place the origin of Yiddish with regard to the history of German, the only sufficiently flexible designation seems to be 'medieval German', with due margin left for defining the particular speech territory. The term has an additional advantage in that it permits the inclusion of linguistic phenomena pertaining to the Old High German period (750–1150). There are at least some phenomena in Yiddish whose analysis might benefit from this extension in time although, in general, the Jewish community did share in the linguistic shifts that are associated with the transition from OHG to MHG.

4. Likewise, conceptual clarity is missing in often encountered statements to the effect that Yiddish should be compared with MHG "and" with modern German dialects.

Except for a limited number of later-day loanwords (and those, of course, came into Yiddish from upper-strata "literary" German), the ties between Eastern Yiddish and German dialects were severed, on the whole, no later than in the sixteenth century; from that time on, only Western Yiddish remained in the German sphere.[6]

[5] Of course, the founders of German historical grammar knew all the facts, but they somehow were disinclined to face them. Only recently a more realistic picture has begun to be drawn. Cf. H. Moser in *Deutsche Philologie im Aufriss* 1 (1949), pp. 810–970.

[6] For the record it must be noted that in Courland, Yiddish was affected by the speech of the German minority which before World War One constituted the upper stratum; but the Yiddish of that province was secluded from that of the neighboring areas and hardly brought any pressure to bear on them. Cf. the present writer's [The Yiddish of Courland] in his *Shtaplen*, 260 pp. (Berlin, 1923), pp. 193–240, 246–249, and Z. Kalmanovitsh: [The Yiddish Dialect in Courland], *Filologishe Shriftn* [*fun Yivo*] 1 (Vilna, 1926), 161–188. Kal-

If the student of Yiddish discovers, say, in Schmeller's *Bayerisches Wörterbuch* some entry that he can correlate with a particular Yiddish item, it will certainly not enter his mind that Yiddish acquired that item from the Bavarian dictionary. But what would he assume? Any of several things. At the time migration to the East was still proceeding on a considerable scale, Bavarian German might have affected a portion of the Yiddish-speaking Jews living in Bavaria, and then those Jews or their descendants might have brought the item in question to Eastern Europe. Or Bavarian Jews, with that item in their speech, might have gone to another region in Germany, where it was incorporated into the local Yiddish and afterwards brought to Eastern Europe by settlers from that other region. Or, to try still another hypothesis which may or may not be valid in a particular instance, the item might have penetrated into Eastern Yiddish from Western Yiddish at a time when these two main regional blocks had already taken shape; such cross contacts are known to have existed. At any rate, for a German regional-speech item to appear in Eastern Yiddish, an earlier Western-Yiddish regional variety must be assumed as an intermediary.

Now, how would the appeal to Middle High German AND modern German dialects help us in arriving at a decision about the regional origin of a particular Yiddish item? With all the gratitude owed to the scholars who have taught us to approach Yiddish with the equipment of German historical grammar and dialectology, the truth may as well be told that at no time were the principles examined on which a medieval German and the modern spoken dialects of that language could be combined to admit of being compared with a different linguistic entity.

5. But the main objection against the orthodox or modified Middle-High-German genealogy lies in the fact that Yiddish cannot be adequately understood and defined in terms of its German component alone, though this is the main component as long as we stick to numbers and have not started weighting.

A great multitude of regional traits of German can, of course, be detected in Yiddish or in parts of it but, as rightly stated by Prilutski forty years ago, there is no Yiddish dialect that can be identified with any German dialect.[7] Small wonder then that even with regard to the same item the emphasis is quite different. Standard German does have the *s* and *z* sounds, but the opposition /s ~ z/ is absent in prevocalic and final positions and relegated to a very humble status intervocalically; in Yiddish, *zamen zikh* 'to be late' ~ *samen zikh* 'to poison oneself', *a royz* 'a rose' ~ *aroys* 'out' form oppositions that cannot be overlooked. Any number of such items, from phonemics as well as from other fields, can be quoted. On the other hand, isoglosses that are of the utmost im-

manovitsh perished in 1943 in a German slave-labor camp in Estonia.—Galician Yiddish became Germanized on its fringes not through the influence of the local German population, which was quite insignificant, but through radiation from afar. The case deserves intensive study; it might be similar to the impact of French on Rumanian.

[7] In a 1915 paper reprinted in N. Prilutski (Prylucki): *Barg aroyf*, 323 pp. (Warsaw, 1917), pp. 289–290. Prilutski was killed by the Gestapo in 1941 in German-occupied Vilna.—In the same vein, R. Loewe in *Indogermanische Forschungen* (*Anzeiger*) 16 (1904) 43–50.

portance to the history of German, like *ik* ~ *ich* or *he* ~ *er* or *us* ~ *uns* play no part in Yiddish; the first forms in those pairs, the northern ones, do not appear in it at all.[8] But clinging to the southern varieties of German ('Hochdeutsch') is no ready solution either. Yiddish has rejected both the southern *Bube* and the northern *Knabe* in favor of *yung* 'boy', cf. Standard German *Junge*. Yiddish has only *ferd* 'horse' (with specific connotations, there is also *sus*, of Hebrew origin) as against the three German synonyms *Pferd, Ross, Gaul*, in spite of the evidence of the *Deutscher Sprachatlas*, maps 8, 32, 68, that all three of them appear on territory which is unquestionably High German.

6. Sometimes Eastern Central German ('Ostmitteldeutsch') is given as the territory from which Yiddish "stems," and Gerzon in his still very useful Heidelberg dissertation of 1902 made the most of the fact that Germanic *p*, just as in Eastern Middle German, appears in Yiddish as *f* in the beginning and as *p* in the middle and final positions; e.g., *ferd* 'horse' ~ *epl* 'apple', *kop* 'head' as compared with Standard German *Pferd, Apfel, Kopf*.[9]

Closer investigation shows, however, that there is a whole bundle of isoglosses cutting through East Central Germany which makes the linguistic texture of the region far from uniform: *gebruchen* ~ *gebrochen, unser* ~ *unse*; *trocken* ~ *drūge, Stückla, -le* ~ *Stückchen*; *(ge)brennt* ~ *gebrannt*; *er ist gekommen* ~ *er kam*; *Brūt* ~ *Brot*; *wo* ~ *wie*, and so on and on.[10] In some of these phenomena Yiddish goes with one region and in others with a different one, and with still others Yiddish is not concerned at all.

Such considerations hardly predispose one to accept the preponderance of "Ostmitteldeutsch" in the formation of Yiddish on the basis of the substantiation presented until now. The probability of such a genealogy by virtue of the extralinguistic factors involved (settlement, routes of further eastward migration, cultural influences, etc.) must be part of the evidence to be introduced.

6.1. Incidentally, even Gerzon conceded: "While we may assume that the consonantal system of Yiddish points to East Central German (Thuringia, Upper Saxony, Silesia) it is not altogether excluded that Jews emigrated to Poland from other parts of Germany, too." Now, there certainly are items in the German component of Yiddish that are reminiscent of German dialects of regions other than the ones mentioned by Gerzon. For instance, the *ets–enk* 'you (nom.)—you (dat., acc.)' in the so-called "Polish dialect" of Yiddish is characteristic of Bavarian German; but again such a typical Bavarian word like *Ertag* 'Tuesday' is completely absent from Yiddish.

6.2. All the days of the week—and here we have come upon a salient point—

[8] Of course, there are a few phenomena in Yiddish with a northern German taint that have to be accounted for, such as *knaypn* 'to pinch' (cf. Standard German *kneifen*) which in the spoken German language is limited to the North, while the Southwest uses *pfetzen* and the Southeast *zwicken* (cf. F. Kluge: *Etymologisches Wörterbuch*$_{14}$, p. 311), or *drist* 'bold', cf. Standard German *dreist*, in the Mława region of northern Poland.

[9] J. Gerzon: *Die jüdisch-deutsche Sprache*, 134 pp. (Cologne–Frankfurt/M., 1902), p. 131.

[10] Cf. W. Ebert, Th. Frings, et al.: *Kulturräume und Kulturströmungen im mitteldeutschen Osten*, 2 vol. (Halle, 1936), 349 pp. + 97 maps; W. Mitzka in *Deutsche Philologie im Aufriss* 1, pp. 655–780.

have Yiddish names reminiscent of the Standard German designations—all the days, that is, except Saturday. In German there is a regional tripartition into *Saterdag* ~ *Sonnabend* ~ *Samstag* with profound implications for linguistic and cultural history: the first term is a loan translation going back to 'dies Saturni', a Roman word imported from the Northwest, and the second a coinage of the Church intended to dislodge the pagan word, while the third, apparently transmitted by Gothic-Arian missionaries, is ultimately derived from Greek *sámbaton* < *sábbaton*.[11] All this is lost on the Yiddish speakers; the only name for the day they have is *shabes*, to which a derivative, *erev shabes* 'the eve of Sabbath' has been added as an equivalent of *fraytik* 'Friday'.

7. This is the point. Yiddish is a fusion language in which, until the transatlantic migrations of Central and Eastern European Jews set in after 1850, four components have to be reckoned with.

Here is a preliminary statement that will set the stage. In the ninth century or so, the Jews began entering the region which they called *Loter*—the territory comprising the basin of the Moselle and the left bank of the Rhine roughly between Cologne and Speyer—where they were to form the nucleus of the Yiddish-speaking (= Ashkenazic) community. They came from France and Italy with vernaculars which we may call Western Loez and Southern Loez respectively[12] and which can be defined as Jewish correlates of Old French and Old Italian; but they also possessed their sacred language, Hebrew, very much in use for specialized purposes. In Loter, they encountered various German dialects which in that period were undergoing rather profound changes.[13]

The fusion of Hebrew, Loez in its two varieties, and dialectal German marked the beginning of Yiddish. Then, with the eastward movement of the Yiddish-speaking community, a fourth component, Slavic, again in different varieties, entered the picture. This new component first must have appeared in the thirteenth century, but possibly earlier, to assume growing proportions as time went by.

7.1. In other words, the emergence of Yiddish cannot be conceived of as the gradual breakaway of a certain German-speaking group from its former language. A description of this kind would fit Transylvanian German in the twelfth century or Pennsylvania Dutch six centuries later, and a Jewish analogue could be construed if we were to fancy a group of Germans in the Rhineland, pagan to begin with and afterwards Christianized, embracing Judaism; the group might then have incorporated into its speech a Hebrew component and later, if subsequent migrations would have led to that effect, also a Loez and a Slavic component.

But this is definitely not the history of Yiddish. The decisive point is that

[11] Th. Frings and J. Niessen: "Zur Geographie und Geschichte von 'Ostern, Samstag, Mittwoch' im Westgermanischen," *Indogermanische Forschungen* 45 (1927) 276–306.

[12] *Loez* is the customary medieval Jewish term for Romance-type languages spoken by the Jews; see §17.1.

[13] It is a moot question whether the newcomers didn't bring with them at least some knowledge of Germanic, i.e. whether Germanic in Neustria had completely died out by that time.

there was NO period in history before the nineteenth century in which any Jewish GROUP had spoken anything approximating "pure German." The Jews who were to form the Yiddish speech community came into what was to become Germany with languages of their own and then created a new language out of the stock that was at hand in their previous languages and in the one that they encountered in their new country.

7.2. Aside from migrations, other extralinguistic factors affecting language, such as religion, social stratification, etc., also were quite different for Yiddish from what they were for Standard German or, for that matter, for any variant of German. Consequently, it is futile to look for a one-to-one relationship between Yiddish (or any of its subdivisions) and German (or any of its subdivisions). The main features of the language as they now appear owe their existence precisely to the fact of fusion. The master patterns of Yiddish were established at its very inception and it is they which determined the subsequent growth along specific lines; it is essentially with the same developmental problems that we are confronted throughout the whole history of the language.[14]

8. The essence of a fusion language is selectivity with regard to any linguistic item and rejection is as important to the compound as is acceptance. One illustration will suffice.

The present-day word for the noun 'blessing' is *brokhe*, of Hebrew origin; but there is no concomitant verb of the same stem. 'To bless' is *bentshn* which ultimately goes back to Latin *benedicere* and thus is of Romance origin. The antonym *maledicere* 'to curse' has not penetrated into Yiddish; the noun is *klole*, of Hebrew origin, while for the verb *sheltn* is used.[15] This, of course, reminds us of German *schelten*, but in Yiddish it means only 'to curse', never 'to scold'; frequently, *farsheltn* is used, with a somewhat intensified meaning. Here we may invoke, for comparison's sake, Bavarian German; Schmeller *Bayr. Wb.*$_2$, 2, p. 416 gives "*schelten* preferably for '*fluchen*'," but no mention is made of a **verschelten*.

Further within the same semantic field, the regular Yiddish word for 'to abuse, to call names' is *zidlen*. It is a cognate of German *sudeln* 'to smirch'. But for the *-u-* in the German word we would expect the *u/i* phoneme in Yiddish just as in *zukhn/zikhn* $\sim$ *suchen* and hundreds of other words; and the history of this *i*, non-existent in German but the only one in all varieties of Yiddish, is most revealing in Yiddish historical phonemics (see §32). The shift in meaning in *sudeln* $\sim$ *zidlen* is easy to explain; still, in the *Deutscher Wortatlas* 2, pp. 27f., which enumerates over nine hundred synonyms for *schelten* on German linguistic territory, *sudeln* does not appear even a single time. Instead, amusingly, *benschen* was listed by a few informants. The Yiddish term for 'to

[14] Cf. the present writer's [Ashkenaz: the Yiddish Era in Jewish History], *Yivo-bleter* 35 (1951) 7–17 and "*Yidishkayt* and Yiddish," *Mordecai M. Kaplan Jubilee Volume* (New York, 1953), pp. 481–514.—In detail, these problems will be presented in the writer's forthcoming The Yiddish Language: Structure, History, Cultural Background, which has been in preparation for many years and now is nearing its final stage.

[15] Sporadically, a so-called "periphrastic verb" related to *klole*, i.e. *mekalel zayn*, appears; the earliest attestation at hand is in the Cracow community bylaws of 1595.

bless' was taken over by German speakers and is used with the reverse meaning, as loanwords often are.[16]

9. Even with regard to developments within every single component, great care should be exercised in claiming direct descent. On the one hand, allowance has constantly to be made for an influence that might have originated in a different component: Y. *gebirt* '(archaic) generation', cf. German *Geburt*, got its specific meaning through the impact of the Loez word going back to Latin *generatio*;[17] Y. *meylits* '(slang) policeman', cf. Hebrew *meliṣ* 'interceder', can be understood only through the interposition of *milits* 'militia', which at various times was the designation for 'police' in Poland. On the other hand, similarity of a certain phenomenon in Yiddish (or a certain section of Yiddish) and in German (or a certain section of German) need not be the result of direct borrowing: we may well deal with a parallel development that has led to analogous results. Thus, as already alluded, the coincidence of some Yiddish features with what is seen in Eastern Central German, unless proved otherwise, may be attributable to the fact that in both cases colonial linguistic entities are involved and that the settlers in the new territories, German speakers in eastern Thuringia, Saxony, Silesia and Yiddish speakers in Polish-Lithuanian-East Slavic territories, came from the same regions in western and southern Germany, where Jewish and non-Jewish speech had many traits in common.

10. It is hoped that the preceding discussion has somewhat shaken the belief in the "purity of descent" which a previous period in Yiddish studies had produced. There is, however, one avenue of research where genealogical concepts seem to be highly serviceable. Each of the four main components—the Hebrew, the Loez, the German and the Slavic—entered at a certain stage of its history and in each case with only a limited part of its resources. The shape and degree of availability of each component to a considerable degree determined the character and further development of the compound. Therefore the point must be granted that while it is the "biography" of the individual language which ultimately counts, biography hinges on genealogy.

It goes without saying that the genealogical questions have to be taken up for each component separately. The subsequent discussion, apart from considerations of a general nature, will deal with the Hebrew component, except when it interlocks with the rest of them; as for the three other components, they have to be reserved, because of limitations of space, for separate studies.

11. Hebrew is a covering name that needs specifying. To begin with it may be expedient to speak of three main periods in the language: (1) Traditional Hebrew (up to the eighteenth century); (2) Modern Hebrew (nineteenth and twentieth centuries); (3) Contemporary (Palestinian, or Israeli) Hebrew. Now,

[16] Also spelled by the informants as *bentschen* and *benzn*.—The list of German synonyms for *schelten* contains at least six more words of Yiddish origin: *baldawern, ballegoje, masseln, scheckern, schlamasseln, däwara* (*döbere*). None of them has the same meaning in Yiddish! Obviously, linguistic borrowing reaches far beyond the introduction of foreign designations where there is no equivalent native term.

[17] Cf. S. Birnbaum: [Dzhudezmo], *Yivo-bleter* 11 (1937) 192–195.

the influence of Israeli Hebrew, at least outside the State of Israel, so far has been only skin deep: *khalúts–khalutsím* 'pioneer(s)' as an alternate to *kholuts —khalutsim* which is no less frequent; *medine* 'state' with reference to Israel,[18] and perhaps a dozen other cases. Modern Hebrew has left its imprint on the vocabulary, but not on morphology or phonology: *maymer* '(newspaper or magazine) article', usually in a pejorative sense; *vikukhim* 'debate', in addition to its older meaning of 'disputations', etc. In contrast, the part played by Traditional Hebrew has been overwhelming.[19]

12. But 'Traditional Hebrew' in itself, extending as it does over two thousand years until the appearance of Ashkenazic Jewry on the historical stage and another thousand since then, is much too vague a term and must be supplanted by other, more specific, designations.

The transmitted biblical texts themselves, of course, reflect different periods and styles. But if we disregard the disparate layers in Biblical Hebrew, there is the paramount fact in the history of Jewish civilization that long before the destruction of the Second Temple in 70 A.D., i.e. while the Second Commonwealth was still in existence, the spectacular expansion of Aramaic had already affected Palestine, and Aramaic had started replacing Hebrew as the spoken and written language of the Jews. Even later parts of the Bible, like the book of Daniel, ascribed in its final form to the second century B. C., contain whole portions in Aramaic.

There is no doubt that Hebrew continued as a vehicle of instruction and discussion for several centuries to come[20] until Aramaic replaced it in this function as well, but there is considerable dissent as to when Hebrew ceased to be the spoken language of the Jews. The great mid-nineteenth century scholars, such as Abraham Geiger, were convinced that Aramaic had been brought into Palestine by those returning from the Babylonian exile in the sixth century and that from the times of Ezra and Nehemiah on, Hebrew was rapidly declining as a vernacular; later Hebraists, including Noeldeke, Schürer and Brockelmann, were not that categorical but they, too, contended that the latest Hebrew portions of the Bible clearly bear the marks of a "dying" language. As opposed to

[18] This is the influence of the official Hebrew name of the State of Israel, *medinát yisraél* (rendered in Yiddish as *medines yisroel*). In pre-1948 Yiddish, *medine* usually meant 'province, country, countryside'; the regular Yiddish term for state is *melukhe*, also of Hebrew origin, but translated in Hebrew-English dictionaries as 'kingdom'.

[19] The situation is quite different when the inverse impact of Yiddish upon Hebrew is considered. From the inception of Yiddish and until the eighteenth century, the influence of spoken Yiddish upon the Ashkenazic version of written rabbinical Hebrew was very strong. It was as a reaction against this "corrupt" language that Modern Hebrew was born; its emphasis on the return to the "sources," notably the Bible, resulted in the diminution of Yiddish influence. In spoken Israeli Hebrew the Yiddish "substratum" makes itself felt so definitely again that even consistent purists have to acquiesce in some of these influences on phonemics, morphology, syntax and vocabulary.

[20] Jewish tradition distinguishes between the 'language of the Torah' (biblical) and the 'language of the sages' (mishnaic); the two may be considered to be different both in style and in time. Most valuable philological research into those differences has piled up and calls for summation and restatement in linguistic terms.

this view, it is being maintained by the school best represented by Ben-Jehuda, the reviver of contemporary Hebrew, that the language was spoken, at least in some sections of Palestine and by some strata of the population, as late as in the fourth century A.D.[21]

13. Of course, in spite of its ceasing to be an "immediate" language, i.e. one which people use in their daily pursuits and in which they give vent to their emotions, Hebrew did not cease to be employed. It survived as the vehicle of the sacred texts, with many derivative writings, and of prayer, and it is safe to assume that it was imbued with even greater holiness when it no longer served any profane purpose.

However, in this holy function which is explicit in the term *lašon hakodeš* 'the language of sacredness', Hebrew was not completely separated from the new vernacular, Aramaic.[22] At a very early time the addition of a publicly read Aramaic translation to the weekly Bible portion recited during the Sabbath service was made obligatory.[23] This translation was called *targum* 'translation'. The spoken tongue, or what may be called a semisacred variant of it, also found its way into the prayers.[24] Gradually, *targum* became the name of "Judeo-Aramaic" among the Jews themselves; it is felt therefore, that in our "approach from within" *Targumic* is a much more appropriate scientific term than "Judeo-Aramaic."[25]

14. As can be seen, the transition from Hebrew to Targumic was by no means a momentary or unilinear event; on second thought it may be added that a linguistic shift probably never is as simple as it looks in retrospect. For centuries it was not either–or, but both–and. Almost every member of the community used Targumic which, to various degrees on different levels, was permeated with Hebrew, and then Hebrew again which might or might not have been "Targumized" in morphology and vocabulary but most probably always was

[21] The views of this school are conveniently summarized, and the pertinent literature quoted, in the article by I. Methmann-Cohen: [Hebrew after the Babylonian Exile], *Lešonenu* 6 (1935–6) 172–188.—J. Cantineau, in his recent "Essai d'une phonologie de l'hébreu biblique," *Bulletin de la Société de Linguistique de Paris* 46 (1950) 82–122 considers Biblical Hebrew "a language . . . dead for over one thousand years at the time the consonantic text was provided with vowels"; it is the eighth century in which he places that event.

[22] Known to us in at least two Jewish versions, the Palestinian and the Babylonian.

[23] I. Elbogen: *Der jüdische Gottesdienst in seiner geschichtlichen Entwicklung*, 619 pp. (Berlin, 1913), pp. 186, 191; Hebrew translation of this book (Tel Aviv, 1924), p. 120.—Since Aramaic ceased to be the vernacular (see §16) its knowledge among non-scholars obviously has been very limited. By weight of tradition, however, the rule holds to this very day that the weekly portion of the Bible should be perused in private twice in Hebrew and once in Aramaic.

[24] An excellent specimen of the Hebrew-Aramaic fusion language is the *kadish* prayer whose nucleus, in the consensus of the scholars, antedates the destruction of the Second Temple.—Elbogen, *ibid.*, 94: "The kadish is not composed in a dialect of the vernacular but in that artificial idiom spoken in the schools, which is known from the officially recognized targumim."

[25] The Aramaic-speaking Jews of present-day Kurdistan invariably refer to their language as *targúm*. In Yiddish tradition, it is *tárgum-loshn*, literally 'the language of the Translation'. As a colloquialism, the term denotes 'unintelligible speech' (cf. English *Greek*).

with regard to pronunciation. The two poles in choosing this or that language would be the exigencies of everyday life and the high-level study of the Torah. But in reality different areas are not held apart that neatly. Linguistic interference, interpenetration and fusion, then, were the only things to be expected.[26]

15. The earliest history of Hebrew itself might have presented a similar picture of fusion at the time the Israelites entered Canaan, and if we knew enough about conditions prevailing at that age, Hebrew, too, would serve to illustrate everlasting Jewish bilingualism. But since the records all but fail us, the Hebrew ~ Targumic relationship has to be quoted as the first exhibit. Here we can observe almost in full light the fascinating process of moving apart and moving together again that is the concomitant of any language shift and results in basically identical problems for Targumic and any of the younger Jewish languages.

16. With the advent of Islam and the subjugation of country after country by the Arabs, Targumic began to recede as the main Jewish vernacular, though Targumic-speaking splinter groups continue to exist to this very day. In the Middle East, *Yahudic*, a new "Judeo-" language with Arabic as its quantitatively principal stock, came into being;[27] it later expanded along the southern shores of the Mediterranean and finally into Spain.

16.1. In Jewish Europe, comparable developments set in. The turmoil of the preceding centuries now gave way to relative stability. New Jewish subculture areas—the term SUBculture is used with relation to Jewish civilization as an unbroken whole—became distinguishable. They were characterized by significant peculiarities of behavior and thinking: by differences in ritual and prayer, by different approaches to the study and interpretation of the Torah and, naturally, by substantial variations in customs and folkways. In part, the differences were due to different antecedents, that is, they depended on the places directly from which the particular Jewish group had come, whether its basic patterns of Jewish living went back predominantly to Palestine or Babylonia (see §§17.1 and 21.1), etc. But it is self-evident that forceful influences also were exerted by the non-Jewish environment, different in each subculture area.[28]

It is no exaggeration to state that around the end of the first and the begin-

[26] Cf. Uriel Weinreich: *Languages in Contact; Findings and Problems*, 148 pp. (New York, 1953), pp. 68f., 106–110, and *passim*.

[27] References to peculiarities of Jewish Arabic are found not later than in the ninth century; cf. I. Goldziher in *Revue des études juives* 42 (1901) 14. At the same time, a distinction is made between Hebrew and *lugat al-Yahûd* 'speech of the Jews'; cf. M. Steinschneider in *Zeitschrift der Deutschen Morgenländischen Gesellschaft* 26 (1872) 766, note 5, and Goldziher, *loc. cit.* It seems therefore that, viewed from inside, Yahudic is the logical name for what is conventionally called 'Judeo-Arabic'.

[28] All over the Middle East and Europe, a profound reverse influence of Jewish culture on non-Jewish ones is traceable as well, and these relationships of give and take, varying as they do as to place, period and emotional or intellectual field, constitute a fascinating object of study for the cultural anthropologist with historical inclinations; but the topic is beyond the scope of the present paper. For an overall picture of what are the beginnings of the European period in Jewish history, cf. S. Dubnow: *Velt-geshikhte fun yidishn folk*, vol. 4 (Buenos Aires, 1951), pp. 13–117, 361–370, 376–380.

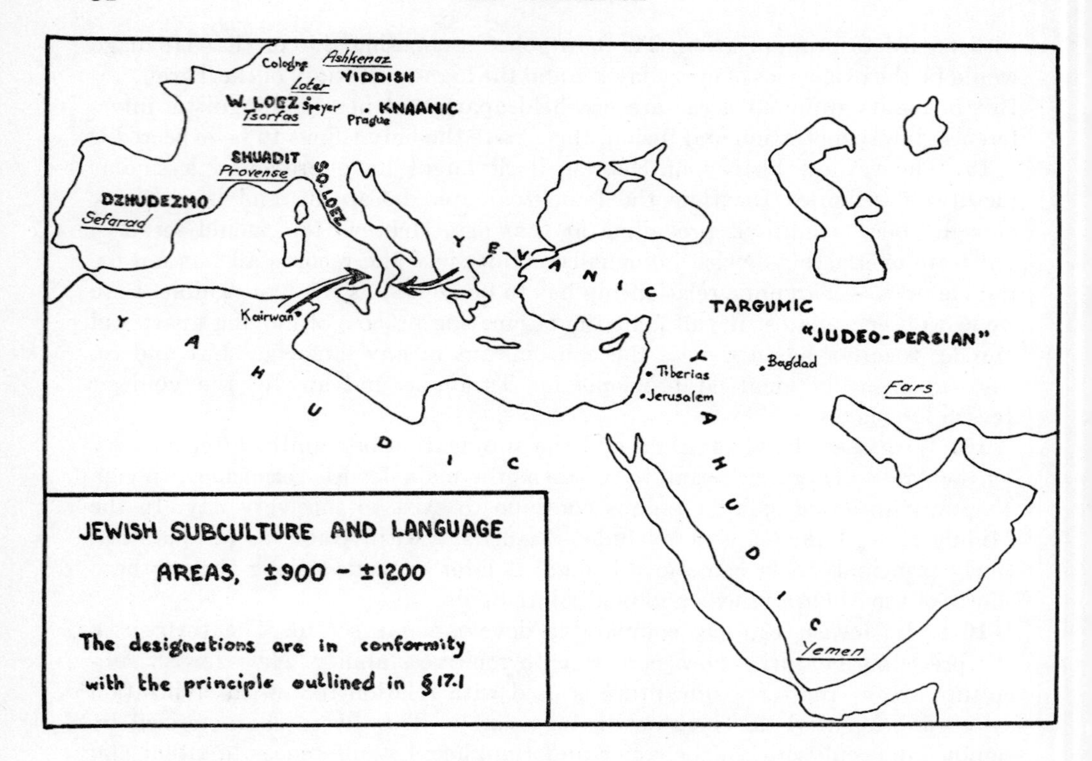

JEWISH SUBCULTURE AND LANGUAGE AREAS, ±900 – ±1200

The designations are in conformity with the principle outlined in §17.1

ning of this milennium a complete realignment of Jewish culture forces in the world took place.

17. As corollaries of those newly delimited subculture areas, new Jewish speech communities emerged. This, let us keep in mind, was the spring of languages in Europe, and new Jewish languages also made their appearance, though only partly produced by the same causes.

Two of them, unequal among themselves to be sure, were destined to play major roles: Dzhudezmo, born in Sefarad (Jewish Spain), and Yiddish, born in Loter which later developed into Ashkenaz. In addition, we have to deal with the area of Yevanic in the Byzantine sphere[29] and that of Knaanic in the Slavic sphere. Then, some of these groupings had "satellites" whose relationships to the major areas remain to be explored, and there were interstitial areas whose cultural-linguistic traits are not as easily perceptible.[30]

17.1. Thus, Jewish Provence (*Provense* in Hebrew sources), contrary to what present-day conditions would make one expect, was attached to Sefarad and not to Tsorfas (in Jewish tradition, the name of Northern France). Ashkenaz

[29] Cf. "*Yidishkayt . . .*" (note 14), pp. 494f.

[30] The adjoining chart lays no claim to full accuracy; it was drawn for orientation purposes only and is to be regarded as preliminary.

The study on the language of the medieval Czech Jews by R. Jakobson and M. Halle, long in preparation, is scheduled to appear in a forthcoming issue of the *Harvard Slavic Studies*.

attracted and gradually absorbed the bulk of the Western-Loez speaking community of Tsorfas, which for a time had seemed stronger than Ashkenaz itself. Knaan was centered in Prague, but a second stable Jewish area in the Slavic sphere, more to the east and the south, may at least be surmised; Knaan ultimately, too, was incorporated into Ashkenaz. Italy, one of the oldest Jewish settlements in Europe, was on the crossroads of Jewish subcultures and its Jewish-culture configuration, therefore, is less transparent, but we do discern here centers of effective cultural diffusion and also a vernacular which conveniently may be called Southern Loez. Calabria and Sicily, as would be expected, exhibited Byzantine-Jewish influences, with a generous infusion of Arabic-Jewish influences in the latter. The Arabic-Jewish area, to close the ring again, was (and still is) joined in the east by its Persian-Jewish neighbor with more than one speech community of the "Judeo-Persian" type.

17.2. Needless to say, the early speakers of those new Jewish languages gave no more thought to their having developed separate linguistic entities than did the early Old-French or Old-Italian or Old-Spanish speakers. Every now and then loose terms like *Loez* (see note 12) or *loshn ashkenaz* 'the language of Ashkenaz' appeared in the texts, and only very rarely, when a distinction was essential, a difference between the speech of the Jews and the coterritorial non-Jews would be mentioned; or the Hebrew author would be content to refer to *lešonenu* 'our language'. People speak prose even without being aware of it. Designations of languages frequently are chosen, both by the group itself and by linguists, in retrospect according to the specificness the languages have attained at later stages; and then the customary division into periods may be applied. Likewise, there should be no doubt that in the case of Western and Southern Loez (see §§7 and 17.1) the attributive adjectives are the linguist's *ex-post-facto* additions, coined from the vantage point of Yiddish.

18. Some of the basic problems in the study of any Jewish language were mentioned in the discussion of Targumic, such as the relationship sacred $\sim$ profane $\rightarrow$ semisacred or the degree to which the vernacular was permeated with Hebrew (see §§13 and 14). Then, another significant line of inquiry came into view: a 'prelanguage', and sometimes more than one, has to be taken into account, that is an older Jewish language that had yielded in a language shift (see §7.1); witness Targumic versus Yahudic, or Western and Southern Loez versus Yiddish. The prelanguage (or prelanguages, as the case may be) may always be presumed to enter the nascent language as one (or more) of its components.

The Hebrew component—and there is no Jewish language without one—is of course no exception. The implications will become manifest after the opposition between 'Whole Hebrew' and 'Merged Hebrew' is discussed.

19. 'Whole Hebrew' seems to be a suitable name for the language of the running Hebrew texts read (from sight or memory) by a speaker of a Jewish language (whose everyday language, by definition, is not Hebrew), while 'Merged Hebrew' applies to the Hebrew component in any of the Jewish languages in which Hebrew, as it were, has taken shelter. The descriptive linguist can object, and immediately score a point, that 'Merged Hebrew' is in a sense misleading because it is no part of Hebrew any more: it has become part and parcel of the linguistic system of another Jewish language. Still the concept is very useful when interest is directed to the genealogical aspect. Moreover, it favors conclusions of a comparative nature since we deal with an element which all Jewish languages have in common.

Usually, the difference between Whole Hebrew and Merged Hebrew is conceived of only in quantitative terms, the first being considered a multiple of the second. Actually, there is a world of difference between the two kinds of Hebrew[31] as used within the same group and even by the same person.[32]

19.1. Perhaps the best way to illustrate the point is to quote a few differences between Hebrew "merged" in present-day Yiddish and its "whole" Ashkenazic counterpart. The after-meal prayer recited by a guest at another person's table contains the phrase *es báal habáyis hazé*, and any Yiddish speaker will immediately identify the two middle words as meaning 'the head of the house', for whom God's blessing is supplicated. But should the guest address the host during the table conversation, it would be absurd for him to say anything but *balebós*, the Merged-Hebrew doublet of the Whole-Hebrew *baal habayis*; this, let us keep in mind, still differs from the Sefardic or Israeli pronunciation *baál habayit*. The biblical feminine name Jochebed is *Yoykheved* and that's the way it is pronounced in reading the Bible or, for that matter, a marriage contract; but the actual name of the girl mentioned in that marriage contract is *Yokhved*. In the speakers' and listeners' consciences there is certainly a more intimate connection between the two members of such opposed pairs than there is for the English speaker between *Swede* ~ *suède* or between *pièce de resistance* on the one hand and *piece*, *resistance* on the other. To a great part of Yiddish speakers nowadays, and in traditional Ashkenazic society to every member, Hebrew was infinitely more familiar than French is even to an educated Englishman, and the fact that the spelling of *báal habáyis* and *balebós* is identical because Yiddish still maintains the age-old unvocalized spelling of the words of Hebrew origin adds to that peculiar identifiability. However, it is not the closeness between the two but the significant differences between Whole and Merged Hebrew that we are after. Chiefly, it is distinctions of degree; but there is almost no

[31] Not the least is the fact that Whole Hebrew is infinitely more susceptible to normative influences; see §27.2. Still, despite strenuous efforts by modern Ashkenazic grammarians for more than two hundred years, no completely set standard in reading the prayers or even the Bible has been achieved. See next note.

[32] The diversities range all the way from deviations in word stress (stressing of the next-to-last syllable instead of the last one) to a blurred pronunciation of unstressed vowels and even the use of vowels other than prescribed by the norm; for instance, in the benediction on wine: *bóyrey* instead of *boyréy*; *boyre* instead of *boyrey*; *hagefen* instead of *hagofen*. One may choose to speak of different pronunciation "styles," but that in itself would not contribute to our understanding of the phenomenon. In most cases, we clearly deal with steps in the direction of Merged Hebrew, i.e. with a inverse influence of the vernacular upon one of the stock languages, and the most revered one at that.

word in the Hebrew component of Yiddish that is pronounced by Yiddish speakers exactly the way it sounds when it occurs in Whole Hebrew: the morning prayer starts with the words *borukh sheomar*, but the equivalent of 'to start *ab ovo*' is *onheybn fun borekh sh(e)omer*; the Hebrew name for the fast on the eve of Purim is *tánis éster*, but the usual Yiddish (= Merged-Hebrew) alternate is *ester-tónes*, and only the latter is used when an ephemeron is described as lasting *fun estertónes biz purim.*[33]

19.2. There is little difficulty in defining what has happened to Merged Hebrew: it has surrendered, at times unconditionally and then again with appreciable face-saving, to the general phonic and morphological structure of the fusion as a whole. As mentioned, Whole Hebrew also, to some degree, has been affected by the vernacular. But to what degree? The answer to this question is made more intricate by the fact that the boundaries between the two kinds of Hebrew are fluctuating rather than rigid: many words and phrases that sound like technical terms and quotations to the man in the street become part of their daily bread to speakers on a higher intellectual level engrossed in the study of the Torah.

Thus, in every Jewish language that came into existence after Targumic two different layers within the Hebrew component have to be considered. One entered from Whole Hebrew directly, as constantly rejuvenated *mots savants;* the other, a much smaller one, might have come via the Merged Hebrew of the prelanguage.[34] Neat separation may prove unfeasible in most cases, but the two strains have to be kept apart theoretically, as a matter of principle. For instance, the key to some deviating phenomena in the Hebrew component of Yiddish, otherwise inexplicable, may well be found in some pre-Yiddish linguistic conditions.

20. The shape of Hebrew in the last quarter of the first millennium and the first quarter of the second, i.e. in the pre-Ashkenazic and early Ashkenazic era, is much less discernible today than it seemed to be about one hundred years ago. Until that time and for centuries, the presentation of the Hebrew sound system[35] had been only in terms of the Tiberian punctuation. As is well known, this punctuation consists to begin with of seven "vowel points": ḥireḳ, ṣere, segol, pataḥ, ḳameṣ, ḥolem, ḳibbuṣ; then, under circumstances that need further elucidation, the original ḳibbuṣ point split up into ḳibbuṣ proper and šureḳ,

[33] *Fun* 'from'; *biz* 'until'.

[34] Cf., in the English speech of contemporary American Jews, the variables *shvuos*, or even *shabuót*, vs. *shvues*, *shabos* or even *shabát* vs. *shabes*, taken from different versions of Whole Hebrew or from Yiddish, respectively. Some words, like *kosher* or *megile*, appear only in their Yiddish version; *kashér* or *megilá* would sound eccentric even if they were understood.—One is tempted to think of a 'Whole Latin' versus 'Merged Latin' when confronted with comparable phenomena concerning the mutual influence of scholarly Latin and the Romance vernaculars. Cf. for instance W. Meyer-Lübke: *Die Schicksale des lateinischen* l *im Romanischen*, 83 pp. (Leipzig, 1934), p. 69.

[35] Would it be judicious to speak of a "phonemic" system in a language at a stage when it is not spoken but read or quoted only for specific purposes?

designated respectively by three dots arranged in a ladder and by a vav with a dot in the middle.[36]

So deeply rooted was the idea of the Tiberian system as the only one that when a manuscript containing a different punctuation—the supralinear one now known as the "Babylonian"—came to light in the middle of the nineteenth century, S. J. Rapoport, one of the most eminent Jewish scholars of the modern period, was quick to brand it a forgery. But more texts with those odd vowel points were unearthed, and in the last decade of the nineteenth century a third system was rediscovered; it is called "Palestinian," even though the city of Tiberias, after which the classical punctuation was named, is in Palestine too. It did not take long to recognize that behind the differences in writing there were also differences in pronunciation. Today, one hundred years after the scholarly world was first confronted with the Babylonian punctuation and after the painstaking research of the last fifty years or so, the system established by the "Sages of Tiberias," most probably in the eighth century,[37] is no longer taken at its face value, though it is still rightfully praised for its ingenuity.

20.1. Be it recalled again: what we can hope to penetrate to is not Hebrew speech of the eighth or ninth or tenth century, because there was none at the time, but Whole-Hebrew pronunciation habits of the period. It may be assumed that those were not completely divorced from actual Hebrew speech as it had existed centuries earlier, but there seems to be for the time being no way of ascertaining exactly how far the correspondence goes.

As for the Tiberian punctuation itself, it is now conceived of as a superb effort of scholars who, on the basis of their own practice in reading but no less of their orthoëpic preconceptions, set up a normative system for the purpose of patching up and bridging divergencies in the way of reading or reciting the sacred texts—above all, the masoretic text of the Bible.[38]

21. Except for minor and comparatively few vacillations, the punctuation of Tiberias is rigidly fixed. But there is no single universally accepted way of pronouncing its seven vowel points. In Europe, tradition has brought down two

[36] There is considerable confusion in Jewish tradition as to the names given to the several vowel points and, particularly, to the point represented by three dots in a ladder and the vav with a dot in the middle. The designations in the text above are the ones accepted, for instance, by H. L. Strack: *Hebräische Grammatik*, 242 pp. (Munich, 1930). As opposed to this, Eastern-European Ashkenazic practice uses the terms *shurek* and *melupn vov*, respectively.

[37] Some students prefer the less definite description "7th–9th century," and their caution may be warranted since the establishment of the norm was certainly no single act but a solidification of a gradually developing tradition.—Cf. W. Chomsky: "The History of Our Vowel System in Hebrew," *Jewish Quarterly Review* 32 (1941–42) 26–49.

[38] Cf. P. Kahle: "Die überlieferte Aussprache des Hebräischen und die Punktuation der Masoreten," *Zeitschrift für die alttestamentliche Wissenschaft* 39 (1921) 230–239; *id.*, §§6–9, in H. Bauer and P. Leander: *Historische Grammatik der hebräischen Sprache des Alten Testaments* 1, 707 pp. (Halle, 1922); *id.:* "Das Problem der Grammatik des Hebräischen," *Indogermanische Forschungen* 45 (1927) 395–410.—Occasionally, earlier scholars with singular insight had also perceived that the Tiberian punctuation was only "a signal for those not expert in reading; the sages never spoke that way" (MaHaRaL of Prague, ±1515–1609).

pronunciation versions, the Sefardic and the Ashkenazic. Ever since the Middle Ages grammarians were concerned with the question of which pronunciation was the "correct" one. For reasons inherent in the development of Hebrew studies in medieval Europe, the Christian Hebraists had always leaned toward the Sefardic version; in the early nineteenth century, it carried the day in the scholarly world. The founders of the "Science of Judaism" headed by Zunz in their works also employed the Sefardic transcription of Hebrew only.[39]

21.1. It was only after the rival Babylonian punctuation was discovered and more light was shed on the Hebrew pronunciation in the Orient that the Ashkenazic version was cleared of the stigma of "corruption." Instead, it was now maintained by such brilliant scholars as Rapoport, Luzzatto and Pinsker that the pronunciation of Hebrew had not been uniform at the time the two main bulwarks of European Jewry were established in Spain and Loter and that the dichotomy Sefardic ~ Ashkenazic was a perpetuation of the dichotomy Babylonia ~ Palestine.

The line that divided those two Oriental centers of Jewish civilization from even before the beginning of the Arab domination well into the twelfth and thirteenth centuries is, indeed, a factor far too little appreciated in Jewish cultural history, and the attempt to trace a crucial difference between the two main branches of European Jewry to a pre-European prefiguration represented a tremendous step forward (see §§27f.). Still, subsequent research has opened new mines of information[40] and the problems, consequently, appear much more complicated now.

Of primary importance is the fact that in neither group have the pronunciation systems been static since the emergence of the Sefardim and Ashkenazim about one thousand years ago, and some signal developments within the Ashkenazic field will be presented later. Our point of departure, however, will be pre-Ashkenazic and early Ashkenazic Whole Hebrew or, rather, one part of it. The consonants will not be inquired into here, although there is material available

[39] Within the cultural context of the period, it seems clear that the issue was decided by the evaluation of the two main Jewish subcultures which prevailed among the non-Jewish intellectuals in Germany and then was taken over by the spokesmen of the German Jews themselves; it was not merely the Sefardic way of reading Hebrew but Sefardic civilization as a whole that was considered superior. It should be stressed, however, that while yielding to the Sefardic pronunciation in transcription, no grouping of the German Jews did so in religious service. There the Ashkenazic pronunciation, albeit in a somewhat modernized form that can bear more intensive study, has been upheld to the last. The Ashkenazim of Eastern Europe adhered to their tradition with equal tenacity. The khasidim in the eighteenth century, in deference to R. Isaac Lurie (the ARI), introduced the Sefardic version of the prayerbook, but there is no trace of their ever even contemplating the acquisition of the Sefardic pronunciation.

[40] Ch. Yalon, to whom we are under obligation for so much of the spadework concerning subtle differences of punctuation and pronunciation in communities as far apart as the Western Ashkenazim and the Yemenites (see note 41), keeps hammering: PUNCTUATION IS PRONUNCIATION. It would be more circumspect to say (and that probably is what is meant): divergencies in punctuation should be watched because they are likely to reflect actual or former divergencies in pronunciation.

on that subject and a definitive exposition obviously would have to deal with it as well. What follows is a discussion of the actual phonic value, and only with regard to quality at that, of the seven conventional Tiberian vowel points.[41]

22. It appears that by the time the Jews began entering Loter (see §7) there existed three systems of pronouncing the vowels in Whole Hebrew. They were regionally defined; instead of the current confusing terms Tiberian, Palestinian, Babylonian we shall designate them Northwestern, Southwestern, and Eastern, respectively.

The focus of the Eastern region was in the yeshives of Babylonia, then the foremost centers of Jewish learning, and it extended to Yemen and to the frontiers of India and China. The Southwestern region included Southern Palestine and the southern shores of the Mediterranean up to the Atlantic, while the Northwestern pronunciation, favored and standardized but not necessarily created by the Tiberias school, was in vogue in northern Palestine, Syria and in adjacent Byzantine territory.

23. The Whole-Hebrew pronunciation systems of one thousand years ago have by now been worked out in some detail and there is reasonable hope that through further patient step-by-step investigation much more insight into them will be gained. Since a great part of the Hebrew component of Yiddish, in all likelihood, actually came from or later was straightened out according to the requirements of Whole Hebrew, it is easy to see the direct bearing of this seemingly remote subject upon our field of inquiry.

23.1. The Eastern region, extending from Babylonia east- and southwards, had six vowels in the reading of Whole Hebrew: [i e ɛ ɔ o u]. The [a] was absent from the system; there was only an [ɛ] where the Tiberian punctuation distinguishes between segol and pataḥ.

Whether the later graphic split of the ḳibbuṣ into two (see §20) was intended just as a kind of reading device or as a distinction of quantity is something to ponder. At any rate, not later than in the twelfth century a notable difference in pronunciation developed in the Eastern region: the šureḳ, i.e. the dotted vav, continued to be pronounced the old way as [u], while the three-dot ladder, ḳibbuṣ, was now pronounced as a palatal [y] (see §§30–32.2). The six-vowel

[41] Older research is summarized in the studies quoted in notes 37 and 38. Kahle's outstanding achievements are fully acknowledged by the following authors who differ with him on relevant particulars: Ch. Yalon: [Review of P. Kahle: *Masoreten des Westens*, 2], *Lešonenu* 3 (1931) 202–207 and Kahle's rejoinder, *ibid.*, 310; *id.:* [Paths of Pronunciation], *Ḳuntresim le'inyane halašon ha'ivrit* 1 (Jerusalem, 1937), 62–78; *id.:* [Orders in Language], *ibid.* 1, 79–86, 2 (1938), 12–14; B. Klar in *Ḳiryat sefer* 15 (1938) 171; Ch. Yalon: [Sefardic Pronunciation in Northern France in the Generation of Rashi and in the Generations After Him], *'Inyane lašon* 1 (Jerusalem, 1942), 16–31, 48; B. Klar: [Problems of Masorah and Pronunciation in the Works of Ḳirḳisani, a Karaite Writer of the Tenth Century], *ibid.*, 2 (1943), 31–38; *id.:* [On the History of Hebrew Pronunciation in the Middle Ages], *Lešonenu* 17 (1950–51) 72–75; Ch. Yalon: [On the Punctuation System of the Mishna] in Albek-Yalon: *Šiše sidre mišnah; seder mo'ed* (Jerusalem, 1952), 13–28.—The "Studies in Historical Phonetics of the Hebrew Language" by Y. F. Gumpertz: *Mibṭa'e śefatenu*, 349 pp. with a xx-page summary in English (Jerusalem, 1953) only in part deal with the topics of the present paper; they merit extensive discussion by specialists in the field of Hebrew.

system thus had become one of seven vowels, but with the [a] still absent: [i e ɛ ɔ o u y].

23.2. The Southwestern region was characterized by a Whole Hebrew pronunciation based on five vowels only. An [a] appears uniformly where Tiberias has pataḥ or ḳameṣ[42] and [e] is read regardless of the distinction made in Tiberias between the ṣere and segol points. The inventory, then, looks like this: [i e a o u].

23.3. In the Northwestern region, the number of differently pronounced vowels is exactly the same as that of the vowel points in the Tiberian punctuation system. This perfect correspondence is hardly accidental. It stands to reason that the normative ideas of the Sages of Tiberias (which city is situated in the region) were based on the actual Whole-Hebrew reading habits of the region and that their orthoëpic instructions were tailored to suit these habits. The pronunciation of the vowel points in the Northwestern area, in the order given in §23.1, is as follows: [i e ɛ a ɔ o u].

23.4. In diagram form, the correspondence between vowel points and vowels may be presented as shown in the adjoining figure.

24. As is easily seen, the three Whole-Hebrew pronunciation regions just described do not coincide with the subculture areas outlined in §§16–17.1: while the former reach with their roots into the past, the latter were the results of subsequent reshuffling processes. But the two setups were by no means irrelative to each other with regard to subsequent development: it was not only geographical location but also culture patterns that were responsible for the ultimate fixing of a certain Whole-Hebrew pronunciation in a certain territory.

25. Essentially, the present-day Ashkenazic Whole-Hebrew pronunciation system is a replica of that of the Northwestern region; variations can be shown (see, for instance, §§19.1 and 31) to be due to the strong influence of Yiddish or its particular territorial variants. By the same token, Modern Sefardic pronunciation does not deviate much from what was ascribed to the Southwestern region. But the studies by Ch. Yalon, B. Klar, Y. F. Gumpertz and a reinterpretation, in their light, of earlier research, seem to have proven beyond doubt that this adherence of Ashkenaz (and of Ashkenaz only) to the prescripts of the Sages of Tiberias is of a comparatively late date and that it began in the thirteenth century. It is the middle of that century which for many other reasons as well, linguistic and extralinguistic, marks the beginning of a new period in the history of Yiddish.[43]

26. The inference is plain: the Whole Hebrew that went into the making of Yiddish in Loter, in the period of Earliest Yiddish, was different from what it is now.[44] Fundamentally, it was the vowel pronunciation pertaining to the

[42] Except for the few cases with the so-called 'ḳameṣ ḳaṭan'. Cf. Strack (note 36), p. 7.

[43] We speak of Earliest Yiddish (–1250), Old Yiddish (1250–1500), Middle Yiddish (1500–1750), Modern Yiddish (1750–).

[44] The limitation to Whole Hebrew is necessary because (see §19.2) some elements of the Hebrew component must have reached Yiddish not from Whole Hebrew but through the intermediary of the prelanguages.

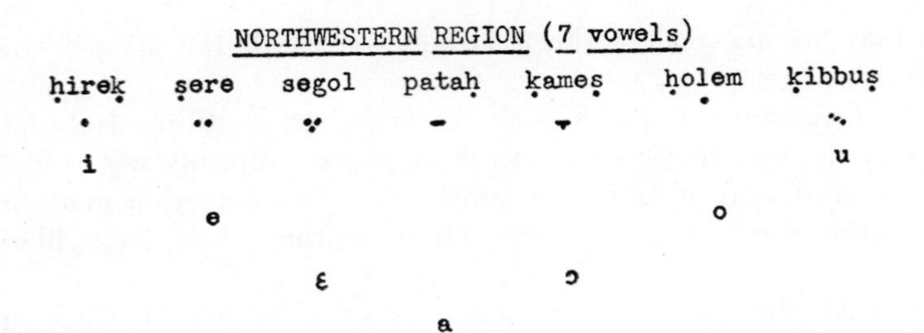

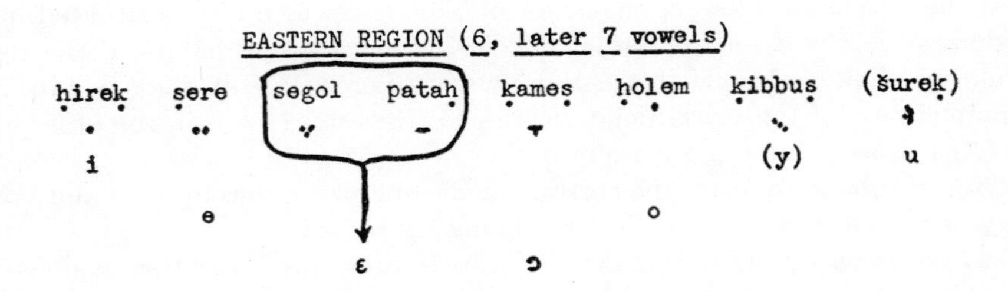

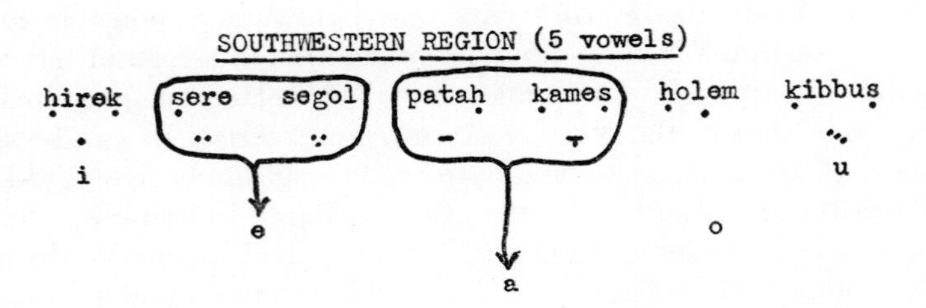

Southwestern region that prevailed among the Loez speakers and also among the Yiddish speakers until, roughly, the middle of the thirteenth century.[45]

There is triple proof for that: (1) in the transcription of Hebrew in non-Jewish sources; (2) in statements on punctuation and pronunciation in the writings of medieval Hebrew grammarians and exegetes; (3) in numerous residues of pre-Ashkenazic pronunciation found in later Yiddish such as *yam* 'sea', *khaver* 'friend'; *meslés* 'day and night', *genem* 'hell'; *Sdom* 'Sodom', *tomer* 'if, maybe', where one would anticipate in the stressed syllables, *o*, *ey* and *oy* respectively.

[45] On the synchronic plane, there is no harm in saying that these Jews pronounced Hebrew the "Sefardic" way. Historically, of course, the case must be stated differently. This pronunciation appears to have originated in southern Palestine at a much earlier date than the emergence of Sefarad; witness the transcriptions of Hebrew in the writings of the fathers of the Church, and even in the Septuagint. It then began moving westward until it hit Spain. Advance guards may be said to have penetrated as far as Tsorfas and Loter and then to have retreated but not without leaving traces in later Yiddish.

The explanation for the linguistic about-face of Ashkenaz is furnished by the history of Jewish civilization.

27. While the Tiberian punctuation dates from not later than the eighth century, its westward march did not start that early. It is only from the tenth century on that reference is made to "teachers who went out from Tiberias to far-away countries and there people . . . urged them to teach their children the Palestinian [way of] reading [Hebrew], and they learned from them the correct reading with great zeal." The earliest testimonies identify the "far-away countries" as Irak (= Babylonia) and Persia,[46] but gradually the system also began expanding toward the west. The Sefardic grammarians led by the Ḳimḥis[47] did not accept the pronunciation, but they reinterpreted the prestige-carrying Tiberian punctuation as distinguishing between long and short vowels, and this lip service to a writing system that was so clearly unsuited for the actual pronunciation of the region has been haunting the students of Hebrew grammar ever since. In distant Europe, a decisive victory for the Northwestern pronunciation was scored in Ashkenaz which was reached through Byzantium and Knaan (see §17.1) as well as through Italy.

Peculiarly, it was teachers of Babylonian and not of Palestinian origin who were responsible for the radical change.

27.1. The oldest Jewish religious-cultural stimuli in Europe obviously had been of Palestinian provenience. But with the rise and expansion of the Arabs, impoverished Palestine was reduced to a more than modest secondary role and the talmudic schools of Babylonia became preponderant. Around the middle of the eleventh century, adversity befell the Babylonian Gaonate too, and the dependence of its far-famed Bagdad yeshive upon outside financial support became greater than ever. Driven by necessity, scholars had to emigrate in growing numbers; when the yeshive had to close down altogether, most of the scholars had to leave. But the precarious state of the Babylonian center of learning resulted in what is comparable to the exodus of Greek scholars from Constantinople after the city had fallen to the Turks: along with the Jewish settlements east and south of Babylonia, Ashkenaz was to gain by what Babylonia lost.

27.2. This "Babylonian renaissance," as it may well be called, in Central (and, by subsequent Ashkenazic migrations, Eastern) European Jewish civilization had far-reaching consequences that are beyond the scope of this paper.[48]

[46] Quoted according to B. Klar in *'Inyane lašon* 2 and in *Lešonenu* 17 (note 41); cf. the sources mentioned there.—P. Kahle: *Masoreten des Ostens*, xxx + 239 pp. (Leipzig, 1913), p. xxviii: "Saadja [892–942, the preëminent Babylonian Gaon] is actually the last Jewish scholar who has real knowledge of the Babylonian tradition of the biblical text. Bible manuscripts punctuated by Babylonian Masoretes at any rate cannot be younger than 900 A.D."

[47] The most prominent of them, David Ḳimḥi (= RaDaK), was born of a family hailing from southern Spain in 1160 in Narbonne and died there in 1235. A critical edition of his principal work is now available: *David Kimhi's Hebrew Grammar* . . . by W. Chomsky, 427 pp. (New York, 1952).—See note 50.

[48] The present writer discussed this problem of cultural ties with regard to interpretation of the Torah, differentials in ritual, etc., in his paper: [The Antecedents of Ashkenazic

Suffice it to say then within our specific context that it was the Babylonian teachers, coached in the Tiberias pronunciation and believing in its superiority over all rival reading systems, who are most likely to have steeped their new charges in the imported orthoëpy. They were the carriers of authority concerning the sacred text of the Torah, so there was no doubt that they also knew better than anybody else how to read it. All scholars, one may assume, tried their best to conform; the younger generation must have been most compliant.

To visualize the process and its effects, there is more than one analogy in recent Jewish cultural experience. In Alsace after 1871, the pronunciation of the ḳibbuṣ and šureḳ in the prayers changed from [y] to [u] under the influence of German-trained teachers, while in the Hebrew component of Yiddish the same words continue to be pronounced as before. In some American Hebrew schools today an effort is made to supersede the traditional Ashkenazic pronunciation of the sacred texts with the Israeli one, and there is no reason why it should not succeed; the reluctance to introduce it on a broader scale stems not so much from linguistic difficulties as from ideological and sentimental attachments. Sentiment works wonders in linguistic change, as can be seen from the conscious introduction of the Palestinian (Sefardized) Hebrew pronunciation into the Hebraist schools of Eastern Europe between the two world wars. For centuries, the community had known nothing but Ashkenazic, and therefore the going was rough at times, but on the whole the teachers and students of those Palestine-oriented schools had made the switch within one generation[49] when the catastrophe of the German war overcame them.

Single Babylonian leaders in education and their native disciples started in the twelfth century, perhaps even by the end of the eleventh; thus, they had much more than one generation to work on; the prestige they displayed was more potent, too. Therefore, no matter how puzzled we are by the tenacity of the relics in Merged Hebrew antedating the Babylonian renaissance, the orthoëpic reform did succeed for all intents and purposes.

28. As already mentioned, the pressure was applied in many places simultaneously.[50] If, ultimately, Ashkenaz was the only area to come through with

---

Jewry: Babylonia or Palestine], read before the twenty-seventh annual conference of the Yiddish Scientific Institute—Yivo on January 4, 1953 (as yet unpublished).

[49] For Alsace, cf. *Jüdisches Literaturblatt* 10 (1881) 120; S. Birnbaum in *Yivo-bleter* 6 (1934) 44 on the authority of Ernest H. Lévy.—Cf. note 32; it may be said that the more articulate, the more centralized, the more sentiment-backed the conscious efforts at linguistic change, the better their chances of succeeding.—Klar was quite right in calling the Tiberian pronunciation imported into Ashkenaz the 'academic' one. The academic pronunciation of Latin in English schools and its introduction instead of the previous Anglicized one might be a good analogy to pursue; cf. Smith, C. G. Moore, "The English Language and the 'Restored' Pronunciation of Latin," *A Grammatical Miscellany . . . Otto Jespersen* (Copenhagen, 1930), 167–178.

[50] One hundred years before David Ḳimḥi, the famous Sefardi Abraham Ibn Ezra of Toledo, in his *Sefer Śaḥut*, stated: ". . . the pronunciation of the ḳameṣ gadol . . . the mouth is compressed when reading that [point] and not open as while pronouncing the pataḥ gadol, as we read it in these places. Only the people of Tiberias and also the sages of Egypt and Africa [a name for Kairwan, near present-day Tunis, in Jewish tradition] know how to

the innovations and to stick to them, there seem to have been at least two extralinguistic reasons for that phenomenon. In no other branch of Jewry was the study of the Torah as deeply rooted and Torah itself made part of the daily routine as in Ashkenaz; consequently, the word of the authoritative teachers from abroad must have carried particular weight. But there was also the factor of geography. The farther back in history, the more the Jewish communities in different lands were dependent upon general communication opportunities, and it can be shown that in the period under discussion the lines of communication from Babylonia to central Europe, via Byzantium and the Slavic countries, were much more open than to Spain.[51]

A third most probable factor, the structural one, which might have been particularly conducive to the acceptance of the Northwestern pronunciation system of Whole Hebrew by the Yiddish-speaking community of Ashkenaz, will be brought up in §33.1.

29. At first glance it may seem like an unwarranted assumption that Babylonian teachers, who in their native Whole-Hebrew reading had no [a] at all and confounded segol and pataḥ in a single [ɛ] should have become the carriers of the Tiberias system that was so different from their own. But the Italian "lingua toscana in bocca romana" is no astounding exception; it just forces the linguist to make normative efforts an integral part of his subject matter. History has repeated itself in the Hebrew of our days, only the tables have been turned: while thousands of non-Ashkenazim in reborn Jewish Palestine learned Yiddish from the Eastern-European settlers, the latter—for extralinguistic reasons, to be sure—switched to a Sefardic-type pronunciation of Hebrew. In present-day New York's Yiddish language schools, teachers who came from Poland, the Ukraine or Rumania impart to American-born children the standard pronunciation of Yiddish with its heavily "Lithuanian" slant. If thousands of people, with various degrees of success, can give up inveterate speech habits for the sake of a superpersonal norm in an "immediate" language, the transition must be even easier in a special-purpose second language.

30. Incidentally, at least on one count the Babylonian local pronunciation habits did deviate from the superimposed Tiberias standard. Reference is made to the split of the ḳibbuṣ into two points, with the corollary split into two

---

read the ḳameṣ gadol." Whether or not "these places" also include Mantua, where the *Sefer* was completed in 1146, the meaning seems to be clear: the "correct" pronunciation that emanated from Tiberias had not reached Spain, but in more closely situated places it had affected at least the "sages," i.e. the scholars who were more susceptible to normative efforts.—The quotation is from the 1769 Berlin edition, p. 26.

[51] With this problem of access routes in mind it may be easier to explain why the Oriental import did not make any appreciable inroads among the Jews of eastern France; cf. P. Mordel in *Lešonenu* 2 (1930) 246; *id.* in *Jewish Quarterly Review* 26 (1933–34) 80–278; Ch. Yalon in *Ḳuntresim* 2 (note 41), 9; *id.* in *'Inyane lašon* 2 (note 41), 26; Gumpertz (note 41) 1–32. On second thought, the attestations concerning the Whole Hebrew of Tsorfas adduced thus far do not reach beyond the middle of the thirteenth century; younger sources, if any, may modify the evidence and show the penetration of the Tiberian system into Tsorfas as well.

sounds, [y] and [u] (see §23.1). And, bewildering as it seems, this twofold pronunciation was carried into Ashkenaz and prevailed there for more than four hundred years;[52] even then it did not disappear but was subsumed under larger categories in a reapportionment that affected the language as a whole and resulted in a different distribution of the [u] and [y] sounds in the Hebrew component as well.

Since a most significant problem of component fusion is posed here, it must be dealt with at some length.[53]

31. Modern Yiddish does not distinguish any more between the pronunciation of ḳibbuṣ and šureḳ though in spelling the two different points continue to be used. Instead, in all of modern Southern Yiddish (the Ukraine, Poland, Western Hungary, Western Slovakia, etc.) EVERY ḳibbuṣ or šureḳ appears as [i] or, in some dialects, as [y], while in Northern Yiddish (White Russia, Lithuania, Courland, and the northern portion of Western Yiddish) EVERY ḳibbuṣ or šureḳ appears as [u].[54]

The "law" applies to Whole Hebrew; it also applies to Merged Hebrew, i.e. to the Hebrew component in Yiddish, except for a few most recent loanwords from Israeli Hebrew. But, as every student or speaker of Yiddish knows, this isogloss between [u] and [y, i][55] reaches out much farther. With amazing regularity, it cuts through the language as a whole and is one of the most conspicuous differentials of the regional varieties as they had more or less congealed by the beginning of the Modern-Yiddish period; cf. *puter* ~ *piter* 'butter', *mekhutn* ~ *mekhitn* 'relative by marriage', *pust* ~ *pist* 'empty'. (The illustrations, which could be multiplied by the hundreds, are taken from the German, Hebrew and Slavic component, in that order.)

32. As soon, however, as we try the diachronic approach, the monolith falls asunder. In the first place, it can be shown that in part of the Slavic component a transition [u] > [i] took place as late as in the late-Middle and early-Modern Yiddish period. Then it turns out that an almost general alternation between [u] and [y][56] must be ascribed to the period of Earliest Yiddish. The facts are

[52] A further shift from [y] to [i], at least in some areas, must have occurred rather early.

[53] The subsequent presentation summarizes a paper (as yet unpublished) read by the present writer before the Linguistic Circle of Yivo on November 29 and December 20, 1953. —An impressive array of pertinent examples going back to the oldest Yiddish manuscripts and of quotations from Hebrew authors and Christian Hebraists, will be found in the pioneering study of Sh. Birnboym (Birnbaum): [The History of the Old *u* Sounds in Yiddish], *Yivo-bleter* 6 (1934) 25–60.

[54] From a field long familiar to the general linguist the off-again-on-again analogy of French *chef* and *(il) aime* may be adduced. They started out with an identical /a/ (cf. Latin *caput, amat*) and at present again have the /ɛ/ in common, but in Old French they had split into *chef* with a monophthong and *áime* with a diphthong. Cf. Leo Spitzer, ed.: *Hugo Schuchardt-Brevier*, 483 pp. (Halle, 1928), p. 69.

[55] The interest here centers in the fact of the palatalization of the old [u]'s; the details of their further fate, the difference in lip rounding between the [y]'s of some regions and the [i]'s of others, or the degree of palatalization (some regions have incompletely palatalized [ɨ]'s) are secondary to our topic. That's the reason for choosing the simple notations [u] ~ [y, i].

[56] And again, as in the case of the ḳibbuṣ coming from the Hebrew, at least in some places a shift [y > i] must have occurred rather early.

too intricate and too numerous to present at this juncture; be it only intimated, therefore, that the universal [i] in *yid* 'Jew' (cf. Standard German *Jude*)[57] or, for that matter, in *zidlen* (see §8) are due to this early alternation.

There is no mistaking that this phenomenon is a particular case of the shift that we best know from French (MURU > *mur*) but which also overtook, to a much greater extent than usually recognized, the adjacent Germanic areas of the Lowlands and the Middle-Rhine basin, in other words, both Dutch and German territories. To be sure, this Germanic phenomenon is conspicuously absent from the household compendia and grammars and even a synthesizing monograph is still a desideratum, but from studies on German and Dutch dialects and from the *Deutscher Sprachatlas* indisputable evidence can be gathered.[58]

32.1. The Western Loez-speaking immigrants into Loter no doubt had the [u > y] tendency (or would it be safer still to speak of allophones for that period and to symbolize them as [y, u]?) in their speech. The question thus may be asked if the [y, u] alternation in Earliest Yiddish is to be considered a carry-over from the prelanguage or whether it was acquired by the nascent speech community as a feature of the German linguistic stock which they found in their new settlement. On general grounds it may be assumed that it was a convergence of the two factors which was responsible. It may well be (this is a line of inquiry to pursue) that the two factors reinforced each other and that, therefore, the tendency towards [y] was stronger in Yiddish than in coterritorial German.

32.2. This assumption is butressed by the fact that convergence can be proved for another phase of the problem, the one affecting the German and the Hebrew component. Confronted as we are with the ḳibbuṣ ∼ šureḳ pronunciation development in the Hebrew component and a concurrent remarkably similar one of [u] ∼ [y] in the German component, the hypothesis may be advanced that the process had started in one component only and afterwards had spread over the language as a whole, just as around the beginning of the modern period the [u > y > i] in the Slavic component must be explained as "contagion" without an intrinsic cause in that component itself.

If we were to accept the hypothesis the decision would still have to be made on whether to look for the initial source in the German or in the Hebrew com-

[57] Lexer's *Mittelhochdeutsches Wörterbuch* offers *jüde* as a parallel form to *jude* and Kluge's *Etymologisches Wörterbuch* rightly allocates the *-ü-* form to "mitteldeutsch." But the implications of the exclusive *i* in Yiddish as against the German doublet have yet to be stated.

[58] Out of the many studies to be consulted, only two will be mentioned here. On the Dutch situation, basic information is contained in M. Schönfeld: *Historische Grammatica van het Nederlands*, 4th ed. (Zutphen, 1947). The study by Th. Frings: "Germanisch ē und ō," *Beiträge zur Geschichte der deutschen Sprache und Literatur* 63 (1939) 1–116, establishes a broad context and successfully couples Dutch and German evidence but lacks perspicuity and sometimes arrives at questionable conclusions. For instance, the dialectal *brüder* 'brother (singular)' on maps 12, 37, 68 of the *Deutscher Sprachatlas* is interpreted as *Bruder* > *Brüderchen* > *Brüder*. However, there is German dialectal material to controvert the proposition that *Brüder* is an isolated phenomenon, and the German component of Yiddish amply proves that the [u > y] shift was a general one. The phonic variants of *Bruder* suggested themselves to Frings as a subject of inquiry merely because the word happened to appear in one of Wenker's forty sentences which lay at the foundation of the *Sprachatlas*.

ponent. But either alternative has to be rejected and with that the hypothesis falls as a whole.

The German component, as shown in §32, experienced the [u, y] alternation by virtue of its appertaining to a wide Romance-Germanic area where no infection from Hebrew need or can be contemplated. But neither is the opposite possible, and that's why the theory of a Babylonian import was presented in such firm terms. The point is that the pronunciation of the ḳibbuṣ as [y] (versus the šureḳ pronounced as [u]) is deeply embedded in the Whole and Merged Hebrew of the entire Eastern region (see §23.1) and, particularly, of Yemen.[59] It has been shown (§§27–27.1) to what degree the whole medieval Jewish Middle East must be considered a dependency of Jewish Babylonia. But with regard to Yemen there is a major contributory fact: since the twelfth century it was most certainly sealed off from both Ashkenaz and Sefarad until the second half of the nineteenth century. Thus, a spread of the phenomenon from Yemen to Ashkenaz, or vice versa, is out of the question.

Had the ḳibbuṣ ~ šureḳ pronunciation split been found in Yemen only, or in Ashkenaz only, an on-the-spot causation would have been feasible and, in the case of Ashkenaz, contagion from the numerically stronger Loez and German component could have been assumed. As matters stand, however, with the identical Whole and Merged-Hebrew phenomenon at the two poles of the Jewish world, it is hardly possible to think of independent identical development in each case. Then the incontestable extralinguistic factors help us to put the pieces of the jigsaw puzzle together and to identify Babylonia as the focus of the ḳibbuṣ ~ šureḳ pronunciation split.

For the field of Yiddish proper, there is no need to delve any further, though the Hebrew scholar and the general linguist may legitimately search for the cause of that split in pre-twelfth-century Babylonian Hebrew. The suggestion is offered for what it may be worth that in this specific case of a non-immediate language a functional causation seems less probable than a normative one; in pursuance of the "read as you write" rule some prestige-carrying grammarians might have come to the conclusion that since there were two different vowel points they should be assigned a different quality.

33. In summing up, several conclusions of a more general nature seem to be justified as a result of the preceding discussion.

The first concerns the relation Whole Hebrew : Merged Hebrew : Yiddish. Chances are that the reception by Ashkenaz of the Babylonian-sponsored Tiberias pronunciation rules was facilitated by the fact that they conformed more closely to the general phonemic picture of Yiddish as it began emerging by the beginning of the thirteenth century. True, the [u ~ y] relationship is but

[59] Idelsohn (note 60); S. D. Goitein in *Lešonenu* 3 (1931) 361; and, with most instructive details, I. Damti: [The Pronunciation of the Yemenite ḳibbuṣ], *Ḳuntresim le'inyane halašon ha'ivrit* 2 (1939) 7–15. Scattered facts from informants outside of Yemen are furnished by Yalon on Bagdad (*ibid.*, 102) and Shiraz (in the province of Fars in Iran, *ibid.*, 1, 76) and by Idelsohn (*op. cit.*, 704) on the Samaritans.—Most promising field work can still be undertaken in Israel, but time is of the essence.

one example and it may be of suggestive value only, but the general outlook strongly points in that direction.

In anticipation of detailed studies it can be said that an affirmative answer to our question will also fit into the pattern of other Jewish speech communities. In a pre-World War I study Idelsohn concluded that wherever a relatively stable pronunciation system of Whole Hebrew exists side by side with a Jewish language, that system can best be understood as a resultant of earlier Whole-Hebrew pronunciation practices and the phonemic system of the language in question.[60]

33.1. This being the case, we may now conceive of the phonemics of Yiddish in any given period and the pronunciation of Whole Hebrew among Yiddish-speaking Jews as of two contiguous systems: they are not identical, but neither are they independent of each other. Though a far-from-negligible number of items in the Hebrew component of Yiddish may go back to the pronunciation system of Whole Hebrew which prevailed in the period of Earliest Yiddish, i.e. before the middle of the thirteenth century, it was the new pronunciation of Whole Hebrew brought to Ashkenaz by the Babylonian renaissance that gave its shape to the bulk of Merged Hebrew in later Yiddish. Conversely, the new pronunciation of Whole Hebrew must have been at least in part conditioned by the phonemic realities of the Yiddish of that period.[61] A detailed analysis would have to demonstrate, and it is hoped it will be able to do so, the reciprocal influence and ultimate outcome of system pressure and a superimposed set of pronunciation rules under the peculiar conditions of Jewish bilingualism.

[60] A. Z. Idelsohn: "Die gegenwärtige Aussprache des Hebräischen bei Juden und Samaritanern," *Monatsschrift für Geschichte und Wissenschaft des Judentums* 57 (1913) 527–545, 697–721. Forty years later, Idelsohn's paper is easily assailable for the lack of subtlety or of proper emphasis, but his factual statements based on first-hand research still stand. It certainly was not his fault that no team of specialists has cared to examine the records which he made for the Phonogramm-Archiv Wien and the Phonogramm-Archiv Berlin. If the discs have survived the wars, it is still not too late.—With regard to the same problem, cf. also: M. Schreiner in *Zeitschrift für die alttestamentliche Wissenschaft* 6 (1886) 259; M. Veynger: [Hebrew Sounds in the Yiddish Language], *Der pinkes* 410 + 68 pp. (Vilna, 1913), pp. 79–84; B. Klar in *Lešonenu* 17, p. 74 (note 41); S. Birnbaum: *Das hebräisch-aramäische Element in der jiddischen Sprache*, 55 pp. (Berlin, 1922).

[61] Ḳirḳisani, a Karaite authority of the first half of the tenth (!) century, stated in so many words: "We find that the reading [of Hebrew] everywhere is close to the language in which the people were brought up, for instance the people of Hejaz and Yemen . . . and something similar to it you find among the people of Bahrein. . . . They are like the people of Hejaz who were born among the Arabs and have adjusted to their language. . . . And the same [refers to] the people of Isfahan; you find that their reading is not like Hebrew at all, and that again because they have become accustomed to the language of [the Iranian province of] Fars, which is the crudest and most corrupt among the languages of the Persians. . . ." Quoted in Hebrew by B. Klar (note 46) after the Arabic edition by L. Nemoy: *Kitab al-anwar wal-maraqib*, 2 vol. (New York, 1939–49).—Even in Tiberias itself, the very seat of the norm setters, the pronunciation of Whole Hebrew is attested to have been, around the year 1000, under the strong influence of Arabic ("Judeo-Arabic" or, in our terminology, Yahudic, would probably be a more realistic description). Cf. J. Mann: *Texts and Studies in Jewish History and Literature* 1, 728 pp. (Cincinnati, 1931), p. 670 and the sources quoted there, and A. Z. Idelsohn in *Hašafah* 1 (1912) 88–92.

34. On a different level of generalization, it must be stated to be in the nature of a fusion language that fusedness is but the result of a steady advance toward unity, in other words the gradual outcome of a process, more often than not a protracted one.

For instance, any student is struck by the remarkable uniformity in the diachronic development of the Yiddish vocalic system: *korev* 'relative', *tsholnt* '(certain kind of) Sabbath dish', *hor* 'hair', *sod* 'orchard', cf. /a/ in some phase of the stock languages; *moyre* 'fear', *antshpoyzn* '(archaic) to betroth', cf. Latin *sponsare*, *boydem* 'attic', *koyletsh* '(certain kind of) white bread', cf. /o/ in the stock languages, etc.;[62] and if we include the regional isoglosses within Modern Yiddish, the regularity of the vocalic alternations is revealed even more clearly. But the discussion of the individual case of [u] $\sim$ [y, i] has demonstrated that ultimate symmetry may prove deceptive: what we now observe in the language and are able to project into some time in the past is likely to be the result of progressively inclusive integrations; it need not always have been as it is at present.

Thus even the student of Yiddish who is historically inclined will start, as a rule, from the contemporary scene, which is easiest of access. While cautiously moving backward, he will constantly be on the lookout for the junctions where a now seemingly uniform phenomenon may be identified as giving off in different directions. In his ultimate presentation, the linguistic historian may be well advised to choose, for didactic reasons, the chronological order; but for his studies and reasoning there seems to be but one way: from the better known to the less known, from more amply attested phenomena to those less amply attested. Then he may be presumed to be on safest ground when he finally reaches the stage of Earliest Yiddish, where all, or virtually all, written record is lacking.[63]

35. If groups of Jews had not settled in Loter one thousand years ago, Yiddish would not have come into being and Jewish cultural history would have taken quite a different turn; although the impact of culture upon language has been studied more often, it is equally true that language is a potent factor in shaping the culture of a group. Whatever the motivation of the settlers—adverse conditions in their former places or the spirit of adventure or what not—they definitely did not set out to create a new language. The rise of that language was a by-product, and its shape would have been quite different if the settlers had happened to come into a different environment. Thus viewed, Yiddish owes its existence to historical conditions imposed from outside. But had the newcomers not brought with them their Jewish civilization or, to put it in more general terms, their peculiar background, they would have taken over the language and culture of the new country and, after a few generations,

[62] Only one example for each vowel in a stressed syllable is given from the Hebrew, Loez, German, and Slavic component, in that order.

[63] It is not difficult to assess the mutual benefit to be derived from allying research into the history of Yiddish with the growing field of diachronic phonemics as exemplified, for instance, in the cumulatively fruitful studies of André Martinet; cf. A. G. Juilland: "A Bibliography of Diachronic Phonemics," *Word* 9 (1953) 198–208.

would have lost their identity as so many other settlers did; and had the newcomers not been carriers of specific prelanguage traits (see §18), the composition and structure of Yiddish would not be what they are.

36. The principle just outlined is not limited to Yiddish though the various Jewish languages vary quite widely as to the degree of their autonomousness. Greater autonomousness may be due to a greater number of speakers, to greater detachment from the non-Jewish majority, to the presence of more than one language group in the non-Jewish population, to transplantation of the Jewish speech community, or a considerable portion of it, to a new territory, to higher attainments in the field of Jewish learning, to refinement through the rise of a sizable literature, and so on. Fundamentally, however, no Jewish language would have come into being if not for a new non-Jewish environment in which a Jewish community found itself. But neither was any of those languages identical with its non-Jewish correlate even in its non-Hebrew stock, where the resemblance was closest. What was shown in §§5–7.1 and 10 with regard to Yiddish must be true of any Jewish language. The Jews never took over the whole stock of the coterritorial non-Jewish language (or languages) indiscriminately; they did take over only certain segments which have to be defined socially or territorially, or both. This was the initial stage. Then, as time advanced and the autonomous Jewish language developed, the component drawn from coterritorial non-Jewish speech was bound further to diverge from the latter in at least two directions. The Jewish language kept some older elements (that's why, for instance, some features of Yiddish, if compared with Modern German, strike the student as "archaic"), but simultaneously it introduced, with much greater ease than its non-Jewish correlate, innovations by analogic change, both in forms and in meaning. Meanwhile, mutual impact of the components on each other, new interference phenomena stemming from new group contacts and advancing uniform development of the whole made the differences between the Jewish languages and their non-Jewish correlates more and more marked.

Hebrew, the oldest among the Jewish languages and simultaneously the youngest again as a vernacular, is essentially no exception, as its history shows. But, as a matter of fact, is there any language in the world that can boast of originating and developing under a motive power completely its own, beyond conditions created by migrations, foreign conquests, social pressure and the like?

Thus the pattern of fusion, which dominated our discussion, can be reinterpreted as the pattern of MID-COURSE FORMATION. Of commanding importance in the analysis of Yiddish, of other Jewish languages and of Jewish culture as a whole, it turns out to prevail on a much wider scale. It is basic to the understanding of language and of culture in general.

DATING THE ORIGIN OF YIDDISH DIALECTS

JUDAH A. JOFFE (New York)

INTRODUCTION

This paper was read in Yiddish on Wednesday, January 22, 1947, at the Twenty-first Annual Conference of the Yiddish Scientific Institute—Yivo in New York under the title "The Origin of Yiddish Dialects." The slight changes stylistically and in the arrangement of material were necessitated by the translation into English and a somewhat different audience (=readers) the author had now in mind. Otherwise the two versions are essentially identical in substance and material.

In matters of transliteration, I have acceded to the desires of the editor for the sake of having as uniform a volume as possible. Transliterations are preceded by the symbol ꜧ. MHG stands for Middle High German. The I. P. A. symbol [ɨ] stands for the sound of Polish *y*, Ukrainian *y*: heavier, more velar than *i* in English (*milk*), but not fully identical with the Russian [ɯ] (*jery*): Yid. [gɨjn, alɨjn] (MHG *gên*, *alein*).

Yiddish Dialects

For the benefit of readers who are not familiar with the dialectal groupings of Yiddish as well as for purposes of easier and clearer marshaling of my material I shall begin with a skeletal outline of the subject.

As a linguistic entity with a physiognomy of its own, Yiddish is over 600 years old:[1] the prior vestiges are so scanty and fragmentary that the stray connected sentences hardly warrant anything beyond blurred outlines of a language.

In 1923 W. Staerk and A. Leitzmann published in Frankfurt a/M. *Die jüdisch-deutschen Bibelübersetzungen* in Latin-letter transcription. The two scholars discuss at great length their quotations from oldest Yiddish manuscripts, but these are the work of copyists (some 100–150 years later) from originals of which the earliest, on proffered linguistic grounds, presumably goes back to the thirteenth century. However, for our immediate task they are of almost no value. Since the change of MHG *â*, *a* into the various guises characteristic of the latter-day final Yiddish dialects had not set in as yet and—most important—there are no *traces* (as far as I have managed to discover) of the vowel-patterns evolved in the early eighteenth century (or at the brink of it, at the earliest), all of them as well as printed records bearing no authenticated author's or printer's name, I shall, accordingly, leave out of consideration.

The generally accepted main dialectal subdivisions in pre-War Yiddish were:

(a) Western (-European) Yiddish, so designated by A. Landau in 1901 (and even earlier)—in Germany, Holland, Alsace, Switzerland, Czechoslovakia, Hungary.

[1] I prefer to err on the side of understatement.

(b) (North-) Eastern or Lithuanian, in former (Tsarist) Russia: Lithuania, White Russia and Baltic Regions.

(c) Polish-Ukrainian, a long zone running midway between (a) and (b) from the Vistula (in the North) to the Black Sea and the Danube (in the South) with the outcropping branches of Bessarabian-Rumanian and Galician—eastward.

This schematic presentation will have to serve as a basis for further discussion.

Study of the History of Yiddish Dialects. The date when Yiddish dialects assumed their final form has naturally been sought during the last several decades, but the results have been rather meager save in a few exceptional cases. The field has not been entirely barren and in the course of my inquiry I shall have to deal with a half a dozen delvers into the past of Yiddish and discuss contributions to the problem in hand, striving to the utmost to be objective in voicing praise or criticism, as deserved in my judgment.

The names most concerned in this field of research are Alfred Landau (1850–1935), Moritz Güdemann (1835–1918), Joseph Perles (1835–1894), Max Grünbaum (1817–1898), Solomon A. Birnbaum, Franz Beranek, Noyakh Prilutski (1882–1944), Mordkhe Veynger (1890–1929), Nokhem Shtif (1879–1933), Max Weinreich and some others enumerated in the footnotes. In his article, "Die Sprache der Memoiren Glückels von Hameln" (*Mitteilungen der Gesellschaft für jüdische Volkskunde*, Heft 7, 1901, pp. 20–68), Landau stated that the criteria of Western Yiddish were: "jd. (=jüdisch-deutsch)[2] *ei* aus mhd. *î*, jd. *ā* aus *ei*, *ā* aus dem alten *ou*—*āg*, *āch* u.s.w." (*ouge*, *ouch*).

And in the Preface (p. xli) to his book, *Jüdische Privatbriefe aus dem Jahre 1619*, edited with Bernhard Wachstein (Vienna and Leipzig, 1911), Landau gave this explicit formula: "Aus dem Vokalismus ist zu erwähnen dass sich die jd. *â* für mhd. *ei* und *ou*, wie *aner*, *agenen*, *ham*, *haligen*, *geklad*, *wast*, *hapt*, *ach*, *lafen*, *tag* (*taugt*) häufiger nur in [the letters, J.A.J.] Nr. 1, 2, 6, 8, 10, 19, 39 und 40 finden. *Im heutigen Jd. kennzeichnet dieses â die westlichen gegenüber den polnischen und russischen Mundarten* (Italics are mine, J.A.J.). Über seine vermutlich fränkische Herkunft, s. M(itteilungen etc.) 34f."

Though my primary concern in this inquiry is the *date* when Yiddish dialects took final shape, I deem it necessary to speak briefly of the *classification* of Yiddish dialects—a subsidiary or side-issue. On several occasions Max Weinreich stated that the real classification (which he follows) was formulated by Noyakh Prilutski.

For reasons best known to himself, in the year 1920, Prilutski quoted anent Yiddish dialects Landau's remarks of 1896[3] and passed by in silence the two above-quoted passages of Landau's of 1901 and 1911.

Prilutski's classification is as follows:[4] (1) *Western Yiddish* (Germany, Bo-

[2] Such was Landau's linguistic term 52 years ago.

[3] "Das Deminutivum der galizisch-jüdischen Mundart," in Nagl's *Deutsche Mundarten* 1 (1896) 46–58; republished in Yiddish in *Yivo-bleter* 11 (1937) 155–172.

[4] Noyakh Prilutski: *Tsum yidishn vokalizm* (vol. 10 of his Works), Warsaw, 1920, §108, pp. 78f.

hemia, Moravia, Hungary and Austria); (2) *Middle Yiddish* (most of Congress Poland and most of Galicia); (3) *Eastern Yiddish* (Lithuania, Russia [White? Great?], Ukraine), all on the basis of (Landau's!) single "ideal" characteristic feature, the treatment of MHG *ei*.

This lumps together the traditional (Northern-) Lithuanian *o*-dialect with the Ukrainian (also with the Rumanian and Galician sub-dialects) and detaches these latter from the Polish *u*-dialect with which every Yiddish speaker normally associates them as "the *u*-dialect," having in mind that an open *o* and an *u* in the North-Eastern = Lithuanian dialect have as their invariable counterparts (1) *u* and (2) [i, i] respectively in the Polish and the other non-Lithuanian sub-dialects. On the contrary, it would occur to no Yiddish speaker to determine a stranger's dialect by finding out how he treats the MHG *ei* sounds, a rather inobtrusive feature which demands knowledge as well as an observing ear to apply in this procedure, because the two Polish-Yiddish subdivisions treat the MHG *î* with a trifling difference in length.

For myself, I prefer the dialectal division into the *o* (= North-Eastern, Lithuanian) and *u* (= Polish-Ukrainian) dialects, the classification accepted also by Solomon Birnbaum.[5]

From Landau we all, younger researchers, obtained our orientation before entering the field of Yiddish dialectal history and Prilutski deserves as little credit for it as do Birnbaum, Mieses, Weinreich, or the writer of these lines. To proclaim anything to the contrary misrepresents the history of Yiddish linguistics and does severe injustice to the memory of the author of this classification, the late Alfred Landau.[6]

Those Yiddish private letters of 1619 were published by Landau in a meticulous reprint verbatim, in square Hebrew characters (pp. 1–60, right side of the book), subjoining a transcript in Latin characters (regular pp. 1–99), and there he added: "The Latin-letter transcription is intended to offer an easily readable and understandable text to readers unfamiliar with the Hebrew script; it therefore deviates from the original only insofar as this purpose requires it" (p. xlvii), and further: "It is apparent from the preceding that a transcription of Judeo-German texts cannot pretend to render the sounds of the original with absolute certainty in every case" (p. xxxviii).

After so explicit and scientifically armor-clad caution it is surprising to see caviling at Landau as in the following lines:

"Besides a very important introduction, a transcription in Latin characters has also been added to the Yiddish texts of the Letters. I have a weighty charge against this transcription. In it, an *a* invariably appears where MHG has *a*: *hat, lasen* (*lozn*), *gezagt* etc. Personally *I am positive that already the Old Yiddish language had o there where the present-day Lithuanian Yiddish has o; but if Dr. Landau thinks otherwise* (*and his opinion is surely the Lord knows how important*),

[5] *Praktische Grammatik der jiddischen Sprache*, Vienna–Leipzig, 1915, §4, p. 16.

[6] Parenthetically I may add that on November 13, 1923, I gave the first lecture to a class in diction and Yiddish dialectal phonetics for young women and men trained in the Dramatic Studio of the Yiddish Theater Society and there *I at least* used Landau's teaching.

it was necessary to prove it, not ignore the whole problem. Moreover, we find *all* transcribers in Germany guilty of the same error: Avé-Lallemant, Grünbaum, etc. *But when an error is repeated many times, it does not thereby cease to be an error*" [All italics are mine, J.A.J.].[7] And again: "In all our older literature we may read the Mod. H. G. *ā* everywhere as *o*, just as in present-day Lithuanian Yiddish. The transcription by German scholars (Grünbaum, Perles, Güdemann, etc.) who always write an *a* in Yiddish texts where Mod.H.G. has *a*, turns out to be not a matter of difference of opinion, but a definite *mistake*" (*ibid.*, p. 137).

"Wherever there is in Wagenseil *♮dz, vvz*, I write *♮d*^{o}*s, vv*^{o}*s*" (*ibid.*, p. 155), this in a Western Yiddish poem, *Dos Vints Hans-lid* of 1616 (describing the anti-Jewish pogrom of August 22, 1614, at Frankfurt a/M.) reprinted by Weinreich in his above-mentioned *Shtaplen*.

Instead of making an effort to visit Amsterdam or Oxford (Weinreich was in Berlin at the time, 1922) to use the editio princeps, Weinreich "reconstructed" it from later prints (p. 154): "If we wish to extract the redaction of the *oldest* [Weinreich's italics] edition, we can set down the following rule: 'if we find in Wagenseil[8] *♮hnt* ['hand'] but *♮h*^{a}*nt* in Schudt,[9] we must presume that in the text the two had before their eyes there was the form which is further away from German, i.e. *♮hnt*'." Try as I might, I cannot grasp how the graphic guise *♮hnt* (i.e. [hant]!) is *further away from German* or conveys anything in text history!

There Weinreich displays an unawareness of the *cardinal principle of Old Yiddish spelling*, at least since 1500: only the interconsonantal *a* (i.e. representing the short *a* sound) is omitted in stems between the consonants: *♮hnt* 'hand', *gnć* 'whole', *zg* 'say', *zagń* 'say (inf.)', *slagń* 'beat', *ds* 'the', *vvs* 'what', and to transcribe by *o* the left-out vowel (*dos, vos*) in any Western Yiddish monument till the latest days is a far more erroneous procedure than the Latin-letter transcriptions which Weinreich so vehemently condemns in the case of others.

The view as to the date of MHG open *a* turning to *o* has been expressed by Weinreich a number of times in print as well as in public lectures, and I shall quote some of these verbatim, to use as my first step in proving that the dates given by Weinreich are wrong.

(a) "Rabbi Elia (Levita) writes in *Shmoys dvorim* (*Šemot debarim;* Isna, 1542) vav (*ḥolem*, the *o* of that spelling) *well-nigh everywhere* [italics are mine, J.A.J.] where we now have *o* in Lithuanian Yiddish and where Fagius writes alef: *♮ˀvdr—Ader*, *♮blvzbˀlq—Blasbalg*, *♮hvr—Har*, *♮nvdl—Nadel*, etc. From this, I hold, it follows that: *where ♮ˀ is written instead of our present-day Lithuanian o* (*♮ˀ could have denoted both an* [a] *and an* [o]) *we must also read* [o]."[10]

(b) On January 24, 1944, in his lecture "Middle High German and Yiddish,"

[7] Max Weinreich: *Shtaplen*, Berlin, 1923, p. 41, footnote.

[8] Johann Christof Wagenseil: *Belehrung der jüdisch-teutschen Red- und Schreib-Art*, Frankfurt/M., 1699, pp. 119–145 in Yiddish and German.

[9] Johann Jacob Schudt: *Jüdische Merckwürdigkeiten*, part 3, Frankfurt and Leipzig, 1714, pp. 9–35: Das Vintz Hanss Lied, in German and Yiddish in parallel columns.

[10] Weinreich: *Shtaplen*, pp. 84f.

Weinreich stated: "In 1500 Yiddish had already penetrated as far East as the river Dnepr," and again, on January 31, 1944: "About 1500, Eastern Yiddish had already formed."

(c) On October 8, 1945, in his talk, "Standard Speech and Dialect": "[Yiddish] dialects are 250–300 years old".

(d) Where Weinreich pushes the change of *a* to *o* definitely further back to 1500: "The long *a*—whether the originally long or later protracted in open syllable—gave *o* (*as a rule*, [italics are mine, J.A.J.] in Western Yiddish, in present-day Lithuanian Yiddish) and *u* (in the Eastern, non-Lithuanian dialects)".[11]

In the history of sounds the problem is not "as a rule," but a rigid separation of *all cases* that come under the rule from those that do not conform with "the rule." All these "out of the rule" cases (what an elementary grammar would conveniently label "exceptions") turn out to be a class by themselves with as much right to the title "rule" as the others have.

(e) "Mod.H.G. *ā* is expressed by ♮ʔ (alef) or by ♮*v* (vav): in the same column we find ♮*dʔzjgi* and ♮*dvzjgj* 'these'. If it were ♮ʔ throughout, there might be a doubt whether it meant *o* or *a*. But when I frequently see a ḥolem (♮*hvσt* '(you) have', *hvt* 'has', *blvtrń* 'boils', *ʔvń* 'without'), whether in lieu of Mod.H.G. *ā* or Mod.H.G. *o* (♮*dv zvlσt* 'you should', *bvtsp̄t* 'message', *mvrt* 'murder'), only one conclusion can be drawn from it: . . . *the pronunciation of Mod.H.G. ā of the author of Sefer šel R. Anšil*[12] *was o.*"[13]

I refrain from discussing the modern German *ā*, because Yiddish does not "descend" from modern German but from MHG, and it would only unnecessarily muddle up matters. But where MHG had *â* (*âder*, *strâfen*, *hâst*, *hât*, *blâtere* —the last three to this day have *hăst*, *hăt*, *blătter* in German!!) there surely was an *o* in *Yiddish long before* 1500.[13a] But proofs that the MHG open *a* remained *a* (*aa*) for centuries in Western Yiddish I shall adduce aplenty later on.

Earliest Dated Yiddish Document (before 1500). *Ksav min kol koykhoys hahakozo vehavridin* (*Ktab min kol koḥot hahaḳazah vehavridin*) 'Treatise of all the Powers of Bloodletting and Bloodvessels', a manuscript of 1396–97 in the Cologne City Archives which Solomon Birnbaum published in *Teuthonista* 8 (1931/32) 197–207, has MHG *âder* spelled with an *o* (i.e. ♮ʔ*v*) in eight sundry places.

Sheyndl(in) (died 1460+), wife of the famous rabbi Isserlin, wrote a Yiddish

[11] This is quoted from §12 (p. 48) of Weinreich's article, "Yiddish," in *Algemeyne yidishe entsiklopedye*, supplementary volume *Yidn B*, pp. 23–90, a section headed "Old Yiddish, 1250–1500."

[12] Cracow, $_{1}$1534; $_{2}$1584.

[13] *Shtaplen*, p. 119.

[13a] Since the paper was delivered to the editor the linguistic world was enriched by a discovery of transcendent importance for the history of Yiddish: the Yiddish Codex of Cambridge. [See pp. 267–277 of the present volume.—Ed.] The two excerpts published so far by Mr. L. Fuks have several dozen very regrettable misreadings and mistranslations. Still, the brief reprints present enough correct material to warrant one in saying without undue hesitation that MHG *â* had definitely turned into Old Yiddish *o* by 1382. [August 27, 1954.]

letter, preserved in full in *Leket yoysher* (*Leḳeṭ yošer*), II, 19–20, her husband's Collectanea, first published by J. Freimann (Berlin, 1903).

In this letter the writer spells 8 MHG *â*'s (*jâr, getân, hân, mâz, nâch, mâl, lâz, wâr*) with ♮*v*: *jvr, gjtvń, hʔvń, mvs,* (*dr*)*nvḱ, mvl, lvs, vvʔr,* (the ♮ʔ imposed by the ♮*v* preceding it). On the other hand, she spells ♮*hʔσt* (5 times), *hʔń* (3 times), *lʔsń* (MHG *hâst, hân, lâz*)—in all 9 ♮ʔ's. The inconsistency does not invalidate the fact that even a woman writer before 1460 discriminated the Old Yiddish sound *o* originating in MHG *â*. This should render it superfluous to argue against Weinreich's general date 1500 of *â* > *o*, save that it is fully a century short of reality.

The cardinal fault of such views is that they deal in centuries and do not cite records whose authors are definitely known or whose dates are securely established.

My Procedure in the Inquiry. With the above caution, I shall confine myself to a more or less limited number of Old Yiddish and later Yiddish prints and manuscripts eschewing the more numerous others which do not contain at all, or merely duplicate unnecessarily, the linguistic facts offered by the group I have selected for my purpose.

Elia Levita and His *Bovobukh*

Elia Levita's (1469–1549) *Bovobukh* is the most famous and widely read Yiddish book on a wordly subject, with known printings in 1909–1910. A poetic recreation of the Toscana edition (most likely of 1497) in *ottava rima* in 1400 stanzas, the *Bovobukh* (composed in 1507–1508) was first (?) published at Isna in 1541, some 7–8 years before the author's death, seemingly under his eyes, by his two grandsons. It contains 650 ottava rima stanzas plus a Prologue and Epilogue, in all 5262 rimed verses. In 1949 I reproduced the first edition, a unicum in the Central Library of Zürich, by offset process, in *Elia Bachur's Poetical Works*, vol. 1. Years of unremitting study and two winters of assiduous labor with Professor N. B. Minkoff have resulted partly in a rime lexicon and the conviction that this old Yiddish romance of chivalry is a precious key to the history of Yiddish (in the Western Yiddish dialect) at the beginning of the sixteenth century.

Barring some two or three dozen obvious printer's slips in a rigidly scientific system of spelling, we find the Yiddish *o* sounds < MHG *â, o,* invariably graphically represented by ♮*v* (the letter vav), while the Yiddish *a* sounds (from MHG *a, ou, ei*) are just as consistently (1) represented by ♮ʔ (the letter alef) or (2) *left out altogether*.

A word of warning about representing initial *i, o, u* sounds in Yiddish. (1) To this day a *silent* alef (♮ʔ) must precede, in writing, the initial ♮*j* or ♮*v* letter: ♮*ʔjbər* [iber], *ʔjḱ* [ix], *ʔjz* [iz], *ʔvndz* [undz], *ʔvntər* [unter]; since the letter ♮*v* represented also [o] in Old Yiddish, this rule held here, too: ♮*ʔvdr* was both MHG *âder* and *oder*, which is no longer necessary now, as the ḳameṣ mark ᴛ beneath the letter alef denotes the *o* sound initially. (2) The MHG letters *v* (fau) and *w* were represented by ♮*v, vv*. Hence such MHG words as *von, vor* (*fun, for*) could not be spelled with ♮*v* for the initial *f* sound as that would have made the words

♮*vvń, vvr* in Old Yiddish: i.e. *wn, wr*, and accordingly, the initial *f* sound had 3 different representatives: ♮*f, v, b̄* to choose from to suit the occasion. On the other hand, MHG words like *wart, wort, wâr, war*, had all to be spelled with an ♮ˀ, as otherwise there would be three consecutive vavs. (3) Another minor supplementary rule must be added, which rooted in *religious scruples. Yahveh* (spelled ♮*jhvh*) is the "ineffable" name for the devout Jews not in speaking only but in writing as well. Accordingly even portions of that "tetragram" are also taboo in pagination of Hebrew books. Hence (a) ♮*jh* (10 + 5 = 15) is replaced by ♮*tv* (9 + 6 = 15); (b) ♮*jv* (10 + 6 = 16) by ♮*tz* (9 + 7 = 16), and MHG *jâr* will often appear as ♮*jˀr* instead of the ♮*jvr* one should expect. In *Bovobukh*, str. 54, 2–4–6: ♮*vr lvrń : jˀrń : qvrń* (*o, â, o*); 98, 7–8: *gjbvrń : jˀrń* (*o, â*); 399, 7–8: *vr lvrń : jˀrń* (*o, â*); (c) ♮*hv* (second and third letter of the "tetragram") appears as ♮*hˀ* in MHG *hâr*: 10, 7–8: *jˀrń : hˀrń* (MHG *jâren, horn*); 93, 1–3–5: ♮*gjvvˀrń : hˀrń : vˀrń* (*o, â, o*); 288, 1–3–5: *hˀr : tvr : vvˀr* (*â, o, â*). Occasionally, of course, there may be slips: 72, 2–4–6: *tvrń : hvrń: gjvvˀrń* (*o, â, o*), but that does not vitiate the general principle.

The test vowels of Western Yiddish: (**1**) MHG *â* > Yid. *o*, written as ♮*v*: 22, 1–3–5: *vrvgń : gjlvgń : vvˀgń* (*â, o, â*); 35, 1–3–5: *gvvjdvń : dvdvń : hvń* (*o, o, â*); 50, 1–3–5; *nvḱ : gvḱ : hvḱ* (*â, â, ô*); 164, 1–3–5: *vvˀgń : vrvgń : gjlvgń* (*â, â, o*) as vs. *trˀgń : slˀgń : zˀgń* (*a, a, a*)—verses 2–4–6 in the same strophe 164!—not as a sextet oe consecutive rimes; 274, 1–3–5: ♮*tjmvń* (Ital. *timone*): *tvń : (dr) b̄vń* (*o, â, o*); 314, 1–3–5; 325, 1–3–5: *dˀ : ˀzv : vrˀ* (*dâ, asô, vrô*). These shall be the last quotations to prove MHG *â* > Yid. *o*, which we have already seen in a document of 1396–97. (**2**) MHG *ô, o* > Yid. *o*, written as ♮*v*, with usual warning: 107, 2–4–6: ♮*ˀvjs dr qvrń : vˀrń : ˀvrń* (*o, vorne, oren*). (**3**) MHG *a* > Yid. *a*: (**a**) written ♮ˀ: 38, 1–3–5: *vvˀrń : bˀrń : vˀrń* (*a, a, a*); 40, 7–8: *gjtrˀgń : zˀgń*; 42, 2–4–6: *zˀmń : ˀmń : qlˀmń* (*a, ammen, a*); 74, 1–3–5: *bˀz : grˀz : vvˀz*; 77, 1–3–5: *bjgrˀbń : lˀbń : qnˀbń*; 104, 2–4–6: *tˀgˀt : rˀgt : zˀgt*; 158, 2–4–6: *hˀnń : drvzjjˀnh : bjgˀnń*; (**b**) left out: 290, 1–3–5: ♮*gjvvˀr : dˀr: gr*; 298, 1–3–5: *ˀń : qˀń : mń*; 41, 1–3–5: *zˀk̄ń : bjzˀk̄ń : mk̄ń*; 75, 1–3–5: *lˀg : tˀg : zg*; 101, 2–4–6: *qnˀbń : hbń : lˀbń*; 138, 1–3–5 : *dˀr : vvˀr : gr* (*gar*); 140, 2–4–6: *zgń : gjslgń : jˀgń*; *stt* 236, 1; 240, 5; 298, 2; 301, 7; 312, 4–6. (**4**) MHG *ou* > Yid. *ā*, spelled: ♮ˀ, *ˀv, ˀvj*; often left out, riming with *a*: (**a**) 22, 7–8: *glbń* (*gelouben*): *hbń*; 8,–2–4–6: *glbń : qnˀbń : hbń*; 70, 1–3–5: *qnˀbń : glˀbń* (*ou*): *sˀbń*; 260, 2–4–6: *dr lˀb* (*ou*): *hinˀb : qnˀb*; (**b**) 7, 2–4–6: *gjzˀgń : trgń : ˀvjgń* (*ou*); 187, 2–4–6: *slˀgń: gˀgń* (*gouge, gaucke*): *trˀgń*; 266, 7–8: *gjslˀgń : gˀgń*; 323, 7–8: *ˀvjgń : trˀgń*; 96, 7–8: *ˀvjgń : slˀgń*; 98, 2–4–6: *gjslˀgń : ˀvjgń : zˀgń*; 108, 1–3–5 *z:gń : trgń : ˀvjgń*; 227, 1–3–5: *lˀg : tg : ˀvjg*; (**c**) 59, 2: *dj trˀḿ* (*ou*); 226, 1–3–5: *qˀḿ : nˀḿ : cˀḿ* (*zoum*); (**d**) 159, 7–8: *rˀp̄ń: qvjp̄ń : lvjp̄ń* (*a*[*ff*], *ou, ou*); (**e**) 102, 1–3–5: *gjsˀḱ : ˀvjḱ* (*ouch*): *ˀń zˀḱ*; 147, 1–3–5: *zˀḱ : ˀvjḱ : sprḱ*; 201, 1–3–5: *sprḱ : ˀvjḱ : zˀḱ*. (**5**) MHG *ei* > Yid. *a* (irregularly): (**a**) article *an* (<*ein*): 208, 6: *ˀń gvt qrń*; 217, 7: *ˀń qrˀnqhjjt*; 241, 4: *ˀń srjjˀ ˀvdr drjjˀń*; 248, 8: *ˀń vvjjl*; 320, 1: *ˀń gvtj vvjjl*; 468, 4: *ˀń ˀndr vvˀzń*; (**b**) 231, 3: *gjmˀjjnt*; 238, 8: *lˀjjdr*; 246, 7: *zjjń hˀljgń nˀmń*; 295, 5: *hˀjjḿ*; 321, 2: *blˀjjk̄ń*.

Finally Levita carefully distinguished and kept apart the MHG *â* and *a* in his *Bovobukh*, save in obvious misprints or slips. This is proven most strikingly by the alternations ♮ʔ/*v* (MHG *a*/*â*) in the preterite singular and plural of the same verb: 471, 2–4–6: ♮*strvsń* 'way': *gjlvsń* 'left': *zʔsń* 'sat' (*â*, *â*, *â*, obvious slip, cf. next passage); 520, 2–4–6 : *strvsń*: *rvσń* 'horses': *zvsń* 'sat' (*â*, *o*, *â*); similarly in other pairs: MHG *sah*, *sāhen*: 405, 1–3–5: *sprḱ* 'spoke': *ʔvjḱ* 'also': *zʔḱ* 'saw' (*a* [left out], *a*, *a*); 102, 1–3–5: *gjsʔḱ* 'happened': *ʔvjḱ*: *ʔń zʔḱ* 'looked at' (*a*, *a*, *a*) as against plural *sâhen*: 603, 7–8: ♮*dr zvhń* 'saw': (*hjntr*) *cvhn* 'withdrew' (*â*, *ô*); 599, 7–8: *stʔk̄ń* 'stuck': *brʔk̄ń* 'broke' (*â*, *â*—before *x*).[14]

The above rimes establish the fact that in 1541 the *a* was still *a* in Western Yiddish—which it remained through the nineteenth century, save a bit prolonged, while *o* < *â* became *ui*/*oi* and is such still in present Western Yiddish.

Another rimed poem, of 75 quatrains, *Hamavdl* (*Hamabdil*) written by Levita in 1514, exists only in two manuscripts: one of 1553, one undated. A summary of data on MHG *â* and *a* should be sufficient now. MHG *â* > Yid. *o*—50 cases; MHG *a* > *a* or left out—60 cases; MHG *o* > Yid. *o* (written as *u*)—70 cases; i.e. not *one* interconsonantal MHG *a* is transcribed as ♮*v* (=*o*, as in the other cases from *â*), and thus, reinforces our thesis.

With Elia Levita's pronunciation of both *a* and *ou* as [ā] so thoroughly documented by some hundreds of quotations, there is no possible justification for transcribing passages of his other *ottava rima* novel, *Pariz un Viene* (Verona, 1594) with the ḳameṣ alef (♮ʔᵒ), i.e. *o* pronunciation, as in the following: *hʔᵒbń* : *glʔᵒ bń* : *gᵉgrʔᵒbń* (*a*, *ou*, *a*), p. 178; *zʔᵃḱ* : *sprʔᵒḱ* : *ʔᵃḱ* (*a*, *a*, *ou*), p. 180; *qnʔᵒbń* : *hʔᵒbń* : *glʔᵒbń* (*a*, *a*, *ou*), p. 182; *qnʔᵒb* : *gʔᵒb* : *hʔᵒb* (*a*, *a*, *a*), p. 183; *glʔᵒbń* : *rʔᵒbń* : *hʔᵒbń* (*ou*, *ou*, *a*), p. 185; *mʔ*[ᵒ]*ń* : *qʔᵒń* : *cʔᵒń* (*a*, *a*, *a*), p. 185.[15]

Shmoys Dvorim (*Šemot debarim*). I deem it necessary to mention a booklet by that name (1542) from Levita's pen, which was highly praised as a document of Levita's own speech. I venture to say, after careful study, that it adds nothing to what we have culled from Levita's *Bovobukh* and *Hamavdl*, save confusion and misleading forms.

It is a piece of hackwork done on order from Fagius for the students in his classes in *Hebrew* (not Yiddish!) elementary composition and grammar—really a German-Hebrew wordbook. Levita was responsible for the columns (1) Yiddish and (2) Hebrew, at the right of the page; (3) Latin and (4) German (in Latin script) were apparently added in (local?) German by Fagius or some one else. The result is a motley of conflicting forms (for the same Hebrew word) in columns (1) and (4), made all the worse by numerous misprints like ♮ʔ*vdrrljσ* (MHG *âderlæze* 'bloodletting'), *ʔvnσjnjqhjjt* (instead of *-zjn-*) 'nonsense', *tjjdsr—ʔsknvz*, *p̄rncvθ* (in Levita's own column!).

Levita manifestly never saw the book until it was off the press. Hence there are such forms as ♮*zvń*, *zvjń* 'sun' and *ʔjń* (=*ein*!) *zvń*, *zvjń* 'son'; *tvjḱ* 'cloth', *lvjng* 'lung'; *cvjng* 'tongue', *svjl* 'school, synagogue', *hvjnger* 'hunger', *brvjdr* 'brother', *dvjrst* 'thirst', *hjjlvjng* 'cure', *mvjtr* 'mother', all with MHG *uo*, *o*, i.e.

[14] I leave out more quotations to the same effect, to save space. In the 1382 manuscript *Yoysef hatsadik* (see footnote 13a) we find *sprvk̄ń* (3. pl. pret.) in 15·1; 16·1; 34·2.

[15] The page references are to Max Weinreich: *Bilder fun der yidisher literatur-geshikhte*, Vilna, 1928.

u (♮*v*) in Levita's other works, and such puzzles as ♮ˀ*jń m*ˀ*jzl* (*mousekin*) 'little mouse', ˀ*ngjjl* (*engel*) 'angel'. Suffice this for the purpose.

Hugerlin

Closely parallel in time and language-forms is another poem (in a manuscript dated Nov. 18, 1516) which consists of 15 Hebrew 13-line strophes alternated with as many strophes in rimed Yiddish translations by the poet himself (?). The poem, an outpouring of the heartbreaking sorrows of a disillusioned inveterate dice-gambler, was completely published by Isaac Rivkind[16] from a photostat copy of the original manuscript.

In all the 15 strophes, there are only the following exceptions: ♮*z*ˀ < MHG *so*, 4, 1; 6, 12; 12, 3; 16, 3 (4 cases), ♮*d*ˀ*ḱ* < MHG *doch*, 6, 12; 16, 11; 24, 13 (3 cases), ♮ˀ*ń* < MHG *âne* 8, 3 (twice), ♮*n*ˀ*ḱ* < MHG *noch*, 12, 5; 14, 13 (twice)—that is, all told, 11 cases without the dot over the alef. But it is possible that, in the original, the dot may have: (1) been inadvertently omitted, (2) faded completely in the course of time, or (3) been too faint to show well in the photostat: after long hours of repeated reading and examination of photostats with a powerful magnifying glass, I discovered over two dozen words where at first I had descried no diacritical marks.

Otherwise, the 192 lines (strophe 12 has 3 verses missing) unerringly denote *o* (1) by ♮*v* (without or with a dot above), or (2) by alef with a dot above, or ḳameṣ below. The *a* is (a) either represented by unmarked alef or (b) left out. As to the sounds *ou* and *ei*, there is no way of judging the poet's pronunciation from the spelling, as they do not occur in end-rimes.

Bar Yokor's Prayerbook

Of Bar Yokor's Prayerbook (Ichenhausen, 1544), only one copy is known. Bar Yokor distinctly states in his Preface (f. 2b) that he "did not translate it from his own head, but merely 'edited' one of several current Yiddish translations" (I have a Ms. of 1520-25, according to the water marks, which is one of these mentioned). Yet several historians of Old Yiddish strove to prove that Bar Yokor had made that statement out of sheer "scholarly modesty."

Bar Yokor possessed a remarkable skill in constructing his own or possibly a pre-existing precise and clear system of diacritical marks for all the vowel sounds in his Old Yiddish speech, and it is thanks to his efforts and those of Bresh (Pentateuch, Cremona, 1560) that we can definitely know the entire Western Yiddish vowel-pattern of the early sixteenth century.

Those who dealt with Bar Yokor's Prayerbook (Max Grünbaum, M. Güdemann, Nokhem Shtif, W. Staerk and A. Leitzmann, and others) never mentioned the system of diacritical marks he employed in his text. In 1934 I obtained from the Munich Royal Library 15 photostats (the first 5, the last 2, and 8 sundry pages of text) of the parts reproduced in Max Grünbaum's *Jüdischdeutsche Chrestomathie* (Leipzig, 1882). To my amazement I discovered that the photo-

16 *Der kamf kegn azartshpiln bay yidn* ('The Fight Against Gambling Among Jews'), New York, 1947; the linguistic notes and translation into present-day Yiddish, on pp. 155–177, were done by me.

stats showed a mass of handwritten interlineary Latin interpolations as well as a wealth of diacritical marks. The written-in translations and what not were clearly not those of Bar Yokor, and the next question was: "Whose were the diacritical marks? Were they also written in by the later annotator?" From the photostats it was impossible to determine it. Around 1937–1938 I approached a New York non-Jewish friend about asking his son in Munich to have the rest of the Bar Yokor book photostated, but my friend refused point blank, as that might cut short his son's stay in Germany long before accomplishing his important task there. Meanwhile World War II broke out and there was no hope of getting anything out of Munich—particularly on a Yiddish prayerbook—in the Hitler era. Downhearted, I was resigned to the inevitable "for the duration." As luck would have it, one day in October 1940 (?) the lamented librarian of the Jewish Theological Seminary, Professor Alexander Marx, asked me to come up and help him settle the source of a single folio of an old Yiddish book. My heart beat fast as I glanced at the rather tattered sheet. "If it were smaller, I could swear it is a page of Bar Yokor, *with the diacritical marks*!" I said, for the Munich librarian had never told me he was sending considerably reduced photostats. The next day I enlarged the prints in my possession to the size of Professor Marx's page unicum—and now had incontestable proof that my original surmise was correct: the diacritical marks were all in the 1544 print.

There were counterpart marks for all MHG vowel-sounds in Yiddish, *u*, *o*, *œ* and all else. But we are concerned only with *â*, *a*, *ô*, *o*, *u*, *ü*, *ei* and *ou*.

The Graphics of Bar Yokor's Yiddish Spelling (*1544*).[17] The standard Western Yiddish of the period is fully reflected in the spelling:

(**1**) The test characteristics: (**a**) MHG *ei* > *a*(*i̯*): ♮*tˀjjlσ* (*teiles*), 2b, 8 and 7; *cˀjjk̄ń* (*zeichen*), *ibid.*; *hˀjjljgń* (*heiligen*), *qlvghˀjjt* (*kluocheit*), *bjrˀjjt* (*bereit*). (**b**) MHG *ou*, *û* > *ā*: ♮*qvjp̄t* (*kouft*), Ia, 4; *ˀvjḱ* (*ouch*), Ia, 5; *drlˀvjbt*, *hˀvjbt* (*erloubt*, *houbt*), last rimed page; *c*^{a}*vjń* (*zoun*, *zun*).

(**2**) *a* is spelled or left out entirely: (**a**) ♮*gˀncń*, *stˀrq*, *mˀrq* (Ia); *ˀl*, *dˀrˀń*, *gˀr*, *ˀndrń*, *mˀk̄ń*, *bjsˀp̄ń*, etc. (**b**) *drˀvḿ*, *vvk̄σń* (*wahsen*), *mń*, *ˀtvvz* (*etewaz*), *hlt* (Ia), etc.

(**3**) *â* > *o*; represented by ḥolem vav (♮*v*^{o}): ♮*ˀv*^{o}*ń* (*ân*[*e*]), *sprv*^{o}*k̄ń* (*sprâche*), *gjtv*^{o}*ń* (*getân*), *hv*^{o}*t* (*hât*), *mv*^{o}*l* (*mâl*); MHG *o* > *o* = ♮*v*^{o}: *nv*^{o}*ḱ* (*noch*), *dv*^{o}*ḱ* (*doch*), *b̄v*^{o}*lˀndˀń* (*vol-*), etc. MHG *ô*: ♮*grv*^{o}*s* (*grôz*), *qrv*^{o}*nń* (*krônen*), *hv*^{o}*ḱ* (*hôch*), *tv*^{o}*rń* (*tôr*[*e*]*n*), *sv*^{o}*ń* (*schône*).

(**4**) MHG *uo*, *u* > *u*, unmarked vav: ♮*ˀvń* (*und*), *drvḿ*, *qvmt*, *zvnst*, *cv*, *gjdrvqt*, *hvndrt* (Ia); etc.

CREMONA PENTATEUCH (1560)

And now I turn to what in my sober opinion is the *most important* (*single page*) *printed document for the pronunciation of sixteenth-century Western Yiddish.* This is the rimed Preface (in some copies, as in mine, it is bound at the *end* of the book) to Yehude b. Moyshe Naftoli Bresh's (Cremona, 1560) reedition of the famous Yiddish version of the *Pentateuch* by Paulus Aemilius (Augsburg, 1544).

[17] In order to simplify the typesetter's task, I shall leave out transcriptions of the Yiddish words wherever the reader should be able to supply them himself without difficulty.

Bresh had the wonderful idea of printing this Preface in *square Hebrew letters* as against the rest of the Yiddish book in cursive Old Yiddish. This enabled him to utilize the full inventory of diacritical marks, reinforced with his own very radical ideas about phonetic spelling, centuries ahead of his times: he had no doubt ♮*v*'s or ♮*j*'s but spelled MHG *wîsheit* as ♮$v^{a}jzq^{a}t$ (*l.* 8), the pataḥ (♮^{a}) denoting the *a* pronunciation, as also in ♮$sr^{a}jbr$ 'writer', $v^{a}jbr$ 'women', $l^{a}jbr$ 'bodies' (*l.* 1), $\dot{b}^{a?}d^{i}j\ v^{e?}lt$ 'both worlds' (*l.* 20), $?^{a}\acute{m}\ m^{a}ns{\cdot}t^{e}jn\ t^{a}g$ (*taug*: 'behooves the most,' *l.* 22), $b^{a}j?$ 'by', $pr^{a}j?$ 'free', $z^{a}j?$ 'be' (*bî, vrî, sî, l.* 4).

The 24 lines reproduced facing pp. 118 are in doggerel-verse (*knüttel-verse*) stemming from ancient Arabic prosody, employed by Dunaš ben Labraṭ for his polemical verse and by Solomon Gabirol in liturgical poems. As the reader may see from the reproduction the final syllable *-fen* (separated in the print, at the left; spelled ♮-*pjń*) was identical throughout. Below I give a partial list of words which the reader can easily identify in the indicated line by the dash-line subscript (pataḥ) denoting the *a* sound.

â > *o*; *ô* = ♮v^{o} (ḥolem vav): *l.* 2: ♮$hv^{o}\acute{n}$ (*â*); *l.* 3: $hv^{o}t$ (*â*); *l.* 7: $?v^{o}\acute{n}$ (*â*); *l.* 9: $gv^{o}t$ (*o*), $hv^{o}t$; *l.* 10: dv^{o} (*â*), $gjs{\cdot}lv^{o}pj\acute{n}$ (*â*); *l.* 11: $?v^{o}\acute{n}$ (*â*); *l.* 13: $hv^{o}\acute{n}$ (*â*), $v^{?o}l$ (*o*), $hv^{o}\acute{n}$ (*â*), $tv^{o}\acute{n}\ qlv^{o}\dot{p}p^{e}\acute{n}$ (*â, o*); *l.* 14: $grv^{o}s$ (*ô*), $nv^{o}\acute{k}$ (*o*), $hv^{o}\acute{n}\ g^{i}js{\cdot}lv^{o}p^{e}\acute{n}$ (*â, â*); *l.* 15: $v^{?o}l$ (*o*); *l.* 17: $s{\cdot}tv^{o}ppj\acute{n}$ (*o*); *l.* 19: $b\dot{v}\acute{n}$ [misprint for $\bar{b}v^{o}\acute{n}$] (*o*); $lv^{o}\acute{n}$ (*ô*); etc. L. 23: $d^{e?}r\ nv^{?}\acute{k}$: misprint for $nv^{o}\acute{k}$ < *nâch*?

a > *a*, spelled ♮$?^{a}$ (pataḥ alef) or left out: *l.* 1: ♮$?^{a}l^{e}j$; *l.* 3: $?^{a}l^{e}j$; *l.* 4: $g^{a}r$ (*gar*); $m^{a}g$ (*mag*); *l.* 5: $?^{a}l$; *l.* 6: $?^{a}l$, $d^{a}z$ (*daz*); *l.* 7: $?^{a}\acute{n}$, $?^{a}l$; *l.* 8: $?^{a}l$; *l.* 9: $d^{a}z\ ?^{a}lz$, $?^{a}\acute{m}$ $h^{a?}lz$; *l.* 10: $d^{a}z$ (*daz*), $d^{a}z\ ?^{a}lz$; *l.* 11: $s{\cdot}ar\acute{p}$; *l.* 12: $?^{a}z$, $\sigma^{a}p^{i}jr$ (*saphir*); $d^{a}z\ \dot{p}^{a}\dot{p}^{i}jr$ (*papier*); $t^{a?}pp^{i}jr$ [sic; *tapfer*], $?^{a}\acute{n}$; etc.

ei > *a*, spelled as ♮^{a} or *?*: *l.* 6: ♮$l^{a}jt$ (*leien* 'to read'); *l.* 8: $r^{a}jjkq^{a}t, v^{a}jzq^{a}t$ (*wîsheit*); $\dot{p}^{e?}r\ n\dot{v}pt^{i}jq^{a}t$; *l.* 9: $?^{a}\acute{n}\ t^{a?}lz$ (*ein teils*); *l.* 11: $?^{a}\acute{n}$; *l.* 15: $?^{a}\acute{n}$ (*ein*); *l.* 16: $m^{a?}d$; $l^{a?}d$, $?^{a}jjg^{e}\acute{n}\ ql^{a?}d$ (*eigen kleid*); *l.* 19: $z^{a?}p^{e}\acute{n}$ (*seifen*); *l.* 20: $\dot{b}^{a?}d^{i}j$ (*beide*); *l.* 21: $q^{a?}\acute{n}$ (*kein*); *l.* 22: $m^{a}ns{\cdot}t^{e}j\acute{n}$ (*meinsten*).

ou > *a*, spelled as ♮^{a} (pataḥ): *l.* 2 (also *l.* 16): ♮$p^{e?}r\ q^{a?}p^{e}j\acute{n}$; *l.* 5: $l^{a?}p^{e}j\acute{n}$; *l.* 9: ditto; *l.* 14: $?^{a}\acute{k}$; *l.* 18: $r^{a}p^{e}j\acute{n}$; *l.* 22: $t^{a}g$ (*taug*).

Bridal Song at End of Minhagim Volume (Venice, 1593)

MHG *â, o, ô* are spelled ♮*v* (i.e. they stand for [o]). Str. III, 1–2: ♮*qrvń* : *gjtvń* (MHG *krôn(e), getân*); str. IV, 10–12: *svń* : *qrvń* : *gjtvń* (MHG *schôn(e), krôn(e), getân*); str. XII, 7–8: *mvl* : *vv?l* (MHG *mâl, wol*); 10–11–12: *g?t* : *nvt* : *gjnvd* (MHG *got, nôt, genâde*).

MHG *a* is usually not spelled out. Str. IV, 4: ♮*tg* : *mg* (MHG *tag(e), mag*); 6: *kl?g* : *tg* : *mg* (MHG *klage, tag(e), mag*); 7: *gr* (MHG *gar*); 8: *hb* : *gr* : *tg* : *mg* : *b̄vr c?g* (MHG *hab, gar, tag, mag, verzag*); 11: *hb*; 14: *vvz* (MHG *waz*).

That is, *in 1593 the MHG a = Yiddish* [a].

Fate of Later Western Yiddish: *Tsukhtshpigl*

Having remained by and large in its original home with outbranchings that had practically ceased in the seventeenth century, Western Yiddish had a subsequent history that may be traced in brief.

In 1610, Zelikman Ulma, of the Gentsbakher family, published a book *Tsukht-shpigl* (*Mar'eh hamussar*) of several hundred Hebrew (Aramaic) aphorisms with graceful rimed translations in Western Yiddish. I have never seen the editio princeps, but copies of (1) Prag 1614 (only 4 years later than the first edition), (2) Frankfurt a/M., 1680, and (3) Sulzbach 1733, have the spelling practically identical as regards the critical *a* vowel.

In the over 1000 rimes we find: *♮ʔgjń* (*eigen*): *zʔgjń* (15a, col. 1, 11); *ʔvjgjń* (*ougen*): *trʔgjń* (4a, 2); *cjjgt* (*zeigt*): *tragt* (23a, 2); i.e. MHG *ei*, *ou*, *a* still rime. Likewise *♮ʔzʔmjń* (present-day Yiddish *tsuzamen*): *namjń* (Preface); *caljń* : *ʔljń* (*allen*) (21b, 2); *bjcʔlt* : *ʔlt* : *hlt* (*ʔ* left out) (16b, 1) all prove that the *a* had not turned into *o* in Western Yiddish by 1733.

But the spelling shows co-existence of later forms: *♮tvt* (*ô*): (*svjń*) *nvjt* (*nôt*) (3b, 1, *l.* 7–8); *nvjt* (*nôt*): *hvt* (*â*) (4b, 1); *brvjt* (*brôt*) (15a, 1; 28a, 1); *grvjs* (*grôz*): *mvs* (*â*) (10b, 1); *grvjs* : *mʔs* (*â*) (5b, 1). And in *ü* = *i*, we find: *p̄vjrń* : *prvbjrń* (8a, 1); *zjnd* (*ü*): *gjsvvjnd* (3b, 1).

In the course of the seventeenth and eighteenth centuries the situation remained nearly stationary, as follows:

o < MHG. *â* changes further in character and ends in *ui/oi*, or very nearly so.

a < *a* gained merely in duration, i.e. approached *ā* (*aa*);

Original *ou* > *a* remained long *ā* (*aa*);

Original *ei* > *a* remained long *ā* (*aa*).

This is practically the situation today in the small terrains where Western Yiddish is still heard as a *rara avis* (Alsace, Switzerland, Slovakia, Hungary). I shall cite some linguistic data from the second edition of Yoysef Herts' comedy in verse, *Ester, oder di baloynte tugnt* ($_1$1828 and $_2$1854, Fürth). I shall briefly mention Arn Halle Volfson's better-known comedy *Laykhtzin un fremelay* (Amsterdam, 1798) which, in this edition (there is another, undated printing) is a travesty of Western Yiddish: the subscript ķameṣ diacritical marks under the alef (♮ʔᵒ) represent all the characteristic monosyllables with *o* sounds: *♮vvʔᵒhσ* (11, 49), *dʔᵒσ* (11, 4), *hʔᵒb* (10), *nʔᵒḱ* (<*nâch*), *dʔᵒ* (<*dâ* 12, 16), *ʕmʔᵒl* (*â*), *hʔᵒbń* (*a*) (37); *zʔᵒg jʔᵒ mjr ʕ mʔᵒhl* (*sag jâ mir ein mâl*) (37, last line), *ʔᵒbbʕr* (<*aber*, 27, 12), *lʔʔhp̄t* (*ou*) (12, 3), and *hʔhḿ* (<*ei* 12, 14).

Ester[18] (also a comedy, which is on a lower level than Volfson's play as a literary effort) is an excellent (though not faultless) embodiment of Western Yiddish in the nineteenth century and I cull the following as illustrating the question we are considering:

(1) MHG *â* = *o* > *ui/oi*, spelled *♮vj*: *mâl* > *♮ʔmvjl* 5. 7, *ʔmvjlʕ* 6. 15, *ʔmvjl* 10. 15; MHG *dâ* > *♮dvj* 3. 21; MHG *tân* > *♮tvjń* 3. 23; MHG *hât dâ* > *♮hvjt dvj* 3. 26; MHG *vrâgen* > *♮p̄rvjgʕń* 3. 3; 36. 13.

(2) *a* > *a*, *aa*; spelled *♮ʔ*, *ʔʔ*, *ʔh*: *zʔʔgt* 1. 5, *zʔʔgʕn* 1. 9; *vvʔʔz*, 1. 15, *vvʔz* 3. 22; 4. 20; *dʔʔz* (twice) 15. 16; (twice) 15. 17; *dʔz* 9. 4; *ʔbʕr* 4. 17; *hʔbń* 3. 22; *gʔr* 4.

[18] Robert M. Copeland has written a Ph.D. dissertation on *The Language of Herz's Esther* for the Department of Germanics at Harvard University (1951).

22; *tʾʾtʿ* ('daddy') 5. 10 and 12; *ʾlʾhń* : *mʾhń* (*ei*, *a*) 2. 16–17; *qʾhń mʾhń* (*ei*, *a*) 2. 20: *mʾń* 2. 7, 8; *qrʾhgʿn* : *trʾgʿń* 20. 1–2.

(3) *ou* > *a*, *aa*; spelled ꜧʾ, ʾʾ, ʾ*h*: *ʾʾgń* 6. 12; *ʾhg* 14. 5; *ʾjbʿrlʾʾp̄ʿń* 30. 5; *lʾʾp̄ʿń* 6. 19; *gʿlʾṕ* 6. 21; *lʾp̄ʿń* 3. 11; *glʾʾb* 29. 7; *dʿrlʾʾbt* 9. 7; *p̄ʿrtʾbt* 9. 8; *ʾʾḱ* 8. 1. 30, 12, 32, 11; *qʾʾp̄ʿń* 18. 10; *qʾhṕ* 18, 7.

(4) *ei* > *a*, *aa*; spelled ꜧʾ, ʾʾ, ʾ*h*: *qlʾʾd* 34. 6; *qlʾdʿr* 3. 5; *hʾʾḿ* 38. 7, *hʾḿ* 33. 1; *tʾʾg* 1. 10; *ʾlʾhń* 5. 3; 31. 2; *qʾhń qjnd*, *qʾhń rjnd* 5. 1; *ʾhń* 16. 3, *ʾhnʿ* 6. 21; 7. 3; *qʾhń qlʾhń* 31. 12; *hʾʾd* 32. 22.

With this I conclude the consideration of Western Yiddish, save for a few words about present Hungarian Yiddish in the closing pages of this study.

Jews in Old Russia and Slavic Lands

The enterprising Western European (=German) Jews who migrated into East European (=Slavic) lands did not come into a Jewish vacuum. In early days after the destruction of the Temple in 70 A.D., the ensuing great mass emigration of Jews split into two streams: one westward—the Balkans, Italy, North Africa, Spain and Provence (later to France and eventually to Germany); the other, via the Black Sea to Crimea and Kiev-Russia, later further north toward Novgorod (Lithuania, present Belorussia) and possibly to Czecho-Moravia. Both L. Zunz and M. Güdemann held the view that in early Middle Ages the bulk of Jews in Slavic lands came principally from Byzantium, the Southeast and the Orient.

The rulers (Kahans) of the Khazars were of Jewish faith, and for centuries the Khazars (their capital, Itil on the Volga, was the outstanding commercial center of the vast Europe-Asia territory) were masters of the southern half of present European Russia.

Jews (or Khazars) were urging Vladimir I to embrace Judaism before he turned to Christianity in 988. They constituted a sizable settlement in Kiev (with a "Jewish Gate" mentioned in 1146 and 1151) and, according to the chronicler, a great conflagration on Christmas Eve, 1124, wiped out all monasteries, 600 churches and all houses in the Jewish quarter of Kiev.

The prince Jaroslav I the Wise, appointed (1036) Luka Židjata ("Jewish offspring") as second bishop of Novgorod, and Jaroslav's successor, Izjaslav, was exhorted (1056–58) by Feodosij Pečerskij not to succumb to the wiles of Judaizing missionaries.

The Judaizing propaganda and the public disputations—*naturally, in the Russian language*—in Kiev in the eleventh century grew apace, and in the fourteenth century the *Heresy of the Judaizers* became a matter of utmost importance to the State. The zealots of the movement were equipped with great erudition: they had the entire Pentateuch and most of the biblical books, and even the *Logic* of Maimonides (1135–1204), in Russian translations, some centuries before the Bible was translated into any Western European tongue.

The court of Jaroslav the Wise harbored many princes of Europe's royal houses who had to flee their native lands. Jaroslav knew five European languages (also taught to some of his children) and became related to six European rulers by marriage of members of his family:[19] (1) granddaughter Evpraksia, wife of Henry IV of the Holy Roman Empire; (2) grandson Vladimir Monomakh (1113–1125) married daughter of Anglo-Saxon king Harold; (3) son Vsevolod—a Byzantine princess; (4) daughter Anastasia—Hungarian king Andrew; (5) daughter Jelisaveta—Harold II, the Stern (1046–1066) of Norway (the story embellished in Nordic sagas with a profusion of poetic embroidery); (6) daughter Anna married the illiterate Henry I of France (1031–1060) and in his stead signed royal decrees in Slavic characters and, after his death as regent—*Anna Reina*.

The Jews of old Rus' naturally spoke the language of their home, Russian, until late in fifteenth century, and the situation was similar in Czecho-Moravia.[20]

The Jews of Czecho-Moravia

From the ninth to the end of the eleventh century Moravia (-Czechia) was perhaps the foremost land of Europe in matters of culture with the principality of Kiev as a close second. The first record of Jews in Moravia belongs to 903–906. In the eleventh-twelfth centuries the Prague group of Jewish savants was in constant correspondence with the elder French scholars and many of them were pilgrims to study in the school in France, stemming from the great biblical and talmudic exegete Raši (initials of RABBI SOLOMON BEN ISAAC) of Troyes, in Champagne (1040–1105). They knew French and in their glosses sometimes used French words, but the glosses themselves were in Slavic ("in the Canaan tongue," "in our tongue"—Canaan meant Slavonia, Czecho-Moravia, "our tongue" meant Czech).

The Moravian Scholars

The tosephtist Abraham ben R. Azriel of Prague (13th cent.), the famous author of *'Arugat Habošem*, wrote *the earliest known treatise on Czech grammar* (antedating by several centuries the works of gentile scholars), dealing with noun and cases, verb-conjugation, transitive—intransitive, mode, tense etc.

His still more famous disciple Isaac ben Moses 'Or Zaru'a (13th cent.), who studied in France, interested himself in *contents*, the *meaning* of words: "in the language of Canaan," "in our language," or simply "what we call" were his usual terms, and frequently he confined himself to the Czech expression and omitted the Hebrew altogether. In one passage 'Or Zaru'a reproduces the talk of Jews in Czech while buying meat in the market for the Sabbath.

These two eminent scholars exhibit such an unfailing and profound sensitivity to the finest nuances of the Czech language, such finesse in the transliteration of Czech sounds, as can be found in the works of none among the non-Jewish scholars who came to study the Czech tongue several centuries later. Pending the possible unearthing of still unknown earlier other works in the field, 'Or

[19] Cf. Genealogical Table of Russian Princes Mentioned in the *Povest' vremennykh let* (Laurentian Chronicle, 1377), vol. 2, Moscow-Leningrad, 1950.

[20] The following pages are based entirely on the study of Roman Jakobson (still in manuscript) which I had in my hands for a number of months as a translator. Needless to add that I am deeply indebted for the information I have used.

Zaru'a and his teacher remain indisputable and inapproachable authorities for the history of old Czech.

If we bear in mind that after the Crusaders' anti-Jewish pogroms in Prague (1096–98), a mass of Jews fled to Hungary and Poland (1150, 1190, 1204) with recorded settlements near Kalisz (1213) and a religious community at Płock (1237), we shall realize some facts that otherwise might be puzzling. It is also of great importance to know that "the first two waves of immigration from Western Europe had hardly fringed the Russian terrains, they settled only *in the central points of Poland*. 'In the sixteenth century *Lithuania* (at that time it comprised *well-nigh all Russian sections* where Jews lived) counted a population of some 10,000–12,000 Jews,'[21] and that would surely have been impossible, had the first two West-European immigrant waves reached as far as Lithuania."[22]

With these data established as matters of history, we can say with a certain amount of assurance that in the East-European non-Germanic (=Slavic) lands the German Jews, those driven as well as the more enterprising, pushing, among them, did not come into a Jew-less language vacuum, but found Russian (Polish?) -speaking Jews with established phonetic habits and linguistic patterns and that, instead of the Slavic element wedging into a completely formed German-Jewish tongue, this latter played the role of the hedgehog (in the fable of the Hedgehog and the Mole). The wide-awake intruders pushed the less bellicose denizens living in more or less compact groups and in the lengthy process of give and take had to absorb a considerable ingredient of Slavic words from their crowded hosts, as well as deeply-rooted sound-habits.

This explains the accelerated transition of all Western-Yiddish /u, ü/ phonemes into /ɨ, i/ in Polish-Ukrainian Yiddish, thus completing the early stages of the process (begun in the original habitat—Germany), so well studied by Birnbaum and Franz J. Beranek. And it also accounts for the absence of the neuter gender in (Northern) Lithuanian Yiddish, conditioned by centuries of living among neuterless Lithuanian and Latvian natives, prior to the arrival of German Jews in that territory.

Fate of the Eastern Yiddish Dialects

The physical (=territorial) parting between Western Yiddish and the future Eastern Yiddish came about in the early sixteenth century when migration of German Jews into Slavic lands in the East assumed mass proportions. At that time the younger linguistic group still shared with the older stay-at-homes the pronunciation of *a* < MHG *a* as /a/. As the Polish-Ukrainian dialect of Yiddish is distinguished from the other two by the *u* sound developed from the original *a*'s, and as this process cannot be consummated save through an intermediate *o*-stage, my first step will be to ascertain, if possible, when that *a* duplicated the fate of *â* and this newly acquired *o* joined the earlier one evolved from *â* in the Western German era.

[21] S. L. Beršadskij: *Litovskije jevreji*, St. Petersburg, 1883, p. 7.

[22] B. Rubshteyn: [The Former Languages of Jews in the Russian Regions], in *Der pinkes*, Vilna, 1913, 21–35.

As far as I know from the material I have been gathering for the greater part of my life, the *earliest clue* to this problem is a "Dirge on Khmelnitski's Anti-Jewish Excesses of 1648"[23] in 76 single-rime quatrains. In this lament by a native Ukrainian Jew who survived and, later, as an eye-witness, penned the horrors of those bloody days of wholesale massacre by sword and fire, we come face to face with the early Polish-Ukrainian dialect.

We find that (ca. 1650):

A. (1) MHG *â* > *o* rimes with *o*: 17. *p̄rvgń : gjp̄lvgń : gjlvgń : bvgń* (*â, o, o, o*); 51. *gjp̄lˀσń : mˀσń : lˀσń : strˀσń* (*o, â, â, â*); 73: *gˀt : spˀt : lˀt : hˀt* (*o, o, â, â*).

(2) Original MHG *â* and *a* rime with each other: 69. *jˁnrˀl : ˀjbrˀl : tˀl : mˀl* (*a, a, â, â*); 72. *p̄rˀgń : plˀgń : gjslˀgń : p̄rtrˀgń* (*â, â, a, a*).

(3) Original MHG *a* rimes with *o*: 45. *♮dˀz : glˀz : grˀz : qrjvv''h nˀ''z* (*a, a, a*, Rus. *Krivonos*); 56. *gjbˀrń : p̄ˀr lˀrń : vvˀr[d]ń : ˀrp̄ˀrń* (*o, o, o, a*).

In the above we find proof that ca. 1650 in Polish-Ukrainian (ergo also in Lithuanian) Yiddish, MHG open *a* had also become *o*, but, so far, nothing to show the characteristic further turning of these former *â, a* into *u*.

B. All [ɨj]—[aj] diphtongs rime each with the other and approach a (half?-)long *ā*, as may be gathered from the following: 21. *♮sjjnń* (*schînen*) : *djˀ mjjnń* (*mannen*) : *qljjnń* (*kleinen*) : *rjjnń* (*reinen*); 60. *svvjjgń : stjjgń : ljjgń : gjjgń* (*swîgen, stîgen, liugen, gougen*).

The same phonetic evolution, as one should naturally expect, is on hand in the Polish-Yiddish proper names of such Polish cities as dial. Yid. *Kruke* < Kraków, *Turne* < Tarnów, *Tsuzmir* < Sandomierz, but just as naturally their "name-days" (or the birth of those names) were not registered by the Jews and we can draw no chronological enlightment from their phonetic garb. It is curious that in his lecture of Monday, March 27, 1944 on "The Formation of Dialects in Eastern Yiddish," Max Weinreich told his students that he had sought in vain to settle the date of the evolution of *a* > *o* > *u* in Polish-Ukrainian Yiddish, in the Amsterdam ($_2$1701) edition of a 5-language phrase-book: *Sofe brure* (*Śafah berurah*) (Hebrew, Yiddish, French, Italian, Latin), because French, Italian, Latin phrases were given in Hebrew-character transcriptions. He evidently did not realize that the ♮*v̇* (H. vav with dot in middle) for all *u*-sounds (save the French *ü*—šureḳ) denoted and still denotes the *standard* and not the Polish dialectal pronunciation, and all the *o*-marked alef-characters could not disclose their *phonetic* value any more than they can today.

For aid in that direction we now turn to a book bearing the date of 1733–34.

Iyun Yitskhok

I have reached the critical point of my study: to determine the exact date (1) when all Yiddish [o]'s—which originated from MHG *â* and the "open" (=interconsonantal) *a*—cleaved away from the [o] sound (in which the Lithuanian has persisted unchanged to this day) and turned into [u] : [štrufn, šlufn,

[23] "Kine gzeyres takh," reproduced on pp. 199–211 of Max Weinreich's *Bilder* . . . (see footnote 15).

bluzn, bluter, šlugn, zugn, hubn] (MHG *strâfen, slâfen, blâsen, blâtere, slagen, sagen, haben*); (2) when every [*u*] sound turned into [i], [ɨ], in all non-Lithuanian Eastern dialects.

The answer to these problems has been provided by the book *Iyun Yitskhok* (*ʿIyyun Yiṣḥaḳ*) (Berlin 1734?) with close to 2,000 rimes in the 772 adages, maxims and proverbs gleaned from Hebrew or Aramaic sources and translated into Yiddish, a poor artisanlike imitation of *Tsukhtshpigl*, its prototype.

As there is no possible means of discovering the *u* pronunciation of any *o* letter (i.e. alef with the kamec beneath it) by a frontal attack at the material, we shall adopt an indirect yet simple way of tackling *our problem number 2*, the date of [u] > [i, ɨ], *first*.

[u] > [i, ɨ]. The author, a roaming native of Lisa (in Great Poland) where he proudly boasts to have had three generations of ancestors, rimes every *u* (Hebrew or Germanic) with any *i* (Hebrew or Germanic):

Hebrew: *♮qhjlh : gdvlh* (44a 11 a f.); *θp̄jlh : gˀvlh* (11a 9–8 a f.);

Hebrew—Germanic: G. *♮ˀvjṕ* (=[ɨf]) : H. *gvṕ* (19b. 15); *mcˀθj* : G. *dᵊrcv* (5b. 14 a f.), H. *xσdjḿ* : G. *p̄rvḿ* (21a, 13 a f.); H. *zxvθ* : G. *ˀjz* (27a, 11–12); H. *mdqd[j]q* : G. *cv/rvq* (46a, 14); G. *mvtr* : H. *dḿ ˀjσvr vhjθr* : G. *pvtr* (53b, 8–7 a f.);

Germanic: *zjtcń : nvcń* (34b. 6–7); *qjndr : vvˀvndr* (Preface 1a 7 a f.); *sjqń : drvqń* (*ibid*., 1b, 5); *brvdr : vvjdr* (2b, 8 a f.); *qrjgń : gjnvgń* (3a, 10 a f.); *bjqvmjń : rjmń* (*rüemen*, 5b, 15); *gvt : njt* (7b, 13); *p̄jndń : p̄[ˀ]r svvˀvndń* (9a, 5–4 a f.); *cvvjngń : ˀvntr drvngń* (12b, l. l.); *bljndr : bjzvndr* (13a, 7 a f.); *jvng : djng* (14a, 13); *grvnd : p̄jnt* (*vindt*, 14a, 7 a f.); *tvst* (*tuon*) : *dᵊr vvjst* (15a, 3 a f.); *gvtć : vvjtć* (18b, 15: *guotes*: *witz*[*e*]); *qjndr : bjzvndr* (20b, 11); *ˀjz : p̄[ˀ]r drvσ* (21b, 5); *gjnjgń : cjgń* (*genuegen*: *zigen*, 25, 16); *lvσdjg*: *gjnvg* (*lustic*: *genuog*, 34b, 4); *zjtcń : nvcń* (34b, 6); *mil : p̄vl* (*müle, volle*, 38a, 12 a f.); *gvtń : sjtń : gjljtń* (41a, 11–12); *bjzvk̄ń* (*besuochen*): *gjsljk̄ń* (*geslichen*, 47b, l. l.); *gvtń : mjtń* (51b, 3); *ˀjjń gjldń : lvbń ˀvn hˀldń* (misprint; MHG *loben und hulden*, 55, 14 a f.); *tvst : gvvjs* (56b, 16); *ˀjjdjḿ* (MHG *eidem*) : *ˀvmndvḿ* (*umbe und umbe*, 66a, 14); *stjq : gjnvg* (70a, 6).

The above establishes a definite date (1733–34; possibly some other document may turn up and set this date some 10—20—30 years back!) of the completion of the process of every non-Lithuanian Eastern Yiddish [u] turning into [i] or [ɨ].

This process began many years earlier. In his article on the history of *u*-sounds in Yiddish,[24] Birnbaum published the results of an unusually penetrating study of many dozens of old grammars of Hebrew-Aramaic, as well as of Old Yiddish books and manuscripts. His conclusions are that (1) some 600 years ago the *u, uo* sounds of Western Yiddish began to turn to *ü*, possibly at first in the šureḳ of the Hebrew element and later, apparently through Bohemia and Moravia, crossed into Poland; by 1500 the process was completed. (2) About the end of the fifteenth century, the *ü* turned further toward *i*.

In Eastern Europe both the new *ü* and the old *ü* became unrounded > *i*. In parts of Slovakia, the new *ü* < *u, uo* remained *ü*.

F. Beranek, in another study,[25] makes Slovakia a microcosm of the above process: *u* in the West, *ü* in the middle, *i* in the East (p. 69).

[24] [The History of the Old *u*-Sounds], in *Yivo-bleter* 6 (1934) 25–60.

[25] [Yiddish in Czechoslovakia], in *Yivo-bleter* 9 (1936) 63–75.

איך דער שרייבער · אלי ווייבער · אין פרום ליבער · טו איך רו · פין :
אין נייעי פרוכט · מיט ערבער צוכט · הון איך גיזוכט · צו פער קא · פין :
אלי ניבוט · די אונזיר גוט · אונז געבין הוט · אונ זיין שטרו · פין :
אין פירוש ביא · פער שטינדר פריא · מן ווער עז זיא · ריך און טרופ · פין :
און אל סדרא · הוט כסברא · איר הפטרה · ביא איד לא · פין : 5
און ווער אל ואוך · ליטרז בוך ווערט · מילך און לעקוד · אים מאל טרי · פין :
אן אים קלעבין · ווערט דער געבין · עביג לעבין · און אל שים · פין :
איר און רייכקט · און אל וויזקט · פער נופט קט · מיט פיל האר · פיך :
אובר דיז אליז · גוט הולד אן טאליז · הוט ער אם האליז · און דרוס לא · פין :
אוז עז ניט שאין · דיז בוך זייא פיין · דיז דו אליז דראין · איז גישלו · פין : 10
אן ואוגדער לייך · זעכט אים בוך מיין · ויא ליטריז זיין · שרף און שליי · פין :
אז דער ספיר · איז דיז ספיר · און אך טאפפיר · אן צו גריי · פין :
איך הון דען פרייז · דיז אלי גרייז · איך ואל דראויז · הון מון קלו[illegible] · פין :
אך מיט גרוש אכט · הב איכש גימכט · דיז טג נוך נאכט · הון גישלו · פין :
אום דיז אליר · אוך אז טאליר · איז דער צאליר · ואל צו שא · פין : 15
אשליכי מאר · זייא עז ניט לאר · איר אינן קלאר · צו פער קא · פין :
איר אל זאבין · גערט צו מאכין · זייא מיט מאכין · און גענד [illegible] · פין :
און גיויגין · מיט דעם שביגין · [illegible] · גענז [illegible] · פין :
און בול די טעש · בין לון דער וועש · די זא טיט עש · נאכט און [illegible] · פין :
אין כאדי וועלט · נוט עז פער געלט · ווער מיט יעם געלט · דיז וערט קא · פין : 20
און דער קוויקין · מיט קאן שריקין · זול ער שיקן · דען [illegible] · פין :
אזו איך זאג · און דען טאג דיז · אם מנשטין טג · [illegible] · פין :
און טריכט און טראכט · דער נואך ביא נאכט · פיר מול מן מאכט · [illegible] · פין :
פין שין כף יאר · איך האש פיר ואר · ליב און גוט פאר · [illegible] · פין :

Rimed Preface to Cremona Pentateuch (1560)

(*See p.* 112)

חד גדיא חד גדיא

ואתא שונרא ואכל לגדיא דזבן אבא בתרי זוזי חד גדיא חד גדיא

[illegible]

ואתא כלבא ונשך לשונרא דאכל לגדיא דזבן אבא בתרי זוזי חד גדיא חד גדיא

[illegible]

ואתא חוטרא והכה לכלבא דנשך לשונרא דאכל לגדיא דזבן אבא בתרי זוזי חד
גדיא חד גדיא

[illegible]

ואתא נורא ושרף לחוטרא דהכה לכלבא דנשך לשונרא דאכל לגדיא דזבן
אבא בתרי זוזי חד גדיא חד גדיא

[illegible]

ואתא מיא וכבה לנורא דשרף לחוטרא דהכה לכלבא דנשך לשונרא דאכל
לגדיא דזבן אבא בתרי זוזי חד גדיא חד גדיא

[illegible]

ואתא תורא ושתא למיא דכבה לנורא דשרף לחוטרא דהכה לכלבא דנשך [illegible]
[illegible] דאכל לגדיא דזבן אבא בתרי זוזי חד גדיא חד גדיא

EARLIEST VERSION OF "KHAD GADYE"
(*See p.* 214)

This view is welcome as far as it concerns the tendency around 1500, but for such forms in Levita's language as ♮ˀ*vjm̍* (in his Psalms, 1545) we find in MHG (Lexer II, 172) *umbe, ümbe, umme, ümme, um, üm,* and for ♮ˀ*vjnz* (1573) in Lexer *üns*, and such forms occur in MHG still earlier. But the unrounding of *every u, ü* sound in Yiddish in its mass impact on the Slavic vowel systems in their new home in Eastern Europe is a different matter.

o > *uo* > *u* > *ü* > *üe* > *i* is a special Slavic linguistic phenomenon which reflects the totality of similar changes, partially present in various non-Slavic languages. The Greek *mūs* (*mȳs*) is *mis* in Mod. Greek; Lat. *inclūtus, lūbet, homo* became *inclytus, libet, humanus* in the course of time; *hortos* > *hortus*.

The Latin heritage *nŏuos, homo, bonus, cor, soror, portus, fons* (*-ntis*), *hora, dolorem* became (1) *nuovo, uomo, buono, cuor*(*e*), *suor*(*a*) in Italian, (2) *nuevo, bueño, cuer, puerto* in Spanish, (3) *neuf, cœur, sœur, heure* in French, and in this latter every open Latin *u* > *ü* : *purus, luna, una* > [pyr, lyn, yn].

The Germanic languages combined some of these phenomena. The Gothic *brôþar, môds, fôtus, blôda* are OHG, MHG *bruoder, muot, fuoz, vuoz, bluot*, OE *bróðor, mod, fôt, blód*, E. *brother, mood, foot, blood*. MHG and E. umlauted forms are *brüeder, gemüt, vüeze, feet, geese* < *goose*.

Yiddish, which started with the MHG (OHG?) forms, went through from *uo* > *u* > *ü* > *i* which we see only in the Slavic languages, IE. *ū* > Sl. *y* [= i, ɯ]: Skr. *dhūmaḥ, sūnuḥ*, Gr. *thymós, mȳs*. Lat. *fūmus, mûs, tū*, OHG *mûs*, Lith. *sūnus, dúmai* (pl.), Slav. *dymŭ, synŭ, myšĭ, ty*. In Czech every palatalized *u* > *i* : l*i*biti, l*i*d, l*i*ty are l′*u*bit′, l′*u*d, l′*u*tyj in Russian. A single illustration from the Ukrainian will show the totality of all changes of *o* > *u* > *ü* > *i* in Germanic and *o* > *uo* > *ue* > *eu* in Romance: the old Slavic k*o*n′ (horse) went through the following successive stages until it reached the present Ukrainian *kin′* (gen. *kon′a*) : ¹ *kon′* > ² *kuòn′* > ³ *kúon′* > ⁴ *kúen′*, ⁵ *kuén′* > ⁶ *kuín′* > ⁷ *kín′* (Cf. Sobolevskij, *Lectures on the History of the Russian Language*, 3rd (4th) ed., 1903, pp. 6–7). (1) *nŏvus, fôtus, gôs, fôt*; (2) *nuovo, fuoz, goose, foot*; (3) *vuoz*; (4) *nuevo, neuf*; (5) *nuevo, vüeze*; (6) *füsse*, Fr. [pyr]; (7) Yiddish, German dialectal *fis*, Engl. *geese, feet*.

The Vocalic Triangle i—a—u[26]

The *vocalic triangle* is also known as the "*law of implication*" (*Folgerungsgesetz*, in German) which says: "Of the five basic vowels usually arranged in a vocalic

```
   a
  / \
 o   e
/     \
u-----i
```

triangle, the *o* and *e* are of a secondary importance and either or both may be lacking in a 'culture' language, but in *all culture languages, without exception, a, u, i* are a *sine qua non*: if there are *a, u*, there must also be an *i*; if there are *a, i*, there must also be *u*; if there are *u, i*, there must also be an *a*."

In accordance with this law, when all the *u*'s in Polish-Yiddish had become

[26] I learned the significance and value of the vocalic triangle in linguistic investigation from the lips of Roman Jakobson in the various courses of lectures he delivered at the Ecole Libre des Hautes Etudes and Columbia University during his stay in New York in 1941–49. For the many things I learned in those years I have a deep sense of gratitude to express here.

i, or *y* sounds (about 1733–34), the vocalic triangle (which thereby lost its left leg) became lopsided and, in order to retain (or regain) its equilibrium (the "sound-pattern"), all the Eastern, non-Lithuanian dialects *had to get* a new *u* to replace the former *u*, now turned [i] or [i]. In other words, those dialects could not function unless *these o* (originally *â*, *a*) sounds were already *u*.

In Rumanian Yiddish, every *a* (as in Rumanian itself) is pronounced *o*, and the case is the same in Hungarian Yiddish (as in Hungarian itself); consequently, when the *a* disappeared in these dialects, the roof of the vocalic triangle caved in, and, in order to retain its equilibrium, Rumanian (Yiddish changed the [aj] in [rajx, vajs, lajt] into half-long *a*: [rāx, vās, lāt] (MHG *rîch*, *wîz*, *liute*), while (Western) Hungarian Yiddish already had an [ā] < MHG *ei*, *ou*: [flāš, kāfen].

Conclusion

And, to clench the above series of proofs I shall resort to an irrefutable piece of visual evidence from a non-Yiddish language. Some 35 years ago I conceived the idea of utilizing historical records in a Slavic language dealing with Yiddish (=Jewish) names. I obtained the bulky Bondy-Dworský book,[27] and turned to it with pleasurable anticipation. But a cursory perusal of its pages convinced me that my expectations were vain: all the Jewish names were given in the records (many in German, mostly in Slavic) in their classical, or biblical, form and remained standard (or well-nigh invariable) throughout the two volumes.

Though checked, I did not give up and sought to secure a similar book (in Russian) of *Registers and Records*,[28] municipal, administrative, juridical documents and decrees in South Russia, Lithuania, Poland and White Russia until 1800. I procured vol. I (until 1670) of the three volumes published. This contained mere crumbs: B*o*rukh (1583), Šmojla N*o*khimovič 1643), Šaj N*o*khimovič (1645), N*o*khim twice (1646), Avram Zr*o*ilevič (1583); useless *A*hron, *A*ronovič and *A*khronovič, against *O*rel (1621), *O*khron Ekhudič (1561), *O*khron Ihudič (1556); S*a*rka, S*o*rka and the questionable S*u*rka (1563); then in Vol. II (till 1740): S*o*ra, Sr*o*l′ (1729), Fr*o*im (No. 1534), Šr*o*l′ (1737).

For twenty years I sought Vol. III (1740–99) and on Thursday, January 16, 1947—six days before my paper (on which this article is based) was to be read—a good friend, Dr. Isaac Rivkind, assistant librarian at the Jewish Theological Seminary, finally unearthed the volume we had been looking for. In this treasured book I found what I had been hoping to find for over twenty years. I had 64 Jewish names with *u* instead of the *a* and *o* invariably used in the first two volumes: the earliest (1746) was N*u*son (Nathan), N*u*sin (3 times) and Vol′ N*u*sinovič (once) (1765); D*a*vid B*u*nemovič (1778); D*u*vid (8 times), Kramar D*u*vid (once) and Šimko D*u*vidovič (in all *10* times, 1765); Naft*u*la (4 times), Herška and Moška Naft*u*levičs (in all 6 times, 1765); N*u*khim (7 times), Herško

[27] *Zur Geschichte der Juden in Böhmen, Mähren und Schlesien von 906 bis 1620*, ed. Gottlieb Bondy and Franz Dworský, Prague, 1906, I: xii + 552 pp.; II: pp. 553–1149.

[28] *Regesty i nadpisi; svod materialov dlja istorii jevrejev v Rossii (80–1800)*, vol. 1 (till 1670), St. Petersburg, 1899.

N*u*khimovič (twice), Mordko N*u*khimovič (1765) and Lejba N*u*khimovič (1749, in all 11 times); Sr*u*l′ (6 times, 1761, 1765); Herška and Jona Sr*u*levičs (1765, in all 8 times); *U*šer (5 times, 1765), Herš *U*šerovič (twice, 1778), and Jos *U*šerovič (once, 1765) in all *8* times; Ts*u*dik Itskovič and David Ts*u*dikovič (1765, in all twice); Š*u*lim (5 times, 1751, 1758, 1765); Fajbiš Š*u*limovič (1778), Davidko Š*u*limovič (1778), Majorko Š*u*limovič (1765, in all 8 times); Š*u*l′ (twice, 1765).

This gives a total of *64* Southern names (Kiev, Zhitomir, Bratslav, Kamenets-Podol′sk, Kremenets, etc). The proof of the pronunciation in the Russian letter *y* (= [u]) is irrefutable, and the co-temporary rimes in *Iyun Yitskhok* settle *the date of the formation of the Polish-Ukrainian dialect at the fourth decade of the eighteenth century.*

RESUMÉ

Yiddish originated in Middle Rhine territory of Germany and showed definite deviations from its parent-language MHG by the last quarter of the fourteenth century: *ā* turned into *o* and that still later became *ui/oi*; while *ei, ou* became *a* (*ă*) and the original *a* > *ā*.

By 1500 a considerable mass of German Jews (from East German border territory?) had migrated to the East European Slavic lands, where they found other Jews who had come there centuries earlier, from the near East and Northern shores of the Black Sea.

In the East, around 1650, *a* duplicated the fate of *â* by also turning into *o*. And then a cleavage came, in the new home, into:

(1) (North-) Eastern, Lithuanian Yiddish where *o* < *â* and *o* < *a* merged with the original closed *o* (kop, dort, dokh, holts), all the three *o*'s remaining unchanged to this day; and

(2) Ca. 1730, i.e. some eight decades later, Polish-Ukrainian which turned every *o* < *â* or *a* into *u*, and every original *u* into *y, i*.

These two non-Western branches had left their original habitats before MHG *ei* > *ā*, i.e. before the loss of the glide *i* element: *ei* was completely merged with MHG *ê—ein, kein, klein* [ɨjn, kɨjn, klɨjn] fully riming with [gɨjn] (*gên*). In stray variants like MHG *beide/bêde, wenec/weinec* and Central German *leim/lem* we have definite proof that in MHG the sounds were nearly alike.

The descendants of MHG *ei* (*ê*) were [ɨj] in Lithuanian Yiddish [ɨjn, kɨjn, klɨjn, gɨjn]; [aj] in Polish Yiddish [ajn, kajn, klajn, gajn], while Ukrainian Yiddish *overlapped with Lithuanian* (and *not with Polish!*) in [ɨj], in some localities with a tendency to an opener (more "back") first element of the diphthong: [ɨjn/ɛjn, kɨjn/kɛjn, klɨjn/klɛjn, gɨjn/gɛjn].

On the last phenomenon (the curious "desertion" of Polish by its subdialect Ukrainian in favor of the Lithuanian) I venture to offer a cautious suggestion as a side-light on the [ɨj/ɛj] matter. The close similarity shown by the (North-Eastern) Lithuanian and (Southern) Ukrainian (Galician, Rumanian) sectors is strikingly identical with the phenomenon shared by the native tongues of Belorussia and the Ukraine: "*V. Traits common to both the Belorussian and the Ukrainian dialects:* (a) *y* and *i* before non-syllabic *i* (i.e. [j]—J.A.J.) in such words as *myju, ryju, šyj* (Rus. *šej*), *šyja* (Rus. *šeja*), *zlyj, xudyj*."[29]

This sharing of the linguistic phenomenon is due to historical conditions: "Owing to the fact that the Belorussians and the Ukrainians had for a long time been integral parts of the same Lithuanian-Russian State, certain common above-mentioned traits developed in the speech of the two peoples."[30]

[29] A. D. Grigorjev: *Russkij jazyk*, Warsaw, 1915, p. 47.

[30] Nikolaj Durnovo: *Očerk istorii russkogo jazyka*, Moscow–Leningrad, 1924, p. 225.

YIDDISH IN HOLLAND: LINGUISTIC AND SOCIO-LINGUISTIC NOTES

H. Beem (Leeuwarden)

The study of the Holland branch of the Yiddish language has been rather neglected to date, especially by Dutch scholarship. The resulting gap in Yiddish historical linguistics is a substantial one, for in the seventeenth and eighteenth centuries Dutch Yiddish occupied a position of unique importance. It was Holland that, for a certain period, functioned as the publishing center of translations into Yiddish. Books printed in Amsterdam exerted a considerable linguistic influence and left their traces even on dialects of Yiddish outside of the Netherlands. Of particular importance are the surviving remnants of this language among Dutch Jews; these vestiges are a goldmine of words and phrases which, as a result of their linguistic isolation from the rest of Yiddish-speaking Jewry, have retained archaic forms that are highly informative of the character of Western Yiddish, now nearly extinct.

Among scholars abroad, only Max Grünbaum[1] and Jacob Shatzky[2] dealt with Dutch Yiddish in any detail. Max Weinreich republished and analyzed a text in Western Yiddish of probable Dutch provenience[3] and recently outlined the place of this dialect in the study of Western Yiddish in general.[4] In Holland proper, the most important work on the subject is J. L. Voorzanger and J. E. Polak's *Het Joodsch in Nederland* (Amsterdam, 1915, 324 pp.). It is notable as a collection of materials, but is full of gaps and extraneous matter, and is rather unreliable in questions of etymology. Unfortunately we can only join in M. Weinreich's verdict that the book "is an example of good material spoiled by nonprofessional 'analysis' "[5] and support his suggestion that the data it contains be screened afresh.[6] Much graver are the faults of the most unsatisfactory study of the well-known linguist J. van Ginneken.[7] It is so overflowing with errors that, except insofar as it was copied from other sources, it was adjudged as overly speculative and misleading.[8] Besides the above treatments, which are either sketchy or inaccurate, there is hardly any research on Dutch Yiddish.

I

If we consider the question of why the Yiddish of Holland has attracted so little attention, the answer is almost self-evident. Eastern Yiddish is to this day a living language spoken by millions, extending, until the recent ca-

[1] Max Grünbaum: *Jüdischdeutsche Chrestomathie* . . . , Leipzig, 1882, *passim.*

[2] Jacob Shatzky: [The Last Outcrops of the Yiddish Language and Literature in Holland], *Yivo-bleter* 10 (1936) 232–265.

[3] The poem "Megilas Vints" (Amsterdam, 1648; Frankfurt $_2$1696), in Max Weinreich: *Shtaplen*, Berlin, 1923, 140–192.

[4] Max Weinreich: [Outlines of Western Yiddish], *Yidishe shprakh* (New York) 13 (1953) 35–69, esp. pp. 57f.

[5] *Ibid.*, p. 57.

[6] *Shtaplen*, p. 51.

[7] *Handboek der Nederlandsche Taal*, vol. 2, Nijmegen, 1914: "De Jodentaal."

[8] Cf. E. Slijper: "Bekattering," *Nieuwe taalgids* 10 (1916) 29–46, p. 46 and passim.

tastrophe, over a vast part of Europe, and reaching into the New World; it possesses a literature on a world scale. In Holland, on the other hand, Yiddish was never spoken by more than a small number of people in a limited area and, after protracted and profound upheavals, ceased to be spoken in the nineteenth century, with some increasingly rare exceptions. No wonder, then, that it was Eastern Yiddish in its several varieties which caught the fancy of so many more scholars. But this still does not explain why the interest of the Dutch Jews themselves for the language of their ancestors has been so slight.

As a matter of fact, Jewish intellectual circles in Holland have, since the Emancipation, avoided the subject to the utmost. One of the reasons was the set of erroneous conceptions about the language which became current in the age of assimilation. The view was then propagated that this language, which for centuries had been the link between widely scattered groups of the Jewish people, did not deserve the name "language" at all, that it was something inferior and degrading, and that all knowledge of it should be eradicated as fast as possible. Many persons who were otherwise scholars of distinction could not help being infected by this attitude. In Germany these views were particularly prominent. Thus Moses Mendelssohn had asserted that "the Jewish language [i.e. Yiddish] bears a large part of the blame for the lack of civilization of the ordinary Jew [*Unsittlichkeit des Mannes aus dem Volke*]." The historian Graetz in his *History of the Jews* expressed himself even more strongly, calling the language "a repulsive babbling and stammering, a loathsome Jew-talk [*Mauscheln*], . . . the language of half-savage people." Similar opinions were expressed by M. Steinschneider, G. Karpeles, L. Zunz, and other German Jewish scholars. In Holland, too, this attitude became common. The real battle against Yiddish was joined in 1797 by a group which, under French influence, was infected by the spirit of assimilation. If the hatred of Yiddish was somewhat less violent here than in Germany, it was because the Emancipation in Holland was considered an accomplished fact and was never again threatened.

Nevertheless, Holland, too, became the scene of contempt and detestation of Yiddish. Under the influence of the progressing assimilation, it was the intellectual circles and the well-to-do bourgeoisie which were most receptive to the anti-Yiddish attitude, while the man in the street obstinately held on to his inherited language until far into the nineteenth century. In the upper strata, speaking Yiddish became a sign of "lack of education." The general desire was to replace the old Jewish culture by a West European, in this case Dutch, culture and to become as Dutch as possible (even though conversion to Christianity was far less frequent in Holland than in Germany). It was especially to those who were desirous both of remaining Jews in a religious sense and of becoming Dutch citizens that the question of language loomed large. The elite felt frustrated in its drive for assimilation by the refusal of the masses to follow them. The continued speaking of Yiddish among the plain people was embarrassing to the members of the elite, for the non-Jewish environment, in mocking the Jewish language and all other peculiarities of Jewish culture, did not differentiate between the upper and lower strata. Among those anxious to assimilate, a Yiddish word became taboo; their mortifying sensitivity was lampooned by the common people in the proverb, *a yidish vort—a dónershloog* 'a Yiddish word is a clap of thunder'.

It took a long time for the ordinary Jew to abandon his resistance to assimilation and, with it, the Yiddish language. Many an Ashkenazic community had its peace disturbed in the nineteenty century by conflicts over this issue. (For the Sefardic communities, of course, Yiddish was no problem.)

II

But misunderstanding and disparagement of Dutch Yiddish did not come from the inside only. The Yiddish of Holland naturally sounds strange to a person familiar with the East European variety, and he may be tempted to dismiss it as a "corrupt Yiddish" if he is not aware of the fact that the Holland dialect is a legitimate brother of Eastern Yiddish. It developed on the same general principles, but in another direction and under other influences. It did not sever its connection with Germanic-speaking areas and did not undergo the influence of Slavic languages, but it was profoundly influenced by Dutch,[9] precisely because as a fusion language it remained more hospitable to foreign influence than other, more homogeneous languages.

The divergence between the two branches of Yiddish was slow in growing. As late as the end of the seventeenth century, one may still speak of a single European Yiddish speech area; witness the publication of Yiddish Bibles for a Europe-wide market. The first complete Old Testament by R. Yekusiel b. Yitskhok Blits, which appeared in Amsterdam in 1676–1679, contains not only declarations of approval by the rabbis of Amsterdam, but also a warning by the rabbis of Lublin, Lemberg, Cracow, and Posen, calling on printers, under penalty of excommunication, to desist for twenty years from reprinting this translation "into the language of Ashkenaz which people use." Whether or not the language of this translation was identical with the spoken Yiddish of Amsterdam, it is clear that a single literary idiom could satisfy the needs of the whole European Yiddish-speaking community. Just as Amsterdam received many Yiddish books from farther east, the bulk of its own book production was marked for export. At the fairs in Leipzig and Breslau, Amsterdam books were sold cheaply; in 1685, the city officials of Breslau advised against the founding of a local Jewish printing shop "because in Holland, at Amsterdam, there are three Jewish printing shops whence the books are brought by sea to Danzig and Memel and supply the Jews in Poland and Lithuania."[10] Many publishers of other cities liked to disguise their books as Amsterdam editions. Thus, the title page of a book of *kines* (*Ḳinot* 'laments') with Yiddish translation, published in 1762, states that it is printed *be'otyot AMSTERDAM* ('in Amsterdam letters,' i.e. type), the first word being in fine print, the latter word displayed large. An edition of the *Ḥobot*

[9] When J. Shatzky, in his otherwise valuable article [*Der diskurs*, a Yiddish Periodical in Amsterdam in 1797–1798], *Zamlbukh lekoved dem 250stn yoyvl fun der yidisher prese, 1686–1936*, New York, 1937, 20–106, speaks of the "superficial" Hollandization of Dutch Yiddish, he is in error, at least from the linguistic point of view.

[10] H. Brugmans and A. Frank: *Geschiedenis der Joden in Nederland*, Amsterdam, 1940, p. 475.

halebabot from Żółkiew (Galicia), dated 1739, lists the place of publication in tiny letters, but notes in display type that one of the type engravers is R. Aharon Halevi, grandson of Uri Fayvush Segal of AMSTERDAM, in order to create the impression that the latter was the place of publication. To this day East European Jews speak of "Amsterdam margins [*ámsterdamer gilyoynes*] and Bershad prayer shawls" as the best.

If written communication between the farflung parts of the Yiddish area was entirely feasible, this was partly due to the fact that certain differences in the spoken language, especially discrepancies in the vowels, were not reflected in the conventional orthography. Special efforts were also made to "de-regionalize" the language lexically. Yoyzl Vitsnhoyzn (Witzenhausen), Blits' great competitor who published a Yiddish Bible translation at about the same time, stated that his edition was intended not only for Amsterdam consumption, and was especially pleased to acknowledge the aid of R. Shabse Bas (Sabbatai Bass) of Prague "who is well versed in the languages [i.e. the Yiddish dialects] of the land of Bohemia" and who helped to eliminate words "which are current [*murgl*] here in Holland or Friesland, for they are not understood elsewhere."[11] But it would be incorrect to interpret this passage as an indication that Dutch Yiddish was at that time already intensely Hollandized. It reflects, in our opinion, merely the beginning of a divergence which subsequently grew in force as a result of the action of Dutch on the isolated westernmost branch of Yiddish and of its independent development.

Vitsnhoyzn's desire to make his text intelligible to Eastern readers by avoiding regional, West European words was no doubt based on commercial considerations. Similar efforts were, after all, made by printers to de-regionalize many other European languages. But there was no systematic effort to unify Yiddish. There was no norm, or rather there were countless norms. Every author considered the Yiddish of his region and his native milieu as *the* Yiddish language. Hence the frequent complaint by editors and publishers about the "bad language" of one's predecessors. Even Yoysef bar Yokor, who published his Yiddish prayer book in Ichenhausen as early as 1544, joined in this complaint.

References of this type were all the more in evidence in a community like Amsterdam, where emigrants from many regions converged and where many varieties of Yiddish could be heard. Both Blits and Vitsnhoyzn speak of the bad language of their predecessors. Yoysef b. Yankev Maarsen (*♮mʔrsjn*) makes a similar comment in the introduction to his Decameron translation of 1710.[12] The preface to *Tsene-rene* (aggadic interpretation of the Pentateuch), Amsterdam, 1711, notes that previous editions "are quite difficult to understand, primarily because of the corrupt language which is not like a translation at all [*♮gʔr bjjʔ qjjń tjjts qᵊń p̄r gljk̄ń vvᵊrń*] and is not at all in order [*♮gʔnć slʔ kσdr*]." In a burst of local pride, the publisher then states: "But in Amserdam it is, thank Heaven, not so."[13] Here the Yiddish of Amsterdam is set up as the only

[11] Cf. Grünbaum, *op. cit.*, p. 111.

[12] H. Brugmans and A. Frank, *op. cit.*, p. 552; Jacob Shatzky: [The Introductions to Joseph Maarsen's Works], *Yivo-Bleter* 13 (1938), p. 382.

[13] *Ṣe'ena u-re'ena*, Khaim Drucker, published by Cornelis van Hoogenhuysen, 1711.

justified model. The book *Birkas hamozn*, 1722, states on the title page: "The songs [♮*zmjrvθ*] have also been translated in an entirely different way, / For in the previous translation [♮*tjjts*] a great deal was lacking. / And everyone complains / That one gets no understanding out of this translation."[14] Finally, here is an example from the rimed preface to a book of Yiddish prayers for women (*tkhines*) published in Amsterdam in 1711: "Since I saw / That the previous prayers are far too crude, / Not only because they were written in bad language, / But failed even in the translation, / I therefore hastily decided / To take a little time / And to do the women a great favor, / So that when they pray for their souls and bodies, / They should understand the prayers, / And not let the words leave their mouths / Without understanding and without devotion. / Whoever heard them had to laugh."[15]

The feeling that users of another type of Yiddish spoke a "corrupt language" was mutual.

III

In reconstructing the Yiddish spoken in Holland in previous centuries, we cannot depend on written or printed documents as our primary or exclusive source. In the first place, older Yiddish spelling made no pretense of being phonetic; the latter *vav*, for example, is found representing regularly both /u/ and /o/, and sometimes other sounds as well. Secondly, there are numerous inconsistencies even within the ambiguous spelling; Yiddish is in this no different from other European languages in their pre-modern stage. We need not be surprised at finding, in an Amsterdam collection of customs,[16] varying spellings which reflect an alternation between *gevest* and *gevezn* 'been', *gehobt* and *gehot* 'had', sometimes even within a single line.

In view of these difficulties, we have to begin the reconstruction from such remnants of the idiom as have survived in spoken form. We cannot enter here into a full characterization of the language; suffice it to point out some of its salient dialectological features. Corresponding to the medieval German diphthongs *ei*, *au*, and *öü*, we have, in many instances in Dutch Yiddish, *aa*; according to a widely accepted classification, this characteristic marks it as Western Yiddish.[17] In the following examples, Dutch Yiddish forms are compared with St(andard) Y(iddish) and with M(iddle) H(igh) G(erman).

Dutch Y.	St. Y.	M.H.G.	
raakh	*roykh*	*rouch*	'smoke'
taap	*toyb*	*toup*	'deaf'
kaafn	*koyfn*	*koufen*	'to buy'
braat	*breyt*	*breit*	'wide'
haas	*heys*	*heiz*	'hot'
vaas	*veys*	*weiz*	'knows'
glaaben	*gleybn*	**glöüben*	'to believe'

[14] *Birkat hamazon*, ed. Proops, Amsterdam, 1722.

[15] *Seder teḥinot*, printed by Moses ben Abraham Mendes Coutinho, Amsterdam, 1711.

[16] *Minhogim Hirts Leyvi Royfe* (*Minhagim H. L. Rofe*), printed by Isaac di Cordua, Amsterdam, 1723.

[17] M. Weinreich: [Outlines] (see footnote 4), pp. 41f.

Two proverbs which are laden with words of this type are: *ver es nit glaabt is aakh e yehude* 'whoever does not believe it is also a Jew' (in answer to a tall tale); *vas aaner nit vaas makht aanem nit haas* 'what one doesn't know doesn't make one hot', i.e. 'what you don't know won't hurt you'. A number of words in which M.H.G. has *î* (*mîn* 'my', *sîn* 'his') also have *aa*.

Both *e* and *ö*, whether originally long or subsequently lengthened, are represented by *ey* (phonetically [ɛj]): *geyn* 'to go', *heybn* 'to lift', *meylekh* 'king,' *sheyn* 'beautiful', *neytik* 'necessary'. These sounds have merged with the regular correspondent of M.H.G. *î*: *reybn* 'to rub, grate'. (There are *ey*'s of still other derivation.) Cf. *ish hob im neytik om kreyn tse reybn* 'I need him for grating horseradish', i.e. 'I wouldn't dream of accepting his offer'.

Quite distinctive is the development of older *u* to *o*: *kokn* 'to look' (St.Y. *kukn*), *mos* 'must' (St.Y. *muz*), *kaals-shtob* 'community house' (St.Y. *-shtub*), *khotspe* 'impudence' (St.Y. *khutspe*), *soke* 'Tabernacle' (St.Y. *suke*), *khope* 'wedding canopy' (St.Y. *khupe*), *meshoge* 'crazy' (St.Y. *meshuge*), *yeroshe* 'inheritance' (St.Y. *yerushe*). Cf. the proverb *vi meer khotspe, vi meer balmazel* 'the more impudence, the greater one's luck'. Old long *ô* or lengthened *o* correspond to Dutch Yiddish [ou]: *brout* 'bread' (St.Y. *broyt*), *voul* 'well' (St.Y. *voyl*), etc. When someone promises to send a gift, he may still hear the comment: *shikn makht houln* 'sending leads to fetching'. This diphthong *ou* is distinct from a long [oo] occurring in such words as *bemoore* 'in fear' (St.Y. *moyre*), *skhoore* 'merchandise' (St.Y. *skhoyre*).

The principal characteristic of the consonant pattern is the merger of the old *ich*-sound with [š]; cf. words like *ish* 'I', *lisht* 'light', *nebish* 'poor thing', *riisht* 'smells', *kíishelish* 'cookies' (St.Y. *kíkhelekh*).

Some of the common word-formation patterns are also of the Western Yiddish type. The suffix *-kat* (St.Y. *-keyt*, *-kayt*) is highly productive: *nárishkat* 'foolishness', *míiskat* 'ugliness', *khálеshkat* (usually) 'unpleasant person', *típeshkat* 'foolishness'. Feminines are formed in *-te*: *khámerte* 'stupid woman' (lit. 'she-ass'), *khaznte* 'cantor's wife', *miise menoblte* 'ugly woman'. Some nouns have double feminine indications: *narnte* 'foolish woman', *meshogéeste* 'crazy woman'; through the blurring of the original meaning, even *óorlte* 'Christian woman' has become possible (*óorl* = literally 'uncircumcised one'). The characteristic East Yiddish derivational suffixes of Slavic origin, like *-nik* or *-ke*, are unknown.

The vocabulary is also typically Western Yiddish: *tetshn* 'to blow (the Shofar)' (St.Y. *blozn*), *harle* 'grandfather' (St.Y. *zeyde*), *fraale* 'grandmother' (St.Y. *bobe*), *ete* 'father' (St.Y. *tate*), *meme* 'mother' (St.Y. *mame*), *mémele* 'aunt' (St.Y. *mume*), *shveyen* 'to marry (jocul.)', *geshvéy* 'brother-in law' (St.Y. *shvoger*), *tsveel* 'tablecloth' (St.Y. *tishtekh*), *shiibert* 'mask' (St.Y. *maske*), *shiir* 'soon' (St.Y. *shir* (*nit*) = 'almost'; 'soon' = *bald*). The Slavic loanwords that have penetrated from Eastern into Dutch Yiddish are extremely few. *Khapn* (St.Y. 'to catch') is used for 'to steal', but in Dutch as well as in Yiddish. *Khotshe* 'although' is also current. Occasionally one hears *zeyde* 'grandfather' instead of *harle*. An oath like *miise-meshine* 'an unnatural death' has Eastern Yiddish vocalism; in Dutch Yiddish, *-meshone* would be expected.

It is entirely plausible that, except for minor details, the Yiddish of Holland which is reflected in the documents of the seventeenth and eighteenth centuries was of the same variety as has survived in isolated remnants. To read the older Dutch Yiddish texts, we must learn to discount the purely conventional spelling, which was of an all-European scope, and realize that a word spelled ♮*qvjp̄ń*, which may have been read *koyfn*, *koufn*, or *keyfn* in the East, stood for *kaafn* in the West; similarly, ♮*p̄ljjs* stood for *flaash*, ♮*vvjjs* for *vaas*, etc.

It is significant that the closer we get to the year 1800, the more the spoken language breaks through the conventional literary language.[18] To put it another way, as the eighteenth century was ending, the all-European Yiddish writing convention was breaking down. The Yiddish language community of Holland was growing more isolated and a more natural relation between speech and writing was emerging.[19] One of the orthographic effects of the colloquialization of written Yiddish was the replacement of the digraph ♮*vj* by ♮*ʔ* (aleph) in representing the sound [aa]. We find this alternation in most Western Yiddish works of the Middle Yiddish period. For example, Glückel von Hameln in her Memoirs[20] regularly writes ♮*vvʔtcjń* 'wheat', ♮*brʔt* 'broad', etc., but alternates between ♮*mjjt* and ♮*mʔt* 'maid', ♮*ʔdjḿ* and ♮*ʔjjdvḿ* 'son-in-law', ♮*ljjqnjń* and ♮*lʔqnjń* 'to deny'.[21]

Incidentally, it is safe to assume an *aa*-pronunciation for Glückel, and in general, in view of many other correspondences with Holland Yiddish, there is no reason to doubt that her pronunciation was close in many important respects to what we know of Dutch Yiddish. Thus new light is thrown on some of the unclear aspects of her seventeenth-century Yiddish. Her spellings ♮*nvjt*, *tvjt*, *grvjs* can safely be read *nout* 'need', *tout* 'death', *grous* 'big'. Without the benefit of comparison with a surviving variety of Western Yiddish, students of Glückel are likely to draw erroneous conclusions. Thus, Landau states that the letter *yud* (♮*j*) may represent *ê*, *ö*, *i* and *ü*, quoting as examples ♮*ʔjbjg* 'eternal' and ♮*tjtjń* 'to kill' (*op. cit.*, p. 33). But if Dutch Yiddish is a clue, Glückel pronounced *ey* in all these words. More problematic is the spelling ♮*vj* in words like ♮*stvjb*, *p̄rvjḿ*, *dvjrḱ*. Landau supposes (p. 34) an *au*-pronunciation; but it entirely possible that this spelling indicated *o*, as in Dutch Yiddish: *shtob* 'house', *from* 'pious', *dorkh* 'through'.

One other feature of Middle Yiddish vocalism which has its equivalent in the spoken Yiddish of Holland is the merger of some long *ô*'s with *ou* (see p. 127 above). Thus, in the "Scroll of Vints" of 1648 (see footnote 3), stanza 39, we find ♮*crh* 'trouble' riming with ♮*mvrʔ* 'fear'; these words do not rime in any Eastern Yiddish dialect (*tsore* : *meyre* or *tsure* : *moyre*), but do so in Dutch Yid-

[18] Cf. the Purim pamphlets of Shlomo Duikelaar and others, listed by Shatzky in the study mentioned in footnote 2.

[19] Significantly, parallel developments were taking place in Eastern Europe at the same time; cf. Judah A. Joffe: [150 Years of Yiddish], *Yivo-bleter* 15 (1940) 87–102, and N. Shtif: [On the Threshold of the Nineteenth Century], *Yidishe shprakh* (Kiev), no. 29–30 (1932), 33–37.

[20] *Die Memoiren der Glückel von Hameln (1645–1719)*, ed. David Kaufmann, Frankfurt/M., 1896, lxxii + 360 pp.

[21] Alfred Landau: "Die Sprache der Memoiren Glückels von Hameln," *Mitteilungen für jüdische Volkskunde* no. 7 (1901), 20–68, p. 35.

dish: *tsoore* : *moore*. (In the Dutch pronunciation of Hebrew, they are *mauro, tsooro*.)

IV

The distinctly Western character of Dutch Yiddish supports the assumption that it was German Jews who were predominant in the formation of the Ashkenazic communities of Holland. Not that the German-Jewish settlement of Holland took place entirely by way of Amsterdam: many smaller but not insignificant communities in the north and east of Holland were also founded by immigrant German Jews. Thus the town of Emden, which is well known as a Portuguese point of transit, seems to have been a jumping-off point for the founding of Jewish communities in the north of Holland; their *mémorbikher* ('memorial books') often reflect Emden traditions, such as an annual memorial prayer for Rabbi Uri Fayvush Halevi who taught Judaism to the marranos of Emden. To be sure, Amsterdam absorbed many Jews from Slavic territories, too, but their influence on Holland Yiddish was slight and did not leave any but the most casual traces. It should be recalled that in the seventeenth century the difference between the two types of Yiddish was in any case not as great as later on.

A word might be said about the influence of Low German on the Yiddish of Holland as a result of the immigration of North German Jews to Holland. Certain Low German loanwords in Dutch Yiddish have been incorrectly labeled as Hollandisms. Grünbaum, for example, classifies *dokters*[22] 'doctors' (occurring in Blits' Bible, but also in the "Scroll of Vints") in this category, yet the form is nothing but the normal equivalent of the Latin plural, *doctores*. The word *shiir* 'soon',[23] which survives in the Passover seder song "El beneh" (*almékhtiger got, nu bau daan templ shiire*), was known in this meaning in medieval German and has little to do with Dutch. Nor are *eiser* 'iron' (p. 118) or *vakher* 'awake' (pp. 112, 379) Hollandisms. Yet these examples have been uncritically cited even in Brugmans and Frank's History (see footnote 7). Van Ginneken cites 18 Hollandisms from an Amsterdam edition of *Yoysifon* (*Yosipon*), when in reality they are old legitimate Yiddish forms. Some so-called Hollandisms are rather Low German forms; *fartseyln* 'to tell', cited by Grünbaum as a Dutch loan because of its prefix, is current not only in Low German and in North German Yiddish (Glückel!), but also in High German and in the bulk of East European Yiddish. The real Hollandization which made the Yiddish of Holland nearly unintelligible to other Yiddish speakers did not take place until the eighteenth century.

For purposes of illustrating this development, we present two fragments from a handwritten record book (*ḥσpr hzkrvnvθ*) of the Jewish community in Leeuwarden.[24] It is written in the typical "chancellery" style of Yiddish, with

[22] *Op. cit.* (footnote 1), p. 107.

[23] *Ibid.*, p. 346, footnote 7.

[24] In the archives of the Jewish community of Leeuwarden. During World War II they were concealed by the then State Archivist Dr. A. L. Heerma van Voss and thus survived, in contrast to the valuable archives of many other Jewish communities.

frequent interspersals of Hebrew and even literary German. We have transcribed the text, for the sake of reconstruction, as it would be read by a surviving speaker of Dutch Yiddish. Transliterated segments are preceded by ♮.

[No. 10] *Hayóum youm olf kaf kheshvon ♮θqt''v lpq hobn hamanhiigiim ♮jcv geresulevíirt das Feys bar Youseyf zol shamesh bik-hiiloseynu zeyn, vorfíir er zol geniisn in es shoone sakh finftsish gildn, und anfang zol nemen meyrosh-khoudesh kheshvon ♮θqt''v vegám ale rosh-khoudesh kislev olf reyshstoler far torf und ale rosh-khoudesh nisn far matses olf reyshstoler vorfíir er zol es shamoshus bediinen vii es geheert, nishts tsu toon bousn order fun manhiigiim ♮jcv vegám ale morgens tehiliim zoogn beveys-hakneses uveím er etvas toot neged hamanhíigiim ♮jcv zoln hamanhiigiim ♮jcv kouakh hobn kefíi reóus eyneyhem und nakhdem zish dii zakhe virt tsutroogn iim tsu knasn und zonstn zish tsu troogn, vii zish eyn shamesh geheert tsu troogn, velshes ish, Feys bar Youseyf, aakh ánneeme tsu toon gleysh darín fermélt ist vegám ouftsuhoulen shtat- un tsedoko-moos, vorfíir veyter nishts zol hobn tsu pretendirn.*

('Today, Sunday, the 20th of Ḥešvan of the year 515, omitting the thousands [i.e. 5515 = 1755 A.D.], the [community] leaders M. R. G. [may their Rock and Guardian preserve them] resolved that Feys [< Phoebus] the son of Joseph should be sexton in our community, for which he should receive annually the sum of fifty gulden, starting with the beginning of Ḥešvan [5]515; and also on the first of every month of Kislev [he should receive] one reichstaler for peat and on the first of every month of Nissan one reichstaler for matzot, in return for which he should serve the sextonship properly, without doing anything unless ordered by the leaders M. R. G., and also recite psalms every morning in the prayerhouse, and if he does something against the leaders M. R. G., the leaders M. R. G. should have the power according to their estimation, and after the matter will have happened, to fine him, and otherwise [he should] behave as a sexton ought to behave, which I, Feys the son of Joseph, also accept to do just as is recorded herein, and also to collect pew fees and charity money, against which I should have no further claims.')

Next is an announcement by the community leaders from the same record book, sixty years later:

[No. 498] *Parnosiim ♮jcv makhn hiirmít beként, das zii tsur gelégnheyt fun dii éynhuldigung min adouneynu haprínts yoorum houdou als meylekh der níiderlande ettsétera velshe pléshtige und gedénkvirdige toog shabes ♮hb℘'l zeyn virt, kaan min haseroore yoorum houdou entfangen hobn eyn gevise sume geld velshe an unzer tsedooke zo voul vii an dii fun ale gezíndhedn tsúgeteylt vert um dii pléshtige toog mit ale zolemnitéet und dánkzoogung an der alerheshsten tsu iberbrengen und unser geliibter monarkh mazkir letouvo tsu zeyn, bekhéyn vern hoalufiim parnosiim ♮jcv heynt oobend um akht auer bekheyder hakohol zitsung haltn und das geld ♮hn'l mekhalek zayn an aniim veevyouniim bik-hiloseynu ♮vh' b''h yivoreykh veyishmour es adouneynu hamelekh ♮j''h veyiteyn loonu toomid kheyn vekhesed be-eynov láasous touvo imoonu veim kol yisrooel oméyn. Leoyvardn, youm hey, yuud olf ooder sheynii ♮θq℘'h, biifekuudas ♮pvḿ jcv, vii aakh ♮pvḿ jcv diizélbige oobend makhalek hobn gevezn leyakhad dii sume fun ♮℘h gildn.*

('The administrators M. G. R. herewith announce that on the occasion of the oath of allegiance of our ruler the prince [of Orange, King William I], M. H. P. E. [may his power be exalted], as king of the Netherlands etcetera, which solemn and memorable day will be on the Sabbath which is coming (to bring us good), here have received from the town council M. H. P. E. a certain sum of money which is assigned to our charity as well as to that of all the denominations for dedicating the ceremonial day with all solemnity and thanksgiving to the All-Highest and to remember our beloved monarch favorably; now therefore the honorable administrators M. G. R. will hold a meeting tonight at eight o'clock in the community chamber and will distribute the above money to the poor and destitute in our community and the Lord, blessed is He, will bless and preserve our ruler the king M. H. P. E. and forever have us find favor and grace in his eyes to do good to us and to all Israel, amen. Leeuwarden, Thursday, 11th day in the Second Adar [5]575 [= 1815 A. D.], by order of the A. & L. [= administrators and leaders] M. R. G.; item, A. & L., M. R. G., on the same evening distributed together the sum of 75 gulden.')

While the first fragment, of 1755, shows the old language relatively well preserved (*bousen* 'without' is not a Hollandism), the second passage, of 1815, shows a considerable number of Hollandisms (*plechtig, solemniteet, gezindheden,* etc.) and other foreign elements. To understand this, let us remember that until 1795 the development of Yiddish was allowed to take its course, while after that year the struggle against Yiddish, by Jews as well as non-Jews, had begun.

The increasing Hollandization of Yiddish after 1700 is probably connected with the fact that in the eighteenth century most of the Dutch Jews were more or less conversant with Dutch. Ashkenazic Jews even published books in this language. The Jewish peddlers and merchants could not make a living without a knowledge of the language of the Christians. Only in Amsterdam, with its large Jewish quarter, were the conditions somewhat different: here, too, the many small merchants who had to seek their livelihood in the non-Jewish streets had to use Dutch, but as for the Jewish quarter, there is an instructive local proverb: *for dii brik retish, hinter dii brik ramenás* 'before the bridge [over the river Amstel, connecting the Jewish Section with the rest of the city] radishes are called [in Yiddish] *retish*, beyond the bridge they are called [in Dutch] *ramenas*.'

V

While most Jews, for better or for worse, spoke Dutch, few of them learned to read or write it. On this point the schools, which functioned as bulwarks of the old *yídishkat* 'Jewish way of life' well into the nineteenth century, also were decisive. The medium of instruction in the Jewish schools had been Yiddish exclusively; and when "Felix Libertate," the organization of political reformers, in 1797 launched its attack upon Yiddish, the *kheyder* (traditional school) and its teachers formed the core of the resistance.

As we said earlier, the bulk of Dutch Jewry at first set little store by emancipation and regarded assimilation with hostility. While the economic position of the Jewish proletariat was precarious, there was reason to be satisfied with the political situation. The Jews did not enjoy full civic rights, yet they were no less privileged than other groups that did not belong to the state church, and they were traditionally treated with favor by the House of Orange. Therefore the political reformers at first found themselves crying in the wilderness as the bulk of the population held to the premise, *mir veln bleybn vas mir zenen* 'we shall remain what we are', a "Hebrew nation" under the protection of Orange. And nothing was further from the thoughts of the masses than the abandonment of Yiddish. Whoever thinks that Yiddish died in Holland without a fierce struggle is completely wrong.

The men of "Felix Libertate," representing the new French ideas, began by forming a "New Community" (*neye kile*) in opposition to the old. In the years 1797–98 they published the periodical *Diskurs* (see footnote 7) in which, among others, Yiddish was attacked. However, they were forced by practical considerations to resort to Yiddish as the medium of their pro-Dutch, anti-Yiddish propaganda; for as Hirsch, one of the *laudatores temporis acti* put it in the *Diskursn, galkhes kenen mir nit laaynen* 'we cannot read Dutch' (lit. 'the Christian language' < *galakh* 'priest').

A passage in *Diskursn* no. 7, 1797, casts an informative light on the language conditions of the day. The adherents of the "New Community" write: "The [old] administrators are crude ignoramuses; they are not only ignoramuses from the Jewish point of view but they are also mute when it is necessary to speak to the Christians. Whatever they have to write in Dutch must be done by a notary public." It appears that even the administrators, who ordinarily consisted of wealthy people, could not then write Dutch.

A few years later, the reformers turned for help to King Louis Napoleon, who ruled in Holland from 1806 to 1810. This king, a brother of Napoleon Bonaparte, wished the Jews well and hoped to help them by supporting their assimilation. He decided to form a Jewish military corps; the decree was promulgated in a kind of Yiddish which is probably unique.[25] In the year 1809 Louis Napoleon ordered the Bible translated into Dutch for the special use of the Jews. The Supreme Consistory called on the Chief Rabbis to promote the Dutch language; uncooperative officials were threatened with the loss of their positions. But in vain: Chief Rabbi Löwenstamm of Amsterdam reported that his command of Dutch was insufficient to check the Bible translation; Rabbi Herzfeld of Zwolle pleaded illness and lack of time; Rabbi Lehman of the Hague refused outright. Only Rabbi Berenstein of Leeuwarden sent in some comments on the subject. The teachers referred to the ban of the rabbis. Thus the translation project failed just as Louis Napoleon's rule came to an end. Napoleon Bonaparte, incorporating Holland into the French Empire after 1810, had other worries and did not pursue the matter. In 1817, William I renewed the royal decree concerning the Bible translation. When, in 1827, the government made available medals for the authors of the best sermons and schoolbooks for the Jews in Dutch, the response was relatively indifferent; until 1840 the sermons and announcements in the synagogues remained in Yiddish, be it of an increasingly mutilated variety. In

[25] The full text is reprinted in Voorzanger and Polak, *op. cit.*, pp. 20–22.

1834, the administrators of the Utrecht community attempted for the first time to have the sexton read an announcement in the synagogue in Dutch; the indignant tumult which arose was so great that the plan had to be abandoned.

In 1844 Koenen, the non-Jewish historian of the Jews of Holland, described the Dutch language among the Jews as a weak plant on sandy soil which could be overturned and uprooted by even a feeble wind.[26] In 1867, the *Kerkeraad* ('Church Council'!) of the "High German [Jewish] Community" of Amsterdam entertained a motion to discontinue annual Yiddish sermons on *šabbat hagadol* and *šabat šuba*, but the administrators replied that the time was not yet ripe. As late as 1850, the house of Proops in Amsterdam considered it worthwhile to publish a calendar for the year 5611 which is, except for a few pages, entirely in Yiddish. Even information on ferry and mail schedules, so easily available elsewhere in Dutch, was here included in Yiddish.

The last Chief Rabbi to preach in Yiddish was Dusnus of Leeuwarden, who officiated until 1886. When, after his death, the new Chief Rabbi for the first time delivered a sermon in elegant Dutch, part of the old guard left the synagogue in dismay, saying: *in shuul veln mir keyn galkhes heern* 'in the synagogue we will not listen to the Christian language.'

Yiddish as a language has disappeared among Dutch Jews, of whom only a small minority escaped the Nazis in the recent war. However, the Dutch language has absorbed numerous loanwords from Yiddish, more perhaps than other languages. There is not a Dutchman who does not know the words *gochem* (< *khookhem* 'clever, shrewd'), *schofel* 'shabby', *lef* 'heart', *balleboos* 'householder', *dalles* 'poverty', *chappen* 'to steal' (see p. 137 above), *schiker* 'drunk', *sof* 'end'. Along with many others, these words have acquired Dutch citizenship and travel with Dutch passports. What is more important is that in the speech of surviving Dutch Jews there are innumerable Yiddish words, locutions, and proverbs still current, as will be demonstrated by a collection which will soon be published by the present writer.

Shtarbt der rebe, lebt es seyfer 'the rabbi dies, the book lives on'.

[26] H. J. Koenen: *Geschiedenis der Joden in Nederland*, Utrecht, 1845, p. 399.

ALTER TERAKH: THE BYWAYS OF LINGUISTIC FUSION[1]

DOV SADAN (Jerusalem)

I

"There is no old man except a wise one; one is not old unless one has acquired wisdom." Thus taught the sages of the Talmud.[2] Yet the epithet *an alter terakh*, meaning 'an old fool', is an extremely common expression in Yiddish, in the spoken language as well as in the literature. Yehuda Avida (Zlotnik), the well-known Jewish folklorist, cites the following usages:[3] *an alter terakh*, occurring in the works of all three major Yiddish writers of the modern period, Mendele, Sholom Aleichem, and Peretz; *fun terakhs tsaytn* 'from the days of Terah', used by Mendele; *a terakh* 'a fool', used by Mendele; and finally the macaronic expression *hoho! prishól terakh na derakh*,[4] first recorded by Bernstein,[5] employed as a humorous comment about someone who, after long deliberations, has at last hit upon the right idea. But Avida provides no explanation of the origin of these expressions, except for noting that *Terakh* was the father of the patriarch Abraham.[6] Many years later Avida returned to the problem,[7] and came to the conclusion, on the basis of the same quotations, that the expression was a corruption of *an alter toyrakh* 'an old burden'. *Toyrakh can be derived from the root *ṭrḥ* (cf. Yiddish *tirkhe*, dial. *terkhe* 'pains, effort'), and actually occurs in a relevant context in a Hebrew song of the 11th-century poet, Abraham ibn-Ezra: *ben šmonim ṭaraḥ 'al banav* 'a man of eighty is a burden to his children'.

We have here, then, either a corruption or a popular pun—*ṭrḥ* being replaced by *trḥ*—which attributes the foolishness of old age to Abraham's father. I had come to a similar conclusion in my book *Ḳa'arat ṣimuḳim* ("A Dish of Raisins," Tel Aviv, 1950). In connection with a joke containing a reference to Terah (no. 36, p. 27) I noted that Yiddish *terakh*, or *alter terakh*—both signifying '(old) fool'—have nothing to do with the biblical Terah. It had been noted by Noyakh Prilutski that German cant (which, as is well known, borrowed many terms from Yiddish) contains the expressions *tarchenen*, *targenen*, *dergen*, *derchen* 'to raise one's hand to beg, to go begging'; *tarchener* 'poor man, peddler, pocket-thief'.[8] To this was appended a remark by the distinguished folklorist A. A.

[1] A summary of the present paper appeared in Hebrew [On the Matter of *alter Terakh*] in *Lešonenu le'am* (Jerusalem) 5 (1954-55), no. 1, 12–16.

[2] Ḳiddušin 32:72.

[3] Yehude Elzet: [Idioms], in *Bay undz yidn*, ed. M. Wanwild, Warsaw, 1923, 187–206, p. 199.

[4] *Prishól*—Russian 'came'; *na*—Russian 'onto'; *derekh*—Hebrew 'road'; thus: 'Ha! Terah has gotten onto the right path [at last]'.

[5] Ignacy Bernstein: *Yidishe shprikhverter un rednsartn*, Warsaw, ₂1908, p. 294.

[6] Genesis 11:27. The Yiddish standard spelling of this epithet —ḥθrx— presupposes that it is the biblical name which is involved.

[7] In his article, [Desserts], in *Haṣofeh* (Tel Aviv), no. 4195 (October 9, 1951).

[8] [The Language of (Jewish) Musicians in Poland], *Rešumot* 1 (1925) 272–291, p. 274, s.v. *aráynterkhenen*.

Druyanov that in Lithuanian Yiddish there is an expression *an alter terkher*, which he interprets as *a zokn a tarkhn* 'an old man [who is] a troublesome person'. By this particular gloss (*tarkhn* is equivalent to Hebrew *ṭarḥan*), Druyanov seems to have been the first to postulate a connection between Yiddish *terakh* and *ṭrḥ* 'to cause trouble'.[9]

Let it be pointed out that readers of Hebrew may long have been aware of this connection. Yehuda-Leb Gordon says of an innkeeper, in his popular story *Ḳefiṣat-haderek*:[10] "I heard that the coachmen called him Reb Terakh, and I also called him that. And when I asked Reb Gershon, the preacher, why the innkeeper was called Terakh [*trḥ*], he said: 'Because he is a very painstaking person [*ṭarḥan*].' The innkeeper was a handy fellow. Because of the pains he took, Reb Gershon again began praising him before the whole gathering and said: 'Why do they call him Terakh? Because everything he took pains to do [*ṭaraḥ*] he did for my sake only.' "

II

The explanation supplied by Gordon is almost the same as Druyanov's and Avida's, except that he interprets *ṭarḥan* 'painstaking person' in a complimentary rather than in a disparaging way. There remains the question as to how the error or the pun originated. How did it happen that scholars and learned writers, no less than the common people, appointed Terah, Abraham's father, as the paragon of age and foolishness? On the score of age, a more likely candidate would have been Methuselah, who exceeded in years his forefather Adam and his grandson Noah. There is, in fact, a German saying, *den alten Adam ausziehen* or *ersaufen*, of Gospel origin, although the adjective *alt* refers here to antiquity rather than to old age.[11] As far as Noah is concerned, there is the famous legend told by the Sages according to which Noah, after having given warning of the flood, "was humiliated and was told: 'Old man, what good is the ark to you?' "[12] Terah, on the other hand, does not seem ever to have been explicitly described as old. Nevertheless, in the midrashic description of the conversation between Abraham and Terah about the idols, there is a clearly implied contrast between

[9] It is interesting to note, on this point, that the expression *terkher* survives in German dialects to this day. In a collection of Tirolian wedding songs (*Quellen und Forschungen zur deutschen Volkskunde*, Vienna, 1908, vol. 3, p. 136) there is a song of a bridegroom who wants to accompany his fiancée continually in order to *sie keinem Hottler, Bettler, Törcher überlassen* 'not to abandon her to a ragdealer, beggar, or tramp'. There is an even more emphatic usage (*ibid.*, pp. 176, 177): *Sautörcher*, and a feminine derivative (p. 183): *Törcherin*. Cf. also J. Andreas Schmeller: *Bayerisches Wörterbuch*, Stuttgart–Tübingen, 1827–37, vol. 1, p. 536 ("derchen"); Hermann Fischer: *Schwäbisches Wörterbuch*, Tübingen, 1908, vol. 2, p. 159; vol. 6, p. 1742 ("derchen").

[10] *Kol kitbe Y.-L. Gordon*, vol. 1, Odessa, 1889, 145–186, p. 182.

[11] In some customs, Adam may have appeared as an actually *old* man; thus the Christians of medieval Halberstadt used to expel a poor criminal, symbolizing Adam, from the local church and force him throughout Lent to beg for food at the church doors in his bare feet until the last meal of Maundy Thursday, when he would again be admitted. See Borchardt–Wustmann: *Die sprichwörtlichen Redensarten im deutschen Volksmund*, Leipzig, 1925, pp. 11f.

[12] *Berešit rabbah* 28; *Midraš hagadol*.

the smart young son and the foolish old father. The contrast between age and wisdom is paralleled in a further incident. An elderly, dignified man who came to buy an idol was asked by Abraham: "How many years do you have?" (*Ben kamah šanim 'atah?*) and he replied: "Sixty years." The question translated into Yiddish gives *Vi alt bistu?* i.e. "How old are you?" with a clear reference to old age. The old age and the stupidity of the customer may have been transferred to the seller, Terah, who was, after all, no longer young himself; we are told that Terah was seventy when his son Abraham was born.

In homiletic literature Terah became imbued with all the shortcomings of old age. But the climax was apparently reached by the poet Shimen Frug, who uses Terah as a comparison for a rickety structure:[13]

Shteyt a brikl shoyn a yor
Zekhtsik–zíbetsik an erekh,
Krum un foyl un alt vi Terakh,
On remont,
Tristshet, treyslt zikh, nor gornit:
Az eyn breyre—vilst nit, for nit.

('A bridge has been standing for approximately sixty or seventy years, crooked and rotten and *old as Terah*, unrepaired; it squeaks and shakes, but nothing is made of it; there is no alternative: if you don't want to, don't cross it.')

Another poet, on the contrary, took pity on Terah. Y. Bovshover, in his poem "Two Worlds: Terah and Abraham,"[14] characterizes Terah as a man who has recognized the hollowness of the idols but does not have the strength to fight for the insight he has acquired and continues to produce stone deities:

Ikh kuk oyf zey mit tsveyfl ruik-shtil,
Shnítsndik bin ikh gevorn alt—
Kh'bin tsu alt tsu shtraytn mit der velt.

('I look at them [the idols] peacefully; in carving them I have *grown old;* I am too old to fight the world.')

A similar conception, though far more profound, is to be found in a poem by H. Royznblat.[15] He describes Terah lamenting his dead idols. The theme is that Terah believes in a single God, but he has compassion for those who do not share this powerful insight and for whom the idols are like sparks of faith for the blind. The poem begins with an emphasis on Terah's age:

A vayser kop geboygn tsu der erd,
Tsvey úmetike oygn mide . . .

('A white head bent to the ground, two sad and tired eyes . . .')

In the light of these references, it is curious to find the epithet of Terah's age transferred to his son. Yet Kalmen Heyzler[16] describes a Purim player in

[13] *Ale shriftn*, New York, 1910, vol. 2, pp. 174f.

[14] Fragment of an uncompleted drama. See his *Gezamlte shriftn*, New York, 1911, p. 85.

[15] [Terah Weeps Over His Dead Idols], *Yidisher kemfer* (New York), 34 (1953), September 11 (Rosh hashanah 5714), p. 77.

[16] *Mayne kumarner, nebekh*, New York, 1953, p. 21.

his home town who, in a play about the sacrifice of Isaac, has the angel say to Abraham: "I am the angel Gabriel; don't be an old fool, then" (*zay zhe nisht keyn alter nar*).

The view of Terah as a symbol of the weaknesses of old age is well established. It can be profusely illustrated in plays reflecting popular usage. In a work by Y. L. Boymvol,[17] a mother who does not want to marry off her daughter to an old widower says to him: "You don't want to take Leah the widow, yet an old Terah like you wants to take my daughter! May these words of mine not count as a sin . . ." Further on, the expression is replaced, but the substitution seems significant: "All right, then, there is no other way, she will have to fall in love with an old sinner [*bal-aveyre*]" (p. 51). In another play,[18] Boymvol says: "An old Terah like that dares to possess such a blossoming rose!" And then (p. 31): "How he kisses her, the old Haman!" And again (p. 53): "If you won't listen to me, you are an old fool [*alter nar*]." Similar usage can be found in the plays of Z. Kornblit, who says of a dancer returning a gift to her old lover:[19] "What a foolish girl! One could extract the very soul from an old Terah like that." Later on (p. 41): "An old half-dead sinner [*bal-avéyrenik*] like you."

III

It is worth noting that the use of 'Terah' as a sobriquet of ridicule has a long tradition in Hebrew letters, beginning at least with Ḳalonymus ben Ḳalonymus, a poet of thirteenth-century Provence, who mobilized a host of biblical names that lend themselves to comical interpretation.[20]

Mehen marat Seraḥ,
Bat harab R. Teraḥ,
Umarat Kazbi,
'Ešet R. Baḳbuḳ hanabi',
Ve'izebel hayfefiyah.

('And among them Madame Serakh [*srḥ* 'stink'], the daughter of the rabbi Reb Terakh [*teraḥ* 'Terah'], and Madame Kazbi [*kzb* 'to tell lies'], the wife of the prophet Reb Baḳbuḳ [= 'bottle'], and Jezebel [*'i zebel* 'oh, what dung!'] the beauty.') Quite a company for Terah!

In more recent times we find Yitskhok Kaminer writing:[21]

AHKaasher kol boey shaar habirzo toykhzeym khalkholo,
Gam hagvir Koyrakh ben Terakh gam rukhoy khubolo.

('When all the stock-exchange people were seized by fright, the rich man Korah, the son of Terah, also became downhearted.') That Korah is the name of the hated rich man should cause no surprise; the Midrash has made "Korah's wealth" proverbial. It is even less surprising that his father's name appears as

[17] *Khatskl kolboynik*, ed. 1926, p. 46.
[18] *Madam-frayln*, 1914, p. 26.
[19] *Motye-malakh der stolyer*, Przemyśl, 1908; ed. 1927, p. 39.
[20] In his book *'Eben boḥen*.
[21] *Šire Iṣḥaḳ . . . Ḳaminer*, Odessa, 1905, p. 225.

Terah, since in the Northeastern (Lithuanian) pronunciation of Hebrew, *Keyrakh* and *Terakh* form an almost perfect rime.

Even Kh. N. Bialik, in adapting—apparently, from the German—a fairy tale about a villain, calls him Terah and utilizes the rime contained in the jocular saying recorded by Bernstein (see p. 134):

AH Darkeynu haderekh
Hooylo beys Terakh.

('Our way is the way that leads to Terah's house.')

Let us cite just one more example from Hebrew poetry. Abraham Shlonski mentions Terah, in a reference which does not seem completely clear, using a similar assonance:[22]

Vehayah kakh be'erekh
Lel kuši zaḳen ke-Teraḥ.

('And it was approximately thus, an Ethiopian [black] night old as Terah.')

The vividness of the epithet 'old Terah' may be illustrated in yet another way. Even though proper names do not normally appear in the plural in Hebrew, we do find Terah so inflected. Amos Mossinson writes:[23] *mipi dod vedodah, "traḥim" zeḳenim* ('from the mouth of uncle and aunt, the old Terahs').

The rime used by Ḳalonymus, *seraḥ—teraḥ*, leads to another possibility: *tarḥan zaḳen—sarḥan zaḳen* 'old stinker', which seems to be reflected in Yiddish *an alter shtinker*, a corruption by folk etymology of German *ein alter Stänker* 'an old idler'.

The well established association between Terah and foolishness served the 19th-century writer Yaknehoz as a basis for creating the mythical town name Terakhovke[24] on the pattern of such formations as Glupsk ('sillytown'; cf. Russ. *glupyj* 'stupid') by Mendele Moykher-Sforim.

IV

We have, then, two versions of the same expression: (1) *an alter terakh*, where *terakh* (*trḥ*) refers to Terah, which is by far the most common, although it remains unexplained as a biblical or midrashic allusion; (2) *an alter toyrakh*, where *toyrakh* (*ṭrḥ*) means 'troublesome person', which can be reasonably well explained etymologically, but which is not very widespread. On the contrary, the Talmud, in the same place where it speaks of wise old men (*loc. cit.*), says: "Whence does it follow that an old man should not be burdensome?" The reader is invited to select either version. But he is also invited to consider a third possibility which may, after all, be the most reasonable. Moshe Shamir, the well known young Hebrew writer, reports that as a boy he had asked at his father's house what Terah had to do with old age and foolishness. He was told that this was a transformation of an older expression, *an alter terk* 'an old Turk' (pronounced in some

[22] *'Alilot miḳi mahu*, Tel Aviv, 1947, p. 60.

[23] Amos Mossinson: *Sefer ḥiyukim*, Tel Aviv, 1952.

[24] [Letters to America], *Yidishe folks-bibliotek*, ed. Sholom Aleichem, vol. 1, Kiev, 1888, 275–294, p. 275.

Yiddish dialects as two syllables: *terək*). 'Turk' has served in Yiddish quite fruitfully as a derogatory epithet: *a geleymter terk* 'a lame dummy', *opton af terkish* 'to play a mean trick on', etc. But these connotations must be of recent date and must be associated with the decline of the Ottoman empire. In previous years, the Turks were rather symbols of power and terror. Thus Mordecai-Samuel Girondi writes:[25] "And the man Moses, the great man of his age, put on his sword like an Ismaelite"—that being the designation originally of an Arab and later of a Turk. The conception of the Turk as a savage, belligerent man fits well into the usage of many other languages. Eduard Damköhler[26] in his book on the dialect of Cattenstedt notes, in connection with the word *tarke:* "Among many old men I still found great fear of the Turks."

Consequently it is not reasonable after all to consider *Ter(e)k* as the basis of our *terakh;* we need to search, rather, for a root word of which *terakh* as well as *toyrakh* and *ter(e)k* are corruptions.

V

In order to discover that root word, it is worth inquiring into the designations for 'fool' in the older German language. For Middle High German, three principal designations are recorded: (1) *narre* (modern German *Narr*); (2) *tôre* (mod. Ger. *Tor*); (3) *giege*, yielding modern German *Geck* or *Gecke*, and Yiddish and Hebrew *yeke*, a disparaging name for 'German Jew', especially common in Israel. The words *narre* and *tôre* were identical in meaning through the Middle Ages, with *tôre* perhaps as the more common one. Brant in his *Narrenschiff etc.* uses both without distinction; but in time—possibly even under his influence—*narre* prevailed. The convergences and divergences of the three words would be worth tracing, but it will suffice for our present purpose to show their one-time simiarity. Johann Lauremberg in *Niederdeutsche Scherzgedichte* of 1652[27] writes:

Man, leidr de Welt is uns so
DÖRICH *und so* GECK.

And Werner der Gartnäre, in his well known *Meier Helmbrecht*, the first German idyll,[28] says:

noch mügt ir hoeren gerne
waz der NARRE *und der gouch*
truoc uf siner huben ouch.

The meaning of *gouch* is 'dummy, fool, demon'; it was subsequently replaced by *gauch* and its cognate, *Geck*.

In the course of time the triad diverged and a differentiation was achieved; in more recent usage *Narr* denotes a fool who is trying to be clever; *Tor* stands

[25] Mordecai Samuel Girondi: [History of the Scholars of Italy and the Rabbis of Padua], *Sefer kerem ḥemed* no. 3, Prague, 1838, 88–96, p. 93.
[26] *Nordharzer Wörterbuch*, Quedlinburg, 1927.
[27] Ed. Wilhelm Braune, Halle/S., 1879, p. 9.
[28] Ed. Friedrich Panzer, Halle/S., 1906, pp. 82f.

for a fool who is naive; and *Geck* designates a fool who dresses up. But *alter Narr*, *alter Tor*, and even *alter Gecke* are basically one and the same; it was Immanuel Kant who observed that, since old age requires the sublime, *so ist ein alter Gecke das verächtlichste Geschöpf* 'therefore an old fop is the most contemptible creature'.

Passing on to *tôre*, *Tor*, we may note that its cognates are very frequent in older Yiddish, especially as adjectives. Thus, the *Kubukh* (ed. 1687, p. 18): *♮ziˀ zˀgtń vvˀz p̄ˀr ˀjjń tˀriktr mˀń ˀjz dˀz*[29] 'They said, what a foolish man is this'; *♮dᵉr ˀlt mˀg vvˀl ˀjjń tˀrjktr mˀń zjjń* 'The old one may well be a foolish man' (*ibid.*); *♮vvᵉr dˀ ˀjz ˀzv tˀrjkt nvń* 'now whoever is so foolish' (p. 27); *♮djˀ dˀzjg tˀrjktj kvˀ* 'this stupid cow' (p. 36). To be sure, this word has become extinct in modern spoken Yiddish, but rudiments survive in idioms to this day, especially in association with *meshuge* 'crazy'. A. A. Avrunin, in his study of folk etymologies,[30] records the saying *mishuge metore ki leoylom khasdoy*, deriving the second word from Hebrew *metoyrof* 'deranged'. Aaron Fürst[31] notes that he heard this expression as a boy from Arminius Vamberi, but does not know how to interpret it. Again, Yomtov Levinski (*ibid.*) relates the following anecdote. A cantor was reciting the great Hallel prayer, one verse at a time, and the congregation was replying after each verse: *ki leoylom khasdoy* 'for eternal is His grace'. At one point someone, in passing the cantor, caused him to drop his prayerbook. The cantor said to him: *binst mishuge tsi meturef?* 'Are you crazy or out of your mind?' The congregation chimed in: *ki leoylom khasdoy*. The expression is supposed to have been current ever since. The interesting point is that all three writers cite the form *metore*; in my own childhood I also heard it, either as *meshige-meture* or as *meshige-metere*. Certainly this form is primary, not the rationalized reconstruction *meturef*, even though the latter also has some currency (either as *metoref* or *meteref*). We have a meaning equivalence: *meshuge* = (*me*)*tore*, almost identical with Middle High German *tôre sîn* 'to play the fool, the madman'.

Another rudiment possibly survives in the word *tures*, *tores*, or *teres* in the expressions *tores traybn*, and especially *tores shpiln*. In the anonymous comedy, *Di genarte velt*, first published in the 1820's, we read (p. 63): *Gleybt mir, es zol do far mir afile tures shpiln, het ikh nisht gekukt* ('Believe me, even if it . . ., I wouldn't look'). The editor of the critical edition[32] notes that the original text had *tures*, and that the meaning of the word is unknown. This is unjustified. *Tores* or *tures* is an expression for 'ridicule' which I, for example, heard many times in Brody; Yoysef Opatoshu, in his personal copy of this book, correctly notes in the margin: 'to ridicule, to make fun of'; *er makht fun im kol-hatores*—i.e. he makes fun of him, for *tores* means a 'comedy'.

At this point we may leave the thicket of explanations of this word, most of

[29] For a key to the transliteration system, see p. vii of this volume.

[30] [Hebrew Words in the Language of the People], *Rešumot* (Tel Aviv), new series 2 (1946) 109–113, p. 112.

[31] *Ibid.*, vol. 4 (1948), p. 198.

[32] Ed. Meyer Viner, Moscow, 1940. This critical edition is based on that of 1863 and the preliminary studies of Nokhem Shtif; page reference is to the 1940 edition.

them along the lines of folk etymology; they led us, on the one hand, back to the medieval tournament and, on the other hand, to the card player's den.

Tores seems to be related, etymologically or by association, with *tôre sîn* 'to make a fool of onseself'. That *kol-hatores* is a humorous allusion to *kol-hatoyres* (< *kol ha-torot* 'all disciplines of learning') is a separate matter.

VI

There remains only one step to be taken from *tôre* to its derived adjective: in older versions, *dörich*, *dorecht*, and more recently *thöricht* or *thörig* (pronounced like *thörich*). We are already at *an alter terikh*, which is the basis of the expressions we have been investigating.[33] Why is the *terekh* old? There might be an allusion to the traditional translation of the words from Ecclesiastes (4:13): "Better is a poor and a wise child than an old and foolish king." But we should anticipate by stating that the process of the displacement of *tôre* by *narre* can be traced both in German and in Yiddish Bible translations. At first the two were not differentiated; even Yehude Leyb Minden, in his glossary *Milim le-'elohah* (Berlin, 1760), translates the same root in two ways: e.g. *'evil* (Hosea 9:7) = ♮*nʔr*, but *'ivelet* (Proverbs 19:3) = ♮*diʔ tʔrhjjt*; or *yiba'aru* (Jeremiah 18:8) = ♮*nʔrjń*, but *ba'ar* (Psalms 92:7) = ♮*tʕrjk̄tʕr*; or else *sakal* (Jeremiah 5:21) = ♮*nʔrjs*, but *ve-śiklut* (Eccl. 1:17) = ♮*tʔrhjjt*. The words of Proverbs 1:4 *latet lifta'im 'armah* 'to give subtlety to the simple' are translated by Mendl Levin (1818) as *tamevate seykhl áyntsugebn*, by *Hamagid* (ed. 1798) ♮*ʔvḿ dʕḿ nʔrjń lj·stjkjjt cv gʔbń*, but an old manuscript, of the 15th century,[34] has (in a Germanizing transcription): *zn geben zu den toren wisheit*. Similarly, for *'evilim bazu* (Proverbs 1:7) 'fools despise', Levin has: *nor naronim kenen mevuze makhn*, while *Hamagid* says: ♮*dj nʔrjń p̄ʔr smʕhń*; the 15th-century manuscript writes: *die doren si ver schmehen*.

Returning to our passage of Ecclesiastes (4:13), the 1679 Yiddish Bible of Yekusiel Blits of Amsterdam has: ♮*ʕs ʔjz bʕsr ʔjjń ʔrjḿ ʔvn' vjjz qjnd vvʕdr ʔjjń ʔltjr qjnjg ʔvn' nrjs*. Levin[35] has: *beser a yunger man un a kluger eyder an alter meylekh un a nárisher*. A popular translation (Ostre [Russ. Ostrog], 1815) runs as follows: *an alter meylekh un a nar*. Another popular translation (Lemberg, 1849): *Der meylekh vos er iz afile alt iz gor a nar*. The translation produced under Moses Mendelssohn's auspices has: *Besser ist ein dürftiger aber ein Jüngling als ein König alt und ein Thor*. Finally, we may contrast the standard version of Martin Luther (*ein alter König der ein Narr ist*) with that of the first German Bible:[36] *Besser ist ein arms kint vnd ein weises eim alten toren kunig*. Here the

[33] To this day the expression is current in modern German. Cf. *Wie es nun zur Abreise kam, wollte der alte thörichte Mann, ich sollte mich entschliessen etc.* (L. Tieck: "Glück giebt Verstand," *Berliner Kalender auf das Gemein-Jahr 1827*, p. 185).

[34] W. Staerck and A. Leitzmann: *Die jüdisch-deutschen Bibelübersetzungen*, Frankfurt/M., 1923, p. 93.

[35] Ed. 1819, photographically reproduced by Yivo, Vilna, 1930.

[36] Ed. William Kurrelmeyer, Tübingen, 1912.

words *alt* and *tor* are very close, and if both were to be adjectivized, we would have *an alter torikhter kinig*, who is, according to the Midrash, the Evil Inclination in all its ramifications, as Satan and as demon. And this old stupid king was degraded to our *alter terakh*.[37]

VII

It is a noticeable feature of Yiddish folk etymology that words of Germanic, Slavic, and other origins are analyzed as Hebrew forms. Curiously enough, this fate befell all three of the medieval synonyms for 'fool'. (1) *nar* became associated with Hebrew *na'ar* 'boy'. A Hebrew-type plural *naronim* (probably formed from an older singular, *narn), has often been spelled in Yiddish ♮*nˀrnjḿ* and the singular has been written ♮*nˀr*. There is a saying, *yeder shmuel is a nar* 'every Samuel is a fool', which is apparently based on the text *vehana'ar šmu'el* (I Samuel 2:21). (2) *Tôre* underwent a development which we have already investigated. (3) *Gecke* or *Jecke* were crossed with the diminutive *Yekl* of the name *Ya(n)kev* 'Jacob' and achieved a definite pejorative meaning, not only as applied to German Jews, but even in the towns of Lithuania.[38] But this would form a separate study.

[37] We cannot leave unmentioned one more possibility—the prince of darkness, Dirach, used by German thieves in their oaths; see A. F. Thiele: *Die jüdischen Gauner in Deutschland*, Berlin, 1841, p. 7.

[38] Illustrations could be cited from the writings of Yankev Dinezon and Ayzik Meyer Dik.

AN EARLY CASE OF STANDARD GERMAN IN HEBREW CHARACTERS

HERBERT H. PAPER (Ann Arbor, Michigan)

In his important work *Die arabische Literatur der Juden*, the master bibliographer M. Steinschneider, in referring to the translation history of Baḥya ibn Paḳuda's *Ḥobot halebabot*, says as follows: "Der I. Tract. erschien 1765 in *hochdeutscher* Sprache, das erste Buch eines jüdischen Verf. in dieser, in welcher das ganze Werk von *Fürstenthal* (1835), *Baumgarten* (1854), M. E. *Stern* (paraphrastisch, 2. Ausg. 1856) erschien. . . ."[1] Elsewhere Steinschneider wrote the following à propos the first item mentioned in the above citation: "Im J. 1765 erschien der Text und die . . . Uebersetzung . . . nebst einer reindeutschen Uebersetzung des ersten Abschnittes von Mose Steinhard, Sohn des Rabbiners Josef Steinhard in Fürth. Dieses Buch führt *Zunz* . . . als die erste unter 'den einzelnen Proben deutscher Arbeiten' auf, nachdem seit 1760 in dem Wörterbuch des Jehuda (b. Joel aus) Minden . . . 'der erste Versuch die hochdeutsche Sprache in die Nationalliteratur einzuführen' gemacht worden."[2] In his catalogue of the Hebrew books in the Bodleian, the great bibliographer recorded a copy of this particular edition and translation of Baḥya's work in the following manner: "—cum Samuel Posen mortui Vers. Germ. [revera eadem ac praec.!] acced. Versio Germ. [pura] et expositio portae I. Mosis fil. Rabbini [Josef Steinhard] 4. Fürth . . . 1765."[3] This is of course a rendition of the material contained on the Hebrew title page.

The volume contains, in addition to the customary approbations of rabbinical authorities and a translator's preface, the Hebrew translation by Judah ibn Tibbon of the Judeo-Arabic original of Baḥya plus a Yiddish translation thereof. The Hebrew text appears on the upper part of each page; the Yiddish translation, on the bottom in the rabbinic script commonly used in Germany at the time. At the end of the book is appended the High German translation (in the same rabbinic script) of the first chapter with comments thereon—both by Moses Steinhard. This is preceded by a short preface in which the latter affirms his belief in the Copernican system of astronomy. This short preface will be presented below in transliteration, and in addition a sample of the first chapter will be given along with a sample of the Yiddish translation in order to show the substantial differences between the two. That the two languages, Yiddish and German, should appear within the covers of the same book in 1765 is an extremely interesting prelude to the German translation of the Pentateuch by Moses Mendelssohn, the first specimen of which appeared in 1778.

The transliteration used here is explained on page vii of this volume. When a particular word appears in the translation in square Hebrew script rather than in the rabbinic script (in order to orient the reader to the original), small capital

[1] M. Steinschneider: *Die arabische Literatur der Juden*, 134.

[2] M. Steinschneider: *Serapeum* 25 (1864) 55.

[3] M. Steinschneider: *Catalogus librorum hebraeorum in Bibliotheca Bodleiana*, Vol. 2 (Auctores), 781, #9.

letters are used according to the above system of transliteration. Paragraph-initial Hebrew words occurring in a much larger type-font to identify the paragraph will be indicated by capitals.

As can be seen from the foregoing explanation, a consistent attempt was made to do nothing more than represent the original accurately. As far as the Yiddish version is concerned, the assignment of phonetic values to the graphic symbols, their phonemic analysis, and a normalized interpretation in the light of the latter is left to some future date when the requisite analysis has been actually made. This transliteration system may possibly produce one tangential effect—it may point up the ease of using a romanized transliteration fully adequate to render any Old or Middle Yiddish text making publication possible without the expensive use of Hebrew type.

Transliteration of the Standard German text:[4]

♮PR RJDJ — GJNJJGTR LˁZJR — ˁZ wjrdj djr ˀjjngr mˀσń vvˀvndrljḱ sjjnń. dˀ ˀjjnj ˀjbr zˁtcvng pvń dˁń gˀncjń bvḱ ˀjbr hvjpt * $_{2}$djzjń vvˁrq svń bjjˀ gp̄jgt vvˀrdń * ˀjḱ dˁnˀḱ mjt mjjnr ˀjb̄r zˁtcvng. cvvˀr nvr dz qˀp̄jtl $_{3}$dˁr mˁdˀphjσjq * ˀvdr pvń dr gˀtljk̄h p̄hjlvsvp̄hjˁ ˀvjṕ gcvjgń qˀḿ. ˀvnd ˀlz ˀjjń ˀnhˀng djzvń $_{4}$vvˁrq ˀjjń p̄ˁr[g]ljjkj. ˀljjń djjń ˁrstˀvnń vvjrdj zjḱ ˁndjgń. vvˁń dv b̄jjˀ gˁgjń zˀmń hˀltvng bjjdj ˀjb̄r $_{5}$zˁctvng[ń] * dˁń ˀvndr sjht bˁˀvbˀktσt * ˀjḱ p̄ˁr ˀk̄tj cvvˀr qjjnσ vvˁgσ dj ˀltj ˀjbr zˁtcvng $_{6}$vnd bjqˁnj p̄jl mˁhr dz zˀlk̄j pr vvjjbσ ˀvnd ˀvngjlˁhrtj p̄ˁrσvnń ˀjnzvndrσ pr dˁnń zˀ qjjń p̄ˀlqvmnń $_{7}$b̄grjpj pvń ˀvnzrj djjtsj mvtr sprˀḱ hˀbń * ˀjjń zˁhr nvtcljk̄σ vvˁrq zjjˀj. ˀvnd grjjkt dˁń pˁr $_{8}$p̄ˀσjr ˀlz p̄ˁr lˁgjr cvr rvhḿ ˀvnd glˀrj. ˀljjń mjt mjjnḿ vvˁrq ht ˁz gˀnć ˀjjnj ˀndrj bsˀpnhjjt. $_{9}$dˁń djˀ ˀvnpˁrpˀlst gˀnć djjtljḱ ˀvnd rjjnj ˀjbr zˁctvng. hˀt dj hˁrń pˁr lˁgjr ˀvḿ djzvz bvḱ $_{10}$pˀlqvmń cv mˀkń : bjvvˀgjń zˀlk̄s ˀjń dˁr drvqj cv bjpˀrdrń:

$_{11}$ˀIḰ rˁqvmˁntjrˁ ˀbr ˀjń sp̄ˁcjˁ. mjjnj bjjˀ gp̄jgtj p̄hjσjqˀljs ˀlz mˁdˀphjsˁ (mxk̄mv $_{12}$htbˁ vp̄hjlsvpjˁ ˀlqjʼ) ˀnmˁrqvng ˀlz mjjnh ˀjjgnj ˀjnvvˁntcjˀhń. dˀ vvjrd cvvˀr mˀnkr $_{13}$zˀ ˀjń bjjdj vvjsnsˀp̄tń ˀvnˁrp̄ˀhrń stvcjń. ˀjnzvndrσ dz ˀjḱ σˁσtˁmˀtˀ qvpˁrnjqvḿ * (bnjń $_{14}$hˁvlḿ lp̄j dˁθ̄ hθ̄vk̄ń hgdvl qvp̄ˁrnjqvḿ). dz dj ˁrdj ˀjjń blˀnˁt ˀvnd b̄jvvˁgljḱ zjjˀj * nˁmljḱ $_{15}$ˀjjnj bjvvˁgvng ˀvḿ zjḱ zˁlb̄stń ˀvdr ˀjhr ˀqσj (qvtrh) tˀg ˀvnd nˀk̄t cv mˀk̄ń. ˀvnd ˀjjnj ˀjń dˁń $_{16}$ tjhr qrjjσ ˀvḿ dˁr zvnj. ˀvmb̄ djˀ p̄jhr cjjtń dˁσ jˀhrσ cv dˁtˁrmjnjrń. pr ˀjjń gvvjshjjt ˀn $_{17}$nˁhmi. ˀjtˁḿ dz ˀjjń qˀmˁt ˀjjń ˀjhr ˁndσ cjhl ˁr rjjktj vvˁlt zjjˀj * dˀ vvjrd mˀnkr mjt ˀvnʼ $_{18}$gjrjjmtj p̄rˀg stvqjń ˀviṕ cv cjhń qvmń. ˁndljḱ mjḱ gˀr ˀjjń ˀvnglvjbjgń sˁltń. ˀljjń dˀ djzr glvjbj : $_{19}$vvˁlkr dˁń gjzˁtć gˀts njkt ˁntgˁgjń : zˁhr p̄ˁr nvnp̄tjg ˀjzt. zˀ ˁr p̄ˀrdrtj mjjnj ˀjjń zjk̄t $_{20}$p̄ˁr nvnp̄t ghˁr cv gˁbń. ˀjk̄ ˀvb̄ljgjrˁ mjḱ hjr mit. jˁdń zˀ vvˀz dˀ gˁgjń ˀjjn cv vvˁndń hˀt. $_{21}$hjnlˁngljkh σˀtjσ pˀqtcjˀhń ˁndvvˁdr srjptljḱ ˀvdr mjndljḱ cv gˁbń. ˁm p̄p̄ˁhlj ˀlzˀ zˀ vvˀhl $_{22}$djzvz vvˁrq ˀlz mjḱ zˁlb̄stń dj gjnjjgthjjt dˁσ lˁzrσ bˁstr mˀσń ˀnd bjhˀrrj. $_{23}$gjnjjgtr lˁzjr ˁrgˁbnstr msh b̄ń hgˀvń hgdvl hmp̄vrσḿ ˀbʼʼd mvhrr jvσṕ mstjjnhrt. $_{24}$p̄jvrdˀ jvḿ ˀʼ ḱʼ tbθ tqk̄ʺh lp̄q

[4] Subscript numbers indicate line divisions; periods, colons, and asterisks are reproduced as in the original.

NOTES

5, 9 *zʕctvng* misprinted for *zʕtcvng*. Note the numerous superfluous rafe's: 2 *ʔjb̄r* for *ʔjbr* 'über'; 6 *p̄ʕrσvnń* for *pʕrσvnń* 'Personen'; 7 *b̄grjpj* for *bgrjp̄j* 'Begriffe'; 15 *zʕlb̄stń* for *zʕlbstń* 'selbsten'; 20 *ʔvb̄ljgjrʕ* for *ʔvbljgjrʕ* 'obligiere'; 21 *ʕm p̄p̄ʕhlj* for *ʕmpp̄ʕhlj* 'empfehle'. Note also the cases where a rafe is presumably required but is not printed: 1 *pvń* for *p̄vń* 'von'; 5 *bʕʔvbʔktσt* for *bʕʔvbʔk̄tσt* 'beobachtest'; 6 *pr* for *p̄r* 'für'; 8 *bsʔpnhjjt* for *bsʔp̄nhjjt* 'Beschaffenheit'; 9 *ʔvnpʕrpʔlst* for *ʔvnp̄ʕrp̄ʔlst* 'unverfälscht'; 10 *pʔlqvmń* for *p̄ʔlqvmń* 'volkommen'; *bjpʔrdrń* for *bjp̄ʔrdrń* 'befördern'; etc. Note also 11 *mʕdʔphjs* for *mʕdʔp̄hjσjs* (cf. the variant *mʕtʔ-*).

So much for the preface. The following is a sample of Moses Steinhard's translation of the first chapter of Baḥya's book which will then be followed by the same section from the Yiddish translation. The Standard German version is given only in normalized transcription; the Yiddish version, in transliteration. The bracketed forms are included for the sole purpose of calling attention to deviations from present-day usage.

Metaphysik: Es sagt der Author: nachdem wir geforscht was zuvorderst zur Haltung des Gesetz[es] des Nötigste[n] seie, haben wir gefunden, dass die Einheit Gottes mit ganzen [ganzem] Herzen zu erkennen der Grund zum Gesetz ist. Mit diesem Glauben werden wir abgehalten, dass wir eine Gottheit zu sein nicht leugnen, wer aber davon abweicht, dessen Werke seien keine Werk[e] und ist in [im] Glauben unbeständig. Eben darum war das erstere Gebot Gottes an uns auf den [dem] Berg Sinai, du sollst kein[e] andere[n] Götter neben mir haben. Wir haben also die Beschaffenheit der Einheit Gottes, dass wir mit ganzen [ganzem] Herzen an Ihm glauben sollen in zehn Faktionen zu betrachten als: a. was Glauben mit ganzem Herzen seie; b. in wieviel Arten die Beschaffenheit der Einheit sich verteilt; c. ob wir mit Nachsinnen nach Ihm zu forschen schuldig seien oder nicht; d. die Art der Erforschung und was zuvorderst zu wissen nötig ist; e. die unumstössliche[n] Gründe wodurch erwiesen wird, dass die Welt ein[en] Erschaffer hat, so sie aus nichts erschaffen; f. wird von die [der] Gegenwart des Schöpfers gehandelt; g. wird mit Vernunftsgründe[n] erwiesen, dass er Ens Entium; h. wird erläutert, was das wahre Ens und vergängliche Einheiten sind; i. dass Gott wahrhaftig Ens Entium und Ihm keiner gleicht; j. was Ihm für Eigenschaften sowohl durch Vernunftsschlüsse als in der Heilige[n] Schrift zugeeignet werden und zeigen die, so man Ihm zueignen kann; auch hinwiederum die, so von Ihm müssen entfernet werden.

In item c. of the above citation the word *ob* is written *♮ʔvjb*, implying a pronunciation [oyb], and may be considered to be a Yiddishism.

The following is a transliteration of the same section of text in the Yiddish version:[5]

[5] Slant lines indicate line divisions.

♮ˀMR ˁr zˀgt dˁr mxbr nˀḱ dˁḿ mjr gjp̄ˀrst hˀbń vvˁlk̄s ds ˀljr njtjgsth ˀjz MPNUΘ p̄vń djˀ grvndń / ˀvn' srsjḿ p̄vń ˀvnzr θvrh hˀbń mjr gjp̄vndń dz dˁr jxvd p̄vń gˀt mjt gˀnćń hˁrćń mjt ˀjr srs ˀvn' / jσvd ds ˀjz dˁr ˁrstr sˁr p̄un djˀ tˀrń dr θvrh ˀvn' dvrḱ dˁḿ jxvd qˁń mń ˀvntr sjjdń dˁr ˀń gˀt / gljjbt p̄vń ˀzv ˀjjnḿ dr x''v ˀń ˀjḿ ljjqnt ˀvn' ds ˀjz dˁr ˀrstr vvˀrhˀp̄tjgr jσvd p̄vń djˀ θvrh ˀvn' dˁr / dˀ p̄vń ˀb vvjjk̄t dˁr qˁń qjjń rˁk̄t vvˁrq p̄vń mcvθ̄ tvń ˀvn' bjjˀ dˁḿ hˀt djˀ ˀmvnh qjjń bjstˀnd ˀvn' / dˀrvḿ vvˀr ds ˁrstj vvˀrt vvˀs gˀt hˀt mjt ˀvns gjrˁt ˀvjṕ dˁḿ bˁrg σjnj smvθ̄ k' (ˀjq bjń gˀt djjń / gˀt dvˀ zˀlst qjjń p̄rˁmdj gˁtr hˀbń) . . . / nvń mvz ˀjḱ bjsjjdń vvjˀ mń / mvz p̄r stjń dˁń jxvd mjt gˁnćń hˀrćń ˀvn' dˀ bjjˀ mvz mń cˁhń ˀrljj zˀk̄ń vvjsń ds ˁrstj ˀjz vvjˀ vvjjt ˁs / gjrjjk̄t djˀ ˀjjnjqjjt mjt gˀnćń hercń ds ˀndrj ˀjz ˀjń vvjˀ p̄jl xlqjḿ djˀ bjtjjtvng p̄jń jxvd p̄rtjjlt / vvˁrt ds drjtj ˀjz ˀvb mjr zjjnń svldjg drvjṕ nˀḱ cv p̄ˀrsń mjt p̄r stˀnd ˀvn' vvˀvl drvjṕ cv trˀk̄tń ˀdr njt / ds p̄jrdj ˀjz ˀjń vvˀs p̄r ˀjjń ˀvp̄ń mń zˀl drvjṕ p̄ˀrsń ˀvn' vvˀs mjr mvzń ˁrst vvjsń ˀj mjr zˀlń p̄ˀrsń nˀḱ / dˁḿ jxvd ds p̄jnp̄tj ˀjz cv bjsjjdń diˀ rˀjvθ̄ djˀ mń ˁrst mvz vvjsń vvˀvrvjs mń qˁń qlˀr bjvvjjzń dz / djˀ vvˁlt hˀt ˀjjń bjsˁp̄r dˁr zjˀ ˀvjs njqs hˀt bjsˁp̄ń ds zˁqstj ˀjz vvjˀ mjr zˀlń zjˀ dr cv brˁngń / ˀvḿ p̄ˀst cv glvjbń dz ˀjjń gˀt p̄r hˀndń ˀjz ds zjbntj ˀjz rˀjvθ̄ cv brˁngń dz ˁr ˀjz ˀjjnjg ds ˀk̄tj ˀjz cv / bjsjjdń vvˁlk̄s hjjst ˀjjnjg HˁVBR ds dˀ p̄r bjjˀ gjt ds ˀjz ˁs bljjbt njt ˀl cjjt ˀjjnjg ˀvn' vvˁlk̄s / hjjst vvˀrhˀp̄tjg ˀjjnjg ds njjntj ˀjz dz gˀt gjlvbt ˀjz ˁr ˀjz vvˀrhˀp̄tjg ˀjjnjg ˀbr qjjnr ˀjz / vvˀrhˀp̄tjg ˀjjnjg njjˁrt gˀt ˀljjnt ds cˁhntj ˀjz p̄vń gˀtljk̄h zˀk̄ń djˀ mń mjt dˁḿ sk̄l b̄jtrˀk̄tń qˁń / ˀvn' djˀ gjsrjbń stjń ˀjn' djˀ rˀjvθ̄ vvˀvrvjs mń qˁń bivvjjzń vvˀs mń gjhˁrt cv tvń p̄vń gˀts vvˁgń ˀvn' vvˀvr / p̄vń mń zˀl zjḱ dr vvjjtrń:

SAINÉAN'S ACCOMPLISHMENTS IN YIDDISH LINGUISTICS

(Preliminaries to a Monograph on the Same Topic)

CHAIM GININGER (New York)

On the occasion of the twentieth anniversary
of L. Sainéan's death.

As many as eight disciplines can, it seems, be listed in which Lazare M. Sainéan (May 5, 1859–May 11, 1934) was at home and to which he made substantial contributions. A Sainéan monograph would have to show the "sufficient conditions" of this division. It would also be necessary to explain on another occasion why Leo Spitzer's apt characterization of Sainéan's fields of interest and of the principal lines of his research is so feebly reflected in my own list. In brief, the reason may perhaps be stated as follows: Spitzer's approach of *Methode ist Erlebnis* (Gundolf) reveals otherwise concealed insights into the interests of a creative personality and presents it in the most appropriate perspective. This puts a new emphasis on the significance of the achievements of a personality. But this approach sometimes implies the result that lesser, secondary accents should disappear altogether. For example, Spitzer knew well of Sainéan's accomplishments for Yiddish linguistics. In summarizing Sainéan's development (*Entwicklungsgang*) in *Literaturblatt für germanische und romanische Philologie*, vol. XLVIII (Leipzig, 1927), 27–36, he notes (col. 34) that Sainéan started as a "Jewish . . . and Rumanian philologist," and cites both variants of Sainéan's study about Yiddish. But in recounting Sainéan's *Hauptwerke* in *Meisterwerke der Romanischen Sprachwissenschaft*, vol. 1 (Munich, 1929), 361, Spitzer makes no mention of this beginning. In the great storm of Sainéan's conquest of linguistic lands it was blown aside. But is the interest of scholarship restricted to storms? On the contrary, science sometimes must consider that which was too weak to withstand the tempest.

These are the eight disciplines and for the sake of illustration, some of the principal works (out of about seventy) that Sainéan contributed to each:

1. GENERAL LINGUISTICS

"Incercare asupra semasiologieĭ limbeĭ române; studie istorice asupra tranziţiuniĭ sensurilor," *Revista pentru istorie, archeologie şi filologie*, Anul III, 6 (Bucharest, 1886?) 211–467. 4⁰. Published also separately with a preface by B. P. Hasdeŭ, Bucharest, 1887, vii + 259 pp. 4⁰.

Raporturile între gramatica şi logica c'o privire sintetică asupra părţilor cuvîntuluĭ; studiŭ de linguistică generală, Bucharest, 1891. xiv + [1] + 193 pp. 8⁰.

2. RUMANIAN LINGUISTICS

Influenţa orientală asupra limbeĭ şi cultureĭ române, Bucharest, 1900. 3 volumes: 8, cccxxxv; viii, 408; viii, 280 pp. 8⁰. Two summaries were published in French journals: (a) "Les éléments orientaux en roumain," *Romania* (Paris), vol. xxx (539–566) and xxxi (82–99; 557–589), 1901–1902; (b) "Le régime et la société en Roumanie pendant le règne des Phanariotes (1711–1821)," *Revue internationale de sociologie* (Paris), vol. x (717–748), 1902.

3. French linguistics

Les sources indigènes de l'étymologie française, Paris, 1925–35. 4 volumes: xii + 448; 519; xi + 602; viii + 653 pp. ("Autour des Sources Indigénes ..."). 8°.

L'argot ancien (1455–1850), ses éléments constitutifs, ses rapports avec les langues secrètes de l'Europe méridionale, et l'argot moderne, Paris, 1907, vii + 350 pp. 8°.

Les sources de l'argot ancien. Vol. 1: *Des origines à la fin du XVIIIe siècle*, xv + 427 pp.; vol. 2: *Le XIXe siècle*, 470 pp. 8°. Paris, 1912.

Le langage parisien au XIXe siècle: facteurs sociaux, contingents linguistiques, aits sémantiques, influences littéraires, Paris, 1920. xvi + 590 pp. 8°.

4. Yiddish linguistics

"Studiu dialectologic asupra graiului evreo-german," *Anuar pentru Israeliţi cu un supliment calendaristic pe anul 5650 (1889–1890)*, anul al XII-lea, sub redacţiunea lui M. Schwarzfeld, Bucharest, 1889, 53–126. Published also separately: Bucharest, 1889, 78 pp. All page references to the Rumanian edition (R.) in the present study are to the *Anuar*.

5. Folkloristics

Basmele române in comparaţiune cu legendele antice clasice şi in legătură cu basmele popórelorŭ invecinate şi ale tuturorŭ popórelorŭ romanice; studiu comparativŭ, Bucharest, 1895. xiv + [1] + 1114 pp. 8°.

Studii folklorice; cercetări în domeniul literaturei populare, Bucharest, 1896, vii + 248 pp. 8°.

6. Philology

Istoria filologieĭ române; studiĭ critice, c'o prefaţă de B. P. Hasdeŭ, Bucharest, 1892, xvi + 455 pp. 8°. ₂1895 (without Hasdeŭ's preface), vii + 356 pp. 8°.

"L'histoire naturelle dans l'œuvre de Rabelais," *Revue du seizième siècle*, Paris, 1915–1921; vol. iii (1915) 187–277; vol. iv (1916) 36–104, 203–306; vol. v (1917–18) 28–74; vol. vi (1919) 84–113; vol. vii (1920) 1–45, 185–205; vol. viii (1921) 1–41. Tirage à part: Paris, 1921, 7–450 pp.

7. Didactic works

Dicţionar universal al limbei române, [Craiova,] 1896, 1906, 1914, 1922, 1925, 1929 (1 + 872 pp. 8°). New ed. in prep. by C. Şăineanu, 1947.

8. Historical essays

Moisi Mendelsohn, viaţa şi activitatea sa; studiu biografic (under his previous name: Lazar Şain), Bucharest, 1880, [3] + 6–76 + [3] pp. 8°. (Previously in *Fraternitatea*, Bucharest, 1880.)

The above selection is sufficient to illustrate the classificatory principles which I used; an exhaustive bibliography would require a great deal of additional research. The grouping is based on external criteria which we might call conventional, but even so it was not easy to make, and I would like to bolster it by reference to some of the motives which led Sainéan to plunge into the several lines of research. "4. Yiddish linguistics," for example, is listed separately for this reason, among others, that it is a clear manifestation of Sainéan's pioneering spirit, of his penchant for venturing into untrodden fields. Item "6. Philology," on the contrary, is only a by-product of Sainéan's vast general knowledge in the philological fields of Rumanian, Yiddish, French, and others: basically he was drawn rather towards "pure" linguistics; I therefore thought it appropriate to combine all his philologies into a single item. "7. Didactic works," and "8.

Historical essays" stand apart because of the quantities of material involved, if for no other reason, but it should be noted that Sainéan invested a great deal of ingenuity in both, for he was not only a well prepared teacher; he also had a strong journalistic temperament. (This "quiet" scholar was quite "vociferous" in settling his accounts with the Rumanians when, in early 1901, he was forced to leave his native country because it would not grant him citizenship and thus interfered with his academic career.[1])

As I stated above, in Yiddish linguistics Sainéan was a pioneer. This point should be constantly borne in mind. I will have to refer to some of his errors; but on entirely new ground a great deal of erring is inevitable. In his achievements for Yiddish linguistics he was practically without a predecessor. In the West the star of Alfred Landau (1850–1935) had appeared, but had hardly had time to rise sufficiently; in the East the lexicographer Yehoyshue Mordkhe Lifshits (1830 [?]–1878)[2] was already casting a brilliant light which did not, however, reach Sainéan, probably because he was entirely oriented toward the West and never looked eastward.

Sainéan's achievements in Yiddish linguistics are concentrated in two variants of a single study. The first variant is in Rumanian. It was printed on pp. 53–126 of vol. XII (Bucharest, 1889) of the famous annuals, *Anuar pentru Israeliţi*, which were published in 19 volumes (from 1877 to 1898) in Bucharest, 18 of them (II–XIX) by the well-known journalist and historian of Rumanian Jewry, Moses Schwarzfeld (1857–1943). In the same year it appeared as a separate booklet, 78 pp. octavo. Here is its title with the headings of its parts: *Studiu dialectologic asupra graiului evreo-german. I.*[3] *Introducere, bibliografie, literatura, elemente lexicale.* I was told by Moses Schwarzfeld on several occasions—the last time in a note to Cernăuţi dated April 7, 1940—that originally Sainéan had planned his Yiddish study as a doctoral thesis. At the last minute he replaced it by a topic in Rumanian folklore. He says: "The materials [for the Yiddish study] were collected in the Imperial Library in Berlin and were then analyzed in Bucharest."[4] But the work was essentially ready for the dissertation deadline, March 1–23, 1889. Its introduction was utilized in a circular on the collection of Yiddish linguistic material in July. And when could it have gone through the process of being written and printed if Hugo Schuchardt's acknowledgment (see below) of a received copy was already written in August of the same year?[5]

[1] See his pamphlet, *O carieră filologică*, Bucharest, 1901, viii + 96 pp.; French ed., Bucharest–Paris, 1901, viii + 56 pp.

[2] Cf. Nokhem Shtif: [Y. M. Lifshits the Lexicographer], in *Di yidishe shprakh* (Kiev), 1928, no. 4–5 (11–12), 3–22.

[3] The very appearance of this "I" is evidence that a continuation was planned.

[4] See Chaim Gininger: [The Correspondence Between Alfred Landau and Lazar Şaineanu], in *Yivo-bleter* 13 (1938) 275–300, pp. 286–7.

[5] It becomes clear also why Sainéan used one of his published studies for his dissertation. He was not working on anything else; having no other choice, he took his small folkloristic essay, "Les jours d'emprunt ou les jours de la vieille," a French version of the later "Zilele babei şi legenda dochiei," published in the same year in *Convorbiri literare*, 1888, 193–220. The dissertation was presented to Leipzig University on March 1, 1889, but even the French

A variant on the same subject, and based almost entirely on the same material,[6] was published by Sainéan a good number of years later, after leaving Rumania, in the *Memoirs de la Société linguistique de Paris* (vol. XII, no. 2, 1901, pp. 90–138; no. 3, 1902, pp. 176–196; also published separately).

His work on Yiddish was not a casual matter in Sainéan's life. It was an achievement which took years to mature as he thought and wrote about Jews and Jewishness. The study, which he had conceived as the first dissertation on the Yiddish language[7] to be presented to a major European university, was to be the beginning of the realization of a comprehensive plan: at last to raze to the ground the remaining walls of contempt for Yiddish, which stood, like antiquated relics of ancient buildings, not only in all manner of cultural and scholarly societies, but also in the noble circles of Western European linguistics, and to put Yiddish research in line with the discoveries of the period. He understood well that this purpose required: (1) a research center, (2) the cooperation of competent and interested co-workers, and (3) the familiarization of the general linguistic world with Yiddish linguistics. It was these three paths that Sainéan followed as long as he continued his work on the subject of Yiddish.

A center for Yiddish research had, apparently, been planned as early as 1886, when the "Iuliu Barasch Historical Society" was created in Bucharest. Sainéan had been one of its founders, and at times also its president (as a student, as early as 1888). He must already have been engaged intensively in Yiddish research at that time; otherwise it would be impossible to understand the broadness and solid basis of his study of two years later, i.e. of 1889. Another of the founders of the society, the above-mentioned Moses Schwarzfeld, in recounting the story of the society's establishment,[8] speaks explicitly of a "historical and folkloristic ['*folclorice*'] society," and "folkloristic" here no doubt refers to Sainéan's interest in Yiddish, although it surely also includes Schwarzfeld's own researches on Yiddish proverbs, which were certainly part of the society's program.[9] About three years after its founding, the leaders of the Barasch Society

---

version had already been finished long ago (published in *Romania* (Paris) 18 (1889) 107–127, with the date underneath the article "Paris, April, 1888"). The only study on which he was at that time at work was the monograph on Yiddish.

[6] The French version gained a new "Appendice" which included: "I. Noms propres" (193–195) and "II. Eléments hébreux dans l'argot allemand" (195–196). But on the last page we read "(A suivre)."

[7] The really first doctoral dissertation about Yiddish was apparently presented at Berlin University by Felix Rosenberg of Posen in 1888 (July 20): *Über eine Sammlung deutscher Volks- und Gesellschaftslieder in hebräischen Lettern*. It was a study in literary history with linguistic comments (82 + [4] pp., 8°. See also: Ludwig Geiger's *Zeitschrift für die Geschichte der Juden in Deutschland* (Braunschweig) 2 (1888) 232–296; 3 (1888) 14–28).

[8] See his book, *Dr. Iuliu Barasch*, Bucharest, 1919, p. 182.

[9] This scholarly body had a third moving force for Yiddish research: Dr. Moses Gaster (1856–1939). But the work of research organization received a heavy blow with the exile from Rumania, in 1885 (October 13), of Dr. Gaster and of Dr. Elias Schwarzfeld (1855–1915). Indicative of this institution's work are some of the footnotes appended to certain printed papers of that time. Cf. the note to Moses Schwarzfeld's "Literatura populară israelită ca element etnico-psichologic," in the same *Anuar* which contained Sainéan's Yiddish mono-

Lazare M. Sainéan (1859–1934)

[Portrait obtained by the author from Constantin Șăineanu, Lazare's brother]

A mon cher frère Constantin
Souvenir de notre séjour à
Ablinz, juillet-août 1922
L. Sainéan

in Bucharest issued a special *apel* of four pages, 8⁰, entitled "The Collection of Materials From the Living Language [*graiu*] for the Study of the Judeo-German Dialect."[10] This appeal was directed above all to the members of the society, but certainly had in mind also a wider audience, since it was reprinted in a number of periodicals.[11] It contained a part of the introduction to Sainéan's *Studiu dialectologic* and a specially written chapter to which were appended concrete directions for collectors. The appeal was signed: "Bucharest, in July 1889. Lazăr Şaineanu." The special part is reproduced here.

[P.3] The execution of a work in such conditions requires the possession of materials collected from the very mouths of those who still speak the dialect. These materials, as an immediate expression of the people's manner of feeling and thinking, offer to the linguist and ethnographer authentic and inestimable means. They are the most solid basis on which it will be possible to build the linguistic edifice of the Judeo-German dialect.

The First Secretary of the Society, Mr. M. Schwarzfeld, has taken the first step on this road, having for ten years been gathering a true paremiological treasure.[12] When this collection of over 7000 Judeo-German proverbs will appear, we will have on hand a precious material for judging the psychic qualities and for studying the particularities of the folk speech.

Taking advantage of a paragraph in our statutes, we take the liberty of drawing the attention of the Members to the other Judeo-German popular-literature materials which will be specified below. Any communication which will concern one of the announced points will be welcomed and published under the collector's name.

The most rigorous fidelity, both with respect to transcribing and content, is the first scientific condition. Indicating the locality and the person from whom the information was taken is no less necessary.

We hope that the Members, persuaded of the great importance of such collections and of the timeliness of our initiative, will hasten to send us as many communications as possible. [P. 4] The Judeo-German speech is moving to a fatal death and it is the duty of science to stimulate the gathering of the psychic testimony, of the beliefs and superstitions, the joys and fears, which have always

graph (pp. 41–52). On p. 41 we read: "This study is a part of a series of lectures given in the 'Barascheum' in the fall of 1882 in conjunction with Doctors M. Gaster, E. Schwarzfeld, and Messrs. Lazar Şaineanu and M. Steureanu"; cf. also the note to Sainéan's paper in *Anuar* 6 (1883) 73–86, p. 73; also pp. 118–119. After the attempt of the German philosopher Rudolf Hermann Lotze (1817–81) in Leipzig in the late 1860's, this was the second serious effort at institutional Yiddish research. A third attempt was made by Alfred Landau in the 1890's in Vienna.

[10] "Stringerea materialelor din viul graiu pentru studiarea dialectului evreo-german." In that period, "Judeo-German" was a common way of referring to Yiddish. We have retained the phrase in all quotations without any further comment.

[11] *Analele Societăţii istorice Iuliu Barasch* 3, no. 1 and 2, pp. 93–96; *Revista israelită* 4, no. 16 (August 15, 1889) 442–446.

[12] This collection, which was never published, eventually reached 8000 items (see *Yeda' 'am* (Tel Aviv), April, 1954, vol. 2, no. 2–3, p. 140). Schwarzfeld himself told me that he had started collecting in 1877. I was therefore surprised that in the standard work, *Catalogue des livres parémiologiques* by Ignace Bernstein, Leipzig, 1900, this collection is not listed, even though this catalogue contains a section on manuscripts and though Bernstein listed other works of Schwarzfeld's.

nursed the human imagination and which have caused the souls of peoples in all zones to shake.

Bucharest, July, 1889 LAZĂR ŞAINEANU.

MATERIALS TO BE COLLECTED:

I. Gathering of *stories* and *fairy tales* ([*mānsę̊*]), retaining peculiarities and explaining unusual words.
II. *Riddles* ([*rētenīš*]), with addition of the solutions.
III. *Songs*, to wit:
1. *Cradle songs* ([*vī'g'nlīdl*]);
2. *Children's songs* ([*k'ī'ndrlīdl*]);
3. *Wedding songs* ([*xå'sęnęlīdr*]), especially for orphans;
4. *Purim songs* ([*pīrmšpīl*]).
IV. *Children's games* ([*k'ī'ndršpīl*]), reproducing the formulas and describing the manner of playing. We could divide them into:

A. religious, like *a*) bow and arrow ([*fålnboig'n*]) for the holiday called Lag be-ʻOmer; *b*) flag ([*fūn*]) for Simhat Torah; *c*) spinning top ([*drēidl*]) for Hannukah and *d*) rattle ([*gragr*]) for Purim, etc.

B. profane, like *a*) the king and the queen ([*dr mēilęx mīt dr mälkę*]); *b*) the rabbi and the rabbi's wife ([*dr rūv mīt dr rebętsn*]); *c*) soldiers ([*xājęls lāt*]); *d*) black ox ([*īn* {*dīm?*} *švartsn oks*]), etc.

V. *Incantations* ([*šprux*]{*šprox?*} or [*ubšprexn*]), with exact citation of the formulas, to wit:
1. *For an evil eye* ([*fīn a g'īt-óig'*] or [*nęhorę*]);
2. *For pain* ([*fīn štéxęnīš*]);
3. *For fright* ([*fīn dršrek'*]), when lead or wax is poured ([*bláigīsn īn váksgīsn*]);
4. *For stepping in*[*to dung*] ([*fīn antrētn*]);
5. *For an ill wind* ([*fīn a šlextn vīnt*]), etc.
VI. *Superstitions and old wives' beliefs* ([*båbsk'ę şaxn*]) concerning: *a*) birth, for example "a child with a caul" ([*g'ęboirn īn a hābl*]); *b*) death; *c*) spirits and demons, for example the werewolf ([*nīpér*]); the house spirit or incubus ([*šrētålę*]), evil spirits ([*šēidīm, rīxęs*]), ghost or homunculus ([*goilm*]), etc.; *d*) animals, for example bat ([*flēdrmouş*]), etc.
VII. *Magic or fortune-telling* ([*k'īšef*]).
VIII. *Folk medicine or old wives' remedies.*

Sainéan was also concerned with evoking increased interest and understanding for Yiddish research in the world of linguistics. In the first place, he was not satisfied with what had been done before him. Secondly, he was certain, as we have seen, that Yiddish was disappearing at a rapid rate; this belief was the result of his views concerning the course of Jewish history in general. And there was a third point, too: he loved the language and wanted to see the study of it on a high level. He therefore looked about him for help, and we know of his joy at establishing contact with Alfred Landau in Vienna, another innovator and pioneer in the study of Yiddish. It was to him that he expressed his views in full.[13] With a third scholar who at that time was interested in these matters, Leo Wiener (1862–1939), later the Slavist at Harvard, Sainéan was not able to establish satisfactory contacts. He entertained some hopes of cooperation with

[13] See Correspondence (footnote 4, above), letters 2 and 4.

the French linguist Victor Henry (1850–1907) of Colmar, who had dealt with Alsatian Yiddish, but this did not materialize either. In the nineties of the nineteenth century the people who had a scholarly interest in Yiddish were few indeed. The first edition of Sainéan's study on Yiddish did not receive a single review. The situation improved somewhat when the French version of his book was published; this time it was reviewed by Alfred Landau, O. Meisinger, and noticed by Richard Loewe.[13a] But Sainéan never completed his work. The plan had been too ambitious: he turned the entire Rumanian version (with a few additions and a small number of changes) into an introduction of a French essay; this was to be followed by a phonetics and a morphology of Wallachian Yiddish, and finally by a collection of texts, mostly of folklore material (?), with an etymological word list. But he no longer felt qualified to perform this task by himself, and no help was in sight; disappointed, he left his work unfinished.

There was something else on Sainéan's mind. In one respect the fusion character of the Yiddish language represents a particularly strange linguistic fact. And yet, though this fact is more striking than any other to Western European linguistics, foreign scholars have always had great difficulties in grasping it correctly. This has always presented Yiddish linguistics with the special problem of bringing the language into the sphere of interest of general linguistics. And every period has had its special difficulties on this point. At the time of Sainéan's linguistic interest in Yiddish, the obstacle was the problem of the mixed nature of language, and the solution of this problem was, for Yiddish, a *Lebensfrage.* At that time the entire problem of language mixture was being put on a new basis (Schuchardt, Paul, Lucien Adam (1833–1918), Georg von der Gabelenz, and others). But Max Müller (1823–1900), with his *Lectures on the Science of Language*, was still master of the field; this book, "in numerous editions, did more than anything else to popularize linguistics and served to initiate a great many students into our science," says Otto Jespersen.[14] Müller stated in no uncertain terms: "A Celt may become an Englishman, Celtic and English blood may be mixed; and who could tell at the present day the exact proportion of Celtic and Saxon blood in the population of England? *But languages are never mixed.*[15] It is indifferent by what name the language spoken in the British Islands be called, whether English or British or Saxon; to the student of language Eng-

[13a] The following are the reviews and the most important critical mentions which Sainéan's preliminaries to Yiddish research stimulated upon their appearance: Alfred Landau in *Zeitschrift für deutsche Philologie* 36, Halle a. S., 1904, pp. 268–269; Othmar Meisinger in *Zeitschrift für hochdeutsche Mundarten*, vol. iii, 6, Heidelberg, 1902, pp. 377–378; Richard Loewe in his essay, "Die jüdisch-deutsche Sprache," in *Ost und West*, iv, 10, Berlin, October, 1904, col. 655–664; Oskar Weise in *Deutsche Erde*, iii, 203, Gotha, 1904, pp. 89–90; Heinrich Meyer in *Jahresbericht über die Erscheinungen auf dem Gebiete der germanischen Philologie*, 24 (1902), Leipzig, 1903, p. 155.

[14] Otto Jespersen: *Language*, London, 1922, $_8$1949, p. 85.

[15] The italics are not in the original, but in the German translation, 2nd ed., Leipzig, 1866: "*Aber Sprachen vermischen sich niemals*" (p. 66).

lish is Teutonic, and nothing but Teutonic."[16] That Sainéan was not entirely free of this view is easily apparent in his Yiddish research. But he was able to penetrate more deeply into the problem of language mixture for this, if for no other reason, that the objects of his linguistic research at the time were such typical fusion languages as Yiddish and Rumanian. And even in the linguistic discussions concerning Yiddish this problem continued for a long time to play a dominant part. In introducing Yiddish onto the arena of general linguistics, its character of a fusion language dominated people's thoughts. No wonder then that one of the first to whom Sainéan sent his (Rumanian) study of Yiddish was Hugo Schuchardt, the "advocate of mixed languages," as he was aptly designated by the other great Yiddish scholar of that time, Alfred Landau. And Schuchardt's reply, which is here published for the first time, shows how right Sainéan was in treating him to a copy of his essay.

Graz 22 [.] Aug.
'89.

Sehr geehrter Herr[,]

Die Schrift welche Sie die Güte hatten mir zuzusenden, hat mir eine ganz besondere Freude bereitet: sie beschäftigt sich mit einem Gegenstande der mich auf's Lebhafteste interessirt, und das in der gründlichsten und kritischsten Weise (auch die Ausstattung des Heftes ist eine sehr ansprechende).

Ich möchte Sie ermuthigen sich nach Abschluss dieser Arbeit mit dem *Ladino*, dem Jüdisch-Spanischen zu beschäftigen. Ich hatte (zuerst durch den Anblick einer in diesem Idiom zu Smyrna gedruckten Bibel, der mir 1879 zu Tetuan zu Theil ward, angeregt) den Plan gefasst, mich dem Studium dieser insbesondere auch für den Romanisten merkwürdigen Sprechart zu widmen und mich desshalb —in Wien mit Dr. Jellinek und mit gewissen Spaniolen in Beziehung gesetzt. Aber ich sah ein dass dazu eine so gründliche Kenntniss des Hebräischen und seiner modernen Gestaltungen gehörte, wie sie nur bei einem Israeliten gesucht werden kann. M. Grünwald[17] ist allerdings ein solcher, aber seine Arbeit über das Jüdisch-Spanische hat mich bitter enttäuscht.

Wenn ich nun auch selbst auf ein tieferes Eindringen in diesen Gegenstand verzichtet habe, so liegt er mir doch immer noch nahe genug. Ich werde vielleicht später einmal Gelegenheit haben, mich an [!] Sie wegen Eines und des Anderen, das mir für meine Studien nach dieser Richtung hin von Wichtigkeit ist, um Auskunft anzugehen. Sehr eigenthümlich ist z.B. das Jüdisch-Französische von Oran, dessen Entstehung mir im Allgemeinen zwar (es ist durch das Jüdisch-spanische beeinflusst), aber nicht in allem Einzelnen klar ist.

Hochachtungsvollst

Ihr ergebener
Hugo Schuchardt

Ich bitte Sie mir zu sagen, *wo* ich behauptet habe, „că inlocuirea genitivului cu dativ ar fi asemenea un slavism".[18] Ich habe ganz im Gegentheil deswegen

---

[16] *Lectures on the Science of Language, delivered at the Royal Institution of Great Britain* . . . by Max Müller . . . From the 2nd London ed., revised. New York, 1875, p. 80, second lecture. See also his *Three Lectures on the Science of Language, delivered at the Oxford University Extension Meeting* with a Supplement, "My Predecessors," Chicago, ₂1895.

[17] Schuchardt is apparently referring to M[ax] Grün*baum*, *Jüdisch-Spanische Chrestomathie*, Frankfurt am Main, 1896, iv, 160 pp. We quote Schuchardt's letter in full detail, including his Romance punctuation in the German text.

[18] *Studiu dialectologic*, p. 115, footnote. In the French version, the footnote was removed.

Jagić zurechtgewiesen (Zeitschr. f. östr. [die österr.] Gymn. 1886 S. 323)[:] "das ist Jovo sein Schmalz" hat *nichts Slavisches* an sich; wäre die *Wendung nicht ganz deutsch*, so würde sie eher ein Magyarismus sein.

[TRANSLATION

Graz [Austria], August 22, 1889.

Dear Sir:

The study which you were kind enough to send me gave me very special joy: it deals with a subject which interests me most acutely, and does so in the most thorough and critical manner (the getup of the brochure is also very attractive).

I should like to encourage you, after completing this work, to deal with Ladino, the Judeo-Spanish [language]. I had made plans (stimulated first by the sight of a Bible printed in Smyrna in this idiom, which I had the privilege to see in Tetuan in 1879) to devote myself to the study of this idiom, which is remarkable especially for the Romance scholar, too, and therefore made contacts with Dr. [Adolf] Jellinek and certain Sephardic Jews in Vienna. But I realized that this required so thorough a knowledge of Hebrew and its modern formations as can be sought only in an Israelite. M. Grünwald [see footnote 17] is indeed one, but his work on Judeo-Spanish disappointed me bitterly.

Even though I myself have thus had to dispense with a deeper penetration into this subject, it nevertheless continues to concern me quite intimately. Later on I may have occasion to turn to you for information about one thing or another which may be important to me for my studies in this direction. For example, the Judeo-French of Oran is very peculiar; true, its origin is clear to me generally (it is influenced by Judeo-Spanish), but not in all details.

With my greatest respect

Yours sincerely
Hugo Schuchardt

I ask you to tell me *where* I stated "that the replacement of the genitive by a dative is likewise a Slavism." Quite on the contrary, I showed Jagić the right way on this point (*Zeitschrift für die österreichischen Gymnasien*, 1886, p. 323): "das ist Jovo sein Schmalz" has *nothing Slavic* in it; were this *turn of speech not entirely German*, it would rather be a Magyarism.]

On his road to general linguistics, Sainéan's study of Yiddish was perhaps the beginning. But his discussions in this matter continued, both in Rumania and later on in France, and he succeeded in drawing into them a series of linguists, including Michel Bréal and Antoine Meillet.

In his linguistic study of Yiddish, Sainéan did not cover all aspects of the language. He was, after all, only making preparations. Therefore a good deal was implicit that was closer or farther removed from the language. Even onomastics: he was the first to approach it from a Yiddish linguistic point of view (Fr. 183, footnote). But he dealt systematically with hardly anything but vocabulary. While a separate phonetics and morphology were at least parts of his plan, syntax was not even included in the scheme; in those years it was not generally held that syntax, too, manifests the specifics of a language. But there is no doubt that Sainéan's study of Yiddish was the first comprehensive treatment of the language on a solid linguistic basis. Any scholarly pronouncements on the subject made before him had been scanty and entirely isolated. Also, the number of linguistic problems of Yiddish on which he did dwell is impressive. I will try here to explore several of them.

1. Middle High German dialects. From the very start of his work, Sainéan realized that the main genetic difficulties were caused by an attempt to derive the Germanic element of Yiddish from some general German. Even serious students of the language had been convinced that Yiddish and German were on the same level, but that the Jews here and there failed to observe the norms properly. (The main stress in this was, of course, on phonetics; after all, seman-

tics was not much more than a provisional edifice in the general linguistics of this period.) Some thought in terms of Old German[19] or Older German;[20] we also find the designations Old High German[21] and Middle High German;[22] but none of these parallels were drawn on the basis of a serious linguistic comparison. Everyone was thinking of what Leopold Zunz, the founder of the Science of Judaism in Germany, had set up as a category back in 1832: *ungebräuchliches, oder fehlerhaftes Deutsch*[23] ('unusable, or erroneous German'). Indeed, it was difficult to think of anything better as long as a methodical comparison did not cause one to look into the direction in which the parallelism with Yiddish is at its greatest: the German dialects. This new perspective, based on the view that the dialects were retarded in their development (i.e. that they "retain the old features with greater tenacity"; R. 88) and corrected by the facts of Jewish history and by further comparison, of necessity leads to Middle High German in general, and, directly hence, to the medieval German dialects. The first to have grasped this and to have realized that "within Yiddish it is again possible to distinguish dialects, among which we only want to stress that of the Lithuanian Jews as the one which is phonetically closest to Middle High German," was Alfred Landau.[24] But it was Lazare Sainéan who supplied the foundations for this conception and bolstered it with the necessary linguistic facts of Old and Modern German dialects. And he was the first who laid down for Yiddish linguistics the fundamental proposition: "It is beyond any doubt that in the Middle Ages the Jews spoke the different provincial dialects [Fr. ed.: "le dialecte de différentes provinces"] of Germany, where they were allowed to take refuge."[25]

[19] Leopold Zunz: *Die gottesdienstlichen Vorträge der Juden, historisch entwickelt; ein Beitrag zur Alterthumskunde und biblischen Kritik, zur Literatur- und Religionsgeschichte*, Berlin, 1832 (₂1892), p. 440, footnote. The second edition was revised according to the author's desk copy; in quoting I will therefore distinguish between Z (ed. 1832) and Z' (ed. 1892).

[20] Zunz, *ibid.*

[21] Zunz, *op. cit.*, 440, 441.; Friedrich Chr. B. Avé-Lallemant: *Das deutsche Gaunerthum*, vol. 3, 1862, p. 207.

[22] Zunz, *op. cit.*, 440, 441; Avé-Lallemant, *loc. cit.*; Max Grünbaum: *Jüdisch-deutsche Chrestomathie*, Leipzig, 1882; Moritz Güdemann: *Geschichte des Erziehungswesens und der Cultur der abendländischen Juden*, vol. 3, Vienna, 1888, 291; Abraham Berliner: *Literatur-Blatt der Wochenschrift "Die jüdische Presse,"* Berlin, 1 (1870), 2; "Die mittelhochdeutsche Sprache bei den Juden," *Jahrbuch für jüdische Geschichte und Literatur*, Berlin (1898), 162–182; Hermann L. Strack: *Theologisches Literaturblatt*, Leipzig, 12 (1882), 89; and others.

[23] Zunz, *op. cit.*, p. 440. This is the designation of the third among the four constituent elements of the German language current among the Jews (*Bestandtheile der bei den Juden üblichen deutschen Sprache*), *op. cit.*, p. 439.

[24] *Die Presse*, no. 32, Vienna, 1882.

[25] *Studiu dialectologic*, p. 60. That by "different provincial dialects" he meant dialects of Middle High German may be concluded not only from the reference to the Middle Ages, but also from the great number of parallel citations and unequivocally from a passage in his criticism of Anton Rée: *Die Sprachverhältnisse der heutigen Juden, im Interesse der Gegenwart*, Hamburg, 1844, in *Studiu dialectologic*, p. 70, where he says: "Instead of considering Judeo-German as a natural evolution from *Middle High German*, analogic to the other German dialects, Rée sees in it an original and independent formation." Sainéan also knew already that only southern and central German dialects need to be considered in Yiddish studies.

Today, of course, we have to regard this achievement of Sainéan's, regardless even of his errors in the selection of etyma, as only half an achievement. As a Germanist in Yiddish linguistics, Sainéan pointed out only what was common with German in the Yiddish material, and with this his intention was exhausted. The other half of the task would have been to show what was different in the specific evolution of Yiddish. But to fulfill this task, Sainéan, like his age, was not sufficiently mature.

2. YIDDISH DIALECTS. Despite regional differences in grammar and vocabulary, the word "dialect" makes one think above all of the sound system. This is true of Yiddish no less than of other languages; Yiddish dialects also differ considerably in other domains; but it is safe to say that the major difference between the dialects of Yiddish is in their sounds. There is a considerable body of evidence in the history of Yiddish that the language was constantly avoiding lexical and morphological divergences. One is therefore confronted with the ever fascinating question as to why the dialectal phonetic differences attracted so little scholarly attention throughout the history of Yiddish linguistics up to Sainéan. We find only stray remarks here and there, and even Sainéan, who was the first to approach the problem of Yiddish dialects systematically, did not grasp this matter fully. It seems as if in former days differences between languages were noted only if they were obstacles to mutual intelligibility. On this basis Sainéan was justified in stating that "the Judeo-German dialect, spreading to this day over a large part of Europe, does not present any fundamental or profound differences which might make it unintelligible in all its dispersion, as is the case for example with the provincial dialects of Germany" (R[umanian ed., p.] 62). And yet Sainéan did his work on Yiddish in the first stage of the launching of phonetics (in the German-speaking sphere, where he did his work, this stage was represented by Sievers and the so-called "German School": Bremer, Techmer, Winteler, Trautmann, Viëtor), which soon led to detailed phonetic descriptions of dialects, and he therefore could not remain incognizant of such "differences," for he realized that if they are "not prominent [Fr. ed, 94: "profondes"], they are sufficiently interesting to divide Judeo-German into a series of dialectal shadings according to the divers regions of its linguistic territory" (*ibid.*). Such material needs classification, and Sainéan set out, "after special research" (*ibid.*), to classify it on the basis of the vocalism; "the consonant system remains invariable or undergoes only insignificant changes" (*ibid.*). Incidentally, this vowel basis for the classification remains undisputed to this day. Of all Yiddish dialectologists, only Veynger operated with a consonantal feature (the use of hissing-hushing fricatives and the corresponding affricates) as a criterion for one subdivision in the dialect scheme.[26]

At the present state of our knowledge about Yiddish dialects, Sainéan's scheme cannot satisfy us. As a matter of fact, he was himself aware of its weak-

[26] See M. Veynger: *Yidishe dialektologye*, Minsk, 1929, p. 56 ("The System Scheme of Yiddish Dialects"). Sainéan was aware of this particular consonantal feature. It is a curious fact that J. Gerzon (*Die jüdisch-deutsche Sprache*, Frankfurt/M., 1902, pp. 14–15) got this fact from Sainéan even though one of his own Yiddish informants was a gentleman who no doubt spoke the "Lithuanian" dialect (Gerzon, p. 18).

ness. The chapter on dialects was the only one where he made substantial changes when he adapted his study into French. In making the changes, he was, in all probability, following Landau's advice.[27] Yet he had no material for anything better, nor did he have any specific guidance for improvement. Let us recall that access even to the appropriate Wenker atlas materials[28] could first be had, at best, no earlier than 1889; it was only then that the decision was reached by which "the Kultus Ministry ordered through Ministry Director Althoff that the state library in Berlin was to receive one copy of every three-sheet handwritten map completed in Marburg by Wenker and his collaborators, Maurmann and Wrede."[29] If the first of Wenker's maps to be received by the Berlin State Library was finished on September 13, 1889, as Walther Mitzka reports (*ibid.*), Sainéan could hardly have profited from it, since he had long ago[30] left Germany where, "in the Imperial Library at Berlin," as he states in a letter to Landau of September 24, 1892, he carried out the bulk of his research on Yiddish. And yet Sainéan deserves the honor of a pioneer in Yiddish dialectology, not only because he made "the beginning of a scholarly division and systematization of the Yiddish dialects,"[31] but even more so because this beginning contained many elements of lasting value. No more than "elements," for Sainéan was still unable, for example, to grasp the meaning of Landau's suggestion (in a letter to him dated October 8, 1892) that Yiddish would be better served if, "instead of assuming definite dialects whose delimitation from one another always raises difficulties, an attempt were made rather to delimit each language phenomenon separately."[32] This meant the method of isoglosses. But Sainéan thought in generalizations, generalizations with a specific direction. He was very anxious to conform to two illusions of that period about Yiddish: (1) that Yiddish, itself a lateral derivative of German, could not be internally differentiated; (2) that Yiddish was maximally identical with certain German dialects. The contradiction between these ideas and his own discoveries about Yiddish can be attributed, as we have said, to Sainéan's split outlook. He was led and kept far astray by his generalizations. Thus he set up an "Austro-Russian" dialect (R. 62) with the following delimitation: "forming a semicircle which, starting with the northern part of Austria, from Bohemia and Moravia, goes through Hungary, continues into Rumania (*Ţara Romănească*), and, through Galicia, ends up in Russia" (*ibid.*). And when Landau wrote him in a letter (October 10, 1892; I quote from the recovered original and see from Sainéan's underscorings

[27] See Correspondence (cf. footnote 4), pp. 289, 291.

[28] Wenker's work of 1881, which is discussed by M. Veynger ([Linguistic Cartography and the Yiddish Linguistic Atlas], *Tsaytshrift* (Minsk), 2–3 (1928), pp. 655 ff.), could also be consulted in Marburg only; see Walther Mitzka: *Handbuch zum deutschen Sprachatlas*, Marburg, 1952, p. 12.

[29] Mitzka, *ibid.*, p. 10.

[30] "Rentré au pays [Rumania] au mois de juin 1889" (*Une carrière philologique en Roumanie (1885–1900)*, Paris–Bucharest, 1901, p. 2).

[31] Leyzer Vilenkin: *Yidisher shprakhatlas fun Sovetn-farband*, Phonetics, Minsk, 1931, Preface, col. ix.

[32] Correspondence (see footnote 4), p. 289.

how Landau's words surprised him) that he cannot agree "to the assumption of an Austro-Russian dialect," because there is a "sharp difference between the dialects of Bohemia and Galicia. The former has a decisively Upper German character, while Galician [Yiddish] is nearer to the Central German dialects. Moravian [Yiddish] seems to form a transitional stage. In Galicia the dialect of the East differs from that of the West, the latter seeming to coincide with that of Russian Poland. Toward the East the political boundary also signifies the beginning of the West and South Russian dialect," Sainéan was upset. He changed the delimitations of the dialect[33] and stated in the French version that "in the absence of any previous research on the varieties of Judeo-German, it is at present impossible to give, even tentatively, a comprehensive picture of its subdialects" (Fr. 94), but he left intact the schematization proper of the dialect (except for a change in two text words and the replacement of the designation "Austria-Hungary" by "Hungary"). Nor did he introduce extensive changes in the schematizations of the other dialects. How unwilling he was to renounce his generalizations is evident from the following detail: the only major alteration with respect to the Rumanian version is the statement that the "Polish" dialect (Fr. 96) has, corresponding to MHG. [*ū*], not [*ū*] but [*ī*]; and this is the truth, but how is this alteration effected? By the addition of a nonchalant "or" after the previous statement: "*ū* = *ū*: *būx*, *gūt*, *ṣūn* (*Buch*, *gut*, *Sohn*); ou bien = *ī* (par *ü*): *bīx*, *git*, *ṣīn*."

This must look out of kilter to anyone familiar with the facts, and as a result no dialectologist of Yiddish (or of German) took account of Sainéan's dialect schemes.[34] But they need not be discarded entirely, and I can see my way clear to salvaging them by reconstructing Sainéan's dialect schemes (at this point only the first three groups; the fourth is beset by special problems of its own) on the basis of the following premises:

a. We dispense with the headings. They are, after all, the crux of the generalizations, and they should be renounced because they contain prejudices of the period. Cleared of the distorting captions, the data reveal Sainéan's true discoveries, which, though they are fragmentary in the extreme (limited geographically and involving only some of the vowels), already stand at a high level of reality, especially if the time at which they were made is kept in mind. We will designate the groups by preliminary, neutral I, II, etc.

b. We obtain the new groupings if we consider the indications in Sainéan's existing groups about geographic sound differences for what they are, viz. representatives of dialects, and if we place them together with all other sounds outside of all indications. We also make use of the general orientations given by

[33] In the French version, the first dialect (originally the "Austro-Russian") has no name at all; instead we read: "Judeo-German, spoken on the one hand in Hungary, and on the other in Rumania and Galicia (as well as in Russia)" (Fr. 95).

[34] Besides that, the readers did not read him properly. The *Yidisher shprakhatlas* (col. ix) found a "Galician-Hungarian" dialect in Sainéan, while in reality the words in Sainéan's description of his first dialect group (Fr. 95) must be read in a considerably different way; see preceding footnote.

Sainéan in his descriptions above the schemes, here taking account of present-day knowledge (this enables us to ignore the errors).

c. Since our approach is synchronic, we place together genetically different sounds which are listed separately by Sainéan.

The further step of assigning the resulting groups to the corresponding dialects which Yiddish dialectology has established since Sainéan, must be left for another occasion. My present task is exhausted by the compilation of the schemes. I use Sainéan's transcriptions (except that *x* is here used in place of Sainéan's χ) despite the fact that the note about them (Fr. 95) is rather scanty. Translations are supplied at the first occurrence of an example and in cases of possibly ambiguous recurrence.

I

ī: ṣīn 'son', *jīd* 'Jew', *šīl* 'synagogue'
i̊: ṣi̊n 'sun', *šti̊m* 'mute', *ṣi̊mr̥* 'summer'
ā: āṣn̥ 'iron', *bāsn̥* 'bite', *vāb* 'wife', *vās* 'white', *tsāt* 'time'; *frānt* 'relative', *nān* 'nine', *lāt* 'people'
a: hant 'hand', *vald* 'forest'
ū: jūr 'year', *nūṣ* 'nose'
ēi: flēiš 'meat', *klēid* 'dress', *nēin* 'no', *štēin* 'stone', *vēis* '(I) know'
oi: broid 'bread', *grois* 'big'; *oig'* 'eye', *boim* 'tree', *koifn̥* 'buy', *loifn̥* 'run', *toib* 'deaf'
ou: boux 'belly', *houṣ* 'house', *toub* 'pigeon', *mouṣ* 'mouse'

II

ī: ṣīn, jīd, šīl
i̊: ṣi̊n, šti̊m, ṣi̊mr̥
ā: flāš, klād, nān 'no', [*štān*], [*vās*] 'know'; *āg, bām, kāfn̥, lāfn̥, tāb* 'deaf'
a: hant, vald
ū: jūr, nūṣ
ai: aiṣn, baisn, vaib, [*vais*] 'white', [*tsait*]; *fraint, nain* 'nine', *lait*
oi: broid, grois
ou: boux, houṣ, toub 'pigeon', *mouṣ*

III

ī: ṣīn, jīd, šīl
i̊: ṣi̊n, šti̊m, ṣi̊mr̥
ā: āṣn̥, bāsn̥, vāb, vās 'white', *tsāt*; *frānt, nān* 'nine', *lāt*
å: hånt, våld
ū: jūr, nūṣ
ēi: flēiš, klēid, nēin 'no', *štēin, vēis* 'know'
oi: broid, grois; *oig', boim, koifn̥, loifn̥, toib* 'deaf'
ou: boux, houṣ, toub 'pigeon', *mouṣ*

IV

ē: brēd, grēs; *ēg', bēm, kēfn̥, lēfn̥, tēb* 'deaf'
ō: jōr, nōṣ, tōg 'day'
u: [*bux*], [*gut*] 'good', [*ṣun*] 'son'; *un* 'and', *fun* 'of', *ṣumr̥*, [*ṣun*] 'sun'
ēi: flēiš, nēin 'no', *vēis* 'know'
ai: aiṣn̥, baisn̥, vaib, vais 'white'; *fraint, nain* 'nine', *lait*
oi: boix, moiṣ, toib 'pigeon'

V

ī: bīx, ṣīn 'son'
ai: šnai 'snow', *klaid; flaiš, gain* 'go', *nain* 'no', *vais* 'know'
oi: [*broid*], [*grois*]; *oig', boim, loifn̥, toib* 'deaf'
ou: houṣ, toub

3. Elements. Classical natural science distinguished "primary matter," "constituent parts." In this sense these terms can be used only in reference to fusion languages. Were they used previously in the same way? In our case, Zunz introduced the concepts into the study of Yiddish in 1832, although not yet in their most used sense. It was Sainéan who first made methodical use of them in their conventional meaning with reference to Yiddish, for Sainéan was the first who in fact realized with complete clarity that in addition to German, other languages also had a part in the formation of Yiddish. In the Rumanian version of his Yiddish study he already had separate chapters: "1. The German Element" (R. 87ff.), "2. The Hebrew Element" (R. 99ff.), "3. The Slavic, Especially the Polish Element" (R. 113ff.). And, as a supplement (only in the Rumanian version, of course), Sainéan had a chapter on "The Rumanian Element" (R. 123ff.).[35]

This part of Sainéan's work, more than any other, reveals the specific intellectual rift which plagued a scholar who could not free himself of an obsession of his age. Two entirely separate thought processes may be observed which remain distinct in their application. On the one hand, it is argued that Yiddish is a pure German dialect, except that, for example, "the Hebrew element [is] the most numerous and most important of the foreign elements, and the Polish element [is] less widespread than the former two, but sufficiently well represented" (R. 87); on the other hand, it is explicitly shown how basically Yiddish is composed of *all* its separate elements, including German.

In what way is Yiddish German? The following are the most important factors which can be cited in brief from Sainéan's work. (My quotations on phonetics and grammar are from the French variant (Fr.).) (a) As far as the German element is concerned, the kinship between Yiddish and German in the domain of sounds is not presented with complete clarity.[36] If we disregard the fact that it is not sounds alone which are involved, we can more or less understand Sainéan's view that in the Yiddish of Lithuania, for example, one can distinguish "the distinctive traits of the Swabian group" (Fr. 93);[37] that "the Bavaro-Austrian dialectal group with its Moravian, Carinthian, and other varieties con-

[35] Elsewhere (R. 86) he includes this in the "Romance element," which comprises also Latin, Italian, and French. He discusses the words *bentšn̩* 'bless', *orn̩* 'pray', *lēinn̩* 'read', *såndi̊k'* 'man holding the child at circumcision', *trop* 'accent', *pen* 'pen', *ni̊tl̩* 'Christmas', *planxe̥nn̩* 'bawl', *sargęnęs* 'cerements', *tšūln̩t* 'Sabbath dish kept warm overnight', *preiẹn̥* 'ask', *pi̊ltsl̩* 'girl', *plet* 'raffle'. Because of *braile̥ft* 'marriage', Sainéan thought it necessary to speak also of "the Dutch element."

[36] Sainéan said that he was reserving "for the second part, devoted to phonetics and morphology, the laws pertaining to the correspondence of sounds and the formation of words" (R. 87).

[37] In the Rumanian variant: "the Alemannic group" (R. 60f.).

stitutes the basis" of the Yiddish current "in Austria-Hungary, in Russia, and in Galicia" (*ibid.*); or that the Wallachian dialect "presents in its vocalism certain peculiarities common to the dialects of . . . [Bohemia and Carinthia] with a general physiognomy in conformity with those of the Bavarian group" (*ibid.*). Sainéan even goes on to say that the other components of Yiddish were Germanized from the phonic point of view. "The Hebrew element has undergone, under the influence of the Germanic stock, . . . a veritable metamorphosis in the sense that its physiognomy has assumed a character which has nothing Semitic in it any more. This transformation was carried out by a triple action: by the pronunciation, by the accentuation, and by the suffixes" (Fr. 180). "The Polish element has in its vocalism undergone, just like the Hebrew element, the phonetic changes which dominate in our dialect . . ." (Fr. 189). (b) On the point of grammar, Sainéan was quite certain: "Judeo-German has retained a basically Germanic grammar" (Fr. 93). (c) German, too, are "the senses of Judeo-German words which are not found in the [German] literary language; [they] are purely and simply medieval, archaic, or common to the German dialects" (R. 88).

In the light of present day Yiddish dialectology, morphology, and lexical study (semasiology), this allegation of identity with German does not hold water. But in this paper, where I am discussing Sainéan's accomplishments, I need not stress this shortcoming particularly. I should like to quote only some of his own statements which stress, even though unwillingly, the specifics of the Yiddish language. These comments were, of course, all offered in defense of Yiddish phenomena which are not in conformity with German. They ought to be freed of their apologetic tone and converted into simple propositions of Yiddish linguistics. Not that their level corresponds to the requirements of modern research; but they do correspond to the height which Sainéan had by then achieved. Wherever possible I will, for comparative purposes, indicate whether a fact cited by Sainéan is also to be found in the cited study of Zunz (Z) and/or in the dictionary (*Yidish-rusisher verterbukh*, Zhitomir, 1876) of Lifshits (L); both were distinguished predecessors of Sainéan's. Leopold Zunz (1794, Detmold —1886, Berlin), the founder and theoretician of the Science of Judaism, should be regarded as a pioneer in the study of Yiddish dialects as well. In Lifshits Yiddish linguistics had its greatest lexicographic pioneer. At each subsequent step Yiddish lexicography should therefore refer to Lifshits if it wants to measure its progress. (A dash means the absence of the word in Zunz or Lifshits, as the case may be.)

I. The specificness of one group of words of German origin is explained by Sainéan on the basis of an argument of Zunz's (*op. cit.*, 440). He calls this group "German words pertaining to religious and ceremonial cult." These are words like *šīl* 'synagogue' (L, Z), *jūrtsāt* 'anniversary of death' (L, Z′), *jī́dîšn̥* 'to circumcise' (L, Z), *kvåtr̥* 'godfather' (L, –), *ı̊'ntr̥fīr̥* 'best man' (L, –), *lērnn̥* 'to study ["restricted to religious life"]' (L, Z), [*ófrīfn̥*] 'call to the reading of the Law' (–, Z).

II. One group of Yiddish words of German origin is identified by Sainéan with its German equivalents completely, except that the German words are "medieval, which have disappeared from the modern language" (R. 89). This is his assertion, but in proceeding to prove this alleged identity, he completely ignores the phonetic and semantic differences which he himself cites.[38] Unwillingly, he thus himself reveals the development of the Yiddish facts. His revelation becomes particularly strange when we consider this group of words in the Rumanian version of his treatise. As if on purpose, he translates both the Yiddish and the (Middle High) German words in the *Rumanian* text into *modern* German; that is, he installs a uniform metalinguistic criterion which permits one to see the differences in the concrete linguistic material on a uniform basis and hence more strikingly. In quoting Sainéan, I have introduced two changes in order to make my conclusion more explicit. I have arranged the words in columns (a Yiddish word with its meaning opposite its German cognate with its meaning); and in the Yiddish words I have made Sainéan's transcription more precise according to the way he perfected it after various attempts and used it in the French version (Fr. 95, footnote 3). All the rest is exactly as in Sainéan. An added column indicates the presence or absence of the particular Yiddish form in Lifshits and Zunz. We have dispensed with Sainéan's etymologies and have omitted several of his examples which are blatantly in error or are referred to other sources ([*goidr̥*] etc.).

[*antplek'n̥*] 'offenbaren':	*entblecken* 'sichtbar machen'	L, –
[*farflēitsn̥*] 'überschwemmen':	*verflözzen* 'übergiessen'	L, –
[*faršārt*] 'muthwillig':	*verschart* 'zerstreut'	L,[39] –
[*farti̊mln̥*] 'verwirren':	*vertumeln* 'betäuben'	L, –
[*fartsi̊k'n̥*] 'räuberisch hinwegführen':	*verzucken* 'schnell hinwegnehmen'	L, Z
[*g'e̥vélti̊k'n̥*] 'herrschen':	*geweltigen* 'überwältigen'	L, –
[*hofr̥di̊k'*] 'stolz':	*hoffertic* 'hoffärtig, stolz'	L[40], –
[*i̊nde̥*][41] 'Welle':	*ende* 'Flut'	–, –
[*lugl̥*] 'Sack':	*lôgel* 'Fässchen'	–, Z
[*šaln̥*] 'jauchzen':	*schallen* 'jubeln mit Gesang und Saitenspiel'	–, –
-[*švexn̥*][42] 'entweihen':	(*ver*)*schwechen* 'herabsetzen, beschimpfen, verderben'	–, –

The difference is apparent, as it has to be when two different languages are involved. And this is only a small sample of the possible evidence, selected without any methodological principle. Theoretically Sainéan was of a completely different opinion; he held that to impute "to the Judeo-German speech that it may have given to many German words acceptations foreign to that tongue . . .

[38] It is immaterial for the present purpose whether Sainéan rendered the forms and the meanings of the two quantities in each equation with sufficient accuracy. What matters more is that he was fully cognizant of their differences.

[39] In a slightly different form.

[40] In a slightly different form.

[41] Thus elsewhere only in Hermann L. Strack: *Jüdisches Wörterbuch*, Leipzig, 1916 (Polish Yiddish). Usually *i̊nd*.

[42] In the colloquial language only *faršvexn̥* 'to profane' occurs. Perhaps Sainéan used the basic stem form as was his habit.

proves a complete ignorance of the historical evolution of the language" (R. 88). *This* evolution, of all things, was supposed to have stood still! But it was in these terms that Yiddish was thought of at the time, and Sainéan proceeded to demonstrate identity with German. What came out, however, was separateness, specificness—exactly what true research must yield. Willy-nilly Sainéan was therefore a pathfinder in this sector, too: the discovery of the peculiarity of the *innere Sprachform* of the Yiddish language even with respect to its sources.

It remains for a further investigation to determine where Sainéan obtained his linguistic material. It is a fact that he consulted printed sources also; it is not always easy to determine what is his own language and what is derived from other sources.

III. It was an innovation of Sainéan's to classify Yiddish words according to internal criteria, i.e. criteria derived from the material proper. Perhaps we have here an early step on the road which he followed so successfully years later "of studying the origins of words . . . by the aid of the resources of the language themselves."[43] In folk-languages, he says, we find "the following three general procedures . . .: [1] the selection, from a series of synonyms, of a single expression for the respective notion; [2] the importance of expressivity in the conceptions of the people; and [3] frequent resort to diminutive forms for expressing the meaning of primitives [i.e. non-diminutives]" (R. 91). The first category is illustrated by the independence of *redn̥* and *šprexn̥*, the latter of which "is restricted in Judeo-German to the recitation of magic formulas for conjuring away charms" (*ibid.*).

A great deal of material is cited by Sainéan in illustrating the second category.[44] It is worth noting in detail what Sainéan has to say about it, not only because we have here the method of work which Sainéan used later on, but also because this approach can still be of great service to Yiddish studies in the future. It is important to remember that the great specificness of Yiddish consists in its "slangy" freshness. This is its indigenous source of innovation and enrichment. Sainéan believed that folk languages everywhere embody "the ideas in expressive, concrete, palpable words. To this tendency the dialects owe their true originality. . . . From this point of view the vocabulary of every dialect should be analyzed in order to catch in it the original conceptions, the ideas on which the attention of the people has been fixed. Some of these conceptions may be old and hence common to various dialects; others [are] more or less modern creations and [are] peculiar to a special way of seeing and considering external things" (R. 91). Here we have Bréal's requirement that the linguist should "se depouiller et se faire peuple." It remains subject to doubt whether all of Sainéan's illustrations passed the test of these considerations. But we are concerned here (and in this paper as a whole) with the principles of Sainéan's

[43] Preface (p. iii) of *Les sources indigènes de l'étymologie française*, vol. 3, Paris, 1930.

[44] He continued to collect examples of this type. The Rumanian version states that the list "does not pretend to be complete" (pp. 91f.); the French (p. 133) version promises that it "will be completed in the glossary appended to this study." The glossary was never published.

conceptions; the detailed criticism of the illustrations must be reserved for another occasion. To quote his illustrations in full would require too much space. Sainéan arranged his materials as follows: the Yiddish word in a German orthography and in a Yiddish phonetic transcription is juxtaposed to a German literary equivalent compared with a German dialectal word (with source references). In the bulk of the cases, the usage of the Yiddish word is illustrated from an 1863 translation of the Psalms, and is cited under the German word. Here we present only the juxtapositions arranged according to the Yiddish word in Sainéan's more correct transcription of 1901–1902, again referring to the presence or absence of the word in Lifshits; in cases where a transcription is not available or is not according to Sainéan's own rules I have supplied it in its correct form in brackets. The letters R.Y. following L indicate that the word is contained in Lifshits' Russian-Yiddish dictionary, but not in his Yiddish-Russian volume. It must be remembered that Sainéan's German translations are primary; the rough English equivalents have been supplied only for purposes of general orientation.

akr̥:Pflug 'plough' L; *aksl̥:Schulter* 'shoulder' L; *bahåltn̥:verbergen* 'to hide' L; *bātn̥:tauschen* 'to change' L; *bēis̥rn̥:zürnen* 'to be angry' L; [*bi̊k'n̥*]:*anbeten* 'to worship' L; *boksr̥n̥*[45]:*Johannisbrod(t)* 'St. John's bread' L; *dīx:Schenkel* 'thigh' L; *di̊l:betäubt* 'stunned' L; *doktr̥:Arzt* 'doctor' L; *dr̥grāxn̥*[46]:*ergreifen* 'to reach' L; *dr̥mann̥:erinnern* 'remind' L; *ēinnextn̥:vorgestern* 'day before yesterday' L; *fānt hubn̥:hassen* 'to hate' L; *farextn̥:herstellen* 'to repair' L; *fars̥īxn̥:schmecken* 'to taste' L; *fartex̥:Schürze* 'apron' L; *far vūs:warum* 'why' L[47]; *fetr̥:Oheim* 'uncle' L; *fīl mūl:oft* 'often' –; *foxr̥:Fächer* 'fan' L; *frānt:Verwandter* 'relative' L; *g'e̥dext:dicht* 'dense' L; [*g'e̥vi̊nn̥*]:*gebären* 'to give birth to' L; *g'e̥vūr vērn:erfahren* 'to learn' L; *grēitn̥:bereiten* 'to prepare' L; *grēt:Wäsche* 'laundry' L; *gring':leicht* 'easy, light' L; *gūrn̥:Stockwerk* 'storey' L; *hārn̥:kümmern* 'to concern' L; [*hoik'r̥*]:*Buckel* 'hump' L; *i̊mi̊di̊'m:überall* 'everywhere' L; *i̊nēinm̥:zusammen* 'together' L; *joux:Suppe* 'soup' L; *kāle̥xi̊k':rund* 'round' L; *k'ēin mul:niemals* 'never' L. R. Y.; [*k'i̊k'n*]:*schauen* 'to look' L; *klērn̥:überlegen* 'to think' L; *kloistr̥:Kirche* 'church' L; *knāpr̥:Käfer* 'beetle' –; *koibr̥:Korb* 'basket' –; *koiti̊k'*[48]:*schmutzig* 'dirty' L; *koul:Kugel* 'sphere' L; *lāle̥x:Bett-Tuch* 'bed sheet' L; *lērnn̥:lehren* 'to teach' L; *materie̥:Eiter* 'pus' L; *m̊oul:Mund* 'mouth' L; *nextn̥:gestern* 'yesterday' L; *of dr̥ naxt*[49]:*Abend* 'evening' L. R. Y.; *ploušn̥:plaudern* 'to chat' –; *pouk:Trommel* 'drum' L; *rēif:Kreis* 'circle' L; *rēte̥ni̊š:Rätsel* 'riddle' –; [*s̥ēig'r̥*]:*Uhr* 'clock' L; *s̥īdln̥:schimpfen* 'to curse' L; [*s̥i̊'mr̥fēige̥le̥*]:*Schmetterling* 'butterfly' L; *s̥ok:Strumpf* 'sock' L; *šmēixln̥:lächeln* 'to smile' L; *šprēitn̥:ausbreiten* 'to spread' L; *štēin:Felsen* 'cliff' L[50]; *štīb:Zimmer* 'room' L; *šti̊pn̥:stossen* 'to push' L; *tåpn̥:tasten* 'to grope' L; *tåte̥:Vater* 'father' L; *tāx:Bach, Fluss* 'brook, creek, river' L; *tenn̥boim:Tanne* 'pine' L; *toitr̥ kop:Schädel* 'skull' –; *trugn̥:schwanger* [*sein*] 'to be pregnant' L; *tsi̊me̥s:Zuspeise* 'dessert' L; *ubfresr̥:*

[45] Rum. ed.: *boksser*.

[46] Probably an error in transcription. It is a Western Yiddish form. The Rumanian version has *dergreichen*; we would expect *dr̥grēixn̥*.

[47] L lists this word only in R. Y. (Zhitomir, 1869): *počtó* 'what for'.

[48] Missing in R.

[49] But cf. [*gitn̥ uvn̥t*] 'good evening'.

[50] Translated only as 'stone'.

Raupe 'caterpillar' –; *unbāsn̥:Frühstück* 'breakfast' L[51]; *unhēibn̥:anfangen* 'to begin' L; [*untīn*]:*anziehen* 'to dress, to put on' L; *untrābr̥:Kutscher* 'coachman' L; [*varẹmẹs*]:*Mittag*[52] 'dinner' L; *vēiti̊k'*:*Schmerz* 'pain' L; *vūrn̥:denn* 'for' L.

box:Faustschlag 'blow with the fist' L; *brēm:Augenbraue* 'eyebrow' L; *g'ẹlēgr̥: Lager* 'bed' L; *g'ẹtselt:Hütte* 'hut' L; *g'īx:geschwind* 'quick' L; *hek'r̥:Metzger* 'butcher' –; *klek'n̥:genügen* 'to suffice' L; *krenk'*:*Krankheit* 'malady' –; *patš* (*flåsk'*):*Ohrfeige* 'slap' (L, L); *šmek'n̥:riechen* 'to smell'.

IV. Sainéan devotes a special section to words which are diminutives according to their form. Here, too, he is an innovator, the first to realize that they are used in Yiddish "to express the primitive notions" (98), i.e. basic meanings rather than smaller versions of normally larger things. It is a "fruitful procedure . . . to come back to certain known forms and to assign them to a new logical application" (*ibid.*). I am not sure whether they should have been placed in a group apart. Are such diminutives anything but a semantic transfer on the basis of an emotional affinity? The following are cited by Sainéan (R. 98/Fr. 176): *šrābpendl̥* : *Bleistift* 'pencil' (L); *bēigl̥* : *Bretze* 'roll shaped like figure 8' (L); *ji̊ngl̥* : *Bube* 'boy' (L); *joiṣl̥* : *Kruzifix* 'crucifix' (–); *rendl̥* : *Dukaten* 'a former gold coin' (L); *bārgl̥* : *Hügel* 'hill' (L: *bergl̥*); *štāgl̥* : *Käfig* 'cage' (L: only *štāg*); *bērdl̥* : *Kinn* 'chin' (–); *fi̊ng'r̥l̥* : *Ring* 'ring' (L); *benkl̥* : *Sessel* 'easychair' (–); *mesr̥l̥*: *Federmesser* 'penknife' (L R.Y.); *koxr̥l̥*:*Kanne* 'pot' (–); *švēbåle̥*:*Zündhölzchen* 'match' (L).

V. Without any explicit reason, Sainéan sets off another group of words, apparently because he deals with them only "in passing" (R. 99). These are what we might call verbal phrases, the "logical transitions of verbs compounded with prepositions," as Sainéan awkwardly designates them (*ibid.*). He realizes that they are "interesting transitions and different from those of the [German] literary language" (*ibid.*). But when it comes to analyzing them, Sainéan stands completely helpless. Had he followed the elementary structural approach to Yiddish as a language in itself, he might have understood that every item of a separate language is separate, whether the reasons for this are known or unknown. I list the words of this group in the same way as the others, although Sainéan arranged them according to a different plan: *ubdånkn̥* : *sterben* 'die (iron.)' (L[53]); *ug'ẹnemn̥* : *gelähmt* 'paralyzed' (L[54]); *ubrextn̥* : *verrichten* 'celebrate, perform' (–); *ubšprexn̥* : *eine Zauberformel hersagen* 'recite a charm' (L); *unmaxn̥* : [*Notdurft verrichten*] 'relieve oneself' (L); *unštoisn̥* : *eine Anspielung verstehn* 'understand a hint' (L).

VI. With regard to the Semitic component of Yiddish, too, Sainéan brought out quite a number of interesting points. I will here refer only to a few.

As a result of his Germanistic approach, Sainéan naturally complained that the proportion of words of Hebrew-Aramaic origin in Yiddish had been exaggerated. The truly "popular" words had not been distinguished from the bookish

[51] L gives the rare meaning 'dinner' (*obéd*), which I have encountered elsewhere only in my own East Galician dialect.

[52] Also: *Mittagessen*.

[53] L translates it by the Russian idiom *prikazat' dolgo žit'*.

[54] L (in passive form) translates: *dostat' paralič v. . . .*, literally 'to get paralyzed in [one's] . . .'.

ones; folk-words had been confused with technical terms; no account had been taken of "whether or not there exist German equivalents" (R. 99). But this very complaint seems to be evidence that the considerable extent of the Semitic component of Yiddish was impressive to Sainéan. He concerned himself with it rather fully, even though according to Leyzer Vilenkin "Sainéan deals scantily with the Hebrew and Slavic" elements.[55] And in spite of himself he had to assert in one place: "Be that as it may, however, the Hebrew element is relatively well represented" (R. 99).

He stresses (and illustrates) the basic fact that "the Hebrew element which has entered the Judeo-German dialect is not derived directly from biblical Hebrew but from a later development of it, as it presents itself to us in the Talmud and in rabbinic literature. Therefore these words in general have a sense which is foreign to the language of the Bible and corresponds to the one of the talmudic writings. Others do not even exist in the Bible, but are original formations: Aramaic or neo-Hebrew Talmudisms" (R. 101). For example, 1. [*antāne̥n*] means 'to charge with guilt, I accuse and defend', 2. [*mi̊ni̊g'*]—'usage, especially religious', 3. [*tsār*]—'suffering, sorrow', 4. [*tsēilm̥*]—'cross, crucifix', 5. [*tšīve̥*]—'expiation'; all these Yiddish meanings are closer to the ones of their talmudic cognates than to those of the biblical ones (1. 'load', 2. 'steering of a wagon', 3. 'small', 4. 'image', 5. 'return'); furthermore, Yiddish does not possess the biblical words 1. *[*moie̥d*] 'holiday', 2. *[*nēg'e̥v*] 'south', 3. *[*jåm*] 'west', but has the talmudic 1. [*jonte̥v*] '(literally) good-day', 2. *dūrm̥*, 3. [*māre̥v*]; the meaning of the Yiddish word [*dåle̥s*] 'poverty' is only talmudic, that of [*tfīse̥*] 'prison' is post-talmudic; etc.

Sainéan also concerned himself with the phonetics of the Semitic component and its historical phonology; he even worked out an approach of his own to this problem. And although phonetics was not a part of this particular study of his, he nevertheless—probably because he considered his approach to be a considerable achievement—could not restrain himself from presenting and illustrating it, at least in its broad outlines. I must leave this matter out of my present study; it would require a great deal of special additional research.

Morphology is also touched on but lightly: Sainéan discusses briefly the formation of the verb, the noun, and the adjective. Since this part of his work is quite clear, it is worthwhile citing here. Again I will indicate the presence or absence of each item in Zunz and in Lifshits, but will, of course, dispense with Sainéan's etymologies. And again I quote from the Rumanian version, because it is the earlier and the more complete, but I have utilized to the greatest possible extent the superior transcription of the French version.

The following verbs are listed:

1. a. [*xånf[e̥n]n̥*] 'flatter' (–, –); [*xåle̥šn̥*] 'faint' (L, –); [*xūlm̥n̥*] 'dream' (L, –); [*daršе̥nn̥*] 'preach' (–, Z); [*gås̥le̥nn̥*] 'rob' (–, –); [*g'etn̥*] 'divorce' (L, –); [*kašr̥n̥*] 'cleanse for Passover' (–, –); [*måsr̥n̥*] 'denounce' (L, –); [*mi̊špe̥tn̥*] 'judge' (L, –); [*pēigr̥n̥*] 'die (of animals)' (L, –); [*påtr̥n̥*] 'spoil' (L, –); [*tsēilm̥n̥*] 'cross oneself' (L, –); b. [*xåsme̥nn̥*] 'sign' (L, –); [*gånve̥nn̥*] 'steal' (L, –); [*harge̥nn̥*] 'kill' (L, –); [*jarše̥nn̥*] 'inherit' (L, –).

[55] *Shprakhatlas* (see footnote 31), col. ix.

2. [*antānę̊n*] (see above); [*farxi̊dę̊šn̥*] 'surprise' (L, –); [*farsåmn̥*] 'poison' (L, –); [*unšik'r̥n̥*] 'make drunk' (–, –); [*ous-*] '—'.

3. [*xoišę̊d ṣān*] 'suspect' (L, –); [*joitsę̊ ṣān*] 'do one's duty' (L, Z); [*måpl̥ ṣān*] 'miscarry' (L, –); [*matrīę̊x ṣān*] 'trouble' (L, –); [*mę̊xåbę̊d ṣān*] 'treat' (L, Z); [*mę̊xāję̊ ṣān*] 'animate' (L, –); [*mę̊jašę̊v ṣān*] 'consider, think over' (L, –); [*mę̊kājm̥ ṣān*] 'materialize' (L, –); [*mę̊kånę̊ ṣān*] 'envy' (L, Z); [*mę̊nådr̥ ṣān*] 'pledge' (L, –); [*mę̊šāę̊r ṣān*] 'assume' (L, –); [*mę̊šaleię̊x ṣān*] 'send off' (–, –); [*mę̊vāję̊š ṣān*] 'shame' (L, –); [*mę̊våṣę̊ ṣān*] 'put to shame' (L, Z); [*mę̊tsāę̊r ṣān*] 'grieve' (L, –); [*moixl̥ ṣān*] 'forgive' (L, –); [*moidę̊ ṣān*] 'confess' (L, –); [*noję̊g' ṣān*] 'be accustomed to' (L, Z); [*noik'm̥ ṣān*] 'avenge oneself' (L, –); [*toję̊ ṣān*] 'be mistaken' (–, Z).

4. The following noun-formation patterns are listed: [*-šåft*] ([*almūnę̊šåft*] 'widowhood' [–, –]), [*-k'ēit*] (*å'ṣę̊sk'ēit* 'insolence' [–, –], *mīsk'ēit* 'ugliness' [L, –]), also the diminutive in *-l̥* ([*ši̊ksl̥*] 'girl' [–, –]), and as a supplement: [*-tę̊*] [*kåptsn̥tę̊*] 'poor woman' (–, –) and the three plural formations in *-i̊m*: [*naruni̊m*] 'fools', [*doktoiri̊m̥*] (these two are labeled as "rather ironical") and [*kaptsuni̊m*] (which Sainéan calls "a Polish word.").

5. The following adjective-formation patterns are listed: a. [*-i̊š*] ([*balbåti̊š*] 'noble' [L, –], [*bę̊hēimi̊š*] 'stupid, dull' [–, –], [*g'ę̊nēivi̊š*] 'thievish' [L, –]), b. [*-(ę̊v)di̊k'*] ([*pēisę̊xdi̊k'*] 'of Passover' [L, –], [*šåbę̊sdi̊k'*] 'of the Sabbath' [L, –], [*xēinę̊vdi̊k'*] 'charming' [L, Z (in a different form)], *emę̊sdi̊k'* 'truthful' [L, –], [*moirę̊di̊k'*] 'fearful' [L, –]).

6. One adverb is cited as an instance of a derivational pattern: [*bašāmpr̥lę̊x*] 'probable' (L, –).

The above section on word formation is beyond doubt at least partly inspired by Zunz. Zunz's second of the four points among the *Bestandteile der bei den Juden üblichen deutschen Sprache* has four types of compositions of Hebrew-Aramaic morphemes with morphemes of Germanic origin; Zunz's type 1 corresponds with our number 3; Zunz's type 2 goes with our numbers 1a and 1b, 2, and 5; our numbers 4 and 6 are entirely new. In the remaining paragraphs, Sainéan merely shares a few illustrative examples with Zunz.

The bulk of his chapter on the Hebrew-Aramaic component is devoted by Sainéan to vocabulary. Since lexical problems remained Sainéan's favorite in later years, it is not surprising that his Yiddish researches contained the roots of this interest. The problem of the relation of Yiddish to the German dialects, which did not cease to trouble the students of Yiddish in the German cultural sphere, created among them a hypertrophic interest for the lexicology of this language. And what paths did they follow to penetrate its specific character? Zunz perceived a relationship (of Yiddish vocabulary) to *yidishkayt* 'the Jewish way of life', though he was not enough of a linguist to understand that this relationship can only be a genetic one before it becomes linguistic. Words can be *introduced* into a language with the help of a function which society assigns to them. But having arrived in language, their linguistic function alone prevails. They have no feature in themselves which might preserve this original "social" function of theirs within the framework of a linguistic system. A social feature is not necessarily a linguistic one. For Zunz's time, the sociological approach was no doubt no mean achievement, and it was the result of the new historical way of thinking. The father of the Science of Judaism could hardly have defined it in any other way; this is Yiddish study from a Science-of-Judaism point of view. Certainly, it barred the way to the language itself, but nevertheless this was the approach which was followed until recently, even by Borokhov, Shtif and their students and supporters, including the Hebraistic students of Yiddish. They can all be subsumed under a single heading. All those who in one way or another looked for the social functions of this part of Yiddish vocabulary were—at least on this point—Scientists of Judaism in contrast to linguists. Sainéan was one of them, too. And even he, the linguist, followed the same approach which he probably learned from Zunz directly: he, too, arranged his material "according to the order of the ideas" (R. 106). But here too he contributed something of his own.

Sainéan divided the Hebrew-Aramaic lexical material into two major domains. He defined them as follows: domain I—words (and here he means rather concepts) of the "*sphere of the religion*, whose multiple rites[56] accompany the Jew from his birth to his grave" (R. 106/Fr. 185, italics supplied); domain II—words from the "*intellectual sphere*, in which nearly all ideas of an abstract order were drawn from the fertile soil of Jewish learning, the Hebrew language being in the domain of ideas of a remarkable abundance" (R. 109/Fr. 186, italics supplied). This is *considerably like Zunz*. Domain I leads to Zunz's point 1, quotations *a* and *b*; domain II parallels Zunz's point 1, quotations *c* and *d*. Yet this is far from being Zunzian in its entirety. Both the number and the selection of words are different in Sainéan's study; moreover, he has subdivisions, additions, and comments which Zunz did not present. I will refrain here from a detailed comparison with Zunz, which would inevitably lead to a great deal of methodological and linguistic refutation. I present merely Sainéan's list of words, without comments, indicating only the extent to which it corresponds with Zunz and Lifshits. In doing so, I will follow Sainéan's order.

One comment only about the synonymic grouping of some words. Sainéan removes them from their alphabetic order (which is, incidentally, now even more disturbed by my more precise transcription) and juxtaposes them. To call attention to this, I have put the abbreviation "vs." in the appropriate places. It will be apparent with what acuteness he sometimes sensed the synonymity on the basis of the specific meaning of the Yiddish word. This conforms to Sainéan's pioneering role in approaching Yiddish. He is also the first student of Yiddish synonymics.

I would like to add that I made an effort to present the meanings of Sainéan's vocabulary as he had set them down, even if this turned out to be a disfavor to some words. In this respect, too, Sainéan's linguistic position should be apparent.

Base forms of "reflexive" verbs are listed, as by Sainéan, without the particle [s̥e̥x].

I. Religious Sphere

A. Calendar. Months of the Jewish year (none listed by L or Z): [*ni̊sn̥*], [*īr*], [*si̊vn̥*], (*tåme̥s̥*], [*ūv*], [*ell̥*], [*ti̊šre̥*], [*xežvn̥*], [*k'i̊sle̥v*], [*tēive̥s*], [*švåt*], [*ūdr̥*], [*vēiūdr̥*]; [*i̊br̥(jūr)*] 'leap year' (L, –), [*xoide̥š*] 'month' (L, –), [*re̥šxoide̥š*] 'beginning of the month' (L, –), [*me̥xåde̥š s̥ān (de̥ le̥vūne̥)*] 'to consecrate the moon' (–, –), [*le̥vūne̥*] 'moon' (L, –), *šū* 'hour' (L, –), (*rēg'e̥*] 'second, moment, instant' (L R.Y., –), [*šåbe̥s*] 'Saturday' (L, Z), [*ēre̥v*] 'eve' (L, –), [*xåle̥*] '[Sabbath bread]' (L, –),

[56] The French version erroneously has *restes* instead of *rites*.

[*k'ȋde̥š*] 'sanctification (on wine)' (–, Z), *sīde̥* 'holiday feast' (L, Z), [*s̥mīre̥*] 'hymn' (–, Z), [*havdūle̥ maxn̥*] 'to finish the Sabbath' (–, –), *jonte̥v* 'holiday' (L, Z), [*re̥še̥šūne̥*] 'New Year's day' (L, –), [*šoifr̥*] 'ritual ram's horn' (–, Z), [*je̥nk'ȋpr̥*] 'Day of Atonement' (L, –), [*kapūre̥*] 'rooster' (L, –), [*sȋke̥s*] 'feast of Tabernacles' (L R.Y., Z[57]), [*līle̥v*] 'palm branch' (L R.Y.[58], Z), [*esrȋg'*] 'cedar citron' (L, Z), [*pīrm̥*] 'Purim' (–, Z), [*šalxamūne̥s*] 'sending of presents' (–, –), [*pēise̥x*] 'Passover' (L, –), [*måtse̥*] 'unleavened cake' (L, Z), [*xume̥ts*] 'dough, leaven' (–, –), [*be̥tln̥*] 'to destroy' (–, –), [*kašr̥n̥*] 'to make clean' (–, –), [*sēidr̥*] 'arrangement of the celebration' (–, –), [*agūde̥*] 'recital of the exodus from Egypt' (–, –).

B. a. COMMUNITY LIFE. [*k'e̥hīle̥*] or [*k'ȋle̥*] 'community' (–, –), *kūl* 'people, folk' (L, Z), [*kūln̥*] 'to take part, to mix in community affairs' (–, –), [*parne̥s*] 'head' (–, –).

b. SYNAGOGUE. [*xås̥n̥*] 'cantor' (L, –), [*nȋg'n̥*] 'melody' (L, Z), [*daršn̥*] (–, –) or [*måge̥d*] 'preacher' (–, –), [*gåbe̥*] 'collector of contributions and charities' (L, –), [*šåme̥s*] 'servant of the synagogue' (–, –), [*tåle̥s*] 'prayer shawl' (L, Z), [*tvȋln̥*] 'phylacteries' (–, –), [*tfȋle̥*] 'prayer' (L, –), [*txȋne̥*] 'prayer for women' (L, –), [*sȋdr̥*] 'prayer book' (L, –), [*maxs̥r̥*] 'prayer book for the cycle of holidays' (–, –), [*ume̥d*] 'cantor's desk' (L, –), *almemor* 'reading desk,'[59] [*ūrn̥*] 'ark' (L[60], –), [*sēifr̥ toire̥*] 'scroll of the Law' (L, –), [*šxȋne̥*] 'divine splendor' (L, –).

c. EDUCATION. [*xēidr̥*] 'elementary school' (L, –), [*talme̥d toire̥*] 'school for the study of the Law' (–, –), [*be̥smedre̥š*] 'id.' (–, –), [*malåme̥d*] 'teacher, master' (L, –), [*je̥šȋve̥*] 'advanced school or rabbinical academy' (L, Z), [*be̥xīrȋm*] 'students' (L[61], –), [*rebe̥*] 'instructor' (L, –), [*låmdn̥*] 'learned person' (L, –), [*xuxm̥*] 'sage' (L, –), [*tåne̥*] 'person erudite in the Talmud' (–, –), [*s̥mån*] 'semester' (L, –), [*tanáx*] 'holy scripture' (L, –), [*toire̥*] 'scroll of the Law' (L, Z), [*xȋme̥š*] 'Pentateuch' (L, –), [*tȋlm̥*] 'Psalms' (L, –), [*dȋk'dȋk'*] 'grammar' (L, –), [*talme̥d*] 'Talmud' (–, –),[62] [*g'e̥mūre̥*] 'advanced section of study' (L, –), [*mȋšne̥*] 'talmudic text' (–, –), [*pȋlpl̥*] 'subtle disputation' (–, –).

d. RITUAL. *rūv* 'rabbi' (L, Z), [*dājn̥*] 'judge' (–, –), [*påsk'e̥nn̥*] 'to decide' (L, –), *mȋšpe̥t* 'judgment, lawsuit' (L, –), [*psak*] 'rabbinical decision' (L, –), [*šāle̥*] 'ritual question' (L, –), [*kaše̥*] 'id.' (L, Z), [*dȋn*] 'religious custom' (L, Z), [*mȋnȋg'*] 'consecrated usage' (L, Z), [*kūšr̥*] 'permitted according to the Law' (–, Z), [*ūsr̥*] 'prohibited according to the Law' (L, Z), [*pūsl̥*] 'interdicted as profane' (L, –), [*tume̥*] 'impure' (L, –), [*trēife̥*] 'not slaughtered according to rabbinical prescriptions' (L[63], Z), [*g'et*] 'bill of divorcement, divorce' (L, Z), [*xēirm̥*] 'excommunication' (L, –), [*šoixe̥t*] 'slaughterer' (L, –), [*koile̥n*] 'to slaughter' (L, –), [*xåle̥f*] '[slaughterer's] special knife' (–, –), *tse̥vūe̥* 'testament' (L, Z), *joire̥š* 'inheriting successor' (L, –).

e. ARGUMENTATION. (1) "LOGICAL" TERMS. [*hetr̥*] 'concession' (L, Z), [*ȋk'r̥*] 'basis, essential thing' (L, Z), [*tāne̥*] 'argument, objection' (L, –), [*tāne̥n*] 'to argue, controvert, dispute' (L, –), [*tere̥ts*] 'pretext' (L, Z). (2) "DIALECTICAL" TERMS. [*áde̥råbe̥*] 'a fortiori, the more so' (L, Z), [*avåde̥*] 'certainly, undoubtedly' (L, –), *afȋle̥* 'even if' (L, Z'), [*be̥fråt*] 'especially, particularly' (L, –), [*be̥k'ȋtsr̥*] 'in short, briefly' (L, –), *xȋts* 'outside, besides' (L, –), [*dåvk'e̥*] 'absolutely, with the whole intention' (L, Z), [*de̥haine̥*] 'namely' (L, –), [*efšr̥*] 'perhaps, maybe' (L, –), [*aklå'l*] 'summa summarum' (–, –), [*ale̥vái*] 'would that . . .' (L, Z), [*k'e̥dēi*]

[57] Only for 'tabernacle'.

[58] In a slightly different form.

[59] This word is listed by Sainéan out of "universal Jewish" considerations, not because it exists in this form in the Yiddish he described.

[60] In a slightly different form.

[61] Listed in the singular.

[62] Cf. footnote 59; not used reciprocally with the next word.

[63] In a slightly different form.

'in order to' (L, –), [*k'ėmåt*] 'almost' (L, –), [*klomr̥š, klompr̥št, klompr̥štn̥*] 'so to speak, as if' (L[64], Z), *koidm̥* 'before, first' (–, –), [*lehaxęs*] 'purposely, in defiance of' (L, Z), [*mękolšk'n̥*] 'the more so' (L, Z'), *pušet* 'pure and simple' (L, –) [*tēik'ęf*] 'at once, instantly' (L, –), *tomr̥* 'maybe' (L, Z), *tumęd* 'always' (L, –),

C. a. FAMILY LIFE. *mėšpuxę* 'family' (L, Z), [*balbūs*] 'head of the family' (L, Z), [*balbūstę*] 'mistress of the house' (L, –), [*g'ęvīr*] 'man of rank' (L, –), [*jīxęs*] 'genealogy of the family' (L, –), [*mejīxęs*] 'noble' (L, –), [*buxr̥*] 'bachelor, young man' (L, –), [*nękēivę*] 'maid' (L, –), *bsīlę* 'virgin, unmarried girl' (L, –), [*brīs*] "covenant" (L, –), [*mīlę*] 'circumcision' (L, –), [*moil*] 'circumciser' (–, –), [*barmītsvę*] 'maturity, at 13, for bearing responsibility before the Law' (–, –).

b. MARRIAGE. [*šådxn̥*] 'match maker' (L, –), [*šīdęx*] 'match' (L, –), [*şīvīg'*] 'companion' (–, –), [*knås*] 'betrothal' (L, –), *kålę* 'bride' (L, Z), *xūsn̥* 'bridegroom' (L, –), [*tnojīm*] 'conditions [of engagement]' (L, –), [*nådn̥*] 'dowry' (L, –), [*ksībę*] 'marriage contract' (L, Z), *xåsęnę* 'wedding' (–, Z), [*xīpę*] 'canopy' (L, Z).

c. DEATH. [*goisęs*] 'dying person' (–, –), [*vīdę*] 'confession of sins' (L, Z'), [*mes*] 'corpse' (L, –), [*taxrīxīm*] 'shrouds' (–, –), [*ūrn̥*] 'coffin' (L, –), [*levāję*] 'funeral' (L, –), [*bęsoilm̥*] 'abode of eternity' (L, –), [*g'ęnēidn̥*] 'paradise' (L R.Y., –), [*şxīs*] 'moral merit', [*şoixę*] 'worthy' (L, –), [*oilm̥åbę*] 'world to come' (L, –), [*k'ēivr̥*] 'grave' (L, –), [*metsēivę*] 'gravestone' (L, –), [*krīę*] 'rupture [in a garment as a sign of mourning]' (L, –), [*šīvę*] 'seven days of mourning' (–, –), [*kådęš*] 'prayer for the rest of the deceased's soul' (L, –), [*almūnę*] 'widow' (L, Z), [*jūsm̥*] 'orphan' (L, Z).

II. INTELLECTUAL SPHERE

a. ABSTRACT NOTIONS OF EVERYDAY LIFE (made more distinct where possible by synonymical grouping). [*anūę*] 'pleasure' (L, –) vs. [*tānīg'*] 'delight' (L, –); [*agmęsnēfęš*] 'grief' (L, –) vs. [*tsār*] 'anxiety' (L, Z) vs. *tsūręs* 'trouble' (L[65], Z) vs. *jęsīrīm* 'pains' (L, –); *tūs* 'error' (L, –) vs. [*åvlę*] 'failure, wrong' (L, –) vs. *nęvēire* 'sin, [it is a] pity' (L, Z);[66] *bakūšę* 'prayer' (L, Z), [*brēirę*] 'choice' (L, –), *bsīrę* 'news' (L, –), [*bętuxn̥*] 'faith, confidence' (L, –), *bīšę* 'shame' (L R.Y., –) vs. [*xarpe* (*xer*–)] 'disgrace' (L, –), [*xājęs*] 'life' (L, –), *xarūtę* 'regret' (L, –), [*xēin*] 'grace, favor' (L, Z), [*xēišīk'*] 'desire' (L, –), [*xēsęd*] 'pity, mercy' (L, –) vs. [*raxmūnes*] 'compassion' (L, –), [*xīdęš*] 'wonder, astonishment' (L, Z), [*xīlīk'*] 'difference, distinction' (L, –), *xoxmę* 'wisdom, wit' (L, –) vs. [*sēixl̥*] 'brains, mind' (L, –), [*xęsūrn̥*] 'defect, fault' (L, –), *xūlm̥* 'dream' (L, –), [*xoişīk'*] 'mockery' (L, –), *dāngę* 'care' (L, Z),[67] [*dålęs*] 'poverty' (L, Z) vs. [*doixīk'*] 'neediness' (–, –) vs. [*madrēig'ę*] 'impoverished conditions' (L, –), [*dēię*] 'opinion' (L, –), [*ēidęs*] 'testimony, witness' (L, Z), [*emęs*] 'truth' (L, –), *nęmūnę* 'faith, religion' (L, –), [*ēitsę*] 'counsel, advice' (L, –), *gānvę* 'pride' (L, –; cf. footnote 67), [*g'ędīlę*] 'gaiety' (L, Z) vs. [*naxęs*] 'delight' (L, –) vs. [*sīmxę*] 'joy, mainly through entertainment' (L, Z), [*goirl̥*] 'lot' (L, –), [*atsluxę*] 'speed, success' (L, –) vs. *måşl* 'luck, fortune' (L, Z), ([*šlęmåşl̥*]) 'ill luck, misfortune' (L, –), [*ažguxę*] 'providence, attention' (L, –), [*jakręs*] 'dearth' (L, Z), [*jędīę*] 'knowledge, news' (L, –), [*klūlę*] 'curse' (L, –) vs. [*toixęxę*] 'all possible misfortunes (according to a biblical passage)' (L, –), [*koięx*] 'strength, power' (L, –), *kol* 'voice' (L, –), *kuvęd* 'honor' (L, Z), [*mānsę*] 'tale, story' (L, –; cf. footnote 67), [*målęx*] 'angel' (L, –), [*maxšuvę*] 'thought, mind' (L, –), [*maskūnę*] 'plan, project' (L, –), [*mīn*] 'sort, kind' (L, –), [*moirę*] 'fear, apprehension' (L, –) vs. [*paxęd*] 'fright, horror' (L, –), [*mīsr̥*] 'ethics,

[64] Only the latter two forms listed.
[65] Listed in the singular.
[66] In a slightly different form.
[67] Neither represents the nasalization.

rebuke' (L, –), [*mūšl̥*] 'example' (L, –) vs. [*rājẹ*] 'lesson' (L, –), [*mĭtsvẹ*] 'good deed' (L, –), [*nēidr̥*] 'vote' (L, –), *nẹduvẹ* 'alms' (L, –) vs. [*tsdukẹ*] 'charity' (L, –), [*nẹkumẹ*] 'revenge' (L, Z), [*nēfẹš*] 'creature' (L, –), [*nes*] 'miracle' (L R.Y., –), [*nẹšumẹ*] 'soul' (L, –), [*oifn̥*] 'manner, way' (L, –), *rẹfīẹ* 'remedy' (L, –), *rẹtsīxẹ* 'cruelty' (L, –), [*sax*] 'multitude, much, many' (L, –), *švīẹ* 'oath' (L, –), [*šēk'r̥*] 'falsehood' (L, Z), *šẹgūn* 'madness' (L, –), [*šūlm̥*] 'peace' (L, –), [*sg'ĭlẹ*] 'hidden quality, inner property' (L, –), [*sẹkūnẹ*] 'danger' (L, –), [*sxar*] 'reward' (L, –), [*sĭbẹ*] 'accident' (L, –), [*ṣẹkūrn̥*] 'memory' (L, Z), [*sod*] 'secret, mystery' (L, –), [*sof*] 'end' (L, –), [*sūtn̥*] 'shade, shadow' (L,[68] –), [*tām*] 'taste, sense, motive' (L, Z), [*txĭlẹ*] 'beginning' (L, –), [*taxlẹs*] 'use' (L, Z), [*tox*] 'perfection' (R. *ispravă*) (L,[69] –), [*tēve*] 'inclination, character' [L, –), *tšīvẹ* 'penance, answer' (L, –), *tsīrẹ* 'face, figure' (L, –).

b. COMMERCE. [*xålfn̥*] 'money changer, banker' (L, –), [*xåvr̥*] 'comrade, companion' (L, –) vs. [*šītẹf*] 'associate, copartner' (L, –), [*xsīmẹ*] 'signature, subscription' (L, –), [*ksåv*] 'writing, letter' (L, –), [*xēilĭk'*] 'share, portion, part' (L, –), [*xežbn̥*] 'calculation, account, bill, note' (L, –), [*xoivẹ*][70] 'debt' (–, –), [*dīrẹ*] 'apartment, dwelling, rooms' (L R.Y., –), [*ērẹx*] 'approximation, around' (L, –), [*etsūe*] 'expense' (L, –), [*jẹrĭd*] 'fair, market' (L, –), *k'ērn̥* 'capital' (L, –), [*koinẹ*] 'customer, client' (L, –), *måsẹmåtn̥* 'commerce, business' (L, –), *soixr̥* 'merchant' (L, Z), [*maškn̥*] 'pawn' (L, –), [*mẹšūrẹs*] 'servant, attendant' (L, –), [*mẹtbēiẹ*] 'coin, money' (L, –), [*mēšẹx*] 'term, course of time' (L, –), [*mẹtsīẹ*] 'rarity' (L, –), [*mẹṣīmn̥*] 'ready money, cash' (L, –), *oirẹv* (cf. footnote 70) 'warrantor' (–, –), *parnūsẹ* 'subsistence' (L, Z), [*rẹvuxẹ*] (cf. footnote 70) 'interest' (–, –), [*šmī(ẹ)s*] 'news, idle talk' (L,[71] –), ([*šmīsn̥*]) 'to talk' (L, –), *sxoirẹ* 'merchandise' (L, –).

c. DESIGNATIONS CONCERNING THE NON-JEWISH WORLD. *bĭlbl̥* 'calumny, slander, imputation, false accusation' (L, Z) vs. *g'ẹṣēirẹ* 'decree against Jews, persecution' (L, Z), *xogẹ* 'Christian holiday' (–, –), *gålẹx* 'Catholic priest, clergyman in general' (L, –), [*goi*] 'non-Jew, Christian' (L, –) vs. [*g'er*] 'stranger, proselyte' (L, Z), *gūlẹs* 'exile' (L, –), [*måmṣr̥*] 'subtle, sly, crafty fellow' (L, –), [*mẹšīmẹd*] 'apostate' (L, Z), ([*šmådn̥*]) 'to baptize, to christen' (L, –), [*mūsr̥*] 'denunciator' (L, –), *nēsẹx* 'illicit wine' (–, Z), *pūrẹts* 'Boyar, nobleman' (L, –), ([*prītsẹ*]) 'noblewoman' (–, –), *rūšẹ* 'bad, wicked man' (L, Z), *šēig'ẹts* 'non-Jewish boy' (–, Z), [*šĭksẹ, šĭksl̥*] 'non-Jewish girl' (L,[72] Z).

d. POLITICAL TERMINOLOGY. [*mẹdīnẹ*] 'country, state' (L, –), [*k'ēisr̥*] 'emperor' (L, –), [*mēilẹx*] 'king' (L, –), [*mas*] 'tribute, impost, contribution' (L, –), [*xājẹl, xāl*] 'army' (L, –), [*maxnẹ*] 'camp' (L, –), [*mẹlxumẹ*] 'war' (L, –), [*soinẹ*] 'enemy, foe' (L, –).

e. GEOGRAPHICAL TERMINOLOGY. [*jåm*] 'sea, multitude' (L, –), [*mĭṣrẹx*] 'east' (L, –), [*mārẹv*] 'west' (L, –), [*tsufn̥*] 'north' (L, –), [*dūrm̥*] 'south' (L, –).

f. SEVERAL ANIMALS (mostly fig.). [*bẹhēimẹ*] 'stupid fellow, blockhead' (L, –), [*xājẹ*] 'animal, mainly beast of prey' (L, –), [*xåmr̥*] fig. 'ass, jack, donkey' (–, –), *xåṣr̥* 'pig, swine' (L, –), [*k'ēlẹv*] fig. 'dog' (–, –), [*of*] 'fowl' (L, –), [*šērẹts*] 'reptile, child' (L,[73] –).

g. SOME PARTS OF THE HUMAN BODY. [*ēivr̥*] 'limb, membrum virile' (L,[74] –), [*dēifĭk'*] 'pulse' (L, –), [*moiẹx*] 'brains' (L, –), [*pūnm̥*] 'face, aspect' (L, Z), [*partsẹf*]

[68] L pronounces like Sainéan, but the latter considers it to be of Hebrew derivation.

[69] With a different meaning.

[70] In this form not encountered elsewhere.

[71] With a slightly different meaning.

[72] Only the first form.

[73] With a slightly different meaning.

[74] With a slightly different meaning.

'sight' (L,[75] –), [*tuxe̥s*] 'the part of the body where the back ceases to bear an honorable name' (L, –).

h. Some other frequently used words. [*xēile̥v*] 'candle tallow' (L, –), [*kle̥smr̥*] 'fiddler' (L, –), [*kos*] 'glass, cup' (L, –), [*me̥tūne̥*] 'gift' (L, –), [*oire̥x*] 'wayfarer, guest' (L, –), [*oitsr̥*] 'treasure' (L, –), [*pēire̥s*] 'fruits' (L,[76] –), *poite̥k'e̥* 'treasure [of money]' (–, –), [*såm*] 'poison' (L, –), [*moiše̥v*] 'toilet' (–, –), [*sı̂mn̥*] 'sign, indication' (L, –), [*šuxn̥*] 'neighbor' (L,[77] –), *tvı̄e̥* 'grain' (L, –), [*mēie̥*] 'hundred' (–, –), (*hı̂ndr̥t*) 'id.' (L, –).

i. Designations of actions, states, qualities, etc. *ne̥hore̥* 'evil eye' (L, –), [*jēitsr̥ hore̥*] 'genius of evil; personified bad inclination' (L,[78] –), [*broig'e̥s*] 'angry' (L, –) vs. [*kās*] 'wrath' (L, –), [*gåne̥v*] 'thief' (L, Z) vs. [*gåsl̥n*] 'robber, highwayman' (L, –), [*re̥tsēie̥x*] 'murderer' (L, –) vs. [*harge̥n*[*n̥*]] 'to kill' (L, –), ([*hoirı̂g'*]) 'one dead to the world', [*hefk'r̥*] 'homeless, ownerless state or thing' (L, –), [*hoile̥x*] 'getup' (L,[79] Z), [*ı̂pe̥š*] 'pestilence' (L, –) vs. [*me̥g'ēife̥*] 'epidemic' (L, –), [*kaduxe̥s*] 'typhus' (L, –), [*k'ı̂še̥f*] 'magic, charm' (L, –), [*le̥ts*] 'buffoon, joker' (L, –), [*make̥*] 'plague, wound' (L, –), *me̥xı̄r* iron. 'beautiful' (–, –), [*me̥šı̂g'e̥*] 'crazy, excessive' (L, –), *mı̄s* 'ugly, nasty' (L, –), [*me̥fı̂nı̂k'*] 'delicate, spoiled (man)' (L, –), [*nēifåle̥*] 'abortion' (L, Z), [*ne̥vēile̥*] 'carcass, carrion' (L, –) vs. [*pēig'r̥*] 'dead body, corpse' (–, –), [*rēie̥x*] 'scent' (L, –) vs. [*sruxe̥*] 'stench' (–, –), *rı̄x* 'devil' (L, –) vs. [*šed*] 'demon' (L, –) vs. *goilm̥* '(clay) dummy' (L, –), [*šı̂k'r̥*] 'drunkard' (L, –), [*šuxr̥*] 'Negro, Gypsy' (–, –), [*šoite̥*] 'stupid fellow' (L, –) vs. [*tı̂pe̥š*] 'dull fellow' (–, –), [*taxše̥t*] 'trinket, sly person' (L,[80] –), [*taljn̥*] 'hangman' (L, –).

j. Preventive expressions. [*kude̥šborxı̄*] 'the Holy One be praised' (–, –) vs. [*šemje̥sbūre̥x*] 'the Name be praised' (–, –) vs. [*reboine̥šl̥oilm̥*] 'the Lord of the world' (–, –), [*blı̄nēidr̥, bl̥nēidr̥*] 'without promise or vow' (–, –), *xåsve̥xulı̄le̥* 'far be it from us' (L, –) vs. [*xåsve̥šūlm̥*] 'God forbid' (L, –), *mērtse̥šém* 'God willing' (–, –), [*lehåvdl̥*] 'with separation, distinction' (–, –), [*šulm̥alēixm̥*] 'peace unto you' (–, –), [*le̥xājm̥*] 'for health' (L, –), [*bure̥xabū, br̥xåbe̥*] 'blessed be he who comes' (L, –).

k. Invectives. *mı̄se̥me̥šı̂'ne̥* 'apoplexy' (L, –), [*je̥maxšmoi* (*ve̥sı̂xroi*)] 'his name (and memory) be blotted out' (–, –).

l. Heresy. [*apı̂koire̥s*] 'heretic, renegade' (L, –), [*mı̄n*] 'heretic par excellence' (–, –).

m. Peculiarities in attitude. [*balšém*] 'miracle worker, cabbalist' (L,[81] –), [*šēime̥s*] 'sacramental names' (–, –), *dr̥xēre̥ts* 'rationalness, politeness, respect' (L, –), *amūre̥ts* 'unlearned, unschooled person' (L, –), [*baskol*] 'voice from heaven, echo' (L,[82] –), [*roš medı̄ne̥*] 'godless tyrant' (L, –), [*sambåtjn̥*] 'seeker of quarrels' (?) (–, –), *såg'e̥nūr* 'blind man' (L, –), (*g'ı̂t-óig'*) '[evil eye]' (L, –), (*nı̂šg'ı̂tr̥*) 'devil' (–, –), *xoiše̥x* 'complete disorder' (L, –), [*hek'de̥š*] 'lumber room full of dirt and moisture' (L,[83] Z).

The Slavic component of Yiddish was treated by Sainéan no less basically than the Hebrew-Aramaic component or the language as a whole, regardless of

[75] In a slightly different form.
[76] Listed in the singular.
[77] With an additional meaning.
[78] With a slightly different meaning.
[79] With a note that it is ironic.
[80] Only with the first meaning.
[81] With a slightly different meaning.
[82] With a slightly different meaning.
[83] With a different meaning.

his conviction of the Germanness of Yiddish. His work was full of contradictions between theoretical attitudes and actual accomplishments. Here, too, he clearly realized how great the Slavic influence was on all the linguistic categories into which it penetrated, and his convictions on this point grew with time. Among the few additions which he made in the French version of his study was the following statement about the particles of Polish derivation: "But there are, above all, the Polish particles which, because of their number and their expansion, merit our entire attention; they bring out [*font ressortir*] the importance of this ingredient in the totality of elements *which have constituted Judeo-German*" (Fr. 190, italics supplied). Of Ruthenian and Russian vocabulary, "only a small part has succeeded in crossing the border of its provenience" (R. 113). When he speaks of the facts, he considers Slavic as a constituent element; in other contexts he refers to it as to a "foreign ingredient" (Fr. 128). How are we to interpret this contradiction? It seems to me that there is only one correct interpretation: the disparagement of Slavic was part of the tradition, but Sainéan realized its constitutive role in the Yiddish language. And it will remain Sainéan's merit to have placed the Slavic component of Yiddish on the proper level of significance and of research conceptualization.

We skip the phonetic speculations in reference to the Slavic elements as well. As with the other components Sainéan went all out to prove the German basis of the formation of the phonology. The problem of phonology is the least clarified of the entire study at that. As we already know he had postponed this problem. I will elicit only the lexical material for the following list.

Let us begin with derivations. These belong partly to the bits of morphology he cites in connection with the elements. Again I draw parallels (only with Lifshits; the Yiddish of Zunz' time and environment still took little account with Slavic) for comparative purposes and omit Sainéan's etymologies.

NOUNS. 1. *-atš*[84] (augmentative, pejorative): *pi̊skátš* 'large and broad mouth' (L), *ji̊ngátš* 'young man' (L), *fomfátš* 'snuffler' (L); *-ak* (with the same function): *prosták* "bêta" (L). b. *-k'e̥* (diminutive): *šåfk'e̥* 'case' (–), cf. *šåfe̥* 'cupboard' (L), *šå'fk'åle̥* 'small case' (–); *kódk'åle* 'small tail', cf. *kode̥* 'tail' (L[85]); *-tse̥* ('id.'): *båbe̥tse̥* 'good old woman' (L), *xåntse̥* 'little Khane' (–); *-[e̥]niu* ('id.'): *şēide̥niu* 'dear grandfather' (–), *bå'be̥niu* 'dear grandmother' (–), *góte̥niu* 'dear God' (–), *må'me̥niu* 'dear mother' (–), *tå'te̥niu* 'dear father' (–). c. *–i̊vk'e̥: kåptse̥ni̊vk'e̥*[86] 'poorness' (–). d. *-k'e̥* (desinence for fem.): *re̥ndark'e* (–), cf. *re̥ndar* "fermier de boisson" (L[87]); *dråbk'e̥* (–), cf. *dråb* (below, p. 177); *šnādr̥k'e̥* 'ladies' tailor' (–). e. *-[n]i̊k': ni̊dni̊k'* '[bore]' (L), *šli̊me̥şålni̊k'* 'unfortunate, negligent man' (L), *şoill̥ve̥sóive̥ni̊k'* 'glutton, greedy person, and drunkard' (L).

ADJECTIVES. a. *-åte̥: smarkåte̥* 'snotty, pretentious [young fellow]' (L), *vule̥xåte̥* 'Wallachian' (–); b. *-ovåte̥, -e̥våte̥* ('ironic'): *horbovåte̥* 'humpbacked' (–), *pi̊sk'e̥våte̥*

[84] It is because of this transcription that I decided to use *tš* instead of *č* throughout this paper. After all, I carried out my uniformization in other cases of the transcription, too. It must be said that we have here the first well-considered transcription system with the clear intention of representing spoken Yiddish.

[85] With a slightly different meaning.

[86] See p. 177(b).

[87] In a slightly different form.

'talkative' (R. 118), "aux lèvres pendantes" (Fr. 190), "bavard" (Fr. 192) (–), *fråntsęvåtę* iron. 'syphilitic' ("en français") (L), *fomfęvåtę* 'snuffling' ("à peu près le même sens que *fomfátš*," Fr.) (L). b. *-sk'ę*: *båbsk'ę* 'anile' (L).

VERBS. verbal particles: *ub*, *un*, *of*, *ous*, *far-*, *tsī*, *tsì-*; *ṣa-*; *ubxåpņ* 'to do in a hurry' (L), *unxåpņ* 'to seize' (L), *ousxåpņ* 'to snatch away' (L), *farxåpņ* 'to forestall' (L), *farblondṣęn* 'to go astray' (L), *tsìrìtšęn* "commencer à pleurer" (Fr.) (L), etc.; *ṣadìšęn* "étouffer" (R. Fr.) (L), *ṣateręmņ* 'to lose, to exterminate, to destroy' ("renverser," Fr.) (L).

PARTICLES ("the most used," Fr. 190). *žę* (also pronounced *tše*) 'then' (L R.Y.), cf. *šluft tšę* "dormez donc" (R. Fr.), *vū(s) žę* "quoi donc" (R. Fr.); *abī* "afin que, au moins" (R.), "afin que" (Fr.) (L), *aṣ* (L) or [?] *až* "jusqu'à ce que, tant que" (R. Fr.), cf. *aṣ dī vest tsìtŗņ až* 'so that you will tremble'; *xotšę* "quoique, bien que" (R.), "quoique" (Fr.) (L), *xošbę* "quand même" (R., Fr.) (–), *tsī* "est-ce que, si, ou" (R.), "ou" (Fr.) (L), cf. *tsī jo tsī nēin* "oui ou non" (Fr.), *tsìmtsìgrūt* (*tsī ìm tsī grūd*) "au pair et impair" (Fr.), *ī* "et" (R., Fr.) (–), cf. *ī ēx ī dī* 'both I and you'; *jakós* "seulement, du moins" (Fr.) (–), *na* "tiens" (R. Fr.) (–), cf. *na dŗ!* pl. *nat ax!* 'here you have'; *nī* 'neither', "pas, ni" (Fr.) (–), cf. *nī be nī me nī k'ìk'ęrìk'ī* "absolument personne" (Fr.); *no* "eh bien" (Fr.) (–), *nū* (–[88]) and *nū žę* "or, donc" (Fr.), *ot* 'see, look', "voici, voilà" (Fr.) (L), [*boibęrìk'*] 'obliquely, sidewise, slopingly' (–), [*popęrék'*] 'across, athwart' (L), *takę* "ainsi, si, oui" (R.); "ainsi, donc" (Fr.) (L), *ṣāręs* "aussitôt, à l'instant" (R. Fr.) (L), *nebęx* '[unfortunately]' (L), *fìn* 'than' [in Yiddish a preposition] (L), cf. *ēr ìṣ jìng'ŗ fìn mīr* 'he is younger than I'.

This construction and the use of *ṣęx* in combinations like [*ēx ṣets ṣęx*] 'I sit down', [*ēx tī ṣęx a rīr*] 'I budge', [*ēx ob ṣęx farkīlt*] 'I caught cold' are called by Sainéan "*grammatical influence*" of Slavic upon Yiddish, in contrast to "*logical influence*" (R. 116), which affects the meaning of words: *krìm* 'unjust, wrong' (cf. [*krìvdę*] 'wrong'). In the French version (p. 191) he already used the term "semantic influence" (corresponding approximately to Schuchardt–Landau's *influence on the inner linguistic form*).

Now for the words of this Slavic influence, and only those "which have achieved a more general use" (R. 118), with the addition, in the French variant (p. 192), of the qualification "in Rumania." I present them without the etymological notes, but in Sainéan's own, "ideological" grouping. It is interesting merely to add that in the Rumanian version, the meanings of the Yiddish words and of their etyma are not the same.

I. KINSHIP. *ṣēidę* 'grandfather' (L), *båbę* 'grandmother' (L), *bratšìk'* 'little brother' (–), (*brīdŗ*) 'brother (L), *liubę* "bien aimé" (R. Fr.) (–).

II. SOME PARTS OF THE HUMAN BODY (cf. Hebrew element g). *pìsk'* fam. 'mouth' (L), *vontsęs*[89] 'mustache' (L[90]), *plēitsę* 'back, shoulders' (L), *pìpìk'* 'navel' (L), (*pempìk'*) 'short and stout man, short thick-set bantam' (L), *k'ìšk'ę* 'intestine' (L), *ṣūdìk'* 'posterior' (L).

III. HOUSE AND HOME. *stelię* 'ceiling' (L), *kobręts* 'carpet' (L R.Y.), *klåmk'ę* 'doorknob' (L), *tsvok* 'nail' (L), *k'ernętsę* 'fountain, spring' (L), *ploit* 'fence' (L), *koimņ* 'chimney' (L), ([*tšåd*]) '[haze, fume]' (L), [*lopętę*] 'shovel' (L), [*kotšęrę*] 'fire shovel' (L), *prì'pętšìk'* 'fireplace, fireside' (L), [*pomēinętsę*] 'sloppail' (L),

[88] But L does list a derived verb.

[89] Not until the French version; in R.—only the singular.

[90] Listed in the singular.

[*dĭšk'e̥*] 'barrel' (L R.Y.[91]), [*koiš*] 'basket' (L), [*pĭdl̥*] 'bandbox, carton box' (L[92]), [*pĭšk'e̥*] 'box, case, can' (L), *šåfe̥* 'cupboard, clothes press' (L).

IV. FOOD. *vetšere̥* 'the evening meal, supper' (L), *koile̥tš* '[twisted] white bread' (L), (*bĭlk'e̥*) "brioche" (Fr.) (L), *håle̥šk'e̥* 'stuffed cabbage' (L), *jĭšk'e̥* 'poor soup' (–), (*joux*) 'vegetable soup' (L), *lokšn̥* 'noodles' (L[93]), ([*tēig'le̥x*]) 'strings of dough' (L[94]), ([*farfl̥*]) 'squares of dough' (–), [*låtk'e̥*] 'Passover potato pancake' (L), [*varenĭk'*] 'cooked filled pockets of dough' (L), [*pīre̥šk'e̥*] 'id.', [*varne̥tšk'e̥*] 'rolled dough pellets for Passover (?)', [*knĭš*] 'baked cheese-filled pastry', *pove̥dl̥* 'preserves of plums' (L), *kåve̥* 'coffee' (L), [*smete̥ne̥*] 'sour cream' (L).

V. CLOTHING. *gate̥s* 'pair of drawers' (L), *kolnr̥* 'collar' (L), [*pôde̥lĭk'*] 'flap' (–[95]), *stån* 'flap of a shirt', *kåftn̥* 'caftan', "justaucorps" (L R.Y.), *jĭpe̥* "jaquette fourrée" (Fr.) (L[96]), [*fe̥tšeile̥*] 'handkerchief' (L), *jármĭk'e̥* 'cap', "calotte" (Fr.) (L), [*spodĭk'*] 'marten hat' (–), ([*štrāml̥*]) 'sable hat' (–), *kå'pe̥lĭtš* 'hat' (L), *k'ĭtšme̥* "bonnet" (Fr.) (L), [*pape̥tše̥*] 'slipper' (L), [*knåfl̥*] 'heel' (L), [*xole̥ve̥*] 'leg' (L), [*låte̥*] 'patch' (L), [*pe̥dešve̥*] 'sole' (L).

VI. ANIMALS. *bĭk'* 'bull' (L), *tsåp* 'billygoat' (L), *barn̥* 'ram' (L), [*ogr̥*] 'stallion' (L), *škåpe̥* 'mare' (L), *lošĭk'* 'foal' (L), *tsouk* 'bitch' (L), *hĭndĭk'* 'turkey-cock', "dinde" (L), *hĭ'ndĭtšk'e̥* '[turkey-hen]', (Fr.) (L), *kåtšr̥* '[drake]' (L), *kåtšk'e̥* 'duck', "canne" (Fr.) (L), [*kanarĭk'*] 'canary-bird' (L), *påve̥* 'peacock' (L), *vrone̥* 'raven' (L), *žåbe̥* 'frog' (L), [*užák* {*ĭžák*}] 'hedgehog' (L), *jaštšr̥k'e̥* 'lizard' (L), [*lempr̥t*] 'leopard' (L), *pjouk'e̥* 'leech' (L[97]), [*mere̥šk'e̥*] 'ant' (L), [*moil*] 'moth' (L), [*soibl̥*] 'sable, mainly the fur' (L).

VII. PLANTS. *kvĭtk'e̥* 'flower' (L), *tsvĭtn̥* [*-te̥n*] 'to bloom' (L), *berĭk'* 'beet root' (L), *tsĭ'bole̥* [*-åle̥*] 'onion' (L), *xrēin* 'horse-radish' (L), *ĭg'r̥k'e̥* 'cucumber' (L), *petre̥šk'e̥* 'parsley' (L), [*ože̥ne̥*] 'blackberry' (–), *róžĭnk'e̥* 'raisin' (L), [*krope̥ve̥*] 'nettle' (L), [*bĭtše̥ne̥*] 'beech' (–), *dembn̥* (*boim*) 'oaken' (L[98]), *sosne̥* 'pine' (L), [*sosnove̥*] '[of pine]' (L), [*troštše̥ne̥*] 'reed' (–), [*verbe̥*] 'willow' (L), [*tå'bĭk'e̥*] 'snuff' (L), *tĭtīn* 'tobacco' (L), ([*lĭlk'e̥*]) '(tobacco) pipe' (L), ([*tšĭbĭk'*]) 'pipe-tube' (L[99]).

VIII. MINERALS. *bruštīn* 'amber' (L[100]), *doit* 'tar' (L[101]), [*sĭrk'e̥*] 'sulphur' (L), *smole̥* 'pitch' (L).

IX. TRADES. [*kotlr̥*] "chaudronnier" (L), *påse̥månĭk'* "passementier" (L), [*stolr̥*][102] 'joiner' (L R.Y.), [*šmĭklr̥*] "Knopfmacher" (L[103]).

X. SLAVIC-ORIGIN WORDS OF HIGH FREQUENCY IN THE LANGUAGE. a. NOUNS: [*bank'e̥*] 'cupping glass' (L), [*blote̥*] 'mud' (L), [*boletšk'e̥*] 'boil' (–), [*xarobe̥*] 'wound (?)' (–), [*brĭtfe̥*] 'razor' (L), [*xmare̥*] 'cloud' (L), ([*xmarne̥*]) 'cloudy' (L), [*xvalie̥*] 'billow, wave' (L), [*dĭšl̥*] 'shaft' (L), [*fĭs*] 'coffee grounds' (L[104]), [*horevanie̥*] "travail penible, labeur" (R.) (L), [*kanåpe̥*] 'sofa' (L), [*armåte̥*] 'cannon' ([105]),

[91] In a slightly different form.
[92] In a slightly different form.
[93] Listed in the singular.
[94] Listed in the singular.
[95] Lacking in the dictionaries, present in my own speech.
[96] With a different meaning.
[97] Slightly different in pronunciation.
[98] Only in an extended form.
[99] Slightly different in form.
[100] Slightly different in form.
[101] Slightly different in form.
[102] Sainéan's transcription notes the palatality of *k'* and *g'*, but not of *l'* or *n'*.
[103] With a different meaning.
[104] With a slightly different meaning.
[105] With a different meaning.

kåp 'drop' (L), *kå'pålę* 'little bit' (–), [*karętę*] 'elegant carriage' (L), [*klēit*] 'store' (L), [*krētšmę*] 'tavern for brandy, beer, and wine' (L), [*kantšīk'*] 'leather whip' (L), [*k'erbḷ*] 'rouble' (L), ([*rendḷ*]) 'ducat' (L), [*k'īpę*] 'pile' (L), [*k'īlīk'*] 'violent blow with a fist' (L[106]), [*k'īvṛ*] 'helmet' (L), [*koldrę*] 'quilt' (L), [*kroxmęl*] 'starch' (L), [*krīvdę*] 'complaint, injustice' (L[107]), [*liarṃ*] 'noise' (L), [*līsk'ę*] 'scale' (L), [*mast*] 'ointment' (L[108]), [*męşīnīk'*] 'youngest child' (–), [*naród*] 'large crowd' (–), [*niank'ę*] 'nurse' (L), [*nīpér*] 'werewolf' (–), [*okręp*] 'boiling water' (L), [*parę*] 'steam' (L), [*påstęx*] 'shepherd' (L), [*plotk'ę*] 'gossip, intrigue' (L), [*poręx*] 'dust' (L), [*prošīk'*] 'powder, pill' (L), [*prītię*] 'rod' (L[109]), [*steng'ę*] 'ribbon' (L), [*stervę*] 'carrion' (L), [*stotšīk'*] 'long black candle' (L[110]), [*špīlk'ę*] 'pin' (L), [*šmåtę*] 'rag' (L), [*tåndēt*] 'ready-made goods' (L), [*torbę*] 'peasant sack' (L), [*tšerīk'*] "abscès" (R.) (L), [*tšeręp*] 'shard' (L), *vūlęx* 'Rumanian' (–).

b. DESIGNATIONS OF (MOSTLY BAD) QUALITIES. (α. NOUNS): [*burlák*] 'rude fellow' (L R.Y.), [*xlåvnīk'*] 'coarse, rude fellow' (–), [*xlop*] 'peasant, boor, rude man' (–), [*dråb*] 'scamp, vagabond' (L), [*dībīk'*][111] 'dummy (?)' (L[112]), [*hīltai*] "vaurien, libertin" (R.) (L), [*horb*] 'hump' (L), [*kálīk'ę*] 'lame person, cripple' (L), [*kåptsṇ*][113] 'needy person' (L), [*karlīk'*] 'dwarf' (L), [*k'īlę*] 'kilogram; hernia' (L[114]), [*kurvę*] 'whore' (L), [*maşour*] 'vigorous, tall,[115] and broad-shouldered man' (–), [*paręx*] 'bald, itchy person, scab' (L), [*pask'ītstvę*] 'filth' (L[116]), [*prosták*] "rustre" (R.) (L), [*slīnę*] 'saliva' (L), [*smark'(atš)*] 'snot' (L), [*tšurpe, tšer-*] 'hussy' (–), [*šoltīk'*] 'naughty, audacious fellow' (L).

(β. ADJECTIVES): [*xūręv*][117] 'unwell' (L), [*drībnę*] 'small' (L R.Y.), [*horbåtę*] "bossu" (R.) (L), [*horbęvåtę*] 'id.' (–), [*līsę*] 'bald' (L), [*nīdnę*] 'boring' (L), [*parxåtę*] 'scabby', [*paršīvę*] 'lousy' (L), [*paskī(d)nę*] 'disgusting, nasty, ugly' (L[118]), [*prīkrę*] 'unpleasant, annoying' (L), [*prostę*] 'common, ordinary' (L), [*pīstę*] 'waste, void' (L), [*skosnę*] 'crosswise' (–), [*k'ęsok*] 'squint-eyed' (L R.Y.), [*temnę*] "finster" (R.) (–), [*pask'ītstvę*] 'filthy'.

c. VERBS. [*blondşęn*] 'to stray' (L), [*farblondşęn*] 'to go astray' (L), [*blonkęn*] 'to ramble' (–), [*arīmblonkęn*] 'id.' (L), [*blīsk'ęn*] 'to glitter' (–), [*blīštšęn*] 'to glisten, to shine' (L), [*xåpṇ*][119] 'to seize, to catch' (L), [*arānxåpṇ*] 'to drop in' (L), [*ofxåpṇ*] 'to wake up' (L), [*xlopęn*] 'to eat noisily' (—), [*xlīpęn*] 'to sob' (L), [*xråkęn*] 'to spit' (L), [*unxråkęn*] '[to spit all over]' (L), [*xropęn*] 'to snore' (L), [*dråpęn*] 'to climb' (L), [*drīmlṇ*] 'to slumber' (L), [*dīšęn*] 'to choke', [*dşībęn*] 'to peck' (–), [*gūlṇ*] 'to shave' (L), [*håmk'ęn*] 'to bark' (L[120]), [*hodęvęn*] 'to feed' (L), [*horęvęn*] 'to labor' (L), [*hīlęn*] 'to amuse oneself' (L), [*kājęn*][121] 'to repent' (L), [*kājęn*] 'to chew' (L), [*katšęn*] 'to roll' (L), [*farkatšęn*] 'to tuck up (sleeves)',

[106] With a slightly different meaning.
[107] Not exactly the same meaning.
[108] In a slightly different form.
[109] Slightly different in pronunciation.
[110] Not exactly the same meaning.
[111] Not Slavic.
[112] With a different meaning.
[113] Slavic?
[114] Only with the second meaning.
[115] But he presents a quotation showing that a *maşour* is short.
[116] In a slightly different form.
[117] Not Slavic.
[118] In a slightly different form.
[119] Slavic?
[120] Pronounced a little differently.
[121] Thinking of homonymy, Sainéan adds, "different from . . . ."

fig. 'to stay too long' (L), [*kåpe̥n*] 'to drop, to trickle' (L), [*koixe̥n*] 'to enjoy much, to long for' (–), [*kontše̥n*] 'to finish, to get through' (L), [*krempe̥ve̥n*] 'to tie together firmly' (L), [*kvi̊tše̥n*] 'to cry, to squeak' (L), [*me̥ri̊k'e̥n*] 'to moo' (–), [*morde̥ve̥n*] 'do a thing to death, to throw oneself' (L), [*mi̊tše̥n*] 'to torment' (L), [*ṣami̊tše̥n*] "fatiguer, épuiser" (R.) (L), [*proše̥n*] 'to dust' (L), [*pråve̥n*] [*po-?*] 'to improve' (L), [*pi̊le̥ve̥n*] 'to take good care of' (L), [*plonte̥n*] 'to become entangled' (L), [*anplonte̥n*] '[to entangle]' (L), [*farplonte̥n*] 'to confuse' (L), [*ousplonte̥n*] 'to disentangle' (L), [*plodṣe̥n*] 'to increase' (L R.Y.[122]), [*unplodṣe̥n*] 'id.' (–), [*råbe̥ve̥n*] 'to plunder' (L), [*ri̊tše̥n*] 'to shout (weeping)' (L), [*unri̊tše̥n*] 'id.' (–), [*žåle̥ve̥n*] 'to economize' (L), [*ši̊še̥n*] 'to dry up' (–), [*ousši̊še̥n*] 'to fall away' (–), [*ši̊šk'e̥n*] 'to whisper' (L[123]), [*skali̊tše̥n*] 'to cut oneself (in the body)' (L[124]), [*štork'e̥n*] 'to push' (–), [*trese̥n*] 'to shake' (L), [*ubtrese̥n*] '[to shake off]' (L), [*tšepe̥n*] 'to pick on (somebody)' (L), [*untšepe̥n*] '[to attach oneself]' (L), [*ṣatšepe̥n*] '[to provoke]' (L), [*våle̥n*] 'to push in, to cram (food)' (L), [*vortše̥n*] 'to grumble' (L).

This concludes a summary review of Sainéan's accomplishments in Yiddish linguistics. It is plain to see that Sainéan represents a large and still unexploited chapter not only in general linguistics, where an appreciation of his work is now in the process of developing, but also in Yiddish linguistics. The perceptive bibliographe· Ber Borokhov, said with regard to Sainéan's Rumanian study of Yiddish:[125] "It is impossible to summarize the content of this booklet, because it does not contain a single superfluous word." This is so true—his study is indeed so filled with substance—that no matter what our objections to Sainéan's various conclusions may be, they have to be formulated on the basis of, and in accordance with, this substance which he presented.

[122] In a slightly different form.
[123] In a slightly different form.
[124] In a slightly different form.
[125] [The Library of the Yiddish Philologist], in *Der pinkes*, Vilna, 1913, no. 119.

AMERICA IN EAST EUROPEAN YIDDISH FOLKSONG

ELEANOR GORDON MLOTEK (New York)

The Yiddish folksong of Eastern Europe has rarely been utilized to present the attitude of that Jewry to particular social phenomena or single events. There have appeared collections of recruit and soldiers' songs, workers' songs, revolutionary, ghetto and concentration camp songs, but seldom have comprehensive analyses of these followed. Generalizations of the sort: "the life of the Jewish people is reflected in their song," or: "to obtain a glimpse of and to understand the daily problems of the Jews one must know the songs they sang," have been many. As a matter of fact, it was usually the everyday matters that occupied the Jews and were recorded in song (e.g. children's songs and games, work, love, dance, even gambling, and so forth) that were subjected to analysis from time to time. However, such has rarely been the case with songs arising from specific historic events or situations. This is certainly a lapse since, to paraphrase the above generalization, the feelings of individuals, as expressed in song, are in some respects comparable to letters, memoirs, interviews or even autobiographies which have been recognized and accepted as source material for historical or sociological studies.

In undertaking this topic, therefore, I was primarily interested in discovering if, and to what extent, America had been treated in the Yiddish folksong, in view of its historic significance for the Eastern European Jews as the land of immigration. And secondly, I hoped to be able to determine, on the basis of the first, in what light America was regarded. The topic suggested itself, in connection with the tercentenary of Jewish life in America, as a link between the Jews on either side of the Atlantic. For as the editors of a symposium on Jewish social research expressed it, "... neither can American Jewish life be rightly understood without reference to Central European and Eastern European antecedents and cross-influences."[1]

In order to limit the material to be examined, which was necessitated by space assigned, I chose to restrict myself to Yiddish East European songs that appeared in Yiddish folksong collections and to unpublished songs of Eastern Europe that are found in the archives of the Yiddish Scientific Institute—Yivo, and to exclude all songs about America that were born in this country, unless they had been widespread in Eastern Europe before the destruction of Jewish life by the Nazis in World War II and had attained the degree of popularity in indigenous creations.

A collection of songs about America has hitherto never been published. Nor has an index of Yiddish songs ever appeared, although an index for my purpose would not have proved too conclusive either, since songs with mention of America, as I expected, were scattered among the various categories, and allusions to

[1] H. L. Lurie and Max Weinreich, ed.: "Jewish Social Research in America: Status and Prospects, A Symposium," *Yivo Annual of Jewish Social Science* 4 (1949), p. 309.

America in a song were not necessarily to be found in its first lines. This meant that the entire inventory of Yiddish songs available in the three aforementioned categories had to be explored.

If we accept the estimate by S. Z. Pipe in 1939[2] of the total number of Yiddish folksongs published up to that time as having been over 2,000, then to date there should be close to three thousand published songs. In the Yivo's unpublished A. Litvin Folksong Collection there are over 300 songs. This means that I have examined about 3,000 songs. Out of these I succeeded in gathering 38 songs with mention of America. Nine songs just carry mention of America with no other import;[3] and 29 songs, in alluding to America, bear connotations that will be presented for analysis.

One reason for this paucity, I would be inclined to believe, is the relative recency, in terms of the folksong, of America's appearance in the ken of the Eastern European Jew. The direct significance that America conveyed to East European Jewry was inchoate with the Jewish mass migration to the United States in 1881. By that time the growing influence of Yiddish literature in East Europe had acted as a deterrent upon anonymous folksong creation. Many folk-like songs of literary origin replaced the anonymous folksong in the repertoire of the East European Jew. By means of publications, the press, traveling folk bards, and the theater, the number of songs was increased and their spread among the communities was hastened. Those songs of traceable authorship were however rejected by folksong compilers, whose rigid definition of a folksong barred the inclusion of any literary compositions. Thus, hundreds of songs originating from the Yiddishfolk poets, E. Tsunzer (Zunser) or M. M. Varshavski, from A. Goldfaden and other playwrights, as well as from the labor poets Morris Rosenfeld, Dovid Edelshtat, Morris Vintshevski and others, which were created in Europe or were transmitted from the United States and dealt with life in this country, were considered unacceptable as authentic folklore material, unless they had undergone thorough transformations. As could be expected, subsequent study nevertheless disclosed the literary derivation of a number of seemingly anonymous songs that were included in the folksong collections. These, particularly the ones describing conditions in America, were altered in the folksong in such a way that they no longer pertained to or mentioned America but reflected the conditions in Europe. Among the folksongs proper, or rather those of unknown literary origin, this situation also occurred; thus, one song will mention America while variants of it will just refer to a distant land.

Obviously, most of the motives quoted by social historians for Jewish emigration to America reappear in the songs, namely poverty, striving for a better livelihood, persecution, the horrors of military conscription in Czarist Russia, imprisonment, unhappy family life. Furthermore, the persons addressed or referred to in these songs seem to reflect the general attitude of the singer to

[2] S. Z. Pipe: [Folklore Songs], *Yivo-bleter* 14 (1939), p. 350.

[3] Three variants of songs describing the sinking of the *Titanic;* three dance songs; two Soviet Yiddish songs; elegy upon the death of Baron de Hirsch.

America. Thus, there is implied mistrust and doubt, criticism, hope and praise of America.

Inasmuch as these songs cannot be arranged chronologically, I have elected to group them according to attitude and type.

"THE BITTER AMERICA..."

In the first place, then, we hear of criticism and unhappiness. America is indirectly considered responsible for husbands' betrayals of wives and the disintegration of families. These sentiments are to be found mainly in the songs of either *agunes* (deserted wives), or of soon to be parted lovers. The *agune*-songs are not rare in Yiddish folklore. They appeared formerly as love songs, lullabies, recruits' and even humorous songs. With the beginnings of Jewish emigration to America in the 60's and 70's of the past century and the later mass emigration at the end of the 19th and the beginning of the 20th century, the *agune* became a more frequent figure, in consequence of the opportunity America presented for desertion. Incidentally, it is the *agune* songs to which I. Orshanski in the 60's referred as the only factual evidence of emigration at that time: "Unfortunately we have no data on the details of this phenomenon, no statistics on its size. As far as I know, nothing about it was ever even mentioned in print up to now. It is therefore interesting to dwell upon those undetermined and not precise data concerning this which we can gather from the Yiddish folksong."[4]

The wife who was left behind with the children ascribed her bitter circumstances to America whose fortunes and temptations brought about her husband's betrayal. Her bitterness was aggravated by the fact that according to Jewish law, only the husband is permitted to send his wife a divorce. Accordingly, the request for a divorce recurs in a number of the *agune* songs.

The translations of the song excerpts that follow are more or less literal and may therefore sound awkward in places. The Yiddish original texts are cited in footnotes only for previously unpublished songs.

1. Oh, my dear husband / May you rot in the earth / And remain without years / How long / Must I beg you / To write me a letter? / I cry and wail at night / I lie awake and think / Perhaps you cannot live without me / I beg you, my husband / To be so good / and send me a reply.

\- - - - - - - - - - -

Listen here, you scoundrel / Oh, you rascal / May you burn like a fire / A curse upon your years / For going off / And refusing to return to me / The children beg for food / And you have forgotten / There is no bread to live on / I have already pawned everything / Even your prayer shawl / And you don't want to send me a reply....

Fat Sore / And black-haired Dobe / Are already fortunate / Their husbands have made them happy / And have sent them money / They have left for New York / While I remain shut in / And sit and wait / I have been ejected from the apartment / Moyshele is sick / I pray to the heavens / And you don't want to send me a reply....

[4] I. G. Orshanski: [Folk Songs of the Russian Jews] in *Hakarmel*, Russian supplement, nos. 31, 32 (1867); republished in his *Jevreji v Rossii* (1877), pp. 391–401, esp. 396f. Quoted by Z. Skuditski in *Folklor-lider*, Moscow, 1936, vol. 2, p. 26.

Perhaps you have there / Another in my stead / I shan't begrudge you those American joys [*glikn*] / Do not suppose / I will weep for you / But a divorce you must send me / May you perish / In the golden land / God will give me a second / And I will be rid of such an affliction / From me, your wife Khaye Sore....[5]

Another variant of this song has additional verses of a more moralizing nature:

2. ... It's already six years / That you're so far away / To America you went to seek your fortune / You left me here / An unhappy wife / And don't want to send me a reply.

I can't understand / What has happened to you / That you should forget your family / Your three small children / To whom you were so devoted / You never would eat without them.

I can't understand / That it doesn't bother you / You have learned such tyrannous ways / You have been away from me / So long / That your character has already changed.

— — — — — — — — —

The bitter America takes away strength / And reduces many wretched to tears / [It takes so long] until you finally raise [*khovet oys*] husbands and wives / Then they are not heard from.

Those who leave, promise / That they will look after their family / A year passes before / They even remember / To send the first letters....[6]

In another song the *agune* sings to her child of her misfortune: "Your father went to America where he drinks the best beer," while she was left behind with two small children. Greater is her pain when she recalls that it was she who saved him from imprisonment. She contrasts his prosperity—drinking beer and wine and dancing at balls—with her own poverty and hard life.

3. Your father went to America / And there drinks the best beer / Me he left with two small children / Like a beggar at a door.

Your father went to America / And there drinks the best wine / I wanted to spare him from all misfortunes / He should not go to prison.

Your father went to America / And there dances at balls / Me he left at Rokhele Shapiro's / To wash her dishes for her.[7]

In a dialogue between a querulous wife and her indifferent husband who is leaving for America, we again learn of the contrast in circumstances following their separation:

4. :Where are you going, Elikl / Elikl, my husband: / To America, my little wife / To America, my little dove / To America, my crown / You remain at home alone.

---

[5] Sh. Bastomski: *Baym kval...*, Vilna, 1923, p. 77, no. 15; variant in *Brivelekh fun rusland*, Warsaw, 1913, p. 3.

[6] Skuditski, vol. 2, p. 120.

[7] *Ibid.*, p. 113; Y. Dobrushin and A. Yuditski: *Yidishe folkslider*, Moscow, 1940, p. 225, n. 40. This song is reminiscent of another *agune* song, one in which America is not mentioned though probably meant, since in it the husband has left for a very distant land to make his fortune (Skuditski, p. 124):

Leaning on her elbow / A young woman sits late at night / Tears pour from her eyes / As she sits alone and thinks.

Children, children, your father no more will you see / (Except) sometimes on paper / Your father left to make his fortune / Alack and alas for me.

Your father left to make his fortune / In a very distant land / May he at least send me a divorce / Lest shame befall me.

Your father left me / At strange homes, before a strange door / By the whole world an *agune* regarded / Alack and alas for me.

:What then will I eat, eat / Elikl, my husband: / Bread, my little wife....
:Where will I get bread, bread / Elikl, my husband: / You will work, my little wife....
Elikl went away / And his wife remained at home / Oh, she suffers hunger / While he prospers there / Oh, farewell, my dear little wife / Oh, farewell, my dear little dove / Farewell, my precious crown / Die at home alone.[8]

A variant of this song speaks of the dishes the wife must prepare for the Sabbath, about which the husband at first seems unconcerned and becomes increasingly annoyed:

5. Where are you going, Elikl, my husband / Where are you going, Elik, you scoundrel / To America, my little wife / To America, my little dove / To America, my crown / My golden beauty.
Where then will I get meat for the Sabbath / Where then will I get meat for the Sabbath / At the butcher's, my little wife....
Where then will I get candles for the Sabbath / Where then will I get candles for the Sabbath / I will tie you up / So you won't have to light candles / And no money do I have.
Where then will I get *tsimes*[9] for the Sabbath / Where then will I get *tsimes* for the Sabbath / If you keep on about *tsimes* / You grow tiresome / And no money do I have.
Where then will I get bread for the Sabbath / Where then will I get bread for the Sabbath / If you keep on about bread / Then go drop dead / And no money do I have.[10]

The following song merely mentions America as the place to which the husband has set out. Actually it is a type of unhappy love song in which the wife recalls the last conversation she had with her husband before he left for America.

6. You are setting off for America, my dear life / While I remain in Russia / Oh, I tell you, my dear sweet life / To write me frequently.
Frequent letters will I write you / But you won't be able to read them / I tell you, my dear sweet life / That you will yet regret your years.
Remember when we went to the wedding canopy / How the moon and stars shone brightly for us / Even then my heart told me / That we would not be together long....[11]

The last song of this group is a love song of parting in which a girl grieves over the ill-fated outcome of her love affair. Weeping over the impending departure of her lover, she tells him that "a girl who would fall in love should foresee the end." She is distrustful of him and feels that he is running off to America in order to break off with her.

7. I stand at the river's edge / And cannot come to you / You with your sweet talk / Have destroyed my life.
My fingers will become pens / And my lips as paper pale / With the tears of my eyes / Will I write love letters to you.
My heart yearns for you / As magnet draws to steel / Whoever begins to play at love / Should see that it is for keeps.
My eyes refuse to dry / And my head is numb from pain / Whoever dares play at love / Should not be made a fool.

---

[8] *Tsaytshrift far yidisher geshikhte, demografye un ekonomik, literatur-forshung, shprakhvisnshaft un etnografye* (Minsk), vol. 2–3 (1928), p. 814.
[9] Fruit or vegetable preserves served on the Sabbath and on holidays.
[10] Skuditski, p. 114.
[11] *Ibid.*, p. 112; Dobrushin and Yuditski, p. 225.

Why do you inflict this torment / Oh, torment and pain / In the finest love affair / The outcome should be foreseen.

You want to go to America with me / For you know I have no money / You want to put an end to my young years / Through you my world is ruined....[12]

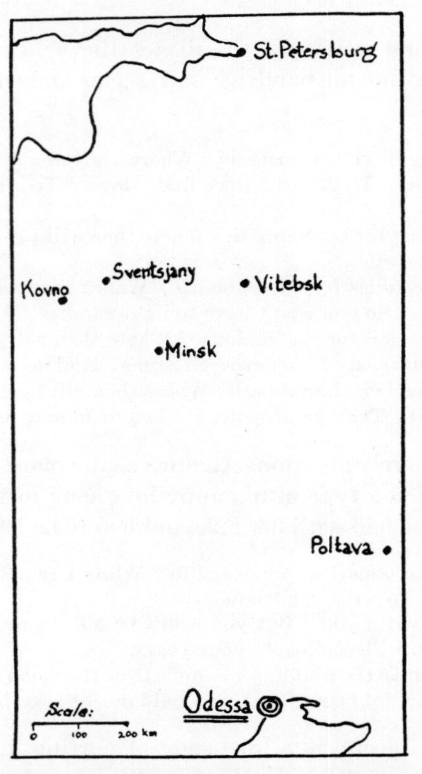

DISPERSION OF SHOLOM ALEICHEM'S LULLABY BETWEEN 1892 AND 1901

"In Amer ica There Is Joy For All"

Of the folksongs collected about America there is a number that presents America in a favorable and optimistic light.[13] In comparing the second group with the former we find that sometimes the same circumstances prevail, the same problems, the same alleged prosperity in America, but the attitude of the singer is an altogether different one. This group looks to America with hope, as to the land of plenty, of milk and honey, of freedom.

One of the most popular and widespread of all songs of this kind is the lullaby *Shlof, mayn kind* ("Sleep, my child"). This is one of the few well-known poems

[12] S. M. Ginzburg and P. S. Marek: *Jevrejskije narodnyje pesni v Rossii*, St. Petersburg, 1901, p. 168.

[13] Incidentally, this aspect was ignored by the Soviet folklorist Z. Skuditski, who only mentioned the first, negative, category (*op. cit.*, p. 26).

written by the great prose writer, Sholom Aleichem, in 1892.[14] That this song became a folksong almost immediately is evinced by the fact that six years later, when the compilers of the first major collection of Yiddish folksongs, Ginzburg and Marek, started to gather their material, this song was sent in by five different correspondents from five different localities and was published in 1901 as one among over 300 Yiddish folksongs (see map). This song is still being sung today with different texts and at least five melodic variants.[15]

A mother rocks her son to sleep and describes the wonders of that distant land America, where his father has gone. "By your cradle your mother sits, sings a song and weeps. You may some day understand what her weeping meant." Her tears are not bitter, as in the songs of the *agunes*, they are not tears of resentment or accusation, but of hope and longing for reunion in America. America for her means the paradise where *khale* (white bread baked only for the Sabbath and holidays) can be eaten every day and where she will prepare broth for her son.

8. Sleep, my child, sweet comfort mine / Sleep now, lyu-lyu-lyu / Sleep, my life, sole *kadish*[16] mine / Sleep, my little one.

By your cradle your mother sits / Sings a song and weeps / Some day you may understand / What her weeping meant.

In America is your father / lyu-lyu-lyu / You are but still a child / So sleep, my little son.

In America there is for all / Real joy [*glik*], they say / And for all a paradise / Something wondrous.

There on weekdays they eat / *Khale*, my little son / Broths will I cook for you / Sleep now, lyu-lyu-lyu.

God bidding, he will send us / Letters, my little one / And will make us happy very soon / So sleep, lyu-lyu-lyu.

He will send us twenty dollars / And his picture too / He will take us—long life to him / Over there.

He will hug us then and kiss us / Even dance for joy / Torrents of tears will I then shed / And weep quietly.

Until the good ticket comes / Sleep, lyu-lyu-lyu / For sleep is a dear remedy / So sleep, my little son.[17]

The original poem by Sholem Aleichem contains certain significant words and stanzas that were omitted or changed in the folksong variants.[18] For example,

[14] Published in *Kol mevaser tsu der yidisher folks-biblyotek*, Odessa, 1892.

[15] According to the author's footnote to the lullaby when it was first printed, it was to be sung to the melody of Lermontov's *Spi, mladenets moj prekrasnyj, bajuški baju*. However, another melody was inserted between pp. 24 and 25, and Sholem Aleichem writes: "After the poem, 'Sleep, My Child,' was already printed, we made the acquaintance of the talented music student, Mr. Dovid Kovanovski (the composer of the 'Notn leshirey tsiyen'), who composed this authentic Jewish melody for us on the spot." This and other melodic variants in A. Z. Idelsohn: "The Folk Song of the East European Jews," *Thesaurus of Hebrew Oriental Melodies*, vol. 9, Leipzig, 1932, nos. 116, 128, 492, 628; Sarah P. Schack and E. S. Cohen: *Yiddish Folk Songs*, New York, 1927, no. 3, p. 18; A. Litvin Collection of Yivo, no. 96.

[16] The son who recites the prayer for the dead parent.

[17] Ginzburg and Marek, p. 73, no. 82; M. Beregovski and I. Fefer: *Yidishe folkslider*, Kiev, 1938, p. 318; Dobrushin and Yuditski, p. 53, no. 26; Schack and Cohen, no. 3, p. 18.

[18] In the anthologies by Jacob Fikhman, *Di yidishe muze*, Warsaw, 1911, p. 90, and M.

instead of "And for all a paradise" the original line reads "And for Jews a paradise" (*yidn* instead of *yedn*). Stanzas that were omitted are the following:

So, in the meantime, let us hope / What else can we do? / I would long have gone to him / But I know not where.

He will provide everything / For our sake / And will come ahead to meet us / So sleep, sleep, lyu-lyu.

These hopes were shared by thousands throughout Eastern Europe. In the cities and towns people waited for letters, for the "twenty dollars," for a "picture" of the loved one across the seas—above all, their dream was that he "... take us over there." Perhaps this is the reason that the song attained such popularity among the Jews of Eastern Europe, who later used the basic theme in a number of workers', revolutionary, and ghetto songs.

Among the Yiddish ballads there is one which describes an accident in a linen factory in Jassy, Rumania, in which a girl met her death. Here America serves to contrast the tragedy: Saturday night she was supposed to go to America for the long-awaited reunion with her father—and on Friday her funeral was held instead.

9. Listen to what has occurred / In the linen factory in Jassy / Oh, when a girl ran back from lunch / The foreman sent her up to work.

As soon as the girl threw down the linen / All the machines remained still / And when they ran over to her / Her head was caught in the machine.

\- - - - - - - - - - - -

As soon as her mother came to the factory / She stood as though stunned / Oh, she caught the dead body to her / And hugged it and kissed.

Saturday night she was to go to America / Eight years had she her father not seen / Oh, Saturday night she was to go to America / And Friday her funeral will be....[19]

We have a song where a man decides to take his fate into his own hands and asks God to help him execute his decision to go to America, where he is ready to sell himself as a slave rather than remain in Russia. This song is interesting since it confirms a report in the 1880's of rumors that the emigrating Jews were to be sold as slaves in America. The Jews were supposed to have replied to this rumor thus: "... but even should we become slaves there ... it is still better to be a slave in America than to live here under such terrible conditions."[20]

10. One thing, God, will I beg of you / That it may be granted me / From Russia I must flee / America will be my goal.

Of no joy do I know / in Russia it is very bad / To America I will set out / And sell myself as a slave....[21]

Basin, *Finf hundert yor yidishe poezye*, New York, 1917, p. 240, the following stanzas are also included in the lullaby: "There they know not of exile, oppression / Persecution, little son / Nor of worry, grief / So sleep, lyu-lyu. — There, they say, Jews are / Rich, no evil eye / Each one lives contendedly / All are equal."

[19] *Yidisher folklor*, Yiddish Scientific Institute, New York, no. 1 (January 1954), p. 10.

[20] M. Friedländer: *Fünf Wochen in Brody under jüdisch-russischen Emigranten*, Vienna, 1882; quoted in *Geshikhte fun der yidisher arbeter-bavegung in di fareynikte shtatn*, vol. 1, New York, 1943, p. 174.

[21] A. Litvin Collection of Yivo, no. 904. The original text:

In the following group of songs light is shed on internal relations existing within the Jewish community, more specifically on the age-old traditionally set conventions of marriage. The *yikhes* (social status) of the prospective bride or groom played the dominant role in arranging a match. The highest status in a groom was considered his own learning or his descent from learned people, while in the bride's case the larger the *nadán* (dowry) she could provide, the better. There were many instances where love affairs, usually carried on clandestinely, had to be severed because of parental standards and objections. By such lovers the happy solution that America presented was also carried over into their song, where we see America as a means of breaking through social barriers.

A girl promises her lover, on the eve of his leaving for service in the army, that she will wait five years for him. If after that time, she frets, his parents disapprove of her, what then? He reassures her; in that event they will simply elope to America and marry there.

11. Oh, my joy, my dearest life / Both are we an equal pair / I swear to you by my very life / That I will wait five years for you.

Five years will I wait for you / Upon the sixth you will be freed / And if I will not please your parents / Ah, my pain will then be great.

Do not fret, my dear life / Lest my parents be not pleased / To America will we run off / And have our wedding there.

We will have our wedding there / In the presence of ten [*minyen*] / God in heaven will be our witness / And 'neath the canopy will bless us....[22]

Eyn zakh vel ikh, got, ba dir betn / Az di zakh zol mir zayn bashert / Fun rusland muz ikh optretn / Keyn amerike vet zayn mayn pakhod.

Fun keyne glikn veys ikh nit / In rusland iz mir zeyer shlekht / Keyn amerike muz ikh opforn / Farkoyfn vel ikh zikh far a knekht....

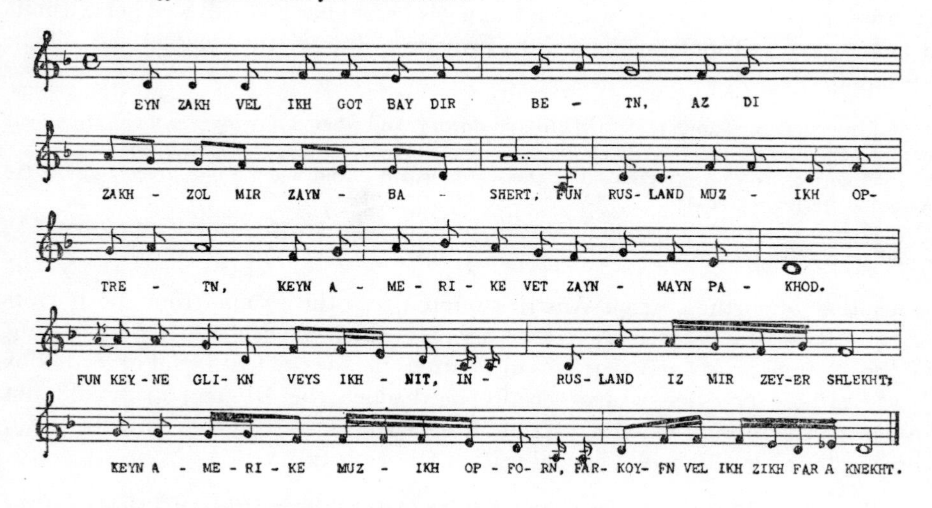

[22] Y. L. Cahan: *Yidishe folkslider mit melodyes oys dem folksmoyl*, vol. 1, New York, 1912, p. 102, no. 12.

In a variant to this song it is the girl that proposes eloping to America:

12. The beginning of our love affair / Was as sugar sweet / But the end of our love affair / Proved very bitter....

If you love me truly / I will ask you something / Sneak away from your parents / And come to see me off.

\- - - - - - - - - - - -

And when you will come out of the army / You will already not want me / Let's both go to America / There we will have our wedding....[23]

A similar motive for going to America is revealed in a song in which a rich girl confides in her mother about her lover and begs her to let her marry him. The mother furiously points out the difference in status between them; she disinherits her, as she says, for "cursing" her parents, and tells her to marry whomever she wishes. The couple in the song take their things and go off to America.

13. Mother love, mother dear / My head aches, I grow ill / Heal the wounds of my heart / And give me the one I want.

Daughter love, daughter dear / Poison would I rather give / When you have a father so rich / A rogue you choose for a husband.

Mother love, mother dear / Do not boast of your wealth / I have seen many richer than we / But we outlive them all. [!]

Daughter love, daughter dear / I cast you off as my child / If you can so curse your father and mother / Then marry whomever you wish.

Sweetheart love, sweetheart dear / To my mother I have spoken / The next day we took our money and things / And for America we left.

As soon as we came to America / We turned rich from poor / With how many boys I went / No one is equal to mine....[24]

In a lighter vein is the song *In amerike forn furn* ("In America wagons ride"). In America, when a boy loves a girl, he kneels before her and will wed her without a penny, i.e., without her having to provide a dowry. In America she will be his equal.

14. In America wagons ride / Up hill and down / And when a boy loves a girl / He kneels before her.

In America *khales* are baked / For the whole world / And when a boy loves a girl / He weds her without a cent.

In America *beygl* are baked / For a whole year / I—your groom, and you—my bride / An equal pair will we be.[25]

Another opportunity that America offered was the escape from the horrors of the Tsarist military service. The agonies which Jewish soldiers underwent in the Tsarist army make up a sad chapter in Jewish history. For orthodox Jewry military service was especially hard since the Russian army did not recognize their right to *kashrut* and those soldiers were forced to subsist for three or four years on a diet of cold water and dry bread.

[23] S. Z. Pipe: [Yiddish Folksongs from Galicia (Sanok)], *Yivo-bleter* 11 (1937), p. 68.

[24] *Der pinkes* (Vilna), 1913, p. 402, no. 8.

[25] Ginzburg and Marek, p. 183, no. 228; Dobrushin and Yuditski, p. 67, no. 18.

The first song is of a recruit who would have fled to America had he had the money. Judging from the terms used and from the first stanza, it would appear that the singer had come to Russia from Austria (Galicia) and there had fallen into the hands of the *khapers* (snatchers of boys for impression into military service).

15. As soon as I came to Russia / With a wail and with a cry / I at once resolved / That I would not become a soldier.

How many tears did my dear mother shed / Until she bore me / Today a [recruiting] board arrived / And made me a soldier.

They took me to the engagement party / Seated me in the middle / Gave me a sabre for a bride / And the emperor became my in-law.

As soon as I came to the squadron / I already thought of escaping / Should I serve three years / Should I run to America?

To America I would escape / And travel throughout the world / But I have, alas, one drawback / There isn't a single penny.[26]

We have here the very popular image, which recurs in many songs, of the recruit's "marriage," i.e. induction, with the sabre becoming his bride and the emperor his father-in-law.

In another song a Jewish recruit enumerates the many hardships to be expected in the army and after each stanza sings a refrain:

16. Well, I ask you, my Lord, is it just / And how is a person to bear it? / Give me your answer to this, my Lord / Should I not run off to America?[27]

The third soldier's song stems from the first World War and is the only one of many variants with mention of America. The song is found in many collections and can still be heard quite often. It is a song of a wounded soldier in World War I. In this variant the soldier has run away and, being wounded, regrets his not having gone to America before his life was ruined.

17. The [19]14th year arrived / To be a soldier I was taken / Three days I lay in the barracks / And no food was given.

Three fled from the regiment / The first bullet struck me / Who will follow my funeral? / Only my faithful horse.

Who will weep and mourn for me? / Who will recite *kadish* after me? / Amidst the woods, in the fields / A soldier lies slain.

My mother wrote to the Red Cross / That her son remained in the field / I should better have gone to America / Before ruining my young life.[28]

---

[26] A. Litvin Collection of Yivo, no. 613. The original text:

Ikh bin nor keyn rusland gekumen / Mit eyn yomer un mit eyn geveyn / In zinen hob ikh mir genumen / Az keyn zelner zol ikh nit zayn.

Vifl trern hot mayn mamenyu geton fargisn / Eyder zi hot mikh gehat / Haynt iz ongekumen a komisye / Un m'hot mikh gemakht far eyn soldat.

M'hot mikh tsu farlobung genumen / Gezetst hot men mikh in der mitn / Dos zeybele far a kale gegebn / Un der keyser blaybt mayn mekhutn.

Vi ikh bin in skadron arayngekumen / Geklert hob ikh shoyn oyf a[nt]loyfn / Tsi zol ikh dray yor dinen / Tsi zol ikh keyn amerike antloyfn.

Keyn amerike volt ikh antlofn / Barayzt di gantse velt / Nor leyder ikh hob a khisorn / S'iz nito keyn graytser gelt.

[27] M. Osherovitsh: *Shtet un shtetlekh in Ukraine*, vol. 1, New York, 1948, p. 20.

[28] Bastomski, p. 108, no. 3.

"A Letter to Mother"

What were the sentiments of the new immigrant in America? According to the songs that were sung in Eastern Europe—disillusionment, bitterness, and loneliness. These were also expressed in the songs by the older Yiddish poets in this country in the early 90's and the beginning of this century: Vintshevski, Edelshtat, Yoysef Bovshover, Rosenfeld, and others; they were also reflected in the Yiddish theater.[29]

The following two songs might well be a product of the Yiddish theater. They describe the transformation and disillusionment of young immigrant girls in America.

18. There came a cousin to me / Pretty as gold was she, the green one / Her cheeks were like red oranges / Her little feet just begged for a dance.

\- - - - - - - - - - - -

She walked not but she skipped / She talked not but she sang / Gay and cheerful was her manner / This is how my cousin once was.

I came in to my neighbor / Who has a millinery store / I got a job for my cousin / Praised be the golden land.

Many years have since passed / My cousin became a wreck / Many years of collecting wages / Till nothing was left of her.

Beneath her pretty blue eyes / Black lines are drawn / Her cheeks, once like red oranges / Have turned completely green already.

Today, when I meet my cousin / And I ask her: How are you, green one? / She'll reply with a grimace / To blazes with Columbus's country.[30]

19. I am a little girl, a green one from Poland / Came to America in search of a good boy / Girls, oh girls, green from Poland / What America is, I will tell you.

I came to New York, a town a delight / And bless the Lord for the land so free / Girls....

Two weeks at my rich uncle's / And they begin to ask me: How do you like America....

They tell me with a smile: You must "ungreen" yourself / And with they they mean: Go out and earn....

I run around from shop to shop, I run senselessly / But because I am green I can't find a job....

---

[29] Perhaps one of the most popular songs describing the hard life of the immigrant of that period was Morris Rosenfeld's *Mayn yingele* ("My little son"), in which a father sings of his little son whom he never has a chance to be with, since he must leave for work at dawn when the boy is still asleep and returns late at night when his son has long been put to bed. Many such songs were widely current throughout Eastern Europe.

[30] A. Litvin Collection of Yivo, no. 227A. The original text:

Es iz tsu mir gekumen a kuzine / Sheyn vi gold iz zi geven, di grine / Di bekelekh vi royte pomerantsn / Fiselekh vos betn zikh tsum tantsn.

\- - - - - - - - - - - -

Nit gegangen iz zi–nor geshprungen / Nit geredt, nor gezungen / Freylekh, lustik iz geven ir mine / Ot aza geven iz mayn kuzine.

Ikh bin arayn tsu mayn nekst-dorke / Vos zi hot a milineri-storke / A dzhab gekrogn hob ikh far mayn kuzine / Az lebn zol di goldene medine.

\- - - - - - - - - - - -

Avek zaynen fun demolt on shoyn yorn / Fun mayn kuzine iz a tel gevorn / Peydes yorn lang hot zi geklibn / Biz fun ir aleyn iz nisht geblibn.

Unter ire bloye sheyne oygn / Shvartse pasn hobn zikh fartsoygn / Di bekelekh, di royte pomerantsn / Hobn zikh shoyn oysgegrint in gantsn.

Haynt, az ikh bagegn mayn kuzine / Un ikh freg zi: "Vos zhe makhstu, grine?" / Entfert zi mir mit a krumer mine / "Az brenen zol kolumbuses medine!"

Found one finally at a relative's, what a joy / Earn almost five dollars a week and work by the piece....

\- - - - - - - - - - - - -

I meet up with a boy, an East Broadway dandy / He pays me many compliments and already asks for my hand....

\- - - - - - - - - - - - -

Ah, in this land, the rich one of all pleasures / You can't get the holiest, the purest here....

This pure love, this truthful life / This Uncle Sam will not give at any price....[31]

The following song is again in the popular form of a letter, in which the singer writes to his mother of his longing to see her again. He would return but his wife, fearing the threat of military conscription in Russia, forbids it.[32] This song, entitled *A briv fun amerike* ("A Letter from America"), is by one of the most popular Yiddish folk poets, M. M. Varshavski, whose songs were the favorites of Eastern European Jewry.

20. Dear mama, dear mother / My dear pure heart / Do you know how I weep so bitterly / And how great my pain is here? / Oh, what would I not give / To look upon you / I would give my life for you / If I could only return to you.

But these are not the years / That we can do everything / Mama, I cannot come to you / Writing this isn't easy for me / Leyenyu forbids it, she is afraid / She trembles at the thought of conscription....[33]

In another song regret is expressed about having left home, for what fortunes were then found in America?

21. Why did I run to America / And what fortunes met me there? / Since I remained alone / So far from my sisters and brothers.

---

[31] A. Litvin Collection of Yivo, no. 228A. The original text:

Bin ikh mir a meydele, a grininke fun poyln / Kum ikh keyn amerike, nokh a boy a voyln / Meydelekh, ay meydelekh, grininke fun poyln / Vos es iz amerike vel ikh aykh dertseyln.

Gekumen bin ikh keyn nyu-york—a shtetl gor a mekhaye / Un bentsh dokh take got far dos land dos fraye....

Opgeven tsvey vokhn bay dem onkl bay dem raykhn / Un men heybt mikh on tsu fregn shoyn: Vi tust amerike glaykhn....

Men zogt mir mit a shmeykhele: darfst zikh geyn oysgrinen / Un in erntst meynt men dos: gey zikh dir fardinen....

Ikh loyf arum fun shap tsu shap, ikh loyf arum on zinen / Nor vayl ikh bin a grininke, ken ikh keyn dzhab gefinen....

Gefunen endlekh, bay a korev, gor a glik / Fardin a vokh finf dolar koym, un arbet mir fun shtik....

\- - - - - - - - - - - - -

Kh'baken zikh mit a bokherl an ist-brodvey[er] *frant / Er git mir komplimentn fil un bet shoyn gor mayn hant....*

\- - - - - - - - - - - - -

Akh in dem land, dem tayern, fun ale fargenign / Dos heylikste, dos herlekhste kent ir do nit krign....

Ot di libe reyninke, ot dos vare lebn / Dos vet dokh aykh far keyn fal "onkl sem" ... nit gebn....

[32] "Some young people who came here in the [18]40's and 50's and returned to Russia already as Americans were arrested by the police as fugitives from the Russian military service." *Geshikhte fun der yidisher arbeter-bavegung*... (see footnote 20), vol. 1, p. 67.

[33] Idelsohn, no. 746; M. M. Varshavski: *Yidishe folkslider*, 2nd ed., New York, 1918, p. 5.

Now my parents beg me to return / And to go back isn't right for me / A fire burns within me / For my dear devoted mother.

And my heart yearns only for her / I know she will give me back / My bread to live / And I sing my dear devoted mother's song.[34]

The question, "Why did I run to America?" appears in a fragment of a variant in which the singer seems to be on a boat going back.

22. Why did I run to America / And what fortune met me there? / : I write a letter and sit on the boat:

When I lie on my bed / I count the hours on the clock / : I moan and weep, for tomorrow I must....:[35]

This sentiment of longing for home and mother found expression in the song *A brivele der mamen* ("A Letter to Mother") written by S. Shmulevitz in America. Although the song is of the mother in the old country who begs her child in America not to forget to write her a letter, it became the beloved song of both sons and daughters in America as well as of lonesome parents left behind.

23. My child, my comfort, you are going away / See that you be a good son / This, with tears and worry / Your devoted mother begs of you.

You are going, my child, my only child / Across distant seas / Oh arrive there in good health / And don't forget your mother....

Yes, depart and get there in safety / See that you send a letter each week / To refresh your mother's heart, my child.

A letter to mother / Do not delay / Write soon, dear child / And give her some consolation / Your mother will read your letter / And will rejoice / You will heal her wounds / Her bitter heart / You will refresh her spirit.[36]

In the last stanza we learn:

In New York City, a rich house / Of hearts without pity / There lives her son / He lives quite well / With divine gifts....

He receives a letter informing him of his mother's death and of her last wish that he recite the *kadish* after her.

"Long Live America With Its Dollars"

The Jews in Eastern Europe suffered acute poverty during the depression following World War I and were largely dependent upon the aid which American Jewry provided, through individuals as well as through specially set-up relief organizations. The American dollar was considered the only stable currency and trading of dollars for other currency was conducted extensively. There arose a number of humorous songs about the American dollar in Poland, where poverty was especially great.

For the sake of dollars, one song reveals, the singer is ready to marry a shrew, a cripple, as long as she has dollars, or even an aunt in America.

[34] Skuditski, p. 112.

[35] Pipe, [Folklore Songs] (see footnote 2), p. 354.

[36] Idelsohn, no. 428; Nathan Ausubel: *A Treasury of Jewish Folklore*, New York, 1948, p. 677.

24. Dollars, give them here to me / Dollars, that is my desire / Let my bride be a shrew / As long as [she has] a full sack of dollars / Dollars, give them here to me....
Let my bride be deformed / As long as [she has] an aunt in America / Dollars....
Let her be without a nose / As long as [she has] a full measure of dollars....
Let her be swollen like a barrel / As long as [she has] a whole street of dollars....[37]

There is irony coupled with bitterness in the songs describing the relief which various American Jewish delegations brought. It often seemed to the Jews in Poland that the visiting delegates didn't possess the necessary understanding for their fundamental needs. They also felt that these delegates often used their positions on the relief committees to their own advantage.

25. Long live America / With her dollars / The delegates arrive / And proceed to fool us / They take the dollars and change them for marks / And achieve thereby the best speculations.
Long live America / When she became aware / That we, in Vashlikov, go naked and in rags / She sent us fancy shoes / With long pointed tips / The girls want to go walking with the boys / And have to stay at home.[38]

This ridicule of the aid which American Jewry sent is again expressed in a variant:

26. Long live America / Long may she thrive / When she learned / That we are in tatters / She clothed us / In satin and plush / And made us up / Like fools in top hats.[39]

Another song praises the American Jews for sending dollars but not for their delegates:

27. Our American brothers send us dollars / Blessed be their deeds / There is only one thing bothering us, brothers / Why must you send us the delegates?[40]

Criticism of the local committees which were created for the purpose of distributing relief was articulated in the following song. The money and clothes that were sent from America, so it seemed to the people, were taken away by the committee men instead of being distributed to the poor.

28. Long live America / For sending us clothes / So that the committee men can have / Rolls to bake [i.e. so they can trade the clothes for bread].
Long live America / For sending us dollars / So that the committee men can have / What to take.
Long live America / For sending us flour / May the committee men / Turn green and yellow.
Long live America / For sending us bread / May the committee men / All drop dead.[41]

---

[37] *Yidishe filologye* (Warsaw), I, 1924, p. 94.

[38] *Ibid.*

[39] *Ibid.*

[40] Sent in by Mr. B. Levin, Los Angeles, 1954. The original text: *Undz're amerikaner brider shikn undz dolarn / Gebentsht zoln zayn ayere tatn / Nor eyn zakh, brider, vos undz tut arn / Tsu vos shikt ir tsu undz di delegatn?*

[41] Received from Mr. L. Ran, New York, 1953, who recorded the song in Vashlikov before World War II. The original text:

Lebn zol amerike / Vos zi shikt undz yakn / Far di komitetnikes / Bulkelekh tsu bakn.
Lebn zol amerike / Vos zi shikt undz dolarn / Az di komitetnikes / Zoln hobn vos tsu sharn.
Lebn zol amerike / Vos zi shikt undz mel / Zoln di komitetnikes / Vern grin un gel.
Lebn zol amerike / Vos zi shikt undz broyt / Zoln di komitetnikes / Krign dem toyt.

The final song which treats of this same situation is a parody on the lullaby by Sholom Aleichem (see no. 8). The images which were used formerly to present hope and optimism are here transformed into pessimism and bitterness. The dollars which the father will send from America will now be used to buy worthless Polish marks. The broth that the mother promised to prepare for her son is now eaten by the American delegates in Warsaw. In this song, criticism of the new Poland of 1918 (which was resurrected following the Versailles Peace Treaty) is revealed, particularly for its worthless currency and its disorder, in which packages get lost. Furthermore, the inability to comprehend the bureaucratic ways of American delegates made the Polish Jews skeptical and critical of the good intentions of the former.

29. Sleep, my child, my comfort, life / Sleep already, lyu-lyu-lyu / Food "shmood", bah, t'is ugly / Shut your little eyes.

From America your father / Dear little child / Has sent us a package / So sleep, lyu-lyu-lyu.

And a few dollars too / Dear little child / Your father, long life to him / Sent us over here.

For a dollar you can get / Whole sacks of marks / And we both, child mine, will grow / Rich without end.

But the package has been lost / Alack and woe is me / And the dollars have been frozen / So sleep, sleep, my child.

And the dollars lie around / Somewhere in the banks / And we both, my child, get / None of it meanwhile.

Someone from America is here / A man called Morgenthau[42] / He nourishes us upon his speeches / Alack and woe is me.

And after him a Doctor Bogen[43] / Who speaks endlessly / The delegates come and go / So sleep, meanwhile, sleep.

They come to ease our troubles / Our worry and our pain / But they sit around like lords / in the Angielski Bar.[44]

There they eat on weekdays / broths with chicken, too / While we, my child, both are ill / So sleep, sleep, my son.

Neither dollars, nor a package / Do we have, my child / Oh we're caught in a trap / So sleep, sleep, my child.[45]

---

[42] Henry Morgenthau, Sr. (1856–1946), head of Woodrow Wilson's commission to investigate the treatment of Jews in the newly created Polish republic.

[43] Boris David Bogen (1869–1929), director-general of the Joint Distribution Committee during World War I.

[44] A Warsaw restaurant.

[45] A. Litvin Collection of Yivo, no. 826. The original text:

Shlof mayn kind, mayn treyst, mayn khiyes / Shlof shoyn, lyu-lyu-lyu / Esn shmesn, fuy, s'iz miyes / Makh di eygelekh tsu.

Fun amerike dayn foter / Tayer kindenyu / Undz geshikt a pekl hot er / Shlof zhe lyu-lyu-lyu.

Un dertsu nokh a por doler / Tayer kindenyu / Shikt dayn tate, lebn zol er / Undz ahertsutsu.

Far a doler kon men krign / Markn gantse zek / Un mir beyde, kind mayns, vern / Raykh gor on an ek.

Nor dos pekl iz farloyrn / Vey iz mir un vind / Un di dolers oysgefroyrn / Shlof zhe, shlof mayn kind.

Un di doler blaybn lign / Ergets in di benk / Un mir beyde, kind mayns, krign / Oy dervayl a krenk.

Epes iz do fun amerike / Eyner Morgntoy / Shpayzt er undz mit zayne droshes / Vey iz mir un oy.

Un nokh im a dokter Bogn / Redt er on a sof / Kumen, forn meshulokhim / Shlof zhe dervayle, shlof.

With the introduction of immigration restrictions in the United States which culminated in the Quota Law of 1924, Jewish mass immigration to this country was virtually ended. As the gates of the golden land were closed to the East European Jews, so were their hopes and aspirations for America extinguished. The songs that arose after that period may have been a reflection of this realization that America had become an unattainable dream, for no new songs about the golden land were composed or imported; or was it that the daily, more pressing, problems took precedence in the songs that were sung? In any event, the Yiddish folksong of Eastern Europe no longer spoke of America—of its golden fortunes for the poverty-stricken, of the refuge for the oppressed, of the solution for unhappy lovers, of homesick letters, of weeping, of dreams, of joys. . . .

Zey kumen lindern undzere tsores / Undzer vey un tsar / Nor zey zitsn vi di srores / In angielski bar.

Dortn est men in der vokhn / Yaykhelekh mit hun / Un mir beyde, kind mayns, zokhn / Shlof zhe, shlof, mayn zun.

Nit keyn dolers, nisht keyn pekl / Hobn mir mayn kind / Oy, lign mir tif in zekl / Shlof zhe, shlof mayn kind.

ON CHILDREN'S NONSENSE OATHS IN YIDDISH

MORDCHE SCHAECHTER (New York)

Words without meaning—perhaps we should rather call them nonsensical sequences of sounds—can be found in children's lore aplenty. In counting-out rimes and in oaths they are paramount. Not only do these two genres swarm with meaningless sound sequences, but even the stray meaningful words that do crop up in them often appear in no sensible relation to one another. They are just plain jabber and gibberish. It is impossible to deduce the function of the whole from its parts, i.e. the sound sequences and the words. Moreover, the purport of the whole is frequently problematic. If we pull a folklore item of this kind from its concrete context (e.g. if one were to write out the text on a piece of paper without noting its function) it is sometimes difficult or even impossible to recognize what it is. In counting-out rimes the rhythm may at least provide a clue to the function of the words and sound sequences. What else could *am dam dey nos, sava rika rey nos* . . . be, if not a counting-out rime? But among oaths, there are many in which the layman cannot even find a glimmering of a hint as to the function of the elements. Here are a few illustrations:

Mrs. L., an informant hailing from Buhúts,[1] Carpatho-Russia, and now residing in New York, who was brought up in a hassidic family, told me of the following oath that had been current in her home town: *moríshko, shokl dekh in nem leyb!* This oath, she reports, was considered vehement. Yet it means precisely nothing. In Hungarian *Mariska* (phonetically [ˈmɔriškɔ]) is a common endearing form of the girl's name, *Mária* (Slovak and Czech: *Mariška*); in Rumanian the same sequence of sounds means 'windmill'. The stress in the Yiddish *moríshko* is on the second syllable, as in Rumanian and Slovak. *Shokl dekh* is, in all probability, to be interpreted as the imperative form of *shoklen zikh*: 'shake yourself'. *In* is either the preposition (rather implausible) or the conjunction (Standard Yiddish: *un*). I believe than *nem* has nothing to do with *nemen* 'to take', but is rather the Hungarian negative *nem* 'not'. In other words, *nem leyb* would signify 'do not live (*imperative*)'. Even so the whole phrase does not seem to make any sense. How can we relate 'do not live' with the shaking windmill or the unfortunate young maid, Mariska? And why is the whole an oath?

The same Buhúts informant cited another oath: *man khlyeptshe borsht!* A refugee from Dubové (Yid. Díbeve), Carpatho-Russia, corrected it: *tsi man khlyeptshe borsht!* It does not take much deliberation to recognize the verb *khlyeptshen* 'to drink noisily' and its object *borsht* 'beet soup'. But what connection is there between these words and swearing?

Another informant from Iršava (Yid. Órsheve), Carpatho-Russia, supplied me with: *kátshkele, físele, hímlshtoyb*, . . . She was certain that this was but a

[1] A tiny community, called in Czech and Rumanian Valeskrad'e, located approximately 5 km NNW of Slatinské Doly (Yid. Solótvine); nearest post office in Středný Apša.

fragment of a longer oath, but try as she did, she was unable to remember the rest of the 'little duck, little foot, sky dust' sequence.

Another oath current in Buhúts was this: *man lóshekl in dan shkápkele, umeyn seyle!* 'my filly and your young mare, amen!'. By what devious means the animal pair got into this, and just how this odd mixture came to function as a protection against being cheated, is a curious problem.

Mr. L. K., an informant from Michalevice, Slovakia, now in New York, recalls his grandmother's admonition that the only permissible oath is: *udem a mentsh, katshke rik dekh!*, literally, 'Adam a man duck move'. Now this hardly analyzable phrase is often used as an answer to a preposterous statement, an immodest claim, and the like; Sholom Aleichem popularized it among many Yiddish speakers. But how did it come to function as a children's oath? Either the derisive idiom is the older and gave birth to the oath, or conversely, the oath, though today restricted regionally, is historically the source of the idiom. It would be worthwhile to consider three well-known facts at this point: (1) Some items in children's folklore are older than is usually imagined. I might even generalize: children's lore is blessed with longevity. (2) Present-day restricted geographic distribution of a fact need not reflect its former degree of dispersion. (3) The affectiveness and derisiveness of a saying are conducive to its wide diffusion. A word or an idiomatic saying that stings and bites can capture entire countries before one can say Jack Robinson.

Let us assume for a moment that the oath is older than the mocking phrase. Perhaps, once upon a time, when *odem a mentsh* . . . as the oath of small fry resounded in Jewish homes, someone was struck by the similarity between the naively solemn posture of children swearing about some trifle and the posture of the nobody who puts on airs. The comparison caught on to such a degree that the oath came to be regularly used in mocking the pretentious. Soon other people, unfamiliar with the original *odem a mentsh* . . . in its oath form, may have followed suit without understanding the reference to the pretentiousness of a child taking an oath. If this hypothesis is invalid, some other explanation remains to be found for the odd parallelism between the combination of 'Adam, the man' with the duck which is asked to move over and the combination of Maria (or the windmill) who is told to get moving but not to live. Other nonsensical children's expressions of a similar construction could be cited.

Be that as it may, we are faced here with instances of artificial speech distortion, and it is apparent that such phenomena are particularly common in the domain of children's oaths. They are motivated, of course, not by mischief, but from the interference of adults in the conduct of the children. The mother, an older sister, or a grandmother (as in Mr. L. K.'s case) forbade the use of the oath *kh'zol azoy leybn!* '[as this is true] so may I live' or other realistic oaths that might, perish the thought, come true. The adults thus supplied all the gibberish forms and stamped them as "proper" oaths in order to restrain the children from using dangerous "real" oaths.

There is, on the other hand, yet another possibility. Mrs. R. W. from Dracineţi, Bukovina, Rumania, told me that in her town, when a child did not believe the statement of another, he would challenge *shver dekh!* 'swear it!'. The standard reply to this was: *bikslekh!* 'rifles (*diminutive*)!' Another variant (cited by Dr. J. G. from Siret, Rumania) runs as follows: *shverdlekh, shikslekh, bikslekh, ptu!* 'swords (*dim.*), gentile girls (*dim.*), rifles (*dim.*), *ptu*!'. (The last element is a Yiddish interjection associated with spitting.) This strange oath and its string of variants probably developed from the pun *shver dekh—shverdlekh*. I doubt whether children's humor alone is responsible for the next step, since the result (*shver dekh–bikslekh*) is an oath, not a joke. I think I detect an adult hand. It's easy to visualize a grown-up who, on being challenged by a child: *shver dikh*, put on his best earnest expression and in a calm voice did swear—with an oath that was all stuff and nonsense. The youngsters, unaware of the adult evasiveness, accepted the so-called oath without appreciating the prank which was behind it.

The diversion of the challenge to swear is even more striking in an oath that found widespread currency in Old Rumania: *eylem, beylem, tu. . ., tseylem!* '*eylem, beylem*, hindquarters, cross!' The first two "words" frequently serve as the beginning line in children's songs. The meaning of the other two is unequivocal. However, the four together are absolute and highly irreverent fiddle-faddle.

In sum then, nonsensical children's oaths should be catalogued either under "humor" or "linguistic taboo" or under both. In any case children are innocent of these creations which are attributed to them. They were either taught them consciously by adults, or the children picked them up from their evasive elders. In either case children did no more than adopt them. But while the adults, either seriously or as a prank, offered the children the linguistic vessel which the little ones filled with deeply felt emotions, they turned nonsensical gibberish into oaths which could weather the most arduous of tests. Some oaths are thus genetically the folklore of adults, while functionally they are children's folklore.

FOUR YIDDISH VARIANTS OF THE MASTER-THIEF TALE

BEATRICE SILVERMAN WEINREICH (New York)

INTRODUCTION

Yiddish folktales have been divided by scholars into two major families: "moral" tales,[1] i.e. those with ethical, religious, or edifying overtones; and "secular" tales,[2] i.e. the non-religious ones told for amusement only. The moral tales have been extensively studied; the secular tales have not shared this good fortune.

A number of attractive research problems are presented by the secular tales. After a thorough study of the individual tales in all their variants there is the task of characterizing the secular tales as a literary genre. Furthermore, individual tales could be compared in form and content with equivalent tales in other Old-World folklores, e.g. with German *Märchen* or Russian *skazki* whose motifs they share. On this cross-folklore level, there is the even broader problem of characterizing the specifics of this Yiddish form of the *Märchen* genre as contrasted, say, with the corresponding Russian genre. But this whole field is still untouched.

Any generalized statements regarding the genre *per se* or in contrast with similar genres in other folklores must, for methodologically obvious reasons, be preceded by detailed structural and content analyses of the individual tales. Here I have analyzed one secular tale, The Master Thief, in four of its variants in a framework that, I hope, will prove useful in a future study of the genre as a whole. I have limited myself to a discussion of plot, episode, and incident structure; plot motivation; and certain stylistic techniques of characterization.[3] As points of departure, I utilized existing surveys of similar genres among other peoples,[4] noting wherever appropriate and feasible, parallels from other folklores

[1] Referred to in Yiddish folkloristics as *moralishe mayses*.

[2] Referred to in Yiddish folkloristics as *sekulere, a-moralishe mayses* or *mayselekh*. The nearest equivalent to this genre of tales is the *Märchen*-type as defined by Stith Thompson, in *The Folktale*, New York, 1946, p. 8. The English term "Fairy-Tale" is unsatisfactory, because it implies the presence of fairies. I have never come across a Yiddish secular tale that has fairies as characters; certainly the variants of the tale to be discussed in this paper have no fairies.

[3] The original paper, written for a highly profitable folklore course with Professor Gladys A. Reichard at Columbia University in 1953, contained much more citation from the variants themselves and studied stylistic features in great detail. Individual and regional differences in narrative technique as well as cultural reflections in the tale remain to be scrutinized.

[4] My principal general sources included: Y. M. Sokolov: *Russian Folklore*, New York, 1950; V. Propp: *Morfologija skazki*, Leningrad, 1928; Max Lüthi: *Das europäische Volksmärchen; Form und Wesen*, Berne, 1947; Stith Thompson: *The Folktale*, New York, 1946. Major sources concerning the Yiddish folktale were: Y. L. Cahan: *Shtudyes vegn yidisher folksshafung*, Max Weinreich, ed., New York, 1952; Angelo S. Rappoport, *The Folklore of the Jews*, London, 1937.

as preliminaries to a full-scale comparison of the Yiddish Master-Thief tale with the same tale as told by other peoples.

The analysis of variants of the same tale has its limitations as well as its advantages. In dealing with versions of a single tale, one may expect *a priori* that more will be constant than in the genre as a whole. Constancy of theme, for example, may produce a certain constancy of characterization which would not necessarily be typical of the genre as a whole. On the other hand, the great advantage of dealing with many variants of one tale (where the variable of theme is kept constant) is that the inner construction of the tale, i.e. the concrete possibilities of handling a theme, emerge with particular clarity. When it comes to such structural questions as the relative freedom or rigor in the sequence of episodes and incidents, or the relationship between motivations and motifs, only a comparison of variants can provide the answers.

The four variants of "The Master Thief"[5] to be discussed here were obtained from the following sources: Variant A appears in Y. L. Cahan's *Yidishe folksmayses* (Jewish Folktales), Yiddish Scientific Institute, Vilna, 1940, as "A mayse fun a geshaytn ganev" (no. 42), pp. 189–205. Variant B appears in the same collection as "A mayse fun a klugn ganev" (no. 31), pp. 129–136. Variant C is no. 3 ("Der kluger ganev") in *Yidisher folklor*, ed. Y. L. Cahan, Vilna, 1938 (=Publications of the Yiddish Scientific Institute, Philological Series 5), pp. 105–107. Variant D appears as no. 5 among the "Märchen und Schwänke in Amerika aus dem Munde russischer Juden aufgezeichnet von Leo Wiener" in *Mitteilungen der Gesellschaft für jüdische Volkskunde* 18 (1906, no. 2), pp. 69–72.

Variant A was recorded from a story-teller hailing from Šeduva (Yid. Sadove), Lithuania; variant B—from Beltsy (Yid. Belts), Bessarabia; variant C—from Sanok (Yid. Sonek), Poland; and D from Teteryn (Yid. Teterin), Belorussia (see map).

It would be of interest to know just how popular and widespread the Master-Thief tale was among Yiddish speakers of Eastern Europe. These four points on the map, though impressively wide apart, cannot of themselves shed light on this problem. All that they tell us is that *at least* in these four far-flung geographical points the tale was known by East European Jews and liked well enough by them in these four spots to have been told by story-tellers in their own language, Yiddish; and, as could be shown, liked well enough in each case for certain specific stylistic and thematic coloring to have been included in the renditions of the tale that make the tale appear very much at home among its tellers. The task of determining the exact dispersion of this tale, however, remains open for future research. With the great majority of East European Yid-

[5] In the international classification system of folktales the four variants to be discussed here would be assigned to the family of crafty fellows and to the class of tales about a master thief. For a theory concerning the relation of the Master Thief to Prometheus tales and solar myths, see R. L. Erlikh: "Skazka o lovkom vore," *Jazyk i literatura* 8 (1932) 195–203.

dish speakers destroyed in the German war against the Jews, and the rest dislocated and cut off by the Iron Curtain, the only way to proceed is by the "memory culture" technique. I feel certain that if this tale really was popular, many more variants of it could be collected in a city like New York, where there are Yiddish speakers hailing from so many different places in East Europe.

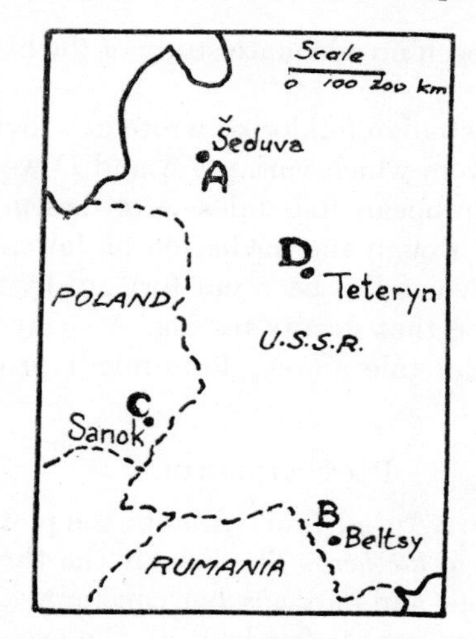

It would also be interesting to know if there is a Lithuanian Master-Thief tale to match variant A, a Rumanian tale to match variant B, a Russian tale for C, and a Polish tale for D, in these very same four geographical points; and if so, to know how similar and different these are in content and formal structure. How, for example, would the different languages and cultures affect the telling of the same prototype? While this comparative problem is beyond the scope of the present paper, I may note that in carefully combing Bolte and Polívka's listing[6] of all variants of the *Meisterdieb* type of folktale as they appeared in collections in the major European languages up to 1914, I found no items *absolutely* parallel in theme to my four versions; only individual motifs that occur in the Yiddish variants are found in Russian, Polish, Lithuanian, and Rumanian versions. It seems that in a tale of this kind where "incidents can be inserted rather freely"[7] a multitude of variants are possible, with no two necessarily alike.

The general dispersion of the Master-Thief tale over the continents of Europe and Asia seems to be wide indeed. In one form or another it appears in nearly every collection of tales from these two continents.[8]

[6] Johannes Bolte and Georg Polívka: *Anmerkungen zu den Kinder- und Hausmärchen der Brüder Grimm*, Leipzig, 1918, vol. 3, pp. 365–406. For additional pertinent Ukrainian parallels, see Osip Rozdol's'kyj in *Etnografičnyj zbirnyk . . . Tov. im Ševčenka* 8 (1900), pp. 25–30.

[7] Thompson, *The Folktale*, p. 175.

[8] *Ibid.*, p. 174.

> It consists first of all of a nucleus, a well defined series of incidents which occurs almost everywhere and which affords a clue by which even fragmentary stories can be identified as belonging to this cycle. [In all cases, the action revolves about a hero's cleverly stealing closely guarded things.] . . . Of this nuclear part of the tale, more than 700 oral versions have been noted from all over the world.[9]

Unfortunately, there has been no adequate study of the history and development of this tale to date.[10]

Walter Anderson, the Estonian folklorist, wrote in a review of Cahan's *Yidishe folksmayses* (the volume from which variants A and D were taken): "It is likely that some of the East European folk tales were disseminated from the Near East to Eastern Europe through the mediation of Jews."[11]

This hypothesis is one which has been put forward by many other prominent folklorists as well, and one that awaits testing. A study of the popularity and dispersion of this particular tale among Jews might prove very useful in this connection, too.

Plot Structure

Factors Unifying Plot. In all four variants the plot hinges on two things: (1) The *constant presence of the hero*. The hero is the thread that runs through the entire tale. He is the one and only *absolute* constant. (2) The similarity in the type of adventures the hero goes through. With the exception of one episode in variant A (Epis. VII) all of the adventures of the hero in all four variants consist of *cleverly stealing closely guarded items*. This unity in type of adventure is as important a factor for the unity of the plot as is the constant presence of one character.

Cumulative Listing of Episodes and Incidents. To enable the visualization of the concrete possibilities of handling a single theme and to facilitate the further discussion of sequence and comparison of similar episodes, the plot of each variant was analyzed into episodes (labeled by Roman numbers) and those were in turn broken up into incidents (identified by Arabic numbers). Even if a certain degree of arbitrariness was unavoidable, the analysis yielded a fruitful comparison. An exhaustive description of the variants in terms of Thompson's *Motif Index*[12] turned out to be impossible, but such international motifs as I did find I have cited in ⟨angular brackets⟩.

Considerations of space prevent me from presenting here the complete analysis of the variants. There follows instead a cumulative listing of the episodes and incidents of all four variants. Alternate lines of development between similar terminal points are printed in parallel columns, each column corresponding to

[9] *Ibid.*, p. 174.

[10] *Ibid.*, p. 175.

[11] *Yivo-Bleter* 3 (1932), pp. 421–424.

[12] Stith Thompson: *Motif Index of Folk Literature; A Classification of Narrative Elements in Folk Tales, Ballads, Myths, Fables, Medieval Romances, Exempla, Fabliaux, Jest Books and Local Legends*, Bloomington, Indiana, 1935–36; = *FFC*, Nos. 106–109, 116, 117.

one of the variants. Minor incidents are enclosed in [square brackets]; relatively insignificant details pertaining to one variant only appear in (parentheses).

I. Introduction of hero and family.

1. Return of three sons of emperor from study trip.
2. Emperor talks to two "wise" oldest sons; disappointed in their lack of "wisdom."
3. [At "stupid" youngest son's request, emperor has a talk with him, too; surprised and pleased that youngest has become "wise";] emperor decides to make youngest son successor to throne. ⟨L21 "Stupid youngest son becomes clever"⟩
4. Childless rabbi and wife desire to have child. [Rabbi's prayers bring an angel.]
5. Faced with choice between prostitute daughter and thief son, rabbi chooses latter.
6. Angel blesses son (hero) to be successful in anything he undertakes.
7. Princess, sister of hero, discusses future of empire with father; advises father to get tutor for dissolute, unlearned brother.
8. Hero and tutor get drunk together; studies of no avail.

II. Hero leaves home.

1. Emperor prepares will;[13] dies.
2. Older brothers find will; hide it from youngest brother.
3. Older brothers cheat hero out of inheritance, sending him away from country with horse and sack of gold. ⟨K2211 "Treacherous brothers" and K170 "Deception through pseudo-simple bargain"⟩
4. Hero grows up; prophecy of his turning thief comes true.
5. Rabbi tries in vain to reform hero.
6. Hero leaves home.

III. Hero demonstrates skill by robbing various individuals.

1. Hero meets bandits in woods. ⟨N765 "Meeting with robber band"⟩
2. Hero outwits them by claiming to be a thief, too, showing sack of gold as proof.
3. Hero
   a. meets robbers' challenge to prove his cleverness as a thief ⟨H1151 "Theft as a task"⟩
   b. demonstrates cleverness to father

   by cleverly stealing: a peasant's horse and cart; cow; and clothes. [Hero drops a boot once, then again, to distract peasant. While peasant seeks "first" boot, hero steals cow,

   c. cuts off its head and floats it in river.
   d. places peasant's cow neck-deep in a river.

   Peasant returns from vain search, sees cow, rushes to save it, removing clothing and jumping into river. Meanwhile hero steals clothing, and horse and cart. ⟨K341 "Owner's interest distracted while goods are stolen"⟩]
4. Hero steals money under pillow of sleeping rich man for robbers. ⟨H1151 "Theft as a task"⟩
5. Hero steals jacket of same rich man for himself. [Thieves quarrel over jacket; hero decides to let an "impartial" person decide; picks the former owner; relates the dispute to him in hypothetical terms; the owner awards the "hypothetical" jacket to hero.]
6. Hero leaves robber band.

---

[13] In the *Motif Index* the only mention of "wills" that I could find was: Z78 "Testament willing rewards and punishments," listed under "conventional endings of story." Here it is certainly not the "ending."

IV. Hero steals things in emperor's palace.

1. Hero meets second robber band; takes on an assignment.
2. Hero intoxicates the soldiers and dogs guarding the palace. ⟨K331.2 "Owner put to sleep and goods stolen" (Cf. V 10)⟩
3. Hero robs emperor's palace. ⟨H1151 "Theft as a task"⟩
4. Hero leaves robber band.

V. Hero (and partner) rob(s) emperor's treasury; emperor tries to trap him (them).

1. Hero talks emperor's contractor into leaving one brick loose in the new palace being constructed, to serve as secret passage to imperial treasury; they become partners.
2. Stealing expeditions successful. ⟨K315.1 "Thief enters treasury through passage made by him as architect of building," a motif very close to our variant A, except that we have "thieves" rather than "thief" and "contractor" rather than "architect".⟩
3. Hero successfully takes up emperor's challenge to "steal jewels in palace without causing damage to anything". [Hero creeps on top of attic; removes lamp screwed to ceiling; puts umbrella through hole; puts loosened bricks into umbrella; makes large enough hole to slip through; takes the jewels; puts everything back in place.]
4. Hero and partner rob treasury by entering through back door.
5. Secret passage discovered by emperor and councillors. [They build straw fire; smoke escapes through loose brick. ⟨J1143 "Thief detected by building straw fire so that smoke escapes through thief's entrance. The secret hole is thus discovered and the thief caught." In our variant (A) the thieves are not detected this way, but their passageway is.⟩]
6. Emperor plans to trap robbers. [Places barrel of pitch in entrance of passageway (or fills pit around treasury with pitch).]
7. Stealing expedition unsuccessful; contractor (partner) caught in trap. ⟨J1146.1 "Detection by pitch trap"⟩
8. Unable to extract contractor (partner) from pitch, hero beheads accomplice: dead men tell no tales; runs away and buries head.
9. Emperor has contractor's (partner's) body hung in center of city to spot next of kin by their reactions. ⟨H50 "Test of recognition by bodily marks or physical attributes"⟩
10. Hero [disguised as drunkard (or water boy)] intoxicates (or distracts) soldiers guarding body; escapes with it. ⟨K331.2 "Owner put to sleep and goods stolen" (Cf. IV 2)⟩

VI. Hero outwits the emperor in his efforts to identify him.

1. Hero cleverly steals gold coins from emperor's banquet hall floor, placed there as a trap. [Hero smears tar onto soles of his shoes; gold coins stick to them; no need for hero's bending down to get coins.]
2. Hero escapes detection.
   a. [Walks out in another pair of shoes.]
   b. [Emperor inspects shoes of all his sleeping guests after ball is over; cuts off sole of hero's shoe to mark him as culprit. Hero arises, cuts off sole of every other guest's shoe, and thus escapes detection. ⟨K415 "Marked culprit marks everyone else and escapes detection" (Cf. VII 6)⟩]
3. Hero takes up emperor's challenge to steal princess' necklace (or to enter princess' chamber).

a. [Hero falls into pit, a trap set by emperor; cleverly manages to get some innocent people into pit, too; escapes and steals necklace. ⟨K415⟩]

b. [Hero cleverly overcomes the first obstacle, a covered pit, by jumping over it onto a chair he throws that gets caught on the princess' door.]

4. As he enter princess' chamber, he meets with a second obstacle: princess splashes his face with paint. Hero takes the paint from princess; splashes paint over all guests; escapes detection. ⟨K415⟩
5. Hero steals box filled with gold. [Hero falls into cellar, a trap set by emperor; is thereby marked as culprit. Hero cleverly escapes after shouting for help and causing other innocent guests to fall into the trap. All are now potentially culprits. ⟨K415⟩]
6. Hero steals golden goblet at emperor's banquet. [He hides it in a priest's pocket during search, knowing that the priest would not be searched because of his social position; hero later takes goblet back.]

VII. Hero successfully performs three (or one) task(s) given him when he comes to claim reward.

1. Hero proves identity by showing gold coins and necklace ⟨H91 "Recognition through precious metal,"⟩ and ⟨H92 "Identification by necklace"⟩; and is given three tasks to perform. ⟨H931 "Tasks assigned in order to get rid of hero"⟩
2. Hero meets old woman and receives magic fiddle and whistle from her. ⟨H971 "Tasks performed with help of old woman"⟩
3. Hero successfully performs first task: sleeps in a room with a bear one night. ⟨H1410 "Staying in a frightful place"⟩ [with help of magic fiddle]
4. Hero successfully performs second task: grazes ten wild hares in meadow; returns them every night for three nights in a row. ⟨H1112 "Herding rabbits"⟩ [with help of magic whistle]
5. Hero successfully performs third task: fills a punctured sack with talk. [In attempt to thwart hero in task no. 2, the emperor on the first day, the queen on the second, and the princess on the third, try to get a hare away from him. He promises each a hare if he/she will dance with no clothes on. They do. As he begins to tell these embarrassing stories, the emperor declares the sacks filled.] ⟨H1045 "Task of filling a sack with lies or truths" is a very close motif to our variant, except that here it is "talk" not "lies" or "truths."⟩
6. Hero successfully removes gold coins from table and floor without being detected. [Hero discovers the powder placed on the table and floor to trap him—powder that removes soles of shoes when stepped on—collects the powder, pours it on shoes of all sleeping guests. All are marked as possible culprits, while he has the gold coins.] Cf. VI 1, 2b. ⟨K415⟩

VIII. Hero rewarded by the emperor.

1. By receiving the princess' hand in marriage. ⟨T68 "Princess offered as prize⟩
2. By receiving half (or all) the empire. ⟨Q112 "One half the kingdom as reward"⟩

SEQUENCE OF EPISODES AND INCIDENTS. We now turn to the structural problem of the relative freedom or rigor in the sequence of episodes and incidents. Note the table on p. 206.

From this table it becomes evident that the sequence of certain episodes (in so far as they do occur in any of the variants) is relatively rigid.

a. Wherever there is an episode placing the hero in his home and family surroundings it occurs *first* in the tale. I tend to believe that this is characteristic of a good many Yiddish secular tales, in contrast to artistic literature, where such an episode can, of course, occur anywhere in the story. (It is interesting to note here, too, that in contrast to many Yiddish moral tales, e.g. the Elijah tales, the hero does not return to these surroundings in any later episode of our

EPISODE	INCIDENT	ORDER OF OCCURRENCE (IF ANY) IN:			
		VAR. A	VAR. B	VAR. C	VAR. D
I. Introduction of hero and family	1	1			
	2	2			
	3	3			
	4		1		
	5		2		
	6		3		
	7				1
	8				2
II. Leaves home	1	4			
	2	5			
	3	6			
	4		4		
	5		5		
	6		6		
III. Robs individuals	1	7	7		
	2	8			
	3	(a, c)9			(b, d)3
	4		8		
	5		9		
	6		10		
IV. Robs imperial palace	1		11		
	2		12		
	3		13		
	4		14		
V. Robs imperial treasury	1	10			
	2	11			
	3		15		
	4			5	
	5	12			
	6	13		6	
	7	14		7	
	8	15		8	
	9	16		9	
	10	17		10	
VI. Escapes identification	1	18	16	2	
	2		(b)17	(a)3	
	3	(a)19	(b)18		
	4		19		
	5			4	
	6			1	
VII. Performs task(s)	1	20			
	2	21			
	3	22			
	4	23			
	5	24			
	6			11	
VIII. Rewarded	1	25	20	12	
	2	26	21		

variant. In the moral tales often the hero, after leaving his home in the first episode, returns again in the last.)

b. Where there is an episode of reward[14] it always comes at the end of the tale, as a conclusion to a series of adventures. Once rewarded, the hero does not embark on new adventures, nor does he discuss past adventures ("flash-back" technique).

[14] The appointment of the Hero as heir, without his knowing it, in variant A, cannot be considered a reward in the same sense.

c. The final sequence of episodes, wherever there is an episode of reward is this: V and/or VI (order here may be inverted as in variant C), followed by VII (lacking in B), followed by VIII. This is the most "logical" order, of course. V and VI may be inverted without disturbing the "logic" of the sequence. VII, where it occurs, must "logically" follow V or VI; and VIII "logically" follows VII.

d. Intermediate episodes of adventure do not have to occur in any fixed way. They may be freely interchanged without disturbing the course of the plot. Each adventure here is an independent unit.

It certainly would be a worthwhile task to check all these conclusions regarding sequence of episodes against other secular tales. Conclusions a, b, and d are very likely to be typical of the entire genre.

Comparison of Similar Episodes and Incidents and International Parallels to These. We now turn to the question of the concrete possibilities for handling similar motifs as reflected in our variants and in international parallels to them. We proceed episode by episode, except for IV, which occurs only in one variant.

I. Introduction of hero and family. While variants A, B, and D all have "pre-plot" episodes (I and II), serving the same function of introducing the hero and his family, none are thematically alike. The details in any of the initial situations affect the following plot but little. Variant C easily launches directly into an adventure.

It is interesting to note, on the other hand, that in the three variants that do have an initial episode, *we find that this is the most important episode for the insertion of culturally familiar details by the teller*. If specific cultural reflections are to be found anywhere in these variants at all, this pre-plot episode seems to be the ideal place for such material because it allows the story teller to immediately establish rapport with his listener. (This may be true of the genre as well, and should be looked into.) Note the details about the "learned rabbi" and his "studying of holy books" of variant B and the culturally significant emphasis on study and learning in variants A and D.[15]

II. Hero leaves home. In variants A and B the adventures do not begin until the hero leaves home; in both of these variants there is a separate episode describing his departing. However, thematically, these two episodes are not alike. Thus A and B seem to share the same formal pattern of episodes: I and II, but not the same thematic pattern. (See the incidents listed for each of the two variants.)

In variant D, which shared a pre-plot episode with A and B, the first (and only) adventure begins *at home*.

III. Hero robs peasant. The first adventure, involving the stealing of a peasant's things, is told in rather similar terms in variants A and D (incident 3). In variant D the cow is not harmed by the hero.

This particular episode is a very popular one in the European *Meisterdieb*

[15] Cf. Mark Zborowski: "The Place of Book-Learning in Traditional Jewish Culture," *Harvard Educational Review* 19 (1949) 97–109.

type of tale. Bolte and Polívka[16] devote three pages to listing European tales that have this episode as a motif. Stith Thompson writes:

> . . . [this] series of incidents (Type 1525D) is so popular that it might well be considered an essential part of the [Master-Thief] type [of tale]. It has been noted in all parts of the world and in considerably more than 300 versions. These incidents always concern the stealing of an animal, usually an ox. One of the best known devices is the putting of shoes in the road separately. The owner of the ox passes the first by, but when later he finds the second, he leaves his ox unguarded while he returns for the first. . . . More rarely in the series of incidents, the thief steals clothes by inducing the owner to take them off and go bathing.[17]

V. Hero robs emperor's treasury. An episode of entering the emperor's treasury by removing bricks occurs in both variants A (incidents 1–2) and B (incident 3). However B is such an encapsulated form of this episode that it would be difficult to prove that both stem from the same motif. On the other hand, in variant C (inc. 4), where there is no mention of *how* (by loose bricks or otherwise) the hero and his partner enter the treasury, the incidents making up this episode are so close to variant A in content and in sequence that there is no doubt that the motif is the same.

This particular episode appears in many Master-Thief variants all over the European continent and can be traced back to the old Egyptian tale of Rhampsinitus (in almost perfect form in variant A!) that has come down to us, in written form, through the writings of Herodotus (Book II, chapter 121).[18] According to Thompson:

> There seems little doubt that all subsequent versions of the story go back eventually to Herodotus. It appears not only in the literary collections of the European Middle Ages and Renaissance but also in the Buddhistic writings of the early Christian era and in the *Ocean of Story* from India of the twelfth century. Moreover, the tale has had a wide acceptance in oral tradition all the way from Iceland across Europe and Asia to Indonesia and the Philippines. . . . Herodotus tells the story in a good deal of detail and the changes that have taken place in the 2400 years since his time consist in minor elaborations. . . . This is one of the best examples of stability in a folktale. Nevertheless a study of the detailed changes should be of great interest in connection with the mutual relations of literature and folklore. It would be interesting to know by what devious routes the story of Herodotus has come to be part of the repertory . . . of simple story-tellers in the farthest reaches of Europe and Asia.[19]

For comparative purposes, variant B, the most distantly related to the Herodotus tale (I am assuming that it is related), is the most interesting precisely because it is much shorter and quite changed. Especially curious is the elaboration of the techniques for entering the emperor's treasury by the use of an umbrella

[16] Bolte and Polívka, *op. cit.*, pp. 390–392.
[17] Thompson, *The Folktale*, p. 175.
[18] Bolte and Polívka, *op. cit.*, pp. 395–406.
[19] Thompson, *The Folktale*, pp. 172f.

(see V 3, p. 204). What an excellent example of freedom in dealing with material! If variant A is an example of the stability of a tale over centuries, variant B is an example of the reverse.

VI. Hero outwits emperor in his attempts to identify hero. Variants A, B, and C have an episode of this type. There is a good deal of similarity in the incidents that make up each of these episodes, but also interesting differences in detail. Thus in incident 3, the hero of variant A must obtain the princess' necklace, while in B he must merely gain entry to her chamber. In variant C it is not the princess' chamber the hero is after but a box of gold (incident 5); and so forth.

VII. Hero performs tasks to prove his identity. In both variants A and C we find episodes where the emperor gives the hero tasks to prove his identity. In A this is a very complex episode composed of three complex incidents (3–5) entirely different from the one-task make-up of variant C (incident 6). Similarity here is purely "formal" and in no way "thematic."

Incident VII 6 in variant C is very interesting, because it is almost a photographic negative of an incident that already occurred in this same variant (VI 1). Whereas in VI 1 the hero puts tar on his shoes so that gold coins will stick to them, in incident VII 6 the emperor, seeking to test the hero in the very same situation, puts some powder over the floor that has the power of removing the soles of any shoes that come into contact with the coins. This second incident is especially remarkable in the light of what Lüthi says about the European folk-tale: "The characters in the tale do not learn anything; they acquire no experience."[20] Yet the emperor here has obviously "learned" something about the manner in which the thief stole the gold coins.

The complex task episode in variant A (incidents 3–5) also merits further attention. This is the first and only episode of exploits in variant A in which the hero does *not* steal closely guarded things. Since this episode does not occur in either of our remaining three variants we may legitimately ask whether this is not a *stray* episode attached to a plot which up to this point demonstrated unity in type of exploit. Neither Bolte and Polívka nor Thompson include this episode in the Master-Thief complex; the latter treats it as a separate tale ("The Sack of Lies") and tells us that as such, "it is rather popular all the way from Iceland to the Caucasus" and that "more than 200 versions have already been noted."[21] When we consider that all of the characters necessary for the "Sack of Lies" tale (viz. hero, king, princess, queen) had already been introduced into the plot, and that some kind of testing of the hero's identity occurs in another variant (C) as an integral part of the tale, it becomes apparent that the combination of this episode with the other Master-Thief episodes was an easy one to make.

VIII. Hero is rewarded. Episodes of reward occur in variants A, B, and C. The rewards seem stereotyped: in all three cases the hero is awarded the princess' hand in marriage. In A he receives, in addition, one half of the empire, and in B he receives the entire empire after the death of the emperor.

[20] Lüthi, *op. cit.* (see footnote 4), p. 49.

[21] Thompson, *The Folktale*, p. 155.

Plot Motivation

As "amoral" tales our four variants do not attempt to exemplify kindness, charity, or other ethical qualities.

The goals of characters which lead them from one episode to the next are one of the most freely varying factors of our variants. The following motivations occur:

1. Initial introductory episode: (*a*) need for selecting heir to throne (variant A, episode I 1–3; variant D, episode I 7–8); (*b*) childlessness and desire for son (B I 4–6).

2. Hero's leaving one place for another: (*a*) expulsion from home, arising from (1) jealousy of brothers (A II 2–3) or (2) realization by hero that he is causing unhappiness to his parents (B II 6);[22] (*b*) robbers (or partners) do not want hero with them any longer (B IV 4); (*c*) no apparent motivation (A V; B III 6).

3. Thieving adventures: (*a*) challenge, by bandits, on penalty of death, to steal (A III 3); (*b*) emperor's decoy (A VI 1, 3; B VI 2; C VI 1, 5); (*c*) open challenge by emperor to steal (B V 3, VI 3); (*d*) hero short of funds (A V 1, 2, 7); (*e*) hero takes a liking to a certain object, a jacket (B III 5); (*f*) hero wants to show off his cleverness to father (D III 3); (*g*) no motivation apparent (B III 1, 4, 5, IV 1–3; C VI 6, V 4, 7).

4. Emperor's attempt to trap thief: (*a*) curiosity aroused as to who this clever thief might be (A V 5, 6, 9, VI 1, 3; B V 3, VI 1–4; C VI 1, 5, V 6, 9); (*b*) sentimental attachment to an object stolen (C VI 6).

5. Hero's treatment of partner: (a) pity (A V 8); see footnote 22; (b) concern about being recognized (A V 8, 10; C V 8, 10).

6. Emperor's hanging of partner's body in city: (*a*) to observe who will cry, and thus deduce headless man's identity (A V 9); (*b*) to display the body and by offering a reward to anyone bringing the head that matches the body, learn the identity of the dead man (C V 9).

7. Emperor's giving hero additional tasks to perform: (*a*) to thwart hero and avoid giving him reward (A VII 1); (*b*) to be entertained (C VII 6).

8. Hero's performing tasks set by emperor: to prove identity and receive reward (A VII 3–5; C VII 6).

9. Hero's being rewarded: to fulfill the promise made by emperor of a reward (A VIII, B VIII, C VIII 1).

What are the relations between motivations and motifs? 1. We find that corresponding episodes and incidents are not always motivated the same way. For example, the incidents 1–4 at the beginning of episode V (robbing of the treasury) are motivated in variant A by the hero's lack of funds (motivation 3*d*), in variant B by the emperor's open challenge to steal (motivation 3*c*), while in variant C no motivation is apparent (3*g*). 2. We also find that new episodes in any one variant do not always imply a new motivation; the same motivation may be employed in the same tale for different episodes and incidents. For example, in variant C, the temptation presented by the emperor's decoy (3*b*) motivates

[22] An instance like this somewhat blurs the line between "moral" and "amoral" tales.

the hero not only to steal gold coins from the banquet hall, but also to steal a box filled with gold.

The motivations appear to be the most expendable element in our tale, a fact which is probably characteristic of the genre.

Stylistic Techniques of Characterization

A very detailed analysis was made of the stylistic techniques used in each variant. On most points I found the tales to resemble the general European folk tale. For example, naming is not used to distinguish characters; they are identified by their profession or social status ("the prince," "the officers," "the contractor's wife").[23] Description of the physical appearance of characters, their mannerisms or gestures is almost nonexistent; items of clothing are specified only if they have a function in the plot.[24] The characters get their individuality above all from their functions, i.e. their actions from the point of view of significance to plot.[25] The Master Thief, of course, appears throughout in a "biographical" function. Secondary characters appear in active functions to complicate the plot and passively in a connective capacity. Among the actively functioning characters we find helpers (including rewarders, information givers, and partners in adventure) and hinderers (cheaters, challengers, guards, and obstacle devisers). There are no secondary characters which appear in all four versions, but we find variations of the following sort: the function of an object of the hero's cleverness is served by a peasant in A and D, by a rich man in B and by a priest in C. It is impossible, for reasons of space, to present the full analysis of character functions here.

If we were to check the characters in other Yiddish secular tales against the functions in this tale many of the types of helpers (rewarders, blessing givers, partners in adventure, information givers) as well as hinderers (cheaters, challengers, guards, etc.) would undoubtedly reappear in other tales.[26] But will rewarders usually be emperors, and cheaters—older brothers? Will the hero usually be the youngest son? Will the father of the hero usually be an emperor or rabbi? These are problems for future research. From these four variants, it would seem that concrete personages are not stabilized. They may change from variant to variant. On the other hand, what is constant for all four variants seems to be the *functions* of the characters.

Sokolov, in describing a parallel genre in Russian folklore, writes: "No matter

[23] I know of one exception to the use of this technique: in one tale in Cahan's collection the two most important characters have personal names: Notke and Ben-Notke.

[24] In its "one-dimensional" style, Lüthi finds (*op. cit.*), the European *Märchen* "does not describe individual things, but rather names them [p. 32]. . . . It is as if the *Märchen* characters were paper cutouts, who could be cut up, without any important changes occurring. . . . The *Märchen* figures cut off body parts without batting an eye-lash [p. 20]. . . . *Märchen* characters are not made of flesh and blood" (p. 48).

[25] In analyzing the function of characters, I followed the system of V. Propp (see footnote 4).

[26] Propp, *op. cit.*, has listed thirty-one basic functions for characters in the Russian magical tale. These "functions" repeat themselves again and again.

how characteristic of the tale its heros and objects may be, . . . still the most important thing, and the most characteristic of the tale as a genre, is the action itself. . . . The acting personages, in the variants of the tale, are less well established than their functions, i.e. the action itself."[27] This holds true for these four variants in the Yiddish secular-tale genre.

Our variants also agree with general European patterns in placing the characters in the dimensions of time and space in a most abstract manner. We find our characters moving in "*a* forest" (var. A, p. 190), "*a* big city in *a* strange land" (var. A, p. 192), and so on;[28] the past of newly introduced characters is never alluded to. This agrees with Lüthi's finding that "the *Märchen* tells us nothing about the town or village in which the hero grew up [*op. cit.*, p. 24]. . . . The flat world of the *Märchen* lacks the dimension of time. There may be young and old people . . . but there are no aging people" (p. 34). The relationships between characters, which may be close within a single incident, are relatively tenuous in episodes and entirely lacking in the tale as a whole. For example, variant C, which is composed of a few episodes around one major adventure, shows rather fleeting relationships between the hero and even the next in importance, the emperor. The latter does not appear in all episodes. Other secondary characters, e.g. the soldier or the priest, appear only once, each in a separate incident, never to reappear in following incidents. This lack of permanent relationships in a tale is considered by Lüthi as another major characteristic of the European *Märchen*: "Parents, siblings, secondary characters disappear out of sight, as soon as they are not important for the plot [p. 25]. . . . The hero of the *Märchen* is not integrated in the family structure. He frees himself from his parents as soon as they are unimportant in the action of the plot, and brothers serve only as contrasting figures [p. 24]. . . . The characters show no relationship to family, nation or any other type of society [p. 39]. . . . The *Märchen* isolates people . . . each figure is as strange to himself as he is to the other characters" (p. 55). The Yiddish tale seems to conform on this point, too.

One stylistic feature which seems to *differentiate* the Yiddish from the general European tale is the amount of emotional description and ratiocination which is introduced. Lüthi finds that the *Märchen* "does not present the realm of feelings at all. . . . *Märchen* characters act in a cool manner" (p. 23). And yet we find in our variants references to definite emotional involvement. In variant A (p. 189), the old emperor on one occasion refers to his youngest son as his *mezinik*, a term full of sentimental connotation. The emperor considers his stupid son's feelings (*ibid.*) in deciding not to *embarrass* him by putting his knowledge to the test. The hero appeals to his older brothers' consciences (p. 190): "What did I do that was wrong? What do you hold against me?" When the hero's partner, the contractor, failed to return home, his wife "started *worrying*. . . . She began to *weep*: 'Where is my husband?' And she *wanted to* run out into the street to

[27] Sokolov, *op. cit.* (see footnote 4), pp. 426f.

[28] Somewhat more definite places occur, too: "*the* imperial palace [p. 193]"; "*the* center of the city [p. 196]"; "*the* pit surrounding the emperor's palace [p. 198]". These places are not described, however.

look for him" (p. 196). As the last day for performing his tasks approaches, the hero "still could find no way out. He became *sad* and started to *pout* about his bad fortune" (p. 200). In variant B, the emperor said: " 'In that case, wait here for a few minutes.' But the tricky fellow got *frightened*, and sat glued to his chair looking like a corpse" (p. 136). In the very brief variant D[29] the emperor's daughter *worries* about her brother (p. 69). Altogether, six instances of emotional description were counted in A, four in B, and one each in C and D.

There is, of course, the possibility that in these variants emotional description happened to be part of the techniques of the individual story-tellers, and not something generally employed. Other Yiddish secular tales should be examined to check this point.

A second possibly significant feature of the tales under consideration is that the narration is occasionally interrupted by "interior monologue." This is a device for reproducing the thought, particularly the decision-making process, of a character without explanatory interventions by the narrator. Thus, in variant A we read:

> The peasant drove by, and noticed a beautiful boot lying in the road. He thought to himself: "Probably some young squire lost it. Only one boot . . . what can I do with it?" And he drove on. . . . The peasant [later] saw another boot [in the road]. He thought to himself: "What a blockhead I am! This boot plus the other boot equals a pair of boots! One ought not to be lazy. I'll [go back] and pick up the other boot" [p. 191].
>
> . . . [The hero] tried to pull him [the contractor] out—but to no avail. He tried again and again—but no sign of success. He thought to himself: "What should I do? Should I run away and leave him here? If I do, he'll be recognized, and I'll be caught, too. Should I try to pull him out of the tar again? There's not enough time. Someone may come along, and I'll be a goner" [p. 195].

And in variant D:

> The peasant thought to himself, "Important people just passed by; if they see me picking up this boot, they'll say I stole it. No; I'm afraid; I shall not take the boot," and he went away [p. 70].

It is interesting that a style which employs no physical description, and little description of emotions, should detail ratiocination at all. Lüthi seems to imply that this technique is never used in European *Märchen*. This may be a technique (though an optional one) characteristic of the Yiddish as contrasted with other-language tales.

A great many more tales will have to be studied in order to verify this and the other broader conclusions which have been suggested here.

[29] Alfred Landau, in his editorial comments on this variant, writes: "Die vorliegende Version, die schon der abrupte Schluss als *Fragment* kennzeichnet. . . ."

THE EARLIEST ARAMAIC AND YIDDISH VERSION OF THE "SONG OF THE KID" (*KHAD GADYE*)

CH. SZMERUK (Jerusalem)

The Passover haggadah[1] in general and the "Song of the Kid"[2] in particular have long been deemed worthy of special interest. Yet all of the problems have not yet been solved regarding the origin of this song and its Jewish variants. On the basis of the text which follows below, we shall try to clarify a few questions that have direct bearing on the genesis of one of the oldest folksongs of the Jews.

There is a handwritten illustrated Ashkenazic haggadah in the Italian Sereni collection now located in the Jewish Historical General Archives in Jerusalem.[3] Experts on paleography and on medieval illustration date the haggadah between the beginning of the fifteenth and the beginning of the sixteenth centuries. The haggadah is written on parchment in black, red, and green india ink. Its margins are illustrated with drawings appropriate to the haggadah text. The haggadah contains 46 leaves, 26 × 18.5 cm. The first page is blank. The last three pages, after the counting of the 'Omer, contain an Aramaic, or rather a quasi-Aramaic, and an Old Yiddish text of the "Song of the Kid."[4] The entire haggadah is written in square script; the "Song of the Kid" is in cursive. The first page of the "Song of the Kid" contains an illustration showing a cat holding a mouse in its mouth (see figure facing p. 119).

Generally it is agreed that the "Song of the Kid" was incorporated into the haggadah between 1526 and 1590, i.e. between the first Prague edition, where the song is still lacking, and the 1590 edition, where the "Song of the Kid" appears for the first time and in the form which has been the model to date.[5] In view of the wide dispersion of this motif in general European folklore, it is conjectured that the song had been known earlier but had not received its official place in the haggadah until the end of the sixteenth century.[6]

[1] I. Rivkind: [The Literature of the Passover Haggadah; Bibliographical List], *Ḳiryat sefer* 12 (1935–36) 230–237.

[2] Čeněk Zíbrt: *Ohlas obřadních písní velikonočních* (*Haggada: Chad Gadja, Echad mi iodea*) *v lidovém podaní*, Prague, 1928, 474 pp.; reviewed by J. Shatzky, *Yivo-bleter* 6 (1934) 150–153. On the song of the twelve numbers, see the recent study by Leah Rachel Clara Yoffie: "Songs of the 'Twelve Numbers' and the Hebrew Chant of 'Echod Mi Yodea'," *Journal of American Folklore* 62 (1949) 382–411.

[3] I should like to express my thanks to the administrators of the Archives for permission to publish the text.

[4] In our haggadah, the songs *'eḥad mi yode'a* 'Who Knows One?' and *'adir hu'* 'Mighty Is He' (in its Old Yiddish version, ♮ˀ*lmktjgr gvt*) are still lacking. In addition to the Yiddish "Song of the Kid," it is worth noting the following instruction in Yiddish for the blessing of bitter herbs: *veyiḳaḥ ḥasa' šeḳorin bilšon aškenaz* ♮*ltvg*ˀ 'and one takes lettuce which is called in Yiddish ♮*ltvg*ˀ [latux? latyx?]'. Cf. Lexer (*Mhd. Taschenwörterbuch*): *latech, lateche, leteche*.

[5] See G. A. Kohut: "Ḥad Gadya," in *Jewish Encyclopedia*, vol. 6, 1904, 127f.; also in *Revue des études juives* 31 (1895) 240–246.

[6] Zíbrt, *op. cit.*, pp. 232ff.

Even the approximate dating of the manuscript haggadah under discussion here allows us to correct some generally accepted views. The penetration of the song into the Jewish world can definitely be moved back to at least the fifteenth century, if not further. As early as the sixteenth century the "Song of the Kid" was associated with the Passover seder. At any rate, we may definitely conclude that we are here dealing with the earliest texts of the song in Aramaic and in Yiddish.

On the basis of the consideration that the Aramaic version of the song is later than the Yiddish, attempts have been made to find the mysterious reason why the song was translated from Yiddish into Aramaic and not into Hebrew. According to one view the intention was to establish a symmetry between the Aramaic beginning, *keha' laḥma' 'aniya'*, of the haggadah and an Aramaic end.[7] Another view holds that it was the popularity of kabbalah mysticism and its main book, the Aramaic *Zohar*, during the sixteenth century that determined the language into which the "Song of the Kid" was translated. This view can also be connected with the symbolic religious interpretation which was read into the literal meaning of the song.[8]

Considering both texts together—the Aramaic and the Yiddish—and assuming that the Yiddish text was the basis for the Aramaic text,[9] a view which is also reinforced by the faultiness of the Aramaic, one can, I believe, arrive at a rather simple answer to the puzzle of the language of translation. All the sound play in the Yiddish text is based on the riming of diminutives. All nouns in the song —except ♮*hqdvs brvḱ huˀ* 'the Holy One, blessed is He'—are given in the diminutive form with the suffix ♮*-ljjń*.[10] The translator of the song sought an equivalent for the Yiddish diminutive which would both transmit the original diminutive form of the noun and make possible the preservation of the rime effect. To translate the song into Hebrew would have meant to give both up. Diminutives did not exist in Hebrew, at least not at that time. On the other hand, Aramaic removes both difficulties. The Aramaic noun-suffix *-a'* permits the rime effect to a large degree. In this connection it is characteristic that the translator, who probably did not know the proper Aramaic terms for ♮*stˁqljjń* 'little stick' or ♮*svxtljjń* 'slaughterer (*dimin.*)' easily got around this by adding the suffix *-a'* to the Hebrew *maḳel* and *šoḥeṭ*. Along with the rime effect, an illusion of the diminutive is achieved in Aramaic. The pseudo-Aramaic *maḳla'* and *'akbara'* (for 'mouse') do sound more like diminutives than the Hebrew *maḳel* or *akbar*. This is especially true for one who is better acquainted with Hebrew than with Aramaic.

I believe that this purely "technical" solution to the "Aramaic" riddle is more reasonable than the earlier theories, although one may and should keep in mind that there did exist a certain familiarity with Aramaic connected with the great popularity of mysticism in this period.

[7] "Chad Gadia" in *Encyclopedia Judaica*, vol. 5 (1930), p. 142.

[8] Zíbrt, *op. cit.*, pp. 229f.

[9] Leopold Zunz: *Die gottesdienstlichen Vorträge der Juden*, Frankfurt/M., 1892, p. 133; in the Hebrew translation (Jerusalem, 1947), p. 300.

[10] The transliteration system is explained on p. vii of the present volume.

Up to now we know next to nothing of the earlier developments of the "Song of the Kid" motif among Jews. We know only the conventional version and some later folk variants in Yiddish whose source must be sought not in the haggadah but in the German Jöckeli-songs and the like.[11]

The version of the "Song of the Kid" we have been referring to here points to an unknown earlier stage in the development of the motif. In regard to content, we find a link here which was heretofore unknown: that of ♮*dz mjjzljjń* 'the little mouse'. It is true, of course, that the mouse occurs in the "Song of the Kid" motif among other ethnic groups;[12] however, it has completely disappeared in Jewish variants. The reason for this may be the poor logic of the mouse devouring the ♮*cjqljjń* 'little goat, kid'. Obviously the original motif had a much larger rodent than the diminutive mouse, e.g. a rat, but when the wholesale diminutivization made the meaning absurd, the first link broke off.

It is also worth looking into the textual peculiarity of the versions in both languages. The Yiddish variant contains some epithets which are lacking in the conventionalized version: ♮*ˀlt vvˁtrljjń* 'grandfather (*dimin.*)' ♮*gjhrgjt svxtljjń* 'killed slaughterer (*dimin.*)'. In the later traditional Aramaic text the erroneous, invented form *maḳla'* has been eliminated and replaced by *ḥutra'*. From all of this we see that before the "Song of the Kid" was put into conventionalized form in the haggadah, it had already gone through a rather special development—both in content and in textual form.

In closing I should like to point out to the Yiddish philologist the uncertainties of the copyist, which reveal some peculiarities in language development. I mean the various ways of writing the same words: ♮*vvˁtjrljjń—vvˀtjrljjń* '. . . father (*dimin.*)' or ♮*gjqvjpt—gjqˀpt* 'bought (*past part.*)'.

There follows the transliterated text. The Aramaic stanza is separated from the Yiddish by a dash.

♮*xd gdjˀ xd gdjˀ*

[1] *vˀθˀ ˁkbrˀ dˀkl lgdjˀ dzbjń ˀbˀ bθrj zvzj xd gdjˀ xdjˀ* [sic] *gdjˀ — dˀ qˀḿ dz mjjzljjń ˀvn ˁsjt dz cjqljjń ds qˀpjt dz ˀlt vvˁtjrljjń ˀvḿ cvvjjˀ ppˁnjgljjń ˀjjń cjqljjń ˀjjń cjqljjń*

[2] *vˀθˀ svnrˀ dnsjḱ lˁkbrˀ dˀkjl lgdjˀ dzbjń ˀbˀ bθrj zvzj xd gdjˀ xd gdj' — dˀ qˀḿ ds q*^{e}*cljjń* [sic] *ˀvn' ˁsjt dz mjjzljjń dz djˀ hˀt gˁsjń ds cjqljjń dz dˀ qˀpjt dz ˀlt vvˀtrljjń ˀvḿ cvvjjˀ ppˁnjgljjń ˀjjń* [*cjqljjń*] *ˀjjń cjqljjń*

[3] *vˀθˀ klbˀ dnsjḱ lsvnrˀ dˀkjl lˁkbrˀ dˀkjl lgdjˀ dzbjń ˀbˀ bθrj zvzj xd gdjˀ xd gdjˀ — dˀ qˀḿ ds hjntljjń ˀvn' bjjsjt dz qˁcjljjń dz ˁsjt dz mjjzljjń dz dˀ hˀt gˁsjń dz cjqljjń dz dˀ qˀpjt dz ˀlt vvˀtrljjń ˀvḿ cvvjjˀ ppˁnjgljjń ˀjjń cjqljjń ˀjjń cjqljjń*

[4] *vˀθˀ mqlˀ vmkˀ lklbˀ dnsjḱ lsvnrˀ dˀkl ˁkbrˀ dˀkjl lgdjˀ dzbjń ˀbˀ bθrj zvzj xd gdjˀ xd gdjˀ — dˀ qˀḿ ds stˁqljjń ˀvn' slv̇g* [*slvjgˀ*] *dz hjntljjń dz dˀ bjs dz qˁcjljjń dz dˀ hˀt gˁsjń dz mjjzljjń ds dˀ hˀt ˀvjṕ gˁsjń dz cjqljjń ds dˀ hˀt gjqvjpt dz ˀlt vvˁtjrljjń ˀvḿ cvvjjˀ ppˁnjgljjń ˀjjń cjqljjń ˀjjń cjqljjń*

[11] S. M. Ginzburg and P. S. Marek: *Jevrejskije narodnyje pesni v Rossii*, St. Petersburg, 1901, no. 126; Noyakh Prilutski [Pryłucki]: *Yidishe folkslider*, vol. 1, Warsaw, 1914, pp. 75–84.

[12] E.g. Zíbrt, *op. cit.*, pp. 309f.; Kohut, *Revue des études juives* 31 (1895), p. 245.

[5] vˀθˀ nvrˀ vˀvqjd lmqlˀ dmkˀ lklbˀ dnsjḱ lsvnrˀ dˀkjl ˁkbrˀ dˀkjl lgdjˀ dzbjń ˀbˀ bθrj zvzj xd gdjˀ xd gdjˀ — dˀ qˀḿ dz pjjˁrljjń ˀun' vvˁr brˁnjt dz stˁqljjń dz djˀ hˀt gjslˀgń dz hjntljjń ˀvn' dz djˀ hˀt gjbjsń dz qˁcjljjń ˀvn dz dˀ hˀt gˁsjń dz mjjzljjń ˀvn' dz djˀ hˀt gˁsjń dz cjqljjń dz djˀ hˀt gjqvjpt dz ˀlt vvˁtrljjń ˀvn [sic] ccvjjˀ ppˁnjgljjń ˀjjń cjqljjń ˀjjń cjqljjń

[6] vˀθˀ mjˀ vmkvvˀ lnvrˀ dˀvqjd mqlˀ dmkˀ lklbˀ dnsjḱ lsvnrˀ dˀkjl ˁkbrˀ dˀkjl lgdjˀ dzbjń ˀbˀ bθrj zvzj xd gdjˀ xd gdjˀ — dˀ qˀḿ dz vvˀsrljjń ˀvn' vvˁr lˁsjt dz vvjjˁljjń dz djˀ hˀt vvˁr brˁnt dz stˁqljjń dz djˀ hˀt gjslˀgń dz hjntljjń dz djˀ hˀt gjbjsń dz qˁcjljjń dz djˀ hˀt gˁsjń dz mjjzljjń dz djˀ hˀt gˁsjń [dz] cjqljjń dz djˀ hˀt gjqˀpt dz ˀlt vvˁtjrljjń [ˀjjń, crossed out] ˀvḿ ccvjjˀ ppˁnjgljjń ˀjjń cjqljjń ˀjjń cjqljjń

[7] vˀθˀ θvrˀ vsθˀ lmjˀ dmkvvˀ lnvrˀ dˀvqjd mqlˀ dmkˀ lklbˀ dnsjḱ lsvnrˀ dˀkjl ˁkbrˀ dˀkjl lgdjˀ dzbjń ˀbˀ bθrj zvzj xd gdjˀ xd gdjˀ — dˀ qˀḿ dz ˁqsljjń ˀvn' trjnqt dz vvˀsrljjń dz vvˁr lˁsjt dz vvjjˁrljjń dz djˀ hˀt vvˁr brˁnt dz stˁqljjń dz djˀ hˀt gjslˀgn dz hjntljjń dz djˀ hˀt gjbjsń dz qˁcjljjń dz djˀ hˀt gˁsń dz mjjzljjń dz djˀ hˀt gˁsń dz cjqljjń dz qˀpjt dz ˀlt vvˁtjrljjń ˀvḿ cvvjjˀ ppˁnjgljjń ˀjjń cjqljjń ˀjjń cjqljjń

[8] vˀθˀ sxtˀ vsxt lθvrˀ dsθˀ mjˀ dmkvvˀ lnvrˀ vˀvqjd [sic] mqlˀ dmkˀ lklbˀ dnsjḱ lsvnrˀ dˀkjl ˁkbrˀ dˀkjl gdjˀ dzbjń ˀbˀ bθrj zvzj xd gdj' xd gdjˀ — dˀ qˀḿ dz gjhrgjt [sic] svxtljjń ˀvn' sˁktjt dz ˁqsljjń dz dˀ hˀt gjtrvnqn ds vvˁsrljjń dz dˀ hˀt vvˁr lˁst dz vvjjˁrljjń dz djˁ hˁt vvˁr brˁnt dz stˁqljjń dz djˀ hˀt gjslˀgń dz hjntljjń dz djˀ hˀt gjbjsń dz qˁcjljjń dz dˀ hˀt gˁsń dz mjjzljjń dz dˀ hˀt gˁsń dz cjqljjń dz dˀ hˀt gjqˀpt dz gjhrgjt [sic] vvˁtrljjń ˀvḿ cvvjjˀ ppˁnjgljjń ˀjjń cjqljjń ˀjjń cjqljjń

[9] vˀθˀ mlˀḱ hmvθ vsxt lsxtˀ dsxt lθvrˀ dsθˀ mjˀ dmkvvˀ lnvrˀ dˀvqjd mqlˀ dmkˀ lklbˀ dnsjḱ lsvnrˀ dˀkjl ˁkbrˀ dˀkjl gdjˀ dzbjń ˀbˀ bθrj zvzj xd gdjˀ xd gdjˀ — dˀ qˀḿ dˁr mlˀḱ hmvθ ˀvn' sˁktjt dˁḿ [sic] svxt dˁr dˀ hˀtg jsˁkt dˁń [sic] ˀqσ[13] ˀvn' dˁr dˀ hˀt gjtrvnqjń ds vvˀsr ˀvn' dz dˀ hˀt vvˁr lˁst dz vvjjˁr dz dˀ hˀt vvˁr brˁnt dz stˁqljjń ˀvn' dz dˀ hˀt gjslˀgń dz hjntljjń ˀvn dz dˀ hˀt gjbjsń dz qˁcljjń ˀvn' dz dˀ hˀt gˁsń dz mjjzljjń ˀvn' dz dˀ hˀt gˁsń dz cjqljjń dz dˀ hˀt qˀpt dz gjhrgjt [sic] vvˁtrljjń ˀvḿ cvvjjˀ ppˁnjgljjń ˀjjń cjqljjń ˀjjń cjqljjń

[10] vˀθˀ qvdsˀ brjḱ hvˀ vsxt lmlˀḱ hmvθ dsxt lsxtˀ dsxt lθvrˀ dsθˀ lmjˀ dmkvvˀ lnvrˀ dˀvqjd mqlˀ dmkˀ klbˀ dnsjḱ svnrˀ dˀkjl ˁkbrˀ dˀkjl gdjˀ dzbjń ˀbˀ bθrj zvzj xd gdjˀ xd gdjˀ — dˀ qˀḿ hqb''h ˀvn' sˁktjt dˁń mlˀḱ hmvθ dˁr dˀ hˀt gjsˁkt dz gjhrgjt svxtljjń dz dˀ hˀt gjsˁkt dz ˁqsljjń dz dˀ hˀt gjtrvnqn dz vvˀsrljjń dz dˁ hˀt vvˁr lˁst dz vvjjˁrljjń dz dˀ hˀt vvˁr brˁnt dz stˁqljjń dz dˀ hˀt gjslˀgń dz hjntljjń dz dˀ hˀt gjbjsń dz qˁcljjń dz dˀ hˀt gˁsń dz mjjzljjń dz dˀ hˀt gˁsń dz cjqljjń dz [dˀ] hˀt gjqˀpt dz gjhrgjt [sic] vvˁtrljjń ˀjjń cjqljjń ˀjjń cjqljjń. xσl σjdvr pσx khlkθv.

'A Kid, A Kid

[1] Then came the mouse and ate the kid which the old father (grandfather ?) bought for twopence, a kid, a kid.

[2] Then came the cat and ate the mouse that ate the kid that the old father (grandfather ?) bought for twopence, a kid, a kid.

[13] Text unclear; possibly ♮ ˀqsń.

[3] Then came the dog and bit the cat that ate the mouse that ate the kid that the old father (grandfather ?) bought for twopence, a kid, a kid.

[4] Then came the stick and beat the dog that bit the cat that ate the mouse that ate the kid . . . .

[5] Then came the fire and burned the stick that beat the dog that bit the cat that ate the mouse . . . .

[6] Then came the water and put out the fire that burned the stick that beat the dog that bit the cat . . . .

[7] Then came the ox and drank the water that put out the fire that burned the stick that beat the dog . . . .

[8] Then came the killed slaughterer (!) and slaughtered the ox that drank the water that put out the fire that burned the stick . . . that the killed (!) father bought . . . .

[9] Then came the Angel of Death and slaughtered the slaughterer that slaughtered the ox that drank the water that put out the fire . . . .

[10] Then came the Holy One, blessed is He, and slaughtered the Angel of Death that slaughtered the killed slaughterer (!) that slaughtered the ox that drank the water. . . . The Passover seder according to traditional law is finished.'

ON FREE RHYTHMS IN MODERN YIDDISH POETRY

Benjamin Hrushovski (Jerusalem)

1. Introduction

1.1. The majority of modern Yiddish poets have undergone the influence of at least two from among a variety of literatures: mainly Russian, German, and American, but also Polish, French, Rumanian, and others—not to speak of Hebrew. In a single generation and often on the same few geographic and socio-cultural bases all these interacting influences have flown, like so many tributaries, into the pool of a common, uniform Yiddish literature. Moreover, for reasons of cultural history, Yiddish literature had not shared the development of its neighbors for hundreds of years; consequently, when the East European Jewish intelligentsia, in one grand leap, landed in the general twentieth century, Yiddish poetry undertook not only to catch up with Europe's deepened appreciation of the classics and the modernistic trends of recent generations, but also to take an active part in the discussion of the most timely cultural problems and in the artistic movements of the environment.

As a result, modern Yiddish poetry, apart from its intrinsic value, may serve as an extraordinary source for the understanding of general literary processes, such as the rise of literary trends, literary forms, and means of expression, especially insofar as the crossing of influences and the degree of their absorption is concerned; the role played by linguistic specificness; the significance of a cultural heritage peculiar to the group and the problem of giving it expression in new forms; the role of the socio-cultural base in deciding the amounts and types of influences admitted; the degree of inertia of conservative forms and patterns and the possibilities of a precipitous organic evolution to culture forms of an entirely different level; the relative roles of the early environment of a writer and of his milieu during his subsequent development, especially against so striking a background as the sudden transition of an entire culture from small town to city, from one country to another—even across an ocean; and many others. Let us keep in mind, too, that despite the eclecticism of these cross-influences and the clashes of cultures and epochs, there has developed, thanks to the power of a specific Jewish culture and a separate Yiddish language, supported by a re-invigorated organized society and the creative personalities of many poets, a good deal that is original and *homogeneous*, including even unique literary trends and expression patterns.

1.2. Rhythmic expression is only one aspect of this set of problems, but it is an organic aspect. "Poetry is the rhythmic expression in rhythmic language of rhythmic poetic emotions."[1] Hence, a true poet's treatment of rhythmic forms in application to a given subject matter reveals both his breathing pattern and

[1] B. Roland Lewis: *Creative Poetry; a Study of Its Organic Principles*, Stanford University, 1931, p. 315.

his adherence to a literary trend.[2] Nor are these revealed patterns isolated or incidental. Rhythm is so organic an expression of a man's whole conception of life, so deeply rooted in the poet's subconscious, that the homogeneous *rhythmic type*[3] both of the individual and of the entire literary period or trend is apparent in *all* his creative patterns of a given period. Only a revolution in the whole poetic and human perception of the world produces changes in the obstinately conservative forms of poetic structure.

For the same reasons, the iambs of a Leyeles (b. 1889) are more similar, by their essential rhythmic expression, to his own free rhythms than to the iambs of another poet—say, Avrohom Reyzin (Reisen, 1876–1953). Therefore the separate treatment of free rhythms, in a non-mechanistic comparative literary analysis, produces one-sidedness and incompleteness of the general picture. We make the separation here artificially, but under methodological pressure: there are still no generally valid classificatory rules in this form domain.

1.3. The classification which we have attempted here proceeds not from any ready-made doctrine, but from the material itself, particularly because of its originality and the importance of linguistic structure in the formation of free rhythms in especial. Rhythm results from the intimate interaction of a great many factors of prosody, syntax, and tonality, and we will touch here on only some of them; even so we will differentiate artificially between the several inseparably bound up factors of a *single poetic breath.* The *rhythmic configuration* is created (not necessarily consciously in all its structural details) by the character, the momentum, the speeds and pauses of this poetic breath as it shapes the linguistic and thematic material. Then this configuration enables the reader to reproduce in his reading similar speeds, pauses, etc. in his breathing *in conformity with the content atmosphere.* The principles of this reproduction are those which have been made familiar by gestalt psychology.[4]

The lack of any specific preliminary research forced me to study virtually every detail; my statements are based on a great deal of experimental material, although limitations of space have allowed me to present only the most important conclusions with a minimum of illustration and without the full apparatus of proof.[5]

[2] For example, Fritz Strich, in his book *Deutsche Klassik und Romantik* (Berne, 1949), distinguishes between the two trends according to their essentially different approaches to man, subject matter, language, rhythm and rime, etc. Not only does the selection of forms differ, but one and the same form may be expressed in quite different language and breathing patterns depending on the author's broader conception of the world and of poetry.

[3] From the Sievers school, I have adopted only the term, not its application.

[4] Unfortunately we cannot dwell here on the application of gestalt psychology to the poetry perception. But it should constantly be kept in mind, because the same form can have an entirely different effect in another context.

[5] The scope of my subject, of course, forced me to take several mental leaps over unexplored points and to make assumptions which may be confirmed or refuted by more specific future research. In this paper it was the overall picture which was important to me, the basic problems, comparisons, and differences which could serve as a perspective for such more detailed studies. I have to state that the accidental nature of the analyzed and quoted material, poetic as well as theoretical, is due to the general difficulties of Jerusalem University, especially the inaccessibility of the great University library on Mt. Scopus, despite the provisions of the Palestine armistice.

1.4. Let us remember: (a) The all-human foundations of rhythm and (b) the interacting foreign and traditional influences (c) on the basis of the specifics of the Yiddish language and in the conditions of its concrete phonetic-prosodic structure have created unique and immanent (and therefore firmly anchored) forms of free-rhythm poetry. Hence also the interest which our problem can have, if pursued further, for general comparative rhythm research. The specific breathing patterns of the Yiddish language group, its own subject matter and symbolism, and, above all, its own environmental atmosphere, its own rhythmic tradition, and the separate development of its rhythm perception have led to the fact that sometimes integral influences of ideas and content are in Yiddish expressed in rhythmic forms entirely different from those of the models (even though their spiritual essence may be similar).

1.5. When I say *free rhythms*, I have in mind (a) freedom from the prevalent metric system, which in the Yiddish case is tonic-syllabic[6] (we will abbreviate it as t.-s.); this "freedom," then, is an inconsistency in the arrangement of a predetermined number of stressed and unstressed syllables in the interior of a line. But free rhythms also imply (b) a poetic language which gives the reader the impression of a rhythmic poem, in contrast to prose. The limits of freedom and the character of the concealed principles of organization of this rhythmic impact—in relation to the essence of the content—are the goal of our research.

It is clear from our definition that for us the domain of free rhythms does not include poems written in unequal but iambic or other t.-s. lines,[7] or poems with a free end of line, free anacrusis, or even freedom of caesura. The last—increase or decrease in the number of syllables in the interior of the line—are made possible by the breathing pause at the caesura, which approaches in its

[6] We speak of poetry that is (purely) SYLLABIC if the only organizational principle is the number of syllables per verse; poetry is TONIC OF FREE-TONIC if the organizational principle is the number of stressed syllables per verse; and finally, poetry is TONIC-SYLLABIC (t.-s.) if the verse is organized into a fixed number of stressed and unstressed syllables in a fixed order. In contrast to Andreas Heusler's *Deutsche Versgeschichte (mit Einschluss des altenglischen und altnordischen Stabreimverses)*, Berlin–Leipzig, 3 vol., 1925–29, I include among the free rhythms those poems which have a fixed number of stresses in the line but a free number and order of the unstressed syllables. I do so for the following reasons: (a) With the number of stresses the same, such poems nevertheless have altogether different rhythms, depending on the number of syllables and on the type and limits of freedom. In this respect Heusler is disqualified because of his strictly isochronistic, musically tainted doctrine. Yet even he often realizes that the boundaries are blurred, that this type of poetry can be found among some of the freer rhythms, too. (b) The procedure is justified historically. The rhythms of this type, together with other free ones, originated in Yiddish in the *modern* era only as the severity of t.-s. metrics was being abolished (similarly in Russia); see below, chapters 3 and 4.

[7] This against B. Risberg (*Den svenska versens teori*, Uppsala, 1905), with whom I do agree on the problem touched on in footnote 6, because free rhythms are free only in relation to the *prevalent* metric system from which they want to liberate themselves. Metric lines of unequal length were a form widespread even in the era of completely t.-s. metrics (e.g. the parables of Eliezer Shteynbarg [1880–1932]; similarly in other languages). We will call these t.-s. poems *free verse*, since their verses are not predetermined, having no fixed number of measures. What differentiates *free rhythms* from all t.-s. verse, including free verse, is precisely the absence of *equal* measures in each verse.

essence the inter-line break.[8] This factor must be considered in connection with certain free rhythms, too.

1.6. The borderline cases also include poems which are written formally in a t.-s. meter, but which as a matter of fact (because of their inner agitation or lexical composition) have a group of stronger stresses as well which decide the real rhythmic impact and are *not* distributed at equal syllabic intervals. For example, "Oyf di fayern" by H. Leyvik (Leivick, b. 1888):

Ōyf dĭ fā̋yĕrn̆ ĭn lū̋ft dĭ tā̋ntsn̆dīkĕ kū̋k ĭkh,
ūn dĭ ō̋ygn̆ mā́ynĕ
vē̋rn̆ vī dĭ fā̋yĕrn̄ ĭn lū̋ft dĭ tā̋ntsn̆dīkĕ.[9]

('I look at the fires dancing in the air, / and my eyes / become like the fires dancing in the air.' All translations of poetic material are in this paper rendered in prose.) Formally these are trochees. But in reality four principal stresses dominate every long line in the poem (due to the long words, the inversion, the lofty mood), and, as a matter of fact, the number of trochees is not the same in every line of the poem, and they are not even all true trochees. For example:

Vī ĕs lō̋yfn̆ | ībĕr shtē̋rn̆ | īn gĕdī̋khtĕr | fī̋ntstĕrnīsh—
dĭ ō̋ygn̆ mā́ynĕ—
tsū dĭ vā̋ytĕ | fāyĕrn̄ | shnā̋ydn̆ zēy zĭkh | dūrkh dĕr fī̋nstĕrnīsh.

('As the stars run across the dense darkness / these eyes of mine / cut through the darkness to the distant fires.') The stronger stresses may lie on every second metric stress, and then a paeonic impression is created; or if they have a mixed distribution, as is true in our case, there result unequal word groups, which are sensed as rhythmically free, but which have not yet dared to liberate themselves from the formally accepted schema. (This may sometimes evoke a scanning trochaic reading, which deadens both the dactylic endings and the entire organic mood of the poem.)

1.7. In order to avoid a dispute about the rhythmic elements themselves, I make use of the most common symbols in my schemas. — stressed syllable (ictus); ◡ unstressed syllable; if the actual reading differs, these two symbols

[8] For example: *ŭn ā* GĔHĒYMĔ / *hānt băshīt // dĭ kēp fŭn* BĒYMĔR / *mĭt yūngn̆ tsvīt. // Ōvn̆t kūmt,* / *shlōft mĕn āyn // bărōysht fŭn kīln̆* / *shtērn̆shāyn* . . . etc. ('And a secret hand pours / young blossoms over the heads of trees. / Evening comes, and one falls asleep / intoxicated by the cool starlight'; from Eliezer Grinberg: *Di lange nakht*, New York, 1946). A feeling of symmetry predominates in every line of the poem. (Here it is enhanced by the internal rime.) The syntactic conditioning of the caesura break is manifest. By means of the deviations from the meter, excessive melodicity is avoided and a certain prosy-narrative tone is attained. But except for the middle of lines, two stressed or two unstressed syllables do not meet head on. That is, the poem is iambic, or to be more precise, written in disyllabic measures.

[9] H. Leyvik (Leivick): *Ale verk*, New York, 1940, vol. 1, p. 67. (All my quotations from Leyvik are from this volume.) When the whole poem is read, the truth of my contention becomes even more apparent. Since the effect of a rhythmic device is achieved only by the *entire* configuration, not accidentally, each of my quotations ought to be checked by reading the source in its entirety and at one stroke.

represent the schema and ″ represents a strong stress, ′ a weaker actual stress (or normal stress when it comes alone); // means the end of the line; / stands for caesura; | marks the colon (between the words, a measure). The conventional concepts like iamb, anapest, etc., are also used only *schematically*. They suffice for the understanding of the problem, while an exhaustive superior procedure is not available anyway. The *measure* (Heusler's *Takt*) is an artificial concept, but this is not the place for proving its invalidity; for convenience's sake we use it to designate the interval between two stresses, without meaning to give it strict limits. The true unit of rhythm is the *colon*—that is, a word grouped around one center-like accent, a word with its auxiliary words, which can be pronounced at one stroke, without an interruption in breathing even in slow reading.

The counting of syllables in free rhythms involves special difficulties, because many syllables can be intended by the poet as elided (or, on the contrary, as stretched).[10] The main indefinite cases involve the sheva in words of Hebrew origin (*melokhe* 'craft'—two or three syllables), elisions at a hiatus,[11] syllabic *n̩* and *l̩* and weak *e* in various other positions,[12] and monosyllables tending toward shortness like *un* 'and', *iz* 'is', *es* 'it', *ikh* 'I', and the like. This is true not only of the folksong or of the Yiddish t.-s. metric system in its early period, when the technique had not yet been firmly mastered, but also of the work of good technicians where their *pronunciation* differs from the grammatical norm.[13] This makes it very difficult to determine the limits of freedom in free rhythms. In general, because of the possible individual nuances in reading and stressing, my symbols refer only to what is essential, and not to an absolutely precise schema in a concrete example.

[10] It is the musical notation which sometimes reveals this treatment. Thus in Y.-L. Cahan: *Yidishe folkslider mit melodien* (*oys dem folksmoyl*), 2 vol., New York, 1912, vol. 1, p. 236 (hereafter we will write A 236), the text has (dial.) *gĕtīn*, while the music has *zĭ hōt ĭm* GĔTĪĔN *ĭn kēyvĕr dĕrmānĕn* 'she did remember him in her grave'—i.e. precise amphibrachs. In another song, the amphibrach is in singing preserved in all lines, despite the syllabic freedom of the text: *ĕs* | *yōgt ă* | *vīnt, ĕs* | *gīst ă* | *rēgn̆, / ă* | *shōydĕr nĕmt* | *dūrkh ălĕ* | *bēynĕr* ('a wind blows, a rain pours, / a shudder goes through all one's bones'; the marks according to the music). It is clear that one reads *yō-ŏgt, vī-ĭnt*, and as many as three notes coincide with one syllable when it stands alone in a measure (*frā-ă-ăynd* 'friend').

[11] For example, *lŏmĭr gēbn̆ ă shvākh tsŭm bōyre‿elŏyhēynŭ* ('Let us give praise to the Creator our God'; Fritz Mordechai Kaufmann: *Die schönsten Lieder der Ostjuden*, Berlin, 1920)—one note for both *e*'s. Under the music, we do in fact read *boir*-E-*lo-hei-nu*.

[12] E.g. *oygn* 'eyes' as one syllables. Tsunzer often slurs over syllables like *ge* in *ōng(ĕ)văksn̆* 'grown'. In Gotlober's "Greberlid" we find many instances of *ōr(ĕ)mĕlāyt* 'poor people', and even *tsĕkrōkhn‿un fōyl* 'slovenly and lazy', to be read as *tsĕ-krōkh-nŭn-fōyl*. And in a folksong (*Der Urquell*, n.s. 1 [1897] 82; parentheses supplied), we read:

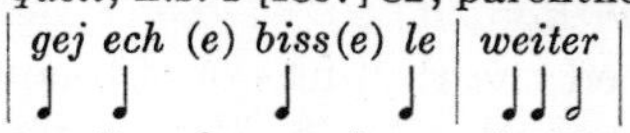

| *gej ech (e) biss(e) le* | *weiter* |
| ♩ ♩ ♩ ♩ | ♩♩𝅗𝅥 |

[13] As conscious a technician as Leyeles reads words like *zeyer* 'their', *ayer* 'your' as monosyllables (*zeyr, ayr*), *zeyere* 'their (pl.)' as a disyllable (*zeyre*). From the many examples in his *A yid oyfn yam* (New York, 1947), I cite but one, from a poem of 6-trochee lines: *mūzt ĭr ōn shŭm brēyrĕ tōn ŭn tōn* ĂYER *tūŭng* ('then you must, without any alternative whatsoever, do and do your deed').

1.8. The free rhythms in Yiddish poetry originated in the various literary trends after World War I. It is possible to distinguish two main groups (although they are not strictly delimited):

a. Those which retain equal numbers of measures per line (and may, at the same time, also preserve a stanza structure) and which are mostly folk-like in a modern way in their tone and language;

b. Those which are free both as to the length of their measures and in the number of measures (and mostly also as to their strophic structure). These are chiefly free-rhythm creations which followed the expressionistic ferment (viewed genetically, not necessarily by their date). Their rhythmic devices are most intimately related to the expression of content atmosphere and therefore differ widely with the authors and the subject matter of their poetry. They fluctuate between highly rhythmicized big-city dynamics and the verge of prose.

c. A third area is the *folksong*, which in its structure resembles the first group and has strongly influenced it, mainly because the folksong is the result of the integration of a natural feeling for the language within the frame of the free-tonic verse, traditionalized for generations. Before we turn to the modernistic free-rhythm means of expression, it is necessary to review the traditional old free forms. (The *literary* forms of older Yiddish poetry, in contrast to those of folklore, had almost no effect on the modern period.)

2. Free Rhythms in Yiddish Folksong[14]

2.1. It is important to consider the rhythm of the texts alone, without their melodies, because:

a. Within the framework of one and the same musical rhythm there have arisen diverse language rhythms, i.e. various ways of filling the melody with syllables and various lengths of lines or speeds of texts, differing especially according to the content genre;

b. The same language rhythms govern folk-proverbs and children's counting-out rimes, even those which have no melodies;

c. Prose, too, can be set to music (we know of prayers with prose texts, or of Prokofieff's opera to L. Tolstoy's prose text of *Peace and War*). It is therefore obviously necessary to see whether, and in what way, the text in itself is a poem. If it is, that means that the choice of words is limited by certain restrictions. Without this we could not turn prose into poetry even by forcing onto it a musical rhythm.

d. Rime is unnecessary to melody, while in the text of the folksong it is an indispensable principle of stanza construction (even though the song would be *sung* in stanza form even without it!).

e. Folksong has influenced the rhythms of subsequent art poetry principally through the rhythm of its *texts*.[15]

[14] I present only those results which are necessary for my purpose here of an extensive study of mine on the rhythmic principles of the Yiddish folksong in its development. The reader will have to trust my conclusions pending the publication of the detailed evidence.

[15] Incidentally, the musical stresses are not always identical with the linguistic ones. Moreover, a language measure missing from the full number may be filled by the melody.

f. There are songs whose language rhythm is distinctly Germanic (i.e. it retains the general conservative feeling of the folksong), while the melody is Slavic.

g. Only a uniform rhythmic system of the texts permits the easy adoption of melodies from song to song as well as the contamination of text fragments and the transfer of conventional locutions and formulas.[16]

2.2. The characteristic *stanza* of the folksong is constructed in the simplest manner, but highly symmetrically (and uniformly): four lines riming *mana*. Every two lines form a syntactic unity, concluded by a rime, and between them, too, the break between the lines is identical with the strongest present break in syntax and content. Every line contains four stresses which are usually divided by a caesura into 2 + 2, unless there are only three stresses (i.e. a catalectic form of the same quadruple framework, which often creates a "lightening" and a pleasant contrast to the "full" lines).[17]

This is the oldest German stanza form. Its source lies in a rimed pair of Old German *Langzeilen* which eventually each split into two (hence the principal rime in the second and fourth lines).[18]

Heusler finds among German folksongs (in the early New German period, beginning of the fourteenth to the beginning of the seventeenth centuries) stanzas of more numerous lines and of different rime patterns.[19] These were no doubt induced by the constant stream of artistic poetic forms of the German

---

Other musical utilizations of time for melismata and other ornaments which draw on the text for sound, but not for content, also occur. (Cf. August Reissman: *Geschichte des deutschen Liedes*, Berlin, 1874, pp. 51–53.)

[16] For details, see M. P. Štokmar: *Issledovanija v oblasti russkogo narodnogo stikhoslo-ženija*, Moscow, 1952. He demonstrates that the whole rhythmic system of the texts of Old Russian songs was essentially different from their later melody rhythm, and conformed to the historical specificness of the sound structure of the Old Russian language. On the non-individual relation between melody and text in German folksong, see Hans Mersmann: "Das deutsche Volkslied" (in *Kulturgeschichte der Musik in Einzeldarstellungen*, Berlin, 1921, p. 32). In contrast to the early sung German lyrics, the distinctive feature of modern folksong is the free filling of syllables. Cf. Heusler, *op. cit.*, §§ 854, 871.

[17] Thus, for example (Cahan, A 48):

Mayne shabosim un mayne yontoyvim —◡◡—◡◡—◡◡—◡
zaynen mir gevorn farshtert; —◡◡◡—◡◡—
zint ikh hob dayn libe derkent —◡—◡—◡◡—
ligt mir mayn ponim in der erd. —◡◡—◡◡◡—

('My Sabbaths and my holidays / have been ruined; / since I recognized your love / my face is in the ground' [i.e. I am downhearted].) Both sentences are constructed in parallel and form one whole, terminated and emphasized by the rime. Additional rimes would be a luxury which would, incidentally, break up the sentences, since they would run counter to the folk conception of rime as a concluding force. The first line gets us used to the normal length of four measures, and so we want to give the second line the same time interval (in order to feel it the same way). Therefore we render a pause after the second line, even without the melody, similar in length to a measure, and this magnificently underscores the syntactic pause. By this and other devices of this type, the stanza structure helps absorb and retain the content of the poem at a minimum effort.

[18] This stanza excellently fits the all-human rhythmic feeling in the face of tonic language material; it originated not only in Germany.

[19] Heusler, *op. cit.*, §§ 872f.

Lied (including the musical *Lied*) into the folk domain.[20] In Yiddish, however an artistic poetry with sophisticated forms arose relatively late; it had little time to be digested by the folk and was all the less capable of causing a change in the uniform and obstinate folk pattern *from the inside.* What is more, the 4-line stanza has remained the main form of the Yiddish literary poem, too, almost until the revolution of expressionism.

Full cross-riming *abab* is rather rare in Yiddish folksong, and is of late literary origin. It is remarkable that where the content of a literary poem has been altered in folksong, the full rimes of the poem have also been discarded.[21] Couplet rimes of the type *aabb* are also infrequent, and occur, incidentally, only in full 4-measure lines (mostly complete sentences) and even so only in certain content forms; there, too, it is the melody which keeps them in the traditional 4-line framework.

The Yiddish folksong does not know of an independent stanza of more than four lines. It seems that such a stanza could not be remembered as a fixed form in which the content is subject to alteration.[22] All stanzas exceeding four lines in the published collections fall into three categories. (a) The notation is incorrect; e.g. the extra lines do not appear in all stanzas of a poem or they represent an accidental accretion,[23] or else a single line is recorded as two lines with two stresses each.[24] (b) Whatever exceeds four lines constitutes a refrain or a group of several additional lines which recur (exactly or with small variations) throughout the song. (c) Quite rarely, the song is not in stanza form but is constructed on a single cumulative or expanding pattern, as exemplified by the

[20] Reissmann (*op. cit.*, p. 37) believes that the songs with artificial stanza patterns which were popular among the folk in the sixteenth and seventeenth centuries were derived from the *Minne-* and *Meistersang.*

[21] For a clearcut example, see Y.-L. Cahan (Kahan): *Shtudyes vegn yidisher folksshafung*, 374 pp. (New York, 1952), pp. 203f.: two poems by Sholem Bernshteyn rimed *abab*, in being folklorized, had their rime scheme changed almost without exception to *mbnb*. The short lines have been lengthened by filling with additional syllables, in accord with the traditional folk line. Consequently it is not true that "a folksong can more easily be recognized by its internal, thought or spiritual [*gedanklekh oder gaystik*] content than by external, formal features" (Cahan, *ibid.*, p. 201).

[22] Unless the form is a pattern in which only two (!) words are changed from stanza to stanza. This is the case in the only stanzaic song recorded by Kahan which was not originally made up of quatrains: the popular 7-line item, known in many versions, "Yome, yome, shpil nor a lidele" (Cahan B 13, B 31; S. M. Ginzburg and P. S. Marek: *Jevrejskije narodnyje pesni v Rossii*, St. Petersburg, 1901, no. 244; etc.).

[23] For example, when the melody repeats the last two lines of each stanza, the repetition being a variation. In one song (Cahan A 208), instead of twice having *der tsigayner, der toter, / er hot mikh umgliklekh gemakht* ('the Gypsy, the Tatar [both figurative], / he ruined me'), we find a variation in the repetition: *der tsigayner, dayn foter, / dortn zitst er un lakht* ('the Gypsy, your father, / there he sits and laughs'). This is the germ of a 6-line stanza, but the 4-line source is apparent.

[24] Sometimes this notation is due to an internal rime. But internal rimes—a result of the mid-line caesura—are not sustained throughout a folksong. Furthermore, in the resulting new stanza *aacbbc*, each *a* and *b* line has only two measures (*c* usually has three). That is to say, with regard to metrics, it is still the original stanza! Nevertheless, the rhythmic form already does make a different impression.

"Song of the Kid" (e.g. Ginzburg–Marek [cf. footnote 22] 1, 5, 6, 7; these in the recent period no longer represented a sung form of great dispersion).

In sum we may state that all of the deviations from the principal stanza structure are forms of address, repetitions of words, refrains, and the like, i.e. playful ornamentations[25] which add life and atmosphere but do not serve the development of the content of the song.

Songs of literary poets, too, are interpreted by the folk as constructed according to the quatrain principle, and if they are assimilated they are so treated and even so reconstructed.[26]

2.3. Conservatism in the field of form is also reflected in the character of the specific song groups. The Yiddish children's play song has retained the special 2-measure form of the Old German children's saying.[27] The Yiddish proverb, within a 4-measure framework, often contains only three measures, and there are also some of two measures (cf. Heusler, §1218).

Furthermore, songs which are adaptations or explicit translations of Slavic t.-s. folksongs (mainly trochees, which already prevailed in the Slavic domain in the nineteenth century) retain only that which is understandable to the old rhythm feeling: the number of stresses, while the number of syllables in the interior of the measure is set free.[28] Even in the t.-s. songs by Yiddish poets, at the slightest alteration, the count of syllables is violated as a superfluous luxury.

The folk alterations are often not accidental; they are intended to attenuate the march-like or urban measured rhythms in the spirit of folk informality and the old free narrative style. Thus the tempo of the amphibrachic stanza of the revolutionary song by M. Sore-Rives (pseudonym of Khaim Miller [Alexan-

[25] See Reissmann, *op. cit.*, p. 43.

[26] An interesting example: "Di mashke" by Mikhl Gordon (1823–1890), containing 18 six-line stanzas *aabbcc*, is recorded by Sh. Bastomski (*Baym kval; yidishe folkslider*, Vilna, 1923, p. 188) "erroneously" (?!) as a folksong containing 19 *four*-line stanzas (*aabb*). It is remarkable that the majority of changes connected with the folklorization of the song, those of content included, were conditioned by the reconstruction of the form. On the conversion of 5-line stanzas to quatrains in another song of Gordon's, see Eleanor Gordon Mlotek: [The Metamorphosis of Mikhl Gordon's Poem *Di bord*], *Yivo-bleter* 35 (1951) 299–311.

[27] Heusler, *op. cit.*, p. 1225. Incidentally, this is true textually also: "A large part of the play and counting-out verses sung by [Jewish] children, certain riddle and wishing songs, were already known in Germany in the fifteenth and sixteenth centuries" (Cahan, *Shtudyes. . .*, p. 16).

[28] For an example, cf. Sh. Lehman: *Ganovim-lider mit melodyes*, Warsaw, 1928, p. 17, and the Polish source of the song published there, *ibid.*, notes, p. 209; cf. also the famous soldier song *Beser tsu lernen khumesh mit rashe / eyder tsu esn di soldatske kashe* ('It is better to study the Pentateuch with Rashi's commentary / than to eat soldiers' pap') and its Belorussian trochaic parallel (see Sh. Z. Pipe: [Folklore Songs], *Yivo-bleter* 14 [1939] 339–367, p. 351). This is true even in those bilingual folksongs in which the original Slavic stanza alternates with a Yiddish translation; e.g. Cahan A 16, no. 9: *gdzīe tĕn chłōpiĕc cō mniĕ chciāł?* becomes *vū ĭz dŏs bōkhĕrl̆ / vōs hŏt mĭkh gĕvōlt?* ('where is the fellow who desired me?'). At least the trisyllabic diminutive did not *have* to be there! (The base form, *bokher*, is disyllabic, like the Polish model *chłopiec*.)

drov], 1869–1909) is softened by the folk[29] through the inclusion of additional syllables in the same melody. The song of Sore-Rives (as sung by the folk) runs as follows:

Brīdĕr, mĭr hōbň gĕshlōsň
ŏyf lēbň ŭn tōyt ă fărbānd.
mĭr shtĕy(ĕ)n[30] *dŏ ĭn shlākht vĭ gĕnōsň,*
dĭ fōnĕ dĭ rōytĕ ĭn hānt.

('Brothers, we have concluded / a pact for life and death. / We stand as comrades here in battle, / the red flag in our hands.')

Now the completely folklorized version (Beregovski, *op. cit.*, no. 65):

Brīdĕr, ŏyb gōt vĭl ŭnz nĭt hēlfň,
lōmĭr zĭkh băfrāyĕn ălēyn.
lōmĭr zĭkh tsĕrāysň fŭn dĭ kēytň
ŭn lōmĭr ălēyn tsŭzămĕn gēyn.

('Brothers, if God does not want to help us, / let us liberate ourselves. / Let us tear ourselves from the chains / and let us go together on our own.')

The metronome records ♩ = 166 in the first case and ♩ = 72 in the second. What a difference in tempo! Yet it is created principally by a "slightly" increased syllable load of the measures. Since for the content to be conveyed the words cannot be slurred, the long line must have more time (unless its great speed is itself determined by the content). *Herein lies the difference between meter and rhythm.* Even when the meter permits a free number of syllables (and even with the same musical rhythm), this number is extremely significant in creating the tempo and the general rhythmic impression of the song; it depends upon the very heart of the poem or the song.

2.4. The melody of the folksong retains the isochronal nature of the measures and permits, in a formal sense, the freedom of syllables. That is to say, if a measure consists of a single syllable, that syllable is stretched, while if it consists of many syllables, the notes are split in order to allot to them smaller segments of time. But too many syllables are not tolerated in a measure because then each syllable would be too short to be heard accurately. For the folksong strives above all to give a clear expression to the content. In deference to the content the melody may be altered; if it is not, the language text is changed.[31]

[29] M. Beregovski: *Yidisher muzik-folklor*, vol. 1, Moscow, 1934, no. 82.

[30] Here, incidentally, is already a folk-like dropping of a metrically compressed syllable.

[31] For example, in the song "Vigndik a fremd kind," published in Ruth Rubin: *A Treasury of Jewish Folksong*, New York, 1950, p. 18, every musical 2/4 measure equals two textual measures (four textual measures per line). At the termination of lines a single syllable occurs alone in a measure, i. e. occupying a 1/4 note all by itself (normally a syllable takes up only 1/8). At the utmost there are in this song four syllables in a single measure, at 1/16 each. If the liberty of a fifth syllable were taken, its duration would have to be 1/32, i.e. it would be slurred over in pronunciation, being eight times shorter than another syllable. Therefore *iz* is abbreviated: *dayn mameshi 'z gegangen in mark arayn* ('your mommy's gone to the market place'). This in spite of the tendency of folksong to reëxpand, for clar-

Heusler notes that in German folksong a single measure ranges from one to five syllables. The described melodic requirements limit the measure to four syllables. Thus a line of the same 4-stress meter may contain from four syllables[32] up to sixteen. But a precise count of syllables in whole volumes of Yiddish folksongs leads to highly interesting observations concerning the manner in which *limitations* upon the permitted range create specific forms and expression devices in consonance with the content tone. The most important groups in Yiddish are these:

a. In the lyric love songs, there is a maximum of three syllables in one measure, producing an iambic-anapestic movement.[33] A major subgroup sticks to a pattern of *two* syllables per measure, except for dactylic words (mainly diminutives) which create 3-syllable measures.[34]

b. In the narrative songs,[35] there is a maximum of four syllables per measure, i.e. freedom up to the limits of melodic acceptability. Here, too, there is a distinct subgroup (consisting mostly of general symbolic, ballad-like songs) marked by a maximum of three syllables per measure, except for measures containing dactylic words which are tetrasyllabic (*ă mēydĕlĕ ă klēynĭnkĕ* 'a little girl' or dactylic enclitic combinations like the first part of KRĪGT MĔN NĬSHT *tsŭ kōyfn̆* 'is not to be had for sale').

c. The bulk of children's songs and counting-out rimes sticks to the maximum of two syllables per measure. These texts would be pure trochees and iambs if not for the existence of 1-syllable measures containing the stress only. The playfulness of the children's songs has brought about close rimes and in

---

ity's sake, the abbreviations of poets, even at the expense of t.-s. regularity; thus, Dovid Edelshtat (1866–1892) reads, amphibrachically, *ir froyen vos shmakhtn in hoyz 'n in fabrik* ('you women who languish at home and in the factory'), but the folk sings UN *in fabrik;* and so forth (see the song in Beregovski, *op. cit.*, no. 80). The collectors of Yiddish folksong have not always taken sufficient heed of this fact and the contradictions between text and musical notation are often evident.

[32] E.g. *mā́yn zī́s lī́b kī́nd* 'my sweet dear child' (Rubin, *op. cit.*, p. 17). Both extremes are rare. But as a rule all lines of a song are similar in structure.

[33] Cf. Cahan A 6: *Ŏy, vōs kh'hŏb gĕvōlt hŏb ĭkh ōysgĕfīrt, // zōl ĭkh āzŏy lēbn̆: // kh'hōb gĕvōlt ă shēyn yīngĕlĕ // hōt mĭr gōt gĕgēbn̆* ('Oh what I wanted I attained, / may I live so [as this is true]: / I wanted a handsome boy / and God gave me one').

[34] A song published by Cahan (A 22) is so constructed down to the last syllable:

Tif in VELDELE *shteyt a beymele* —◡—◡◡/—◡—◡◡
un di tsvaygelekh blien; —◡—◡◡ —◡
un bay mir, orem SHNAYDERL, —◡—(◡)/—◡—◡◡
tut dos HERTSELE *tsien.* —◡—◡◡ —◡

('Deep in the forest stands a tree / and its branches are blooming; / and in me, poor tailor, / my heart is drawn'.)

[35] With linguistic expressions characteristic of a narrative tone: *Hert nor oys, mentshn, vos s'hot zikh getrofn* ('Listen, folks, to what happened'), *azoy vi men hot* ('as they. . . '), etc. In general, Heusler observes, "the (mostly more voluminous) historical and political folksongs stand out on this account, as well as the saga-like narrative songs ('folk ballads and romances'). They incline above all to a longer anacrusis (up to five syllables) and to heavy internal measures" (*op. cit.*, §874).

most children's games and counting-out rimes the regular 4-stress line has split into 2-stress lines, just like those of German children's games. Frequently it is precisely the 2-measure form which has retained the accumulation of unstressed syllables typical of German.[36]

d. The German 5-syllable freedom is rarely utilized in Yiddish and appears only in narrative songs where the event related bears a rather concrete, local, *individual* or group character (e.g. in the thieves' songs, which concern concrete heros).[37] By the same token, the inclusion of the song and its events in the common stock of folksongs leads to a blurring of its local or incidental character and it is resung in 4-syllable form (i.e. group b). Five-syllable measures force the slurring of syllables or an imprecise filling of the melody; it is so difficult to feel a song rhythm in them that they border on the recitative.

No theoretical framework has been set up by the folk; even scholars, because of their musically influenced theories, have not paid proper attention to this matter. But the general thematic character of the song has decided the stream of its language: heavy narrative epics have been rendered in long lines; lyricism has been treated lightly, in a manner approaching metric uniformity; children's songs have stressed the beat and not the flow of language or the content, so that rime and sound and a minimum of syllables are important. In the folk feeling there has developed a firm tradition of rhythmic types (not only of metrics), supported by wandering established versions of songs.[38]

2.5. Among other form properties of Yiddish folksong, the following are also pertinent to the present topic. Despite syllabic freedom in the interior of the line and at the line end (e.g. two parallel lines having, respectively, a male and a dactylic ending; see footnote 33), certain strict limitations are sometimes observed. Heusler notes them without interpreting them, yet they are quite significant. One example out of many: In the song Cahan A212, which formally has three stresses per line in the text, every odd line is feminine, every even line masculine. The reason is clear: the first line must have an additional syllable in which the missing fourth stress could be placed; the second line, according to the folk-feeling, must deviate from the first but must usually be shorter in order to create a feeling of pause on account of the end of the sentence; hence a masculine 3-measure line is the only possible length.

The distribution of short and long measures is also important. Thus Cahan A194:

A shem hob ikh gehat far an erlekh meydl	∪–∪∪∪–	–∪∪∪–∪
der shem iz mir geven tayerer fun gelt.	∪–∪∪∪–	–∪∪∪–
Yetst bin ikh orem, elnt un baleydikt. . .	– ∪∪–∪	–∪∪∪–∪
Ay, durkh dir hob ikh farshpilt mayn velt.	–∪∪∪–∪∪∪–	

[36] But by and large the Slavic trochee already predominates here, too, especially in texts borrowed from Slavic.

[37] Cf. Lehman, *op. cit.*, p. 63, the song "Donershtik in der fri bin ikh mir in gas aroysgegangen" ('Thursday morning I casually walked into the street').

[38] See also Štokmar, *op. cit.*, p. 400.

('I had the reputation of a respectable girl, / this reputation was worth more to me than money. / Now I am poor, lonesome, and humiliated. . . / You have caused me to lose my world.')

Paeonicity is characteristic of narrative songs. But here the breath pause at the caesura is obvious. According to Andrej Belyj (cf. footnote 95) the length of the line determines the breath load. Our song is not long-breathed. The line divides itself into two, as is the case with a whole group of 2-measure songs (Cahan A148, 150, 170, 214 et al.). Instead of a wave flowing forward, the basis here is an *arc*, resting on two stresses at each end of the line, with as many unstressed syllables as possible in the interior of the measure. The full measure preserves the narrative content. But the short line is light and lyrically agitated. Its playful tone (textually, too: the seducer is called *yingele* 'little boy' with 'blue little lips') conveys the levity of the song and the tension between the long measure and the short line, or the tension of the arc, emphasize the tragic content. (*Ĭkh hōb gĕshpĭlt ă lībĕ / kh'hōb gĕfĭrt ă rōlĕ; / kh'hŏb tsūgĕzŏgt ă yĭngĕlĕ / ăz īkh vĕl zăyn zăyn kālĕ*. . . etc. 'I carried on a love-affair / I acted my part / I promised a boy / that I would be his fiancée.')

Incidentally, midway between this paeonic arc and the trochaic dipod pattern of the children's game lies, with respect to both technique and content tone, the *dactylic arc* of the game song of the adults.[39]

2.6. None of these inner forms, however, carried the Yiddish folksong to t.-s. metrics. Even the big city had no such effect: most of the thieves' songs are also constructed in the old manner. More subject to change was the old stanza pattern: deviant rime schemes (mainly *abab* and *aacbbc*) penetrated the folksong from the theatrical hits and the popular literary songs. But the rhythm resisted change. Even the Slavic environment did not transmit its t.-s. pattern to Yiddish directly (see §2.3), despite the adoption in Yiddish of Slavic motifs in content and melody. It was in the Yiddish children's song, which took in sequences of Slavic sounds as such, that t.-s. metrics first penetrated into Yiddish folklore.[40] This group was then expanded to include t.-s. refrains and couplets (in particular from the theater reportoire), i.e. again segments in which pure *sound* plays a dominant role were the channels for t.-s. importation.

In its *content-laden* segments, the Yiddish folksong experienced a new and

[39] Note the structure of the characteristic ending of a Purim play: *Hāynt ĭz pūrĭm, / mōrgň ĭz ōys, / gīt mĭr ă grōshň / ŭn vārft mĭkh ărōys* ('Today is Purim, / tomorrow it will be over, / give me a groshn [coin] / and throw me out'.) Similarly, in the "Gazlen-shpil" ('Robber Game') recorded by Lehman in *Arkhiv far der yidisher shprakh-visnshaft, literatur-forshung un etnologye*, Warsaw, 1923–33, p. 287: *Kūkt ăykh nŏr ūm / ĭn ālĕ fĭr zāytň, / dĕr gāzlĕn vĕt bāld / kūmĕn tsŭ rāytň* ('Come, look around you / on all four sides, / the robber will soon / come riding'). The rhythm of many dance songs is similar, e.g. *shpīl mĭr ă sēmĕnĕ, / nīt kĕyn kŏzātskĕ, / īkh bĭn ăn ōrĕmĕ / ōbĕr ă khvātskĕ* ('Play me a *semene* [kind of dance], / not a *kozatske*, / I am poor / but snappy'; Cahan, *Shtudyes*. . . , p. 90; concerning the *semele* dance, see *ibid*., pp. 90f.).

[40] See, for example, the first of the [Two Foreign-Language Counting-Out Rimes of Jewish Children of Samogitia], by J. Brutskus, *Yivo-bleter* 26 (1945) 336.

stricter ordering under the influence of the political pprincipally Socialist) mass song. The anthem, the marching song, and the chorus song generally, required the strict general organization of hearing. The thematic influence of the Russian workers' song also made itself strongly felt. Thus Beregovski's collection contains many nearly t.-s. songs, even of a narrative local type.[41]

Only when the Yiddish-speaking group began to sing a great many songs by its own new poets, the folk ear became accustomed to the requirements of a syllable order and gradually introduced it into the old song stock. (A similar change took place in the Russian folksong in the nineteenth century under the influence of the literary song.) Even the irrepressible rimester—the potential first creator of a folksong—begins to write t.-s. poetry. At the last stage, during the tragic disappearance of the folksong together with its singers—t.-s. forms were the most widespread type.[42]

3. Historical Survey

The main periods in the rhythm history of the Yiddish poem are the following:

3.1. *The Middle Ages.* In the secular epic poem (mostly sung) the meter is free-tonic under German influence, but not without the support of native tradition, since Hebrew liturgical poetry outside of Spain continued the biblical tonic pattern (consisting mostly of 4 + 4 stresses). Few unstressed syllables were used in this period.[43]

[41] Cf., for example, the strong paeonicity of the song about *yisker*. But this was not yet a hard and fast rule; hence the alterations in the t.-s. works of the poets.

[42] T.-s. meters prevail in the hundreds of Yiddish folksongs of the German ghettos and concentration and extermination camps of World War II. See Sh. Katsherginski: *Lider fun getos un lagern*, New York, 1948. In Sh. Goldshmid's collection of Soviet Yiddish World War songs (*Folkslider fun der foterlendisher milkhome*, Moscow, 1944), all texts are t.-s. There is no doubt in my mind, incidentally, that this book has some real folksongs, quite remote from the official style of Soviet poetry. The narrative stanza has four primary stresses per line, just as it used to in the old folksong, but the completely paeonized lines have decomposed into seven precise trochees: 4 + 3 divided by a caesura: *fun der hayntiker milkhome vel ikh lider zingen, // az se zol di gantse velt mit di lider klingen, // vi s'iz forgekumen dort mit Yashke dem odeser, // az er hot geshlogn zikh mitn daytsh oyf meser* ('I shall sing songs of the present war, / so that the whole world may resound with these songs, / how it happened there with Yashke the Odessan, / he fought the German at knife's point'). In terms of style this is the old Odessa (the names of the heros already occurred in 1905; cf. the preface); the images and locutions are, except for the name Hitler, old traditional (. . . *vi er hot derzen* 'as he noticed. . .', etc.; cf. footnote 35), yet one misses the flexible and direct, free language of the folksong unforced by a t.-s. meter.

[43] In Elyohu Bokher's (Elijah Levita's) *Bovo-bukh* (1508), the 4-measure lines are mostly "iambic." According to Heusler, §638, Old German lyric poetry had measures mostly up to two syllables long. If in the *Bovo-bukh* Italian influence was a factor, then we may cite the freer *Vints-Hans-lid*, published by Max Weinreich in his *Shtaplen*, Berlin, 1923, which has an average of less than 2.5 syllables per measure (according to 15 sample stanzas out of 103). In the Akhashveyresh (Ahasuerus) play of 1718, the 4-stress lines of the *meylits* do not exceed three syllables per measure, while most measures have only two syllables ("iambic"); some characters, however, do have longer lines (Max Weinreich: [Contribution to the History of the Older Yiddish Akhashveyresh Play], *Filologishe shriftn* [*fun Yivo*] 2 [1928] 423–451).

3.2. *The nineteenth century in Eastern Europe.* This was the flourishing period of the briefer lyrical and balladic folksong. The sophisticated and popular maskilic poetry is free-tonic (4-measure lines throughout) under the influence of the folksong, and in turn influences the folksong thanks to its wide dispersion. The filling of measures grows in diversity in proportion to the literariness of the songs: often the entire song approaches iambs, and even more frequently it tends towards amphibrachs.

The official Haskalah poetics is syllabic. It is in this way that the maskilim write in Hebrew, and so Shloyme Etinger (±1801–1856) writes in Yiddish. Yet all this goes against the strongly tonicized quality of speech. In Hebrew the syllabic pattern (an Italian heritage) persists until the eighties and nineties of the nineteenth century. Patently the *read* language needs above all a meter for the eye. But the spoken language, Yiddish, needs a meter for the ear. Therefore these poets write their poems in Yiddish *tonically*.[44] Subconsciously this is supported by the folksy type of language of these authors. But the Yiddish poems are written to be sung to a melody—hence their syllabic freedom *in contrast to the poetry read by the same poets*, which is mostly German (later also Russian), and entirely t.-s.

Characteristically, Shloyme Etinger, the man of fine literary tastes, could construct complicated stanzas, but he *counted the syllables* in translating, e.g. in his adaptation of Schiller's "Das Lied von der Glocke."[45] And Gotlober, who was influenced by the folk pattern, on the contrary *weighed* the same "Glocke," retaining only its stress count; though he already knew in theory what a t.-s. meter was, he tried it out in some poems but did not use it consistently to the end. To a smaller degree, t.-s. lines and stanzas occur also in the works of other poets,[46] but the melody permits freedom.

Even the works of the most folk-like of the poets are distinguished from folksong, if by no other feature, by the almost constant riming of *all* lines: Berl Broder's stanza is *abab* and not, as in the genuine folksong, *mana*. This criterion permits one to detect in the collections of folksongs individual creations of this period (subsequently their sources may be located or other "literary" features discovered). The rimed lines with unequal numbers of measures of the *badkhonim* (wedding jesters) continue the free line-length of the recitative (of the medieval Hebrew and Yiddish laments and occasional songs). Their verbose, sermonizing type of language often lacks an inner rhythm, and since no rules

[44] No wonder that Avrohom-Ber Gotlober (1811–1899), the first of the profoundly bilingual Jewish poets, was also the first in Eastern Europe to attempt to write a Hebrew poem in t.-s. meter.

[45] Even in translating a free-tonic ballad ("Walheid" by Theodor Körner) he sets himself a uniform syllabic pattern according to one of the stanzas of the original.

[46] Even Yehude-Leyb Gordon (1831–1892), the Hebrew *syllabic* poet who expressed himself against tonic meter, in Yiddish writes only tonic or even purely t.-s. poems. The tendency of other writers to lapse into t.-s. meters may be due to the fact that they *wrote* their poems, that is, in abstracting themselves momentarily from the melody, they needed the inner balance furnished by a t.-s. meter in order to feel the isochronism. Such poems also lack the effects of being digested and transformed by the folk.

are observed, we often have simply rimed prose, carried by the melodic phrasing. The *badkhn* "says" them only at the wedding. His "song" can therefore be separated from the wedding occasion and become a regularly sung piece only if it is pressed into the framework of lines up to four measures and of uniform stanzas, as was done by Eliyokum Tsunzer (Zunser, 1836–1913).[47]

3.3. *The classical period of Yiddish literature.*[48] In the eighties and nineties of the nineteenth century, in Yiddish as well as in Hebrew, poetry *all at once becomes t.-s.* For decades the maskilim had been reading t.-s. poems, but it was a *silent* and *passive* reading: they were not fully at home either in German or in Russian, and did not hear the sound of the poetry in a deeper sense. If they understood it they could not actively absorb the greater poets (even as to subject matter!). Therefore their attempts to approach this read poetry in sound and to write t.-s. poems themselves remained isolated. Only as wider strata of the Jewish intelligentsia joined the general culture the experiencing of Russian literature in an active, creative sense could begin. This led to an upheaval in *all the fundamentals* of Jewish poetry in both languages simultaneously, i.e. it was socio-culturally determined; it was a leap to a new artistic level, in rhythm as well as in other respects.

A contributing factor was the decisive turn from the sung poem to the poem for reading and recitation, which needs substantial isochronal features in place of the melody. But the new doctrine penetrated even the song: Tsunzer, who could do without measures of equal numbers of syllables, nevertheless began to sing t.-s. songs as early as in the 1880's.

There is as yet no individual rhythmic approach to a poem. Even the consciously artistic poetry is in this sense subordinated to internal uniform driving forces which primarily determine the *ear* of the hearer and the creator. And since rhythm is experienced only tonically-syllabically, even Heine is in this period interpreted and adapted in Yiddish in a t.-s. pattern (just as previously the t.-s. poetry of Schiller was reinterpreted syllabically or only tonically). Avrohom Reyzin, Kh. N. Bialik (1873–1934), Sholom Aleichem (1859–1916), Yitskhok Katsenelson (b. 1886; perished at the hands of the Germans in 1944), even the folk singer Mordkhe Gebirtig (b. 1877; perished at the hands of the Germans in 1942), and many others create folksongs which are genuine as to content, but take the form of the trochees of the Russian *častuška*![49]

3.4. *After World War I.* If at the beginning of the twentieth century Jewish poetry was exposed to classical European literature, the upset of the first World War finally cast it into the stream of problems of the contemporary modernistic trends. The previous isolated attempts ceased to be accidental. A new language, new imagery, new subject matter, new rhythms appeared on the scene.

[47] Tsunzer, to be sure, was unable to express a thought in four lines, yet his large stanzas are each composed of several quatrains with folk rimes.

[48] This was, in its beginning, a brief transitional period of scanty artistic value in the poetic field. But it did prepare a mass reader and developed a poetic technique. Tsunzer's poem "Shives-tsien" ('Return to Zion') of 1884 was already in iambs.

[49] This is not restricted to the Yiddish field, of course. Even Goethe understood and adopted the 'Knittelvers' of Hans Sachs in a form different from the source.

With respect to rhythmics there was a sharp reaction against the melodic character of the impressionistically, symbolically colored poem of the beginning of the century (e.g. the *Yunge* 'young ones' in America). This was an expression of the time: even the representatives of the earlier trend opened themselves to free rhythms (Leyvik).[50]

It is interesting to note that upon the first signs of approval from the outside a whole series of poets was aroused to writing in the linguistically immanent rhythms of the folksong (though not according to their external free forms): Moyshe-Leyb Halpern (1886–1932), Itsik Manger (b. 1901), Ber Horovits (b. 1895; perished at the hands of the Germans, 1941), et al. Their poems were not intended to be folkloristic, but close to the folk in their linguistic expression. This stylistic trend was more inherently Jewish than its predecessor and burst into full bloom actually only after true expressionism had ended its seething. But since all these events took place within the span of a single generation, we will consider this trend first as one which is genetically closer to t.-s. metrics. It is notable that true expressionism in Poland in the 1920's, of all trends, did not import from Germany a liberation from the t.-s. meter.[51] The expressionists made their revolution in rhythmics within the old framework, by exploding the symmetric and uniform limits of line and stanza, by giving an extraordinarily dynamic character to the sentence, by developing metric contrasts, and by executing a stirring paeonization of the iambs. Storms rather than melodies were forged from the iambs. Similar to this was the solemnly fervent (in Yiddish: *patetish*) poetry of Ukrainian Yiddish revolutionary lyricism.

While expressionism tore down the uniformity in the number of measures and the round 4-line stanza structure, and the folk-like trend in turn dispensed only with the equality within measures, the specific Yiddish introspective trend (*Inzikhizm*) united in it both these tendencies and created truly modern expressions of free rhythm, differing as the several participating poets differed. These expressions were *created*, i.e. they were not written as free prose, but great attention was paid to constructive devices of the poem other than the meter which shape its specific rhythmic impact. Here much more was accomplished in combatting the inertia of older patterns and in giving greater individual expression to each poem. Yet the general linguistic-rhythmic tone of one writer is palpable in all his work.

[50] The date is clear: In the works of Leyvik, poems of this type first crop up in the book *In keynems land* (written in 1916–20). His "Oyf di fayern" (1916), quoted above, is his only free-rhythmic poem prior to *In keynems land*, but it, too, was meant as t.-s. (see §6). In M. Basin's anthology, *Finf hundert yor yidishe poezye* (New York, 1917), free rhythms do not yet occur. Moyshe-Leyb Halpern's *In Nyu-york* (published 1919) is—despite German free-rhythmic influences—purely t.-s. But his second book, *Di goldene pave* (1924), is almost entirely free-rhythmic.

[51] Out of 270 poems in the expressionistic anthology *Menschheitsdämmerung* by K. Pinthus (Berlin, 1920), 133 are free-rhythmic (free in number of measures, too), but only 31 of them are rimed (figures according to Heusler). On the other hand, the Yiddish *Mefisto* (Lemberg, 1921) by Uri-Tsvi Grinberg (b. 1894) is purely t.-s., but the general rhythm is closely related to the free ones.

The true free rhythms did not prevail in the bulk of Yiddish poetry, although the influence of the new rhythm feeling went far beyond the borders of the free rhythms. Only some poets refrained entirely from t.-s. metrics. The introspectivist Leyeles renewed in Yiddish the severest metric forms (rondeau, villanelle, sonnet ring, etc.). Like his free rhythms, this return to strict forms reflected his reaction to the monotony of the preceding poems which were little differentiated in form,[52] in which the words were blurred in one fluid euphonious gentle tunefulness. Instead, the distinction of the free rhythms was to emphasize the *single word* in its full denotative and connotative meaning while the strictly constructed, non-fluid but architectonic forms make apparent the compressed thought in its construction.

All this makes it clear that the difference between this period and that preceding the t.-s. meters, even where similar forms are involved, consists in the fact that the modern poets and their readers experience and feel the t.-s. order profoundly. The new free rhythms are supported by this perception, basing themselves on the t.-s.-metric inertia, utilizing its proportions as a background, and emphasizing the contrasts and their violation of these patterns.

4. Group One: Free Rhythms with Bound Number of Measures

4.1. The most widespread form of Russian poetry in the second decade of the twentieth century[53] (Akhmatova, Jesenin) was the so-called *pauznik*. This is essentially a triple amphibrachic line with a free anacrusis in which unstressed syllables are occasionally missing.

Type A: Interrupted Trisyllabic Mesh		
	Ikh veys nisht mit velekhe shleser	◡–◡◡–◡◡–◡
	farshlist men a harts fun payn,	◡–◡◡–O◡–
	nor efsher, nor efsher iz beser	◡–◡◡–◡◡–◡
	vos umet iz haynt mayn fraynd.	◡–◡◡–O◡–
	(Arn Kushnirov, 1891–1949)	

('I don't know with what locks / a heart is locked off from anguish, / but perhaps, but perhaps it is better / that sadness is my friend today.') After we have become used to the amphibrachic mesh, where a syllable is missing our metric inertia supplies a pause in its place (or stretches or emphasizes the existing syllables, depending on the content and the concrete syntactic construction; schematically we represent this by O) in order to preserve the accustomed time interval from stress to stress. The syllabic pauses occur unpredictably, without a set order; this yields a pleasant variation, making it possible to avoid a stirring anapestic ardent flow, separating words for the purpose of emphasizing

[52] Critics who are astonished at such inconsistency on the part of a poet should realize that his rhythmic innovations are reactions to a previous *prevalent rhythm*, not to metrics. The meter is a mere scheme and may in various periods serve various ends, while the rhythm of a poem is the linguistic expression of a particular life rhythm. Consequently the New York free-rhythm patterns of Leyeles are akin to M. Kulbak's big-city rhythms of Berlin.

[53] According to Vladimir A. Pjast: *Sovremennoje stikhovedenije* (Leningrad, 1931), it was no less widespread than the 4-iamb line even in the nineteenth century.

them, interrupting the breathing and creating a mood. The characteristic *emotional*-lyric tone may be varicolored, according to the place and number of interruptions, and is sensed even when there are accretive syllables:[54]

Type B: Augmented Trisyllabic Mesh

Type B: Augmented Trisyllabic Mesh	*Vemen betn, tsu vemen zikh vendn*	◡◡–◡ ◡ –◡◡–◡
	in heymlekhkeyt fun tsimern shtile—	O◡–◡◡|◡–◡◡–◡
	harts aza farshayts un nisht shtendiks	O O–◡◡ ◡–◡◡–◡
	hot haynt farbenkt zikh nokh friling.	O◡–O ◡ –◡◡–◡
	(Kushnirov, 1922)	

('Whom to ask, to whom to turn / in the privacy of quiet rooms— / [my] heart so wanton and inconstant / has today been seized by a longing for spring.')

The preserved amphibrachic mesh clings to the reader and forces him to fit the "abnormal" places into the pattern by speeding up the breathing or by interrupting it according to the will of the writer, i.e. in a way that resembles the writer's breath fluctuations during the composition of the poem. The word *harts* is emphasized both because it occupies a place equivalent to three syllables in the first line and because an interruption is necessary after it in order to pass on to the unstressed trisyllabic sequence without violating the metric feeling; but no less significant rhythmically is the lack of an article or adjective, which elevates the noun to a generic symbol.[55] It was this prominence of the word *harts* in the feeling of the poet which created the rhythmic devices, and they now work back on the reader in leading him to reproduce in his feeling the original structuring of the poet's experience.

The interruptions are not always functional, bound to the concrete word. Their purpose is to create the general atmosphere of the poem. In type B they are intended to give a definite hint that one cannot float along the line like a wave. The several syllabic accretions accustom us to separating every colon as a unit of rhythm and content, in contrast to the mesh of measures on which the new image is weaved. The differences in the lengths and endings of the colon are thus sensed more vividly and create a lively rhythmic shading (cf., for instance, the effect of the dactylic *in heymlekhkeyt*.)[56]

4.2. In Yiddish poetry, this form is rather rare even among the writers of Russia, with the exception of Kushnirov. But in Hebrew it is widespread (among poets influenced by the same Russian poetry, such as N. Alterman [b. 1900], Raḥel [1890–1931], I. Bat-Miryam [b. 1901], and others). Although in the tonic patterns of the Bible the number of syllables was quite free, modern Hebrew offered no direct stimulus for such freedom (within a

[54] In which case it is called in Russian *udarnik* (*udarenije*—'stress')—unjustly so, I think, because it is not just the number of stresses that is decisive in it, but also the fixed syllabic mesh which is deviated from.

[55] August Closs: *Die freien Rhythmen in der deutschen Lyrik* (Berne, 1947), writes (p. 85): "... We would like here to point again at the nouns without articles, by which the word gains force and personification ... "

[56] Incidentally, similarity rather than identity is characteristic not only of meter, but also of the assonant rime. In other words, the entire feeling of writer and reader has become freer; there is a tendency to contrasts and tensions even in the most elementary structural principles. (Note the sentence suspense in the last two lines.)

fixed number of measures); the Yiddish ear, on the other hand, experienced the liberating effect of the living folksong.[57] Without the latter it would have been most difficult to abandon the t.-s. feeling without lapsing altogether into prose. Let us compare the former cases with a stanza by Itsik Manger:

Type C. Length of Measure Free Within Limits		
	Yankev ovinu zitst alt un mid	—◡◡—◡◡— ◡—
	oyf der grozbank farnakht.	—◡ —◡◡—
	Er filt di beyner tuen im vey	◡— ◡—◡ —◡◡—
	nisht far keyn shum yid gedakht.	◡◡— ◡— ◡—

('Jacob our Patriarch sits old and tired / on the bench of grass in the evening. / He feels his bones aching, / may all Jews be spared [such pain].') Manger is not beyond producing iambs and sonnets, too, but in *Medresh Itsik* (Paris, 1951 = *Khumesh-lider*, 1935) he strives to stay quite close to the folk feeling, to persuade the folk of the naive truths of his characters. All poems in that book are composed in the symmetric folk stanza *mana*[58] (see §2.2).[59] The freedom within the measures attempts to avoid any order and keeps us from becoming accustomed to one mesh. But since there is no isochronal melody, Manger keeps within the limits of *two unstressed syllables per measure, at a maximum.*[60] The whole construction of the stanza forces us into an isochronal perception of measures without making us feel all *syllables* as equal time units (as in the ordered sample of §4.1); that is, our reading is less forced, the syllables being of various durations, as in direct narration.[61]

[57] In Hebrew it was only a Jewish folk-like "Diaspora" subject matter which occasionally brought with it a comparable freedom (e.g. David Šim'oni [b. 1884] in poems of the catastrophe; in a somewhat different manner, U.-Ts. Grinberg—poets not influenced by the above-mentioned Russian moderns).

[58] The sole exception—the couplet-rimed "Lid funem loyfer" (*aa bb* . . .)—does not belong to the period described, but is an intrusion from the *present* time (hence mostly trochaic). Manger is aware of how strangely a fully rimed *abab* pattern strikes the folk ear.

[59] The even lines mostly have three stresses each and are in lively alternation with 4-measured odd ones. But with all this freedom, the observance of inner laws is characteristic. The rime is (with a few exceptions in the *megile* poems) *masculine*, even though in Yiddish the feminine rime is easier, and firmly terminates the stanza (a function formerly served by the melody). In one group of poems (on Hagar) all lines are 3-measured, but then the first and third lines never have masculine terminations. This interdiction seems on one hand to be due to the alternation with the masculine even lines and on the other to be a vestige of the folksong of the same type, where the unstressed last syllable bore the fourth stress of the melody. (In German folksong, too, the masculine 3-measure line—the *k*-type, according to Heusler—does not occur in the odd lines.) Cf. §2.5.

[60] So too in Manger's book *Briv fun Velvl Zbarzher tsu Malkele di sheyne* (1937). Although Zbarzher, the real-life poet who is the prototype of these poems, was close to such a limitation (which governed the love lyrics of folksong), he often failed to sustain it because his hearing lacked a t.-s. orientation. Manger has it, hence his quantitatively limited freedom. Though a melody is absent, he *essentially* transmits the same folk rhythm. On the contrary, an excess of unstressed syllables would disturb the perception of the fixed number of stresses in the line, i.e. the similarity of the lines (except for their syntactic parallelism) and the poem's rhythm as a whole would be obscured.

[61] The nearly rigid order in type A causes every disturbance to produce a dramatic tension between itself and the meter. Here in type C the deviations are not perceived as

The framework of the same 4-measure line puts into prominence various thematically conditioned manners of feeling the rhythm. For example, the quietly lyrical poems are very close to iambs, being interrupted only occasionally by an extra syllable, in a way resembling Heine's love lyricism.[62] It is unlike the interrupted anapest of type A, because there the missed syllable is filled by a syllabic pause, while here, on the contrary, the normal flow is disturbed by an extra "burdening." Thus a seemingly prosaic character and a simplicity is created in the lyrical, somewhat *excited* mood.

Against this background the stark contrast of Manger's "Avishags troyer" is apparent. This poem exceeds the bounds of the book by its long heavy lines as well as by its measures of more than three syllables, the antisymmetric contrast between sentence and line, the enjambement, and the sharp line cuts which not only obliterate, in a free reading, the last symmetric basis of the poem—the equal lines—but even blur the rime.

Here, by way of background, is a stanza from the poem "Avishag," which is in keeping with the rest of the book (though more markedly iambic):

Zĭ lēygt tsvĕy fīngĕr tsū tsŭm mōyl
ŭn fāyft dĭ shōf tsŭnōyf;
tsāyt ăhēym, văyl mōrgn̆ făr tōg
fōrt zĭ ĭn mēylĕkhs hōyf.

('She puts two fingers to her mouth / and whistling, gathers her sheep; / time to go home, for tomorrow before dawn / she is going to the king's court.')

And now an excerpt from the very different "Avishag's troyer":

Ăz lĕkōvĕd īm dĭ gōldĕnĕ ōyrĭnglĕkh
ĭn māynĕ ōyĕrn̆. / Ŭn dŏs gĕblīml̆tĕ shābĕs-klĕyd
vŏs kh'trōg ĭn dĕr vōkhn̆. / Ŭn dŏs rēytlĕn zĭkh
fŭn ālĕ măynĕ rōyzn̆ ŏyf dĕr bēyt.

('. . . that in his honor [are] the golden earrings / in my ears. And the flowery Sabbath dress / which I wear on weekdays. And the blushing / of all my roses in the flowerbed.')

4.3. Two paths lead from the last example. One of them permits full syllabic freedom in a fixed number of measures:

Type D: Syllabically Free 4-Measure Line

S'ĭz ēmĕs, ĭkh bīn tăkĕ vāyt fŭn dīr
Nŏr dāynĕ tsērtlĕkhkăytn̆ / ĭn dĭ brīv tsŭ mĭr
Dĕrmōnĕn ŏn gāntsĕ tshātĕs mĭt zūmĕr-fĕygl̆
Vŏs zūkhn̆ blūmĕn-hŏnĭk tsvīshn̆ krōpĕvĕ.
(Moyshe-Leyb Halpern)[63]

"disturbances" because no such order is present. No sooner do we get accustomed to the trisyllabic pattern than we lapse into disyllabics, and so on. There is thus no tension but an easygoing flow.

[62] Thus in the poems "Khaves viglid," "Neomi zogt 'Got fun Avrom,' " "Neomi geyt shlofn," the Avishag poems.

[63] Moyshe-Leyb Halpern: *Di goldene pave*, p. 69. Our tendency to feel the lines as equal makes possible the accumulation of unstressed syllables. A secondary stress disturbs us because it would raise the normal number of stresses.

('It is true, I am indeed far from you / but your tendernesses in your letters to me / recall whole hosts of butterflies / seeking flower nectar among nettles.') This pattern avoids the frequent oscillation between iambic and anapestic lines. (Manger does the same, though as a rule not consistently over a whole stanza.)

The other path (type E) breaks open the symmetric folk stanza. Only the equal number of measures in all lines remains to transmit a connected feeling. But the sentences overflow the line boundaries, and what is most important, the lines are not symmetrically paired. In the last example the riming in the stanza interior was already blurred, as it were.[64] Moyshe-Leyb Halpern does this even more effectively in his favorite 5-line stanza *manao*,[65] and continues this later on in blank-verse or freely rimed stanzaless poems which are based only on an equal number of measures per line, i.e. on freedom within the fixed folk *verse* but without the perfection of the symmetric folk *stanza*.

Needless to say, as the freedom of structure increases, so does the number of variant types and of combined types, while the effect of each grows less specific, since it is the *type* that makes the impression.

Thus the folksong, with its overall natural rhythm feeling, having influenced first the stanza structure (in t.-s. metrics) and then the general rhythm configuration (within the limits imposed by the abandonment of melody, as in Manger), now inspires a form of poetry which keeps only the verse structure, with all its freedom, while violating the stanza pattern. Finally, folksong stimulates a type based on intra-measure freedom alone, abandoning the fixed number of measures altogether (see chapter 7).

5. Specificness of the Yiddish Language as a Rhythm Factor

5.1. Even from a formal point of view, there is one type of Yiddish folksong which is unknown in German. To Heusler's four cadence types we must add, for Yiddish, the 4-measure line with a dactylic ending (*ĭkh hōb mĭkh fărlībt* | *īn ă shĕyn yīngĕlĕ* 'I fell in love with a handsome boy'), which is so characteristic of the Russian song. Recalling also the rhythmic specifiness of the dactyls in the interior of the verse (see §2.4, a and b), let us state immediately that the dactyl or hyperdactyl (— ◡◡◡) permit the voice to sweep over the beat and allow an arc of unstressed syllables (as in the example of type D, or in the Russian *bylina*).

The Slavic influence on Yiddish poetry *from above* was a late one (coinciding with the adoption of t.-s. metrics), but *from the inside* the strong effect began

[64] The rhythmic value of rime is most significant. Even a 4-line stanza sounds quite different—not "like a poem" at all, even though the lines be short—if the rimes are not on the folksong pattern. When Ber Horovits (*Fun mayn heym in di berg*, vol. 1, Vilna, 1929, p. 41) writes: *Bay nakht farmakh ikh di oygn / oyf mayn shlof-geleger, / flaterndik, royshndik kumen / malokhim fun himl gefloygn* ('At night I close my eyes / in my bed, / flutteringly, noisily there come / angels flying from heaven'), he makes 3-measure lines riming *amna*. While his patterns vary, Horovits is in general closer to the folk narrative and to the overall spirit of folklore than to the folksong.

[65] Only the second and fourth lines rime. This is, in fact, a folksong stanza with an accretive line. The rime has an almost unnoticed effect, like that of internal rimes.

much earlier, in my opinion, particularly in the non-artificial folksong. The formal framework obstinately remained old Germanic (see §2.3), i.e. purely tonic, but the distance from one stress to the other increased in Yiddish as a result of the widening phrasal wave under the influence of the Slavic environment.

The average interval between stresses in present-day Russian is 2.8 syllables,[66] and was even greater in Old Russian (according to Štokmar, 4.0, or at least 3.8); it is also greater in Ukrainian, by which Yiddish was considerably influenced, while in German this interval is far smaller (closer to 2 than to 3). In Yiddish the phrasing patterns have in this respect come under the complete sway of Slavic. While there is no exact research on this point and the proof must be left to the linguists, I do want to point out several phenomena which have accompanied this development in Yiddish and discuss their reflection in poetry.

5.2. Since the number of stresses per line in the folksong did not change, the number of syllables can serve as evidence of the said broadening of the phrasing pattern. Within Yiddish proper the change is clear. In the *Bovo-bukh* (1508), we have nearly iambic lines; in the epic *Vints-Hans-lid* (1616?)—despite the complete freedom of measure length, up to five syllables—the average is still only 2.5 syllables per stress (see footnote 43). In the more recent narrative Yiddish folksong, on the other hand, the average exceeds three syllables[67] with a definite tendency toward the paeonic. The German folksong, like the older Yiddish, tends to the prevalence of iambs, i.e. it contains fewer syllables per stress.[68]

[66] See Štokmar, *op. cit.*, part 3, chap. 1. He observes that in order to change this average (his term is *koefitsjent slogoudarnosti*, i.e. 'coefficient of syllabic accentuality') by as much as 0.1, a distinct change of vocabulary is necessary. In Russian syllabic poetry the average was still as high as 3.2.

[67] Exact research is still lacking. Moreover, the classification problem is difficult, because lyrical love songs even as episodes in the ballad-like songs display a much lower average (as is clear from §2.4). In Cahan's collection (vol. 1), the section "Ballad-like Songs" yields the following ratios: no. 1—on the average 3.0 syllables per stress; no. 15—3.5; no. 8 (in the characteristic narrative style: *a motiv, mentshn, vel ikh aykh zingen* 'Folks, I will sing you an air')—3.7. In the long song no. 16, the first four stanzas (a dialogue) have 2.7; the last four (a lyrical love song) have 2.6, but even there the typical narrative stanza *Azoy vi Leybele iz in shtub arayn gekumen* ('As soon as L. entered his house') rises to a ratio of 3.5!

[68] Comparing a German free-tonic song with a Yiddish transformation of it (one in a related style, at that), we find:

Es war einmal ein junger Knabe ◡–◡–◡ –◡–◡
der liebt sein SCHÄTZLEIN *sieben Jahr,* ◡–◡–◡ –◡–
und als der Knab in die Fremde kam, ◡–◡–◡◡–◡–
da ward ihm sein Schätzlein krank. –◡–◡ –◡–

('There was once a young lad, / he loved his sweetheart for seven years, / and when the lad left home, / his sweetheart became sick.')

Ikh hob gelibt a MEYDELE *fun akhtsn yor,* ◡–◡◡◡–◡◡◡–◡ –
gelibt hob ikh ir a dray-fir yor. ◡–◡◡ – ◡–◡ –
Ikh hob gevolt visn tsi zi hot mir lib, ◡–◡◡ –◡ ◡–◡◡–
bin ikh AVEKGEFORN *fun ir shtub.* ◡–◡–◡–◡ –◡ –
Vi der yunger KNABE *iz opgeforn* ◡◡–◡–◡◡◡–◡–◡
azoy iz di gelibte krank gevorn. ◡–◡◡◡–◡–◡–◡

Thus modern Yiddish makes possible greater rhythmic diversity by means of alternating the number of syllables in a given number of measures. The same is true of modern free rhythms: in English they display a strong bent for the iambic, while in Yiddish the number of syllables per measure ranges quite widely, as we will show below, and in a text which is normally "prosaic" it is, on the average, amphibrachic, with many paeonic leaps.

This length of the phrasing contour in the Yiddish sentence is created by means of (or, as I prefer to see it, this tendency in the spoken language has supported) the following phenomena:

a. Yiddish has a multiplicity of long words, particularly with dactylic and hyperdactylic terminations. (1) In the folksong, we are struck by the frequency of the dactylic diminutive with the disyllabic suffix (*yīng-ĕlĕ* 'boy', *ālt-ĭtshk-ĕ* 'old', *yūng-ĭnk-ĕ* 'young'—all diminutives), which generally exceeds the modern German equivalent by a syllable.[69] (2) There are markedly longer suffixes and prefixes, which have also spread to bases of Slavic origin (with the stress usually falling on the prefix): *bă-rēd*-ĔVDĬK-Ĕ 'talkative', *glīvĕr*-DĬK-Ĕ 'jelly-like', *lāykht-ń*-DĬK-Ĕ 'shining' (cf. German *lēuchtĕndĕ*), *shtēyn*-ĔR-ĬK-Ĕ 'stony', *trōyĕr-ĭk-ĕ* 'mournful' (cf. German *trāurĭgĕ*), TSŬNŌYF-*lĕyg-ń* 'to put together', *ōp-lĕy*KĔN-ĔN 'to deny (perfective)', *pārmĕt*-ĔN-Ĕ 'of parchment', *āndĕr-ĕr* '(the) other', *kŭtshĕr*-ŌVĔ 'curly', *kŭdlĕ*-VĀTĔ 'shaggy', etc.

b. Yiddish does not have the German requirement of a secondary stress on the syllable of a long word second from the one bearing the primary stress; at least such secondary stresses are much weaker in Yiddish and are therefore not necessary in poetry. Even when the primary stress is on the prefix of a long word, the root does not receive a stress. Witness the folksong passages: *dŭ hōst mĭr dŏkh* TSŪGĔZŎGT *brīvĕlĕkh tsŭ shrāybń* 'you have promised me, after all, to write letters', *rōzhĭnkĕs mĭt māndlĕn* 'raisins and almonds', *bīn ĭkh* ĂVĒKGĔ-FŎRŃ *fūn ĭr shtūb* 'so I left her house'.[70]

('I loved a girl of eighteen, / I loved her for three or four years. / I wanted to know if she loved me, / So I left her house. / As soon as the young fellow left, / His beloved fell ill.' According to Alfred Landau: [Notes on Yiddish Folklore], *Filologishe shriftn [fun Yivo]* 1 [1926] 13–22, pp. 18f.) In the German text the syllable-stress ratio is 2.1, while in the Yiddish text, which has a 2.7 ratio, the many-syllabled measures are prominent. The difference may be symbolized by the passage from a disyllabic *Schätzlein* to a trisyllabic *meydele*.

[69] On the German dialectal basis of some Yiddish diminutives, see Alfred Landau: [The Diminutive in Galician Yiddish], *Yivo-bleter* 11 (1937) 155–172. But there remain the questions whether in German the suffixes were not stressed, and why it was precisely the disyllabic diminutive suffixes which were accepted in Eastern Yiddish. From the standpoint of rhythmic effect, it is sufficient to compare the Yiddish with the later German folksong.

[70] To be sure, in riming position the stress sometimes continues to fall on the root of the complemented verb (a heritage from German?): *vĭ ăzōy vĕl ĭkh ĕs kĕnĕn ībĕrshtēyn* 'how will I be able to bear it' rimes with *shteyn;* occasionally the proper primary stress is completely overshadowed by the prominence of the riming ("secondary") stress: *ŏnklīn-gĕn* 'to ring the bell' (instead of *ōnklĭngĕn*) riming with *zīngĕn*, dial. *ŏyskīmĕn* (rather than *ōyskĭmĕn*) riming with *shvīmĕn*. But diminutives remain dactylic even in riming position

c. The same law is manifested in the sentence in collocations of "small words" and in idioms: *kĕn ĭkh nĭt* 'and so I can't', *vĭl ĭkh nĭt* 'and so I don't want to', *vĭfl ĭz dĕr zēygĕr* 'what time is it' (paeonic arc without a stress on *iz*).

d. There are additional minor phenomena, such as the lack of the German-type preterite for expressing the past tense. Instead Yiddish has only the compound tense (frequent in narrative folksong) with a single stress in the participle. Cf. the German *ĕr gīng wēg* with Y. *ĕr ĭz* AVĕ*kgĕgăngĕn*, which has an extended prefix to boot. (In everyday German speech, the equivalent perfect participle would have two stresses corresponding to the single stress of Yiddish, despite the greater number of syllables.)

5.3. With expressionism, as we noted, a new manner of feeling rhythm was brought into Yiddish poetry. It was a new feeling for the language as well. Leyb Naydus (1890–1918) could still rime *bŭrshtīn* ('amber') with the 4-iamb line *dĕm klēnstň bānd fŭn kēnĭgīn* ('the smallest ribbon of the queen'; in "Dos lid fun shklaf," *Lirik*, Warsaw, 1926, p. 118). But modernistic Yiddish poetry does not tolerate a secondary stress in a dactylic ending (*kēnĭgĭn*), and this type of rime is interdicted. More than that, expressionism has introduced, along with the wide use of long and composite words with single stresses in their paeonized iambs[71] *many new enclitic combinations* as well.[72] On the whole the long words and in general the rhythm of broadly spaced stresses (which are consequently all the stronger) produce a large-breathed fervor in the paeonized *metric* framework of Yiddish expressionism,[73] but in its *free* rhythms they make for momen-

---

(see §5.1); so also enclitic combinations at the end of unrimed lines: *ŭn hāynt bĭn ĭkh* BĂRĒDT GĔVŎRŇ / *dūrkh ă fălshň yīngĕlĕ* ('Today I was slandered / by a faithless lad'—Cahan A 196); also *vestu flien in der vāyt ăhĭn* 'you will fly there, into the distance') in a song in which every remaining odd line terminates in a dactylic word (Rubin, *op. cit.*, p. 28).

[71] The paeon in general becomes a favorite in this period. For example, Gebirtig's folklike song (melodically supported): *shlōf zhĕ mĭr shŏyn, Yānkĕlĕ măyn shēynĕr, / dĭ ēygĕlĕkh dĭ shvārtsĭnkĕ măkh tsū*... ('Go to sleep now, my handsome Yankele, / close your dear black little eyes'; *Mayne lider*, Cracow, 1936, p. 21). The long words, even in iambic poems, are so spaced that only every other iamb is a pyrrhic, resulting in overall paeons.

[72] By inversions of former proclitic combinations, as in a poem by Perets Markish (b. 1895; disappeared without trace in the Soviet Union after 1948) in his book *Nakhtroyb* (1922): *Ŭn klāngĕn brēklĕn zĭkh* FŬN TĀYKHŇ ŎYS / *ŭn vīntlĕkh ĭn* ĔK-VĒLT MĬT ZĔY *nŏkh ŏvňtĭkň tŏy gĕyĕn* (riming with *fărtsŏygň!*) 'and sounds crumble out of rivers / and breezes go with them after dew to the end of the world'; KŪMĔN ZĔY FŬN ĀLĔ ZĀYTŇ TŌG *ĭn ēynĕm* SHTĪL ŎN (: *Dlīlĕn*) 'they arrive quietly together from all ends of the day'; *kh'zŏl ărŏys-shtĕkň* DĔM TSŪNG ZĬKH; *ăz frāy zŏl ă shtŏybĭkĕ* SHVĒL ZĀYN (: *rēlsň*) 'that I may stick out my tongue at myself, that a dusty doorstep may be free'. Incidentally, an inversion of this sort brackets the whole end of the sentence in one single-breathed expression. As Moyshe Nadir (1885–1943) put it: *azelkhe brēytĕ ĭkh-vĕl-ăykh-nĭsht-lŏzň-khăpň-dĕm-ōtĕmdĭkĕ līdĕr!* ('such broad I-won't-let-you-catch-your-breath poems!'), and as Der Nister (b. 1884; disappeared without a trace in Soviet Union after 1948) wrote even in prose: *A mayse mit eynem, vos hot grŏysĕ ōygň gĕhăt* ('A story of one who had big eyes').

[73] To put it more exactly, only the solemn fervor of the content prevents paeons from decomposing into iambs or trochees, while the lack of a constant iambic mesh in the free rhythms permits large unstressed ("paeonic" and "pentonic") arcs.

tum, agitation, dynamism (Leyvik, Leyeles, and others), and not necessarily solemn fervor.

5.4. A study of the vocabulary of the poetry of Milton, Pope, Tennyson, and other English poets[74] shows 17 percent disyllabic words and 80 percent monosyllables, i.e. only 3 percent trisyllables and longer words. In Yiddish the percentage of long words is incomparably greater;[75] the proportion of 4- and 5-syllable words in the total number of syllables is particularly great, although the precise calculations are still lacking.

Clearly the number of long words is not in itself decisive for the rhythm. In analyzing one of the most solemnly stirring passages in the German expressionist anthology *Menschendämmerung* (see footnote 51), I found 27 percent "long" words, but an average of only 2.9 syllables per stress.[76] On the contrary, in the beginning of H. Leyvik's "Der volf" (p. 180) we have an average of 3.9 (!) syllables per stress,[77] though the "long" words constitute no more than 13 percent. Of even greater importance to the free rhythms is the intricate combination of lines whose stresses are broadly spaced with other kinds of lines.

A big role in the rhythmic impact is also played by the character of word composition. In "Di bobeshi oleho-hasholem iz oysgegangen" (see footnote 75) by Moyshe Kulbak (b. 1896; perished in a Soviet concentration camp in the 1940's), in the works of Gebirtig, and in folksongs of a similar type, the paeonicity is "smooth" because all cola are constructed in the same manner. In other poems, however, long words create great tensions thanks to the contrast with preceding lines or with the surrounding types of word composition. In Yiddish poetry significance is attached to the opposition between *descending* long words and *ascending* word collocations. These are, incidentally, usually proclitic in

[74] See B. R. Lewis, *op. cit.*, p. 301.

[75] In M. Kulbak's folk-like *Ăz dĭ bōbĕshĭ dĭ āltĭtshkĕ ĭz ōysgĕgăngĕn* ('When dear old grandmother passed away,' "Raysn," *Ale verk*, vol. 2, Vilna, 1929 p. 49), the words of three and more syllables constitute 21 percent (of which 68 percent in turn have dactylic and hyperdactylic terminations). In his poem "Vilne" (1926), the corresponding proportion is 13 percent (of which 53 percent have dactylic and 22 hyperdactylic terminations, mostly as a result of descriptive adjectives). This, together with the many compounds, prevents us from feeling that the poem is written iambically; for this reason, too, the number of iambs per line is not fixed. But a solemn fervor is avoided because it is not necessarily every second iamb that is stressed. Here the percentage of long words is normal. For examples of much higher percentages, see the illustrations of chapter 6. In Leyvik's linguistically "normal" poem, "Der volf," the long words also amount to 13 percent.

[76] J. Becher: "Klage und Frage" (the beginning); *Jāgdgrŭndĕ* was counted as single-stressed. Many sample tests in the book give, at best, the same results. Karl Otten favors long compounds like *Blütenfrühlingspracht*, *Wandervogelschwärm*, but since they contain many bases, it is hard to avoid secondary stresses, even relatively weak ones. In Yiddish, on the other hand, one-base words of up to five syllables are frequent, e.g. the plural adjectives *ōpgĕrĭsĕnĕ* 'torn off', *bărēdĕvdĭkĕ* 'talkative', *ōysgĕlĕydĭktĕ* 'emptied', *fărăyōrĭkĕ* 'last year's', and even *shtērñgŏld* 'star gold', *vēltñnăkht* 'night of worlds' (U.-Ts. Grinberg), *āltshvărtsĕr* 'old-black' (Kulbak), *līkht-gĕbŏyrĕnĕ* '(of) light born', *vēlt-fărshtăndĭkĕ* 'world-understanding', *shvĕr-ōtĕmdĭkĕr* 'heavy-breathed' (Leyeles)—all read as single-stressed.

[77] Or, at a minimum, 3.5. See also the figures on the epic folksong (footnote 67) and on the following illustrations.

Yiddish; the broad distance between stresses has apparently been adopted from East Slavic like the penchant for dactylic word types, but the Old Slavic tendency to enclitic combinations (*nē ză čtŏ, nē bўlŏ*) has not been emulated; cf. Y. *nĭshtŏ făr vōs* 'not at all' (rejoinder to 'thank you'), *nĭsht gĕvēn* '(has) not been' (see also Štokmar, *op. cit.*). Yet the Yiddish modernists, particularly those of the Russian sphere, have for purposes of variation formed new enclitic combinations. If, for example, a dactylic word is followed by an anapestic proclitic formation, a polysyllabic curve is formed; even the simplest case, like *ōpgĕbrĕnt măynĕ līpň* 'burned my lips', is already a "penton" (5-syllable measure) if it is metrically sustained.[78] The opposite leads to a sudden clash of two strong centerlike stresses, each carrying many unstressed syllables: *ĭn dăyn hāldz āynshtshĕmĕn zĭkh* 'to claw your throat' almost demands a dash between the two stresses and the descent following the clash is also highly effective.

5.5. Because of linguistic its specificness, certain important findings of the general science of rhythm are inapplicable to Yiddish. Jünger[79] finds that the maximum length in excess of which it is difficult to retain a line as an organized verse is six measures and 17 syllables. And this is understandable: in German it is nearly impossible to have a syllable-to-stress ratio in excess of 3. In Yiddish, however, there are much longer lines which hold up well and are not even split into two parts by a fixed caesura. Consider, for instance, the 22-syllable line, *ŭn mĭt ūntĕrgĕbrŏkhĕnĕ knī zĭkh tsūgĕshlĕpt tsŭ dĭ trēp fŭnĕm ŏrň-kōydĕsh* ('and with collapsed knees pulled [him]self to the steps of the [synagogal] ark'; Leyvik, "Der volf," p. 180), which contains five measures (i.e. a syllable-stress ratio of 4.4!) in an environment of mostly long, 4-measure lines. Such a verse is possible because it is the number of stresses that is decisive, not the number of syllables. The resulting possibility of forming especially long lines without transgressing the limitation on the number of stresses endows Yiddish with a definite advantage from the point of view of rhythmic impact. More broadly streaming than hexameter are these lines from Leyvik's "Ferzn" (p. 144):

Mit an oysgeshtrektn kop tsum himl heyb ikh zikh aroys fun unter dem bafalndikn vorem,
treysl op fun zikh dem reyekh fun di ongeklepte shtiker royen leym,
un hekher fun mayn kop ariber shtrekt zikh tsu der heykh mayn vayser orem,
un shpreyt zayn vayse likhtikayt oyf mentsh un khaye, groz un boym.

('With head stretched to the sky I lift myself from under the attacking worm, / shake off the odor of the glued-on chunks of clay, / and above my head my white arm stretches upward, / and spreads its white brightness over man and

[78] Heusler, *op. cit.*, §1081, cites a hexasyllabic measure from Klopstock: *schīmmĕrtĕ dĭe brāut! sānftĕn tōn, fēstlĭchĕ mĕlŏdīen, / frēudĭgĕrĕs gĕfūhl, strōmtĕt īhr, dōnnĕrĕr ĭn dĕm gĕrīcht* (stress marks mine). But the great distance between stresses is achieved because they stand at opposite ends of the dipodal colon; hence the movement has to be interrupted at the clash of the stresses. The line decomposes into three independent, detached groups. And indeed the syllable-stress ratio is only 2.5. But in Yiddish the flow can continue throughout; see Streaming Rhythm, §6.6.

[79] Friedrich Georg Jünger: *Rhythmus und Sprache im deutschen Gedicht*, Stuttgart, 1952.

beast, grass and tree.') In the first line, there are as many as 26 syllables. Yet it holds together; and the rime, too, which demands that it be reached, forces one to read the line in one breath.

Heusler and Jünger both believe that the length of one colon is restricted to a maximum of six syllables. (Both accept the monopodic character of rhythm.) But in Yiddish, the long words make possible the existence of longer monopodic cola: *ĕr ĭz ībĕrgĕblĭbn̆* 'he remained', *ĭn ăn ōysgĕhărgĕtĕr* 'in a slaughtered . . . . ', *mĭt ă tsŭnōyfgĕprĕstn̆* 'with a clenched. . . ', etc.; these are especially perceptible in long lines. We must conclude that this restriction, too, is not all-human, but linguistically conditioned. In this respect, Yiddish has definitely left the Germanic sphere behind it.

6. Group Two: Free Dynamic Rhythms

6.1. This group includes poems (a) whose rhythmic impact is unlike that of normal spoken language, but (b) which have no predetermined ordering device. It does not follow that they contain no such devices at all; quite the contrary, their effect is ordinarily rather strong. But we do not know in advance when they will appear and how long they will last. Hence their integral interaction. Sentence and period structure, length of lines, internal rimes, word collocations and repetitions, extraordinary aggregations of syllables in a measure, metrically similar groups, parallelism or contrast of devices of the same type or of different types—all these together produce the rhythm. We cannot in the available space analyze all these principles and the relations between them. There are as many peculiarities as there are genuine poems, but the general character of the poet is quite prominent in each of them. We will analyze examples from the works of several specific poets with only an outline of a commentary.

6.2. Here is an episode from A. Leyeles' "In sobvey, II," and three lines that precede it (*Rondos un andere lider*, p. 43; the figures indicate the syllable-to-stress ratio):

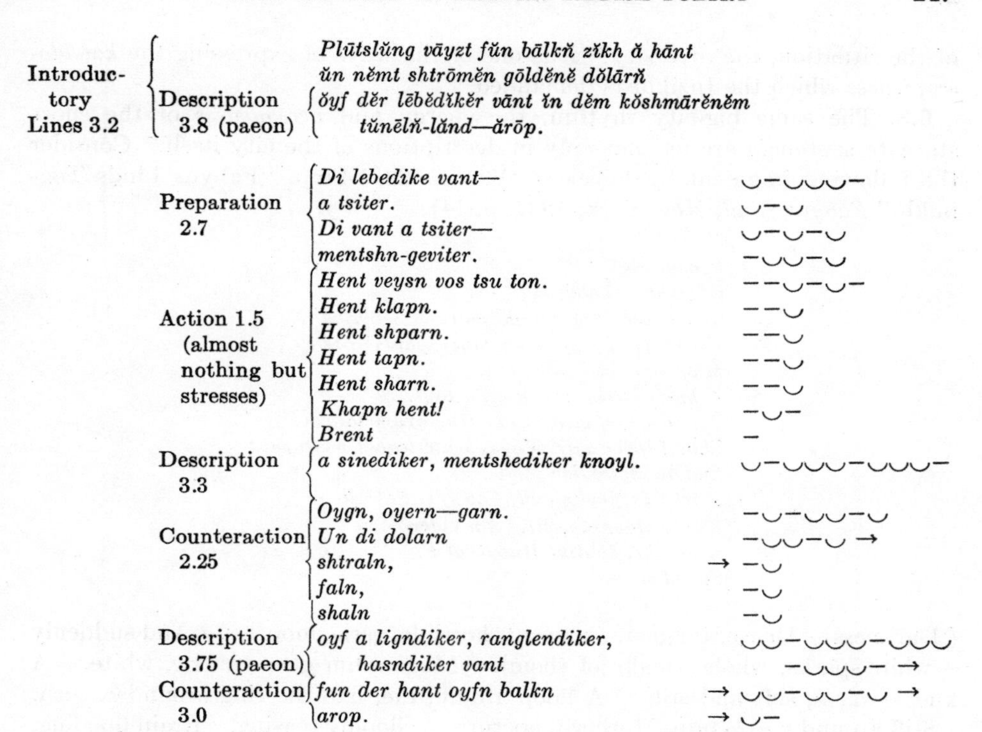

Section	Line	Meter
Introductory Lines 3.2	*Plŭtslŭng văyzt fŭn bālkn̆ zĭkh ă hănt*	
	ŭn nĕmt shtrōmĕn gōldĕnĕ dŏlārn̆	
Description 3.8 (paeon)	*ŏyf dĕr lēbĕdĭkĕr vănt ĭn dĕm kŏshmārĕnĕm*	
	tŭnēln̆-lănd—ărōp.	
Preparation 2.7	*Di lebedike vant—*	∪–∪∪∪–
	a tsiter.	∪–∪
	Di vant a tsiter—	∪–∪–∪
	mentshn-geviter.	–∪∪–∪
Action 1.5 (almost nothing but stresses)	*Hent veysn vos tsu ton.*	––∪–∪–
	Hent klapn.	––∪
	Hent shparn.	––∪
	Hent tapn.	––∪
	Hent sharn.	––∪
	Khapn hent!	–∪–
	Brent	–
Description 3.3	*a sinediker, mentshediker knoyl.*	∪–∪∪∪–∪∪∪–
Counteraction 2.25	*Oygn, oyern—garn.*	–∪–∪∪–∪
	Un di dolarn	–∪∪–∪ →
	shtraln,	→ –∪
	faln,	–∪
	shaln	–∪
Description 3.75 (paeon)	*oyf a ligndiker, ranglendiker,*	∪∪–∪∪∪–∪∪∪
	hasndiker vant	–∪∪∪– →
Counteraction 3.0	*fun der hant oyfn balkn*	→ ∪∪–∪∪–∪ →
	arop.	→ ∪–

('Suddenly there appears from the ceiling a hand / and [it] begins to pour a stream of golden dollars / downward onto the live wall in the nightmarish tunnel land. / The live wall— / a shiver. / The wall a shiver— / human storm. / Hands know what to do. / Hands knock. / Hands push. / Hands grope. / Hands scoop. / Hands snatch! / There burns / a malicious, human clump. / Eyes, ears—yearn. / And the dollars / radiate, / fall, / roar, / onto a supine, struggling, hating wall / from the hand on the ceiling / down.') Big-city tempo. Short, choppy sentences. No articles, no auxiliary verbs. Remarkable are the dramatic, thematically determined shifts from long paeonic lines to the staccato of almost nothing but stressed syllables. Each part has its own meter and only the sharp differences can emphasize the effect.

The hymnal treatment of the big city is effected by periods of long-breathed lines of many syllables with stirring, short-lined terminations.[80] But the *rhythm* of the metropolis is transmitted chiefly by the multifarious staccato. The short sentences themselves and the aggregation (not the symmetry!) of parallel linguistic units of whatever type produce the movement, the abrupt shifting

[80] *Zol ikh bazingen dayn nakht, / ven mit der endlozer shure fun baloykhtene oytos un troks, / mit di elektrishe blitsn bay dayne ripn fun shtol / finklstu, reytsstu, vi a ring fun monster-brilyantn, / du farknaserin fun di tsvey zikh yogndike shtet?* ('Shall I sing of your night, / when with the endless line of lit up cars and trucks, / with the electric flashes at your ribs of steel / you glisten, you tease, like a ring of monster diamonds, / you betrother of the two cities in pursuit of each other?')—"Manhetn-brik," *Rondos...*, p. 39.

of the situation, the diversity;[81] it is one of the ways of expressing the *kaleidoscopicness* which the Inzikhists demanded.

6.3. The same big-city rhythm, the energy and *nervousness* of the short staccato sentences are felt not only in descriptions of the city itself.[82] Consider the following fragment by Leyeles ("Yanuar 28," From "Fabyus Linds Togbukh," *Fabyus Lind*, New York, 1937, p. 14):

> *Finsternish.*
> *Gĕdīkhtĕ,* ' *knōylĭkĕ,*
> *ūrăltĕ, grōylĭkĕ,* / *ŭmhēymlĕkhĕ, mōylĭkĕ.*
> *Un plutslung—funken vayse, gantse pasn.*
> *Magnium-gli—vays, vays.*
> *A kni—varem, veykh un shtayf.*
> *A reyf arum mir, vi der ring arum saturn.*
> *Shtayf arum mir. Vays. Muterlekher nokturn.*
> *Sumne reytsenish.*
> *Markh-farfleytsenish. Fal—fli. Fal—fli.*
> *Knī.* / *Măgnĭŭm-glī.* / *Ŭn vīdĕr—*
> *Knōylĭkĕ, kōylĭkĕ fīntstĕrnĭsh.*
> *Fărfālĕnĭsh.*

('Darkness. / Dense, tangled, / ancient, horrible, eerie, mouthy. / And suddenly —white sparks, whole streaks [of them]. / Magnesium glow—white, white. / A knee—warm, soft and stiff. / A hoop around me, like the ring around Saturn. / Stiff around me. White. Motherly nocturn. / Gloomy teasing. / Brain flooding. Fall—flight. Fall—flight. / Knee. Magnesium glow. And again— / Clumpy, coaly darkness. / Lostness.') Almost every word is by itself, and every word is an image. Thirteen punctuation marks in 13 lines. And, interestingly enough, there is not a single verb! The situation is depicted in terms of attributes (adjectives and adverbs) and nouns of action (*fal—fli*). The internal rimes underscore the parallelism of the links and the continuity. The general frame, based on a similarity of words of an amphibrachic pattern (disregarding the accretions at the caesura), lends coherence to the poem. But the choice of words is also vital: 33 percent are long (i.e. three or more syllables). This is not a sign of a piling up of unstressed syllables, for there is no long *sentence* with auxiliary words. The function of the long words is different: they enable 40 percent of the cola to terminate in dactyls or hyperdactyls. And this is sharply emphasized

[81] In "Sobvey, I" there is more action than in the above example, yet it is rendered without the use of a single verb! (Of all words, the three verbs in the introduction describe no real motion.) Instead of verbs we have nouns (*rir-rir*), participles, comparatives, interjections; their order and rhythm transmit the movement to us; that means that the deviation from the normal (as well as its character, its density, its extremity) is more important than the material of the deviation.

[82] Big-city "impulses of emotion" were introduced by Leyeles into the formerly melodic t.-s. metrics as well. In the sonnet "Vinklen" (*Yungharbst*, Warsaw, 1922) we read: *Trepn. Masn. Shtaygn. Faln. Fintster. Nakht.* etc. ('Stairs. Masses. Ascend. Fall. Dark. Night.')— 43 punctuation marks (37 sentences) in 14 lines!

by the contrast of monosyllabic stress-sentences,[83] which is all the more apparent because the few feminine cola are concentrated in almost one spot (line 3).

6.4. A further example from Leyeles ("Etyud," from *Rondos...*, p. 77):

In vayse krayzn fun naygerikayt
forsh ikh a shvaygiker dayn loyter gezikht.
A helzikhtike likhtikayt shpreyt zikh mit mistishkayt
fun dir
iber der vistenish fun mayn velt.
Bistu nisht alts far mir?
Dokh bahaltstu fun mir dayn vore geshtalt.
Ikh ken gornisht dikh.
Bist nit oysbrengerish
mit dayn genod.
Nor fun dayne tsufelike shtralungen
ver ikh, der farfalener, getreyst un geleyzt.
O minutn zeltene,
ven fun zeyer baheltenish
laykhtn aroys di shtraln fun dem sod,
vos halt undz, baveltikte, mistish tsuzamen.
Dan viklen oykh dikh spiraln fun naygerikayt.
Dan brenen tsvaygiker, brenen durkhzikhtiker
di knospn fun dayn likhtikayt,
un vilst mikh derkenen—
vi ikh dikh.

('In white circles of curiosity / I study in silence your pure face. / A clairvoyant brightness diffuses with mysticity from you / over the wastes of my world. / Are you not everything for me? / Yet you hide from me your true shape. / I know not you at all. / You are not extravagant / with your grace. / But by your accidental emanations / I, the lost one, am consoled and saved. / O minutes rare / when from their hiding / the rays emanate from the secret / which keeps us, overcome, mystically together. / Then there burn more branchily, more translucently / the buds of your brightness, / and you want to know me thoroughly / as I want to know you.') The rimes are concatenated, without terminating lines, but on the contrary, occurring inside the lines, leaning over the full stops. It is, on the contrary, the true end of the line which remains without a rime. Out of 60 cola, 36 participate in the rimes and assonances.[84]

[83] What does the fact that 47 percent of all words are monosyllabic tell us? Of much greater interest is the finding that of the 25 monosyllables, 18 are stressed, i.e. 72 percent (!) in comparison with the 25 percent (15 out of 61) of the next example, "Etyud." Even in an iambic poem, in which the meter requires stressing wherever possible, so high a percentage is not to be found. (In the adjoining poem, "Yanuar 29," we have 42 stressed words out of 102 monosyllables, i.e. 41 percent.)

[84] Similarly in the poem "Dos lid" (*A yid oyfn yam*, p. 7): in the first two strophes, 39 out of the 47 cola participate in sound ties (rimes and rich alliteration). Characteristic is the fact that the riming there is more adjoining than concatenating, i.e. internal rimes occur in *every* line (or combination of lines as a whole). In this poem we also find almost pure amphibrachs, and their disturbance creates a syntactic pause.

The rime causes a kind of metric, non-syntactic cut in the line, thanks to which the pattern in all segments is amphibrachic almost throughout. According to F. Strich, the love of rimes is a distinct trait of romanticism, and if such historical parallels can be made, it is the romantic principle in Leyeles.[85] The rimes produce enclises of short words: *Bīstŭ nĭsh*[86] *ālts făr mĭr?* (riming doubly with *vīstĕnĭsh* and with *băhāltstŭ fŭn mĭr*; incidentally, we see here how immaterial is the number of syllables in the dactylic descent: even a rime need not contain the same number of syllables); *ĭkh kēn gŏrnĭsh : ŏysbrēngĕrĭsh*. Long words here constitute 22 percent (in English poetry only 3%!), and of those, 77 percent are dactylic and hyperdactylic; the dactyls take up 35 percent of all cola. This is a great deal if we consider that most short words are connected proclitically with others. The average is 3 syllables per stress.

6.5. Rather than representing concatenations of sound, the poetry of H. Leyvik is characterized by a concatenation of sentences and words. By this means he creates a uniform, religiously lyrical, mood-filled atmosphere:

Ahinter Nyu-york farkayklt zikh di zun,
farkayklt zikh di zun un lompn tsindn zikh on.
Az lompn tsindn zikh on falt a gel-vayse shayn,
falt a gel-vayse shayn oyf alemen on.
("Di gel-vayse shayn," p. 112)

('Behind New York the sun rolls away, / rolls away the sun and the lamps go on. / When the lamps go on a yellow-white light falls, / falls a yellow-white light onto everyone.') Instead of terminal rimes, we have a parallelism of sentences; but as a primary device this is relatively infrequent in the work of either poet, nor is it entirely sufficient, in the absence of a fixed stanza, especially where an organic wholeness of the poem is desired. Hence it is connected with the internal repetition of sounds and words.

Forhangen fun tsimern—vi funandergerisene fliglen,
vi funandergerisene fliglen fun derkoylete feygl—
un der tog iz nokh likhtik, un der tog iz nokh freylekh—
far vos fargeyt er nisht? Far vos fargeyt er nisht?
Dine finger tsien zikh nokh diner,
dine finger frirn oyf gefroyrene felder—
vayse betn—vi gefroyrene felder—
bloye finger oyf gefroyrene felder.
("Nisht gezetikte tayves," p. 133)

('Curtains of rooms—like wings torn apart, / like torn-apart wings of birds thoroughly slaughtered— / and the day is still bright, and the day is still gay— / why doesn't it pass? Why doesn't it pass? / Thin fingers are drawn even thinner, / thin fingers freeze in frozen fields— / white beds—like frozen fields— / blue fingers in frozen fields.') An alliterative spell in *f*, repetitions, symbolically

[85] It is characteristic, too, of his mystically colored romantic love poems and the like, but it depends on the *character* of the rimes. It can also be grotesque, as in "Februar 29" (see §8.7, c).

[86] *Nish* 'not', with *sh* and without *t;* so Leyeles reads, as is shown by all his rimes.

detached images. The unsaid wants to develop and receives a new, unsaid symbol; a mystic mood results; the lofty tone is due to the high syllable-stress ratio (average 3.4); thus a wholeness of strophe (or rather, of line-group) is also achieved.[87]

From the extreme *concatenation*—by tying each new period to a preceding central word—we have passed on to the *ring*, which encloses the newly created line-group (replacing the stanza of a fixed number of lines) into a homogeneous whole or brackets such line-groups as parts of a complete, coherent poem. Consider Leyvik's in "Iber di shlofndike oygn" (p. 132), of whose rhythmically interesting periodic structure we can unfortunately cite only one strophe, without even comparing it with the rest, despite the fact that the total structure is here vital:

ī̆ber dĭ shlōfn̆dĭkĕ ōygn̆ ǀ *fŭn ālĕ mēntshn̆,*	2 paeons + 2 iambs
frēmdĕ mēntshn̆ ǀ *ĭn frēmdĕ hāyzĕr,*	2 + 2 iambs
trōgt zĭkh dūrkh dĕr bărīr fŭn măyn hānt,	3 anapests
fŭn măyn hānt, vŏs dĕkt tsū măynĕ ēygĕnĕ ōygn̆.	4 anapests
Ōngĕglĭtĕ fāyĕrdĭkĕ rīngĕn	3 paeons
kāyklĕn zĭkh ĭn gĕdrēy	1 "penton"
ŭn mā̆ynĕ ōygn̆ ǀ *vērn̆ nĭsht mīd*	1 paeon (2 iambs?) + 2 dactyls →
fŭn tsŭ kūkn̆ ŏyf zēy.	→ 2 dactyls
Zē, ǀ *mēntshn̆ līgn̆ zĭkh ĭn dĭ hāyzĕr ŭn shlōfn̆.*	——

('Over the sleeping eyes of all people, / strange people in strange houses, / there floats by the touch of my hand, / of my hand which covers my own eyes. / Glowing-hot, fiery rings / roll in a whirl, / and my eyes do not tire / of looking at them. / See, people casually lie in their houses and sleep.') We will not dwell on the construction of thematic motives and word threads. Thanks to the syntactic suspense (e.g. the late arrival of the main sentence units), we cannot interrupt our reading until the end of the fourth line (the following strophes have even longer periods). It is notable, incidentally, that the *metric segments* wind and grow (in pure metric groups) gradually from disyllabic to pentasyllabic measures and start anew. The transitions are easy; the same meter is sustained and is continued in the thematically most closely related lines (first and second, third and fourth, seventh and eighth). The two instances of transition from one meter to another in *mid-line* are connected with an emotional pause which in both cases follows the central word, *oygn*. It is this internal order which makes so acute the contrast with the isolated prosaic last line (*ze, mentshn . . .*), in which *every* measure is of different length (1, 2, 4, 3, and 2 syllables).[88] In this rhythmic type, it is not the concluding sentence alone, but the *arc-like sentence periods* which create the closed, perfect circles. The periods stretch from line to line, with an inner suspense which is rhythm-building. The suspense

[87] It must be observed that but for the fifth 3-measure line, all lines have four measures. Yet because of the lack of rime and the many-syllabled measures, this is felt not directly, but through the internal caesura which divides every line into two parallel parts.

[88] The line recurs thrice as a leitmotiv. Another example is Leyvik's "Der geviksiker tate" (p. 144), where all stanzas begin with a certain variation of the heading.

is produced both by leaving important syntactic units unsaid at the beginning of sentences and by the interspersion of mutually parallel sentence parts.

6.6. *Streaming Rhythm.*[89] As one passes from staccato rhythm through the concatenated pattern to the periodic arc which is closed like a strophe, the internal pause points become more widely spaced. If the smaller circles are successfully broken in the process and period is piled on period (without word or sound repetition), as in the *flowing* classical "musical" poem, while the stress intervals increase (i.e. the number of syllables grows) and the long-breathed epic lines are maintained, a *streaming rhythm* results. There is no Yiddish hexameter, and the width of its measures would not create a particularly lofty effect in this language. The corresponding stream bed of Yiddish poetry therefore consists of chiefly polysyllabic measures, and secondarily of many-measured lines (with multi-line sentences):

	Number of Stresses	
. . . ŭn ĕs ī̆z gĕvēn ŏyfn̆ drītn̆ frĭmōrgn̆,	3 (4)	
vĕn dĭ zūn ĭz ōyfgĕgăngĕn ĭn mīzrăkh-zăyt	3	
ĭz fŭn dĕr gāntsĕr shtōt shŏyn nĭsht gĕblībn̆ kĕyn zēykhĕr.	4	
Ŭn dĭ zūn ĭz gĕshtīgn̆ ălts hēkhĕr ŭn hēkhĕr	4	great stress contrasts
bĭz vānĕn zĭ ĭz tsūgĕkŭmĕn tsŭm mītn̆ hīml,	4	
ŭn ĭrĕ shtrāln̆ hŏbn̆ zĭkh băgēgn̆t mĭt dĕm rōvs ōygn̆.	4	
Un der rov iz gelegn oyf a barg ash un shteyner,	4	
mit a tsunoyfgeprestn moyl un oysgeglotste shvartsaplen,	4	
un in zayn neshome iz geven shtil un fintster un mer gornisht.	4	
Un ven zayne oygn hobn derfilt oyf zikh di heyse shtraln	4	
hobn zey zikh funandergeshpreyt un gekukt un gekukt,	3	
biz vanen zayn guf hot ongehoybn zikh rirn un oyfkumen.	4	

(Leyvik, beginning of "Der volf")

('. . . And it was on the third morning, / when the sun had risen in the east / not a trace of the whole city remained. / And the sun climbed ever higher and higher, / until it reached the middle of the sky, / and its rays met the rabbi's eyes. / And the rabbi lay on a mountain of ashes and stones, / with pressed mouth and staring pupils, / and his soul was quiet and dark and nothing else. / And when his eyes felt the hot rays upon them / they spread wide and looked and looked, / until his body began to move and rise.') Because of the great differences in the order of stressed and unstressed syllables, the poem is not "melodic." There is no organizing factor like rime. And yet this is not prose, but lofty epic poetry, for the sentences spread over several lines, the syllable-stress ratio is high (3.9), and the epic language devices, by requiring this lofty tone, avoid minor secondary stresses (note the frequent *un . . ., un az . . ., un ven . . .*). The line terminations are also rarely masculine and the number of measures per line remains quite fixed.[90]

[89] With respect to this concept, I am close to Wolfgang Kayser: *Das sprachliche Kunstwerk*, Berne, 1948, p. 260; *idem: Kleine deutsche Versschule*, Berne, 1946.

[90] For more numerous measures, see the streaming-rhythm example from Leyeles (in footnote 80), but note that a line of more than five measures is decomposed by a caesura

7. Group Three: Free "Speaking" Rhythms

7.1. The assignment of forms to content groups is bound to be misleading, yet for the explication of a particular poem, its essential thematic grouping is more significant than its accidental constructional details. Since the preceding two groups dispense with any *predetermined* organization (even in the poetry of Leyeles, so full of rimes, one cannot anticipate the moment or type of a rime), the rhythm is produced mainly by linguistic means, i.e. linguistic expression is called upon to solve the rhythmic problems at each concrete spot. Thus the center of attention shifts to language. It is not by chance that the non-rimer and composer of free rhythms (free, at least, to the German ear, if not to the eye), Friedrich Gottlieb Klopstock, spoke of a special poetic *language* in contrast to that of prose ("Von der Sprache der Poesie").

On the whole, linguistic expression in the third group resembles the forms of the spoken language, while the preceding group achieved its special rhythmic effect by a marked (or at least a perceptible) deviation from the rhythms of the spoken language. The deviations of Group Two were principally in two directions: (a) departure from the normal speech flow by increasing the stress interval[91] and by special diction, or by producing special contrasts (in terms of syllable-stress ratio) between the several portions of one poem; (b) modification of normal sentence structure and erection of articificially sharp rhythmic differences between sentences, both by the use of abrupt, very short sentences, and by the construction of tense, inversive periods to hold a series of lines together, thus producing the impact of a strophe. In the present group, the "speech-like" one, if a sentence does extend over several lines, these ordinarily form parallel or continuing parts of that sentence; we can interrupt at the end of almost any line without being left in syntactic suspense.[92] The forms, of course, are mixed, the boundaries vague.

(as in Leyvik's "Volkns hintern vald," p. 411). A streaming rhythm is realized also in officially metric poems if their linguistic construction allows a reading with a reduced number of principal stresses. (The long line stimulates one to reduce the number of measures, i.e. to emphasize the number of main stresses.) This occurs e.g. in Kulbak's "Vilne" (see footnote 75). But if the main stresses form a new metric mesh (paeons), the streaming rhythm is lofty in a solemnly fervent rather than an epic way.

[91] By and large, in the "speaking" rhythms we may consider as normal a syllable-stress ratio of somewhat less than 3 (about 2.8); in the dynamic rhythms, this ratio is strongly differentiated, but always exceeds 3 (i.e. it is above normal; about 3.4). My statistics, however, are too limited to justify definitive conclusions.

[92] But there must be continuity. If the lines are not interconnected, the poem does not give a rhythmic effect even if a formal meter exists. Thus Yankev Glatshteyn's "Eybik" (in his book *Kredos*, New York, 1929, p. 64): *Fuftsn knoytn ongetsundn, / a mitnvokh faryontevt. / Ale reder opgeshtelt. / Ale royshn ayngeshtilt. / Ale gasn oysgetsirt— / Far vemen makh ikh khoge? / Far mir, vayl ikh bin eybik. / Vi petrishke iz eybik. / Vi marantsn-sholekhts, / vi a shtoybele, / vi a funk, / vi a vintlbloz, / vi a vaser-tropn. . .* etc. ('Lighted fifteen wicks, / turned a weekday into a feast. / Stopped all wheels. / Subdued all noises. / Adorned all streets— / For whom am I making a profane holiday? / For me, because I am eternal. / As parsnips [in Yiddish, symbol of triviality] are eternal. / Like orange peel, / like a particle of dust, / like a spark, / like the blow of a breeze, / like a water drop'). Does any-

A more moderate form of language, too, has been given rhythmic expression in this group with its unexaggerated tempos. By virtue of their temperament and, in particular, their folk-like language style, these poets came under the influence of the folksong; the dividing line between them and the poets of Group One (chapter 4) are often vague with respect to *word flow*. Not so, however, with regard to measure construction: the lack of fixed stanzas in Group Three is intimately connected with the lack of a fixed line length; therefore the stresses are not particularly prominent because they are not set apart as a constructive device of the line. In short, the "singable" poem has come to an end with the elimination of pure isochronism; only in minor syllabically organized groups does isochronism continue to be perceptible.

7.2. The group under discussion is quite widespread in various forms. The Yiddish poets of the United States, especially, under the liberating influence of modern American poetry, have avoided "songiness" by violating all symmetric forms, avoided solemn fervor by eschewing polysyllabic gallops, and avoided dynamism by employing a language style which requires everything to be calmly *said* rather than "made conscious" (*bavustikn* was Kushnirov's term) in an epically-lofty manner or mystically hinted. Their syllable-stress ratio is low.

In the work of Yankev Glatshteyn (Glatstein; b. 1896)—the second clearcut *Inzikhist*—we find different forms, depending on the period of his development and the particular poem. Since to him the individual verse is important, he is—or at least his language segments are—tonically-syllabically measured. There is a great deal of calm iambicness, but it is broken, willy-nilly as it were, now by a disturbing accretion, now by a segment of another t.-s. meter which we are hindered from perceiving as such by our metric inertia induced by the preceding segment. In the truly speech-like poems of the Bratslaver even the segments are not metric. And with the lines unequal, there is no danger of the beat "overcoming" the disturbances in the reader in a metric way (or even simply in a truly isochronal way).

In his new period Glatshteyn creates profoundly folk-rooted, maximally non-melodic rhythms, heavily laden with folk locutions; his principal device is his synthetic, intensely Jewish style (*reboyne dealme hayitokhn, daváy a bísele nakhes* 'Lord, please, let's have a little satisfaction': words derived from four languages—Aramaic, "Slavic," German, and Hebrew—and yet a phrase so profoundly Yiddish!). His poetry is tantamount to slow, weighty, well-considered, wise speech; the phrasing of it is governed, aside from the language, by the length of his lines (which are also his sentences). His characteristic riming pattern connects the end of one line with the beginning of the next (a form often used by Leyeles), yet the line-initial rime is not the end of an expression, but a beginning, and is thus blurred, as it were. However, the close rimes are a mainstay of his poem and, additionally, a means of arranging words of neighboring lines in a metrically parallel way and of sliding from one line to the next.

---

one feel that these are pure trochees, the "same" trochees as those of the so melodic poems of the preceding generation? There is no billowing forward movement here, but a mere monotonous list.

7.3. In such epic poets as Berish Vaynshteyn (Weinstein; b. 1905) or Eliezer Grinberg (Greenberg; b. 1896), a *single* (ordinarily trisyllabic) t.-s. background is felt in entire poems. Connected with this is their tendency to stanza form. The free tone is achieved by the disturbances in the trisyllabic mesh which are ordinarily related to syntactic or reading pauses; and by the intercalation of "iambic" segments, mostly in the interior of lines, in order to cancel the metric impact.

Pāntsĕrs fŭn shīfn̆ tsĕshlōgn̆ dĭ khvālyĕs ĭn shōym ŭn tsĕrūdĕrn̆(˘) dĭ bōrtn̆s.
Shtrīk mĭt gĕānkĕrtĕ shīfn̆× *rīrn̆ dĭ brēgn̆.*
Hāfn̆s× *rōyshn̆ mĭt ōpgĕrĭsĕnĕ klētsĕr fŭn hīltsĕrnĕ vēnt.*
Ŏyf dĭ klētsĕr dĕr shōymĭkĕr mōkh× *grĭnt vīld*× *ŭn kīl.*
(B. Vaynshteyn: *Lider un poemes*, New York, 1949)

('Armor of ships smashes the waves into foam and agitates the coast. / Ropes with anchored ships move the shores. / Harbors hum with beams torn from wooden walls. / On the beams the frothy moss greens, wild and cool.') At × there are syllable omissions which are connected with thematic or phrasal breath interruptions. A few "detached" words like *opgerisene* in line 3 suffice to cancel the metric feeling. In comparison with the previously cited "streaming" poetry, Vaynshteyn's epic work is calmer; his syllable-stress ratio is only 2.9.

7.4. The third subgroup comprises lyric poems, individual and mostly brief ones (e.g. the free lyricism of Y. L. Teler [J. L. Teller; b. 1912], Ber Horovits, several women poets, etc.), which do not maintain a fixed number of measures in the line but whose shorter lines permit one to feel the measures more vividly and contribute to the creation of atmosphere. The frame of the poem and of the strophe is also often linguistically rigid. Here is an example by Malke Kheyfets-Tuzman (b. 1896):

ˈ *Nēm mĭkh ărŭm,* ˈ *măyn lībĕr,*
nēm mĭkh ărūm.
Mĭt dōrn̆s īn dĭ fīngĕr ˈ *nēm mĭkh ărūm.* ˈ
Mĭt shtōlshplĭntĕrs ˈ *ĭn dĭ ōrĕms*
nēm mĭkh ărūm.
Mītn̆ fīntstĕr fū̆n dăyn ōysgĕhăkt ōyg,
mī̆t dăyn gōr tsĕvūndĭkt lēbn̆,
nēm mĭkh ărūm.[93]

('Embrace me, my dear, / embrace me. / With thorns in your fingers embrace me. / With steel splinters in your arms / embrace me. / With the dark of your knocked-out eye, / with your entire life, all wounds, / embrace me.')

7.5. The boundary between this form and prose is not always clear,[94]

[93] The reiterations also act as a rhythmic leitmotiv prominent against the background of differently ordered lines (formally, almost pure iambs).

[94] Ber Horovits composed a free-rhythmic poem in which the rime does not come until the end of the exceedingly long periods (*Reyakh fun erd*, vol. 2, Vilna, 1930, p. 83), e.g. *In zeyere salons iber klavirn iz zayn maske gehangen, bakrentst mit blumen un lorber*-BLETER. / *Er flegt tsu zey kumen in zisn kholem bay nakht vi Zeus tsu Eyropen, vi der shvan tsu Leden, vi Yohanes tsu Salomen, un vi tsu andere shterblekhe, oysgebenkte bsules—kumen* GETER

especially where there are no definite rimes. The very vagueness of the stress distribution, the subjective perception of unequal semi- or quasi-stresses is a sign of proximity to prose.

But this type of work is not prose, not even in its most unorganized passages. The poem's typographical arrangement makes us read it as a poem, with a special suspense in each line, with a will to compare the lines and equate them, with a uniform stressing. According to A. Belyj[95] the line determines our breath load. That is, a great depends on its length alone. Every line is an "aural image" (Arno Holz), and only genuine poets know, or rather feel, how it should be constructed, especially in the difficult conditions of full freedom. "... Free verse ... is an additional instrument ... but its scope, I think, will never be otherwise than very restricted, both because it is only suited for certain moods and certain matter, still more because to write successfully without meter needs stronger inspiration, more mastery of rhythm, and a severer sense of form, not less discipline, but a greater discipline than to write in meter."[96]

The absence of meter has the advantage of creating more immanent rhythm for the poem in an age which no longer believes in the suggestive possibility of metrically and phonically rocking the reader into a lofty mood. Now that the content of the word is in the center, the word must not be smoothed over by melodic undulation.[97] But a unique wholeness must be *created* which does not permit the replacement of the poem by prose. The difference between such un-

---

('In their salons over pianos his mask hung, wreathed in flowers and laurel leaves. / He used to come to them in sweet dreams at night like Zeus to Europa, like the swan to Leda, like John to Salome, and as gods come to other mortal, yearning maidens'). Yet the arc of the sentences stretches the half-period with the help of the *expected* rime (if the reader knows that it is coming) and differentiates it from outright prose.

[95] Adrej Belyj: *Ritm kak dialektika. . .* , Moscow, 1929.

[96] L. Binyon: *Tradition and Reaction in Modern Poetry,* The English Association, Pamphlet no. 63, 1926, p. 13.

[97] Jünger indicates that in Hölderlin's hexameters there are already many trochees, i.e. instances of slowed down movement in which all parts of the verse strive toward independence. But melodicity can also be broken simply by passing from one group of meters to another in mid-line, i.e. simply by breaking the inertia. Quite "prosy" is the appearance of the following lines by Leyeles (from his poem "Lodzh," *A yid oyfn yam*, p. 220):

Tsŭ zēn dĭ ērshtĕ zŭn | *fŭn ĕlēktrĭshĕr prākht*
hŏt īn ă frāyĕr nākht | *nŏkh măyn tātĕ gĕfīrt mĭkh.*
Dĕm ērshtň ĕlēktrĭshň trāmvăy |*—vūndĕr, khōlĕm, shēd—*
bĭn īkh ĭn dĕr zēt fŭn tsĕn-yōrĭkň nāygĕr
ălēyn gĕlōfň zēn.

('To see the first sun of electric splendor / my father on a night off took me. / The first electric streetcar—miracle, dream, demon— / I, in the satiety of my ten-year-old curiosity / myself ran to see.') Schematically this may look like a collocation of pure iambic and anapestic segments, even of similar length and order, but the feeling is free-rhythmic and anti-melodic. The internal ordering, of course, has its effect, but it is subtly induced, and the reader is enticed into the rhythmic pattern, as it were, through the back door. The metric nature of every thematic segment attracts attention to it and helps it stand out independently.

metered poetry and prose consists, besides its arrangement in short lines, of (a) unusual speech movement, rhythmically governed word order (or avoidance of "unsuitable" word order), and (b) partial, non-subduing t.-s. feeling.

Characteristic of the "freedom" of the group is Ber Horovits' declaration:

Vĕr s'hŏt līb
gĕrēgĭtĕ vāsĕrn̆—
ī̆kh hŏb līb
frāyĕ, rāshĕ
rāysn̆dĭkĕ bārgvăsĕrn̆ . . .

Ŭmgĕbūndn̆,
nī̆sht gĕkōvĕt
shvīm măyn gĕzāng!
Vĭ ă bārgvăsĕr shvīm
ĭn vĭld-ēygĕnĕ brēgĕs![98]

('Some people like / regulated waters— / I like / free, rapid / gushing mountain streams . . . / Untied, / unshackled, / swim, my song! / Like a mountain stream, swim / within savage banks of your own!') A glance at the scheme shows the t.-s. feeling to be so strong that from meter to meter we glide into pure anapests![99] To be sure, the short line helps.

8. Principles in the Organic Structure

8.1. The differentiation between rhythm and beat by the psychologist Klages is ingenious, but dangerous in a practical sense.[100] From the pure beat, which is most precise in a machine, through the scanned verse which, with all its members, dominates a poem, to the poem of pure flowing rhythm, where only the sentence prevails, as in prose, there is a range of countless intermediate combinations. On the whole it can be stated that the folksong is sung *flowingly*, such approaches to order as do occur being blurred; the dance song, on the other hand, and even more so the children's song, underscore the beat. In t.-s. metrics "melodic" impressionistic poems are separated in this way from the declamatory and political poems and marching songs. In the truly free rhythms, the *content* is decisive, and the rhythmic effects, too, are achieved above all on a content basis. In the absence of a fixed order of syllables, sharp cuts are effected not by an emphatic beat but by dense sentence points, while the continuous flow results not from freedom within a fixed number of measures, but principally from long sentence periods.

Whether the decisive role is played by the verse of the sentence, whether the unit of rhythm is the word or the measure, whether long units (lines) or short ones (cola) are involved—all these are not general theoretical questions. The answer depends on the subjective general approach of the reader as well as on

[98] *Fun may heym in di berg*, vol. 1, Vienna, 1919, p. 5.

[99] A similar declaration by U.-Ts. Grinberg in Hebrew (in *Keleb bayit*) against "foreign iambs" itself lapses into iambs.

[100] Ludwig Klages: *Vom Wesen des Rhythmus* (Zurich, 1934). He is followed by Hans Hellenbrecht: "Das Problem der freien Rhythmen mit Bezug auf Nietsche" (*Sprache und Dichtung* no. 48, Berne, 1931). If one sees rhythm as connected with experience (*Erlebniss*) and beat (*Takt*) with consciousness, it is difficult to understand the appearance of strong beats in the behavior of small children and the free-rhythmic flow of intellectual poetry of the twentieth century. But the problem is not quite as simple for these scholars, either, and their errors require extended clarification.

the objective force relationships of each concrete poem, which usually put forward one (or several) of the elements as the bearer(s) of the basic rhythmic form. Whether or not the same bearer is formally sustained in the entire poem, it puts the other elements in the shade, even if their accompishment in forming the nuances of the shade is significant and impact-changing. And the stricter the rules, the more weighty and perceptible is every deviation.

The freer the predetermined frame, the more important the organic interaction of the rhythmic principles and their mutual influences. Consequently, all that has been said outlines a trend and does not lay down fixed limits. Let us sum up with a few general remarks.

8.2. According to syllabic relations, the poems can be divided into the following kinds.

a. A single t.-s. metric mesh in the whole poem, interrupted by syntactic or emotional pauses. Here an important role is played by the limits of freedom and the degree of order of the higher principles (e.g. types A and B in §4.1).

b. One prevalent meter in most of the major word groups. Emphasis is usually on continuity and there are no fixed stanza or line dimensions.[101]

c. One rhythmic leitmotiv (i.e. occasional cola of a fixed rhythmic group) permeates the entire poem or an entire strophe. Occasionally there also occurs a manifest struggle of two leitmotivs, or—in the case of highly distinct individual strophes—of a leitmotiv with an opposing mesh (thus, in different ways, Tuzman in §7.4, Leyeles in footnote 97).

d. Following concatenated t.-s. metric groups which change their basis from one instance to the other, but in such a way that in passing from line to line in one sentence, there is no interruption; either the end and beginning of lines are segments of a single mesh or they grow naturally into each other. This occurs in concatenated rhythms when the poet has difficulty in freeing himself from the t.-s. feeling at every concrete instant, but it cancels the t.-s. pattern as a poem-building principle (thus, e.g. Leyvik, footnote 88; Leyeles, §8.3; Horovits, §7.5).

It is rare (except in strongly agitated streaming rhythms) for any t.-s. background to be absent. (We are speaking, of course, of *modern* poetry, not of folk-like literature in which the number of measures is retained.) The implicit t.-s. schema provides a grounding effect which does not reach the surface. Only where an extensive t.-s. order is present does it dominate the line; only then,

[101] The prevailing dimensions are furnished by the fixed number of unstressed syllables *between* every two stresses in each colon and content-determined word-group; the homogeneous pattern does not necessarily, however, exceed the boundaries of content groups. For example, in "Dos lid" by Leyeles (see footnote 84), trisyllabicity prevails, but among the individual "inexactnesses" we find stanza beginnings such as the following: *ĭn ōnhĕyb ĭz dĕr nīgṅ* ('in the beginning is the melody') and *ĭn ōnhĕyb vēkt zĭkh dĕr nīgṅ* ('in the beginning the melody awakes'). It is evident that the author makes a significant breathing pause after *in onheyb* (that is, associating it with the biblical "In the beginning"), although there is no comma. The prevailing trisyllabic measure forces us in reading to reproduce the same pause in order not to permit a single utterance-segment to contain more (or less) than two unstressed syllables between every two stresses. Freer instances in the same group are Leyeles' "Etyud" (§6.4) and the fragment by Vaynshteyn (§7.3).

too, can it be perceived and may act as a disturbance, forcing more frequent stresses than the content would require. The genuine poet strives with the help of his delicate sense to avoid such a state of affairs. A line like *ŭn rūĭkĕr fŭn ālts ĭz dōkh dŏs ōnkŭmĕn fŭn ūntĕrgāng* ('and calmer than anything is after all the approach of downfall') is fatally liable to slip into an iambic beat, i.e. by inertia it forces superfluous, mechanizing secondary stresses onto the long words. But when Leyvik removes the word *dokh* and places the line in a frame where every line (nearly all iambs) is interrupted by a metric caesura and in the forward-moving (i.e. rhythmically preparatory) line the second part is suddenly anapestic, the result is paeonicity, i.e. the preservation of the widely spaced stresses of the long words becomes a requisite (at most, perhaps, the word *rūĭkĕr* receives a secondary stress in the poem):

Un az ikh zog nor aroys dos vort—vert mir gut
vayl ruiker fun mir iz der kalter klang fun vort
un kelter funem klang fun vort iz dos ponim fun gornisht
un ruiker fun alts iz dos onkumen fun untergang.

◡◡◡–◡◡–◡– | –◡–
◡–◡–◡– | –◡–◡–◡–
◡–◡–◡–◡– | ◡◡–◡◡–◡
◡–◡–◡– | ◡◡–◡◡◡–◡◡

('And as soon as I utter the word, I am relieved / because the cold sound of the word is calmer than I / and colder than the sound of the word is the face of nothing / and calmest of all is the approach of downfall.') The schema is, according to my reading, carefully constructed down to the last details, and how prudently! (Note the missing syllable in the middle of each line.) And the overall effect of the entire configuration is one of genuine free rhythm.

It must also be remembered that syntactic pauses may occur at the expense of unstressed syllables, but this does not mean that the increased stress density (with respect to time) is then also perceived in the actual rhythm.[102]

8.3. The effect of syllable order in the subconscious becomes manifest during sharp transitions from mesh to mesh. In "Shotns" (*Rondos...*, p. 76), Leyeles writes:

Far mayn fentster shteyen beymer	–◡–◡–◡–◡
erntst, shvaygik, fartrakht.	–◡–◡ | ◡–
Zey(e)re yunge tsvaygn, pleferishe bleter	◡◡–◡–◡–◡◡◡–◡
rirn zikh, regn zikh	=◡◡–◡◡
vign zikh, bavegn zikh,	–◡◡ | ◡–◡◡
in di FLIR*tn*DIKE *vintlekh*	◡◡–◡◡◡–◡
fun der FRIL*ing*DIKER *nakht.*	◡◡–◡◡◡–

---

[102] In Kulbak's "Khanke—a fayerdike kale" (see §8.4), the syllable-stress ratio of the first nine lines is 3.4, but without the first line it is 3.7. The difference is due to the many stresses in that first line: *Khānkĕ, ēy, Khānkĕ, kūm tsŭ mīr făr nākht* ('K., hey, K., come to me in the evening'). But this is the result only of a formal syllable count. The *time intervals* between stresses here are—due to the intonational phrasing—no smaller than in the many-syllabled sequel. And conversely, the relative lack of unstressed syllables helps to create a feeling of sentence interruption. This, incidentally, is required by the mood-determined phrasing, aside from all theories.

('Before my window trees stand / serious, taciturn, absorbed in thought. / Their young branches, stupefying leaves / stir, start, / sway, move / in the flirtatious breezes / of the spring night.') The special rhythmic effect of this formally non-metric passage is achieved by the gradual and plain increase in stress intervals: from a precise trochee, through disyllabicity in every colon, formal trochaicness, dactyls, trisyllabicity in the cola—up to true paeons. Only the preceding dense mesh can so impressively emphasize the airy, buoyant effect of the last two paeonic lines (and of the next-to-the last dactyls). Their unusualness is their merit. Thus, the *economizing* of words and structures of one kind is often more of a gain than a farfetched piling up of a pattern extending over a whole poem.

In this connection it is important to realize that the avoidance of secondary stresses in long words is made possible first and foremost by the fact that the paeons occur not next to iambs (which would "iambicize" the paeons, too), but to longer (trisyllabic) measures. If, in reading, we wish to compare the new measures with the already established measure intervals, we cannot do it by crumbling a measure into two pieces; the measure becomes more heavily loaded —for an instant this is unusual—and then the mesh widens (from three to four syllables).[103] Thus, in the free rhythms the metric conditioning of diction is one of the most complicated and significant accomplishments of the truly poetic ear. To go into details here is impossible.

8.4. Truly paeonic poems do not stick to pure t.-s. meters (unless supported by a melody or a highly stirring declamation). We are speaking only of a tendency to paeonization; a slight iambic (or trochaic) secondary stress is always present. But in the free rhythms paeonic lines are rather strong, especially so after a trisyllabic preparation.

Even as many as five unstressed syllables can be maintained after an appropriate preparation, i.e. one which does not permit the reader to fall into a denser mesh. In Kulbak's "Khanke—a fayerdike kale," already quoted, we read:

Ĭkh bēt ĕs băy dīr, Khānkĕlĕ, kūm tsŭ gēyn.
Ă shtīlĭnkĕr ' vĕl ĭkh līgn̆.
Ōt ăzŏy shtīl vĭ ă shēpsĕlĕ.
Dū vĕst zītsn̆ ŏt dō ŏyfn̆ shvēl.
Īkh—ŏyf dĕr ērd vĕl ĭkh līgn̆ ōysgĕtsŏygn̆.
Mĭtn̆ kōp ŏyf dĭ hēnt vĕl ĭkh līgn̆.
Ō̆t ăzōy.
Ĭkh vĕl dĭr frēgn̆: Khānkĕlĕ, hŏstŭ shŏyn ōysgĕmŏlkn̆ dĭ bĕhēymĕs dăynĕ?

---

[103] This effect of metric inertia is the main factor requiring a *single* meter in an entire t.-s. poem (cf. footnote 97). Just as in Germany the strict forms of the Greek odes had a liberating influence because of their non-uniform pattern (see, primarily, F. Strich, *op. cit.*, but also Closs, *op. cit.*), in Yiddish poetry, too, mixed (but predetermined) meters are essentially closer to free rhythms than to metric poems. In Leyeles' strophe (Rondos..., p. 46): *Blas-gelblekhe royz. Aromat / fun shtile, fayerlekhe ritualn, / fun gotdinung in veykhe zayd-sandaln, / fun gloybn mit vayzhayt shoyn zat* ('Palely-yellowish rose. Aroma / of quiet, solemn rituals, / of divine service in soft silk sandals, / of faith already sated with wisdom'), is it felt that the lines are written in a strict form, the first and last being amphibrachic, while the middle two are iambs (and so throughout the poem).

('I ask it of you, K., come to me. / I will lie still. / As still as a lamb. / You will sit here on the doorstep. / As for me—I'll lie stretched out on the ground. / With my head on my hands will I lie. / This way. / I will ask you: K., did you milk your cows yet?') The syllable-stress ratio of the last line goes all the way to 5.2! And yet, in another frame, it could be read iambically. The trisyllabic mesh with its several skips forms the preparation for the swing. The beginning of the last line contains two independent cola—the introduction. The long word *ōysgĕmŏlkň* accustoms us to the hyperdactylic and makes possible the enclisis: *dĭ bĕhēymĕs dăynĕ*. When we read the line detached from the poem, we usually find more stresses, especially since the possibility of iambic order is so attractive.[104]

8.5. When it exists, the t.-s. meter prevails over the cola in the line. Similarly, when the number of measures in the line is fixed, the line is usually a stronger unit than the syntactic group. On the contrary, when the syntactic groups become stronger, they cancel the line symmetry, and the stresses are weakly felt because of their irregularity; consequently the number of stresses is also less perceptible even if fixed.

Given a free number of stresses, there are possibilities of: (a) regularity of line, frequently containing up to four stresses, with few deviations from four or three; the number then does not exceed five, or—in the case of six—the line is divided by a fixed, permanent caesura, or else it ceases to be a line of a poem;[105] (b) great, tangible differences in line length; in that case, lines with a great many stresses also occur. In this group, too, we find poems with stress-rhythm leitmotivs, i.e. sentence sections with a fixed number of stresses and a given syllable order which recur several times in the vicinity of each other.

The more regular the number of stresses, the more apparent are the deviations.

[104] Only by taking account of the interaction factors can a poet create an impact by his selection of long words. Thus, if we were to insert, in a poem composed on an iambic mesh, the phrase *zay sheferishe drayst* 'be creative boldness', it would mostly be read as an iamb, but when several phrases so constructed come in parallel and, in addition, the first violates the iambic pattern, there results a free-rhythmic fervor like the following (Eliezer Grinberg, *op. cit.*, p. 69):

Ver hofndike fargebung!
Zay sheferishe drayst!
Ver eybike balebung.
Zay otem fun gayst!
Ver likhtike bafrayung,
zay eybike banayung!
Un du herst
yerst
un verst!

('Become hoping forgiveness! / Be creative boldness! / Become eternal animation. / Be breath of spirit! / Become bright liberation, / be eternal renewal. / And you hear / ferment / and become!') Incidentally, only the preceding many-syllabled arcs (due to the Yiddish long descending words) allow such a bold emphasis of the three energetic stresses (rimes!) at the end.

[105] Similarly Hellenbrecht, *op. cit.*, p. 11: "The number of rises usually fluctuates between one and six." When the line becomes excessive, we lose our sense of the poetic rhythm. Even when it is written in trochees, like N. B. Minkov's rimed periods in "Der letster tsug" (*Undzer Pyero*, New York, 1927), it is hard to feel the measures. The rhythmic value of the rime also goes almost entirely to waste.

An extraordinarily long line ordinarily produces heaviness, while a short line adds weight to its words:

Blotike, blutike balade fun Balut—
kemerlekh daled oyf daled, vebshtul, betn, kinder,
mit oremkayt blinder, mit aza ashires noyt,
mit aza shmaltsgrub noyt—
Lodzh.
(Leyeles: *A yid oyfn yam*, p. 220)

('Muddy, bloody ballad of Bałut [Jewish section of Lodz]— / cubicles four [ells] by four, weaving loom, beds, children, / with blind poverty, with such a wealth of want, / with such a goldmine of want— / Lodz.') Our tendency to equilibrium and to unexaggerated (large or small) dimensions inclines us on the one hand to give greater force to the stresses of the short lines and, on the other, to read as few main stresses as possible in a long line, provided it is felt as a line (see footnote 105). Therefore a relatively small proportion of long words suffices to create loftiness, for example in a streaming rhythm.[106] Therefore, too, we hear as prose those lines in which it is difficult, because of the perceptible gradation, to determine the number of stresses. Too many stresses destroy it as a (comparable) unit, and only a t.-s. meter allows an alternate ordering principle. (Hence the accepted rule: in poetry the stresses are more uniform.)

8.6. In all this one thing is clear: we are intent only on perceiving a short line in a way similar to the preceding long one. But this does not mean equating the two. The same applies to the syllables. Isochronism, too, does not necessarily mean equal duration of measures, but merely similar duration which can be experienced by the human interpreter as equivalent. But frequently it is hard to know whether the author intended isochronism (it is omitted, often purposely, even in certain t.-s. poems, in the immediate linguistic expression; especially when the lines have unequal numbers of measures) and the reader, too, fails to give precise supplemental durations to the descending syllables (or vice versa). But the *tendency* to equate (especially with the last established inertia) is always present and causes the preceding text to affect the manner of reading a line in a poem.

On the whole two principal forces contribute to the creation of rhythm in a

[106] For example, Leyvik's poem "Unter di trit fun mayne fis" (p. 121):

ŭ̄ntĕr dĭ trīt fŭn mā̆ynĕ fīs,
ī̆n dĭ tīfĕ tīfĕnī̆shn̆ fū̆n dĕr ērd,
hĕr ĭkh dŏs ŭmōyfhĕrĭkĕ gĕrōysh-gĕzăng fŭn măyn lēbn̆
shtrōmĕnvăyz—ōdĕrn̆văyz.

('Under the steps of my feet, / in the deep depths of the earth, / I hear the incessant noise song of my life / in streams—in veins.') The sound-repeating emphasis on the proximity of the stresses in *tīfĕ tīfĕnishn* makes an excellent (iambicizing) backdrop for the strongly contrasting third line. We see an interaction of all principles: syntactic suspense (main clause not until the third line); long, hyperdactylic words in a long line; and a chord in the two parallel (almost rimed) dactylic single words which bear the main sense of the sentence: *shtromenvayz—odernvayz*. The real syllable-stress ratio is 3.8.

poem: order and contrast. The more order, the more metric the pattern, and the more basis for the effect of the contrasts. But while "in a work of art, a rhythm *is* only by its constants," at least in the ordered parts (segments), "it *lives* only by its variables,"[107] that is by contrast to the normal. The contrasts with *order* create the suspense of a poem. In the free rhythms, where the order is not predetermined, the rhythmic effect is achieved by (a) *contrast with the surrounding context;* (b) *opposition to ordinary linguistic expression.* Therefore word order and inversion are so vital in this type of poetry. The linguistic specificness consequently here plays a larger role than in metric writing.[108]

8.7. On different bases certain devices produce similar effects, depending on the total structure. For example, the emphasis of words and intensification of cuts between them can be carried out in three ways: (a) by syntactic pauses; (b) by breaks in a metric mesh;[109] (c) by internal rimes (often accompanying b, supporting it). Thus, after lines of pure disyllabic mesh, we find in Leyeles' "Februar 27" (*Fabyus Lind*, p. 47): *ālĕ shpīl-pămălyĕs ŭn gĕzāng-kăpălyĕs— / shpīlt trīlt trēlt kvēlt pōykt ŭn ōygt*[110] ('all playing hosts and singing ensembles[111]— / play trill warble swell drum and act like 'Og [Deut. 3:11'). Commas are unnecessary: every syllable is stressed, every word is separate.[112] Incidentally, the same poem shows how an exaggerated piling up of rimes, especially when symmetrically grouped, can be an excellent device for grotesqueness,[113] in

[107] H. Rambaud: "Rhythme et littérature," in his book *Les rhythmes et la vie*, Paris, 1947, p. 286.

[108] Cf. for instance the rhythmic prominence of enclitic combinations in Yiddish due to their rarity in relation to proclitic sequences. This is also apparent in that no-man's land of metric poems, the ends of lines, as well as in metric patterns which violate the equality of lines and stanzas and are indeed closer in spirit to the free rhythms (see §5.3). Only a book on Yiddish metrics will be able to summarize all phenomena and consider them from this point of view. In the present paper we have cited a number of cases without pointing out this general theoretical rule; but in analyzing texts it should always be borne in mind.

[109] For example in Leyeles' "Februar-nakht" (*Rondos*..., p. 82), after a series of precise anapests, the last line divides words in a strongly emotional way: *un di februar-nakht iz tsu sheyn // afile tsu zayn tsertlekh* ('and the February night is too beautiful / even to be tender').

[110] A clash of stresses is almost impossible in the flow of speech; it demands a break between the stresses. If the Greeks combatted the molossus (three subsequent stresses, ´ ´ ´), it was retrieved again by this poet's style of manifesto-like phrasing (A. Belyj), i.e. a style of free dynamic rhythms which allow themselves to be read with a highly marked phrasing. But a basic rhythmic law remains unavoidable in the poem; the constant stresses are made possible only because in this style, interruptions are actually made between stresses in reading. This is accomplished either by a break in content atmosphere or—especially where stresses are numerous—by auxiliary interruption devices such as commas or rimes (as in our example).

[111] A grotesque distortion of the normal *kapelyes*.

[112] Two rimed cola are felt as rhythmically parallel. In the previously mentioned trisyllabic mesh of Leyeles' "Dos lid" (footnote 84), there is another deviation in *ă nĭsht-dāytlĕkhĕr ōyfshpĭl, ă vāytlĕkhĕr tsŭnōyfshpĭl* ('an indistinct striking-up, a rather distant playing together'), but due to the rime no imperfection is felt.

[113] Practiced also by Glatshteyn, as in "Shir—a gezang" (*Shtralndike yidn*, New York, 1946, pp. 5f.).

contrast to the asymmetrical interweaved abundance of rime in the same poet's seriously lyrical "Etyud" (§6.4).

Jünger has observed that the rime delivers the solution to the verse-sentence conflict into the hands of the verse. But this is true only of the final rime. Leyeles' internal rimes, in blurring and cutting up both the verse and the sentence, assign the dominating role to the colon, i.e. to the *word meanings*, as well as to the non-predetermined, ever sudden rime itself, i.e. the transcendent power of the poet's rhythmic impulse (inspiration).

Jünger has further stated that the rime lifts symmetry above rhythm (i.e. above the forward flow). As far as the line-final rime is concerned, this is doubtless true. But in Leyeles' work the question is solved in each concrete spot, and often the decision is not in favor of symmetry. That means a genuinely free-rhythm approach to riming. Since his is formally "blank verse," he can afford to rime so much and to animate his works as poems, yet remain no less free-rhythmic than a Walt Whitman or a German expressionist.

Experience with Russian, a language containing many long words, has shown that the more syllables, the stronger the pauses between words (Belyj). But clearly the converse is also true: the stronger the pauses between the words, as e.g. in dense riming, the more syllables can be read at once, or (if there are few syllables) the more weight is given to the existing stress, and the more strongly underscored is the emphasized colon; for a strengthening of the pause leads to an increased potential energy of the phrasing (in Belyj's terminology), and as a result the intonation (the kinetic energy) proper also is strengthened.

Generally the opposition between rime and logic (Closs, *op. cit.*, p. 13) is manifested in Yiddish poetry both in the dense rimes of the children's song and in the impulsive riming of Leyeles (as one expression of his mystifying approach to the wonder of poetic experience), but *not* in the symmetrical final rime, which is abundant in the most judicious metric songs of the day.

9. Between Languages and Literatures

A few supplementary hints need to be added to the preceding discussion, especially chapters 3 and 5.

9.1. With respect to *linguistic* properties and their role in rhythm formation, many data are lacking, especially about order and sentence structuring. My lay remarks are intended to stimulate the linguists to proceed in this direction. All in all Yiddish free-rhythm poetry stands, *linguistically*, between the East Slavic pattern with its many long words and the strengthened pauses (and pause differences) between them, and the Germanic pattern, with its many enclitic and proclitic combinations and its possibility of denser stressing and thus differentiation of stress level. The interaction of these two bases makes possible the great elasticity of the Yiddish free rhythms in contrast to both the uniformity of phrasing of the Russian *bylina* (at one pole) and the nearly prosaic (because stress-varying) "iambicity" of modern English free rhythms (at the other pole). Yet we often feel that Yiddish free rhythms lean in one direction or the other, not only because of personal rhythmic or thematic inclinations (as we have shown up to now) but also because of the influence of the surrounding manner of feeling the language. In a most general sense, *this*—other factors aside—is the cause of the "speechlike" and "iambic" character of more recent Yiddish free-rhythm poetry in the United States, just as the influences of the Russian language multiplied the number of dactylic endings (in the line interior, too) in the Yiddish poetry of the Russian sphere. In both cases, the statement applies mainly to the period between both World Wars, i.e. to Yiddish writers deeply rooted in the respective languages of the non-Jewish environment.

9.2. Concerning the manner in which the influence of foreign *literatures* was experienced, we should add that the stimulus which upset the old melodic equilibrium did indeed come from German expressionism and Russian modernism (in addition to the changes in Jewish life). But true free rhythms were created in Yiddish in a significant degree primarily in America. The influence of the American moderns is strongly in evidence, especially among the younger generation, both in contents and in means of expression, and even more perhaps in the manner of poem construction in the free rhythms.[114] It was only in America that the Yiddish poem freed itself of counted measures and equal stanzas.[115] We must remember, in this connection, that Polish and Russian poetry, after a short ferment between the wars, mostly went in the direction of t.-s. metrics (or something close to t.-s.),[116] and this development was joined by the principal Yiddish poets in those countries. Thus, the *Yung-Vilne* group was completely t.-s. or free-tonic (Elkhonon Vogler), while the same generation in America was free-rhythmic.

9.3. The influence of *Hebrew* in this domain is quite feeble. This is because Hebrew was not a living territorial language; the surrounding phonetics affected it so strongly that in its history Hebrew poetry passed through every metric doctrine.[117] To be sure, its forms have been highly inert and the Yiddish folksong has preserved certain specifically Hebrew properties (particularly in Jewish religious and national subject matter, where Hebrew words, word pairs and rimes occur aplenty, often taken over from medieval translations). In terms of rhythm, the Bible had the same import as the surrounding German system; on the other hand, it had no device by which to counter the German *stanza system*. For this reason the Hebrew features in Yiddish are basically an addition

[114] I refrain from mentioning names because the question of concrete influences in this domain is still almost unexplored. But in addition to direct personal infuence, general atmosphere is also important.

[115] It is interesting that, in the same environment, American Hebrew poetry long held on to the t.-s. system, drawing inspiration from English *classical* poetry, not from the contemporary environment. The reason is inherent in differences of language and cultural history which require a separate analysis.

[116] In Russia, a contributing factor of this development (besides the official line) was the possibility of rich alternation of language rhythm in the same metric framework. In Poland, the t.-s. system was still felt to be in a fresh contrast to the syllabic pattern of classical Polish poetry.

[117] Tonic in the Bible and early liturgical poetry (*piyuṭim*), quantitative in the Arabic era, syllabic in Italy and during the Enlightenment, and t.-s. in the recent period.

within the framework of the general metrics. Their impact is either linguistic or conscious rather than directly aural: this is true especially of the various acrostically concatenated lines.[118]

It was only modern poetry which could, with its *conscious* approach, adopt biblical rhythmics, for the genuine free rhythms sought not the formal metrics but the deeper inner rhythmic properties. Leyvik (in "Der volf"; see §5.5) and Leyeles (e.g. in "Ruvn"—*A yid oyfn yam*, p. 85) each displayed their peculiar individualities in biblical material, but in the works of both we detect the biblical rhythm in the *linguistic expression*. On this point Leyeles, who is metrically further removed from the Bible, is closer to it in essence thanks to his Hebraizing diction, sentence structure, and parallelisms.

The same goes for the Russian *bylina*: the area of its dying existence was far from the Jewish Pale of Settlement and did not affect its poetry directly. But the deepened appreciation of the structure of rhythmic configurations enabled Yiddish poets to live themselves even into rhythms that were historically passé and to revive them in Yiddish, too. Leyeles writes ("Di almone un er," *Fabius Lind*, p. 99; see also p. 105):

> *Nisht keyn shvartse khmare oyfn himl rayt,*
> *nisht keyn dunerblits di heykh tseshnaydt.*
> *S'ligt di gore erd itst a fartayete,*
> *Di mentsh-getretene—a tsetumlte,*
> *A tsetumlte, a tseruderte, erev tsiternish, erev shoydernish.*

('Not a black heavy cloud rides the sky, / not a thunderflash cuts the high. / The whole earth now lies concealed, / the man-trodden one lies confused, / confused, upset, on the verge of quaking, on the verge of shuddering.') Only the organic rendition of rhythm, diction (dactyls), sentence structure and literary figures of the Russian *bylina* (as formerly of the Bible) creates the desired impact on the reader; and its effectiveness is all the greater if the Yiddish reader *knows* the model according to which the poem was created and reads it as this rhythm atmosphere requires.

[118] It is interesting, however, that the environment penetrated even into the "Hebrew" devices themselves. For example, in a double-acrostic song (Ginzburg and Marek, *op. cit.*, no. 26), we read under the letter tav: *nit keyn Toyre, nit keyn gelt / vos zhe Toyg mir gor di velt?* ('Neither learning nor money, / what good is the whole world to me?'). *Toyg*, though spelled with a ṭet, has entered into an alliterative combination with *toyre*, spelled with tav; hearing triumphed over an alphabetic device.

ON THE OLDEST DATED WORK IN YIDDISH LITERATURE

LEO FUKS (Amsterdam)

During a visit to England in the fall of 1953 I had the unusual privilege of discovering at the University Library of Cambridge a manuscript which, upon investigation, turned out to be the oldest Yiddish manuscript known to date. It comprises a collection of literary works, particularly epic poems. One exception is a list of the Pentateuchal sections (*sidrot*) and a Yiddish glossary of the names of the stones in the breastpiece worn by the High Priest. The manuscript also contains a rimed fable about a dying lion which ends with the explicit date, 3 Kislev [5]143 (November 9, 1382).

That the pedigree of Yiddish literature goes back to the thirteenth and fourteenth centuries has been the view of almost all modern students of the Yiddish language and literature.[1] But this conclusion was arrived at on the basis of the philological or literary analysis of copies of the sixteenth century, since, except for a Yiddish translation of the psalms which goes back to at least 1490 and is found in the Berlin State Library,[2] no literary works of previous periods had been known to this day.

The manuscript under discussion here was brought to Cambridge in 1896 by Professor Solomon Schechter from the Fostat Genizah in Egypt. In my opinion it contains the repertoire of a Jewish minstrel.

The manuscript consists of 42 folios approximately 18.8 × 13.7 cm and includes four epic poems based on Jewish literary motifs borrowed from the Bible and from post-biblical aggadic literature. They are:

1. Folios 1a–2a. An epic poem about which it can be concluded almost with certainty that it treats of Moses. Only three out of 13 pages of this poem have been preserved.
2. Folios 2a–6b. Song of Paradise.
3. Folios 6b–17a. The Patriarch Abraham.
4. Folios 17b–18b. The Pious Joseph.[3]
5. Folios 19a–19b. Untitled. A Fable of a Dying Lion.[4] This fable can be considered a literary no-man's land in the transition from works with Jewish content to works whose contents reflect a cultural sphere outside of Jewish life.
6. Folio 20b. List of the Pentateuchal sections and glossary of the breastplate stones.

[1] L. Landau: *Arthurian Legends, or Hebrew-German Rhymed Version of the Legend of King Arthur*, Leipzig, 1912 (introduction); B. Borokhov: [The Tasks of Yiddish Philology], in *Der pinkes*, Vilna, 1913, p. 4.

[2] M. Steinschneider: *Die handschriftlichen Verzeichnisse der Kön. Bibliothek zu Berlin*, Berlin, 1878, vol. 2, no. 50.

[3] Published by me in *Yidishe kultur* (New York), February, 1954, p. 33.

[4] Published as part of my article, "The Oldest Literary Works in Yiddish in a Manuscript of the Cambridge University Library," *Journal of Jewish Studies* 4 (1953) 176–181, pp. 180f.

7. Folios 21–42. The Duke Horant (♮ *dvkvσ hvrnt*). An epic poem displaying in its principal features considerable similarity with the nuclear portion of the Gudrun Epic, the so-called Hilde Saga.

One of the numerous questions arising in connection with the Yiddish Codex of the Cambridge University Library (*C.Y.*) concerns its language. Are we justified in considering this language as Yiddish? The fact that it is written in letters of the Hebrew alphabet is in itself not sufficient proof that the language is Yiddish; an English or Dutch text transliterated into Hebrew letters would not convert these languages into Yiddish or vice versa. We are therefore correct in asking this question about the text whose language resembles a medieval German dialect and which was recorded by a writer or scribe in Hebrew letters.

There are on the whole two types of criteria for establishing the identity of a language. One set of criteria, strictly linguistic in nature, requires that a language manifest certain peculiarities of form or structure to differentiate it from some other similar language.[5] From this point of view the text at hand contains few *prima facie* lexicological or phonetic features that would identify it as definitely Old Yiddish;[6] the only words of Hebrew derivation are ♮*θjplh* 'church' and the proper names contained in the titles of the works.

The other set of criteria are of a socio-linguistic nature, and in my opinion they should be decisive in establishing the identity of a language.

I should like to illustrate the validity of socio-linguistic criteria by three examples. (1) Afrikaans is generally treated as a language separate from Dutch, yet not because of any number of features in its phonology, grammar, or vocabulary, but merely because the South Africans of Dutch descent, with the rise of their language movement about 1850, recognized Afrikaans as their own language and gave it that name. (2) The following incident occurred to me during the late war. In the course of the German occupation of Holland I spent some time in hiding in a small village located very close to the German border. One evening, while we were watching through the windows of our attic the city of Emden burning after a heavy air raid, the conversation turned, as it so often did, to the senselessness of the war. I wondered aloud whether the Germans across the border understood the speech of their Dutch neighbors. My host answered: Not only do we understand one another but we talk the same language. I suggested that in that case the local Dutch population spoke German. With ill-concealed indignation, he replied that they definitely spoke Dutch, not German. (3) To a number of Dutch Jews of the old and the young generation, I read a sentence and asked them to judge whether it was Yiddish or Dutch. The sentence ran: *Doe hem een mitsve en breng dit Chommesj naar de Chazzen in sjoel* 'do him a favor and bring this Pentateuch to the cantor in the synagogue'. Despite the fact that the

[5] The most recent defense of linguistic criteria in establishing the identity of Yiddish was made by N. Süsskind: [How Yiddish Originated], *Yidishe shprakh* (New York), 13 (1953) 97–108, p. 99.

[6] On the characteristics of Old Yiddish, see Max Weinreich: "Yiddish," in *Algemeyne yidishe entsiklopedye,* supplementary volume *Yidn B*, 1940, 23–90; pp. 23–53.

sentence contained a number of Yiddish words, the unanimous verdict was that it was Dutch.—For reasons like these I am firmly convinced that it is the sociolinguistic criteria which are decisive. The question of the separateness of a language or dialect is "not of a linguistic nature, but of a socio-political or perhaps a culture-political character. For language is one of the first forms which permits a human group to define itself in contrast to others. What is decisive is the awareness that one speaks one's own language or that the language is regarded as different by outsiders."[7]

In what period did the Ashkenazic Jews accept the Germanic language they were speaking as "Yiddish"? In other words, when was it that they became aware of speaking a specific language, or when was it noticed by outsiders that the language of the Jews was in some ways peculiar? The answer to this question is concealed in both Jewish and non-Jewish sources. In the Hebrew writings of the noted commentator Rashi (1040–1105), we find the term "the language of Ashkenaz" in reference to the language used by the Jews in German-speaking regions.[8] But if there is any doubt as to what Rashi meant by this designation, it disappears when we compare another Hebrew source, a manuscript from the year 1290, where the label "language of Ashkenaz" is paralleled by *leshonenu* 'our language'.[9] In subsequent generations, as shown by sources e.g. of the sixteenth century, both terms are in use, and we find explicit indications that the "language of Ashkenaz" as well as "our language" means "the language used among us" or "the language which we speak."[10] The same applies to the term *taytsh,* which remains in use at least until the eighteenth century.[11] As for the designation "Yiddish," traces of it lead us back to the sixteenth century.[12]

That the native inhabitants of German-speaking countries were aware of the difference in the speech of the Jews is a fact for which we seem to find hints as far back as the fifteenth century.[13]

Another interesting problem is to determine how our manuscript got to an Egyptian Genizah. I need not dwell here on the enormously important role played by Egypt in Jewish history. It was in this country that, according to biblical tradition, the children of Israel took their first steps to peoplehood; it was here that a new and glorious branch of Jewish culture, the Judeo-Hellenistic philosophy, came to bloom; it was here, too, that the Jewish intellect reached the previously unattained heights symbolized by Maimonides. It is probably safe to say that

[7] I owe the formulations appearing in quotation marks to Professor W. Gs. Hellinga of Amsterdam.

[8] N. Shtif: "Loshn ashkenaz—taytsh, leshoyneynu, yidish, undzer shprakh," *Yidishe filologye* (Warsaw), 1 (1923) 386–388. On the names of Yiddish, see also E. Spivak: [The Principal Names of Yiddish], *Fragn fun yidisher shprakh* (Moscow), 1 (1938) 71–86.

[9] Shtif, *op. cit.*

[10] Quoted by N. Shtif, *op. cit.*, from *Mirkebet ha-mišneh,* Cracow, 1584.

[11] Max Weinreich: *Studien zur Geschichte und dialektischen Gliederung der jiddischen Sprache,* unpublished Ph.D. dissertation, Marburg, 1923, vol. 1, p. 5.

[12] J. Shatzky: [On the Names of Yiddish], *Yivo-Bleter* 8 (1935) 148–154, p. 148.

[13] *Ibid.*, pp. 152f.

there has not been a single period in Jewish history in which Jews did not live on Egyptian soil.

But not only in Hellenistic, Roman, and Byzantine times were there large communities of Jews in Egypt; there are sufficient indications that even in the Middle Ages under Arab rule the Jewish inhabitants of that country were not without significance. They enjoyed, under the circumstances, a relatively large measure of freedom and equality and even possessed an extensive autonomy.[14] But their status was seriously aggravated when the Mameluke dynasty came to power (1250 A.D.). Like the rest of the population they were subjected to oppressive tax burdens, and like the Christian section of the population were exposed to humiliations, discriminations, and outright persecution. The result was that the Jewish community in Egypt declined seriously, both economically and culturally.[15]

Even the unfavorable circumstances experienced by the Egyptian Jews under the Mameluke rule seem ideal in comparison with those prevailing in the Christian lands of Europe at the same time, that is after the Crusades and the Black Death.[16] There they were subjected not only to humiliations but to the most brutal physical attacks by the Christian rulers and by the populace roused to blind hatred by religious fanaticism.[17] While the Black Death in the Christian lands of the West brought with it the extermination of large numbers of Jews, these consequences of the epidemic remained unknown in the countries of the Crescent.[18] No wonder then that many of the surviving Jews of the West sought a haven in the countries of the Near East, including, according to our opinion, Egypt. To be sure, the documents known to us from the Genizah do not inform us about the life of Ashkenazic Jews in Egypt in the fourteenth century. Nevertheless we may assume that the country was not only a point of transit for them on their way to Palestine, but that some of them settled there for the simple reason that there they were never driven to the desperate state of having to kill, burn, or drown their own children or themselves in self-defense.[19]

Starting with the latter half of the fourteenth century a stream of Jewish immigrants flowed from the West into the Balkan countries, then under Turkish occupation, and continued to flow until the end of the Middle Ages.[20] We even know of a proclamation issued at the beginning of the fifteenth century by the Rabbi of Adrianople, Isaac Ṣarfati, "to the sacred Jewish community in Ashkenaz . . . in the cities of Swabia, the Rhineland, Styria, Moravia, and Hungary," pointing out the advantages of Turkey and the Kingdom of Ishmael, explaining

[14] S. Dubnow: *Weltgeschichte des jüdischen Volkes* . . . , Berlin, 1926, vol. 4, §§60, 61; A. Straus: *Toldot ha-Yehudim be-Miṣrayim ve-Surya taḥat šilton ha-Mameluḳim*, Jerusalem, 1944, vol. 1, pp. 26–47.

[15] J. Shiper: *Toldot ha-kalkala ha-yehudit*, Tel Aviv, 1937, vol. 2, pp. 582–84.

[16] *Ibid.*

[17] M. Güdemann: *Yidishe kultur-geshikhte in mitl-alter* . . . , Yiddish translation by N. Shtif, Berlin, 1922, p. ii.

[18] J. Starr: *Romania; the Jewries of the Levant after the Fourth Crusade*, Paris, 1949, p. 10.

[19] S. Dubnow, *op. cit.*, vol. 4, §§33, 34; vol. 5, §44.

[20] *Ibid.*, vol. 5, 66.

that there they could settle and "breathe freely, unlike Germany and its neighboring countries where one misfortune follows another. . . . Do not remain there with hands folded and come to the country shown to us by the Lord."[21]

Egypt, too, belonged in the first half of the fourteenth century to the places of refuge for the persecuted Jews of the European West.[22] As one of the principal commercial centers of the world it attracted a stream of emigrants from Spain and North Africa until after the Middle Ages. There is no reason to doubt that because of the persecutions in the German-speaking countries an Ashkenazic Jewish settlement was established in Egypt just like in the Turkish countries. The Egyptian historian Makrisi relates that during the first half of the fifteenth century there were no less than twelve synagogues in Cairo and Fostat, of which only two belonged to the Karaites and one to the Samaritans.[23] From the travel journal of R. Meshullam Volterra, who visited Egypt in 1481, we learn that in the first decades of that century, Alexandria and Cairo were inhabited by thousands of Jewish families. He also notes that his companion in Cairo was a certain Joseph bar Yehezkiah Ashkenazi.[24]

Together with the circumstances described above, the manuscript under discussion here may also serve in support of the hypothesis that there was an important Yiddish-speaking community in Egypt in the second half of the fourteenth century. The chemical analysis of the paper on which *C.Y.* is written indicates with the highest probability that the paper is of Oriental manufacture.[25] This would indicate that the collection was written down in Egypt itself rather than brought there from Germany. It is not likely, besides, that it should have been brought from Germany to Egypt; an individual or family fleeing from imminent death would take with them, if anything, only serious religious writings in Hebrew, and not the literature of entertainment in Yiddish. It is this circumstance, after all, which is cited as the principal explanation for the fact that no Yiddish manuscripts of the fourteenth or fifteenth centuries in Germany have come down to us.[26] If *C.Y.* was actually written down in Egypt, then it did not have to undergo

[21] S. A. Rosanes: *Dibre yeme Israel be-Togarma,* Tel Aviv, 1930–38, vol. 1, pp. 19–21, 163–175.

[22] A. Straus, *op. cit.* (footnote 14), p. 221.

[23] S. Dubnow, *op. cit.*, vol. 5, p. 486.

[24] J. D. Eisenstein: *Ozar massaot; a Collection of Itineraries by Jewish Travellers to Palestine, Syria, Egypt . . .*, New York, 1926, pp. 90–92.

[25] The Vezelinstituut T. N. O. of Delft, Holland, states that it is improbable that the paper was made in Germany. Mr. E. J. Labarre, founder and secretary of the "Paper Publications Society," writes: "Frankly, my general opinion is that this cannot be European paper. In the fourteenth century most excellent paper was made in Italy and before then in Spain and it seems to me most improbable that the paper had suffered so much from damp, etc., that we only see a small mass of fibres. The fibres do not appear to have been damaged by fungus; they are quite clean and in my microscope resemble most the fibres of linen. . . . Is it not possible that this paper is of Oriental origin? That is to say from North Africa etc.?" This opinion is shared by the paper expert Dr. A. Horodisch of Amsterdam.

[26] Maks Erik: *Di geshikhte fun der yidisher literatur (fun di eltste tsaytn biz der haskole-tkufe)*, Warsaw, 1928, p. 29.

the tribulations of a long trip and thus became the sole specimen of fourteenth century Yiddish literature which has survived to date.

The next consideration—concerning the date mentioned in the manuscript—also serves to support the hypothesis of its Egyptian origin.

The story of the dying lion is the only work in the Codex which is dated at all (November 9, 1382). Unlike the usual story of the sick lion, this fable is extremely hostile to the lion. In it the lion receives the ultimate punishment from God because of his criminal behavior and his unjust treatment of the other animals. The author even justifies the right of the former victims of the lion to rejoice over his downfall. This acutely personal emphasis in the reference, as well as the date, which is so unusual for a medieval poem, leads one to suppose that the fable was composed under the impact of an important event which was witnessed and deeply experienced by the author himself.

What happened in the month of November, 1382 A.D., which could have evoked from the poet the impassioned words (in Hebrew) with which he closes his poem in jubilation: "the conceit of the wicked is dressed in tattered clothes"? The answer, it seems, is contained in the political events which took place in Egypt at this particular time.

In November, 1382, the rule of the Mameluke-Baharid dynasty, which had not been particularly favorable to the Jews, as we have said above, came to an end. Let us follow the events of that time as described by a French historian: "Finally Barkouk became the master, and the young king [i.e. the legitimate successor] was hardly an obstacle: the plague felled him on May 8, 1382. Taken by surprise, the powerful officer did not dare to have himself proclaimed sultan, and entrusted the supreme power to a brother of the young Ali, called Hadjdji, still a child of eleven. However, the Mamelukes were not fooled and it was against Barkouk that they began scheming. Barkouk therefore decided to have himself crowned. But he acted politely and it was the Council of Magistrates, presided over by the Caliph, which, in view of the necessity of an energetic sultan, deposed the last descendant of Kalaoun and unanimously designated Barkouk as a sultan. . . . Barkouk ascended the throne, called on by the Council of Magistrates and the Caliph to restore order in the empire. His enthronement, on November 26, 1382, took place . . ." etc.[27]

In other words, in the month of November the political developments in the country came to a head, and it became clear to all, including our poet, that the energetic Barkouk was seizing power. A dark period in the life of the Egyptian Jews was coming to an end, and as usual in such days, the hopes for a brighter day ran high. It is in this atmosphere, I think, that our fable came into being; at least it is dated in those days. This could serve as the clinching proof of the fact that the entire Codex, which is written in the same hand and on the same type of paper, of Oriental origin, was written in Egypt. It was there that a Jewish minstrel copied it. Possibly some of the poems were his own works, but they

[27] Gaston Wiet: "L'Egypte arabe . . . ," in G. Hanotaux: *Histoire de la nation égyptienne*, vol. 4, Paris, 1937, pp. 510f.

could not all be the products of a single man, for some of them cite the names of the writers (or, perhaps, the copyists) Isaac (♮ˀ*jzq*) and Abraham.

The indication that in the late Middle Ages there was a Yiddish speaking community in Egypt, which was not without literary fruits, is an important fact for Jewish cultural history, and for the history of Yiddish literature in particular it is an entirely novel insight.

Fate was not very favorably disposed to the largest epic poem of *C.Y.*, that of Duke Horant. It is a pity that the last portions of the poem have not come down to us, for they would have given us the solution to the plot, which is concerned with the abduction of Hilde, the daughter of King Hagen. But even the surviving portions of the poem are enough to show that, apart from certain general motifs which Duke Horant shares with the Hilde saga as we know it from the Ambross manuscript written by Hans Ried (1502–1515),[28] the two works differ considerably in their details.

The common motifs are the following:

(1) Young Eten, better known under the name Hetel, hearing of Hilde's rare beauty, undertakes to equip a fleet and to send it to the country of this woman he desires in order to capture her and bring her to his own land. He does this because Hilde's father, the wild king Hagen, has all emissaries coming for Hilde's hand killed.

(2) The expedition is equipped with much care and great luxury.

(3) Horant's song is the decisive factor in the cunningly devised scheme for the capture of Hilde.

(4) Horant and his companion make believe that they are refugees from the German lands because they have lost the favor of King Hetel.

The two poems are different in that in *C.Y.*:

(a) The plot in connection with the capture takes place not in Ireland but in Greece; Hilde's father Hagen is king of that country.

(b) The advice to take a wife is given to Hetel by Horant and by his brother Marung (who incidentally plays a very minor role in *C.Y.*).

(c) Horant is the leader of the entire expedition and is alone responsible for it, and does not have the secondary function of a merchant. While in the Ambross manuscript the principal part is played by Fruote, his name is not even mentioned in *C.Y.*

(d) Horant attempts to gain favor with the Greeks, not as a merchant dealing in expensive wares, but as a charitable man. He proclaims that "the poor people" should come to him, in order that "they too should live in joy."

(e) Horant does not hide his two hundred knights in the hold of the ship and does not bring them secretly into forty houses, but brings them to the city openly, and finds a lodging for them in the house of the richest merchant in town.

(f) Horant does not use cunning in order to approach Hilde, to seduce her with his beautiful songs, and to win her for his scheme. Rather he sings at his lodging, and when Hilde wants to hear him, all her presents and even a "sleeping partner"

[28] E. Martin, ed.: *Kudrun*, Halle/S., $_2$1902.

which she has for Horant are of no avail; she must take the trouble to come to him, "under the linden tree trunk," near the inn.

(g) It is not a chamberlain but a minstrel who appears to be the confidant of Hilde and Horant in helping them carry out the elopement.

(h) It is Horant who gives Hilde a golden ring as a token of their agreement, and not vice versa.

In addition, Duke Horant contains three narrative motifs which are not to be found in the Hilde saga at all. They are the following:

(i) The motif of the three forest giants (Vitold with the steel prong; his brother Asprian, and Vate the "Greek").

(ii) The motif of the king's lion killed by Vitold during Hagen's meal.

(iii) The street scene during the royal procession to Whitsun Mass.

It is evident from this very sketchy outline that Duke Horant occupies a literary place of its own. One could say that it is located between the Hilde saga and the Rother epic,[29] although a motif so general as the abduction of a chosen woman is not unknown in other Germanic epic works of the Middle Ages (Oswald, Salomon and Morolf, and others). Note that Greece, the scene of the plot in the abduction of Hilde, is close to Constantinople, where Rother was active; compare also the narrative motifs cited as (i) and (ii) above, which are common to both Duke Horant and Rother. But there is also the possibility that Duke Horant is an older version of the Hilde saga which was not available to Hans Ried, and was adapted for a Jewish audience by a Jewish minstrel who was no stranger to the German minstrel repertoire (he is familiar with, and refers to, Tristan and Isolde). But we will deal with this aspect of Old Yiddish literature in the introduction to *C.Y.*, which will soon be published in Amsterdam.

[29] J. de Vries, ed.: *Rother*, Heidelberg, 1922.

A NOTE ON THE YIDDISH HORANT

CHAIM GININGER

[In connection with the preceding article by Leo Fuks, "On the Oldest Dated Work in Yiddish Literature," the Editor was pleased to receive the following Note by Mr. Gininger which, apart from its relation to Mr. Fuks' discoveries, deals with a matter of independent significance for the history of Yiddish linguistics.]

In the years 1948–49 in Paris, I devoted myself to collecting materials for a biography of Ernest-Henri Lévy. Lévy was a well known professor of German in France who acquired a reputation, among others, by several fundamental studies in Yiddish linguistics. Since he occupied, especially in his later years, a German chair at the University of Strasbourg, I thought it advisable to consult first Professor Edmond Vermeil, a Strasbourg Germanics scholar then lecturing at the University of Paris. A twenty-minute conversation with Professor Vermeil succeeded in shifting the lines of my interest in Lévy, which was concerned chiefly with discovering as much as possible about his work on Yiddish. I learned that Lévy had been working on a doctoral dissertation on a Yiddish subject; that it had been considered to be of great significance; that he had completed it but had never submitted it to the appropriate authorities in order to receive his doctorate. My problem now was to find Lévy's dissertation. The search turned out to be a veritable odyssey. Together with my friend Gerson Epstein, I imposed on the patience of Lévy's sister, Mme. Léopold-Lévi, and his sick brother, Dr. F. Lévy. By special permission from the Ministry of Education to disregard the legal time limit before which the personal files of the deceased could not normally be examined, I searched through the Lévy materials in the National Archives and in the Ministry itself. It stood to reason that Lévy would have attached his thesis, or parts or excerpts from it, to his applications to the Ministry concerning teaching positions. The search proved futile.

Meanwhile I learned that a student and friend of the late Lévy was the present professor of German philology at Strasbourg, M. Jean Fourquet, and I noted that M. Fourquet's doctoral thesis, *L'ordre des éléments de la phrase en germanique ancien* (Paris, 1938), was dedicated "à Monsieur Ernest-Henri Lévy, Professeur Honoraire de l'Université de Strasbourg," and expressed (p. 2) his great appreciation of Lévy. The ensuing correspondence with Professor Fourquet brought out two new facts in connection with this matter, which are, I think, worth citing in detail.

1. In a letter of February 25, 1949, Professor Fourquet informed me that a friend of Ernest-Henri Lévy, Isidore Lévy, was living in Paris and was among those "who knew about the papers hidden in the Ecole des Hautes Etudes. These papers may have been taken along by Rabbi Hermann Weil, who succeeded in getting an American visa and who is supposed to have died during the [Atlantic] crossing." This indicated a new search at the Ecole and an inquiry concerning the mysterious Hermann Weil. Isidore Lévy, Professor Emeritus of the Collège de

France, told me that Rabbi Weil, a German refugee, had been interested in E.-H. Lévy's work; that he, I. Lévy, had permitted Weil to remove it occasionally from its place of deposit in order to consult it. Weil then left for America and it was reported that he perished when his ship was sunk. The dissertation itself should still have been concealed in the secretariat of the Ecole des Hautes Etudes. Professor I. Lévy, despite his very advanced age, took the trouble of joining me in a perusal of a mass of fascicles in the files and drawers of the secretariat, but again to no avail.

2. Professor Fourquet was able to furnish me with information about E.-H. Lévy's study proper. It might be best to let M. Fourquet himself speak, quoting his letter to me of March 21, 1949. But I might preface this with a pertinent quotation from M. Fourquet's necrology of Lévy (apparently the only one published about this great scholar). In the special necrology volume issued by the Faculté des Lettres of Strasbourg University (vol. 103 of its Publications), entitled *Mémorial des années 1939–1945* (Paris, 1947), pp. 59–63, we read on pp. 60f.: "An unexpected event turned this relentless scholar in yet another direction. Among the manuscripts of the Genizah of Cairo, purchased by an English scholar for the University of Cambridge, there were found texts in German of the fourteenth century, recorded according to Jewish custom in Hebrew characters." And then: "These are probably wordings recorded from memory by Jews who fled from Swabia to Egypt. One of these summarizes the literary versions of German epic legends. . . . Ernest Lévy transcribed these texts in Latin characters for the purpose of editing them in normalized Middle High German. It was a delicate problem and one which had never yet been posed."

When, accordingly, I questioned Professor Fourquet concerning the mentioned Genizah document, his answer revealed that he was himself quite deeply absorbed in the matter; it would be worthwhile to take him up on his promise (expressed in the previous letter) to "gladly contribute my help in the possible editing and publication" of these texts. Regarding the Genizah manuscript and Lévy's study of it, he wrote as follows: ". . . The text is heavily damaged; only several pages permit the reconstruction of a more or less coherent text. It consists partly of biblical subjects (Abraham, fables), partly (about ten folios) of Middle High German verses from a poem whose hero is *Horant*, known from the Kudrun saga—all in Hebrew letters. The language is late Middle High German (fourteenth century?) with central German peculiarities (*nummer* instead of *nimmer*).—The spelling offers great difficulties as a result of the lack of consistency in the notation of the vowels.—In the cursive form of the letters, mem and alef . . . , reš, dalet . . . can hardly be distinguished. . . .

"According to what E. Lévy told me, he had the intention of publishing the poem fragment from the Kudrun cycle, namely under the title *Dukus Horant*; for this purpose he had invented his own system of rendering a transcription which would be readable by Germanic scholars, but which would distinguish the reconstructed vowels and the consonant values which were based on his conjectures from those which were really attested; e.g. $w^{å}s^{se}r$ for ♮ *vvsr*."[1]

[1] For a key to our transliteration, see p. vii of this volume.

To my question concerning the source of his knowledge that the text came from the Fostat Genizah, M. Fourquet replied that he had heard it "from my former colleague Dr. Ginsburger; I know nothing else—I first heard the word at that time." His reference is to the well known historian of the Alsatian Jews and late "professeur de littérature judéo-araméenne postbiblique," Moïse Ginsburger (1865–1949).

In his letter, Professor Fourquet enclosed a fragment of the Horant poem "from one of the few entirely legible passages." He transcribed it, as he puts it, in a " 'normalized' Middle High German spelling," and we cite it here in that form, for lack of the only proper thing, an unravelled Yiddish original:

. . . . Vil manegen pfellel schône | und manegen samit rîch
Gewirket alle mit golde | und vun gesteine rîch
Und ouch vum schônen hermelin
Die nummer besser mochten sîn.

Ouch hieß er in gewinnen alles des genuoc
Und pfert und harnesch, ouch spîse man in dar getruoc
Zuo deme schiffe hin în // daz in in der reise sulde sîn.

Vun silber un vun golde wart in das schiff geslagen
Daz die marner muosten sprechen: es mac nummê getragen.
Do er genam si innen (?) schiffe sân
Horant und alle sîne man,

Der stolze künec Eten gienc mit in ûf das mer
Ime folgten vun vrouwen und vun mannen ein grôz kreftigez her

Do si quâmen ûf des meres trân
Di risen giengen vur den künec stân.

These stanzas are from folio 26a of the manuscript.

It is thus apparent that essentially E.-H. Lévy could claim consideration as the first discoverer of the Cambridge treasures. In the same letter, Professor Fourquet wrote: "Nothing makes possible the identification of the manuscript." Apparently he meant the copyist, the place, and the date, for he knew now that the manuscript was located in Cambridge. Perhaps the present rediscovery by Mr. Fuks will be more successful than Ernest-Henri Lévy's prediscovery in unraveling these questions, too. The great problem is the linguistic and literary-historical analysis of the document. It constitutes an "important discovery" not only for German research,[2] but also for Yiddish studies.

[2] *Muttersprache* (Lüneburg), 1954, no. 3, p. 117, calls it a "bedeutende Entdeckung."

LITERARY BIBLIOGRAPHIES

by U. W.

1. SHOLOM ALEICHEM (1859–1916): PRINCIPAL RESEARCH SOURCES

The present tentative bibliography was originally prepared for a Columbia University course, Yiddish 151 ("Sholom Aleichem and His World"). It represents a selection from the thousands of items by and on Sholom Aleichem which would be included in a complete listing. It is intended as a first guide for graduate students and others embarking on research projects concerned with this major figure in Yiddish literature.[1]

The abbreviation S. A. stands for "Sholom Aleichem." The language of each item is identified by the following initials: *E*—English, *H*—Hebrew, *R*—Russian, *Y*—Yiddish.

a. General

The basic reference on S. A., as on most Yiddish writers, is the pertinent article in Reyzen's Lexicon:

1. "Sholom Aleichem," in *Leksikon fun der yidisher literatur, prese un filologye*, ed. Zalmen Reyzen, Vilna, 1929 (2nd edition), vol. 4, 673–736. *Y*. Combines biographical and critical material and is supplemented by the fullest available (although non-exhaustive) bibliography of S. A.'s works and of critical writing on S. A. up to 1929.

The other major collections of materials on S. A. are the following (detailed references to their contents will be found below):

2. *Tsum ondenk fun S. A.* [In Memory of S. A.], ed. Y. Tsinberg and Sh. Niger, Petrograd, 1917, 176 pp. *Y*. Memoirs, correspondence, criticism.

3. *Dos S. A.-bukh* [The S. A. Book], ed. Y. D. Berkovitsh, New York, 1926, xvi + 312 pp. *Y*. Greatest compilation of correspondence, unfinished works from S. A.'s files; many important biographical monographs; photographs and facsimiles. An indispensable tool for the study of S. A.

b. Works

No authoritative bibliography of S. A.'s works is available. Reyzen's article (see **1** above) lists collected works up to 1929, but does not attempt to cover all first editions. Much useful information will be found in the chronology of S. A.'s life:

4. Berkovitsh, Y. D.: [Dates in S. A.'s Life and Work], in *Dos S. A.-bukh* (see **3** above), 361–369. *Y*.

5. Doyv ben-Moyshe (pseud. of Ber Borokhov): [The Bibliography of S. A.], in *Di tsukunft* (New York), 21 (1916) 721–723, 801–803, 893–895, 1062–1064. *Y*. Utilized by Reyzen (**1**), but not entirely superseded.

The publication of a complete collection of S. A.'s works was undertaken at least three times, but two attempts were not completed; a third is in progress. So far, all series entitled *Ale verk* ('All Works') are, in fact, selections only. The basic edition, planned for about forty volumes, only got as far as volume 28:

6. *Ale verk fun S. A.* [All Works of S. A.], New York, published by the S. A. Folksfond ("People's Fund"), 1917–1925. 28 volumes. This edition was planned and prepared with the participation of S. A. himself, who did not, however, live to see it in print. *Y*.

Other popular American and European editions are based on the above. For example:

7. *Ale verk fun S. A.*, special *Morgn-frayhayt* edition, New York, 1937. 28 volumes. *Y*. Order of volumes different; otherwise identical with **6**.

Another complete collection, planned for twenty volumes, was launched in the Soviet

---

[1] It is a pleasure to thank Messrs. S. Niger and L. Kahn, and especially Miss Dina Abramowicz, librarian at the Yiddish Scientific Institute—Yivo in New York, for their aid.

Union after World War II, but only three volumes had appeared when all Yiddish publishing was suppressed in that country. The following are available:

8. S. A.: *Ale verk*, compiled and annotated by N. Oyslender and A. Frumkin, Moscow, 1948. *Y*. Vol. 1 (533 pp.): Works of the years 1883–1886; vol. 2 (360 pp.): "Kindershpil," "Sender Blank," and S. A.'s poems; vol. 3 (328 pp.): "Stempenyu" and "Yosele Solovey." Volumes 1 and 2 are particularly valuable because S. A.'s earliest stories and poems had never been reprinted elsewhere. The annotations are devoted to important differences between first editions and later variants of works as S. A. himself revised them.

The third complete collection has been launched in Argentina. It is to include previously unpublished works of S. A. obtained from his private archives; the reprinted works are taken from the Folksfond series (**6**) and the post-War Soviet series (**8**).

9. *Ale verk fun S. A.* [All Works of S. A.], Buenos Aires, published by Ikuf (Icuf). Vol. 1 (1952, 346 pp.): "Taybele," "Kindershpil," "Sender Blank un zayn gezindl," "Stempenyu." Vol. 2 (1952, 412 pp.): "Yosele Solovey," "In shturem." Vol. 3 (1952, 372 pp.): "Menakhem Mendl," all of "Tevye der milkhiker." Vol. 4 (1953, 342 pp.): "Motl Peyse dem khazns." Vol. 5 (1953, 375 pp.): "Mayses far yidishe kinder, I and II." Thirty volumes (bound as fifteen) are planned.

A number of important works not (yet) included in either of the above series are the following:

10. S. A.: *Blondznde shtern* [Wandering Stars], e.g. New York, 1912; New York, 1920. Possibly S. A.'s most important novel.

11. S. A.: "Di goldgreber" [The Golddiggers], in *Di tsukunft* (New York), 32 (1927), 555–568, 618–623, 682–687. *Y*. This play, known in an earlier version as "Der oytser," is widely considered to be S. A.'s best.

12. S. A.: *Fargesene bletlekh* [Forgotten Leaves], comp. I. Mitlman and Kh. Nadel, Kiev, 1939. 338 pp. *Y*. Contains works not included in the standard collections.

13. "Fun S. A.'s literarishn iberblayb" [From S. A.'s Literary Estate], in *Dos S. A.-bukh* (**3**), 324–350. *Y*. A number of posthumous fragments.

Some of S. A.'s critical and political pamphlets are cited in Reyzen's article (**1**, esp. 723f.) and in Berkovitsh's chronology (**4**). His most famous critical enterprise—apparently never reprinted—deserves to be listed separately:

14. *Shomers mishpet, oder der sud prisyazhnykh oyf ale romanen fun Shomer, stenografirt vort am vort fun S. A.* [Shomer's Trial, or the Jury Trial of All the Novels by Shomer, Literally Recorded in Shorthand by S. A.], Barditshev, 1888, 104 pp. *Y*. An attack on the extremely popular dime-novels of the period written by Shomer (N. M. Shaykevitsh) and his imitators, together with a plea for serious realistic literature in the genre of Mendele Moykher-Sforim.

A bibliography of S. A. translations does not yet exist. Within his lifetime, S. A. was translated at least into Hebrew, Russian, Polish, German, English, Rumanian, Dutch, and Slovak. Many languages have been added since, including French, Flemish, Bulgarian, Ukrainian, Latvian, Hungarian, Chinese, Japanese, and Esperanto. Interesting brief essays on S. A. translations are:

15. Shatzky, Jacob: "Slavonic Slant on S. A." and "The Untranslatable Translated," in *S. A. Panorama* (**17**), 51–57 and 57–59, resp. *E*.

Soviet translations into Russian, Ukrainian, and Belorussian have been reviewed by:

16. N. R.: [S. A. Translations in the Soviet Union Since the October (1917) Revolution], in *Tsaytshrift far yidisher geshikhte, demografye un ekonomik, literatur-forshung, shprakh-visnshaft un etnografye* (Minsk) 5 (1931) 88–90. *Y*.

Further information on translations will be found in Reyzen (**1**), 726–728. A tentative listing of English translations is included in the present volume (pp. 285ff.).

A bibliography of S. A. illustrations is also unavailable. Some indications are given by Reyzen (**1**), 727. A great deal of illustrative material is contained in:

17. *S. A. Panorama*, ed. M. W. Grafstein, London (Ontario), 1948. 416 pp. *E*.

c. Biography

The best and most accessible brief biography is contained in Reyzen's article (**1**), 673–693. The chronology by Berkovitsh (**4**) is also worth consulting. More detailed accounts are:

18. Gurshteyn, A.: *S. A., zayn lebn un shafn* [. . . His Life and Work], Moscow, 1946. 63 pp. *Y*. Russian version: A. Gurštejn: *S. A.; kritiko-biografičeskij očerk*, Moscow, 1946. 40 pp. *R*.

19. Bilov, Shloyme: *S. A.; biografishe fartseykhenung* [. . . Biographical Note], Kiev, 1939, 83 pp. *Y*. Russian version in Bilov, Š., and Druker, I.: *S. A. (1859–1939); biografičeskij očerk i kritičeskije etjudy* [. . . Biographical Essay and Critical Studies], Kiev, 1939, 168 pp.; 5–79. *R*.

A partly fictionalized biography is:

20. Finkel, Uri: *S. A., 1859–1939* [i.e. upon the occasion of the 80th anniversary of his birth], Moscow, 1939, 382 pp. *Y*. Written according to the Communist party line of the day. For an adverse Soviet review, see B. Slutski: [On U. Finkel's Book . . .], in *Sovetishe literatur*, 1940, no. 9, 125–130.

Archival materials concerning Tsarist police surveillance of S. A. in 1903 were published by:

21. Galant, I. V.: [The *okhranka* and S. A.], in *Jevrejskij vestnik* (Leningrad), 1928, 184f.

Many valuable autobiographical notes, as well as monographs on S. A.'s relations with his family and friends, are contained in *Dos S. A.-bukh* (**3**). Recollections about S. A. by historian-critic S. Dubnov, writers M. Spektor, Y. Kh. Ravnitski, M. Kaufman, educator Shimoyni, and sculptor B. Patlazhan are contained in *Tsum ondenk fun S. A.* (**2**). A rewarding biographical source is the memoirs of S. A.'s brother:

22. Rabinovitsh, Volf (Vevik): *Mayn bruder S. A. (zikhroynes)* [My Brother S. A. (Memoirs)], Kiev, 1939, 233 pp. *Y*.

Important, too, is the work by a close collaborator:

23. Berkovits[h], Y. D.: *Harišonim kibne-'adam; sipure zikronot 'al S. A. ubne-doro* [The Early Ones as Human Beings; Memoirs About S. A. and His Contemporaries], Tel Aviv, 1938–1943, 5 volumes. *H*.

Memoirs about S. A., especially about his visits to various cities, are listed (although not exhaustively) in Reyzen (**1**). See also **26** below.

A phonograph record of S. A. reading "If I Were Rothschild" and "A Joyful Holiday" (?) in Yiddish was issued by RCA Victor in January, 1917 (no. 60144), but discontinued in January, 1920. While the master record is no longer available at the company, a copy is in the possession of the archives of the Yiddish Scientific Institute—Yivo in New York.

d. Correspondence

S. A. as a writer of letters has been characterized by Niger:

24. Niger, Sh.: [S. A. as a Letter Writer], in his *S. A.* (**72**), 215–226. *Y*.

The major collection of S. A.'s correspondence is contained in *Dos S. A.-bukh* (**3**), which comprises letters to his family, friends, colleagues, publishers, and admirers.

A selection of his letters is the following:

25. S. A.: *Oysgeveylte briv (1883–1916)* [Selected Letters . . .], compiled and annotated by I. Mitlman and Kh. Nadel, Moscow, 1941. *Y*. [Library of Congress Catalog, Supplement, vol. 30, 413.]

Smaller but no less interesting compilations of S. A.'s correspondence are the following:

26. Dubnov, S.: [Recollections About S. A. and His Literary Correspondence], in *Jevrejskaja starina* (Petrograd), 9 (1916) 227ff. *R*. Includes 27 letters to historian-critic Dubnov (1880–1890). Yiddish translation in Sh. Dubnov: *Fun "zhargon" tsu yidish*, Vilna, 1929, 53–63 (recollections), 64–98 (letters).

27. *Tsum ondenk* . . . (**2**), 83–128. Contains letters to Mendele Moykher-Sforim, Y. Kh. Ravnitski, maecenas Sh. Shrire, educator Sh. Dobin (Shimoyni), drama director M. Vorkel.

28. [Six Letters from S. A.], in *Tsaytshrift* . . . (for full title, see **16**), 1 (1926) 250–252. Letters connected with his publications, 1889–1900.

29. [Thirty Unpublished Letters from S. A.], in *Filologishe shriftn* [*fun Yivo*], Vilna, 3 (1929) 153–172. To contemporary literary figures.

30. Mayzl, N.: [142 Letters to (writer) Yankev Dinezon], in *Yivo-bleter* 1 (1931) 385–403; 2 (1931) 13–31; 3 (1932) 337–353. *Y*.

31. Seven letters from S. A., in *Rešumot* (Tel Aviv) 5 (1927) 426–430. *H*. Five letters to writer Dovid Frishman (1901–1914), one to writer Sh. Tshernovits (1914), and one to Y. Kh. Ravnitski and Kh. N. Bialik (1909).

32. Nadel, Kh., and Leyptsiker, M.: [S. A. and the Yiddish Theater; Six Letters by S. A. on the Theater (to Sam Adler and I. Spivakovski)], in *Sovetishe literatur*, 1940, no. 8, 109–121.

33. [Letters from S. A. to (His Brother) Mikhl Rabinovitsh], reprinted from *Ha'olam*, no. 55/56, September 22, 1938. *H*.

34. "S. A. in Exile," in *Commentary* (New York) 8 (December, 1949) 582–587. Four letters to British journalist-author Israel Cohen (1906–1908). "S. A. in Sickness," in *Commentary* 10 (October, 1950) 379–383. Fifteen more letters. Only the English translation is published. *E*.

35. [A Note from Peretz and a Card from S. A.], in *Yivo-bleter* 29 (1947) 151–152. *Y*.

Extremely interesting letters from Mendele Moykher-Sforim *to* S. A. are also available:

36. [Letters from Mendele Moykher-Sforim], in *Shriftn fun der katedre far yidisher kultur bay der alukrainisher visnshaftlekher akademye, literarishe un filologishe sektsyes* (Kiev), 1 (1928) 247–282. *Y*. Letters nos. 21–62. Annotated by N. Shtif.

37. [A Letter from M. to S. A.], in *Di yidishe shprakh* (Kiev), no. 7 (1927), 1–2. *Y*.

A number of letters from a minor contemporary writer to S. A. are the following:

38. [Letters from Paltiel Zamoshtshin to S. A.], in *Yivo-bleter* 11 (1937) 20–52, 199–231. Annotated by J. Shatzky. *Y*.

A collection of letters from Y. L. Peretz to S. A.:

39. Mayzl, N.: [Letters from Y. L. Peretz to S. A.], in *Filologishe shriftn* [*fun Yivo*] 3 (1929) 379–410. *Y*. Reprinted in his *Briv un redes fun Y. L. Peretz*, New York, 1944, *passim*.

On correspondence, see also **58** and **83**.

e. Literary Development

No comprehensive study of S. A.'s literary development has yet been written. (For a sketch, see Reyzen (**1**) 693–718.) However, a number of valuable analyses of particular periods of his life or of certain types of his work have been made.

A monograph discussing a variety of 19th-century Yiddish humorous writing by which S. A. was probably influenced is:

40. Niger, Sh.: [Elements of S. A.-Type Humor Before S. A.], in *Pinkes fun Amopteyl fun Yivo* (New York) 1 (1927) 1–12. *Y*. Reprinted in Niger's *S. A.* (**72**) 227–254. *Y*.

Polemics concerning this study:

41. Prilutski, Noyakh: [Concerning the Sources of S. A.'s Humor], in *Di yidishe velt* (Vilna), no. 4 (July, 1928) 138–147. *Y*.

Rejoinder:

42. Niger, Sh.: [Polemics and Scholarship], in *Di yidishe velt*, no. 7 (October, 1928) 137–143. *Y*.

The most important analyses of S. A.'s literary beginnings are the following:

43. Oyslender, N.: [The Young S. A. and His Novel, *Stempenyu*], in *Shriftn* . . . (for full title, see **36**) 1 (1928) 5–72. *Y*. The subtitle, "Materials for a Characterization of S. A.'s Development as an Artist," does fuller justice to this brilliant study. Cf. also **83**.

44. Nusinov, Y.: [S. A.'s Writings in the Newspaper *Yidishes folksblat*], in *Di royte velt* (Kharkov), 1926, no. 5–6, 104–125. *Y*. An analysis of two early works, showing S. A.'s fluctuation between sentimentalism and sober realism.

45. Oyslender, N.: [Notes on Mendele], in *Di royte velt* (Kharkov), 1928, no. 1, 109–119. *Y*. Discusses S. A.'s efforts to establish Mendele as a model writer in Yiddish literature.

Mendele Moykher-Sforim's influential preface to S. A.'s *Folks-bibliotek* no. 2 (1889) is reprinted, with commentary, in:

46. *Visnshaft un revolutsye* (Kiev), 1936, no. 1 (8), 105–140.

47. Niger, Sh.: [S. A.: General Characterization], in his *S. A.* (see **72**); 19–68, especially, deal with S. A.'s beginnings in literature and his search for a suitable literary form.

The gradual maturing of S. A.'s conception of Menakhem-Mendl—one of his major characters—has been studied by:

48. Erik, Maks: [On the Trail of Menakhem-Mendl], in *Bikhervelt* (Warsaw), 1928, no. 1, 3–10, and no. 2, 13–17. *Y*.

The real-life prototypes of several characters in S. A.'s early works have been identified by:

49. Rabinovitsh, A. Sh.: [Concerning Several of S. A.'s Characters], in *Tsaytshrift* . . . (for full title, see **16**), 1 (1926) 252–253. *Y*.

S. A.'s development as a playwright has been studied by:

50. Dobrushin, Y.: [S. A.'s Playwriting; an Attempted Preliminary Study], in *Tsaytshrift* . . . (for full title, see **16**) 2–3 (1928) 405–424. *Y*. Reprinted in his *In iberboy* (**55**), 199–227. *Y*.

Also important:

51. Oyslender, N.: Commentaries on several plays, in S. A.: *Dramatishe shriftn*, vol. 1, Kharkov–Kiev, 1932, 229–315. *Y*. Covers the plays "A dokter," "Der get," "Di asife," "Yaknehoz," "Mazltov," "Farbitn di yotsres," and—in considerable detail—"Tsezeyt un tseshpreyt" (270–293, 299–315).

52. Erik, M[aks]: [Concerning S. A.'s *Ksovim fun a komivoyazhor* ("Railroad Stories")], in *Visnshaft un revolutsye* (Kiev), no. 3–4 (1935), 161–172.

A stimulating study of the social setting from which S. A.'s humor was derived is:

53. Viner, M.: [The Social Roots of S. A.'s Humor], written as an introduction to the 1932 Soviet edition of *Motl Peyse dem khazns*, and reprinted in his *Tsu der geshikhte fun der yidisher literatur in 19tn yorhundert*, New York, 1946, vol. 2, 235–280. *Y*. While based on a Marxist analysis of Jewish society around the turn of the century, this essay contains many brilliant insights, acceptable even to those who do not agree with its premises.

An earlier, more sketchy essay along somewhat similar lines:

54. Hurvits, Kh. D.: [Socio-Economic Types in Modern Yiddish Literature], in *Di tsukunft* (New York) 16 (1911) 185–195, 246–254, 315–321, 366–375. *Y*.

The text history of the following works by S. A. has been studied:

55. Dobrushin, Y.: [Two Basic Editions of S. A.'s *Kleyne mentshelekh mit kleyne hasoges*], in his *In Iberboy*, Moscow, 1932, 228–254. *Y*.

56. Holdes, A.: Introduction to S. A.'s *Blondznde shtern*, Part I (vol. 4 in a series of *Ale verk*), Kiev, 1936, 7–156. *Y*. Contains both a critical evaluation of the novel and important factual background material. Cf. also **83**.

57. Viner, M.: Variants of *Motl Peyse dem khazns*, in the 1932 Soviet edition of this book (vol. 5 in a series of *Gezamlte verk*), Kharkov–Kiev, 367ff. *Y*. Cf. also **83**.

See also **51** above.

Some of S. A.'s own views on his writings are revealed in his correspondence with his Russian translator:

58. Erik, M.: [S. A. and His Translator], in *Tsaytshrift* . . . (for full title, see **16**) 5 (1931) 79–88. *Y & R*.

S. A.'s relations with his great contemporary in Yiddish literature, Y. L. Peretz, were not always cordial. They have been analyzed by:

59. Mayzl, N.: [Peretz and S. A. in Their Personal Relations], in *Filologishe shriftn [fun Yivo]* 1 (1926) 263–283. *Y*. Similar versions of this material in the same author's *Peretz (lebn un shafn)*, Vilna, 1931, 175–204; his *Y. L. Peretz, zayn lebn un shafn*, New York, 1945, 248–273; and his *Y. L. Peretz un zayn dor shrayber*, New York, 1951, 271–297. See also **39**.

S. A.'s works in Hebrew have been briefly reviewed by:

60. Malakhi, A. R.: [S. A. As a Hebrew Writer], in *Di tsukunft* (New York) 21 (1916) 797–801. *Y*.

f. Style and Language

61. Oyslender, N.: [Word and Form Changes in (Successive Variants of) S. A.'s Novel, *Stempenyu*], in *Di yidishe shprakh* (Kiev), no. 2 (1927), 1–10. *Y*.

62. Zaretski, A.: [Linguistic Playfulness in S. A.], in *Di royte velt* (Kharkov), 1926, no. 5–6, 126–135. *Y*.

63. Spivak, E.: [S. A. and the Yiddish Literary Language], in *Afn shprakhfront* (Kiev), no. 4 (S. A.-zamlung), 1939, 5–17. *Y*.

63a. Spivak, E.: [Notes on S. A.'s Syntax], in *Sovetishe literatur* (Moscow) 1939, no. 1, pp. 150–164. *Y*.

64. Loytsker, Kh.: [Humor in S. A.'s Language], *ibid.*, 17–66. *Y*. The best concrete analysis of S. A.'s humorous technique.

65. Maydanski, M.: [On the Epithet in S. A.'s Works], *ibid.*, 67–80. *Y*.

66. Spivak, E.: [Idioms and Locutions in S. A.'s Diction], *ibid.*, 80–100. *Y*.

67. Lerner, R.: [Intonational-Stylistic Peculiarities of S. A.'s Language], *ibid.*, 101–126. *Y*.

68. Shapiro, M.: [Peculiarities of Construction in Popular Yiddish According to the Language of S. A.'s Characters], *ibid.*, 127–148. *Y*.

69. Shulman, M.: [What S. A. Offers to a Phonetic-Dialectological Study of Yiddish], *ibid.*, 149–160. *Y*.

70. Zaretski, A.: [On S. A.'s Word Order], in *Di yidishe shprakh* (Kiev), no. 1 (1927), 5–10. *Y*.

70a. Spivak, E.: *S. A.'s shprakh un stil* [S. A.'s Language and Style], Kiev, 1940, 167 pp. *Y*. Includes **63**, **63a**, and additional studies. The most important work in its field.

See also **58** above.

71. Kachuck, Rhoda S.: "S. A. in English; a Study in Translatability," M.A. essay in progress at Columbia University, expected to be completed in 1954.

g. Criticism

The following volumes of criticism are devoted to S. A. in their entirety:

72. Niger, Sh.: *S. A., zayne vikhtikste verk, zayn humor un zayn ort in der yidisher literatur* [. . . His Principal Works, His Humor, and His Place in Yiddish Literature], New York, 1928, 254 pp. *Y*. Contains, among others, a major essay on "Jewish and Universal Elements in *Tevye der milkhiker*" (118–157) and an extended discussion of *Funem yarid*, S. A.'s unfinished autobiography (158–178).

73. Trunk, Y. Y.: *S. A., zayn vezn un zayne verk* [. . . His Essence and His Works], Warsaw, 1937, 443 pp. *Y*. Concentrates on S. A.'s treatment of the Jewish personality as a resultant of cultural tradition and socio-economic environment. Contains a discussion of S. A.'s monologues (161–226), his novels and dramas (227–312), his portrayal of children (313–374), and the biographical background of the writer as a limitation on his artistic capabilities (375–443).

74. Trunk, Y. Y.: *Tevye un Menakhem-Mendl in yidishn veltgoyrl* [English title: Tevye and Menakhem-Mendl as Expressions of Eternal Jewish Fate; Studies of S. A.'s Main Characters], New York, 1944, 302 pp. *Y*. An original, though at times difficult, interpretation of these two major characters of S. A.'s as the embodiments of historical and cultural processes: Tevye as the dying order of the bourgeoisie, Menakhem-Mendl as the morbidly imaginative spirit of Jewish economic development made impotent by the surrounding social order.

75. Druker, I.: *S. A.; kritishe etyudn* [. . . Critical Studies], Kiev, 1939, 98 pp. *Y*. Russian version in Bilov and Druker (**19** above).

76. Samuel, Maurice: *The World of Sholom Aleichem,* New York, 1943, 332 pp. *E.* Rather than supplying a background for S. A.'s works from external sources, this book draws most of its evidence from within S. A.'s works. It thus provides no perspective for the evaluation of S. A. as a creative person or of his works as portraits of anything but themselves. Nevertheless it is an excellent introduction for the uninitiated reader.

76a. Dubilet, M.: [Basic Features of S. A's Realism], in *Sovetishe literatur* (Moscow) 1939, no. 1, pp. 124–149. *Y.*

Essays on S. A. have appeared in Yiddish newspapers and periodicals in the hundreds; a partial listing up to 1929 is offered in Reyzen's bibliography (**1**). The following studies are among those which seem to be of particular lasting importance:

77. Oyslender, N.: *Grundshtrikhn fun yidishn realizm* [Basic Features of Yiddish Realism], Kiev, 1920, 152 pp. 2nd ed., Vilna, 1928. *Y.* The chapter on S. A. (199–152) brilliantly discusses S. A.'s relation to Mendele Moykher-Sforim, the concept of Kasrilevke, the treatment of children, and the characters of Menakhem-Mendl and Tevye—all as expressions of the awakening realistic trend in 19th-century Yiddish literature.

78. Bal-makhshoves (pseud. of I. Eliashev): *Geklibene shriftn* [Collected Works], vol. 1, Warsaw, 1929. On S. A.: pp. 89–109. Of particular importance is the evaluation of Menakhem-Mendl as a socio-psychological type.

79. Mezheritski, M.: [Menakhem-Mendl by S. A.; a Tentative Sociologico-Formal Analysis], in *Di royte velt* (Kharkov), 1926, no. 5–6, 136–150. *Y.* Cf. also **83.**

80. Glatshteyn, Yankev: *In tokh genumen,* New York, 1949. *Y.* Pp. 469–484: "Menakhem-Mendl." An excellent piece of criticism, bringing out faults as well as merits of the book.

81. Oyslender, N.: Critical introduction to *Funem yarid,* Moscow, 1934, v–xxi. *Y.*

82. Viner, M.: *Vegn S. A.'s humor* [On S. A.'s Humor], Moscow, 1941, 87 pp. *Y.* Reprinted in his *Tsu der geshikhte . . .* (for full title, see **53**), vol. 2, 281–378. *Y.* The most ambitious attempt to elicit the lasting values of S. A. as a classic in the world's humorous literature.

h. Brief Appreciations in English

For a first introduction to S. A., the following may serve:

77. Madison, Charles A.: "S. A.," in *Poet Lore* 33 (1922) 563–594. *E.* The most extensive and informative essay on S. A. in English.

78. Niger, Samuel: "The Gift of S. A.," in *Commentary* 2 (1946) 116–123. *E.*

79. Goldberg, B. Z.: "S. A.," in *Universal Jewish Encyclopedia,* vol. 9 (1943), 516–518. *E.*

A number of brief articles in English are contained in *S. A. Panorama* (**17**).

S. A.'s place in Yiddish literature is discussed in both of the following histories:

80. Niger, Sh.: "Yiddish Literature," in *The Jewish People, Past and Present,* New York, vol. 3 (1952), 188f., 194. *E.*

81. Roback, A. A.: *The Story of Yiddish Literature,* New York, 1940, 107–124. *E.*

A few brief notes on the same subject will also be found in:

82. Mark, Yudel: "Yiddish Literature," in *The Jews,* ed. Louis Finkelstein, New York, 1949, vol. 2, 880–881. *E.*

Addendum

83. The journal *Shtern* (Minsk) carried the following studies of more than passing importance: 1935: previously unpublished letters by S. A.; Rivke Rubin on *Motl Peyse dem khazns;* M. Erik on *Menakhem-Mendl;* 1937: Y. Dobrushin on *Blondznde shtern*; 1938: H. Reminik on S. A.'s struggle for realism in the 1880's; L. Dushman on S. A.'s struggle for author's rights.

2. GUIDE TO ENGLISH TRANSLATIONS OF SHOLOM ALEICHEM[1]

Part I: English-Yiddish

After the title of a story, play, or poem, the Roman and Arabic numbers indicate the volume and pages, respectively, of the 1917–1925 "Folksfond" edition of S. A.'s collected works (see no. 6 in the bibliography, p. 278) where the Yiddish original of the piece may be found. SAB refers to *Dos S. A.-bukh* (no. 3 in the bibliography, p. 278). Translators are identified according to the following symbols occurring in parentheses:

aar A. A. Roback
ab Adda Birman
bfw Bessie F. White
et Elsa Teitelbaum
fb Frances Butwin
gj George Jeshurun
hb Hannah Berman
hfa Helen Froma
hfk Helena Frank
hg Henry Goodman
ig Isidore Goldstick
igb Isaac Goldberg
ign Isaac Golding
j&fb Julius and Frances Butwin
jk Joseph Kling
jl Joseph Leftwich
md M. Danish
mlrb M. L. R. Bresslar
msm Maurice Samuel
msp Moshe Spiegel
msw Mark Schweid
na Nathan Ausubel
nhl Nathan H. Lemowitz
pj Pinchos Jassinovsky
rs Rene Sylva
tk Tamara (Berkovitch) Kahana
? Unidentified

AH *Apples and Honey*, ed. Nina Salaman, New York: Doubleday, 1922; Richards, 1927.
(*hb*) Elijah the Prophet—XXIII 117–124.

ATJF *A Treasury of Jewish Folklore*, ed. Nathan Ausubel, New York: Crown, 1948.
(*j&fb*) Tit for Tat—I 145–168; In Haste—XXII 17–31.

ATJH *A Treasury of Jewish Humor*, ed. Nathan Ausubel, New York: Doubleday, 1951.
(*na*) Menachem-Mendel, Fortune Hunter—X 66–80; On the Twin Horns of a Dilemma—SAB 349; Business—SAB 350; One of Two Things—SAB 348; Aphorisms According to the Hebrew-Yiddish Alphabet—SAB 348; Free—?; Rabchik—VIII 79–94; My Brother Eliyahu's Drink—XVIII 93–104; The Parable of a Bundle of Straw—SAB 349; Superlatives in Yiddish—SAB 347. (*fb*) Gy-Ma-Na-Si-A—XXVIII 173–193.

BFW *Nine One-Act Plays from the Yiddish*, ed. Bessie F. White, Boston: Luce, 1932.
(*bfw*) Gymnasiye—[Dramatized version of] XVIII 173–193.

EW *East and West* (a magazine), New York, 1916.
(*msm*) The Song of Songs—II 9–20. (*rs*) The Knife—VIII 7–32. (*hfa*) If I Were Rothschild—VI 129–133; They All Love Us—?. (*md*) Scraps of Paper—X 43–80. (*msm*) Another Page from the Song of Songs—II 21–30. (*nhl*) [Authorship mistakenly attributed to Jonah Rosenfeld] Station Baranowitch—XXVIII 39–59.

FJA *The Jewish Anthology*, ed. Edmond Fleg, New York: Harcourt, Brace, 1925.
(*msm*) The Marriage Broker—V 102–104; The Poor Student—V 97–99.

GJL *Gems of Jewish Literature*, by Elsa Teitelbaum, New York: Pardes Publishing House, 1953.
(*et*) Three Little Heads—XXIII 133–143.

[1] Several of the references were found in Sylvia Ray Miller's *Bibliography of American Yiddish Literature, With a Critical Introduction*, unpublished M. A. Thesis (Columbia), 1944. A number of additional items were taken from the extensive supplement to Miss Miller's list, compiled by Lucy S. Dawidowicz and available at the Yivo library. Corrections and additions will be gratefully received by the present compiler.

GPA *Golden Peacock Anthology*, ed. Joseph Leftwich, London: Anscombe, 1939.
(*jl*) Epitaph—XXVII 293.

GSAN *Great Stories of All Nations*, ed. M. Lieber and B. C. Williams, New York: Brentano's, 1927; Tudor, 1934.
(*jk*) Eva—V 121–140.

GSSW *Great Short Stories of the World*, ed. M. Lieber and B. H. Clark, New York: McBride, 1926.
(*hfk*) A Passover Guest—XXIII 103–115.

GT *Golden Treasury of Jewish Literature*, ed. Leo W. Schwarz, New York: Farrar & Rinehart, 1937.
(?) Passover Fugue—XXIII 103–115.

IK *Inside Kasrilevke*, by Sholom Aleichem, New York: Schocken Books, 1948.
(*ig*) A Guide to Kasrilevke—XIII 61–128; The Poor and the Rich—XIII 9–60; Epilogue—XIII 131–141.

IL *International Literature* (a magazine), Moscow, February, 1939.
(?) The High School—XXVIII 173–193; Berel Isaac Tells Wonders of America—VI 247–254; The Happiest Man in Kodnya—XXVIII 23–38; A Man from Buenos Aires—XXVIII 69–88; Accepted—XXVIII 60–68; Three Little Heads—XXIII 133–143; Conscription—XXVIII 195–211.

JC *Jewish Children*, from the Yiddish of "Shalom Aleichem," authorised version, New York: A. A. Knopf, 1920, 1922, 1926; Bloch, 1937.
(*hb*) A Page from the "Song of Songs"—II 9–20; Passover in a Village—An Idyll—XXIII 161–178; Elijah the Prophet—XXIII 117–124; Getzel—XXIII 53–67; A Lost "L'Ag-Beomer"—XXIII 77–88; Murderers—XXIII 145–160; Three Little Heads—XXIII 133–143; Greens for "Shevuos"—IX 121–133; Another Page from the "Song of Songs"—II 21–30; A Pity for the Living—VIII 193–200; The Tabernacle—IX 135–150; The Dead Citron—XXIII 19–38; Isshur [*sic!*] the Beadle—XVII 165–177; Boaz the Teacher—XVII 178–189; The Spinning-Top—IX 175–203; Esther—IX 205–215; The Pocket-Knife—VIII 7–32; On the Fiddle—VIII 33–61; This Night—II 31–53.

JD *Jewish Digest* (a magazine), New York, December, 1940.
(?) Issar the Beadle—XVII 165–177.

JF *Jewish Forum* (a magazine), New York.
1919, pp. 969–974: (*hb*) Greens for Shevuos—IX 121–133.
1920, pp. 148–152, 235–242: (*gj*) The Story of Eve—V 121–140.

JFR *Jewish Fraternalist* (a magazine), New York, 1946.
(*hg*) Robchick—VIII 79–94 (abridged); Epitaph—XXVII 293.

JS *Jewish Spectator* (a magazine), New York.
1938, Oct.: (?) The Spoiled Ethrog—XXIII 19–38.
1939, Apr.: (*hfk*) The Passover Guest—XXIII 103–115; May: (*msm*) Another Page from the Song of Songs—II 21–30.
1940, Aug.: (?) Isser the Beadle—XVII 165–177.
1941, Apr.: (?) In the Village— XXIII 161–178.
1942, May: (?) A Spoiled "L'Ag Beomer"—XXIII 77–88.
1943, Apr.: (?) The Passover Guest—XXIII 103–115; May: (?) A L'Ag Beomer Adventure—XXIII 145–160.

JSS *Jewish Short Stories*, ed. Ludwig Lewisohn, New York: Behrman House, 1945.
(*hfk*) Fishel the Teacher—XXII 33–57.

MJLL *Modern Jewish Life in Literature*, by Azriel Eisenberg, New York: United Synagogue Commission on Jewish Education, 1948.
(*hb*) Greens for *Shavuot*—IX 121–133.

MMP *Memoirs of My People*, ed. Leo W. Schwarz, Philadelphia: Jewish Publication Society, 1943.
(*tk*) Life of a Humorist—XXVII 273–281.

NQ *Notes and Queries* (a magazine), London, July 29, 1916.
(*mlrb*) Sholoum Aleichem: His Will and Epitaph—(Will) XXVII 283–289; (Epitaph) XXVII 293.

REF *The Reflex* (a magazine), New York, December, 1928.
(?) The Clock—VIII 63–75.

SAP *Sholom Aleichem Panorama*, ed. M. W. Grafstein, London (Ontario): Jewish Observer, 1948.
(*ig*) From Drayman to Dairyman—V 13–40; The Younger Generation—V 67–91; Chaveh—Tevye's Third Daughter—V 121–140; A Match for Shprintzeh—V 143–163; The Man from Kodny—XXVIII 23–38; I Am Lucky—I'm an Orphan—XVIII 31–40; What'll Become of Me?—XVIII 41–58; My Brother Elyeh Is Getting Married—XVIII 59–70; My Brother Elyeh's Beverage—XVIII 93–104; Our Chum Pinny—XVIII 139–150; We're Off to America—XVIII 151–164; Dad and Brat—VIII 157–170; College—XXVIII 173–193; Sixty-Six—XXVIII 153–171; Tit for Tat—I 145–168; The Town of Tiny Folk—VI 9–17; The Miracle of Hoshana Rabbah—XXVIII 111–126; Menachem Mendel and Shayneh Shayndel—X 43–80; Berl Isaac and the Wonders of America—VI 247–254; Epitaph—XXVII 293. (*fb*) The Pocketknife—VIII 7–32. (*aar*) Who Is Itsik?—XXVIII 195–211; Going to the Country—XII 12–16; It's a Lie—XXI 153–161. (*ab*) A Premature Passover—XXII 149–168. (*msp*) A Consultation—XXI 71–91; If I Were Rothschild—VI 129–133. (*msw*) Heaven—XXIV 263–280; It's Hard to Be a Jew—XXV 7–164. (*ign*) She Must Marry a Doctor—IV 99–115. (?) Letters—SAB, passim.

SMC *Sleep, My Child*, Renanah Music Co., 1923. 5 pp. (*pj*).

SPYT *Six Plays from the Yiddish Theater*, ed. Isaac Goldberg, Boston: Luce, 1913.
(*igb*) She Must Marry a Doctor—IV 99–115.

ST *Stempenyu*, by Shalom Aleichem, authorised version, London: Methuen, 1913.
(*hb*)—XI 121–254.

TD *Tevye's Daughters*, by Sholom Aleichem, New York: Crown, 1949.
(*fb*) The Bubble Bursts—V 41–63; If I Were Rothschild—VI 129–133; Modern Children—V 67–91; Competitors—XXVIII 11–21; Another Page from the Song of Songs—II 21–30; Hodel—V 95–118; The Happiest Man in Kodno—XXVIII 23–38; A Wedding Without Musicians—XXVIII 127–137; What Will Become of Me?—XVIII 41–58; Chava—V 121–140; The Joys of Parenthood—VI 33–40; The Littlest of Kings—VIII 227–245; The Man from Buenos Aires—XXVIII 69–88; May God Have Mercy—VI 51–58; Shprintze—V 143–163; The Merrymakers—XVII 225–259; An Easy Fast—XIII 165–177; The Little Pot—XXI 7–25; Two Shalachmones, or a Purim Scandal—VI 85–103; Tevye Goes to Palestine—V 167–195; Gy-Ma-Na-Si-A—XXVIII 173–193; The Purim Feast—XXIII 89–102; From Passover to Succos, or The Chess Player's Story—I 185–199; Get Thee Out—V 199–220; The Passover Expropriation—XIII 141–153; The German—XVI 131–147; Third Class—XXVIII 293–303.

TJC *The Jewish Caravan*, ed. Leo W. Schwarz, New York: Farrar & Rinehart, 1935.
(*hb*) Another Page from the Song of Songs—II 21–30.

TK *Adventures of Mottel, the Cantor's Son*, by Sholom Aleichem, New York: Schuman, 1953.
(*tk*)—XVIII (all but 71–82); XIX (all).

TOC *The Old Country*, by Sholom Aleichem, New York: Crown, 1946. New, illustrated ed., 1953.
(*j&fb*) The Town of Little People—VI 9–17; The Inheritors—VI 137–154; Tevye Wins a Fortune—V 13–40; A Page from the Song of Songs—II 9–20; Two Dead Men—XIII 179–199; The Clock That Struck Thirteen—VIII 63–75; Home for Passover—XXII 33–57; The Enchanted Tailor—XVI 7–68; A Yom Kippur Scandal—VI 211–221; In Haste—XXII 17–31; Eternal Life—XVI

211–245; Hanukkah Money—IX 27–50; Tit for Tat—I 145–168; Modern Children—V 67–91; You Mustn't Weep—It's Yom-tev—XVIII 9–30; I'm Lucky—I'm an Orphan—XVIII 31–40; Dreyfus in Kasrilevka—VI 59–68; The Convoy—XVII 51–100; The Fiddle—VIII 33–61; The Day Before Yom Kippur—XVII 191–223 (passim); Three Little Heads—XXIII 133–143; A Country Passover—XXIII 161–178; The Lottery Ticket—XVII 7–50; The Miracle of Hashono [*sic!*] Rabo—XXVIII 111–126; Hodel—V 95–118; A Daughter's Grave—XXVIII 89–101; Cnards—XXII 199–222.

WS *Wandering Star*, by Sholom Aleichem, New York: Crown, 1952. (*fb*)—Original not included in S. A.'s collected works.

WSA *The World of Sholom Aleichem*, by Maurice Samuel, New York: A. A. Knopf, 1943. *These are adaptations, not translations.*
(*msm*) One Man to Be Envied—VI 77–84; The Two Shalachmonuses—VI 85–103; A Seat by the Eastern Wall—VI 137–154; Old and New Kasrielevky—XIII 141–153; The Skullcap and the Bowler Hat—I 75–78; The Reconciliation—XXIII 161–178; Kozodoievka and Kasrielevky—VI 155–210; A Special Kind of Anti-Semite—XVII 51–100; Kasrielevky in Dissolution—XVII 7–50; Superstitions of Kasrielevky—II 121–136; Rabbis and Rabbis—I 145–168; Fringe Types: Yashka Vorona—VII 47–49; Cnards—XXII 199–222; What Is Channukah—II 185–208; The Cheder—XXIII 145–160.

YIS *Yisroel, the First Jewish Omnibus*, ed. Joseph Leftwich, New York: Beechhurst Press, (2nd ed.) 1952.
(*hb*) Passover in a Village—XXIII 161–178.

YT *Yiddish Tales*, transl. Helena Frank, Philadelphia: Jewish Publication Society, 1912.
(*hfk*) The Clock—VIII 63–75; Fishel the Teacher—XXII 33–57; An Easy Fast—XIII 165–177; The Passover Guest—XXIII 103–115; Gymnasiye—XXVIII 173–193.

Part II: Yiddish-English

The initials and numbers following the title of a story refer to the volume or journal in the above list and the pages in that volume.

Vol. I: *Fun Kasrilevke*
75– 78 Kasrilevker progres—WSA 127–129 (adapted fragment).
145–168 A vort far a vort—TOC 200–217; SAP 148–152; ATJF 288–299.
185–199 Fun peysakh biz sukes—TD 247–256.

Vol. II: *Fun peysakh biz peysakh*
Shir-hashirim:
9– 20 Buzi—EW 37–39; JC 9–19; TOC 42–50.
21– 30 Mir raysn grins—EW 307–309; JC 89–98; JS 1939; TJC 348–353; TD 46–52.
31– 53 In der doziker nakht—JC 241–268.
121–136 Latkes shel khanuke—WSA 231–234 (adapted).
185–208 Vos iz khanuke?—WSA 275–278 (adapted).

Vol. III: *Mayses un fantazyes*
None

Vol. IV: *Dramatishe shriftn*
99–115 A dokter—SPYT 91–118; SAP 230–234.
151–256 Dos groyse gevins—reported to be in preparation by Tamara Kahana.

Vol. V: *Tevye der milkhiker*
13– 40 Dos groyse gevins—TOC 21–41; SAP 75–80.
41– 63 A boydem—TD 1–19.
67– 91 Hayntike kinder—TOC 218–238; TD 20–37; SAP 81–87.

95–118 Hodl—TOC 382–401; TD 53–68. Fragments (97–99)—FJA 346–348; (102–104)—FJA 340–342.
121–140 Khave—JF 1920; GSAN 851–863; TD 93–108; SAP 88–92.
143–163 Shprintse—TD 145–161; SAP 93–98.
167–195 Tevye fort keyn Erets-yisroel—TD 203–224.
199–220 Lekh-lekho—TD 257–272.

Vol. VI: *Kleyne mentshelekh mit kleyne hasoges*
9– 17 Di shtot fun kleyne mentshelekh—TOC 1–7; SAP 154–157.
33– 40 Nakhes fun kinder—TD 109–113.
51– 58 Nisht far keyn yidn gedakht—TD 141–144.
59– 68 Drayfus in Kasrilevke—TOC 260–264.
77– 84 Im meg men mekane zayn—WSA 50–52 (adapted).
85–103 Tsvey shalakhmonesn—TD 192–202; WSA 92–101 (adapted).
129–133 Ven ikh bin Roytshild—EW 61; TD 16–19; SAP 153–154.
137–154 Di yorshim—TOC 8–20; WSA 102–108 (adapted).
155–210 Di groyse behole fun di kleyne mentshelekh—WSA 139–144 (summarized).
211–221 Oysgetreyslt—TOC 138–145.
247–254 Berl-Ayzik—SAP 172–173; IL.

Vol. VII: *In shturem*
47– 49 Yashke Vorona—WSA 278–280 (adapted).

Vol. VIII: *Mayses far yidishe kinder I*
7– 32 Dos meserl—EW 47–51; JC 187–209; SAP 99–104.
33– 61 Oyfn fidl—JC 210–240; TOC 301–318.
63– 75 Der zeyger—YT 115–124; REF; TOC 67–74.
79– 94 Rabtshik—JFR (abridged); AJTH 489–499.
157–170 Pesele dem rebns—SAP 132–136.
193–200 Tsar-bale-khaim—JC 99–105.
227–245 Der yingster fun di melokhim—TD 114–127.

Vol. IX: *Mayses far yidishe kinder II*
27– 50 Khanuke-gelt—TOC 183–199.
121–133 Grins oyf shvues—JF; JC 79–88; MJLL.
135–150 Shoyn eyn mol a suke—JC 106–118.
175–203 Dos dreydl—JC 153–177.
205–215 Ester—JC 178–209.

Vol. X: *Menakhem-Mendl*
43– 80 Papirlekh—EW 150–152, 179–181, 215–218; SAP 162–171. Fragment (66–80)—ATJH 24–34.

Vol. XI: *Yidishe romanen*
121–254 Stempenyu—ST.

Vol. XII: *Zumer-lebn*
12– 16 (Fragment of) Goles datshe—SAP 136.

Vol. XIII: *Alt-nay Kasrilevke*
9– 60 Kasrilevker nisrofim—IK 71–118.
61–128 Dos naye Kasrilevke—IK 11–70.
131–140 Kasrilevker moyshev-zkeynim—IK 119–127.
141–153 A peysakhike ekspropriatsye—TD 273–280; WSA 118–121 (adapted).
165–177 A gringer tones—YT 143–152; TD 172–179.
179–199 Tsvey toyte—TOC 51–66.

Vol. XIV: *Yosele Solovey*
None

Vol. XV: *Yidishe shrayber*
None

Vol. XVI: *Oreme un freylekhe I*
7– 68 Der farkishefter shnayder—TOC 93–137.
131–147 Der daytsh—TD 281–291.
211–245 Oylem-habe—TOC 158–182.

Vol. XVII: *Oreme un freylekhe II*
7– 50 A "vigrishne bilet"—TOC 347–370 (abridged); WSA 161–167 (adapted).
51–100 Mitn etap—TOC 265–300; WSA 146–155 (adapted).
Opgeshlogene hoyshanes:
165–177 Iser der shames—JC 131–142; JS 1940; JD.
178–189 Boyez der melamed—JC 143–152.
191–223 Men iz zikh moykhl: Noyakh-Volf der katsev, Azriel der filyer, Getsi-Gubernator—TOC 319–328.
225–259 Me hulyet: Elik der mekhanik, Kopl bal-moyakh, Mendl der blekhener—TD 162–171.

Vol. XVIII: *Motl Peyse dem khazns I*
All TK (except 71–82: Ikh hob a raykhe shtele)
9– 30 Haynt iz yontev—me tor nit veynen—TOC 239–253.
31– 40 Mir iz gut, ikh bin a yosem—TOC 254–259; SAP 120–122.
41– 58 Vos vet zayn fun mir?—TD 83–92; SAP 122–124.
59– 70 Mayn bruder Elye hot khasene—SAP 124–125.
93–104 Mayn bruder Elyes getrank—SAP 126–129; ATJH 556–562.
139–150 Undzer khaver Pinye—SAP 129–130.
151–164 Shat, mir forn keyn Amerike—SAP 130–132.

Vol. XIX: *Motl Peyse dem khazns II*
All TK

Vol. XX: *Yugnt-romanen*
None

Vol. XXI: *Monologn*
7– 25 Dos tepl—TD 180–197.
71– 91 An eytse—SAP 113–116.
153–161 S'a lign!—SAP 146–147.

Vol. XXII: *Lekoved yontev I*
17– 31 Bekhipozn—TOC 146–157; ATJF 418–420.
33– 57 Oyf peysakh aheym—YT 143–152; TOC 75–92; JSS 20–41.
149–168 A frier peysakh—SAP 109–112.
199–222 Knortn—TOC 412–428; WSA 272–275 (adapted).

Vol. XXIII: *Lekoved yontev II*
19– 38 Der esreg—JC 119–130; JS 1938.
53– 67 Getsl—JC 38–49.
77– 88 A farshpilter lag-boymer—JC 50–57; JS 1942.
89–102 Tsu der sude—TD 239–246.
103–115 Der oyrekh—YT 153–161; GT 342–349; GSSW 725–729; JS 1939, 1943.
117–124 Eliyohu hanovi—JC 33–37; AH 191–195.
133–143 Dray keplekh—JC 71–78; TOC 329–335; GJL 184–7; IL.
145–160 Gazlonim—JC 58–70; JS 1943; WSA 307–310 (adapted).
161–178 A peysakh in dorf—JC 20–32; JS 1941; TOC 336–346; YIS 455–461; WSA 132–134 (adapted).

Vol. XXIV: *Komedyes*
263–280 Oylem-habe—SAP 226–230.

Vol. XXV: *Fun tsvey veltn*
7–164 Shver tsu zayn a yid—SAP 235–266.

Vol. XXVI: *Funem yarid I*
Reported to be in preparation by Tamara Kahana.

Vol. XXVII: *Funem yarid II*
Reported to be in preparation by Tamara Kahana.
273–281 Tsu mayn biografye—MMP 243–247.
283–289 S. A.'s tsavoe—NQ.
293 Epitafye—JFR; GPA 799; SAP 183; NQ.

Vol. XXVIII: *Ayznban-geshikhtes*
11– 21 Konkurentn—TD 38–45.
23– 38 Der gliklekhster in Kodne—TD 69–77; SAP 117–119; IL.
39– 59 Stantsye Baranovitsh—EW 349–353.
60– 68 Tsugenumen—IL.
69– 88 A mentsh fun Buenos-Ayres—TD 128–140; IL.
89–101 Keyver-oves—TOC 402–411.
111–126 Der nes fun hoyshane-rabe—TOC 371–381; SAP 158–161.
127–137 A khasene on klezmer—TD 78–82.
153–171 A zeks-un-zekhtsik—SAP 143–145.
173–193 Gimenazye—YT 162–180; BFW 219–235 (dramatized); TD 225–238; SAP 137–141; ATJH 605–617; IL.
195–211 Funem priziv—SAP 104–108; IL.
293–303 Drite klas—TD 292–297.

Not included in S. A.'s Collected Works:
Blondzhnde shtern (see bibliography, no. 10, p. 279)
All WS.

Dos S. A.-Bukh (SAB; bibliography, no. 3, p. 278)
Letters (passim)—SAP 340–346.
348–350 [Dilemma]—ATJH 126.
[Three Kinds of Fair]—ATJH 155.
[One of Two Things]—ATJH 201.
Aforizmen loytn alefbeyz—ATJH 252–254.
A moshl mit a kulye shtroy—ATJH 398.
Undzer loshn—ATJH 670–671.

3. GUIDE TO ENGLISH TRANSLATIONS OF YITSKHOK LEYBUSH PERETZ (1851?–1915)[1]

Part I: English-Yiddish

After the title of a story, play, or poem, the Roman and Arabic numbers indicate the volume and pages, respectively, of the 11-volume edition of *Ale verk*, New York, Central Yiddish Culture Organization (C.Y.C.O.), 1947. Translators are identified according to the following symbols occurring in parentheses:

aar	A. A. Roback	*jl*	Joseph Leftwich
ae	Azriel Eisenberg	*jr*	Jacob Robbins
asr	Angelo S. Rappoport	*jra*	J. Rabinovich
bab	B. A. Botkin	*js*	Jacob Sonntag
bfw	Bessie F. White	*lw*	Leo Wiener
eb	Etta Block	*lwl*	Leah W. Leonard
em	Elly Margolis	*mf*	Mark Feder
et	Elsa Teitelbaum	*mh*	Maximilian Hurwitz
hc	H. Champvert	*mr*	Max Rosenfeld
hcn	Henry Cohen	*msm*	Maurice Samuel
hfk	Helena Frank	*na*	Nathan Ausubel
hg	Henry Goodman	*rr*	Rebecca Rogoff
hmk	Horace M. Kallen	*sl*	Sol Liptzin
hsk	Harry S. Klein	*spr*	S. P. Rudens
hts	H[enry] T. S[chnittkind]	*tf*	Tehilla Feinerman
ig	Isidore Goldstick	*wc*	W. Champvert
jej	Joseph and Emma Jasin	*?*	Unidentified
jk	Joseph Kling		

AH *Apples and Honey* (see p. 285).
(*hfk*) The Fast—II 54–57.

AJF *Australian Jewish Forum* (a magazine), Sydney, 1944, December, no. 34.
Bontsie Shvayg—II 412–420.

AMJP *Anthology of Modern Jewish Poetry*, ed. Philip M. Raskin, New York: Behrman House, 1927.
(*jr*) I Am a Rainworm—I 246; The Two Brothers—I 223–227. (*lwl*) In Alien Lands—I 239.

AOWW *As Once We Were; Selections from the Works of I. L. Peretz*, transl. Elly Margolis, Los Angeles, 1951.
(*em*) Perhaps Even Higher—IV 98–102; The Needy Bride's Portion—IV 13–19; In the Basement Dwelling—II 221–228; Domestic Bliss—II 101–105; Brina's Mendl—II 87–94; Not Good—III 163–174; The Higher Morality—II 525–532; A Jewess' Fury—II 229–235; With Downcast Eyes—V 118–131; Four Generations, Foure Tstaments—III 175–180; Swine—III 117; Scoundrel —III 116; A Girl Reads—II 108; Betwixt Two Mountains—IV 103–117; The Courier—II 30–39; Downgrade—III 147–162; Venus and Shulamith—II 10–17; The Crazy Bahtlen—II 18–29; Seven Prosperous Years—V 105–109; The Miracle on the Waters—V 139–146; Silent Bontsia—II 412–420; The Hermit and the Bear—III 402–406; The Pious Cat—II 295–298; Ransom—V 367–371; By the Dying Man's Bed—V 73–80; The Conjuror—V 147–151; Three Gifts—V 81–92.

ATJF *A Treasury of Jewish Folklore* (see p. 285).
(*asr*) The Cabbalists—IV 20–25; Bontshe the Silent—II 412–420.

---

[1] It is a pleasant duty to thank Professor A. A. Roback and Miss Dina Abramowicz, Yivo librarian, for their help. Philip Goodman's *Peretz Sourcebook* (see SB on p. 295) and the Yivo bibliography of translations (see note on p. 285n.) were useful references.

ATJH *A Treasury of Jewish Humor* (see p. 285).
(*na*) The Hanukkah Lamp—III 301–305; But You've Got to Pray, No?—III 299–300; The Pious Cat—II 295–298.

B 1 *One-Act Plays from the Yiddish*, transl. Etta Block, Cincinnati: Stewart Kidd, 1932.
(*eb*) Champagne—VI 321–334.

B 2 *One-Act Plays from the Yiddish, Second Series*, transl. Etta Block, New York: Bloch, 1929.
(*eb*) After the Funeral—VI 315–320; Of an Early Morning—VI 281–296; The Sisters—VI 37–54.

BFW *Nine One-Act Plays from the Yiddish* (see p. 285).
(*bfw*) The Sewing of the Wedding Gown—I 213–228.

BJT *A Book of Jewish Thoughts*, sel. and arr. Joseph H. Hertz, New York: Bloch, 1926.
(*hfk*) Bontzye Shweig—II 412–420; If Not Higher—IV 98-102.

BS *Bontche the Silent* [*and Other Stories*], by I. L. Peretz, transl. A[ngelo] S. Rappoport, London: Stanley Paul, Philadelphia: David McKay, 1927.
(*asr*) Bontche the Silent—II 412–420; What Is the Soul?—II 40–53; The Messenger—II 30–39; Married—II 469–493; The Repudiated Daughter—III 129–132; Domestic Peace—II 101–105; In the Basement—II 221–228; The Poor Boy—II 400–411; Four Generations, Four Wills—III 175–180; The Devout Cat—II 295–298; The Cabbalists—IV 20–25; He Who Gives Life—IV 43–65; Moonpearls and Old Wares—III 407–411; Deviating from the Right Path—III 502–504; Jochanan the Gabbay—V 310–314; Yenkel the Pessimist—II 3–5; Ormuzd and Ahriman—VIII 137–141; If Not Higher—IV 98–102; The Crazy Beggar-Student—II 18–29; During the Epidemic—II 354–380; The Miracle of Hanouka—II 393–399; The Sick Boy—II 533–538; The Stagnant Pool—II 283–285; Venus and the Shulamite—II 10–17; Shammai Ratman—III 120–128.

BSSW *Best Short Stories of the World*, ed. Konrad Bercovici, Boston: Stratford, 1925.
(*hts*) Bontye the Silent—II 412–420.

EW *East and West* (see p. 285).
(*jra*) The Sick Boy—II 533–538. (*rr*) The Case Against the Wind—V 359–366; Drooping Eyelids—V 118–131. (*jr*) I Am a Rainworm—I 246; Venus and Shulamith—II 10–17. (*?*) Three Sewers—I 153–154. (*hsk*) The Mongrel—II 436–439. (*lwl*) Why Build a House of Prayer?—?. (*hc*) He and She—VI 33–36. (*wc*) Three Sisters—VI 37–54. (*jrk*) Consolation—?. (*hg*) After Burial—VI 315–320; Hope and Faith—I 98. (*spr*) Miracles on the Sea—V 139–146; Three Gifts—V 81–92.

FJA *The Jewish Anthology* (see p. 285).
(*?*) The Kabbalists—IV 20–25; (*msm*) The Rabbi of Nemirov—IV 98–102.

GJL *Gems from Jewish Literature* (see p. 285).
(*et*) Two Brothers—III 286–289; The Prince—IV 139–140; On the Boundaries—III 87–88; Three Cakes—V 359–366; Two Sculptors—III 519–521; The Piece of Glass—V 264–272; If Not Higher—IV 98–102 (condensed); Silence—II 86; Stars—III 384–385; Trees—II 312–313; Seven Lucky Years—V 105–109; The Crow—III 382.

GPA *Golden Peacock Anthology* (see p. 286).
(*jl*) Monish—I 3–27; King Solomon's Throne—I 113–120; A Living Picture from Vilna—I 43–45; From the Prophets— ? ; From Ezekiel—I 144–145; All Through the Stranger's Wood—I 239; Which Is Worse?—I 99–100; Little People—I 91; In the Silent Night—I 194; Sadly Are My Songs Imploring—I 195; A Tear—I 192; It Often Seems to Me—I 193; I Am a Rainworm—I 246; The Two Brothers—I 223–227; The Three Seamstresses—I 153–154; Eternal Sabbath—VI 124–127; From the Old Market Place at Night—VI 273.

GSAN *Great Stories of All Nations* (see p. 286).
(*jk*) A Reincarnated Melody—IV 118–135.

GSWW *Great Short Stories of the World* (see p. 286).
(*hfk*) A Woman's Wrath—II 229–235.

GT *Golden Treasury of Jewish Literature* (see p. 286).
(*spr*) Three Gifts—V 81–92.

HYL *History of Yiddish Literature in the 19th Century*, by Leo Wiener, New York: Scribner's, 1899.
(*lw*) Bontsie Silent—II 412–420.

JA *Jewish Advocate* (a magazine), Boston.
1911, Mar. 3–10: (?) The Klesmer—II 95–98.
1912, Sep. 27: (?) Bonzye Schweig—II 412–420.

JD *Jewish Digest* (see p. 286).
1940, Oct.: (?) If Not Higher—IV 98–102.

JF *Jewish Forum* (see p. 286).
1919, Jan.: (*hb*) The Helmer "Melamed"—II 6–9.
1923, May: (*bab*) Folk Motif—I 212.

JL *Jewish Life* (a magazine), New York, 1954, March.
(*mr*) A Weaver's Love—II 494–515.

JO *Jewish Observer* (a magazine), London, Ontario, December, 1945. (Cf. SAP, p. 287).
(*ig*) The Bass Viol—V 183–197; Domestic Bliss—II 101–105; The Magician—V 147–151; Maybe Even Higher—IV 98–102; The Apron—V 298–309; The Treasure—V 198–201. (*mh*) Opinions and Reflections—IX 137–139, 162–164, 193–194, 214–215, 403–405; (*jr*) I Am a Rainworm—I 246; The Two Brothers—I 223–227. (*jl*) Little People—I 91. (*lwl*) In Alien Lands—I 239.

JQ *The Jewish Quarterly* (a magazine), London, vol. 1 no. 1, Spring, 1953.
(*js*) Brothers—I 96–97· The World is No No-Man's Land—I 268 (condensed); The Rabbi's Hat ("The Shtreimel")—II 249–261; The Golden Chain—V 107–129.

JQR *The Jewish Quarterly Review* (a magazine), London, vol. 20, 1908, pp. 640–646.
(*hmk*) The Eighth Circle of Gehennom—III 181–188.

JR *The Jewish Review* (a magazine), London, vol. 1 (1910), pp. 274–275.
(*hfk*) The Ghetto Alms Collector—I 43–45.

JS *Jewish Spectator* (see p. 286).
1936, Dec.: (*hfk*) If Not Higher—IV 98–102.
1938, Oct.-Dec., 1939, Jan.: (?) Wedlock—II 469–493.
1939, Aug.: (?) Married Bliss— 101–105.
1939, Sep.: (?) The Fast—II 54–57.
1939, Nov.: (?) What Is the Soul?—II 40–53.
1940, July: (*hfk*) Bontzye Shweig—II 412–420.
1942, March: (?) The Purim Player—V 380–386.
1944, Sep.: (*msp*) If Not Higher—IV 98–102.

L *Peretz*, transl. and ed. Sol Liptzin, New York: Yiddish Scientific Institute—Yivo, 1947.
(*sl*) Self-Sacrifice—V 207–251; Seven Years of Plenty—V 105–109; The Magician—V 147–151; The Treasure—V 198–201; An Idyllic Home—II 101–105; Miracles on the Sea—V 139–146; If Not Higher—IV 98–102; Three Gifts—V 81–92; Beside the Dying—V 73–80; Thou Shalt Not Covet—V 132–138; Cabbalists—IV 20–25; Migrations of a Melody—IV 118–135; Four Generations, Four Wills—III 175–180; Hope and Fear—IX 101–104; A Trip into the Future—IX 26–32; On History—VIII 40–47; Poets, Books and Readers—VII 283–298; Education—VIII 3–18 (condensed); Our Platform—VIII 89–92; Advice to the Estranged—IX 123–137; Escaping Jewishness—IX 160–200 (condensed).

MAC *The Maccabean* (a magazine), New York.
1908, June: (*hmk*) Eighth Circle of Gehenna—III 181–188.
1909, Dec.: (*jej*) History—VIII 40–47.

MEN *Menorah* (a magazine), New York.
1902, Feb.: (*hcn*) Four Wills—III 175–180.
1904, Nov.: (*hfk*) The Fast—II 54–57.

MJLL *Modern Jewish Life in Literature* (see p. 286).
(*ae*) Even Higher—IV 98–102.

MYP *Modern Yiddish Poetry: an Anthology*, ed. Samuel J. Imber, New York: East and West Publishing Co., 1927.
(*?*) Three Seamstresses—I 153–154 (prose rendition).

NE *New Era* (a magazine), South Framingham, Mass.
1904, Dec.: (*?*) Michel the Klesmer—II 95–98.

POG *Prince of the Ghetto*, by Maurice Samuel, Philadelphia: Jewish Publication Society of America, 1948.
(*msm*) Devotion Unto Death—V 207–251; All for a Pinch of Snuff—V 254–263; Thou Shalt Not Covet—V 132–138; A Chapter of the Psalms—V 169–182; A Bass Viol for Heaven—V 183–197; The Three Gifts—V 81–92; Stories—III 462–477; Mendel Brainnes—II 87–94; The Poor Boy—II 400–411; [We Chassidim and *They*]—IV 137–138; [He of Nemirov]—IV 179–181; [Joy Within Joy]—IV 252–257; [The Baal Shem]—V 157–159; And Even Beyond—IV 98–102; At Home With the Almighty—IV 209–222; [But a Jew Has to *davven*]—III 299–300; [Reb Yechiel and the Thief]—IV 72–74; [The Billy-Goat]—IV 202–208; Between Two Cliffs—IV 103–117; Transmigrations of a Melody—IV 118–135; The Kabbalists, or The Kiss of Moses—IV 20–25; Silent Bontche—II 412–420.

PPL *I. L. Peretz: Psychologist of Literature*, by A. A. Roback, Cambridge: Sci-Art, 1935.
(*aar*) Precipice, or A Morning in a Cellar-House—II 221–228. (*lwl*) Three Seamstresses—I 153–154. (*jr; bfw*) The Two Brothers—I 223–227.

REF *The Reflex* (see p. 287).
1929, Dec.: (*?*) Three Gifts—V 81–92.
1930, Jan.: (*?*) Miracles on the Sea—V 139–146.

SB *I. L. Peretz: A Sourcebook on Programming*, ed. Philip Goodman, New York: National Jewish Welfare Board, 1951.
(*msm; mf*) At Home With the Almighty—IV 209–222 (dramatized); (*mf*) The Trial of Bontche—II 412–420 (dramatized). (*bfw*) The Sewing of the Wedding Gown—I 213–228. (*na*) But You've Got to Pray, No?—III 299–300; The Little Hanukkah Lamp—III 301–305. (*jl*) A Living Picture from Vilna—I 43–45; All Through the Stranger's Wood—I 239; A Tear—I 192; Little People—I 91; Which is Worse?—I 99–100; In the Silent Night—I 194. (*hg*) Hope and Faith—I 98. (*sl*) On History—VIII 40–47; On Education—VIII 3–18 (condensed); On Jewishness—IX 162–164.

SBJV *The Standard Book of Jewish Verse*, comp. Joseph Friedlander, ed. George Alexander Kohut, New York: Dodd, Mead, 1917.
(*hg*) Hope and Faith—I 98.

SDD *Sabbath: the Day of Delight*, by Abraham E. Millgram, Philadelphia: Jewish Publication Society of America, 1944.
(*hfk*) Domestic Happiness—II 101–105; The Treasure—V 198–201.

SP *Stories and Pictures*, by I. L. Peretz, transl. Helena Frank, Philadelphia: Jewish Publication Society of America, 1906, 1907. . . .
(*hfk*) If Not Higher—IV 98–102; Domestic Happiness—II 101–105; In the Post-Chaise—II 67–85; The New Tune—II 109–111; Married—II 469–493; The Seventh Candle of Blessing—II 112–116; The Widow—II 106–107; The Messenger—II 30–39; What is the Soul—II 40–53; In Time of Pestilence—II

354–380; Bontzye Shweig—II 412–420; The Dead Town—III 75–86; The Days of the Messiah—II 516–524; Kabbalists—IV 20–25; Travel Pictures—II 119–191; The Outcast—III 129–132; A Chat—IV 141–149; The Pike—II 287–291; The Fast—II 54–57; The Woman Mistress Hannah—III 32–72; In the Pond—II 283–285; The Chanukah Light—II 393–399; The Poor Little Boy—II 400–411; Underground—II 221–228; Between Two Mountains—IV 103–117; The Image—II 310–311.

TC *The Three Canopies*, by I. L. Peretz, New York: Shoulson Press, 1948.
(*tf*) The Three Canopies—V 14–72.

TG *Three Gifts and Other Stories*, by I. L. Peretz, New York: Book League of the Jewish People's Fraternal Order, I. W. O., 1947.
(*hg*) If Not Still Higher—IV 98–102; Domestic Bliss—II 101–105; Bontche Shweig—II 412–420; At the Fakir's—II 242–248; Three Gifts— V 81–92; Trust—II 120–121; The Little Boy—II 147–149; The Rebbitzin of Skul—II 166–169; Sisters—III 258–261; The Moralist—II 525–532; The Basement Lodging—II 221–228; The Magician—V 147–151; At the Head of the Dying Man—V 73–80.

TJC *The Jewish Caravan* (see p. 287).
(*?*) Bontche Shweig—II 412–420; If Not Higher—IV 98–102.

YIS *Yisroel* (see p. 288).
(*jl*) The Miracle on the Sea—V 139–146.

YT *Yiddish Tales* (see p. 288).
(*hfk*) A Woman's Wrath—II 229–235; The Treasure—V 198–201; It Is Well—V 152–156; Whence a Proverb—V 202–206.

Part II: Yiddish-English

The initials and numbers following the title of a story, poem, play, or essay refer to the volume or journal in the above list and the pages therein.

Vol. I: *Lider un poemen*

3– 27 Monish—GPA 56–70.
43– 45 Der yidisher kvestar—GPA 77–79; JR; SB 36.
91 [Kleyne mentshn]—GPA 81–82; JO 86; SB 37.
98 Hof un gleyb—EW 353; SB 37; SBJV 625.
96– 97 [Ale mentshn zaynen] brider—JQ 56.
99–100 Vemen iz erger—GPA 81; SB 37.
113–120 Kisey-shloyme—GPA 70–77.
144–145 Fun Yikhezkl l''g—GPA 79–80.
153–154 Dray neyterins—EW 74; GPA 87–88; MYP 239–241 (prose); PPL 235.
192 [A volkn hot fardekt dem himl]—GPA 83; SB 36.
193 [Teyl mol dakht zikh mir]—GPA 83.
194 [In der shtiler nakht]—GPA 82; SB 37.
195 [Troy'rik fregn mayne lider]—GPA 82.
212 [Shteynerne palatsn]—JF.
213–228 Baym fremdn khupe-kleyd—BFW 119–39; SB; Fragment (223–227)—AMJP 123–127; GPA 84–87; JO 54; PPL 232–233.
239 Ikh gey arum in a fremdn vald—AMJP 123; GPA 80; JO 90; SB 36.
246 Ikh bin a regn-vorem—AMJP 122; EW 71; GPA 83; JO 43.
268 Meyn nisht—JQ 57 (condensed).

Vol. II: *Dertseylungen, mayselekh, bilder* (up to 1899)

3– 5 Yenkl pesimist—BS 159–161.
6– 9 Der khelemer melamed—JF.
10– 17 Venus un shulamis—AOWW 171–178; BS 237–243; EW 101–102.
18– 29 Der meshugener batlen—AOWW 179–191; BS 175–185.

30– 39 Der meshulakh—AOWW 140–152; BS 37–48; SP 103–116.
40– 53 Vos heyst "neshome"—BS 23–36; JS 1939; SP 119–134.
54– 57 Der tones—AH 132–135; JS 1939; MEN 1904; SP 327–333.
67– 85 Inem postvogn—SP 29–52.
86 Halt s'moyl—GJL 177.
87– 94 Mendl Braynes—AOWW 48–58; POG 155–162.
95– 98 A klezmer-toyt—JA; NE.
101–105 Sholem-bayis—AOWW 42–46; BS 77–81; JO 42–43; JS 1939; L 146–152; SP 23–29; SDD 257–261; TG 18–22.
106–107 Di almone—SP 95–97.
108 Di lezerin—AOWW 119–121.
109–111 Der nayer nign—SP 53–55.
112–116 Dos zibete bentshlikhtl—SP 89–92.
119–191 Bilder fun a provints-rayze—SP 223–303; Fragments (120–121, 147–149, 166–169)—TG 47–55.
221–228 In kelershtub—AOWW 31–41; BS 83–91; PPL 301–326; SP 417–426; TG 68–76.
229–235 Der kaas fun a yidene—AOWW 81–89; GSSW 722–725; YT 55–61.
242–248 Baym fakir—TG 31–36.
249–261 Dos shtrayml—JQ 57–66.
283–285 In gemoyzekhts—BS 233–235; SP 385–388.
287–291 Hekht—SP 323–329.
295–298 Di frume kats—AOWW 227–231; ATJH 87–89; BS 111–114.
310–311 Der goylem—SP 449–450.
312–313 Beymer—GJL 179–180.
354–380 Beshas mageyfe—BS 187–217; SP 135–170.
393–399 Nes-khanuke—BS 219–225; SP 389–398.
400–411 Dos oreme yingl—BS 93–103; POG 164–170; SP 399–413.
412–420 Bontsye shvayg—AJF; AOWW 209–220; ATJF 507–513; BJT 109–116; BS 13–22; BSSW 61–73; HYL 333–352; JA; JS 1940; POG 75–83; SB 15–19 (dramatized); SP 173–184; TG 23–30; TJC 342–348.
436–439 Kol boy—EW.
469–493 Khasene gehat—BS 48–72; JS 1938–39; SP 61–88.
494–515 Veber-libe—JL.
516–524 Moshiakhs tsaytn—SP 203–212.
525–532 Muser—AOWW 72–80; TG 61–67.
533–538 Dos kranke yingl—BS 227–232; EW.

Vol. III: *Dertseylungen, mayselekh, bilder* (from 1900)
32– 72 Hoisho moras Khano—SP 337–382.
75– 86 Di toyte shtot—SP 187–200.
87– 88 Oyf der grenets—GJL 104–105.
116 Padlyets—AOWW 118.
117 Shvayn—AOWW 117.
120–128 Shamay ratman—BS 245–252.
129–132 Di farshtoysene—BS 73–76; SP 307–312.
147–162 Meshupe—AOWW 153–170.
163–174 Nisht gut—AOWW 59–71.
175–180 Fir doyres, fir tsavoes—AOWW 110–116; BS 105–110; L 266–274; MEN.
181–188 Di akhte opteylung in gehenem—JQR 640–646; MAC.
258–261 Shvester—TG 56–61.
286–289 Tsvey brider—GJL 66–68.
299–300 Ober davnen muz men dokh—ATJH 266–267; POG 205–208; SB 29–30.
301–305 A khanuke-lempl—ATJH 73–77; SB 31–33.
382 Fligl—GJL 195.
384–385 Shtern—GJL 178.

402–406 Der poresh mitn ber—AOWW 221–226.
407–411 Levone-perl un altvarg—BS 145–149.
462–477 Mayses—POG 133–150.
502–504 Fun veg arop—BS 150–154.
519–521 Der bildhoyer—GJL 137–139.

Vol. IV: *Khsidish*

13– 19 Hakhnosas-kale—AOWW 21–30.
20– 25 Mekubolim—ATJF 194–198; BS 115–120; FJA 320–321; L 224–233; POG 256–263; SP 213–219.
43– 97 Yoykhonon melameds mayselekh: 1. Ver es git lebn, git fun vanen tsu lebn (43–65)—BS 121–143; 2. Vos a mol veyniker: Fragment (72–74)—POG 211–213.
98–102 Oyb nisht nokh hekher—AOWW 14–20; BJT 230–233; BS 169–173; FJA 348–352; GJL 156–158 (condensed); JD; JO 46–47; JS 1936, 1944; L 174–180; MJLL 26–29; POG 191–196; SP 13–20; TG 13–17; TJC 388–391.
103–117 Tsvishn tsvey berg—AOWW 122–139; POG 223–239; SP 427–446.
118–135 A gilgl fun a nign—GSAN 846–851; L 234–264; POG 240–255.
137–140 Shehasimkho bemeoynoy: Fragment (137–138)—POG 179; fragment (139–140)—GJL 98–99.
141–149 A shmues—SP 313–318.
179–186 Mishnas-khsidim: Fragment (179–181)—POG 179–181.
202–208 Hisgales, oder di mayse fun tsignbok—POG 215–222.
209–222 Berl der shnayder—POG 119–205; SB 10–14 (dramatized).
252–257 Simkhe shebesimkhe—POG 181–188.

Vol. V: *Folkstimlekhe geshikhtn*

14– 72 Dray khupes—TC.
73– 80 Baym goyses tsukopns—AOWW 240–249; L 200–210; TG 83–89.
81– 92 Dray matones—AOWW 257–270; EW 303–306; GT 217–225; L 182–198; POG 110–120; REF; TG 37–46.
105–109 Zibn gute yor—AOWW 192–198; GJL 191–194; L 120–126.
118–131 Aropgelozte oygn—AOWW 90–109; EW 67–71.
132–138 Loy sakhmoyd—L 212–222; POG 65–73.
139–146 Nisim oyfn yam—AOWW 199–208; EW 355–357; L 154–168; REF; YIS 449–455.
147–151 Der kuntsn-makher—AOWW 250–256; JO 44–45; L 128–136; TG 77–82.
152–156 S'i gut—YT 67–72.
157 Der hintisher seyder: Fragment (157–159)—POG 189–190.
169–182 A kapitl thilim—POG 83–96.
183–197 Shma-yisroel, oder der bas—JO 38–42; POG 96–110.
198–201 Der oytser—JO 51–52; L 138–144; SDD 261–265; YT 62–66.
202–206 A gants yor shiker, purim nikhter—YT 73–79.
207–251 Mesiras-nefesh—L 30–106; POG 13–45.
254–263 Iber a shmek tabak—POG 54–64.
264–272 Dos glezl—GJL 140–146.
298–309 Dos fartekh—JO 47–51.
310–314 Reb Yoykhenen gabe—BS 155–158.
359–366 Der din-toyre mitn vint—EW 41–43; GJL 125–131.
367–371 Pidyen-shvuyim—AOWW 232–239.
380–386 Der shpiler—JS 1942 (condensed).

Vol. VI: *Dramatishe shriftn*

33– 36 Er un zi—EW 149.
37– 54 Shvester—B2; EW.
101–180 Di goldene keyt: Fragments (124–127)—GPA 88–90; (107–129)—JQ 67–75.

181–280 Bay nakht oyfn altn mark: Fragment (273)—GPA 90.
281–296 A frimorgn—B2.
315–320 Nokh kvure—B2; EW 347–348.
321–334 Shampanyer—B1 1–15.

Vol. VII: *Literatur un lebn*
283–298 Der dikhter, dos bukh un der lezer—L 310–326 (condensed).

Vol. VIII: *Gedanken un ideen* (up to 1902)
3– 18 Bildung—L 328–338; SB 44–46 (condensed).
40– 47 Vegn geshikhte—L 296–308; MAC; SB 39–44.
89– 92 Vos viln mir?—L 340 (fragment).
137–141 Hormoz un Akhrimon—BS 163–167.

Vol. IX: *Gedanken un ideen* (from 1903)
26– 32 A rayze in der tsayt—L 284–294.
101–104 Hofenung un shrek—L 278–282.
123–139 Tsu di tsurikgekumene geyrim—L 342–350 (condensed); fragment (137–139)—JO 60.
160–200 Vegn vos firn op fun yidishkayt—L 352–378; fragment (162–164)—SB 46–47; JO 61; (193–194) JO.
213–216 Klal un prat: fragment (214–215)—JO 61.
403–405 Eysev shpilt—JO 61 (condensed).

Vol. X: *Finf megiles*
None

Vol. XI: *Zikhroynes, briv un redes*
None

CONTRIBUTORS TO THIS VOLUME

H. Beem of Leeuwarden, the Netherlands, has been collecting vestiges of Western Yiddish in his country. He is the author of *De verdwenen mediene; kol hokohol hakodousj hazee*, Amsterdam, 1950 (a description of the culture of the exterminated Jews of provincial Holland), and has prepared for publication a volume of Dutch Yiddish proverbs.

Solomon A. Birnbaum, professor at the School of Oriental and African Studies, University of London, is a well known Yiddish linguist and philologist as well as the author of studies on other Jewish languages.

Leo Fuks is the head of the Rosenthaliana, the Jewish division of the University Library in Amsterdam. He is the author of a number of bibliographical and philological articles.

Chaim Gininger is Lecturer in Yiddish at Columbia University in New York. Before World War II he was for several years a research fellow in Yiddish linguistics at the Yiddish Scientific Institute—Yivo. He is the author of a number of articles in this field.

Florence Guggenheim-Grünberg of Zurich has devoted many years to a study of the language and culture of Swiss Jews. Dr. Guggenheim's articles have appeared in *Jüdisches Wochenblatt* (Zurich) and as separate booklets.

B. Hrushovski is an assistant in Hebrew and Yiddish literature at the Hebrew University at Jerusalem, where he is working for his doctorate. Known as H. Binyomin, he is one of the leading young Yiddish poets in Israel and has translated several volumes of Yiddish poetry into Hebrew.

Judah A. Joffe, whose eightieth birthday was celebrated in 1953 by the appearance of two special issues of the journal *Yidishe shprakh* in his honor, has published numerous studies in the field of Yiddish philology. Professor of Yiddish at the Ecole Libre des Hautes Etudes in New York, he is a founding member of the Linguistic Circle of New Xork.

Yudel Mark, chairman of the Yiddish Linguistic Circle at Yivo and editor of the Yivo journal *Yidishe shprakh*, is the author of many descriptive studies in Yiddish grammar and a specialist in problems of the standardized Yiddish language.

Eleanor Gordon Mlotek, for many years assistant to the research director of Yivo, is a member of the Y. L. Cahan Folklore Club, co-editor of the journal *Yidisher folklor*, and a specialist on Yiddish folksong.

Herbert H. Paper is assistant professor of Near Eastern Languages at the University of Michigan.

Dov Sadan, professor of Yiddish at the University of Jerusalem, is a specialist in Yiddish folklore and popular literature.

Mordche Schaechter, linguist and folklorist, wrote a doctoral thesis on "Aktionsn im Jiddischen; ein sprachwissenschaflicher Beitrag zur vergleichenden Bedeutungslehre des Verbums" (Vienna, 1950) and has published articles in *Yidishe shprakh*.

CHONE SZMERUK, assistant in Yiddish at the University of Jerusalem, is working for his doctorate in history.

BEATRICE SILVERMAN WEINREICH, member of the Y. L. Cahan Folklore Club and co-editor of the journal, *Yidisher folklor*, is working for an anthropology degree at Columbia University.

MAX WEINREICH, associate professor in charge of Yiddish courses at the City College of New York and for many years research director of the Yiddish Scientific Institute, has published widely in the field of Yiddish linguistics, folkloristics, and literary history.

URIEL WEINREICH, assistant professor of Yiddish language, literature, and culture on the Atran Chair at Columbia University, is co-editor of *Word* (Journal of the Linguistic Circle of New York) and of *Yidisher folklor*.

INDEX OF WORDS

Words which are familiar in present-day standard Yiddish are listed here in their standard forms, regardless of the dialectal variants which may be cited in the text. Words which are only dialectal or archaic are listed as cited in the text and are preceded by the symbol ◎.

Names of Persons

Place Names

Appellatives (Words and Affixes)

INDEX OF PERSONS

INDEX OF PHONOLOGICAL DEVELOPMENTS

INDEX OF SUBJECTS

L. C. N. Y. Publications

MONOGRAPH SERIES

The *Linguistic Circle of New York* publishes occasional Monographs as Supplements to various volumes of WORD. These Monographs are distributed gratis to members *at the time of publication*. They are available thereafter only on specific order and at the prices listed.

Monograph No. 1, Supplement to volume 7, WORD
KARL HEINRICH MENGES—The Oriental Elements in the Vocabulary of the Oldest Russian Epos, The Igor Tale **$2.00**

Monograph No. 2, Supplement to volume 9, WORD
YURY ŠERECH—Problems in the Formation of Belorussian **$2.00**

SPECIAL PUBLICATIONS

1. URIEL WEINREICH—*Languages in Contact* **$3.50**
   For members and subscribers **$2.80**
2. *Linguistics Today* (1954), 280 pp. **$5.00**
   Equivalent to *Word*, vol. 10, no. 2–3, but with hard-cover binding and separate pagination. For members and subscribers **$4.00**
3. *The Field of Yiddish; Studies in Language, Folklore, and Literature*, ed. URIEL WEINREICH (1954), about 320 pp. **$5.00**
   For members and subscribers **$4.00**

In preparation:
EUGENE DORFMAN—An introduction to phonemics

Individuals and libraries interested in obtaining *a complete set* of back numbers of WORD are urged to send in their orders *at once* in order to avoid inconvenience and delay, since several numbers are almost exhausted. The complete set from volume 1 (1945) through volume 10 (1954) is avail- ·le at $43.00; Monographs 1 and 2, each $2.00 additional.

UGENE DORFMAN, 401 Philosophy Hall, Columbia University,
New York 27, New York